LOCATION MAP

MAP 4 NORTHERN EUROPE

MAP 18 SOUTHERN EUROPE AFRICA AND MIDDLE EAST

MAP 36 FAR EAST AND AUSTRALASIA

- North Cape
- Oslo
- London
- Ushant
- Gibraltar
- Istanbul
- Port Said
- Dakar
- Aden
- Ascension Is.
- Mumbai
- Singapore
- Hong Kong
- Shanghai
- Busan
- Tokyo
- Cape Town
- Cape of Good Hope
- C. Leeuwin
- Sydney

THE SHIPS ATLAS

9th Edition

Shipping guides LTD

The Port Information Specialists

75 Bell Street | Reigate | RH2 7AN | United Kingdom
Tel: +44 1737 242255 | *Fax:* +44 1737 222449 | *Telex:* 917070 Shipg G
email: info@portinfo.co.uk | *internet:* http://www.portinfo.co.uk/

UPDATING AND AMENDMENTS

Shipmasters, Shipowners or Managers, Port Authorities, Administrators and Agents, are earnestly requested to assist our work in up-dating The Ships Atlas by providing information, amendments or corrections, plus additional details of any ports or terminals, to the following address.

SHIPPING GUIDES LTD
75 BELL STREET
REIGATE
RH2 7AN
UNITED KINGDOM

Tel: +44 1737 242255
Fax: +44 1737 222449
Telex: 917070
Email: info@portinfo.co.uk
WWW: www.portinfo.co.uk

Ninth Edition:
December 2001

Eighth Edition:
December 1999

Seventh Edition:
February 1998

Sixth Edition:
January 1996

Fifth Edition:
1st Impression – February 1994
2nd Impression – July 1994

Fourth Edition:
September 1991

Third Edition:
November 1989

Second Edition:
March 1987

First Edition:
1st Impression – April 1984
2nd Impression – March 1985

ISBN 0 9536 105 2 7

All rights reserved. No part of this publication may be reproduced, stored in a retrieval system or transmitted in any form or by any means, electronic, mechanical, photocopying, recording or otherwise without the prior permission of the publishers.

© Shipping Guides Ltd 2001

Typesetting by Shipping Guides Ltd., Reigate, England.
Printed in Great Britain by Bath Press Colourbooks, Blantyre, Glasgow, Scotland.
Bound in Great Britain by Bath Press, Bath, England.

PREFACE

Thank you for purchasing this the Ninth Edition of **The Ships Atlas**. As always we have extensively revised, checked and updated both the "Map Section" and the "Single Index" which we know users have found most useful in previous editions. We hope that the new atlas meets with your approval and that you find it of assistance in your daily work.

The Ships Atlas now contains over twelve thousand marked ports, terminals and places. This includes over one hundred new entries in this edition. Nearly three thousand of these facilities are accompanied by details of port data extracted from **Guide to Port Entry** and the latest port information we have to hand.

In this Ninth Edition of **The Ships Atlas** we have included an updated MARPOL Map. We would suggest that users refer to the full text of the MARPOL Regulations as the map is Shipping Guides' interpretation of the rules. New inset maps for the Caspian Sea, Shannon Estuary, Faroe Islands, Gulf of Kutch and the Gulf of Thailand have also been added.

For many years, a number of prestigious organisations within the shipping industry have been using **The Ships Atlas** as a useful presentation gift for their clients and customers, and in this respect we remind purchasers that we can arrange to have their company name, logo and contact details gold blocked on the front cover for a small additional charge.

Due to advances in technology and our in-house production techniques, it is now possible for individual maps to be reproduced and customised to your requirements. Should this service be of interest, we would welcome further enquiries.

Editorial/Production Staff

Robert Pedlow
Feargal Hogan
Andrew Hamilton
Mark Barnes
Ruth Knight
Nigel Grieve
Stephen O'Callaghan

Reigate
December 2001

CONTENTS

Map No	Map Title
	THE WORLD - LOCATION MAP
	(See inside front cover)
1	MARPOL MAP
2	WORLD OCEAN CURRENTS AND PREVAILING WINDS
3	WORLD LOAD LINE AND INTERNATIONAL TIME ZONES
4	**NORTHERN EUROPE**
5	BRITISH ISLES
6	UNITED KINGDOM RIVER AREAS
	Belfast Lough Bristol Channel
	Clyde Humber
	Mersey Tay/Forth
	Thames Estuary Tyne/Tees
7	ENGLISH CHANNEL/NORTH SEA
8	NORTH EUROPEAN COASTAL AREAS
	Belgium - Netherlands / Schelde to Borkum
	France - Seine France - Gironde
	Norway - Oslo Fjord Shannon Estuary
9	EUROPEAN INLAND WATERWAYS
	Caspian Sea
10	SCANDANAVIA
11	THE BALTIC
12	ENTRANCE TO THE BALTIC
13	SAIMAA CANAL AND LAKES
14	KIEL CANAL
15	NORTHERN SCANDANAVIA
	Faroe Islands
16	WHITE SEA/BARENTS SEA
17	GREENLAND / ICELAND
	Svalbard - Spitzbergen
18	**SOUTHERN EUROPE, AFRICA & MIDDLE EAST**
19	BAY OF BISCAY
20	BISCAY TO GIBRALTAR
	Azores
21	THE MEDITERRANEAN
22	WESTERN MEDITERRANEAN
23	SOUTH EUROPEAN COASTAL AREAS
	Bosporus and Approaches Gulf of Genoa
	Gulf of Naples Marseille District
	Piraeus District Strait of Gibraltar
24	CENTRAL MEDITERRANEAN
25	AEGEAN SEA
26	EASTERN MEDITERRANEAN / BLACK SEA
27	WEST AFRICA / CAPE VERDE ISLANDS
28	SOUTH WEST AFRICA
	Gamba to Luanda (Offshore Terminals)
29	GULF OF GUINEA
30	EAST AFRICA
31	GULF OF ADEN / ARABIAN SEA
32	RED SEA
33	SUEZ CANAL
34	SUEZ CANAL APPROACHES
	Northern Entrance Southern Entrance
35	THE GULF REGION

Map No	Map Title
36	**FAR EAST AND AUSTRALASIA**
37	THE GULF TO MALACCA STRAITS
	Gulf of Kutch
38	WESTERN INDONESIA, MALAYSIA AND BRUNEI
	Sunda Strait
39	SOUTH CHINA SEA
	Gulf of Thailand Mekong Delta
40	MALACCA STRAITS
41	SINGAPORE
42	YELLOW SEA / EAST CHINA SEA
43	JAPAN / SEA OF OKHOTSK
44	JAPANESE COASTAL AREAS
	Kanmon Ko Kobe / Osaka
	Tokyo Bay
45	SOUTHERN JAPAN AND INLAND SEA
46	PHILIPPINES / EAST INDIES
47	PHILIPPINE ISLANDS
48	GUANGZHOU / HONG KONG / MACAU
49	CENTRAL / SOUTH PACIFIC
50	AUSTRALIA
51	AUSTRALIAN COASTAL AREAS
	Australia - N.E. Coast / Coral Sea Spencer Gulf
	Australia - N.W. Coast Melbourne to Hobart
52	NEW ZEALAND
	Chatham Island
53	**NORTH AMERICA**
54	ALASKA / SIBERIA
55	UNITED STATES OF AMERICA
56	NORTH AMERICA – NORTH WEST COAST
	Vancouver / Seattle Area
57	NORTH AMERICA – WEST COAST
58	SAN FRANCISCO / LOS ANGELES AREAS
	San Francisco Bay
	Los Angeles / San Pedro Channel
59	HUDSON BAY
60	GULF OF ST. LAWRENCE / NEW ENGLAND
61	ST. LAWRENCE SEAWAY
62	NORTH AMERICA – THE GREAT LAKES
	Welland Canal
63	USA – EAST COAST
	New York Bermuda
64	CAPE COD CANAL
65	CHESAPEAKE AND DELAWARE BAYS
66	USA – GULF COAST
	Freeport to Lake Charles
67	MISSISSIPPI RIVER
68	**CENTRAL AND SOUTH AMERICA**
69	THE CARIBBEAN
	Galapagos
70	NORTHERN CARIBBEAN
71	EASTERN CARIBBEAN
72	SOUTH AMERICA – NORTHERN PART
73	PANAMA CANAL
74	MARACAIBO LAKE REGION
75	ORINOCO RIVER
76	SOUTH AMERICAN COASTAL AREAS
	The Guianas South East Brazil
77	SOUTH AMERICA – SOUTHERN PART
78	RIVER PLATE
79	THE ARCTIC
80	THE ANTARCTIC
81	INSTITUTE WARRANTIES
	(See inside back cover)

INDEX – Alphabetical by Port Name, etc, and including islands, Seas, Rivers, Canals and other features.

Note: **Bold** type indicates "Key Maps"   *Italic* type indicates "Inset Maps" or "Coastal Area Maps"

THE SHIPS ATLAS

MAPS

Map 1

This map is a representation of Shipping Guides Limited interpretation of the MARPOL 73/78 Regulations. Users are advised to consult the appropriate regulations for complete text.

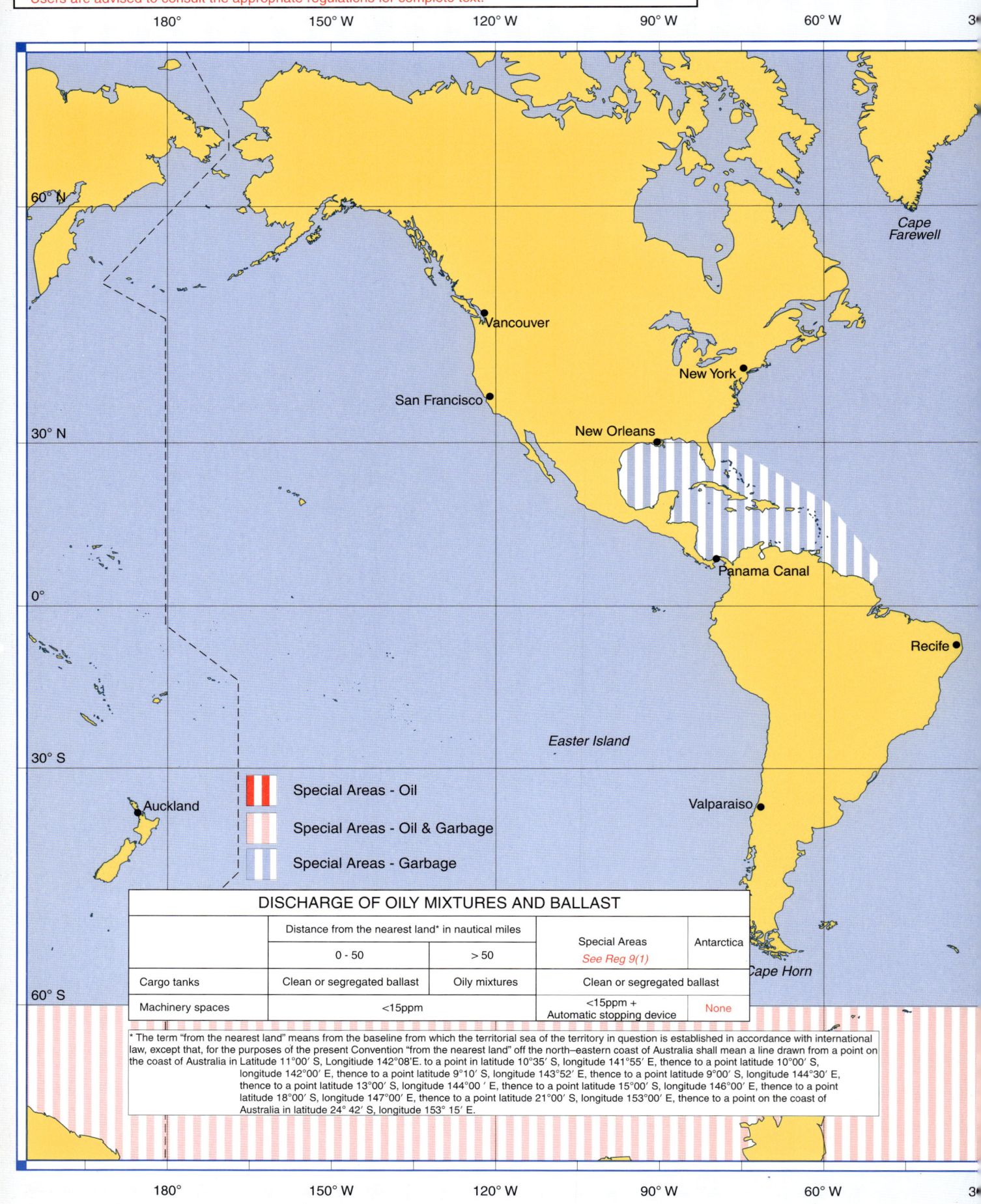

Legend:
- Special Areas – Oil
- Special Areas – Oil & Garbage
- Special Areas – Garbage

DISCHARGE OF OILY MIXTURES AND BALLAST

	Distance from the nearest land* in nautical miles		Special Areas *See Reg 9(1)*	Antarctica
	0 – 50	> 50		
Cargo tanks	Clean or segregated ballast	Oily mixtures	Clean or segregated ballast	
Machinery spaces	<15ppm		<15ppm + Automatic stopping device	None

* The term "from the nearest land" means from the baseline from which the territorial sea of the territory in question is established in accordance with international law, except that, for the purposes of the present Convention "from the nearest land" off the north-eastern coast of Australia shall mean a line drawn from a point on the coast of Australia in Latitude 11°00′ S, Longitiude 142°08′E. to a point in latitude 10°35′ S, longitude 141°55′ E, thence to a point latitude 10°00′ S, longitude 142°00′ E, thence to a point latitude 9°10′ S, longitude 143°52′ E, thence to a point latitude 9°00′ S, longitude 144°30′ E, thence to a point latitude 13°00′ S, longitude 144°00 ′ E, thence to a point latitude 15°00′ S, longitude 146°00′ E, thence to a point latitude 18°00′ S, longitude 147°00′ E, thence to a point latitude 21°00′ S, longitude 153°00′ E, thence to a point on the coast of Australia in latitude 24° 42′ S, longitude 153° 15′ E.

© Shipping Guides Ltd., Reigate, United Kingdom

MAP 1
MARPOL 73/78

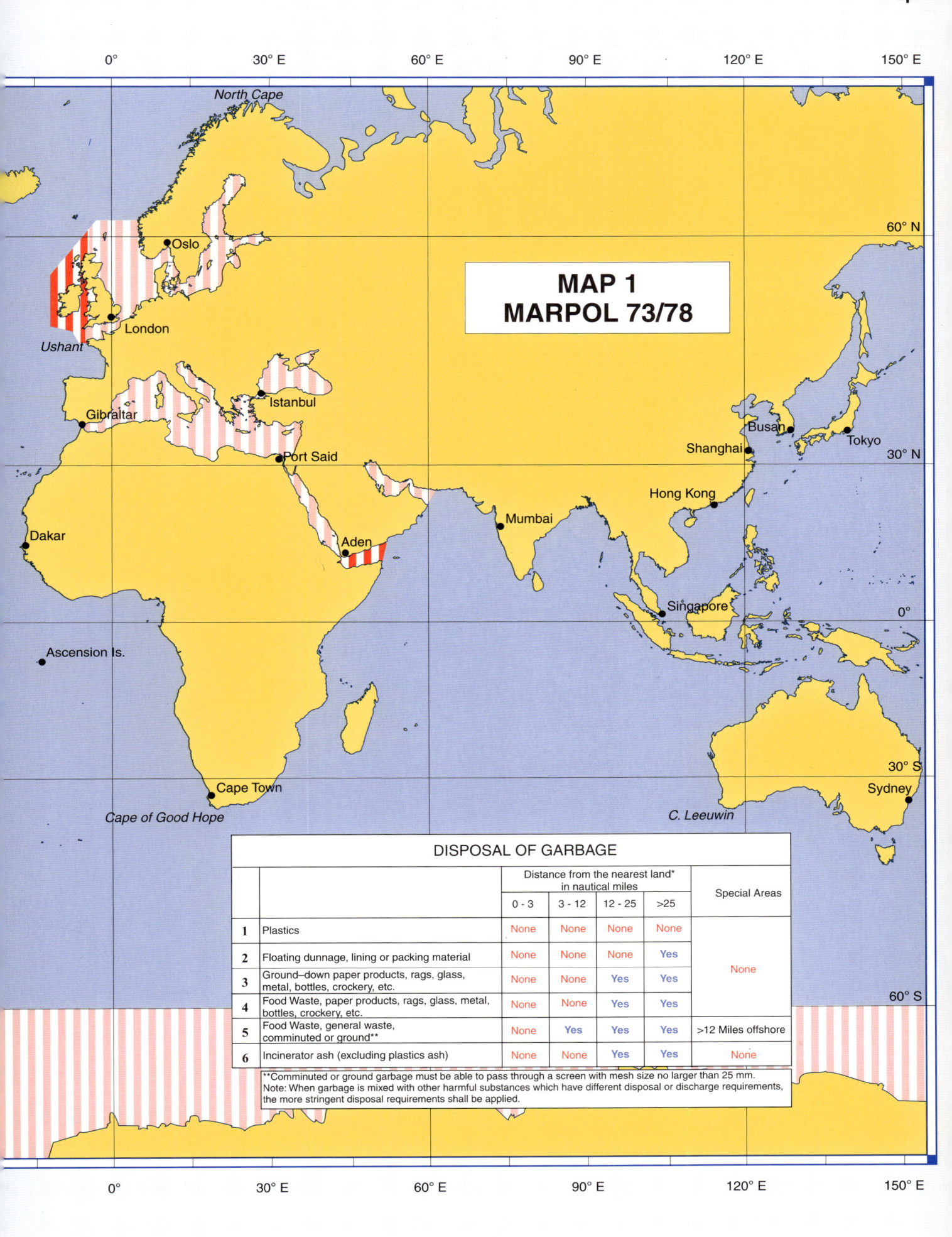

DISPOSAL OF GARBAGE

		Distance from the nearest land* in nautical miles				Special Areas
		0 - 3	3 - 12	12 - 25	>25	
1	Plastics	None	None	None	None	None
2	Floating dunnage, lining or packing material	None	None	None	Yes	None
3	Ground–down paper products, rags, glass, metal, bottles, crockery, etc.	None	None	Yes	Yes	None
4	Food Waste, paper products, rags, glass, metal, bottles, crockery, etc.	None	None	Yes	Yes	None
5	Food Waste, general waste, comminuted or ground**	None	Yes	Yes	Yes	>12 Miles offshore
6	Incinerator ash (excluding plastics ash)	None	None	Yes	Yes	None

**Comminuted or ground garbage must be able to pass through a screen with mesh size no larger than 25 mm.
Note: When garbage is mixed with other harmful substances which have different disposal or discharge requirements, the more stringent disposal requirements shall be applied.

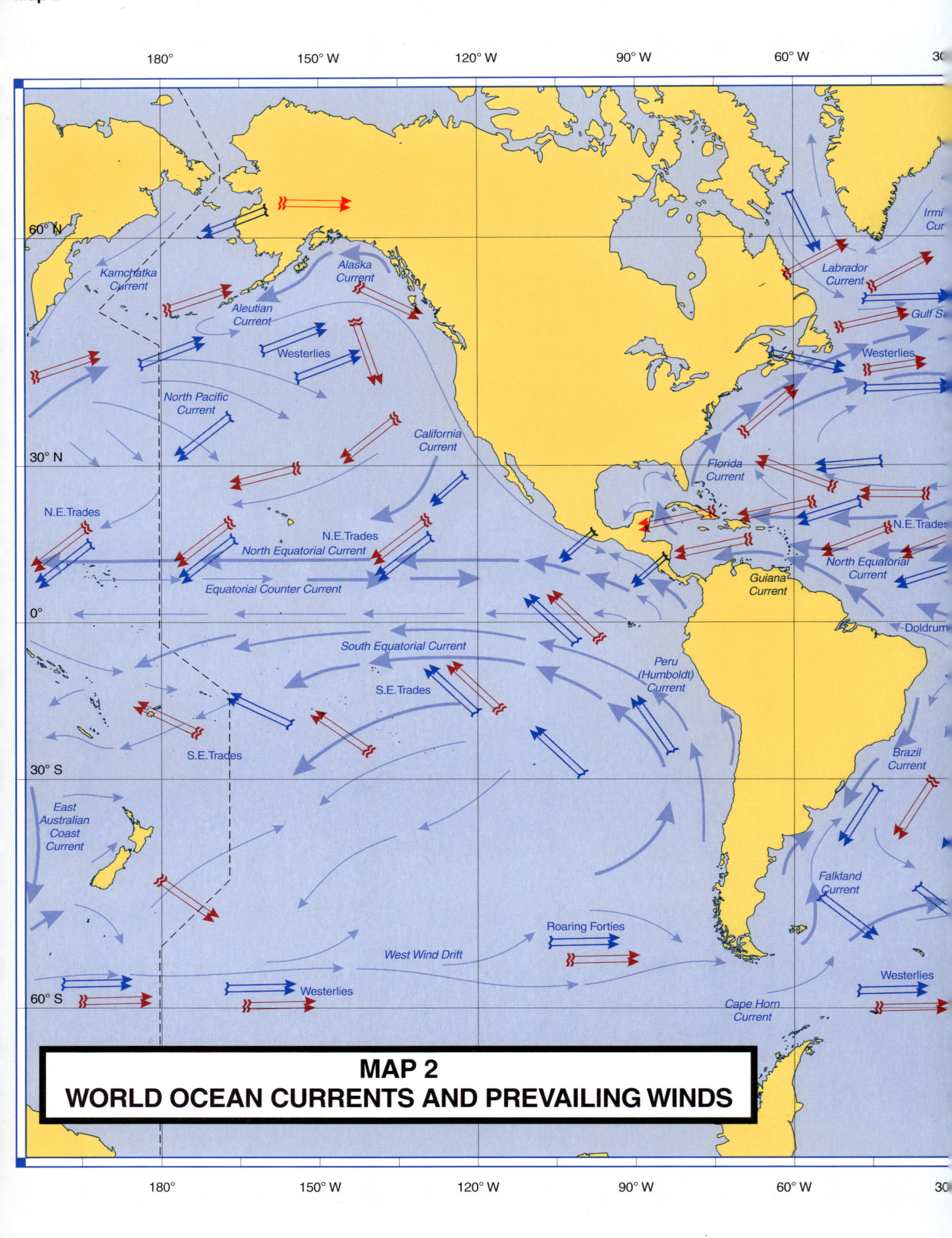

**MAP 2
WORLD OCEAN CURRENTS AND PREVAILING WINDS**

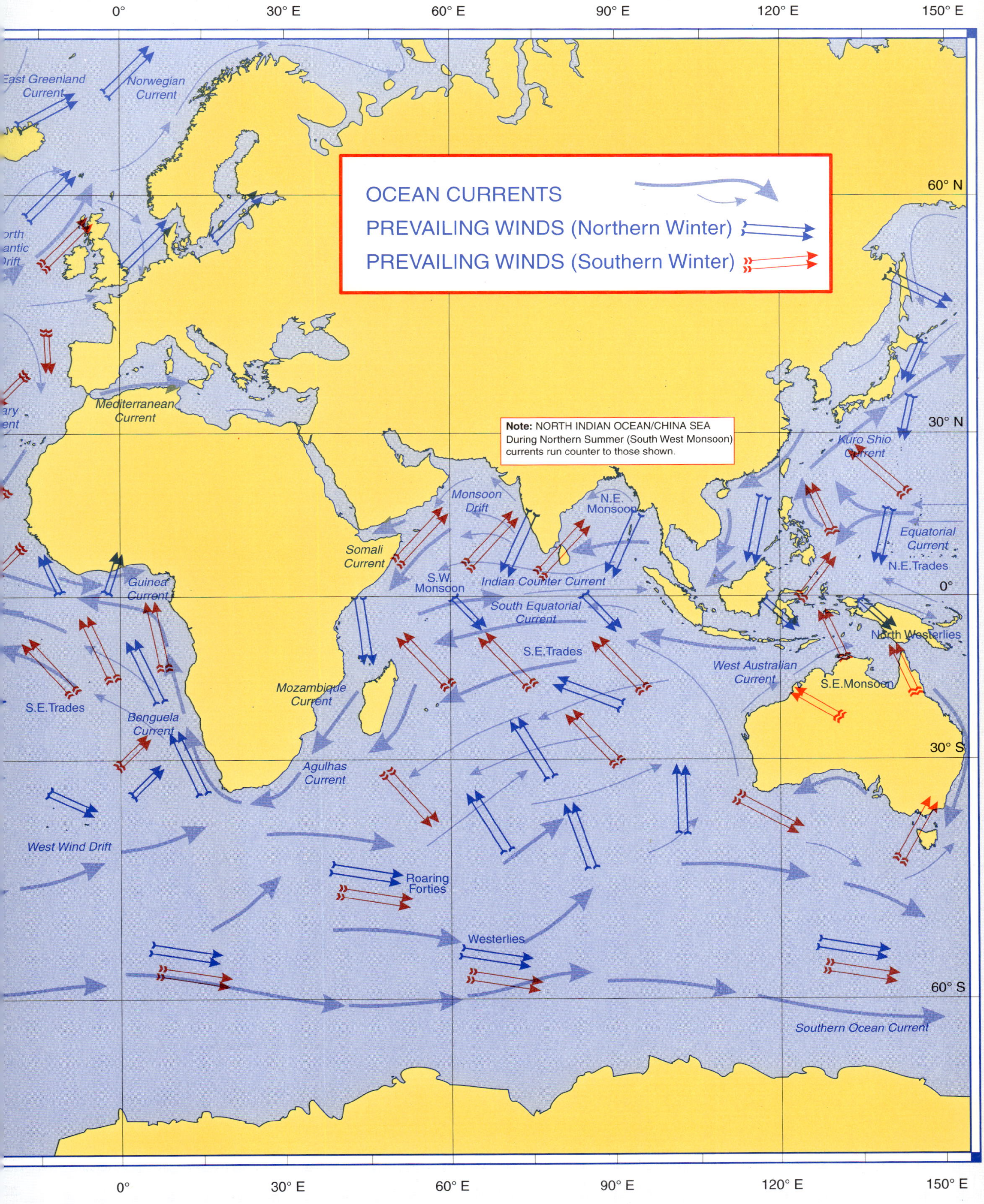
0°
30° E
60° E
90° E
120° E
150° E
OCEAN CURRENTS
PREVAILING WINDS (Northern Winter)
PREVAILING WINDS (Southern Winter)
Note: NORTH INDIAN OCEAN/CHINA SEA During Northern Summer (South West Monsoon) currents run counter to those shown.
60° N
30° N
0°
30° S
60° S
East Greenland Current
Norwegian Current
Mediterranean Current
Guinea Current
S.E.Trades
Benguela Current
West Wind Drift
Somali Current
Monsoon Drift
S.W. Monsoon
N.E. Monsoon
Indian Counter Current
South Equatorial Current
S.E.Trades
Mozambique Current
Agulhas Current
Roaring Forties
Westerlies
Kuro Shio Current
Equatorial Current
N.E.Trades
North Westerlies
West Australian Current
S.E.Monsoon
Southern Ocean Current

Map 3

Note: International Time Zones are based on the fact that 1° Longitude = 4 minutes of time (15° = 1 hour). It should be noted, however, that many individual countries operate a Summer Time, or Daylight Saving Time system, which may vary from the International Zone time.

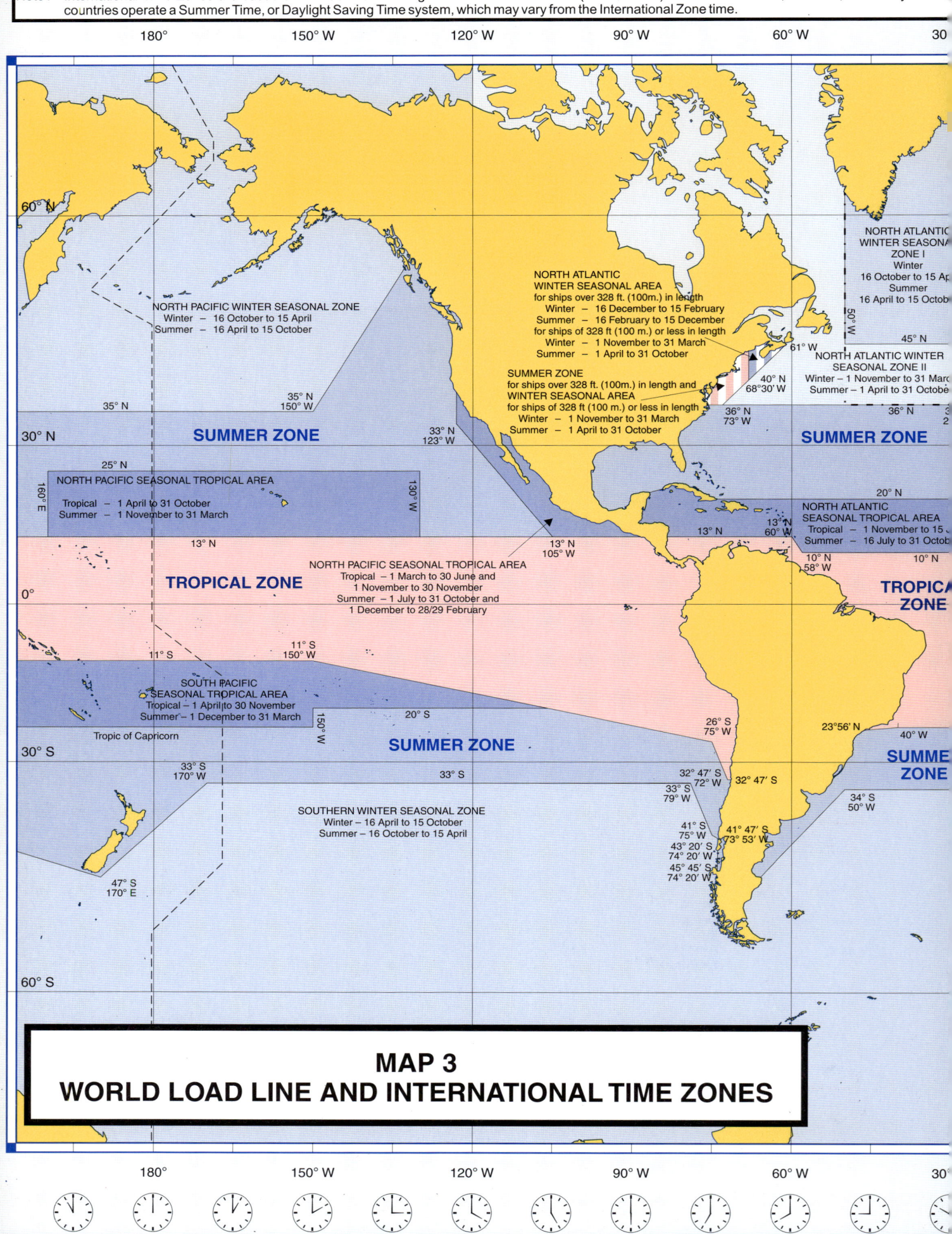

NORTH PACIFIC WINTER SEASONAL ZONE
Winter – 16 October to 15 April
Summer – 16 April to 15 October

NORTH ATLANTIC WINTER SEASONAL AREA
for ships over 328 ft. (100m.) in length
Winter – 16 December to 15 February
Summer – 16 February to 15 December
for ships of 328 ft (100 m.) or less in length
Winter – 1 November to 31 March
Summer – 1 April to 31 October

SUMMER ZONE for ships over 328 ft. (100m.) in length and **WINTER SEASONAL AREA** for ships of 328 ft (100 m.) or less in length
Winter – 1 November to 31 March
Summer – 1 April to 31 October

NORTH ATLANTIC WINTER SEASONAL ZONE I
Winter – 16 October to 15 April
Summer – 16 April to 15 October

NORTH ATLANTIC WINTER SEASONAL ZONE II
Winter – 1 November to 31 March
Summer – 1 April to 31 October

SUMMER ZONE

NORTH PACIFIC SEASONAL TROPICAL AREA
Tropical – 1 April to 31 October
Summer – 1 November to 31 March

NORTH ATLANTIC SEASONAL TROPICAL AREA
Tropical – 1 November to 15
Summer – 16 July to 31 October

NORTH PACIFIC SEASONAL TROPICAL AREA
Tropical – 1 March to 30 June and
1 November to 30 November
Summer – 1 July to 31 October and
1 December to 28/29 February

TROPICAL ZONE

SOUTH PACIFIC SEASONAL TROPICAL AREA
Tropical – 1 April to 30 November
Summer – 1 December to 31 March

Tropic of Capricorn

SUMMER ZONE

SOUTHERN WINTER SEASONAL ZONE
Winter – 16 April to 15 October
Summer – 16 October to 15 April

MAP 3
WORLD LOAD LINE AND INTERNATIONAL TIME ZONES

| GMT+11 | GMT±12 | GMT -11 | GMT -10 | GMT -9 | GMT -8 | GMT -7 | GMT -6 | GMT -5 | GMT -4 | GMT -3 | GMT |

© Shipping Guides Ltd., Reigate, United Kingdom

Map 3

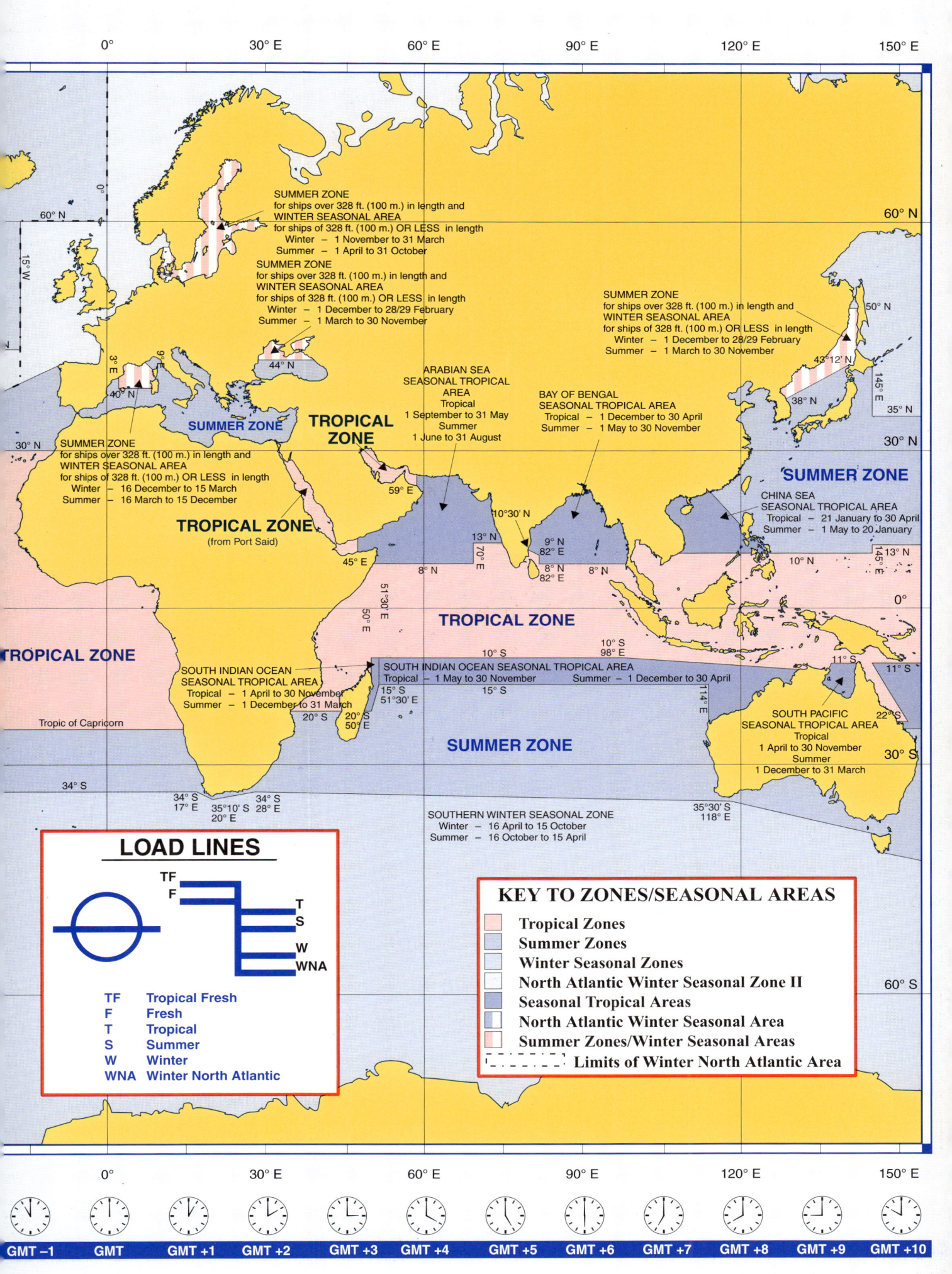

LOAD LINES

- TF — Tropical Fresh
- F — Fresh
- T — Tropical
- S — Summer
- W — Winter
- WNA — Winter North Atlantic

KEY TO ZONES/SEASONAL AREAS

- Tropical Zones
- Summer Zones
- Winter Seasonal Zones
- North Atlantic Winter Seasonal Zone II
- Seasonal Tropical Areas
- North Atlantic Winter Seasonal Area
- Summer Zones/Winter Seasonal Areas
- ----- Limits of Winter North Atlantic Area

Zone and Seasonal Area Annotations

SUMMER ZONE for ships over 328 ft. (100 m.) in length and **WINTER SEASONAL AREA** for ships of 328 ft. (100 m.) OR LESS in length
- Winter — 1 November to 31 March
- Summer — 1 April to 31 October

SUMMER ZONE for ships over 328 ft. (100 m.) in length and **WINTER SEASONAL AREA** for ships of 328 ft. (100 m.) OR LESS in length
- Winter — 1 December to 28/29 February
- Summer — 1 March to 30 November

SUMMER ZONE for ships over 328 ft. (100 m.) in length and **WINTER SEASONAL AREA** for ships of 328 ft. (100 m.) OR LESS in length
- Winter — 1 December to 28/29 February
- Summer — 1 March to 30 November

SUMMER ZONE for ships over 328 ft. (100 m.) in length and **WINTER SEASONAL AREA** for ships of 328 ft. (100 m.) OR LESS in length
- Winter — 16 December to 15 March
- Summer — 16 March to 15 December

TROPICAL ZONE (from Port Said)

ARABIAN SEA SEASONAL TROPICAL AREA
- Tropical — 1 September to 31 May
- Summer — 1 June to 31 August

BAY OF BENGAL SEASONAL TROPICAL AREA
- Tropical — 1 December to 30 April
- Summer — 1 May to 30 November

CHINA SEA SEASONAL TROPICAL AREA
- Tropical — 21 January to 30 April
- Summer — 1 May to 20 January

SOUTH INDIAN OCEAN SEASONAL TROPICAL AREA
- Tropical — 1 April to 30 November
- Summer — 1 December to 31 March

SOUTH INDIAN OCEAN SEASONAL TROPICAL AREA
- Tropical — 1 May to 30 November
- Summer — 1 December to 30 April

SOUTH PACIFIC SEASONAL TROPICAL AREA
- Tropical — 1 April to 30 November
- Summer — 1 December to 31 March

SOUTHERN WINTER SEASONAL ZONE
- Winter — 16 April to 15 October
- Summer — 16 October to 15 April

Reference coordinates shown on map
60° N, 50° N, 43°12′ N, 38° N, 35° N, 44° N, 40° N, 30° N, 13° N, 10°30′ N, 9° N 82° E, 8° N 82° E, 8° N, 0°, 10° S, 11° S, 15° S 51°30′ E, 15° S, 20° S 50° E, 22° S, 30° S, 34° S 17° E, 34° S 20° E, 35°10′ S 28° E, 35°30′ S 118° E, 60° S
3° E, 9° E, 45° E, 51°30′ E, 59° E, 70° E, 98° E, 114° E, 145° E

Tropic of Capricorn

Time zones: GMT −1, GMT, GMT +1, GMT +2, GMT +3, GMT +4, GMT +5, GMT +6, GMT +7, GMT +8, GMT +9, GMT +10

Load Line Zones information is from the Merchant Shipping (Load Lines) Regulations 1968

Map 4

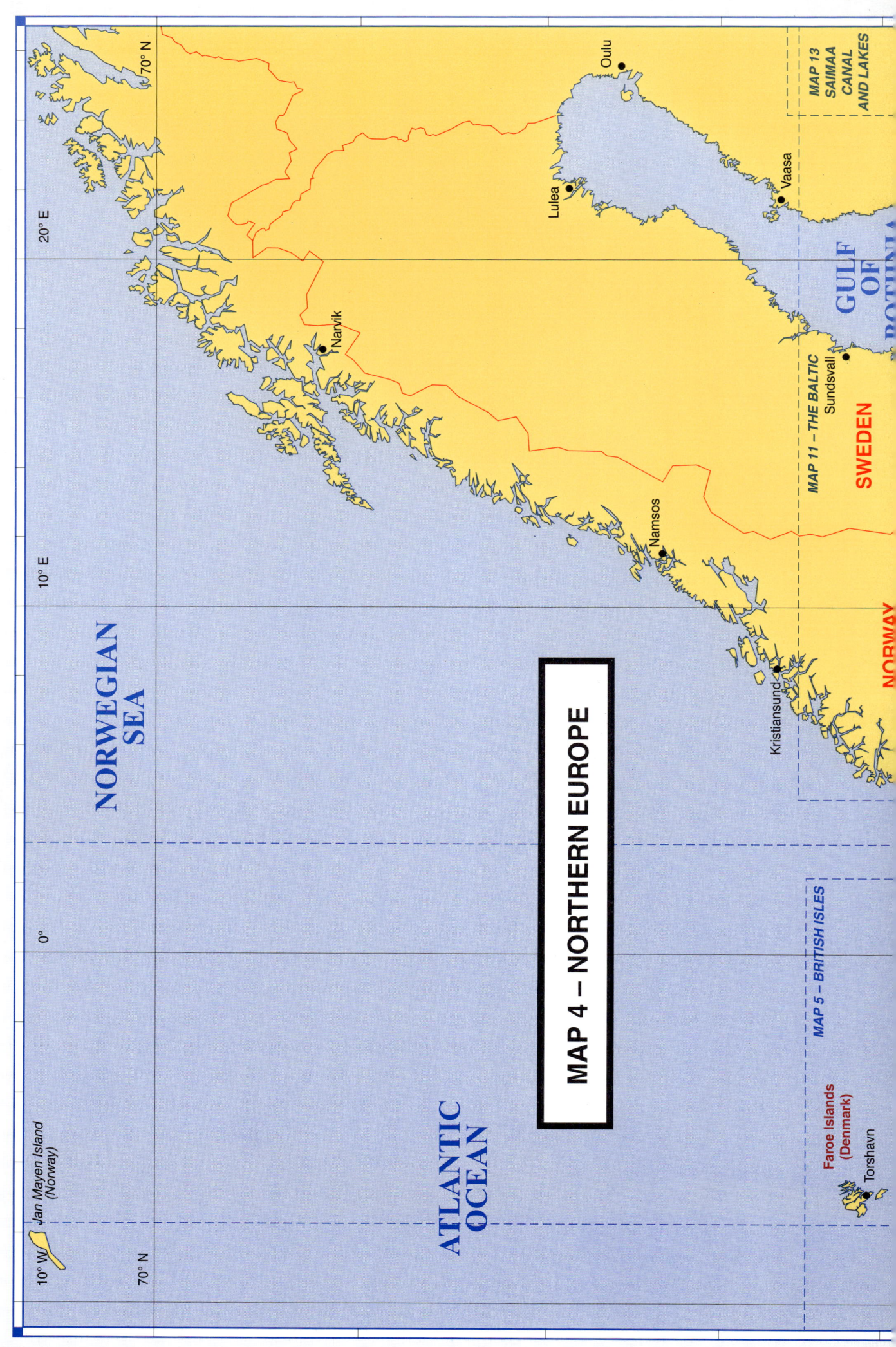

MAP 4 – NORTHERN EUROPE

- Oulu
- Vaasa
- Luleå
- Narvik
- Sundsvall
- Namsos
- Kristiansund
- Torshavn, Faroe Islands (Denmark)
- Jan Mayen Island (Norway)

NORWEGIAN SEA

ATLANTIC OCEAN

GULF OF BOTHNIA

SWEDEN

NORWAY

MAP 11 – THE BALTIC
MAP 13 – SAIMAA CANAL AND LAKES
MAP 5 – BRITISH ISLES

© Shipping Guides Ltd., Reigate, England

Map 4

MAP 5 – BRITISH ISLES

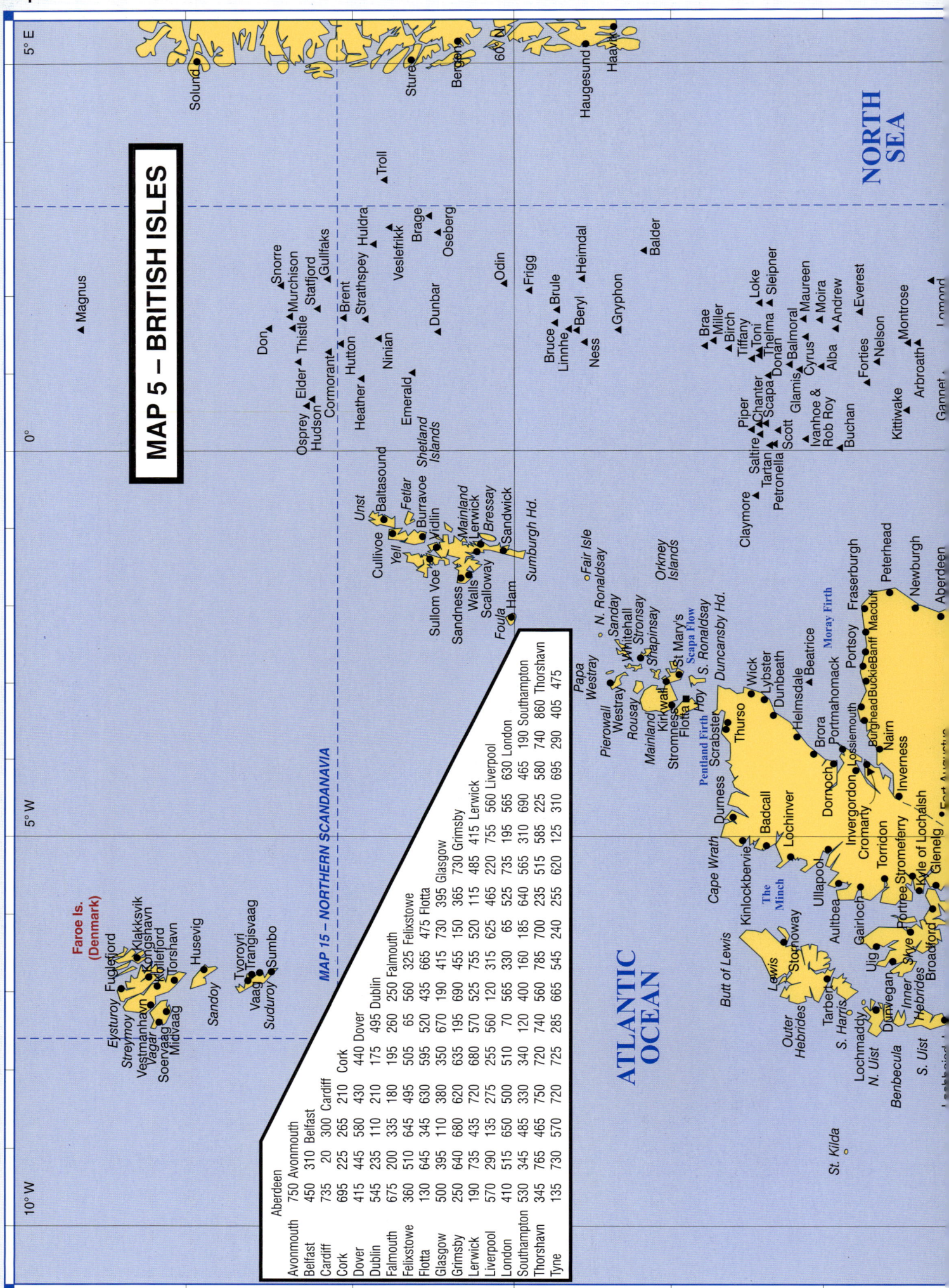

	Aberdeen	Avonmouth	Belfast	Cardiff	Cork	Dover	Dublin	Falmouth	Felixstowe	Flotta	Glasgow	Grimsby	Lerwick	Liverpool	London	Southampton	Thorshavn
Avonmouth	750																
Belfast	450	310															
Cardiff	735	20	300														
Cork	695	225	265	210													
Dover	415	445	580	430	440												
Dublin	545	235	110	210	175	495											
Falmouth	675	200	335	180	195	260	325										
Felixstowe	360	510	645	495	505	65	560	325									
Flotta	130	645	345	630	595	325	435	665	475								
Glasgow	500	395	110	380	350	580	190	415	630	395							
Grimsby	250	640	680	620	635	195	690	455	150	365	730						
Lerwick	190	735	435	720	680	415	525	755	565	115	485	415					
Liverpool	570	290	135	275	255	560	120	315	625	465	220	755	560				
London	410	515	650	510	510	70	565	330	65	330	735	195	565	630			
Southampton	530	345	485	330	340	160	400	120	185	515	530	310	690	225	190		
Thorshavn	345	765	465	750	720	785	560	740	700	240	615	565	310	695	740	860	
Tyne	135	730	570	720	725	285	665	545	240	255	620	125	310	695	290	405	475

MAP 15 – NORTHERN SCANDANAVIA

Map 5

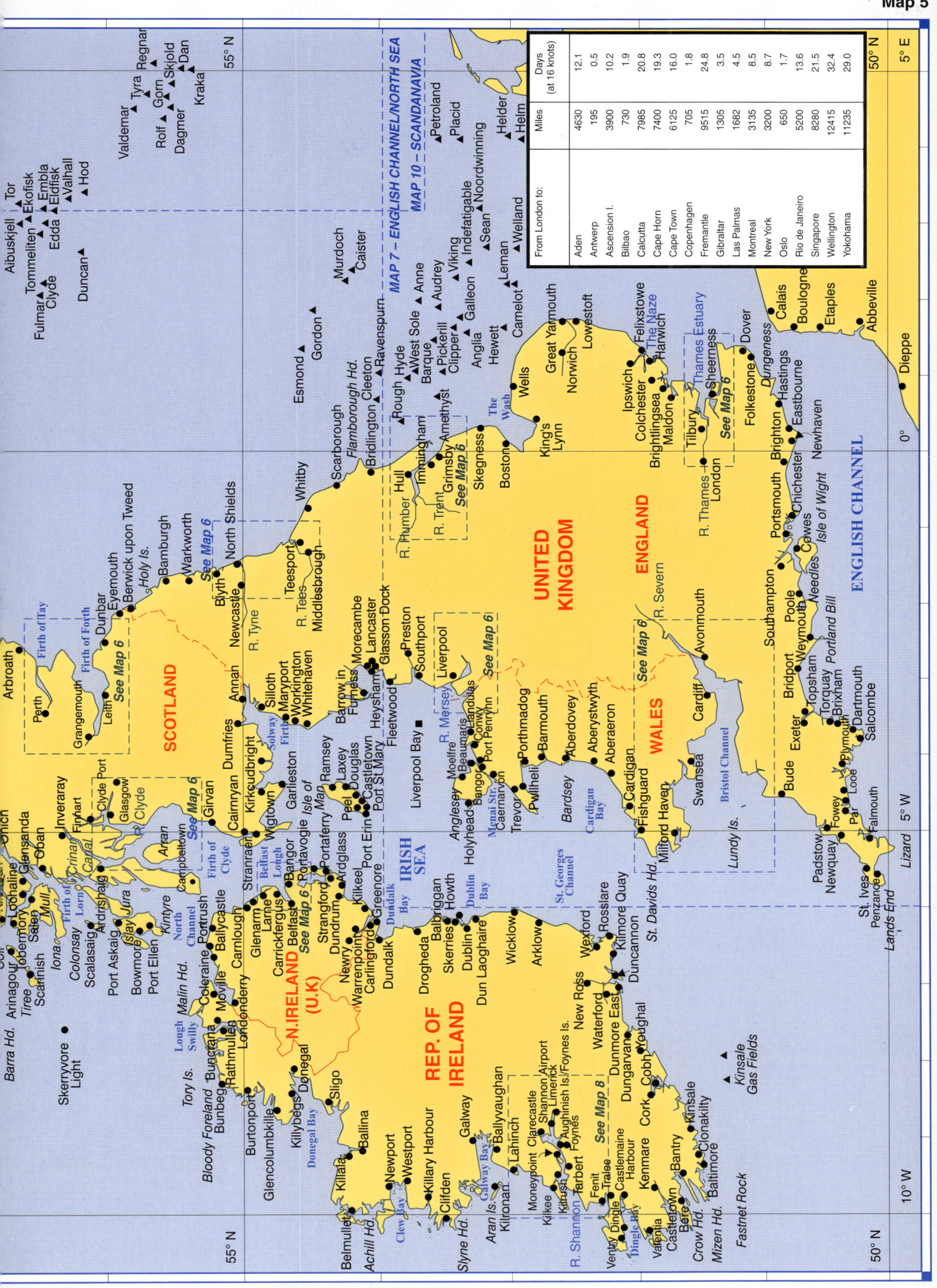

From London to:	Miles	Days (at 16 knots)
Aden	4630	12.1
Antwerp	195	0.5
Ascension I.	3900	10.2
Bilbao	730	1.9
Calcutta	7985	20.8
Cape Horn	7400	19.3
Cape Town	6125	16.0
Copenhagen	705	1.8
Fremantle	9515	24.8
Gibraltar	1305	3.5
Las Palmas	1682	4.5
Montreal	3135	8.5
New York	3200	8.7
Oslo	650	1.7
Rio de Janeiro	5200	13.6
Singapore	8280	21.5
Wellington	12415	32.4
Yokohama	11235	29.0

MAP 7 – ENGLISH CHANNEL/NORTH SEA
MAP 10 – SCANDANAVIA

Oil/gas fields (North Sea): Aibuskjell, Tor, Tyra, Regnar, Tommeliten, Ekofisk, Fulmar, Clyde, Embla, Eldfisk, Edda, Valhall, Duncan, Hod, Valdemar, Rolf, Gorm, Skjold, Dagmer, Dan, Kraka, Murdoch, Caister, Esmond, Gordon, Ravenspurn, Rough, Hyde, West Sole, Anne, Audrey, Viking, Indefatigable, Barque, Pickerill, Galleon, Sean, Noordwinning, Clipper, Anglia, Hewett, Camelot, Leman, Welland, Petroland, Placid, Helder, Helm

SCOTLAND – Arbroath, Perth, Firth of Tay, Grangemouth, Firth of Forth, Leith, Dunbar, Eyemouth, Berwick upon Tweed, Holy Is., Bamburgh, Warkworth, Blyth, North Shields, Newcastle, R. Tyne, Teesport, Middlesbrough, Whitby, Scarborough, Flamborough Hd., Bridlington, Cleeton, Hull, R. Humber, Immingham, Grimsby, R. Trent, Amethyst, Skegness, The Wash, Boston, King's Lynn, Wells, Great Yarmouth, Lowestoft, Norwich

UNITED KINGDOM / ENGLAND – Ipswich, Colchester, Felixstowe, Harwich, The Naze, Brightlingsea, Maldon, Tilbury, R. Thames, London, Thames Estuary, Sheerness, Dover, Folkestone, Dungeness, Hastings, Eastbourne, Newhaven, Brighton, Chichester, Portsmouth, Cowes, Isle of Wight, Needles, Poole, Southampton, Weymouth, Portland Bill, Bridport, Exeter, Topsham, Torquay, Brixham, Dartmouth, Salcombe, Plymouth, Looe, Fowey, Par, Falmouth, Penzance, Lands End, St. Ives, Newquay, Padstow, Bude, Avonmouth, R. Severn, Bristol Channel

WALES – Cardiff, Swansea, Milford Haven, Fishguard, Cardigan, Cardigan Bay, Aberaeron, Aberystwyth, Aberdovey, Barmouth, Porthmadog, Pwllheli, Bardsey, Trevor, Caernarvon, Menai Str., Bangor, Anglesey, Moelfre, Holyhead, Beaumaris, Conwy, Port Penrhyn, Landudno

Liverpool, R. Mersey, Liverpool Bay, Southport, Preston, Fleetwood, Heysham, Morecambe, Glasson Dock, Lancaster, Barrow in Furness, Isle of Man, Ramsey, Laxey, Douglas, Peel, Castletown, Port St. Mary, Port Erin, Whitehaven, Workington, Maryport, Silloth, Annan, Dumfries, Solway Firth, Kirkcudbright, Wigtown, Garlieston, Cairnryan, Stranraer

See Map 6 (various locations)

N. IRELAND (U.K) – Portpatrick, Portavogie, Ardglass, Kilkeel, Strangford, Strangford Lough, Portaferry, Bangor, Belfast, Belfast Lough, Carrickfergus, Larne, Glenarm, Ballycastle, Portrush, Coleraine, Moville, Londonderry, Lough Foyle, Warrenpoint, Newry, Carlingford, North Channel, Malin Hd., Lough Swilly, Bloody Foreland, Bunbeg, Burtonport, Tory Is., Rathmullen

REP. OF IRELAND – Donegal, Killybegs, Donegal Bay, Sligo, Ballina, Killala, Belmullet, Achill Hd., Clew Bay, Newport, Westport, Clifden, Slyne Hd., Aran Is., Killary Harbour, Ballyvaughan, Galway, Galway Bay, Inishmore, Lahinch, Aughinish Is./Foynes Is., Kilrush, Kilkee, Fenit, Tralee, Moneypoint, Clarecastle, Shannon Airport, Limerick, Foynes, R. Shannon, Ventry, Dingle, Dingle Bay, Castlemaine Harbour, Valentia, Castletown, Bere, Crow Hd., Mizen Hd., Kenmare, Bantry, Baltimore, Clonakilty, Kinsale, Cobh, Cork, Youghal, Dungarvan, Dunmore East, Waterford, New Ross, Duncannon, Kilmore Quay, Rosslare, Wexford, St. Georges Channel, Arklow, Wicklow, Dun Laoghaire, Dublin, Dublin Bay, Howth, Skerries, Balbriggan, Drogheda, Dundalk, Dundalk Bay, Greenore, St. Davids Hd., Lundy Is., Fastnet Rock, Kinsale Gas Fields

(Western islands) Barra Hd., Skerryvore Light, Tiree, Arinagour, Coll, Mull, Iona, Scalasaig, Colonsay, Jura, Scarinish, Tobermory, Glensanda, Salen, Oban, Lochaline, Lismore, Firth of Lorn, Crinan, Canal, Inveraray, Ardrishaig, Fyne, Firth of Clyde, Clyde, Glasgow, Port Ellen, Bowmore, Port Askaig, Islay, Kintyre, Campbeltown, Aran, Girvan

IRISH SEA, **ENGLISH CHANNEL**

55° N, 50° N, 10° W, 5° W, 0°, 5° E

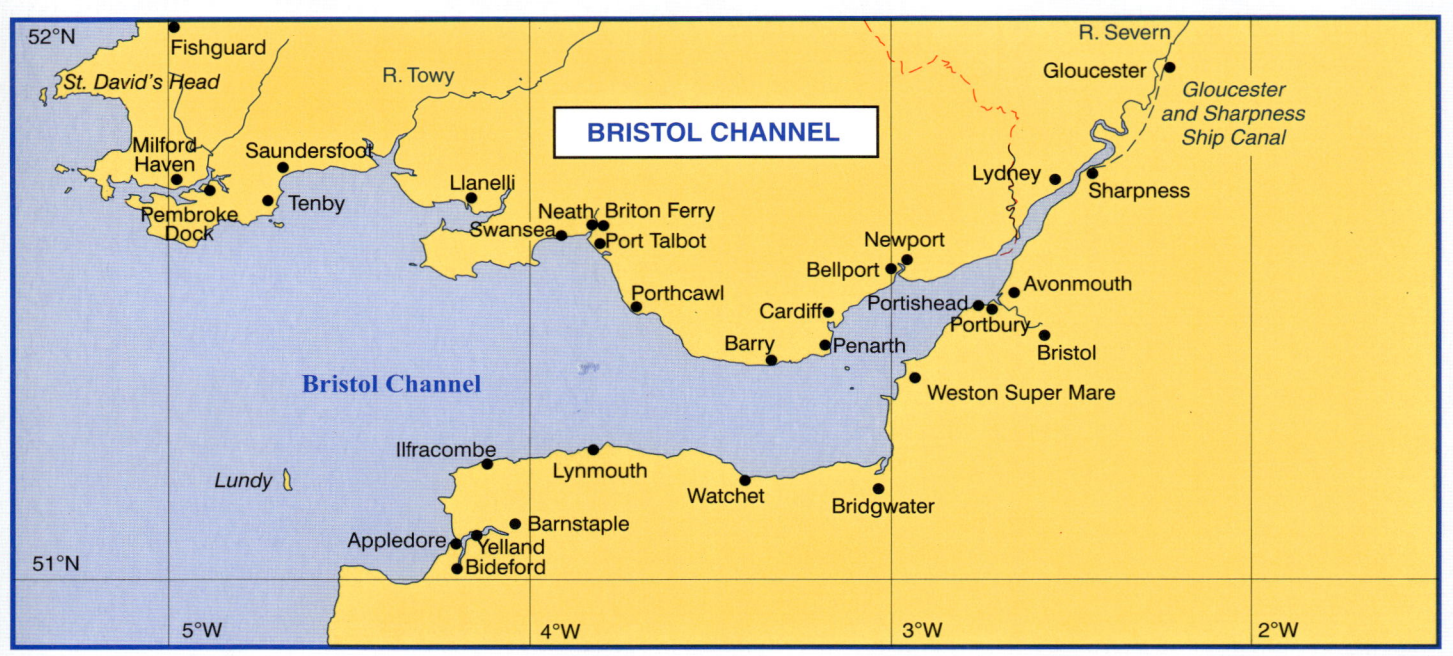

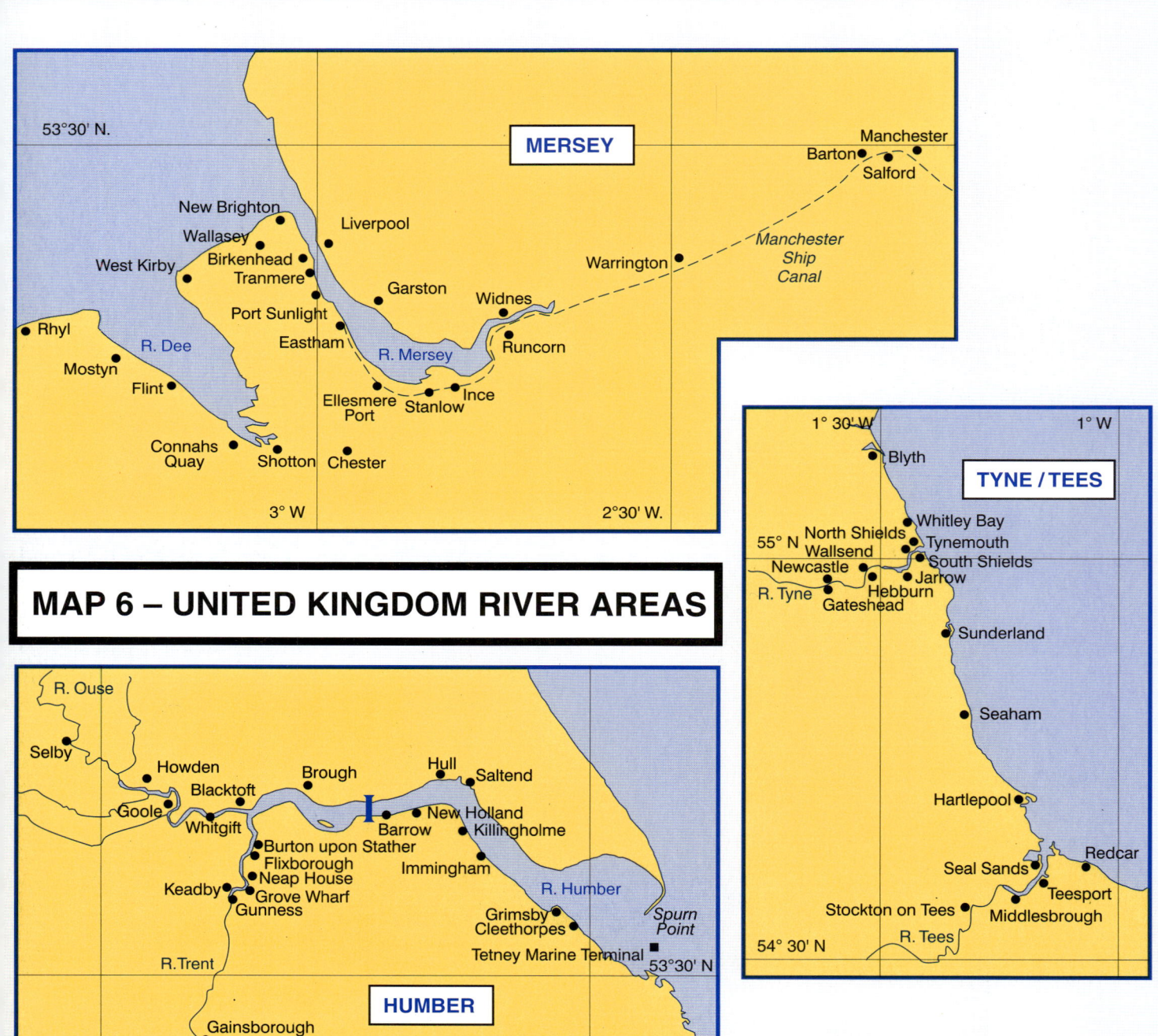

Map 6

MAP 6 – UNITED KINGDOM RIVER AREAS

BRISTOL CHANNEL

Fishguard, St. David's Head, Milford Haven, Pembroke Dock, Saundersfoot, Tenby, R. Towy, Llanelli, Neath, Briton Ferry, Swansea, Port Talbot, Porthcawl, Cardiff, Barry, Penarth, Newport, Bellport, Portishead, Portbury, Avonmouth, Bristol, Weston Super Mare, R. Severn, Gloucester, Gloucester and Sharpness Ship Canal, Lydney, Sharpness, Bristol Channel, Lundy, Ilfracombe, Lynmouth, Watchet, Bridgwater, Appledore, Yelland, Barnstaple, Bideford

52°N, 51°N, 5°W, 4°W, 3°W, 2°W

MERSEY

53°30' N., New Brighton, Wallasey, West Kirby, Birkenhead, Tranmere, Port Sunlight, Eastham, Liverpool, Garston, Widnes, Runcorn, Ince, Stanlow, Ellesmere Port, Chester, Rhyl, Mostyn, Flint, R. Dee, Connahs Quay, Shotton, Warrington, Manchester Ship Canal, Barton, Salford, Manchester, R. Mersey

3° W, 2°30' W.

TYNE / TEES

Blyth, Whitley Bay, North Shields, Tynemouth, Wallsend, South Shields, Newcastle, Jarrow, Hebburn, Gateshead, R. Tyne, Sunderland, Seaham, Hartlepool, Seal Sands, Redcar, Teesport, Stockton on Tees, Middlesbrough, R. Tees

1°30' W, 1° W, 55° N, 54°30' N

HUMBER

R. Ouse, Selby, Howden, Blacktoft, Goole, Whitgift, Brough, Hull, Saltend, New Holland, Barrow, Killingholme, Burton upon Stather, Flixborough, Neap House, Grove Wharf, Keadby, Gunness, Immingham, R. Humber, Grimsby, Cleethorpes, Spurn Point, Tetney Marine Terminal, R. Trent, Gainsborough

1° W, 0°, 53°30' N

© Shipping Guides Ltd., Reigate, England

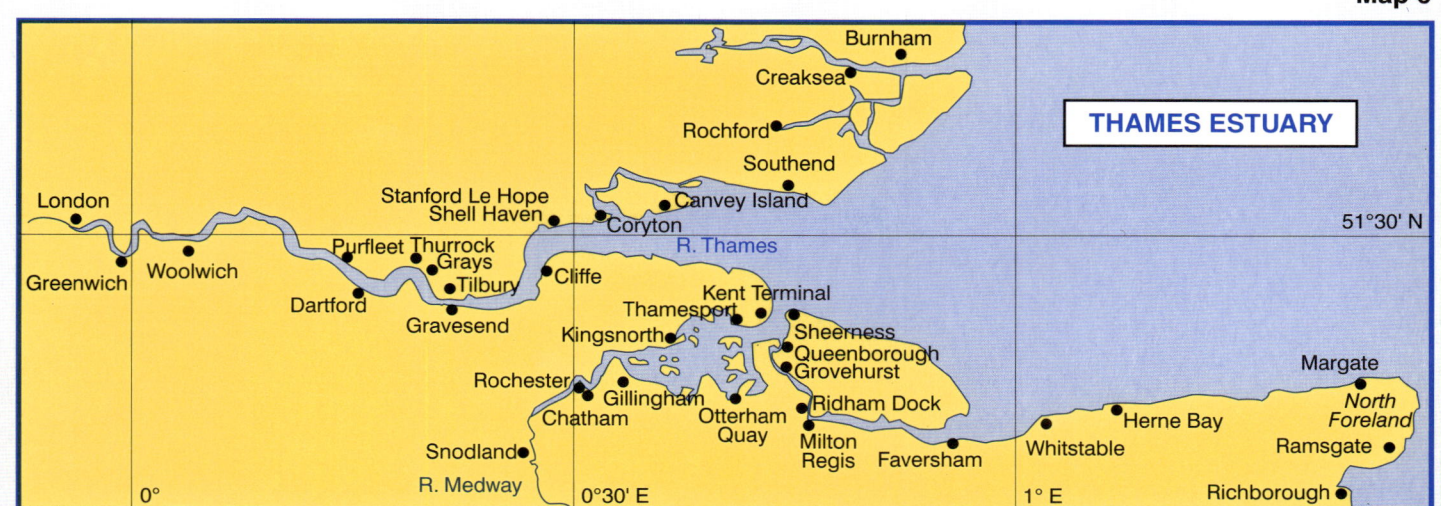

Map 6

THAMES ESTUARY

- London
- Greenwich
- Woolwich
- Purfleet
- Dartford
- Thurrock
- Grays
- Tilbury
- Gravesend
- Stanford Le Hope
- Shell Haven
- Coryton
- Cliffe
- Canvey Island
- Southend
- Rochford
- Creaksea
- Burnham
- R. Thames
- Kent Terminal
- Thamesport
- Kingsnorth
- Sheerness
- Queenborough
- Grovehurst
- Ridham Dock
- Rochester
- Gillingham
- Chatham
- Otterham Quay
- Milton Regis
- Faversham
- Snodland
- R. Medway
- Whitstable
- Herne Bay
- Margate
- North Foreland
- Ramsgate
- Richborough

51°30' N
0° 0°30' E 1° E

CLYDE

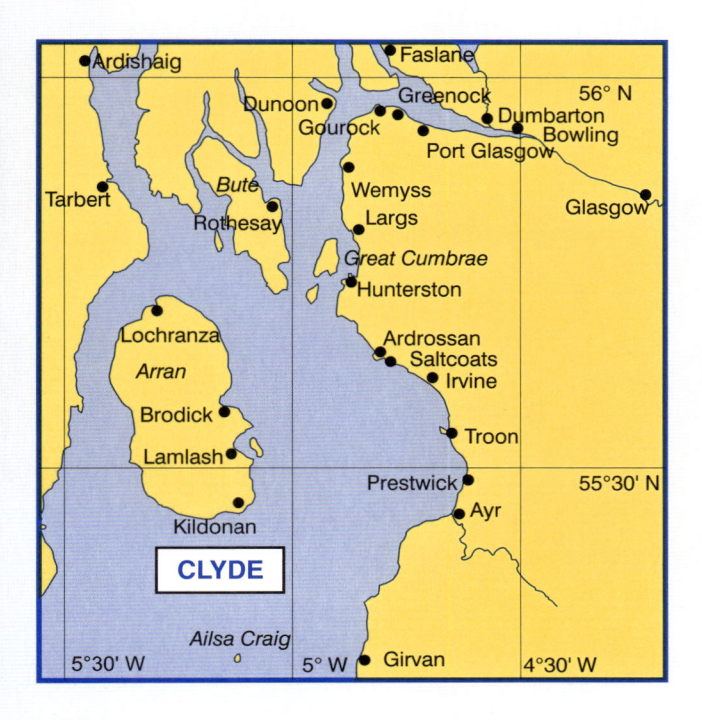

- Ardishaig
- Faslane
- Dunoon
- Greenock
- Gourock
- Dumbarton
- Bowling
- Port Glasgow
- Glasgow
- Tarbert
- Bute
- Rothesay
- Wemyss
- Largs
- Great Cumbrae
- Hunterston
- Lochranza
- Arran
- Ardrossan
- Saltcoats
- Irvine
- Brodick
- Lamlash
- Troon
- Prestwick
- Ayr
- Kildonan
- Ailsa Craig
- Girvan

56° N
55°30' N
5°30' W 5° W 4°30' W

BELFAST LOUGH

- Larne
- Whitehead
- Carrickfergus
- Kilroot
- Bangor
- Belfast
- Strangford Lough
- Portavogie

6° W 5°30' W
54°30' N

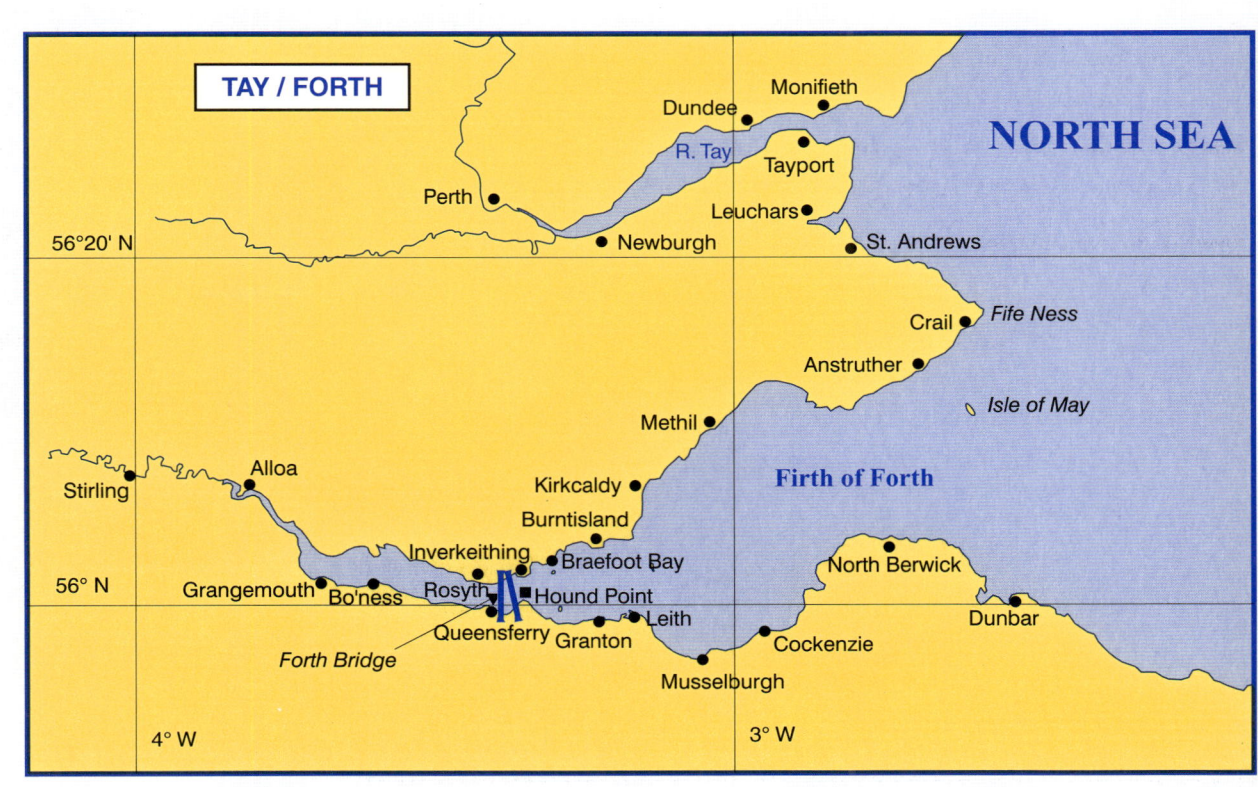

TAY / FORTH

- Dundee
- Monifieth
- R. Tay
- Tayport
- Perth
- Leuchars
- Newburgh
- St. Andrews
- Crail
- Fife Ness
- Anstruther
- Isle of May
- Methil
- Stirling
- Alloa
- Firth of Forth
- Kirkcaldy
- Burntisland
- Inverkeithing
- Braefoot Bay
- North Berwick
- Grangemouth
- Bo'ness
- Rosyth
- Hound Point
- Queensferry
- Granton
- Leith
- Cockenzie
- Dunbar
- Forth Bridge
- Musselburgh

NORTH SEA

56°20' N
56° N
4° W 3° W

Map 7 – English Channel / North Sea

From Dover Strait to:-	Miles	Days (at 16 knots)
Cape Horn	7310	19.0
Cape Leeuwin[1]	9485	24.7
Cape of Good Hope	6060	15.7
Genoa	2080	5.4
Gibraltar	1235	3.2
Lombok Strait[1]	8970	23.3
Malta	2220	5.7
Montreal	3160	8.2
New York	3255	8.4
Panama Canal (Cristobal)	4675	12.1
Port Said	3145	8.1
Singapore	8160	21.2
Sunda Strait[1]	8355	21.7
Yokohama[2]	11055	28.7

[1] via Suez Canal
[2] via Suez Canal and Singapore

© Shipping Guides Ltd., Reigate, England

Map 7

From Antwerp to:-	Miles	Days (at 16 knots)
Archangel	2090	5.4
Bombay	6325	16.5
Copenhagen	705	1.8
Dakar	2590	6.7
Gibraltar	1370	3.6
Halifax	2805	7.3
Lisbon	1090	2.9
Manila	9635	25.1
Melbourne	11115	28.9
Montevideo	6250	16.3
New York	3390	8.8
Panama Canal (Cristobal)	4805	12.5

	Amsterdam										
Antwerp	175	Antwerp									
Avonmouth	605	580	Avonmouth								
Calais	160	130	460	Calais							
Cherbourg	305	275	320	155	Cherbourg						
Den Helder	50	185	630	165	320	Den Helder					
Dover	160	135	445	20	145	185	Dover				
Europoort	53	135	560	115	260	67	115	Europoort			
Le Havre	275	245	385	115	75	300	115	230	Le Havre		
London (Gravesend)	190	175	515	85	215	205	70	150	185	London (Gravesend)	
Rouen	345	320	455	190	140	370	185	300	70	255	Rouen
St.Helier	390	365	310	215	64	390	205	320	130	275	200	St.Helier
St.Malo	390	365	325	240	90	415	230	345	155	300	225	50	St.Malo
Southampton	285	255	345	140	84	305	120	235	105	190	175	50	165

Map 8

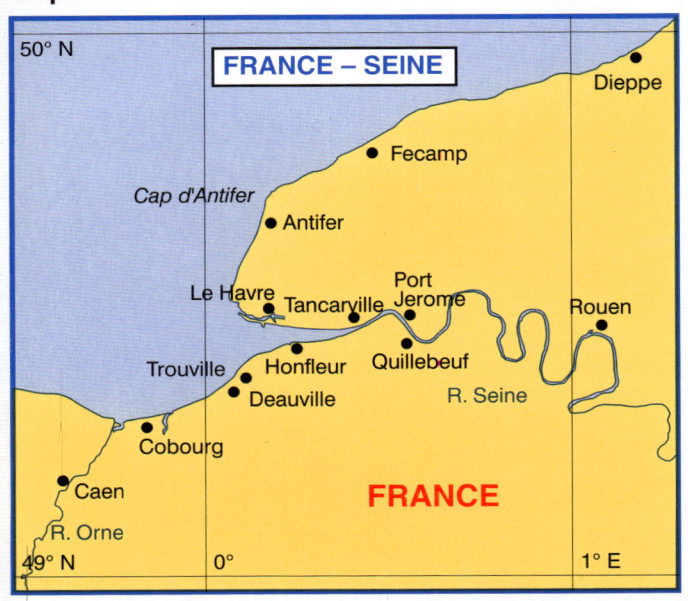

MAP 8
NORTH EUROPEAN COASTAL AREAS

FRANCE – SEINE

- Dieppe
- Fecamp
- Cap d'Antifer
- Antifer
- Le Havre
- Tancarville
- Port Jerome
- Rouen
- Trouville
- Honfleur
- Quillebeuf
- Deauville
- R. Seine
- Cobourg
- Caen
- R. Orne

FRANCE

50° N, 49° N, 0°, 1° E

BELGIUM/NETHERLANDS SCHELDE TO BORKUM

NORTH SEA

NETHERLANDS

- Norderney
- Borkum
- Norrdeich
- Eemshaven
- Delfzijl
- Emden
- Leeuwarden
- Harlingen
- Groningen
- Eems Canal
- Den Helder
- Lemmer
- Ijsselmeer
- Enkhuizen
- Alkmaar
- Hoorn
- Kampen
- Beverwijk
- Purmerend
- Zwolle
- Ymuiden
- Zaandam
- Velsen
- Amsterdam
- Harderwijk
- Deventer
- Katwijk
- Scheveningen
- Leiden
- Zutphen
- The Hague
- Utrecht
- Hook of Holland
- R. Lek
- Europoort
- Vlaardingen
- Rotterdam
- Arnhem
- Maassluis
- Schiedam
- Haaften
- Tiel
- Emmerich
- Ouddorp
- Dordrecht
- Gorinchem
- Nijmegan
- Brouwershaven
- Middelharnis
- Willemsdorp
- R. Rhine
- Moerdijk
- R. Maas
- Zierikzee
- Willemstad
- Oosterhout
- Domburg
- Wemeldinge
- Tilburg
- Westkapelle
- Yerseke
- Bergen Op Zoom
- Middelburg
- Hansweert
- **GERMANY**
- Flushing
- Borsele
- Bats
- Duisborg
- Ruhrort
- Zeebrugge
- Terneuzen
- Krefeld
- Sluiskill
- Sas van Gent
- Antwerp
- Bruges
- Ghent
- Dusseldorf
- Hemikem
- Neuss

BELGIUM

53° N, 52° N, 3° E, 4° E, 5° E, 6° E, 7° E

© Shipping Guides Ltd., Reigate, England

Map 8

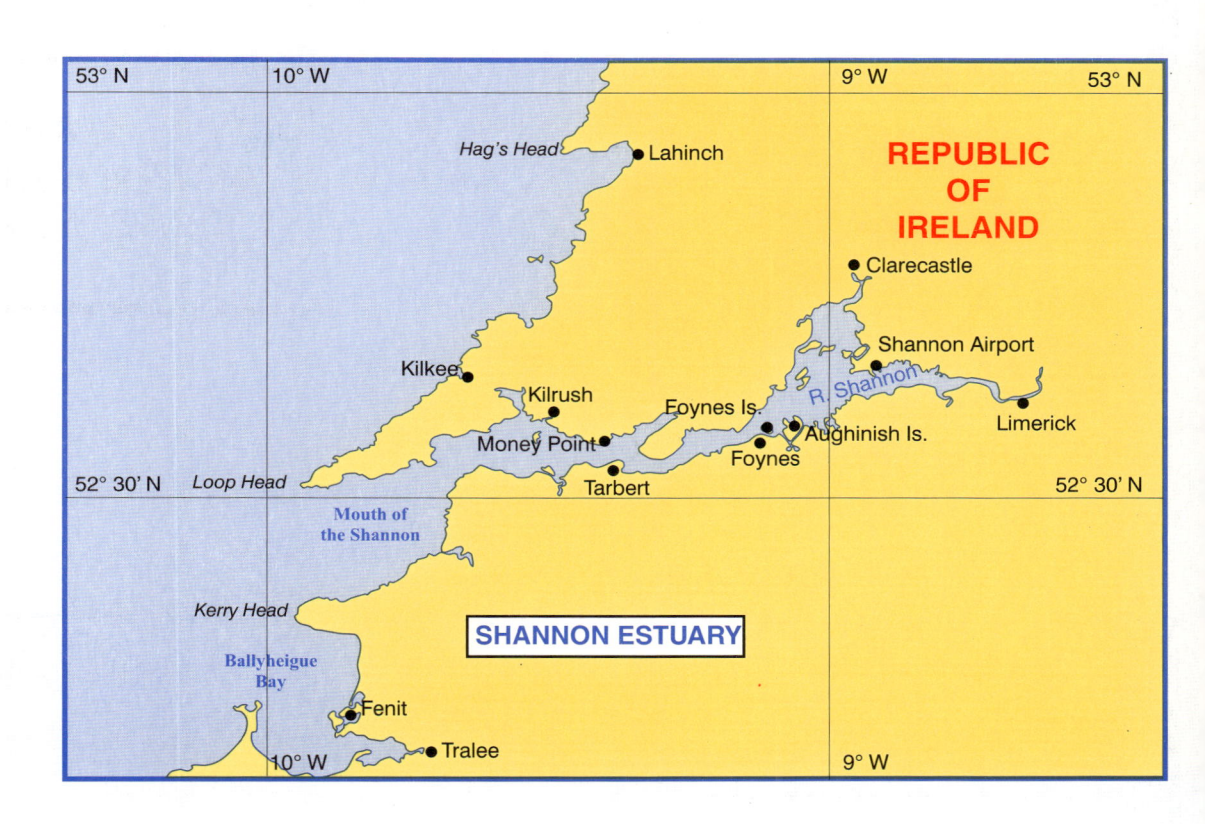

Map 9

Map 9 – European Inland Waterways

MAP 10 – SCANDANAVIA

Map 10

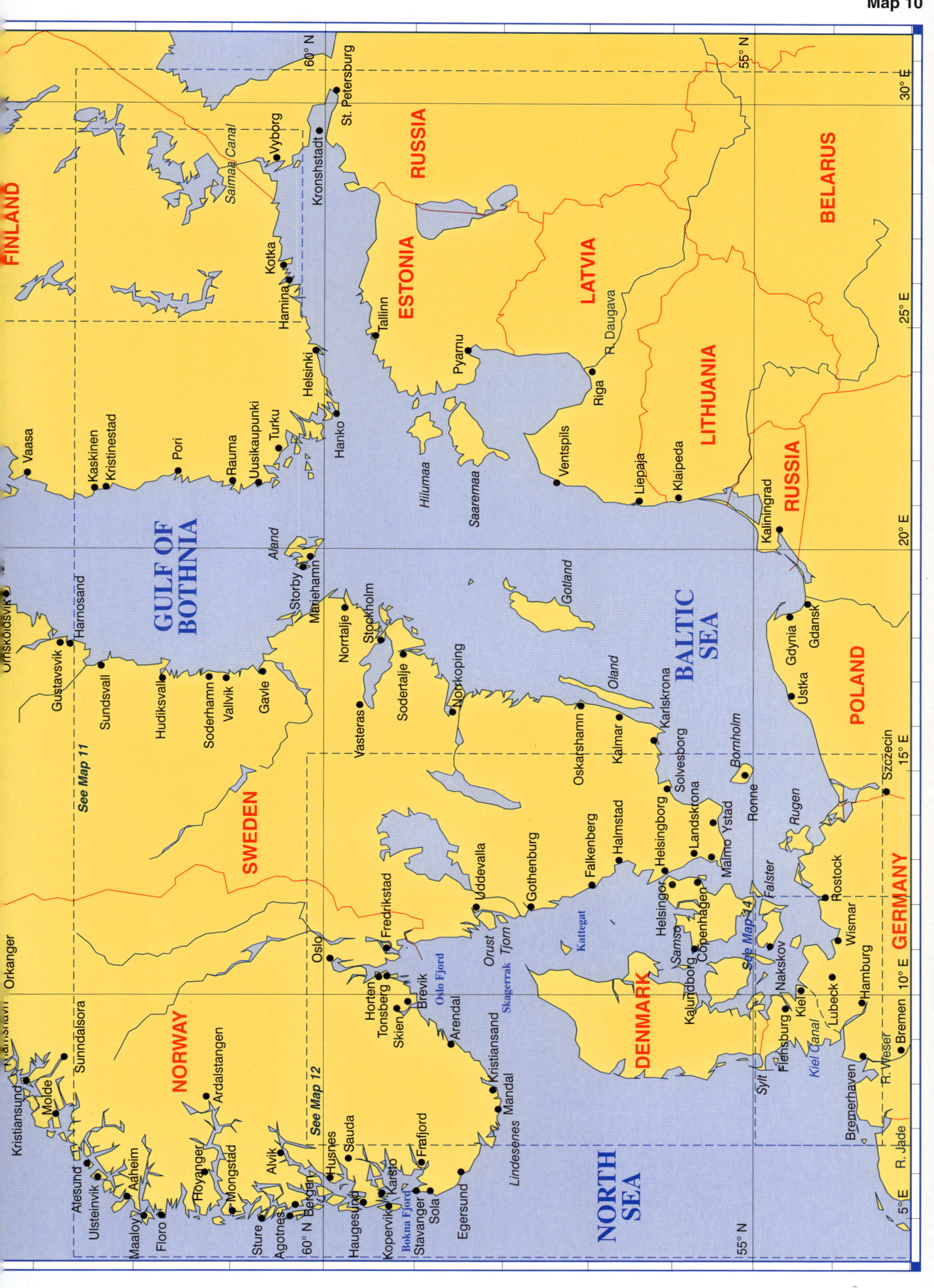

MAP 11 – THE BALTIC

Map 11

Map labels

GULF OF BOTHNIA

FINLAND
- Kaskinen
- Kristinestad
- Pori
- Rauma
- Uusikaupunki
- Naantali
- Turku
- Pargas
- Nagu
- Stromma
- Korpo
- Skinnarvik
- Bromarv
- Ekenas
- Dalsbruk
- Rilaks
- Skogby
- Lappohja
- Hanko
- Koverhar
- Inkoo
- Kantvik
- Porkkala
- Helsinki
- Tolkkinen
- Porvoo
- Isnas
- Lovisa
- Valko
- Kotka
- Hamina
- Baltijeto (Vilia)
- Vyborg/Vysotsk
- Sovetsky
- Primorsk
- Saimaa Canal

Aland, Geta, Saltvik, Kumlinge, Vardo, Storby, Foglo, Mariehamn

GULF OF FINLAND
- Gogland
- See Map 13
- Sestoretsk
- Kronstadt
- Lomonosov
- Petrodvorets
- St. Petersburg
- 60° N

ESTONIA
- Paldiski
- Kopli
- Vanasadam
- Tallinn
- Kesklinna
- Muuga
- Loksa
- Kunda
- Ustluga
- Narva Joessu
- Osmussaar
- Vasalemma
- Kardla
- Vermsi
- Hiiumaa
- Haapsalu
- Emmaste
- Muhu
- Saaremaa
- Nasva
- Roomassaare
- Kihnu
- Pyarnu
- Ruhnu
- Ainazi
- Salacgriva

Swedish coast:
- Johannedal, Lubikenborg
- Utskar, Karlholm, Graso, Oregrund
- mark, Kallero, Hallstavik, ammar, gshamn
- Herrang, Grisslehamn
- Norrtalje, tuna, Flaxenvik, Vaxholm, Stockholm, Sandhamn, ertalje, Dalaro, Orno, Musko, Uto, Nynashamn
- Furusund
- Gotska Sandon
- Faro, Storugns, Farosund, Visby, Slite, Gotland, tehamn, gsvik, Ronehamn

LATVIA
- Mazirbe
- Roja
- Ventspils
- Uzava
- Sarnate
- Pavilosta
- Liepaja
- Mersrags
- Engure
- Jurmala
- Lielupe
- Skulte
- Saulkrasti
- Milgravis
- Riga
- Bolderaja
- Gulf of Riga
- R. Daugava

BALTIC SEA

LITHUANIA
- Butinge
- Palanga
- Klaipeda
- Neringa

RUSSIA
- Kaliningrad
- Baltysk
- Braniewo
- Gulf of Danzig

Polish coast:
- dyslawowo, Puck, Hel, Gdynia, Sopot, Gdansk (Danzig), Nowy Port, Elblag
- R. Nogat
- R. Vistula

From Copenhagen to:

From Copenhagen to:	Miles	Days (at 16 kts)
CAPE HORN	7999	20.8
CAPE TOWN	6715	17.5
HALIFAX	3030	7.9
GIBRALTAR	1915	5.0
LERWICK	565	1.5
NEW YORK	3675	9.6
NEWCASTLE	590	1.6
NUUK	2305	6.0
PANAMA	5355	14.0
RIO DE JANEIRO	5795	15.1
TORSHAVN	760	2.0

Distance table

	Bergen	Copenhagen	Gdansk	Gothenburg	Hamburg	Helsinki	Kiel	Narvik	Oslo	Pitea	Riga	St. Petersburg	Stavanger	Stockholm	Trondheim	Vaaso	Vardo
Copenhagen	460																
Gdansk	725	275															
Gothenburg	350	137	405														
Hamburg	490	255	435	325													
Helsinki	1010	555	425	690	720												
Kiel	505	162	350	235	90	630											
Narvik	630	1060	1325	955	1080	1610	1095										
Oslo	380	275	545	160	445	820	355	975									
Pitea	1225	780	680	900	950	535	860	1830	1040								
Riga	925	480	335	610	640	320	550	1530	745	590							
St. Petersburg	1150	700	565	830	870	171	780	1750	965	680	460						
Stavanger	106	385	650	270	410	935	425	715	300	1150	850	1075					
Stockholm	880	430	345	555	590	240	500	1480	695	400	265	385	805				
Trondheim	310	755	1020	645	765	1305	785	410	675	1520	1225	1445	400	1175			
Vaaso	1135	685	590	815	855	435	765	1740	950	155	495	580	1060	305	1430		
Vardo	1000	1440	1705	1325	1455	1990	1470	440	1355	2210	1910	2130	1085	1860	760	2115	

MAP 12 – ENTRANCE TO THE BALTIC

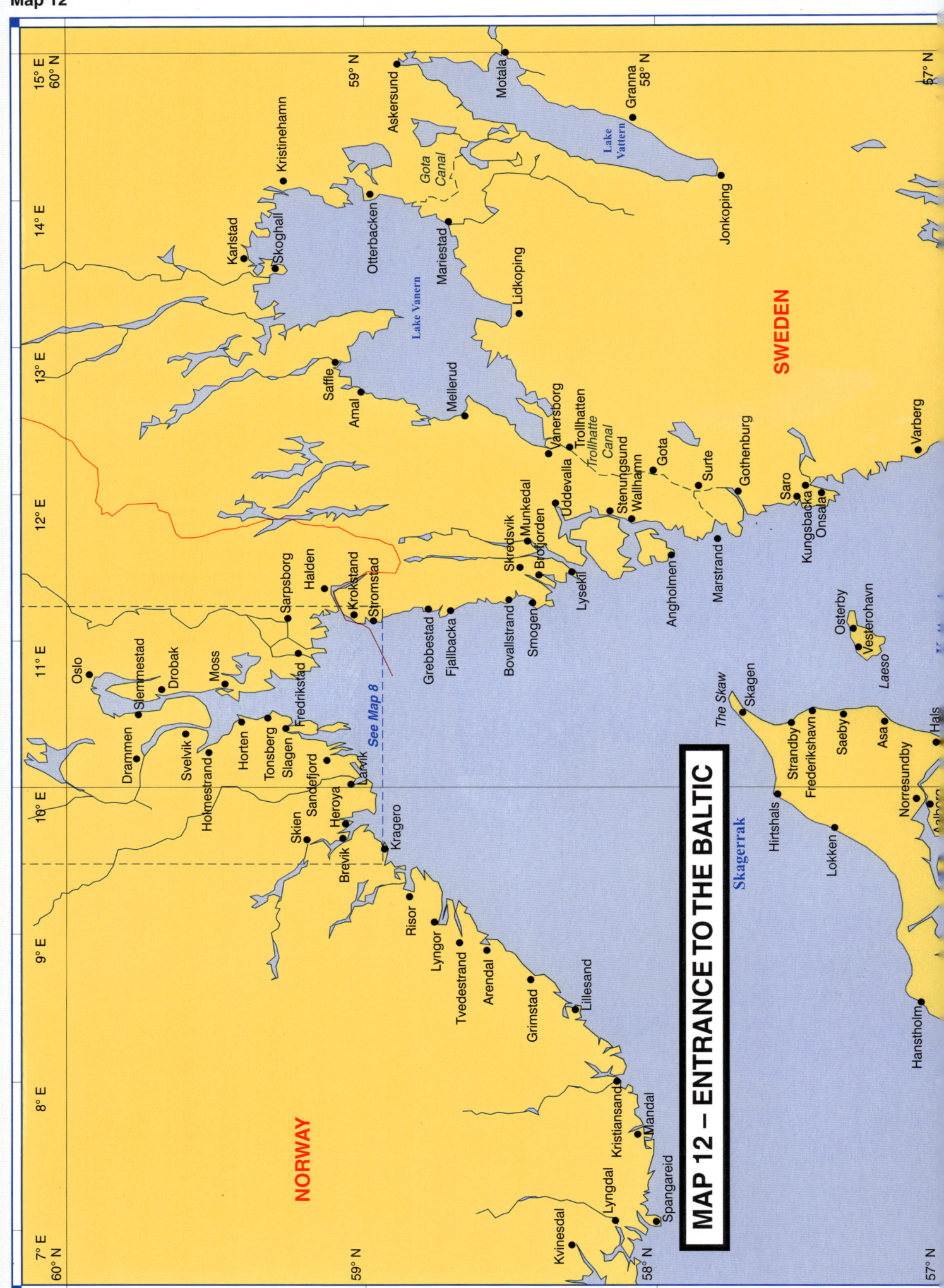

DENMARK
GERMANY
POLAND
BALTIC SEA
Jutland
Zealand
Funen
Lolland
Falster
Mon
Langeland
Als
Aero
Samso
Sejero
Fehmarn
Fano
Romo
Sylt
Fohr
Amrum
North Frisian Islands
Anholt Is.
Bornholm (Denmark)
C. Arkona
The Sound
Samso Belt
Great Belt
Little Belt
Langeland Belt
Fehmarn Belt
Kiel Bay
Mecklenburg Bay
Kiel Canal
R.Elbe
See Map 14
56° N
55° N
54° N
8° E
9° E
10° E
11° E
12° E
13° E
14° E
15° E
Thyboron
Lemvig
Torsminde
Ringkobing
Nymindegab
Skive
Hobro
Kongsdal
Hadsund
Mariager
Udbyhoj
Voer
Randers
Grenaa
Studstrup
Knebel
Ebeltoft
Aarhus
Norsminde
Hov
Horsens
Juelsminde
Vejle
Fredericia
Strib
Middelfart
Lyngsodde
Skaerbaek
Kolding
Haderslev
Arosund
Aabenraa
Ensted
Augustenborg
Sonderborg
Mommark
Grasten
Flensburg
Hojer
Esbjerg
Ribe
Nordby
List
Hornum
Wyk
Husum
Tonning
Busum
Schleswig
Rendsberg
Kappeln
Gelting
Eckernforde
Holtenau
Kiel
Laboe
Heiligenhafen
Orth
Puttgarden
Fehmarnsund
Grossenbrode
Neustadt
Lubeck
Travemunde
Wismar
Warnemunde
Rostock
Ribnitz
Barth
Zingst
Stralsund
Barhoft
Lauterbach
Sassnitz
Wolgast
Peenemunde
Zinnowitz
Swinoujscie
Wolin
Ueckermunde
Police
Szczecin
Itzehoe
Gluckstadt
Brunsbuttel
Cuxhaven
Hamburg
Stadersand
Butzfleth
Bremerhaven
Nordenham
Brake
Bremen
Wilhelmshaven
Emden
Eemshaven
Delfzijl
Assens
Faborg
Svendborg
Troense
Soby
Aeroskobing
Marstal
Rudkobing
Spodsbjerg
Bagenkop
Nyborg
Odense
Bogense
Lindoe
Kerteminde
Reerso
Korsor
Skaelskor
Gulfhavn
Stignaesvaerkets
Kaerbaekominde
Lohals
Naestved
Vordingborg
Masnedoevaerket
Kragenaes
Bandholm
Nakskov
Rodby
Sakskobing
Guldborg
Nykobing
Nysted
Gedser
Orehoved
Visgnaes
Stubbekobing
Stege
Kalvehave
Praesto
Fakse Ladeplads
Rodvig
Koge
Roskilde
Holbaek
Kyndby
Nykobing
Rorvig
Hundested
Frederiksvaerk
Lynaes
Frederikssund
Kalundborg
Asnaes
Havnso
Ballen
Maarup
Kolby Kas
Gilleleje
Helsingor
Snekkersten
Niva
Vedbaek
Tarbaek
Tuborg Havn
Copenhagen
Kastrup
Amager
Dragor
Molle
Arild
Torekov
Bastad
Halmstad
Angelholm
Jonstorp
Hoganas
Helsingborg
Raa
Landskrona
Lomma
Malmo
Limhamn
Klagshamn
Trelleborg
Falsterbo
Ystad
Kivik
Simrishamn
Ahus
Solvesborg
Stilleryd
Kolo
Ronneby
Karlshamn
Sandvig
Allinge
Hasle
Svaneke
Ronne
Nekso
Anholt

Map 13

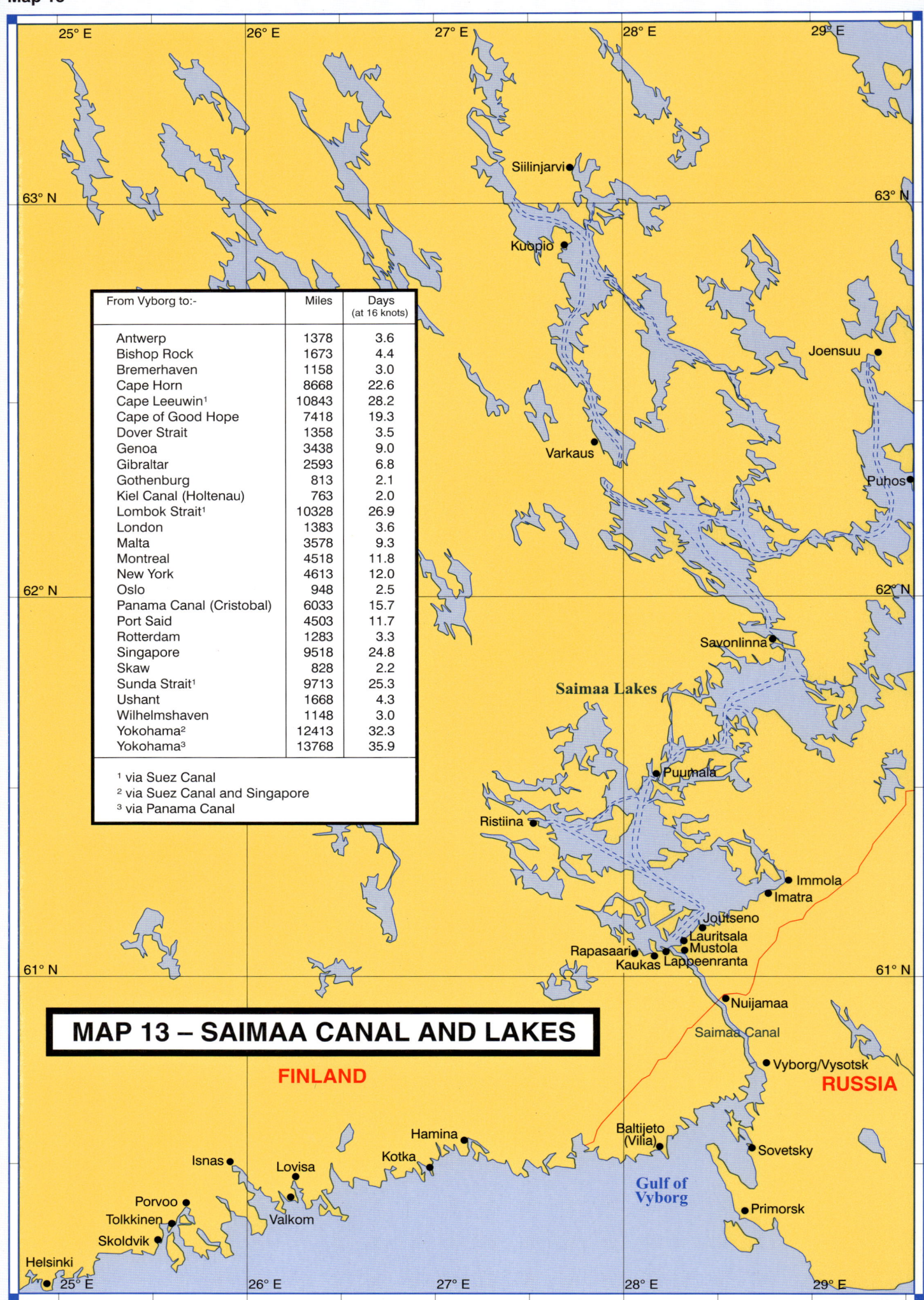

MAP 13 – SAIMAA CANAL AND LAKES

FINLAND | **RUSSIA**

Gulf of Vyborg

Saimaa Lakes

Saimaa Canal

From Vyborg to:-	Miles	Days (at 16 knots)
Antwerp	1378	3.6
Bishop Rock	1673	4.4
Bremerhaven	1158	3.0
Cape Horn	8668	22.6
Cape Leeuwin[1]	10843	28.2
Cape of Good Hope	7418	19.3
Dover Strait	1358	3.5
Genoa	3438	9.0
Gibraltar	2593	6.8
Gothenburg	813	2.1
Kiel Canal (Holtenau)	763	2.0
Lombok Strait[1]	10328	26.9
London	1383	3.6
Malta	3578	9.3
Montreal	4518	11.8
New York	4613	12.0
Oslo	948	2.5
Panama Canal (Cristobal)	6033	15.7
Port Said	4503	11.7
Rotterdam	1283	3.3
Singapore	9518	24.8
Skaw	828	2.2
Sunda Strait[1]	9713	25.3
Ushant	1668	4.3
Wilhelmshaven	1148	3.0
Yokohama[2]	12413	32.3
Yokohama[3]	13768	35.9

[1] via Suez Canal
[2] via Suez Canal and Singapore
[3] via Panama Canal

Places labelled on map: Siilinjarvi, Kuopio, Joensuu, Varkaus, Puhos, Savonlinna, Puumala, Ristiina, Immola, Imatra, Joutseno, Rapasaari, Kaukas, Lauritsala, Mustola, Lappeenranta, Nuijamaa, Vyborg/Vysotsk, Baltijeto (Vilja), Sovetsky, Primorsk, Hamina, Kotka, Lovisa, Valkom, Isnas, Porvoo, Tolkkinen, Skoldvik, Helsinki

© Shipping Guides Ltd., Reigate, England

Map 14

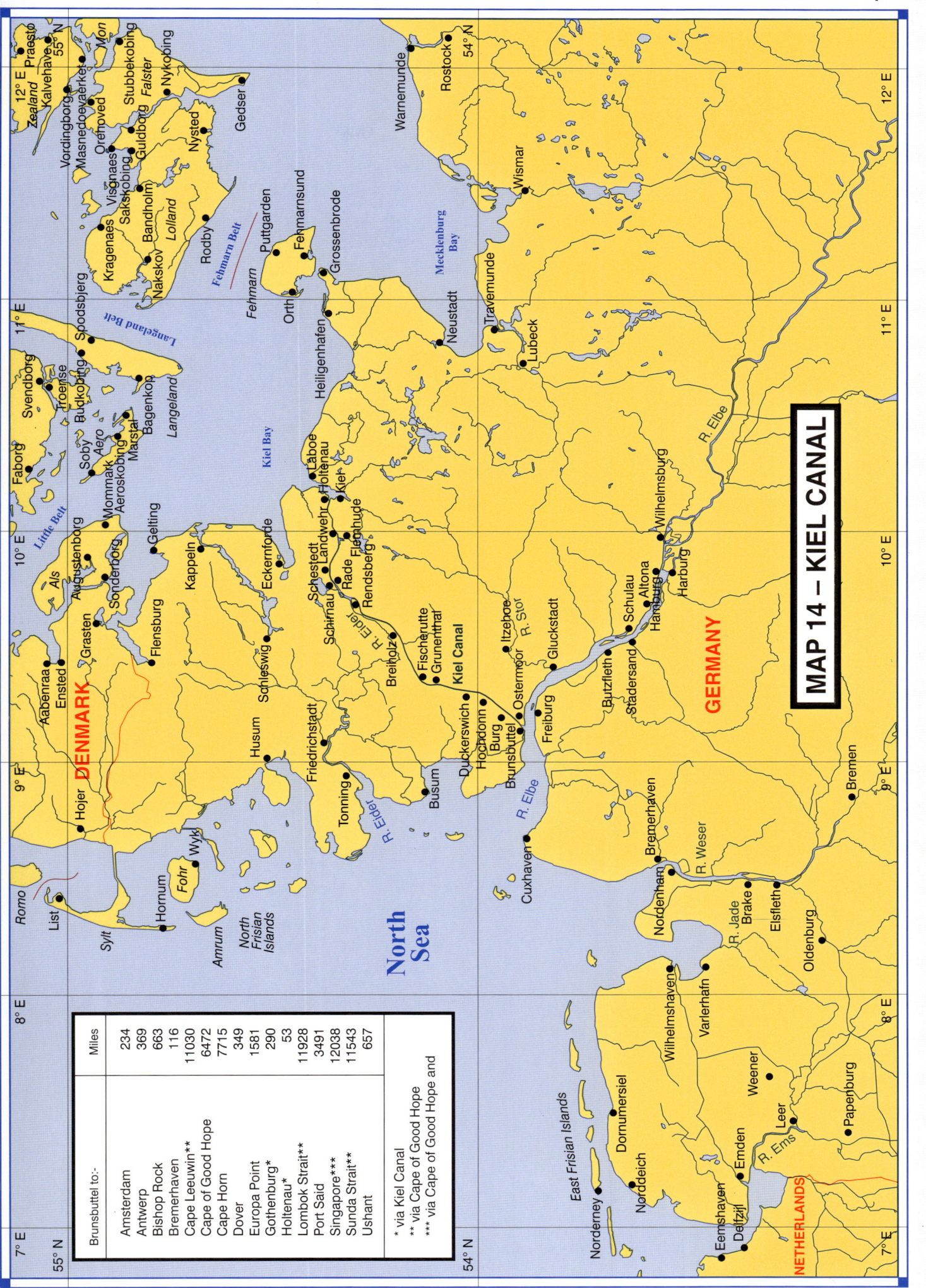

MAP 14 – KIEL CANAL

Brunsbuttel to:-	Miles
Amsterdam	234
Antwerp	369
Bishop Rock	663
Bremerhaven	116
Cape Leeuwin**	11030
Cape of Good Hope	6472
Cape Horn	7715
Dover	349
Europa Point	1581
Gothenburg*	290
Holtenau*	53
Lombok Strait**	11928
Port Said	3491
Singapore***	12038
Sunda Strait**	11543
Ushant	657

* via Kiel Canal
** via Cape of Good Hope
*** via Cape of Good Hope and

© Shipping Guides Ltd., Reigate, England

MAP 15 – NORTHERN SCANDANAVIA

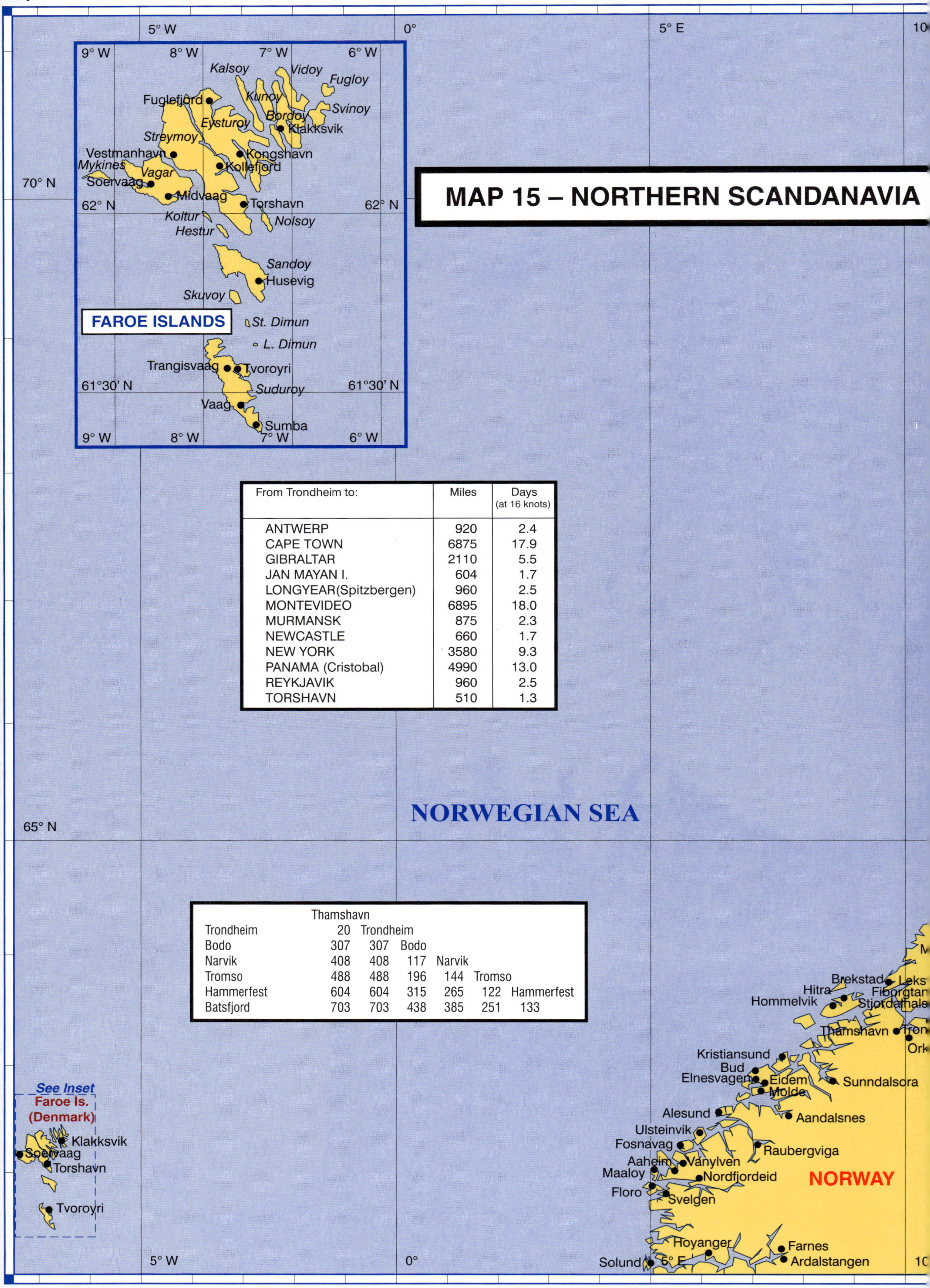

Faroe Islands

Kalsoy, Vidoy, Fugloy, Fuglefjord, Kunoy, Svinoy, Eysturoy, Bordoy, Klakksvik, Streymoy, Kongshavn, Vestmanhavn, Kollefjord, Mykines, Vagar, Soervaag, Midvaag, Torshavn, Koltur, Nolsoy, Hestur, Sandoy, Husevig, Skuvoy, St. Dimun, L. Dimun, Trangisvaag, Tvoroyri, Suduroy, Vaag, Sumba

FAROE ISLANDS

From Trondheim to:	Miles	Days (at 16 knots)
ANTWERP	920	2.4
CAPE TOWN	6875	17.9
GIBRALTAR	2110	5.5
JAN MAYAN I.	604	1.7
LONGYEAR (Spitzbergen)	960	2.5
MONTEVIDEO	6895	18.0
MURMANSK	875	2.3
NEWCASTLE	660	1.7
NEW YORK	3580	9.3
PANAMA (Cristobal)	4990	13.0
REYKJAVIK	960	2.5
TORSHAVN	510	1.3

NORWEGIAN SEA

	Thamshavn				
Trondheim	20	Trondheim			
Bodo	307	307	Bodo		
Narvik	408	408	117	Narvik	
Tromso	488	488	196	144	Tromso
Hammerfest	604	604	315	265	122	Hammerfest
Batsfjord	703	703	438	385	251	133

See Inset Faroe Is. (Denmark)
Klakksvik, Soervaag, Torshavn, Tvoroyri

NORWAY

Brekstad, Leks, Hitra, Fiborgtan, Hommelvik, Stjordalms, Thamshavn, Tron, Ork, Kristiansund, Bud, Elnesvagen, Eidem, Sunndalsora, Molde, Alesund, Aandalsnes, Ulsteinvik, Fosnavag, Raubergviga, Aaheim, Vanylven, Maaloy, Nordfjordeid, Floro, Svelgen, Hoyanger, Farnes, Solund, Ardalstangen

© Shipping Guides Ltd., Reigate, England

Map 15

	Vallvik	Hudiksvall	Ornskoldsvik	Skelleftehamn
Hudiksvall	44			
Ornskoldsvik	141	127		
Skelleftehamn	272	258	160	
Lulea	315	308	210	64

MAP 16 – WHITE SEA / BARENTS SEA

From Murmansk to:	Miles	Days (at 16 knots)
Antwerp	1725	4.5
Cape Horn	8895	23.2
Cape Town	7670	20.0
Copenhagen	1530	4.0
Gibraltar	2895	7.5
Halifax	3545	9.2
Longyear (Spitsbergen)	710	1.9
Oslo	1450	3.8
Panama (Cristobal)	5660	14.7
Rio de Janeiro	7000	18.2
Vladivostock	12825	33.4
Tyne	1465	3.8

Map 16

Kara Sea

- Cape Nassau
- Cape Zhelaniya
- Whitney Cove
- Russkaya Gavan
- Novaya Zemlya
- Uyedinyeniya Is.
- Arkticheski Institut Is.
- Sverdrup Is.
- R. Pyasina
- Belyy Is.
- Vilkitski Is.
- Dikson Is.
- Port Dikson
- R. Paira
- Skuratov Point
- Malygin Strait
- Shokalski
- Kuzkin Is.
- Kapitana Varzugina
- Yeniseyski Bay
- Tambey
- Golchikha
- Oshmarino Point
- Yuribei
- Gulf of Ob
- Vaigach
- Yugorski Strait
- Nosok
- Karaul
- Ust Port
- Varneka
- Amderma
- Khabarovo
- Kara
- R. Yenisey
- Gulf of Tazovskaya
- Dudinka
- R. Dudinka
- Novvy Port
- Tazovskoye
- Potapovo
- Igarka
- Yar Sale
- Poloi
- Labytnangi
- Salekhard
- Nyda
- R. Ob
- Nadym
- R. Taz
- Turukhansk
- R. Nadym

RUSSIA

MAP 17 – GREENLAND / ICELAND

SVALBARD-SPITZBERGEN (NORWAY)

- North East Land
- Hinlopen Strait
- Barents Is.
- Olga Strait
- Edge Is.
- Hopen
- West Spitsbergen
- Magdalena Bay
- Kings Bay
- Ny Alesund
- Prins Karls Foreland
- Longyear
- Barentsburg
- Isfjord
- Sveagruva
- Braganza Bay
- South Cape
- Bear Island (Bjornoya)

GREENLAND SEA

Southern Limit Permanent Ice

- Shannon Is.
- Nanok
- Eskimonaes
- North Star Bugt (Thule)
- Savigssvik

© Shipping Guides Ltd., Reigate, England

Map 17

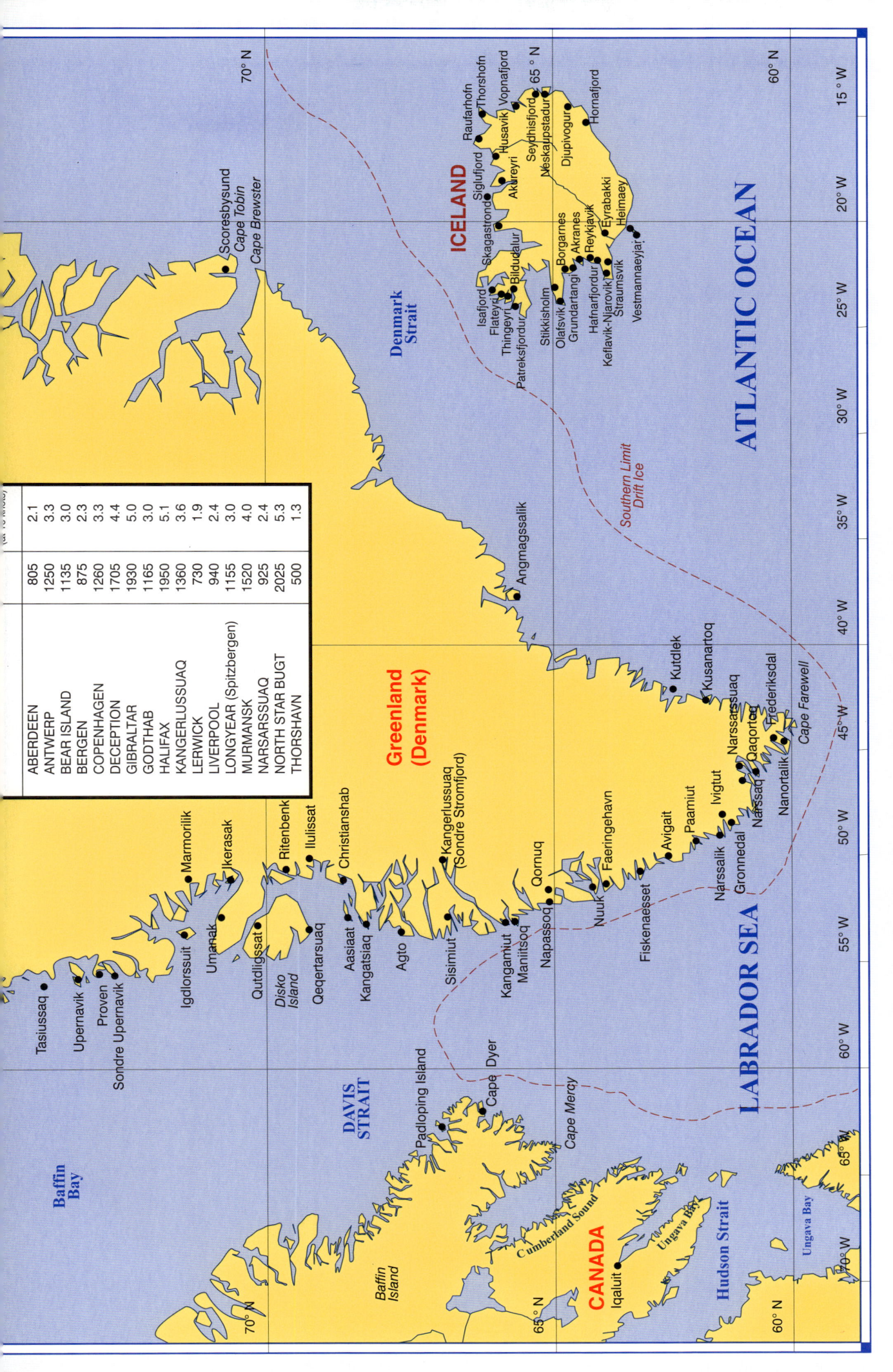

ABERDEEN	805	2.1
ANTWERP	1250	3.3
BEAR ISLAND	1135	3.0
BERGEN	875	2.3
COPENHAGEN	1260	3.3
DECEPTION	1705	4.4
GIBRALTAR	1930	5.0
GODTHAB	1165	3.0
HALIFAX	1950	5.1
KANGERLUSSUAQ	1360	3.6
LERWICK	730	1.9
LIVERPOOL	940	2.4
LONGYEAR (Spitzbergen)	1155	3.0
MURMANSK	1520	4.0
NARSARSSUAQ	925	2.4
NORTH STAR BUGT	2025	5.3
THORSHAVN	500	1.3

Map 18

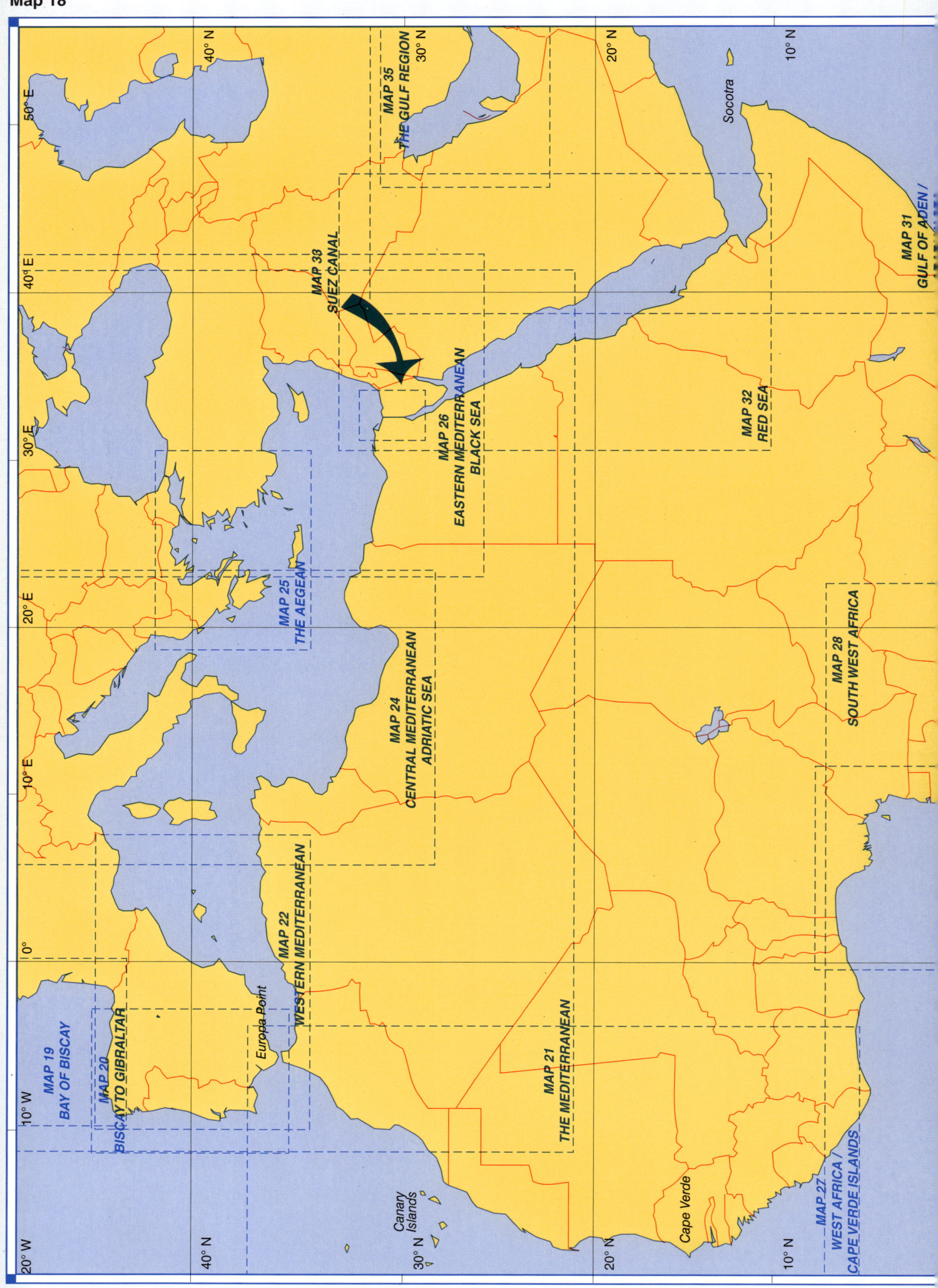

MAP 19 BAY OF BISCAY
MAP 20 BISCAY TO GIBRALTAR
MAP 21 THE MEDITERRANEAN
MAP 22 WESTERN MEDITERRANEAN
MAP 24 CENTRAL MEDITERRANEAN / ADRIATIC SEA
MAP 25 THE AEGEAN
MAP 26 EASTERN MEDITERRANEAN / BLACK SEA
MAP 27 WEST AFRICA / CAPE VERDE ISLANDS
MAP 28 SOUTH WEST AFRICA
MAP 31 GULF OF ADEN
MAP 32 RED SEA
MAP 33 SUEZ CANAL
MAP 35 THE GULF REGION

Europa Point
Canary Islands
Cape Verde
Socotra

© Shipping Guides Ltd., Reigate, United Kingdom

Map 18 — Southern Europe, Africa & Middle East

MAP 19 – BAY OF BISCAY / WESTERN APPROACHES

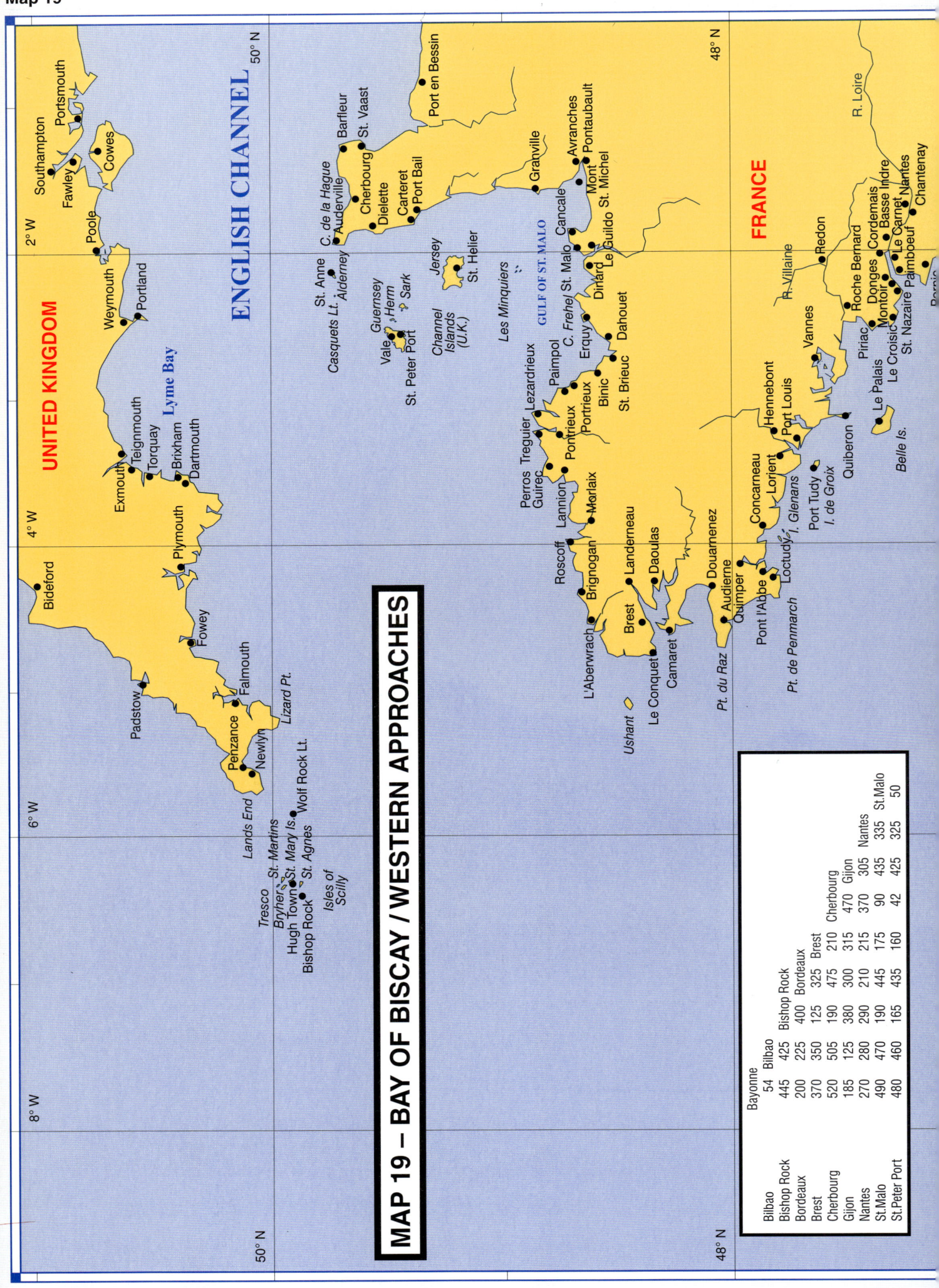

	Bayonne	Bilbao	Bishop Rock	Bordeaux	Brest	Cherbourg	Gijon	Nantes	St.Malo
Bilbao	54								
Bishop Rock	445	425							
Bordeaux	200	225	400						
Brest	370	350	125	325					
Cherbourg	520	505	190	475	210				
Gijon	185	125	380	300	315	470			
Nantes	270	280	290	210	215	370	305		
St.Malo	490	470	190	445	175	90	435	335	
St.Peter Port	480	460	165	435	160	42	425	325	50

© Shipping Guides Ltd., Reigate, United Kingdom

Map 19

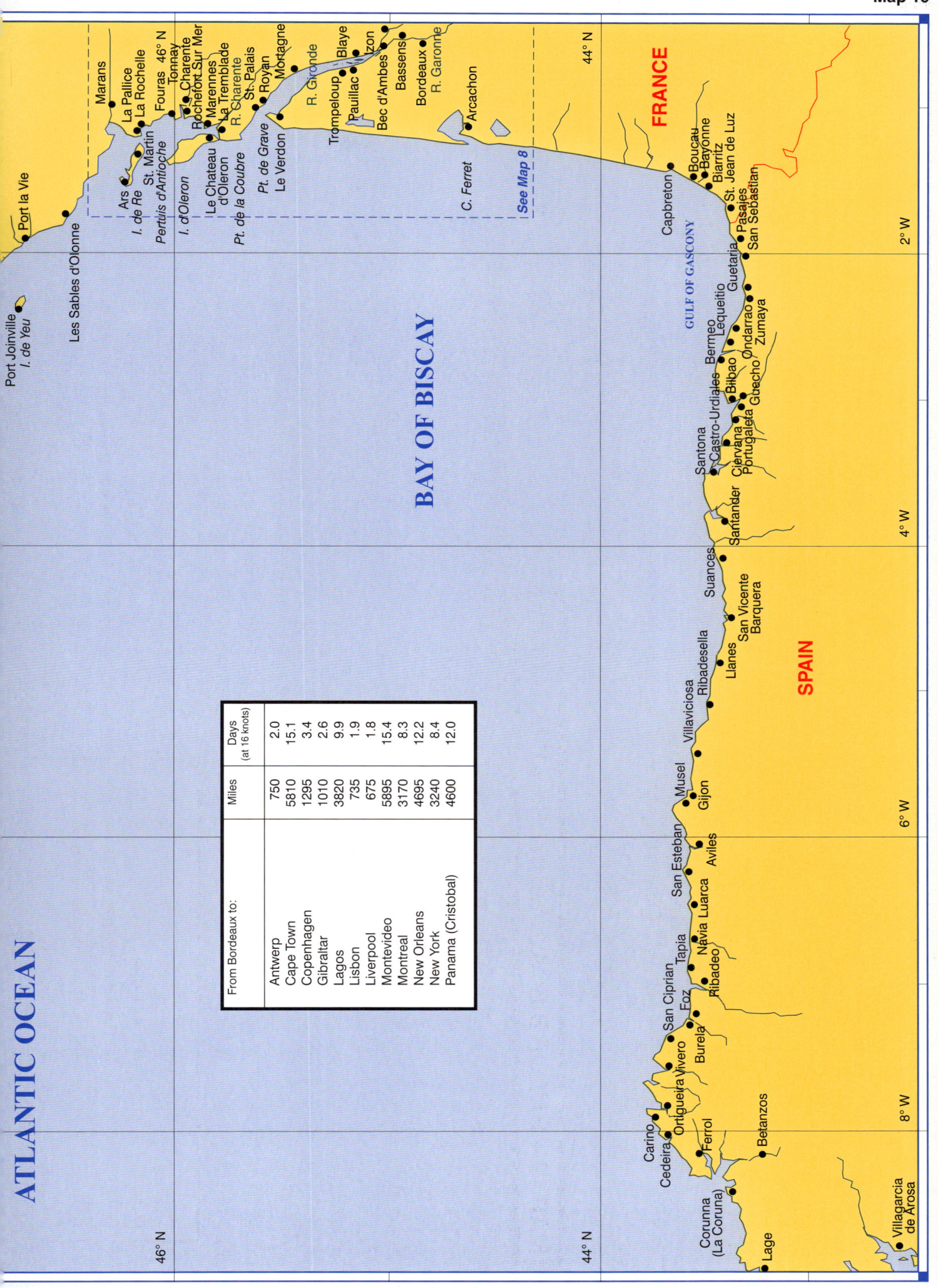

ATLANTIC OCEAN

BAY OF BISCAY

GULF OF GASCONY

FRANCE

SPAIN

Port la Vie
Port Joinville
I. de Yeu
Les Sables d'Olonne
Marans
La Pallice
La Rochelle
Fouras 46° N
Ars
I. de Ré
St. Martin
Pertuis d'Antioche
Charente
Rochefort Sur Mer
Tonnay
Marennes
La Tremblade
R. Charente
I. d'Oleron
Le Chateau d'Oleron
St. Palais
Royan
Pt. de la Coubre
Mortagne
Pt. de Grave
R. Gironde
Trompeloup
Blaye
Pauillac
Le Verdon
Bec d'Ambes
Bassens
Bordeaux
R. Garonne
Arcachon
C. Ferret
See Map 8

Capbreton
Boucau
Bayonne
Biarritz
St. Jean de Luz
Pasajes
San Sebastian
Guetaria
Zumaya
Ondarroo
Lequeitio
Bermeo
Gvecho
Bilbao
Portugaleta
Ciervana
Castro-Urdiales
Santona
Santander
Suances
San Vicente Barquera
Llanes
Ribadesella
Villaviciosa
Musel
Gijon
Aviles
San Esteban
Luarca
Navia
Tapia
Ribadeo
Foz
Burela
San Ciprian
Vivero
Ortigueira
Cedeira
Carino
Ferrol
Corunna (La Coruna)
Betanzos
Lage
Villagarcia de Arosa

From Bordeaux to:	Miles	Days (at 16 knots)
Antwerp	750	2.0
Cape Town	5810	15.1
Copenhagen	1295	3.4
Gibraltar	1010	2.6
Lagos	3820	9.9
Lisbon	735	1.9
Liverpool	675	1.8
Montevideo	5895	15.4
Montreal	3170	8.3
New Orleans	4695	12.2
New York	3240	8.4
Panama (Cristobal)	4600	12.0

MAP 20 – BISCAY TO GIBRALTAR

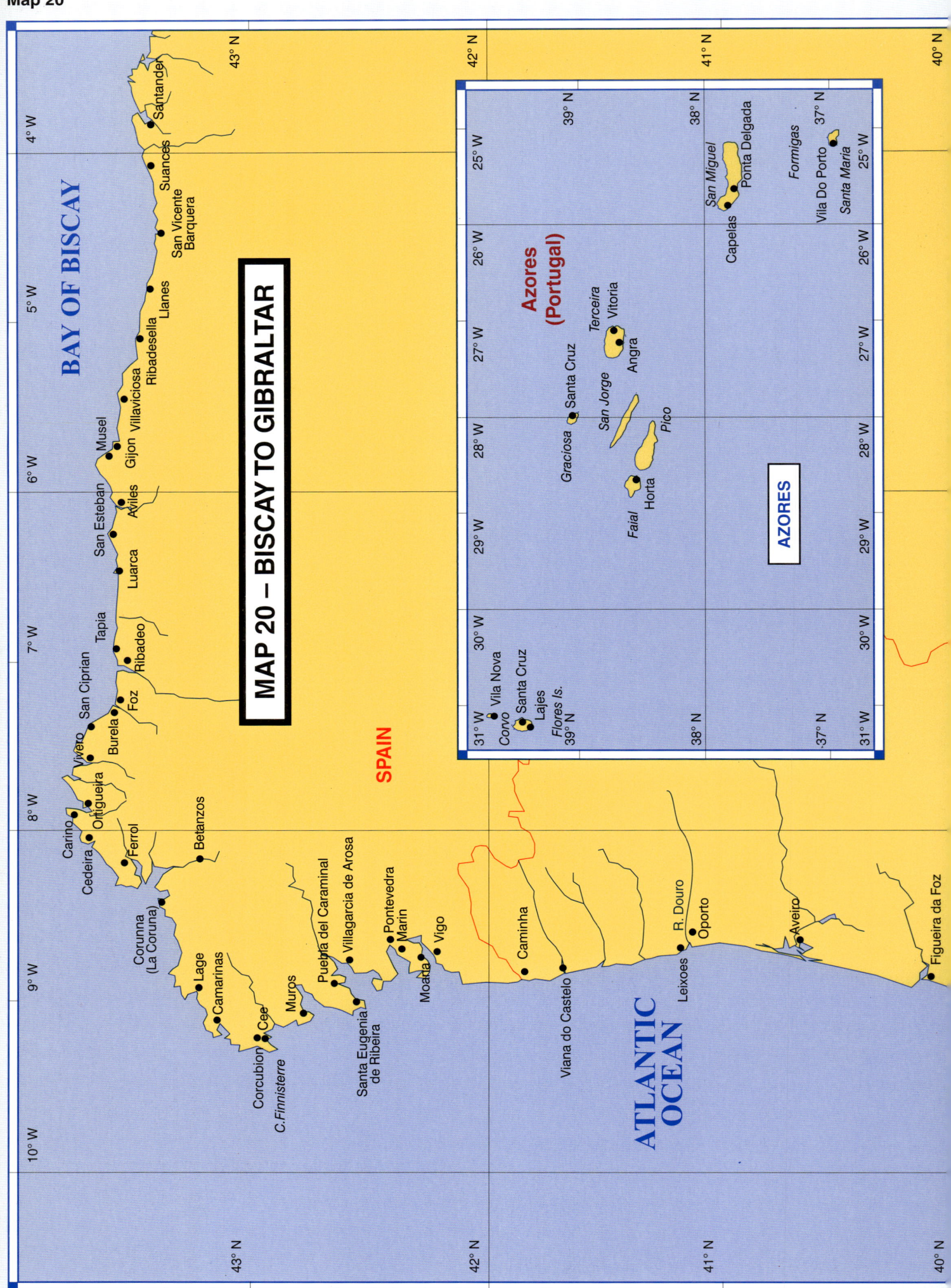

Map 20

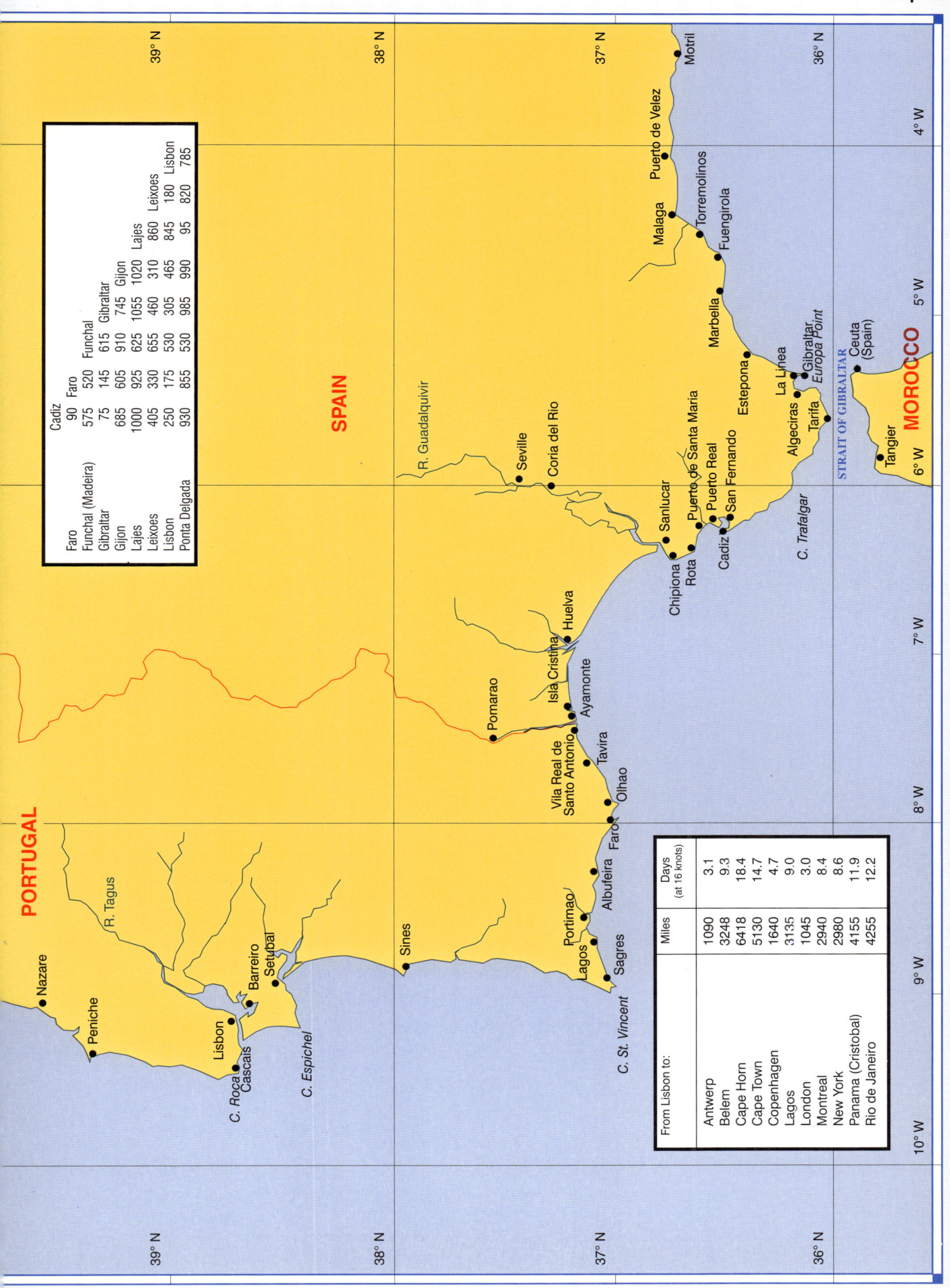

Distance Table (nautical miles)

	Cadiz	Faro	Funchal	Gibraltar	Gijon	Lajes	Leixoes	Lisbon
Faro	90							
Funchal (Madeira)	575	520						
Gibraltar	75	145	615					
Gijon	685	605	910	745				
Lajes	1000	925	625	1055	1020			
Leixoes	405	330	655	460	310	860		
Lisbon	250	175	530	305	465	845	180	
Ponta Delgada	930	855	530	985	990	95	820	785

From Lisbon to:

	Miles	Days (at 16 knots)
Antwerp	1090	3.1
Belem	3248	9.3
Cape Horn	6418	18.4
Cape Town	5130	14.7
Copenhagen	1640	4.7
Lagos	3135	9.0
London	1045	3.0
Montreal	2940	8.4
New York	2980	8.6
Panama (Cristobal)	4155	11.9
Rio de Janeiro	4255	12.2

PORTUGAL — Nazare, Peniche, R. Tagus, Lisbon, Cascais, C. Roca, Barreiro, Setubal, C. Espichel, Sines, C. St. Vincent, Sagres, Lagos, Portimao, Albufeira, Faro, Olhao, Tavira, Vila Real de Santo Antonio

SPAIN — Ayamonte, Isla Cristina, Pomarao, Huelva, R. Guadalquivir, Seville, Coria del Rio, Sanlucar, Chipiona, Rota, Puerto de Santa Maria, Puerto Real, Cadiz, San Fernando, C. Trafalgar, Tarifa, Algeciras, La Linea, Gibraltar, Europa Point, Estepona, Marbella, Fuengirola, Torremolinos, Malaga, Puerto de Velez, Motril

STRAIT OF GIBRALTAR

MOROCCO — Ceuta (Spain), Tangier

Map 21

	Algiers														
Bordeaux	1425	Bordeaux													
Dubrovnik	985	2400	Dubrovnik												
Gibraltar	415	1010	1390	Gibraltar											
Istanbul	1385	2810	885	1800	Istanbul										
Jeddah	2230	3650	1750	2640	1510	Jeddah									
Lisbon	720	735	1695	305	2105	2945	Lisbon								
Marseilles	410	1700	945	690	1380	2240	995	Marseilles							
Naples	580	1990	545	980	975	1835	1285	460	Naples						
Odessa	1725	3155	1225	2145	345	1855	2450	1720	1315	Odessa					
Piraeus	1070	2490	570	1480	355	1320	1785	1065	660	695	Piraeus				
Port Said	1505	2925	1025	1915	785	725	2220	1515	1110	1130	595	Port Said			
Taranto	825	2245	250	1235	805	1665	1540	790	385	1145	485	940	Taranto		
Trieste	1240	2660	340	1650	1155	2020	1955	1205	800	1495	840	1295	510	Trieste	
Tripoli (Libya)	665	2085	660	1075	950	1715	1380	745	505	1290	635	990	505	915	Tripoli (Libya)
Valletta	575	1995	470	985	830	1665	1290	635	325	1175	520	940	315	730	195

© Shipping Guides Ltd., Reigate, England

Map 21

MAP 21 – THE MEDITERRANEAN

Countries: HUNGARY, SLOVENIA, CROATIA, BOSNIA, YUGOSLAVIA, ALBANIA, GREECE, ROMANIA, MOLDOVA, UKRAINE, BULGARIA, TURKEY, RUSSIA, CYPRUS, SYRIA, LEBANON, ISRAEL, JORDAN, EGYPT, LIBYA, SAUDI ARABIA

Seas: Adriatic Sea, Ionian Sea, Aegean Sea, Mediterranean Sea, Black Sea, Sea of Azov, Red Sea

Cities and locations:
- Zadar, Split, Dubrovnik, Barletta, Bari, Brindisi, Taranto, Kerkira, Argostoli, Patras, Messina, Reggio, Syracuse
- Durres, Thessaloniki, Kavalla, Volos, Piraeus, Syros, Iraklion (Crete), Rhodes, Rhodes Is., Mitylene, Izmir
- Galatzi, Constantza, Varna, Bourgas, Istanbul, Eregli, Giresun
- Odessa, Kherson, Sevastopol, Kerch, Berdyansk, Mariupol, Novorossiysk, Tuapse
- Mersin, Lattakia, Famagusta, Tartous, Limassol, Beirut, Haifa, Port Said, Suez Canal, Ismailia, Suez, Alexandria, Nile Delta, Zaafarana, Eilat, Aqaba, Haql, Safaga, Yanbu, Jeddah, Benghazi

See Map 24, See Map 25, See Map 26, See Map 32, See Map 33

25° E, 30° E, 35° E, 20° E
45° N, 40° N, 35° N, 30° N, 25° N

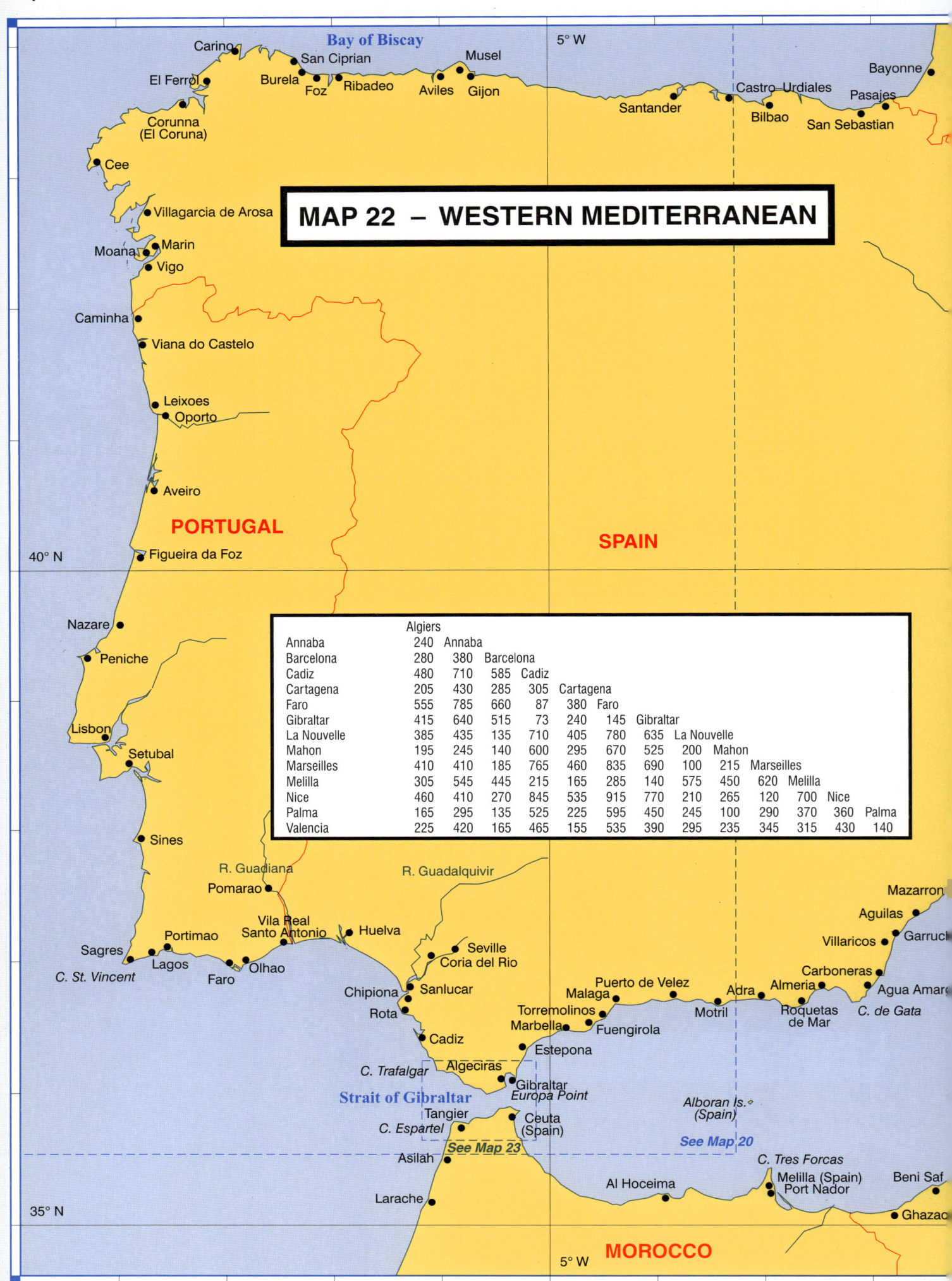

MAP 22 – WESTERN MEDITERRANEAN

	Algiers	Annaba	Barcelona	Cadiz	Cartagena	Faro	Gibraltar	La Nouvelle	Mahon	Marseilles	Melilla	Nice	Palma
Annaba	240												
Barcelona	280	380											
Cadiz	480	710	585										
Cartagena	205	430	285	305									
Faro	555	785	660	87	380								
Gibraltar	415	640	515	73	240	145							
La Nouvelle	385	435	135	710	405	780	635						
Mahon	195	245	140	600	295	670	525	200					
Marseilles	410	410	185	765	460	835	690	100	215				
Melilla	305	545	445	215	165	285	140	575	450	620			
Nice	460	410	270	845	535	915	770	210	265	120	700		
Palma	165	295	135	525	225	595	450	245	100	290	370	360	
Valencia	225	420	165	465	155	535	390	295	235	345	315	430	140

© Shipping Guides Ltd., Reigate, England

MAP 22

From Marseilles to:	Miles	Days (at 16 knots)
Buenos Aires	5985	15.6
Cape Horn	7080	18.4
Cape Leeuwin	7855	20.5
Cape of Good Hope		
via Gibraltar	5815	15.1
via Suez Canal	6820	17.8
Dover Strait	1925	5.0
Fremantle	7820	20.4
Gibraltar	690	1.8
Houston	5465	14.2
Lombok Strait	7340	19.1
London	2015	5.2
Montreal	3875	10.1
New York	3900	10.2
Osaka	9230	24.0
Panama Canal (Cristobal)	5020	13.1
San Francisco	8315	21.7
Santos	5075	13.2
Singapore	6530	17.0
Suez Canal (Port Said)	1515	3.9
Sunda Strait	6725	17.5
Ushant	1615	4.2

From Gibraltar to:	Miles	Days (at 16 knots)
Aden	3310	8.6
Ascension Island	2860	7.4
Cape Horn	6390	16.6
Cape Town	5095	13.3
Dublin	1200	3.1
Hampton Roads	3365	8.8
Lagos	3100	8.1
Montreal	3185	8.3
New Orleans	4575	11.9
Panama (Cristobal)	4330	11.3

FRANCE

R. Rhone, Arles, Sete, Agde, La Nouvelle, Fos, Berre, St. Louis, Cassis, Marseilles, Port De Bouc, Ciotat, Hyeres, Toulon, Ste. Maxime, St. Raphael, St. Tropez, Hyeres Is., Port Vauban (Antibes), Villefranche, Cannes, Nice, Menton, Monte Carlo (Monaco), San Remo

See Map 23

Gulf of Lyons

Port Vendres, Port Bou, Rosas, C. Creus, Palamos, Sant Feliu de Guixols, Blanes, Badalona, Mataro, Barcelona, Vallcarca, Vilanova I La Geltru, Tarragona, R. Ebro, San Carlos de la Hapita, C. Tortosa, Alcanar, Vinaroz, Burriana, Castellon de la Plana, Sagunto, Valencia, Albufera, Gandia, Denia, Javea, C. San Antonio, Altea, C. Nao, Benidorm, C. Huertas, Torrevieja, C. Palos, Cartagena

Gulf of Valencia

Minorca, Ciudadela, Fornells, Mahon, Pollensa, Alcudia, Soller, Dragonera, Anoraitx, Palma, Majorca, Cabrera, BALEARIC ISLANDS (Spain), S. Antonio, Ibiza, Formentera

MEDITERRANEAN SEA

ALGERIA

Oran, Arzew, s-El-Kebir, Mostaganem, Tenes, Gouraya, Port Briera, Cherchel, Algiers, Dellys, Bejaia (Bougie), Djen-Djen, Jijel, Les Falaises, C. Bougaroni, Collo, Skikda, Chetaibi, C. de Fer, Annaba

map 23

STRAIT OF GIBRALTAR

- Barbate
- 36°10' N
- *Cape Trafalgar*
- Los Barrios
- San Roque
- La Linea
- Algeciras
- Gibraltar (U.K.)
- *Europa Point*
- SPAIN
- MEDITERRANEAN SEA
- 36° N
- *Punta Marroqui* • Tarifa
- ATLANTIC OCEAN
- Strait of Gibraltar
- *Punta de la Almina*
- Ceuta (Spain)
- 35°50' N
- *Cape Espartel* • Tangier
- MOROCCO
- 6° W · 5°50' W · 5°40' W · 5°30' W · 5°20' W

MARSEILLES DISTRICT

- FRANCE
- 43°30' N
- *Etang de Lavaiduc*
- *Etang de Berre*
- Berre
- *Etang de L'Estomac*
- *Etang D'Engrenier*
- Rhone/Fos Canal
- Fos
- Fos/Bouc Canal
- Marseilles–Marignane Airport
- *Gulf of Fos*
- Caronte
- Martigues
- Port de Bouc
- La Mede
- *Pointe de la Gracieuse* • Lavera
- Caronte Canal
- St. Louis du Rhone
- Port de la Coribierre
- Port de Lave Estaque
- 43°20' N
- Cap Couronne
- Marseilles
- R. Rhone
- MEDITERRANEAN SEA
- *Marseilles Roads*
- *I. Ratonneau*
- 4°50' E · 5° E · Gulf of Lion · 5°10' E · 5°20' E

GULF OF GENOA

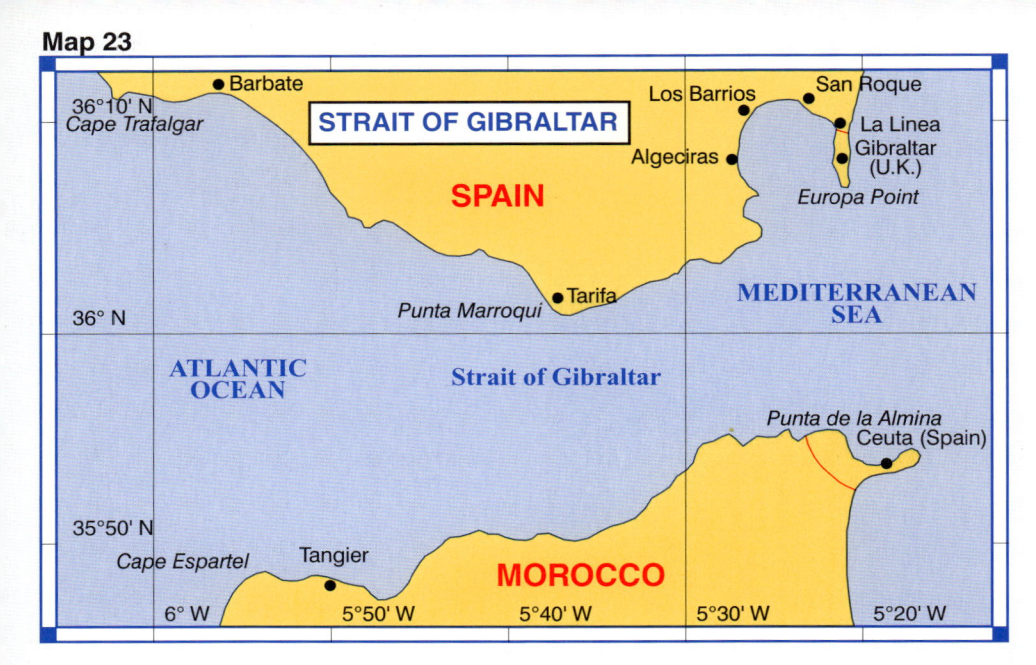

- Voltri
- Genoa (Genova)
- Multedo
- Rapallo
- Camogli
- Sta. Margharita
- Savona
- Quiliano
- Portofino
- Sestri
- ITALY
- Vado Terminal
- FRANCE
- 44° N
- Alassio
- Gulf of Genoa
- La Spezia
- Marina di Carrara
- Menton
- San Remo
- Imperia
- Viareggio
- Bordighera
- Monte Carlo
- Pisa
- Livorno (Leghorn)
- Ligurian Sea
- Vada
- *Gorgona*
- *Capraia*
- 43° N
- *C. Corse*
- Piombino
- Follonica
- MEDITERRANEAN SEA
- *Canale di Piombino*
- *Gulf of Follonica*
- *Gulf of St. Florent*
- Portoferraio
- Bastia
- *Elba*
- Rio Marina
- Calvi
- Ile Rousse
- Porto Azzuro
- Corsica (Fr.)
- *Pianosa*
- 8° E · 9° E · 10° E · 11° E

MAP 23 SOUTH EUROPEAN COASTAL AREAS

© Shipping Guides Ltd., Reigate, United Kingdom

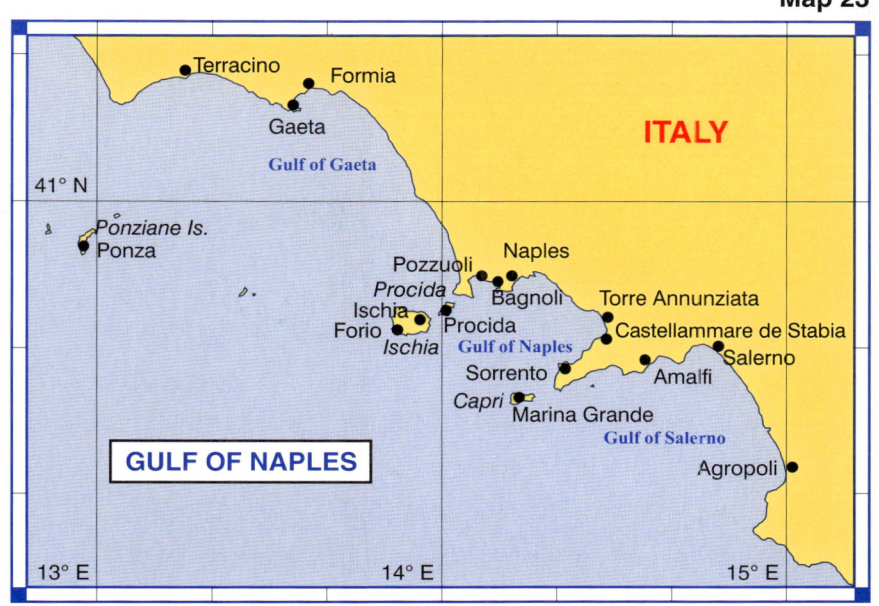

Map 23

GULF OF NAPLES — ITALY

- Terracino
- Formia
- Gaeta
- Gulf of Gaeta
- 41° N
- Ponziane Is.
- Ponza
- Pozzuoli
- Naples
- Procida
- Bagnoli
- Ischia
- Procida
- Torre Annunziata
- Forio
- Castellammare de Stabia
- Ischia
- Gulf of Naples
- Salerno
- Sorrento
- Amalfi
- Capri
- Marina Grande
- Gulf of Salerno
- Agropoli
- 13° E, 14° E, 15° E

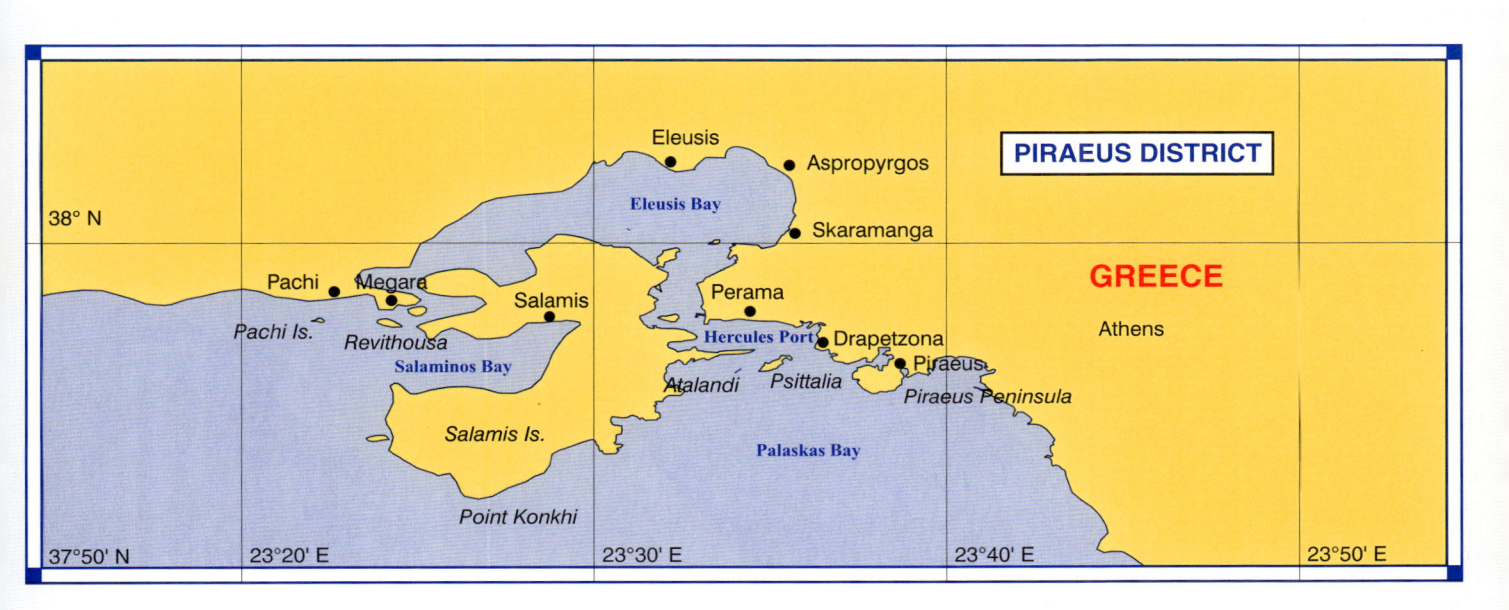

PIRAEUS DISTRICT — GREECE

- Eleusis
- Aspropyrgos
- 38° N
- Eleusis Bay
- Skaramanga
- Pachi
- Megara
- Perama
- Pachi Is.
- Salamis
- Athens
- Revithousa
- Hercules Port
- Drapetzona
- Salaminos Bay
- Atalandi
- Psittalia
- Piraeus
- Salamis Is.
- Piraeus Peninsula
- Palaskas Bay
- Point Konkhi
- 37°50' N, 23°20' E, 23°30' E, 23°40' E, 23°50' E

BOSPOROUS AND APPROACHES

- Bosporous
- Black Sea
- Sariyer
- Sile
- Buyukdere
- Istinye
- Beykoz
- Anadolu
- Silivri
- Istanbul
- Buyukcekmece
- Haydarpasa
- 41° N
- Ambarli
- Yesilkoy
- Bakirkoy
- Erenkoy
- Haramidere
- Maltepe
- Kartal
- Heybeli
- Fercom Terminal
- Buyukada
- Beldeport
- Hereke
- Yarimca
- Tuzla
- Derince
- Gebze
- Diliskelesi
- Tutuncifilik
- Izmit
- Golcuk
- Sea of Marmara
- Gulf of Izmit
- Yalova
- Imarali
- 28° E, 29° E, 30° E

MAP 24 – CENTRAL MEDITERRANEAN

From Genoa to:	Miles	Days (at 16 knots)
Algiers	530	1.4
Beirut	1500	3.9
Corinth	995	2.6
Gibraltar	845	2.2
Istanbul	1285	3.3
Leghorn	80	0.2
London (Gravesend)	2150	5.6
Messina	485	1.3
Naples	335	0.9
New York	4055	10.6
Panama (Cristobal)	5175	13.5
Port Said	1420	3.7
Thessaloniki	1180	3.1
Trieste	1110	2.9
Venice	1125	2.9

© Shipping Guides Ltd., Reigate, United Kingdom

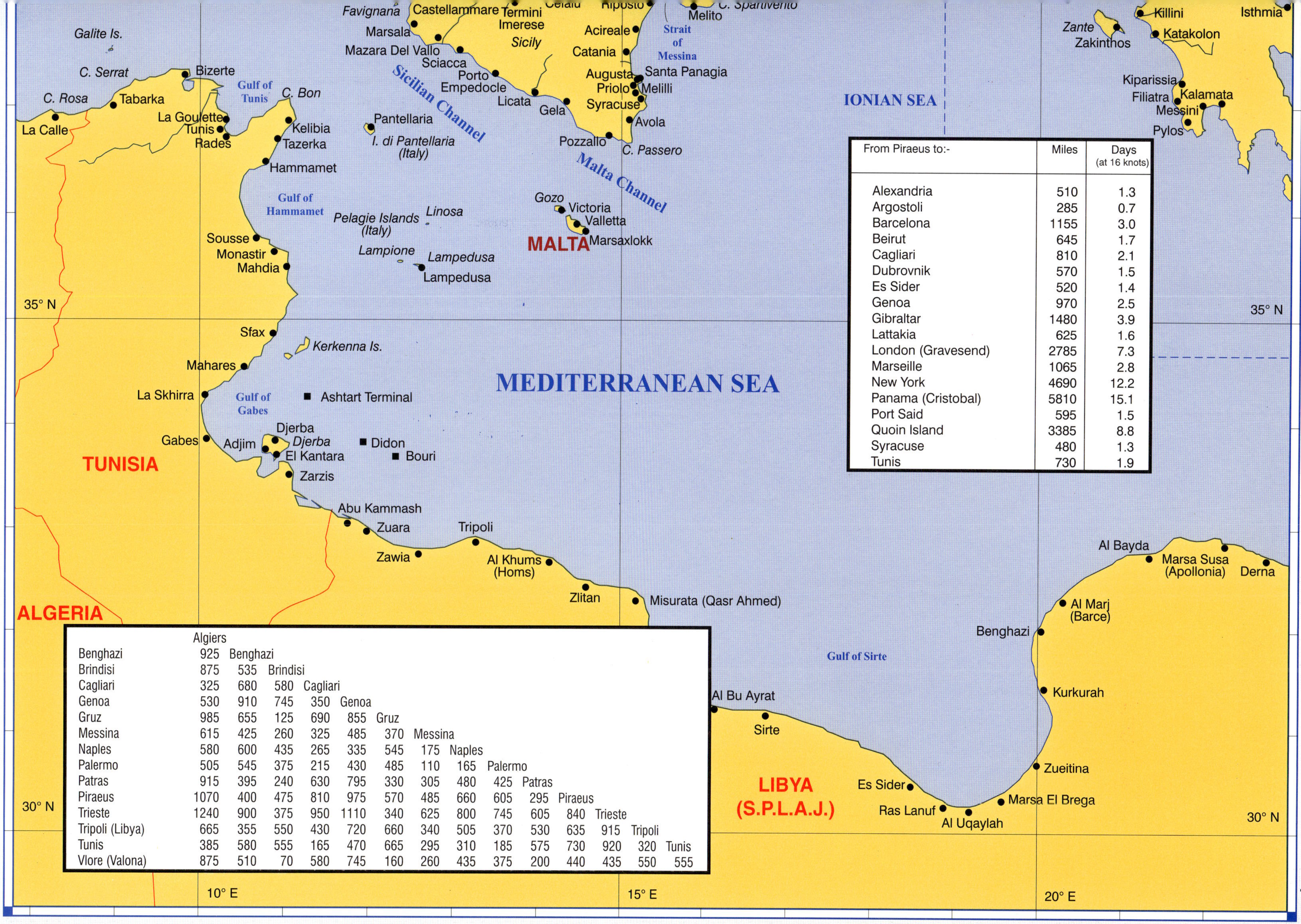

Map 24

From Piraeus to:-	Miles	Days (at 16 knots)
Alexandria	510	1.3
Argostoli	285	0.7
Barcelona	1155	3.0
Beirut	645	1.7
Cagliari	810	2.1
Dubrovnik	570	1.5
Es Sider	520	1.4
Genoa	970	2.5
Gibraltar	1480	3.9
Lattakia	625	1.6
London (Gravesend)	2785	7.3
Marseille	1065	2.8
New York	4690	12.2
Panama (Cristobal)	5810	15.1
Port Said	595	1.5
Quoin Island	3385	8.8
Syracuse	480	1.3
Tunis	730	1.9

	Algiers	Benghazi	Brindisi	Cagliari	Genoa	Gruz	Messina	Naples	Palermo	Patras	Piraeus	Trieste	Tripoli	Tunis
Benghazi	925													
Brindisi	875	535												
Cagliari	325	680	580											
Genoa	530	910	745	350										
Gruz	985	655	125	690	855									
Messina	615	425	260	325	485	370								
Naples	580	600	435	265	335	545	175							
Palermo	505	545	375	215	430	485	110	165						
Patras	915	395	240	630	795	330	305	480	425					
Piraeus	1070	400	475	810	975	570	485	660	605	295				
Trieste	1240	900	375	950	1110	340	625	800	745	605	840			
Tripoli (Libya)	665	355	550	430	720	660	340	505	370	530	635	915		
Tunis	385	580	165	555	665	470	295	310	185	575	730	920	320	
Vlore (Valona)	875	510	70	580	745	160	260	435	375	200	440	435	550	555

MAP 25 – AEGEAN SEA

From Piraeus to:	Miles	Days (at 16 knots)
Dover Strait	2715	7.1
Genoa	975	2.5
Gibraltar	1480	3.9
Malta	520	1.4
Montreal	4665	12.1
New York	4690	12.2
Panama Canal (Cristobal)	5810	15.1
Port Said	595	1.5
Singapore	5610	14.6
Ushant	2405	6.3
Yokohama	8505	22.1

© Shipping Guides Ltd., Reigate, United Kingdom

Map 25

	Adamas													
Andros	76	Andros												
Cannakale	235	165	Cannakale											
Corinth	330	380	540	Corinth										
Edincik	315	245	78	620	Edincik									
Iraklion	120	155	315	375	395	Iraklion								
Izmir	200	145	140	520	220	255	Izmir							
Izmit	405	335	170	710	120	490	310	Izmit						
Kerkyra	340	390	550	200	630	385	530	720	Kerkyra					
Kos	154	150	225	470	305	140	175	400	480	Kos				
Mitilene	170	107	67	475	145	230	85	240	485	160	Mitylene			
Nauplion	100	120	270	335	350	175	250	445	350	235	210	Nauplion		
Piraeus	85	70	220	360	300	185	205	390	370	195	160	90	Piraeus	
Rhodes	200	205	290	515	370	170	235	460	525	62	225	285	260	Rhodes
Souda	95	155	315	340	395	52	275	490	350	185	250	150	160	215	Suda Bay
Syros	58	30	185	375	265	130	145	355	385	120	120	125	80	180	130	Syros
Thassos	255	185	97	555	175	330	200	270	565	275	120	295	240	335	330	210	Thassos
Thessaloniki	270	195	200	570	280	350	255	370	580	330	180	310	255	385	350	225	152	Thessaloniki
Volos	215	140	190	510	270	290	225	365	520	270	155	250	195	330	290	165	165	140

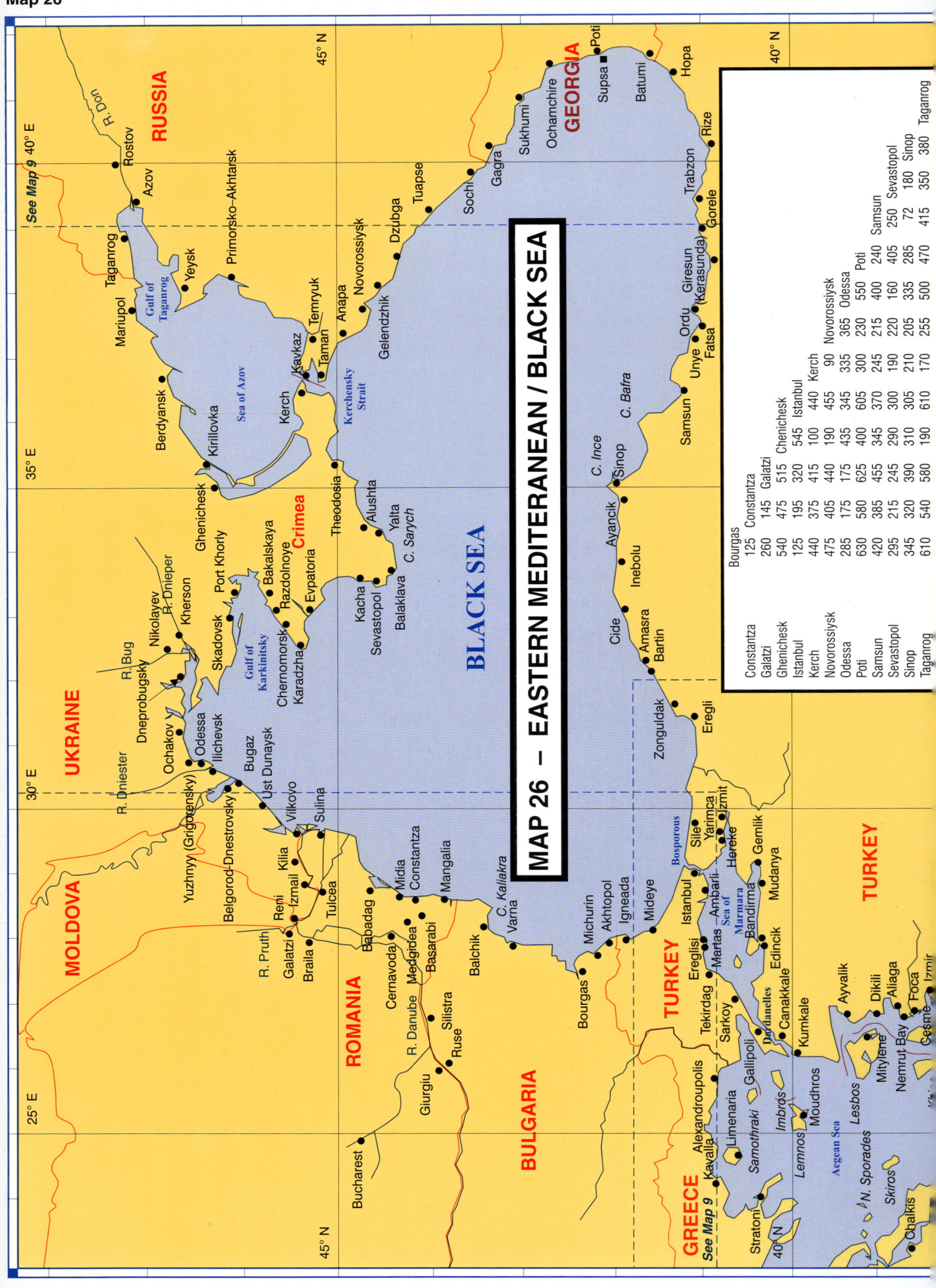

Map 26 – Eastern Mediterranean / Black Sea

Distance Table (nautical miles)

	Bourgas	Constantza	Galatzi	Ghenichesk	Istanbul	Kerch	Novorossiysk	Odessa	Poti	Samsun	Sevastopol	Sinop	Taganrog
Constantza	125												
Galatzi	260	145											
Ghenichesk	540	475	515										
Istanbul	125	195	320	545									
Kerch	440	375	415	100	440								
Novorossiysk	475	405	440	190	455	90							
Odessa	285	175	175	435	345	335	365						
Poti	630	580	625	400	605	300	230	550					
Samsun	420	385	455	345	370	245	215	400	240				
Sevastopol	295	215	245	290	300	190	220	160	405	205			
Sinop	345	320	390	310	305	210	205	335	285	72	250		
Taganrog	610	540	580	190	610	170	255	500	470	415	350	380	

© Shipping Guides Ltd., Reigate, United Kingdom

Map 26

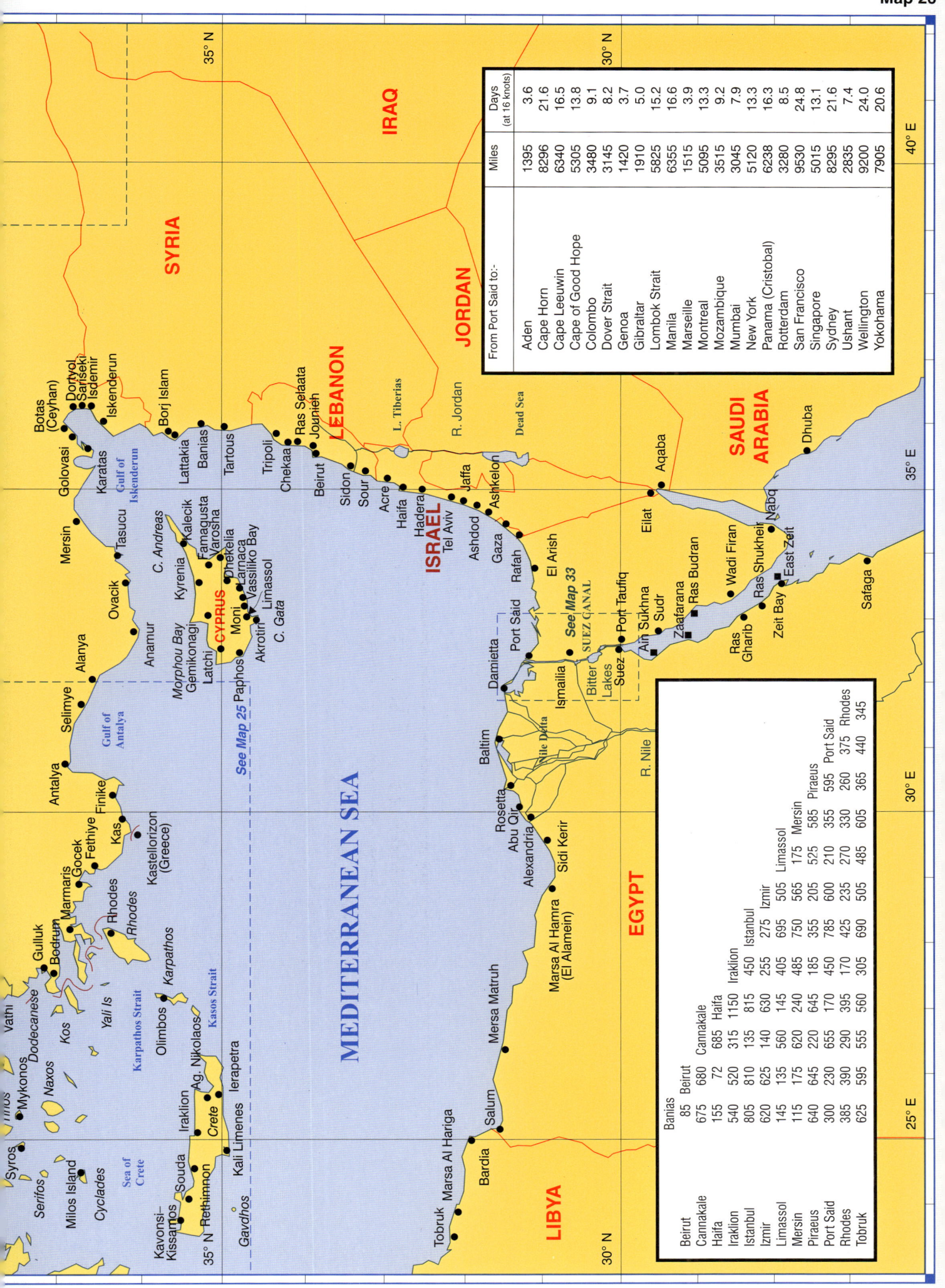

From Port Said to:-	Miles	Days (at 16 knots)
Aden	1395	3.6
Cape Horn	8296	21.6
Cape Leeuwin	6340	16.5
Cape of Good Hope	5305	13.8
Colombo	3480	9.1
Dover Strait	3145	8.2
Genoa	1420	3.7
Gibraltar	1910	5.0
Lombok Strait	5825	15.2
Manila	6355	16.6
Marseille	1515	3.9
Montreal	5095	13.3
Mozambique	3515	9.2
Mumbai	3045	7.9
New York	5120	13.3
Panama (Cristobal)	6238	16.3
Rotterdam	3280	8.5
San Francisco	9530	24.8
Singapore	5015	13.1
Sydney	8295	21.6
Ushant	2835	7.4
Wellington	9200	24.0
Yokohama	7905	20.6

	Banias	Beirut	Cannakale	Haifa	Iraklion	Istanbul	Izmir	Limassol	Mersin	Piraeus	Port Said	Rhodes
Beirut	85											
Cannakale	675	680										
Haifa	155	72	685									
Iraklion	540	520	315	685								
Istanbul	805	810	135	815	450							
Izmir	620	625	140	630	255	275						
Limassol	145	135	560	145	405	695	505					
Mersin	115	175	620	240	485	750	565	175				
Piraeus	640	645	220	645	185	355	205	525	585			
Port Said	300	230	655	170	450	785	600	210	355	595		
Rhodes	385	390	290	395	170	425	235	270	330	260	375	
Tobruk	625	595	555	560	305	690	505	485	605	365	440	345

Map 27

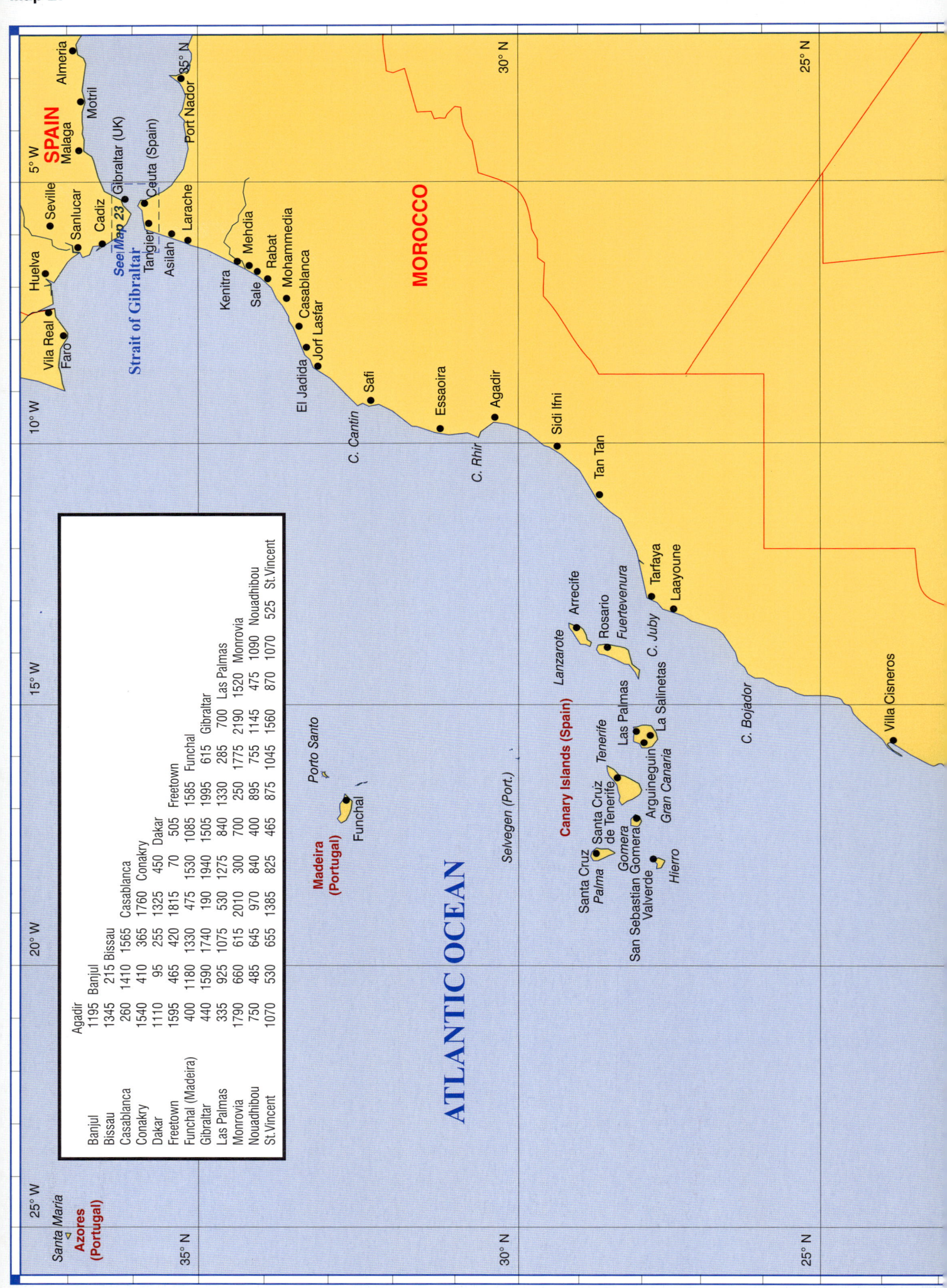

Distance Table

	Agadir	Banjul	Bissau	Casablanca	Conakry	Dakar	Freetown	Funchal (Madeira)	Gibraltar	Las Palmas	Monrovia	Nouadhibou
Banjul	1195											
Bissau	1345	215										
Casablanca	260	1410	1565									
Conakry	1540	410	365	1760								
Dakar	1110	95	255	1325	450							
Freetown	1595	465	420	1815	70	505						
Funchal (Madeira)	400	1180	1330	475	1530	1085	1585					
Gibraltar	440	1590	1740	190	1940	1505	1995	615				
Las Palmas	335	925	1075	530	1275	840	1330	285	700			
Monrovia	1790	660	615	2010	300	700	250	1775	2190	1520		
Nouadhibou	750	485	645	970	840	400	895	475	1145	475	1090	
St. Vincent	1070	530	655	1385	825	465	875	1045	1560	870	1070	525

© Shipping Guides Ltd., Reigate, United Kingdom

MAP 27 – WEST AFRICA / CAPE VERDE ISLANDS

From Dakar to:	Miles	Days (at 16 knots)
Antwerp	2590	6.7
Ascension I.	1370	3.6
Cape Horn	4940	12.9
Cape Town	3605	9.4
Fremantle	8300	21.6
Gibraltar	1505	3.9
Liverpool	2490	6.5
Montevideo	3765	9.8
New Orleans	4310	11.2
New York	3335	8.7
Panama (Cristobal)	3690	9.6

Countries: MAURITANIA, MALI, SENEGAL, GAMBIA, GUINEA BISSAU, GUINEA, SIERRA LEONE, LIBERIA, IVORY COAST, CAPE VERDE

Locations: Nouadhibou, Point Central, C. Blanc, Nouakchott, Port de l'Amitié, St. Louis, C. Vert, Dakar, Rufisque, M'bao Terminal, Fatik, Foundiougne, R. Saloum, Kaolack, Kuntaur, Georgetown, R. Gambia, Banjul, Ziguinchor, R. Casamance, Carabane, Cacheu, Bissau, Bolama, Bubaque, Bijagos Arch., Boke, Port Kamsar, Conakry, Pepel, Freetown, Sherbro Is., Sherbro, Sulima, Robertsport, Monrovia, Marshall, Buchanan, Cess River

Cape Verde: Santo Antao, St. Vincent, Porto Grande, Santa Lucia, S. Nicolau, Sal Rei, Palmeira Bay, Sal, Santa Maria, Boa Vista, S. Tiago, Maio, Porto Inglez, Fogo, Porto Praia, Brava, San Filipe

ATLANTIC OCEAN

Map 28

From Cape Town to:	Miles	Days (at 16 knots)
Aden	3960	10.3
Ascension I.	2395	6.3
Cape Horn	4215	11.0
Colombo	4365	11.4
Darwin	6140	16.0
Dublin	6000	15.6
Dunedin	7225	18.8
Fremantle	4715	12.3
Jakarta	5185	13.6
Karachi	4670	12.2
Melbourne	6105	15.9
Montreal	7115	18.5
New York	6790	17.7
Panama (Cristobal)	6425	16.7
Recife	3320	8.6
St. Helena	1695	4.6
Singapore	5610	14.6
South Sandwich I.	2640	6.9
South Georgia	2660	6.9
Tristan da Cunha	1515	3.9
Yokohama	8350	21.7

© Shipping Guides Ltd., Reigate, United Kingdom

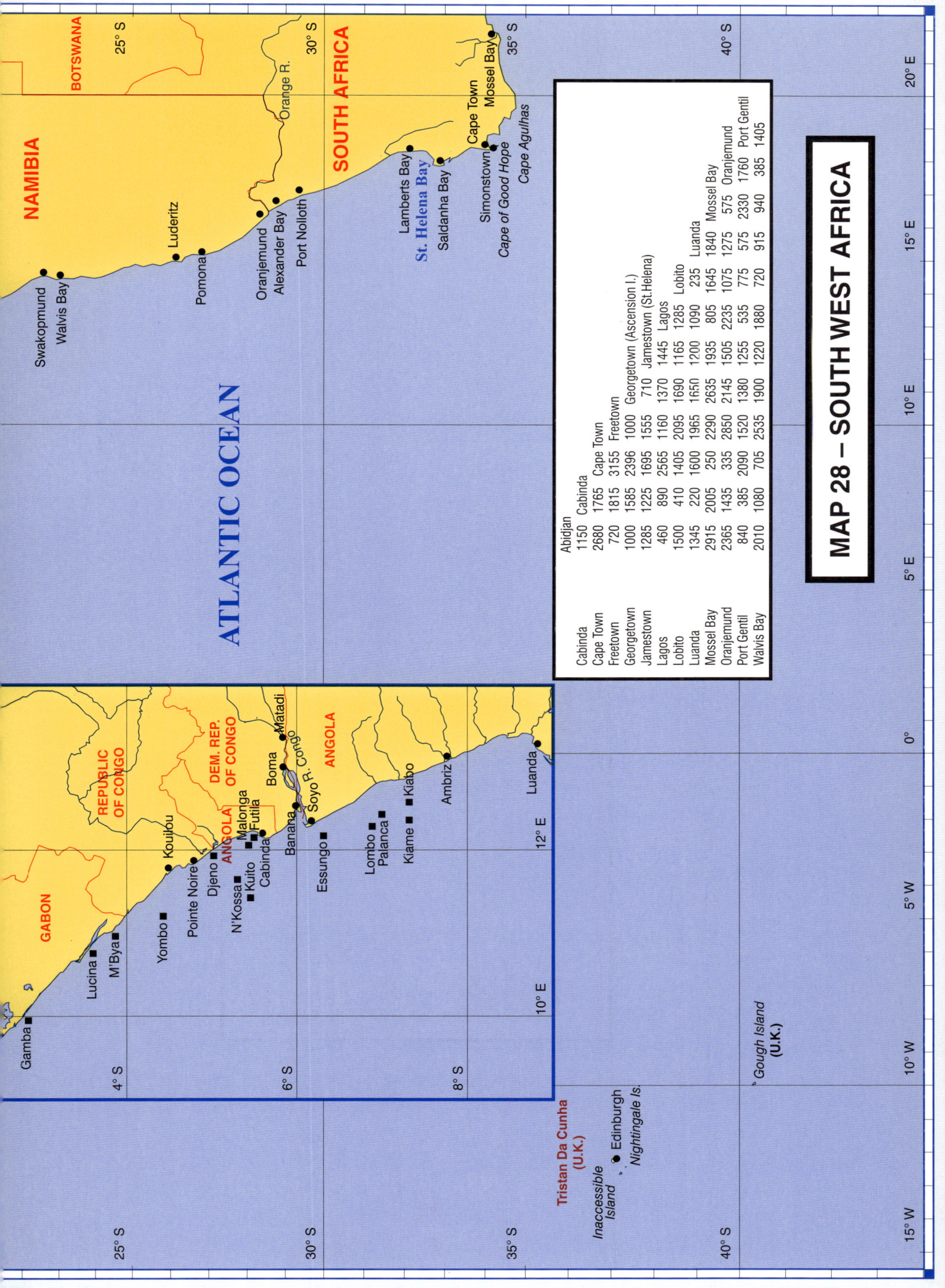

MAP 28 – SOUTH WEST AFRICA

	Abidjan	Cabinda	Cape Town	Freetown	Georgetown (Ascension I.)	Jamestown (St.Helena)	Lagos	Lobito	Luanda	Mossel Bay	Oranjemund	Port Gentil
Cabinda	1150											
Cape Town	2680	1765										
Freetown	720	1815	3155									
Georgetown	1000	1585	2396	1000								
Jamestown	1285	1225	1695	1555	710							
Lagos	460	890	2565	1160	1370	1445						
Lobito	1500	410	1405	2095	1690	1165	1285					
Luanda	1345	220	1600	1965	1650	1200	1090	235				
Mossel Bay	2915	2005	250	2290	2635	1935	805	1645	1840			
Oranjemund	2365	1435	335	2145	2850	1505	2235	1075	1275	575		
Port Gentil	840	385	2090	1380	1520	1255	535	775	575	2330	1760	
Walvis Bay	2010	1080	705	2535	1900	1220	1880	720	915	940	385	1405

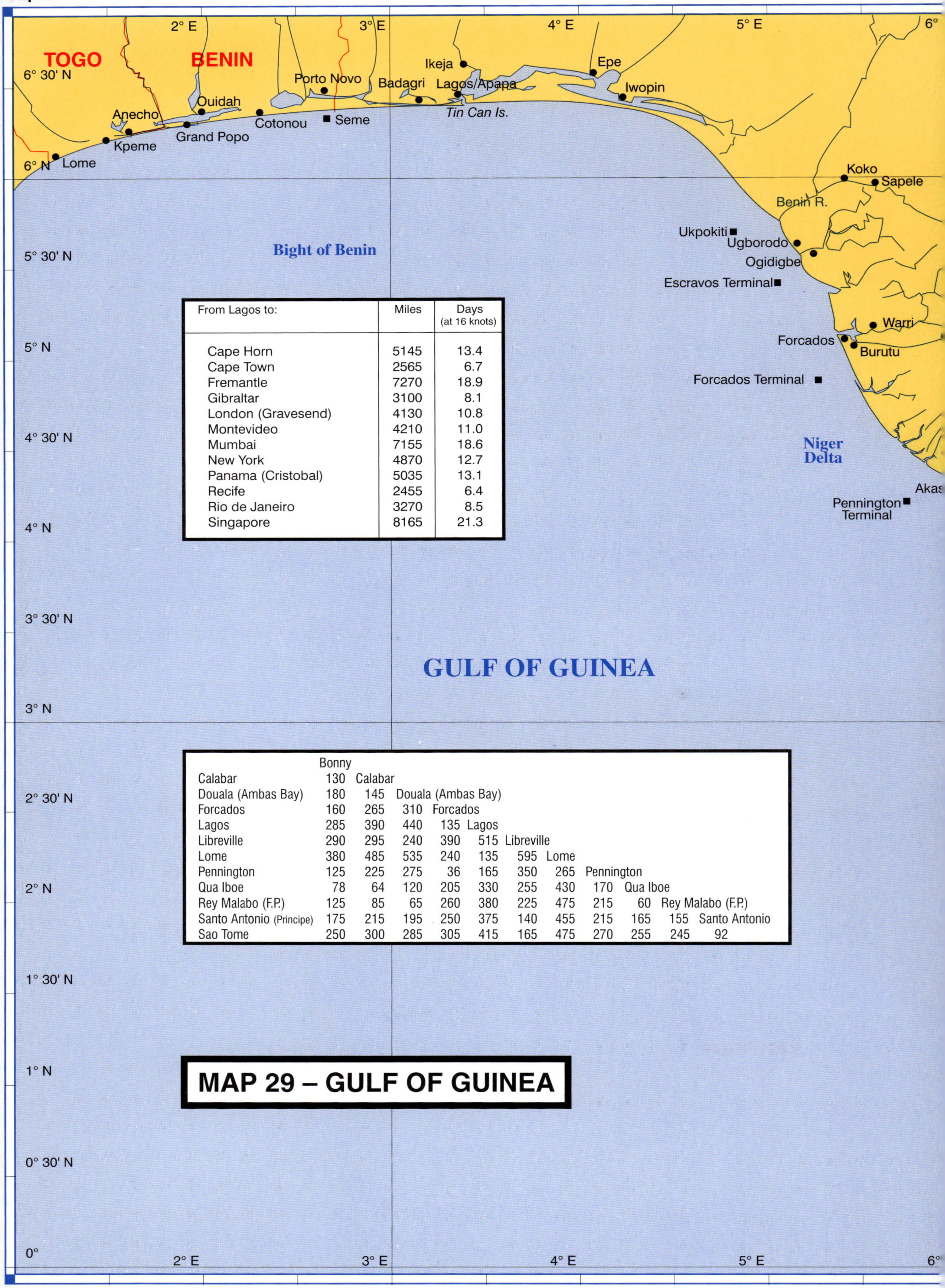

MAP 29 – GULF OF GUINEA

From Lagos to:	Miles	Days (at 16 knots)
Cape Horn	5145	13.4
Cape Town	2565	6.7
Fremantle	7270	18.9
Gibraltar	3100	8.1
London (Gravesend)	4130	10.8
Montevideo	4210	11.0
Mumbai	7155	18.6
New York	4870	12.7
Panama (Cristobal)	5035	13.1
Recife	2455	6.4
Rio de Janeiro	3270	8.5
Singapore	8165	21.3

	Bonny									
Calabar	130	Calabar								
Douala (Ambas Bay)	180	145	Douala (Ambas Bay)							
Forcados	160	265	310	Forcados						
Lagos	285	390	440	135	Lagos					
Libreville	290	295	240	390	515	Libreville				
Lome	380	485	535	240	135	595	Lome			
Pennington	125	225	275	36	165	350	265	Pennington		
Qua Iboe	78	64	120	205	330	255	430	170	Qua Iboe	
Rey Malabo (F.P.)	125	85	65	260	380	225	475	215	60	Rey Malabo (F.P.)
Santo Antonio (Principe)	175	215	195	250	375	140	455	215	165	155	Santo Antonio
Sao Tome	250	300	285	305	415	165	475	270	255	245	92

NIGERIA
CAMEROON
EQUATORIAL GUINEA
GABON
SAO TOME & PRINCIPE
Bight of Bonny
Corisco Bay
Onitsha
Obubra
Niger R.
Cross R.
Calabar
Itu
Oron
Ikang
Port Harcourt
Okrika
Degema
Bugama
Abonnema
Opobo
Bonny
Brass River
Ima Terminal
Bonny Terminal
Brass (Off Shore) Terminal
Odudu Terminal
Zafiro Terminal
Qua Iboe Terminal
Antan Terminal
Kole Terminal
Moudi Marine Terminal
Cape Limboh
Limbe
Tiko
Douala
Manoka
Souellaba
Cameroon R.
Sanaga R.
Nyong R.
Edea
Malimba
Little Batanga
Longuy
Kribi
Ebome
Campo
Punta Europa Marine Terminal
Malabo
Bioco (Fernando Poo)
San Carlos (Luba)
Conception
EQUATORIAL GUINEA
Pta. Santiago
Puerto Nuevo
Bata (Puerto Macias)
Rio Benito
Ceiba
Muni R.
Cabo San Juan
Puerto Iradier
Elobey Is.
Corisco
Cocobeach
La Mondah
Kenje
Libreville
Owendo
Ekuata
Kango
Principe
Santo Antonio
Sao Tome
Sao Tome
7° E
8° E
9° E
10° E
11° E
6° 30' N
6° N
5° 30' N
5° N
4° 30' N
4° N
3° 30' N
3° N
2° 30' N
2° N
1° 30' N
1° N
0° 30' N
0°

MAP 30 – EAST AFRICA

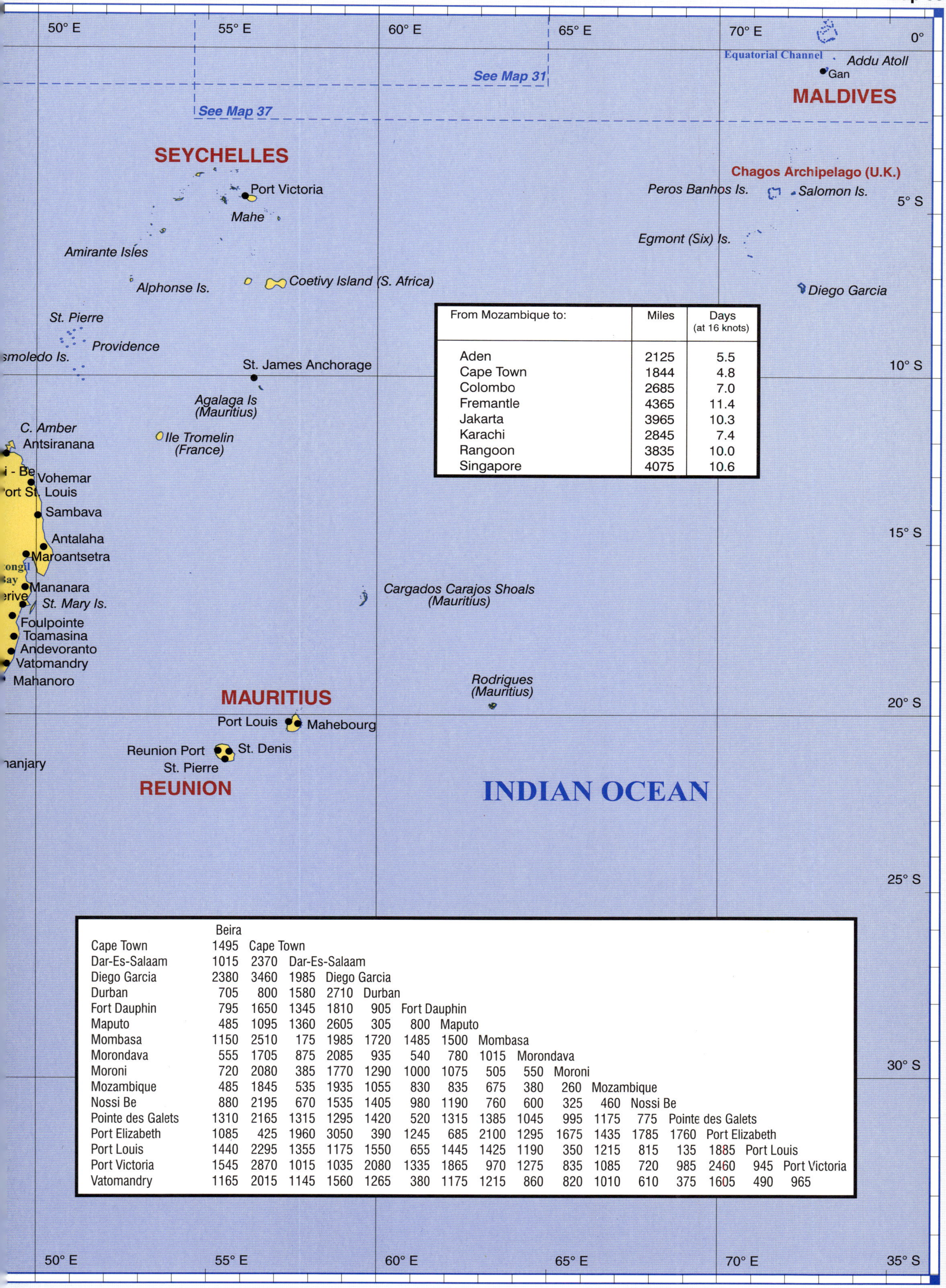

Map 30

MALDIVES
- Equatorial Channel
- Addu Atoll • Gan

SEYCHELLES
- Port Victoria
- Mahe
- Amirante Isles
- Alphonse Is.
- Coetivy Island (S. Africa)
- St. Pierre
- Providence
- ...moledo Is.

Chagos Archipelago (U.K.)
- Peros Banhos Is.
- Salomon Is.
- Egmont (Six) Is.
- Diego Garcia

See Map 37
See Map 31

St. James Anchorage

Agalaga Is. (Mauritius)
Ile Tromelin (France)

C. Amber
Antsiranana
...i - Be
Vohemar
...ort St. Louis
Sambava
Antalaha
Maroantsetra
...ongil
...ay Mananara
...erive St. Mary Is.
Foulpointe
Toamasina
Andevoranto
Vatomandry
Mahanoro
...anjary

Cargados Carajos Shoals (Mauritius)

MAURITIUS
- Port Louis • Mahebourg

REUNION
- Reunion Port • St. Denis
- St. Pierre

Rodrigues (Mauritius)

INDIAN OCEAN

From Mozambique to:	Miles	Days (at 16 knots)
Aden	2125	5.5
Cape Town	1844	4.8
Colombo	2685	7.0
Fremantle	4365	11.4
Jakarta	3965	10.3
Karachi	2845	7.4
Rangoon	3835	10.0
Singapore	4075	10.6

	Beira	Cape Town	Dar-Es-Salaam	Diego Garcia	Durban	Fort Dauphin	Maputo	Mombasa	Morondava	Moroni	Mozambique	Nossi Be	Pointe des Galets	Port Elizabeth	Port Louis	Port Victoria
Cape Town	1495															
Dar-Es-Salaam	1015	2370														
Diego Garcia	2380	3460	1985													
Durban	705	800	1580	2710												
Fort Dauphin	795	1650	1345	1810	905											
Maputo	485	1095	1360	2605	305	800										
Mombasa	1150	2510	175	1985	1720	1485	1500									
Morondava	555	1705	875	2085	935	540	780	1015								
Moroni	720	2080	385	1770	1290	1000	1075	505	550							
Mozambique	485	1845	535	1935	1055	830	835	675	380	260						
Nossi Be	880	2195	670	1535	1405	980	1190	760	600	325	460					
Pointe des Galets	1310	2165	1315	1295	1420	520	1315	1385	1045	995	1175	775				
Port Elizabeth	1085	425	1960	3050	390	1245	685	2100	1295	1675	1435	1785	1760			
Port Louis	1440	2295	1355	1175	1550	655	1445	1425	1190	350	1215	815	135	1885		
Port Victoria	1545	2870	1015	1035	2080	1335	1865	970	1275	835	1085	720	985	2460	945	
Vatomandry	1165	2015	1145	1560	1265	380	1175	1215	860	820	1010	610	375	1605	490	965

Map 31

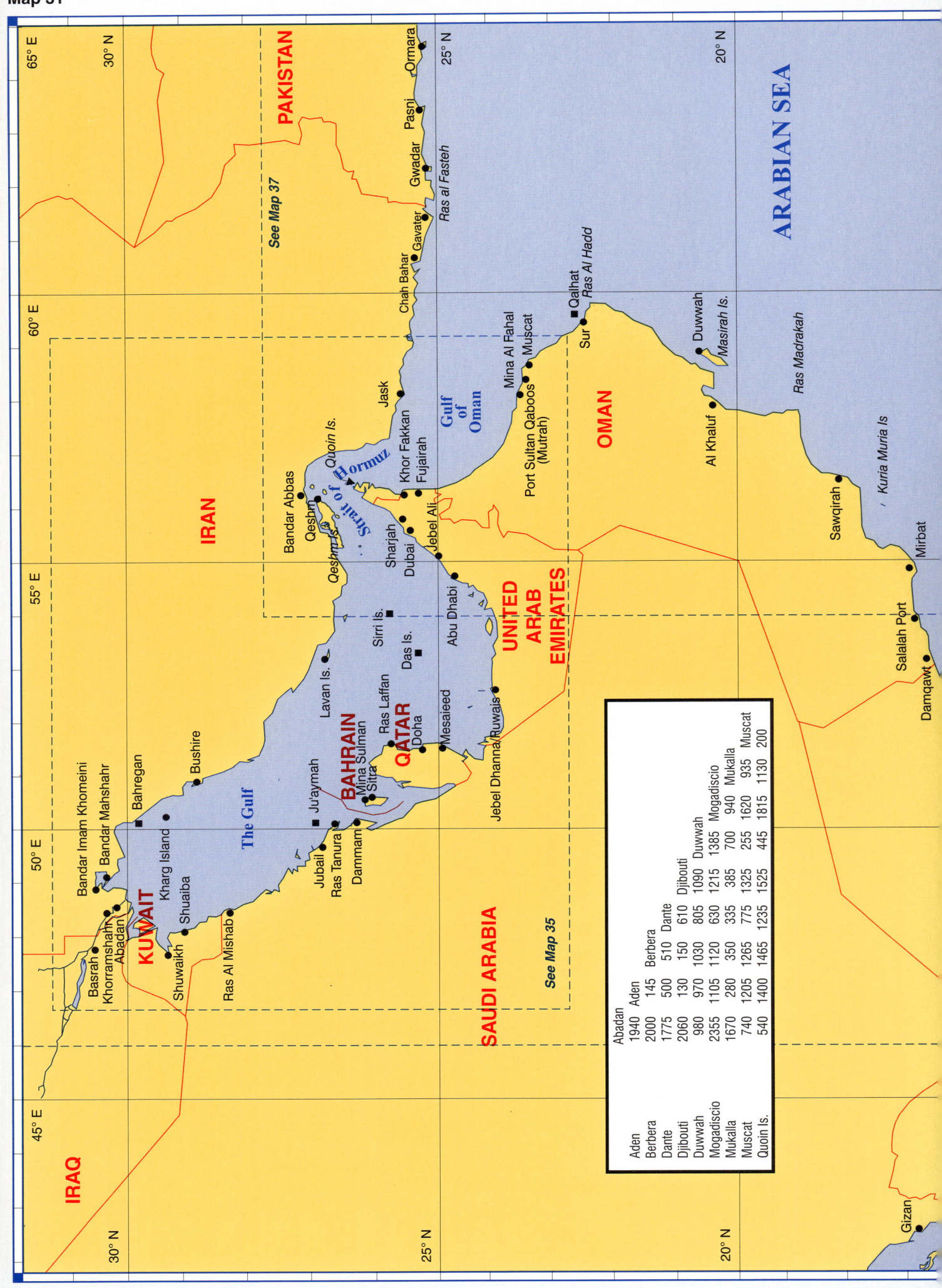

	Abadan	Aden	Berbera	Dante	Djibouti	Duwwah	Mogadiscio	Mukalla	Muscat
Aden	1940								
Berbera	2000	145							
Dante	1775	500	510						
Djibouti	2060	130	150	610					
Duwwah	980	970	1030	805	1090				
Mogadiscio	2355	1105	1120	630	1215	1385			
Mukalla	1670	280	350	335	385	700	940		
Muscat	740	1205	1265	775	1325	255	1620	935	
Quoin Is.	540	1400	1465	1235	1525	445	1815	1130	200

© Shipping Guides Ltd., Reigate, United Kingdom

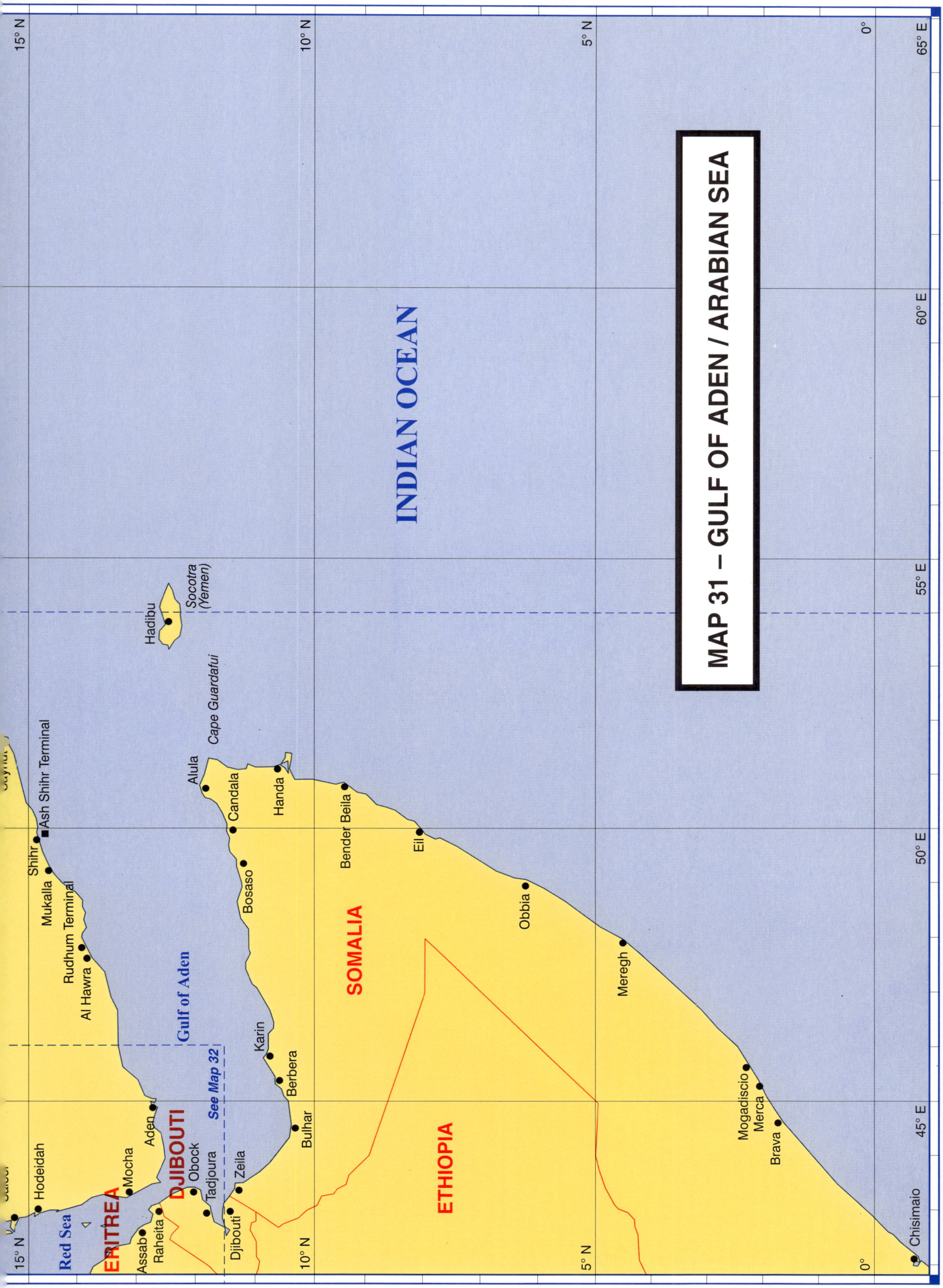
MAP 31 – GULF OF ADEN / ARABIAN SEA
INDIAN OCEAN
Gulf of Aden
Red Sea
See Map 32
ERITREA
DJIBOUTI
SOMALIA
ETHIOPIA
Hodeidah
Mocha
Aden
Assab
Raheita
Obock
Tadjoura
Djibouti
Zeila
Bulhar
Berbera
Karin
Bosaso
Candala
Alula
Cape Guardafui
Handa
Bender Beila
Eil
Obbia
Meregh
Mogadiscio
Merca
Brava
Chisimaio
Al Hawra
Rudhum Terminal
Mukalla
Shihr
Ash Shihr Terminal
Hadibu
Socotra (Yemen)
15° N
10° N
5° N
0°
45° E
50° E
55° E
60° E
65° E

Map 32

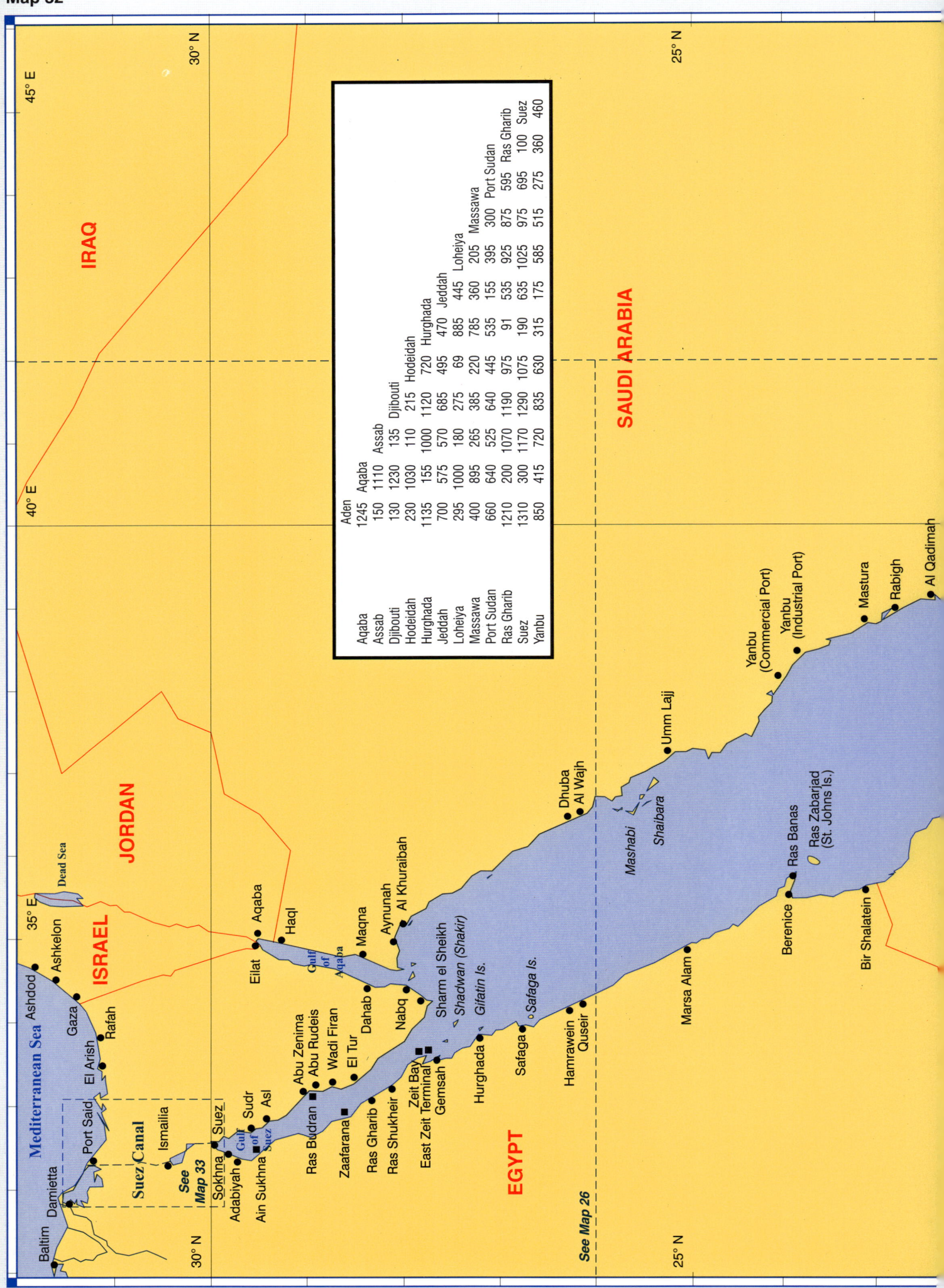

	Aden	Aqaba	Assab	Djibouti	Hodeidah	Hurghada	Jeddah	Loheiya	Massawa	Port Sudan	Ras Gharib	Suez
Aqaba	1245											
Assab	150	1110										
Djibouti	130	1230	135									
Hodeidah	230	1030	110	215								
Hurghada	1135	155	1000	1120	720							
Jeddah	700	575	570	685	495	470						
Loheiya	295	1000	180	275	69	885	445					
Massawa	400	895	265	385	220	785	360	205				
Port Sudan	660	640	525	640	445	535	155	395	300			
Ras Gharib	1210	200	1070	1190	975	91	535	925	875	595		
Suez	1310	300	1170	1290	1075	190	635	1025	975	695	100	
Yanbu	850	415	720	835	630	315	175	585	515	275	360	460

MAP 32 – RED SEA

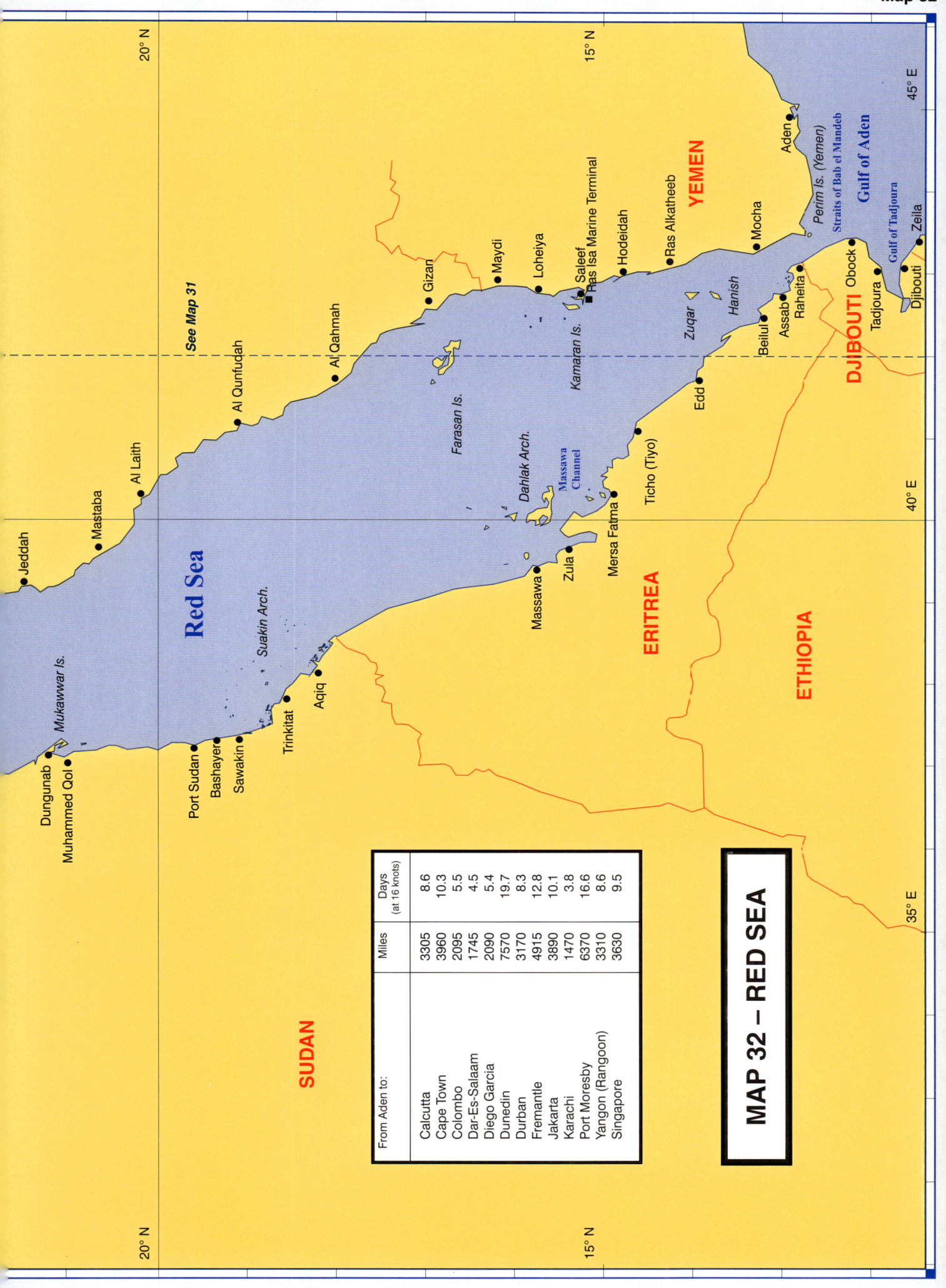

From Aden to:	Miles	Days (at 16 knots)
Calcutta	3305	8.6
Cape Town	3960	10.3
Colombo	2095	5.5
Dar-Es-Salaam	1745	4.5
Diego Garcia	2090	5.4
Dunedin	7570	19.7
Durban	3170	8.3
Fremantle	4915	12.8
Jakarta	3890	10.1
Karachi	1470	3.8
Port Moresby	6370	16.6
Yangon (Rangoon)	3310	8.6
Singapore	3630	9.5

Map 33

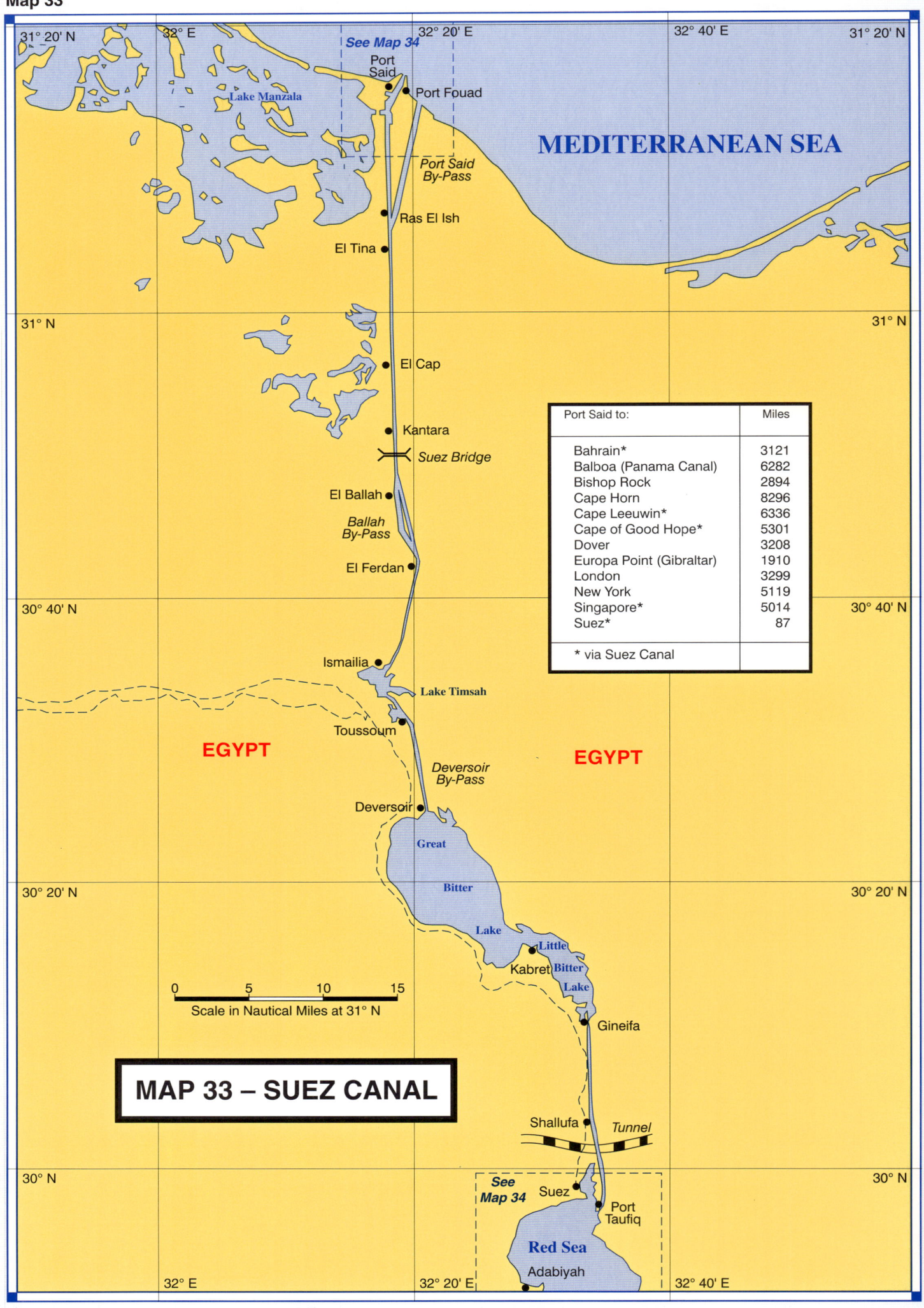

MEDITERRANEAN SEA

See Map 34
Port Said
Port Fouad
Port Said By-Pass
Ras El Ish
El Tina
Lake Manzala
El Cap
Kantara
Suez Bridge
El Ballah
Ballah By-Pass
El Ferdan
Ismailia
Lake Timsah
Toussoum
Deversoir By-Pass
Deversoir
Great Bitter Lake
Little Bitter Lake
Kabret
Gineifa
Shallufa — *Tunnel*
See Map 34
Suez
Port Taufiq
Adabiyah
Red Sea

EGYPT

Port Said to:	Miles
Bahrain*	3121
Balboa (Panama Canal)	6282
Bishop Rock	2894
Cape Horn	8296
Cape Leeuwin*	6336
Cape of Good Hope*	5301
Dover	3208
Europa Point (Gibraltar)	1910
London	3299
New York	5119
Singapore*	5014
Suez*	87
* via Suez Canal	

Scale in Nautical Miles at 31° N
0 5 10 15

MAP 33 – SUEZ CANAL

© Shipping Guides Ltd., Reigate, United Kingdom

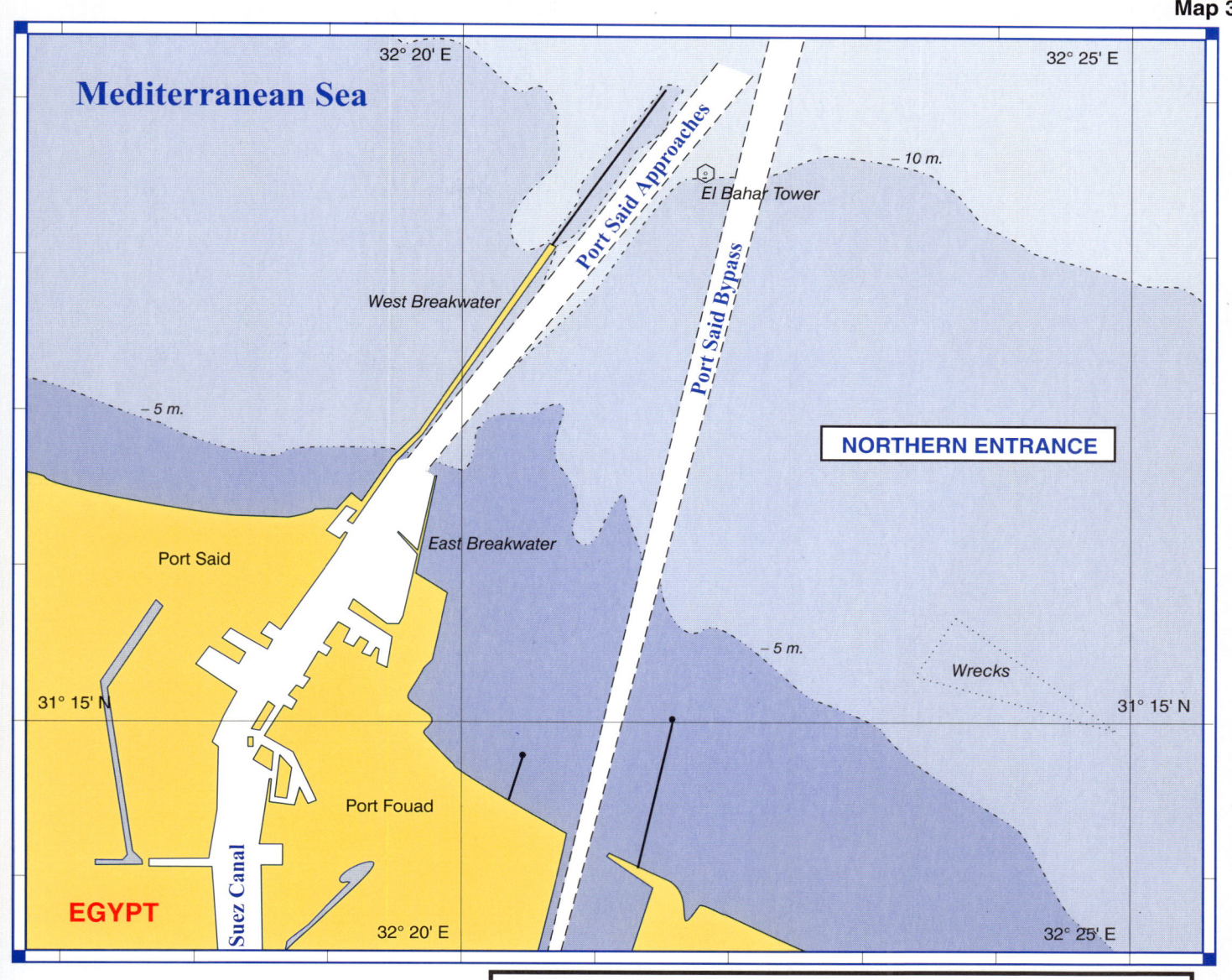

MAP 34 – SUEZ CANAL APPROACHES

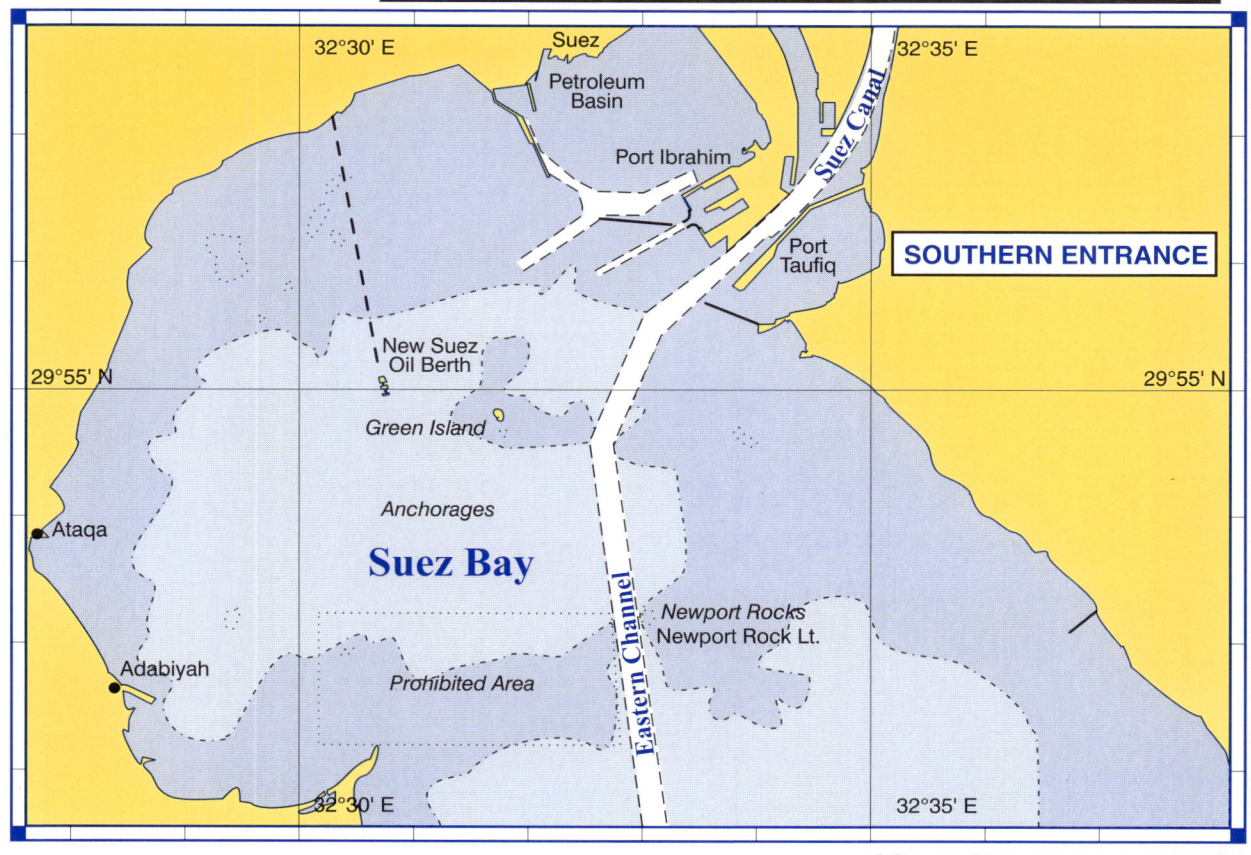

Map 35

From Quoin Is. to:	Miles	Days (at 16 knots)
Cape Town	4655	12.1
Colombo	1785	4.7
Dakar	6200	16.2
Fremantle	4875	12.7
Jakarta	3600	9.4
London (Gravesend)	6025	15.7
Mozambique	2820	7.3
Mumbai	1020	2.7
New Orleans	9275	24.2
Port Said	2790	7.3
Singapore	3330	8.7
Wellington	7810	20.4
Yokohama	6225	16.2

© Shipping Guides Ltd., Reigate, United Kingdom

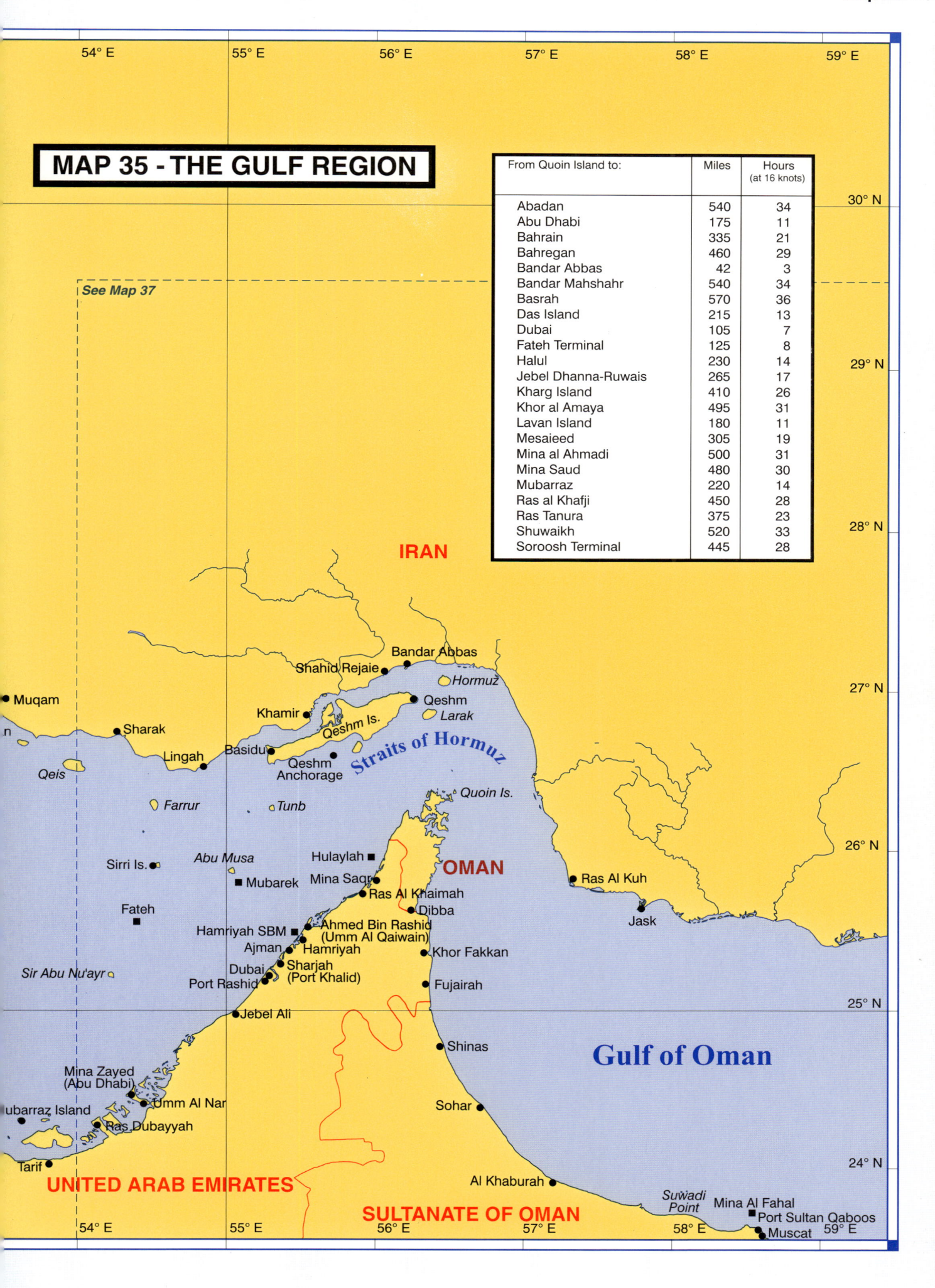

MAP 35 - THE GULF REGION

From Quoin Island to:	Miles	Hours (at 16 knots)
Abadan	540	34
Abu Dhabi	175	11
Bahrain	335	21
Bahregan	460	29
Bandar Abbas	42	3
Bandar Mahshahr	540	34
Basrah	570	36
Das Island	215	13
Dubai	105	7
Fateh Terminal	125	8
Halul	230	14
Jebel Dhanna-Ruwais	265	17
Kharg Island	410	26
Khor al Amaya	495	31
Lavan Island	180	11
Mesaieed	305	19
Mina al Ahmadi	500	31
Mina Saud	480	30
Mubarraz	220	14
Ras al Khafji	450	28
Ras Tanura	375	23
Shuwaikh	520	33
Soroosh Terminal	445	28

MAP 36 – FAR EAST AND AUSTRALASIA

- Bering Sea
- Aleutian Islands
- Sea of Okhotsk
- MAP 54 ALASKA/SIBERIA
- MAP 49 CENTRAL / SOUTH PACIFIC
- MAP 43 JAPAN/SEA OF OKHOTSK
- MAP 45 SOUTHERN JAPAN & INLAND SEA
- MAP 42 YELLOW SEA/EAST CHINA SEA
- MAP 48 GUANGZHOU

© Shipping Guides Ltd., Reigate, United Kingdom

Map 36

Map 37

MAP 37 – THE GULF TO MALACCA STRAITS

IRAN
- Bandar Abbas
- Sirri I.
- Sharjah
- Jask
- Khor Fakkan
- Fujairah
- Dubai
- Jebel Ali
- Abu Dhabi

U.A.E.

Strait of Hormuz
Gulf of Oman

- Chah Bahar
- Gavater
- Gwadar
- Pasni Ormara

PAKISTAN
- Karachi
- Port Muhammed Bin Qasim
- Keti Bandar
- R. Indus
- C. Monze
- Indus Delta
- Lakhpat
- Jakhau

See Inset

- Mina Al Fahal
- Port Sultan Qaboos
- Muscat
- See Map 35
- Sur
- Ras Al Hadd

OMAN

ARABIAN SEA

- Kandla
- Mundra
- Navlakhi
- Mandvi
- Jamnagar
- Vadinar
- Gulf of Kutch
- Okha
- Bedi Bunder
- Cambay
- Dwarkar
- Sikka
- Salaya
- Dahej
- Porbandar
- Bhavnagar
- Baruch
- Mangrol
- Pipavay
- Surat
- Veraval
- Magdalla
- Muldwarka
- Diu
- Gulf of Cambay
- Daman

IND

- Al Khaluf
- Duwwah
- Masirah Is.

20° N

- Ras Madrakah
- Mumbai (FPSO)
- Mumbai
- Jawaharlal Nehru Port
- Sawqirah
- Alibag
- Vikram Ispat
- Murud
- Srivardhan
- Bankot
- Kuria Muria Is.
- Ratnagiri
- Mirbat
- Vengurla
- Port Redi
- Panjim
- Mormugao
- Karwar
- Belekeri
- Kumta
- Honavar
- Bhatkal
- Coondapur
- Malpe
- New Mangalore
- Mangalore
- Kasaragod
- Cannanore
- Tellicherry
- Badagara
- Calicut
- Beypo
- Kiltan I.
- Laccadives (India) (Lakshadweep Is.)
- Amini
- Androth
- Ponnani
- Kavaratti I.
- Kalpeni
- Cochin
- Alleppey
- Neendakara
- Nine Degree Channel
- Quilon
- Minicoy
- Trivandrum
- Eight Degree Channel
- Kolache
- Nager
- C. Com

	Visakhapatnam												
Calcutta	430	Calcutta											
Calicut	1240	1615	Calicut										
Chennai	345	775	960	Chennai									
Cochin	1155	1530	85	875	Cochin								
Colombo	870	1245	390	590	310	Colombo							
Gan	1365	1740	735	1085	665	605	Gan						
Kandla	2105	2480	875	1825	955	1255	1515	Kandla					
Karachi	2190	2565	960	1910	1040	1340	1585	260	Karachi				
Karikal	470	885	860	135	775	490	985	1725	1810	Karikal			
Mangalore	1350	1725	115	1070	195	500	825	763	850	970	Mangalore		
Mormugao	1520	1895	285	1240	365	670	980	605	690	1140	170	Mormugao	
Mumbai	1740	2115	505	1460	585	890	1215	415	501	1360	395	240	Mumbai
Trincomalee	585	975	690	290	605	320	795	1555	1640	185	800	970	1190

Socotra (Yemen)

INDIAN OCEAN

GULF OF KUTCH (Inset)

24° N
70° E 72° E

- Lakhpat
- Jakhau
- Kandla

INDIA

- Mundra
- Navlakhi
- Mandvi
- Vadinar
- Bedi Bunder
- GULF OF KUTCH
- Okha
- Sikka
- Jamnagar
- Cambay
- Salaya
- Porbandar
- Bhavnagar
- Dahej
- Pipavav
- Veraval
- Magdalla
- Muldwarka
- GULF OF CAMBAY
- Daman

INDIAN OCEAN

20° N

See Map 31

- Faddiffolu Atoll
- Male

MALDIVES

- One-and-a-half Degree Channel
- See Map 30
- Equatorial Channel
- Addu Atoll
- Gan

© Shipping Guides Ltd., Reigate, England

From Colombo to:	Miles	Days (at 16 knots)
Cocos I.	1540	4.0
Dunedin	5825	15.2
Durban	3615	9.4
Fremantle	3120	8.1
Muscat	1595	4.2
Port Moresby	4325	11.3
Port Said	3480	9.1
Port Victoria	1645	4.3
Yangon (Rangoon)	1250	3.3
San Francisco	8925	23.3
Singapore	1570	4.1

Map 38

	Api Api													
Bangkok	1000	Bangkok												
Calcutta	1900	2480	Calcutta											
Cocos I.	955	1950	2170	Cocos I.										
Dampier	1445	2440	3185	1270	Dampier									
Haiphong	1495	1375	2975	2330	2735	Haiphong								
Hong Kong	1630	1490	3110	2450	2775	640	Hong Kong							
Jakarta	305	1290	2170	715	1205	1670	1790	Jakarta						
Kota Baru	800	1675	2595	1355	1075	1920	1765	655	Kota Baru					
Labuan	810	1130	2385	1595	2010	1310	1150	935	1110	Labuan				
Macassar	960	1805	2755	1445	1025	2000	1825	765	230	1175	Macassar			
Pontianak	330	1015	2005	1080	1465	1340	1465	420	725	588	850	Pontianak		
Port Blair	1180	1760	775	1450	2455	2255	2390	1450	1875	1665	2035	1285	Port Blair	
Yangon (Rangoon)	1370	1950	780	1755	2740	2445	2580	1645	2065	1855	2225	1475	385	Yangon
Sandakan	1115	1440	2690	1960	1745	1300	1115	1250	720	415	800	900	1970	2160	Sandakan
Singapore	250	830	1650	1170	1660	1325	1460	525	945	735	1105	355	930	1120	1040	Singapore
Surabaya	585	1485	2405	1090	990	1820	1940	385	370	1080	440	545	1685	1870	1075	760	Surabaya
Tarakan	1255	1685	2935	1815	1520	1550	1320	1110	480	690	555	1150	2215	2405	285	1285	820

© Shipping Guides Ltd., Reigate, England

MAP 38 – WESTERN INDONESIA, MALAYSIA AND BRUNEI

Map 39

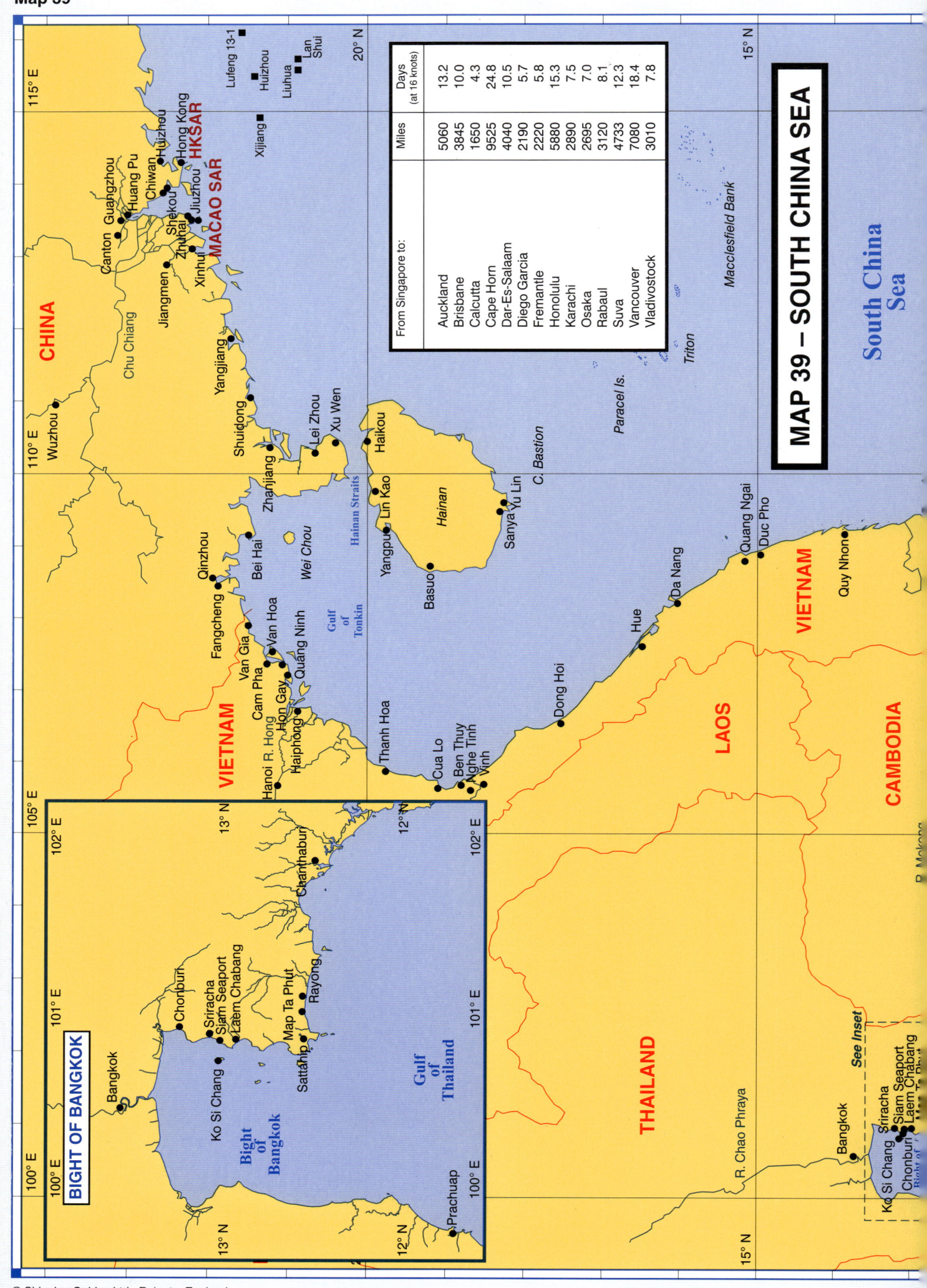

MAP 39 – SOUTH CHINA SEA

From Singapore to:	Miles	Days (at 16 knots)
Auckland	5060	13.2
Brisbane	3845	10.0
Calcutta	1650	4.3
Cape Horn	9525	24.8
Dar-Es-Salaam	4040	10.5
Diego Garcia	2190	5.7
Fremantle	2220	5.8
Honolulu	5880	15.3
Karachi	2890	7.5
Osaka	2695	7.0
Rabaul	3120	8.1
Suva	4733	12.3
Vancouver	7080	18.4
Vladivostock	3010	7.8

BIGHT OF BANGKOK

© Shipping Guides Ltd., Reigate, England

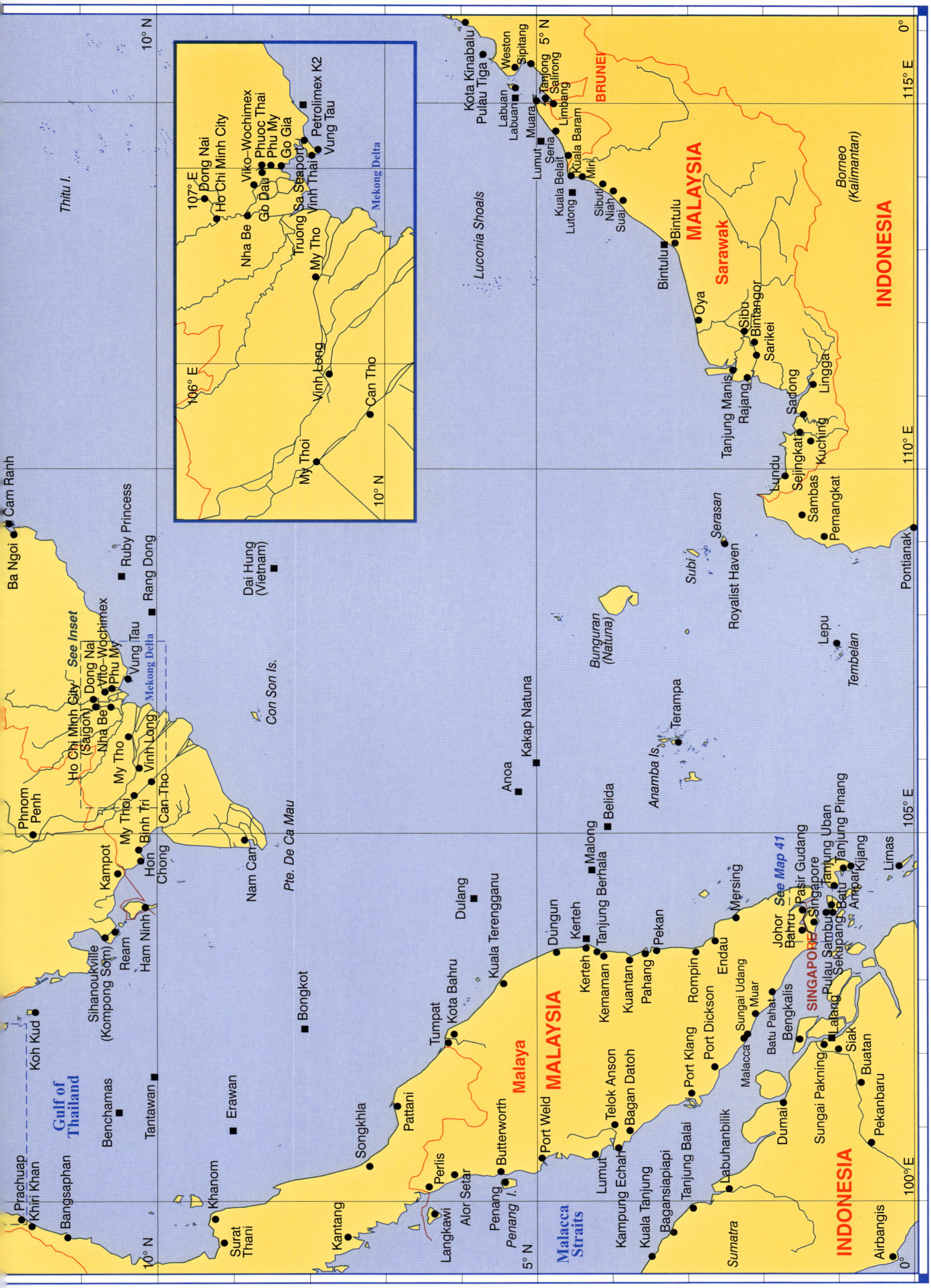
Gulf of Thailand
Prachuap Khiri Khan
Bangsaphan
Koh Kud
Benchamas
Tantawan
Erawan
Khanom
Surat Thani
Kantang
Songkhla
Pattani
Langkawi
Perlis
Alor Setar
Penang
Penang I.
Butterworth
Malacca Straits
Port Weld
Lumut
Malaya
MALAYSIA
Tumpat
Kota Bahru
Kuala Terengganu
Dulang
Dungun
Kerteh
Kemaman
Tanjung Berhala
Malong
Belida
Kuantan
Pahang
Pekan
Rompin
Endau
Mersing
Telok Anson
Bagan Datoh
Kampung Echah
Kuala Tanjung
Bagansiapiapi
Tanjung Balai
Labuhanbilik
Port Klang
Port Dickson
Malacca
Sungai Udang
Muar
Batu Pahat
Bengkalis
Dumai
Sungai Pakning
Lalang
Siak
Buatan
Pekanbaru
Airbangis
Sumatra
INDONESIA
SINGAPORE
Johor Bahru
Pasir Gudang
Singapore
Pulau Sambu
Sekupang
Batu Ampar
Tanjung Uban
Tanjung Pinang
Kijang
Limas
See Map 41
Sihanoukville (Kompong Som)
Ream
Ham Ninh
Hon Chong
Kampot
Phnom Penh
Binh Tri
My Thoi
Can Tho
Vinh Long
My Tho
Nha Be
Ho Chi Minh City (Saigon)
Dong Nai
Vito-Wochimex
Phu My
Vung Tau
See Inset
Mekong Delta
Rang Dong
Ruby Princess
Ba Ngoi
Cam Ranh
Nam Can
Pte. De Ca Mau
Bongkot
Con Son Is.
Dai Hung (Vietnam)
Thitu I.
Anoa
Kakap Natuna
Anamba Is.
Terampa
Bunguran (Natuna)
Subi
Serasan
Royalist Haven
Lepu
Tembelan
Pontianak
Pemangkat
Sambas
Sejingkat
Lundu
Kuching
Sadong
Lingga
Rajang
Tanjung Manis
Sarikei
Bintangor
Sibu
Oya
Bintulu
Sarawak
MALAYSIA
INDONESIA
Borneo (Kalimantan)
Suai
Niah
Sibuti
Miri
Lutong
Kuala Baram
Kuala Belait
Seria
Lumut
Muara
BRUNEI
Limbang
Labuan
Weston
Sipitang
Tanjong Salirong
Pulau Tiga
Kota Kinabalu
Luconia Shoals
Dong Nai
Ho Chi Minh City
Viko-Wochimex
Phuoc Thai
Phu My
Go Gia
Nha Be
Go Dau
Sa Seaport
Truong
Vinh Thai
Petrolimex K2
Vung Tau
Mekong Delta
My Tho
Vinh Long
Can Tho
My Thoi
106° E
107° E
10° N
5° N
0°
100° E
105° E
110° E
115° E

MAP 40 – STRAIT OF MALACCA

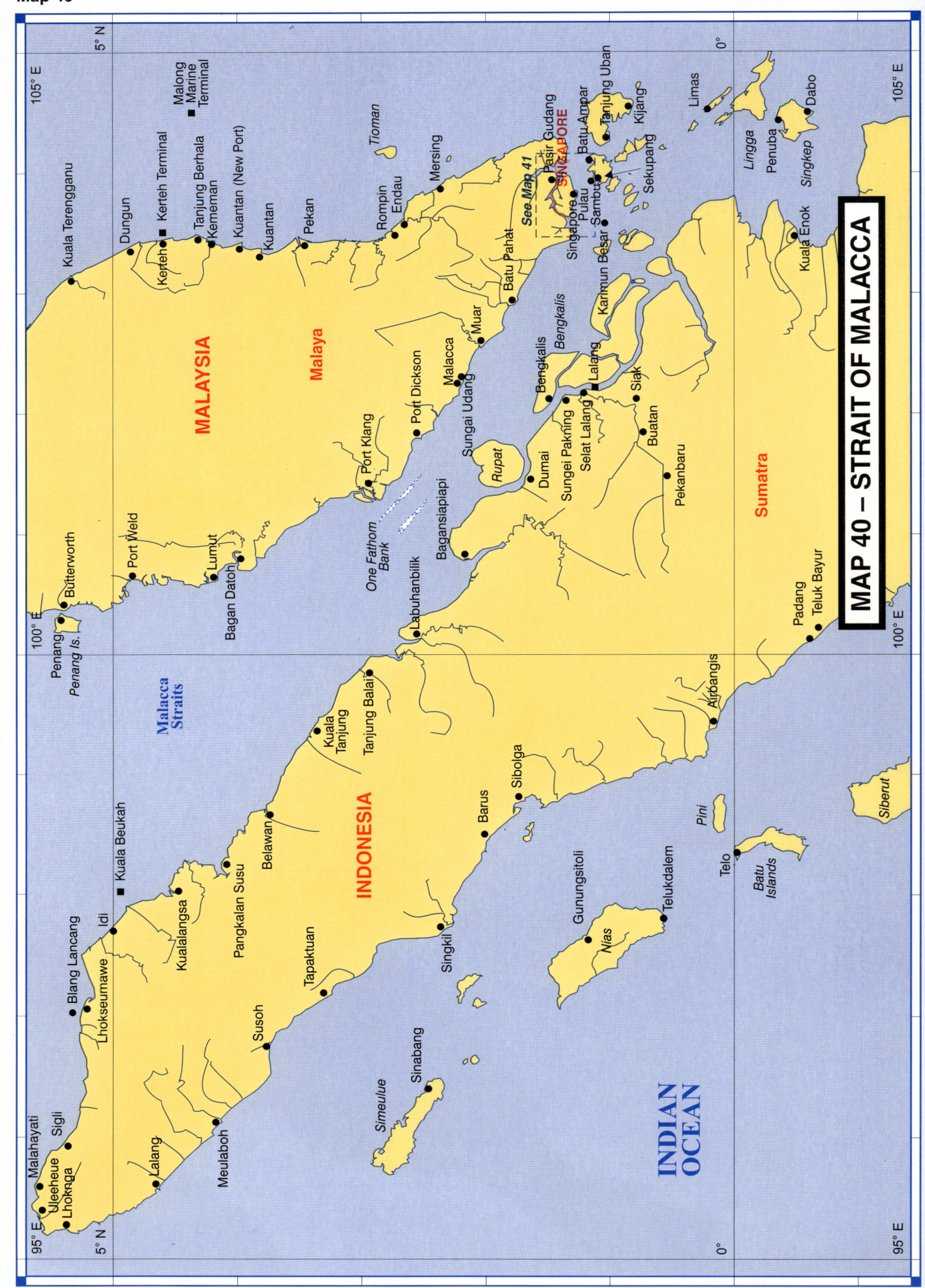

MAP 41 – SINGAPORE

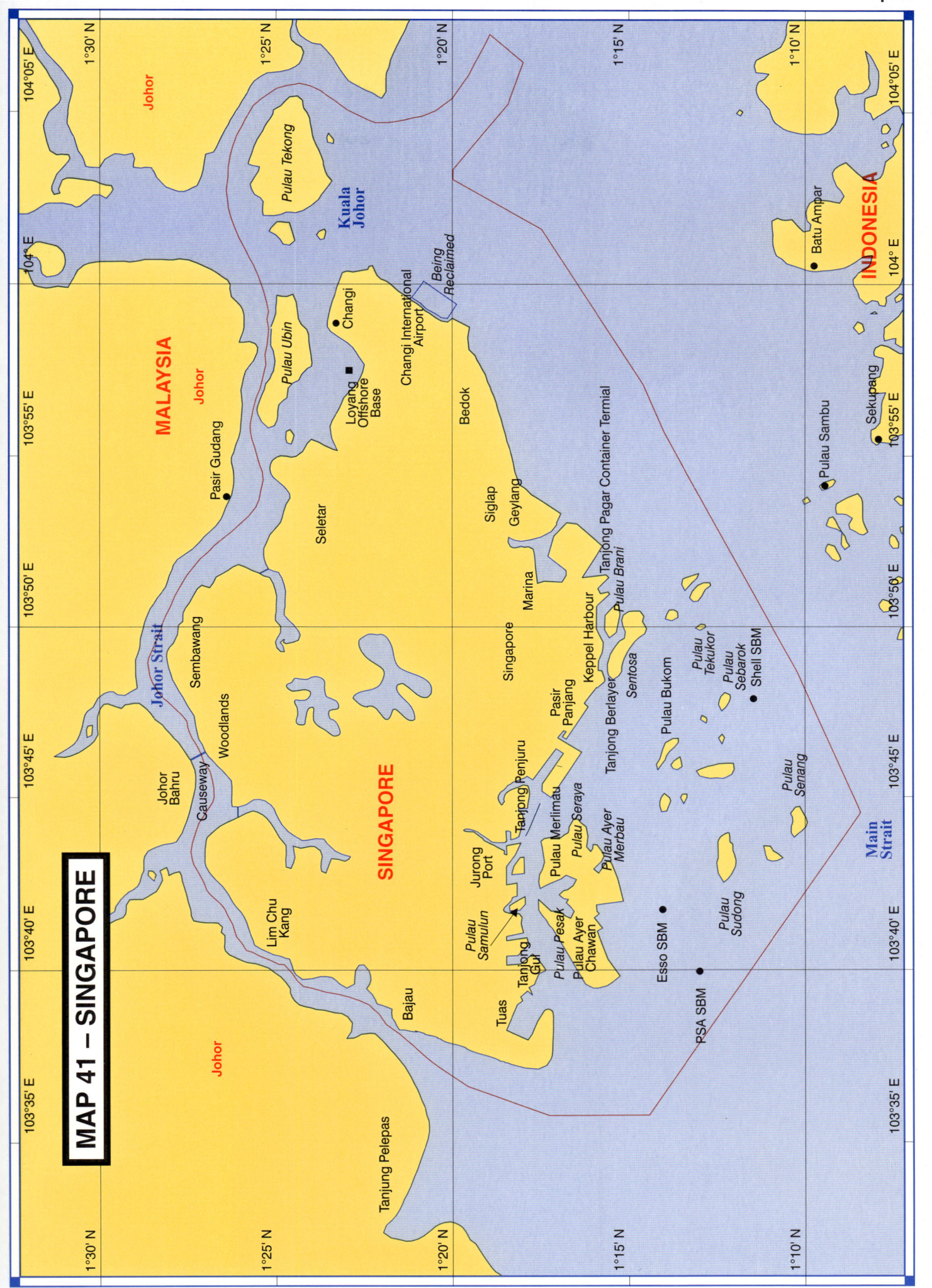

Map 42

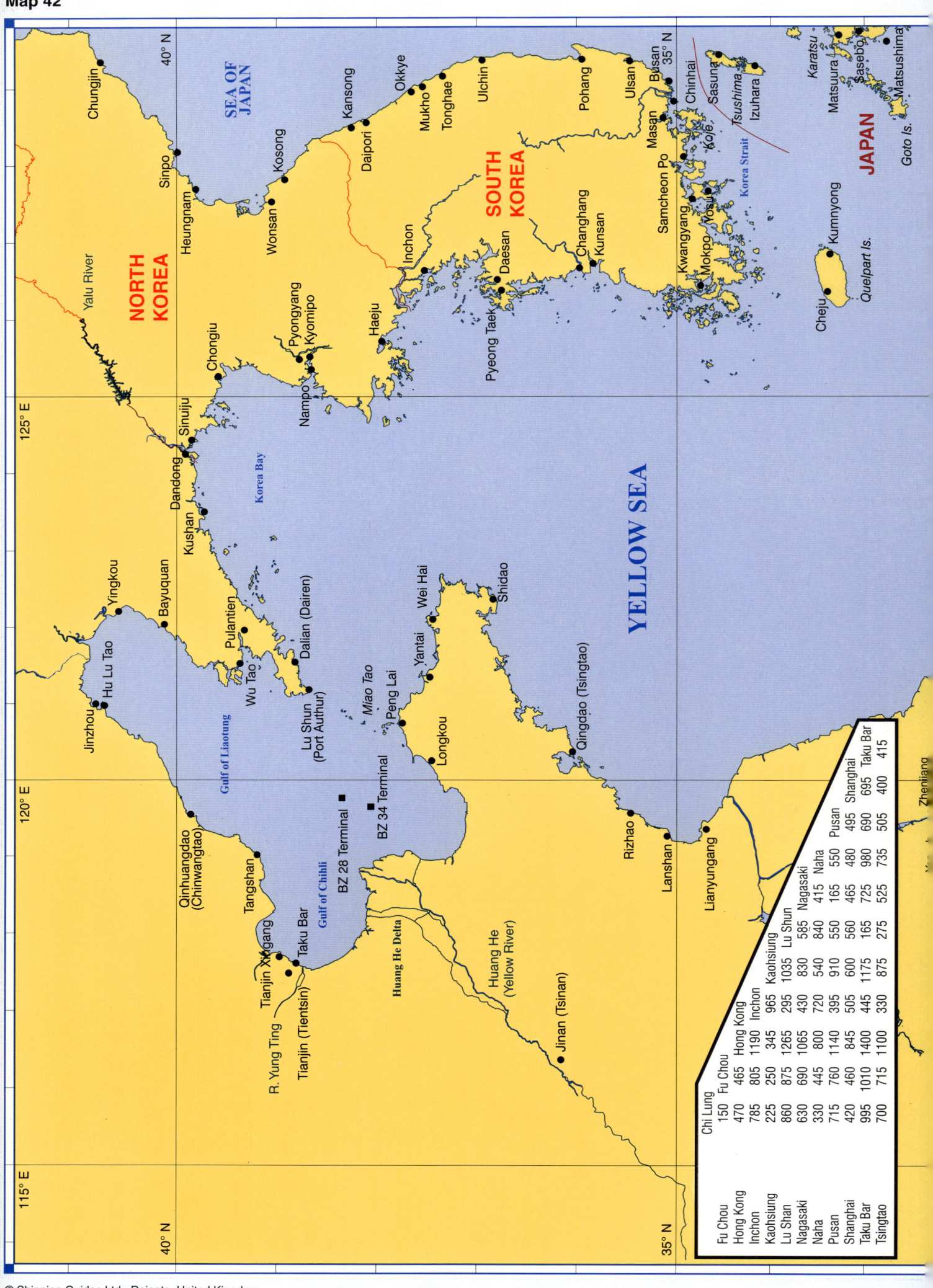

Distance Table

	Chi Lung	Fu Chou	Hong Kong	Inchon	Kaohsiung	Lu Shan	Nagasaki	Naha	Pusan	Shanghai	Taku Bar
Fu Chou	150										
Hong Kong	470	465									
Inchon	785	805	1190								
Kaohsiung	225	250	345	965							
Lu Shan	860	875	1265	295	1035						
Nagasaki	630	690	1065	430	830	585					
Naha	330	445	800	720	540	840	415				
Pusan	715	760	1140	395	910	550	165	550			
Shanghai	420	460	845	505	600	560	465	480	495		
Taku Bar	995	1010	1400	445	1175	165	725	980	690	695	
Tsingtao	700	715	1100	330	875	275	525	735	505	400	415

Locations shown on map:

North Korea: Chungjin, Sinpo, Heungnam, Kosong, Wonsan, Chongju, Pyongyang, Kyomipo, Nampo, Sinuiju, Dandong, Yalu River

South Korea: Kansong, Daipori, Mukho, Tonghae, Okkye, Ulchin, Pohang, Ulsan, Busan, Chinhai, Masan, Samcheon Po, Kwangyang, Yosu, Mokpo, Kumnyong, Cheju, Kunsan, Changhang, Daesan, Pyeong Taek, Inchon, Haeju

Japan: Karatsu, Matsuura, Sasuna, Izuhara, Tsushima, Sasebo, Matsushima, Goto Is., Korea Strait, Quelpart Is.

China: Jinzhou, Hu Lu Tao, Yingkou, Bayuquan, Kushan, Pulantien, Wu Tao, Dalian (Dairen), Lu Shun (Port Arthur), Miao Tao, Peng Lai, Longkou, Yantai, Wei Hai, Shidao, Qingdao (Tsingtao), Rizhao, Lanshan, Lianyungang, Zhenjiang, Jinan (Tsinan), Huang He (Yellow River), Huang He Delta, Tangshan, Qinhuangdao (Chinwangtao), Tianjin Xingang, Taku Bar, Tianjin (Tientsin), R. Yung Ting, BZ 28 Terminal, BZ 34 Terminal, Gulf of Liaotung, Gulf of Chihli, Korea Bay, Yellow Sea, Sea of Japan

© Shipping Guides Ltd., Reigate, United Kingdom

MAP 42 – YELLOW SEA / EAST CHINA SEA

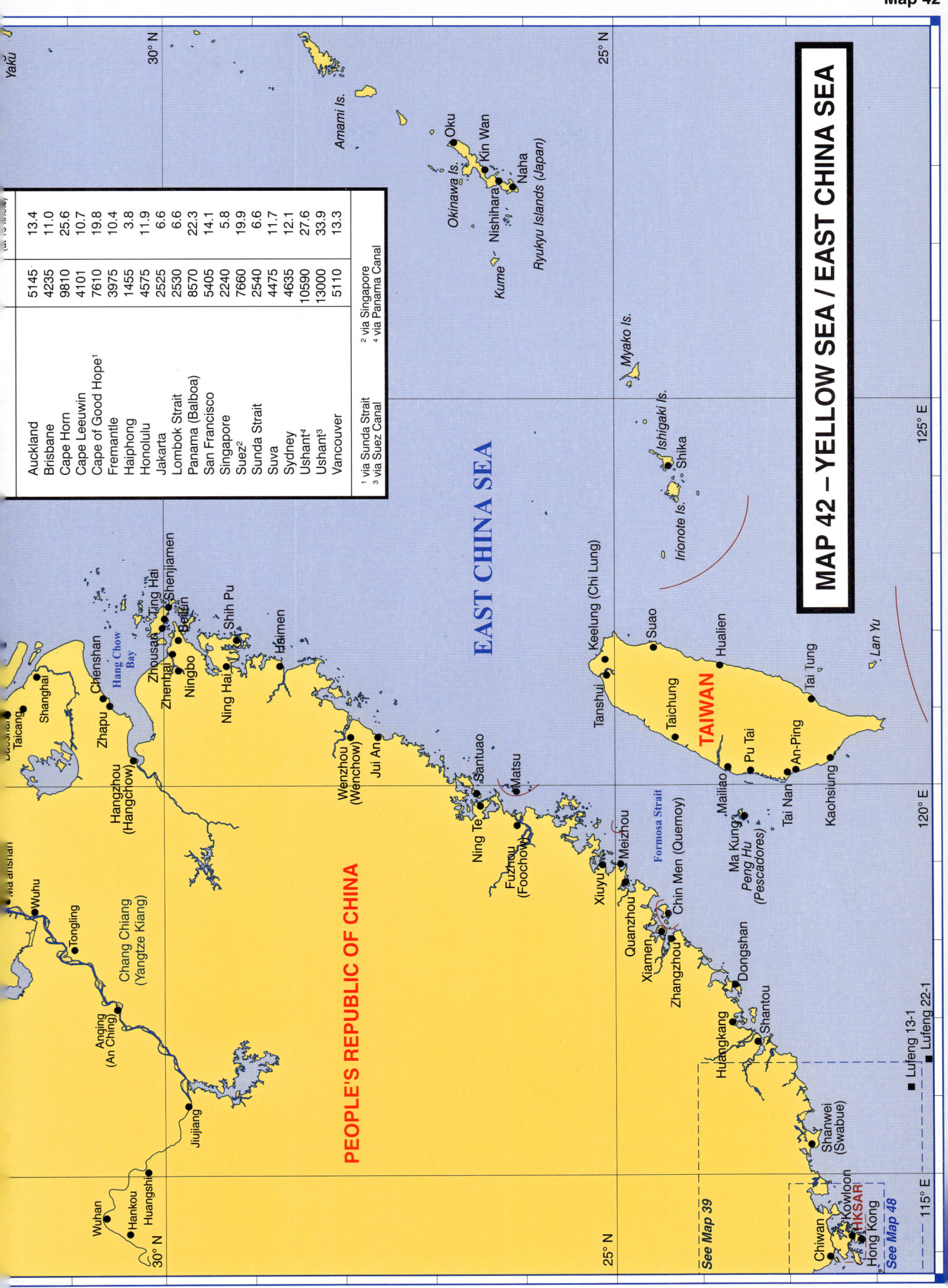

Auckland	5145	13.4
Brisbane	4235	11.0
Cape Horn	9810	25.6
Cape Leeuwin	4101	10.7
Cape of Good Hope[1]	7610	19.8
Fremantle	3975	10.4
Haiphong	1455	3.8
Honolulu	4575	11.9
Jakarta	2525	6.6
Lombok Strait	2530	6.6
Panama (Balboa)	8570	22.3
San Francisco	5405	14.1
Singapore	2240	5.8
Suez[2]	7660	19.9
Sunda Strait	2540	6.6
Suva	4475	11.7
Sydney	4635	12.1
Ushant[4]	10590	27.6
Ushant[3]	13000	33.9
Vancouver	5110	13.3

[1] via Sunda Strait
[2] via Singapore
[3] via Suez Canal
[4] via Panama Canal

PEOPLE'S REPUBLIC OF CHINA

EAST CHINA SEA

TAIWAN

Ports and locations: Yaku, Amami Is., Okinawa Is., Oku, Kume, Nishihara, Kin Wan, Naha, Ryukyu Islands (Japan), Myako Is., Ishigaki Is., Shika, Irionote Is., Lan Yu, Tanshui, Keelung (Chi Lung), Suao, Hualien, Taichung, Pu Tai, Tai Tung, An-Ping, Tai Nan, Mailiao, Kaohsiung, Ma Kung, Peng Hu (Pescadores), Chin Men (Quemoy), Formosa Strait, Matsu, Meizhou, Xiuyu, Fuzhou (Foochow), Ning Te, Santuao, Jui An, Wenzhou (Wenchow), Xiamen, Quanzhou, Zhangzhou, Dongshan, Shantou, Huangkang, Shanwei (Swabue), Chiwan, Kowloon, HKSAR, Hong Kong, Lufeng 13-1, Lufeng 22-1, Xiamen, Shih Pu, Ning Hai, Beilun, Ningbo, Zhenhai, Shenjiamen, Zhoushan, Ning Hai, Hang Chow Bay, Chenshan, Zhapu, Hangzhou (Hangchow), Shanghai, Taicang, Wuhu, Tongling, Anqing (An Ching), Chang Chiang (Yangtze Kiang), Jiujiang, Huangshi, Hankou, Wuhan

See Map 39
See Map 48

Map 43

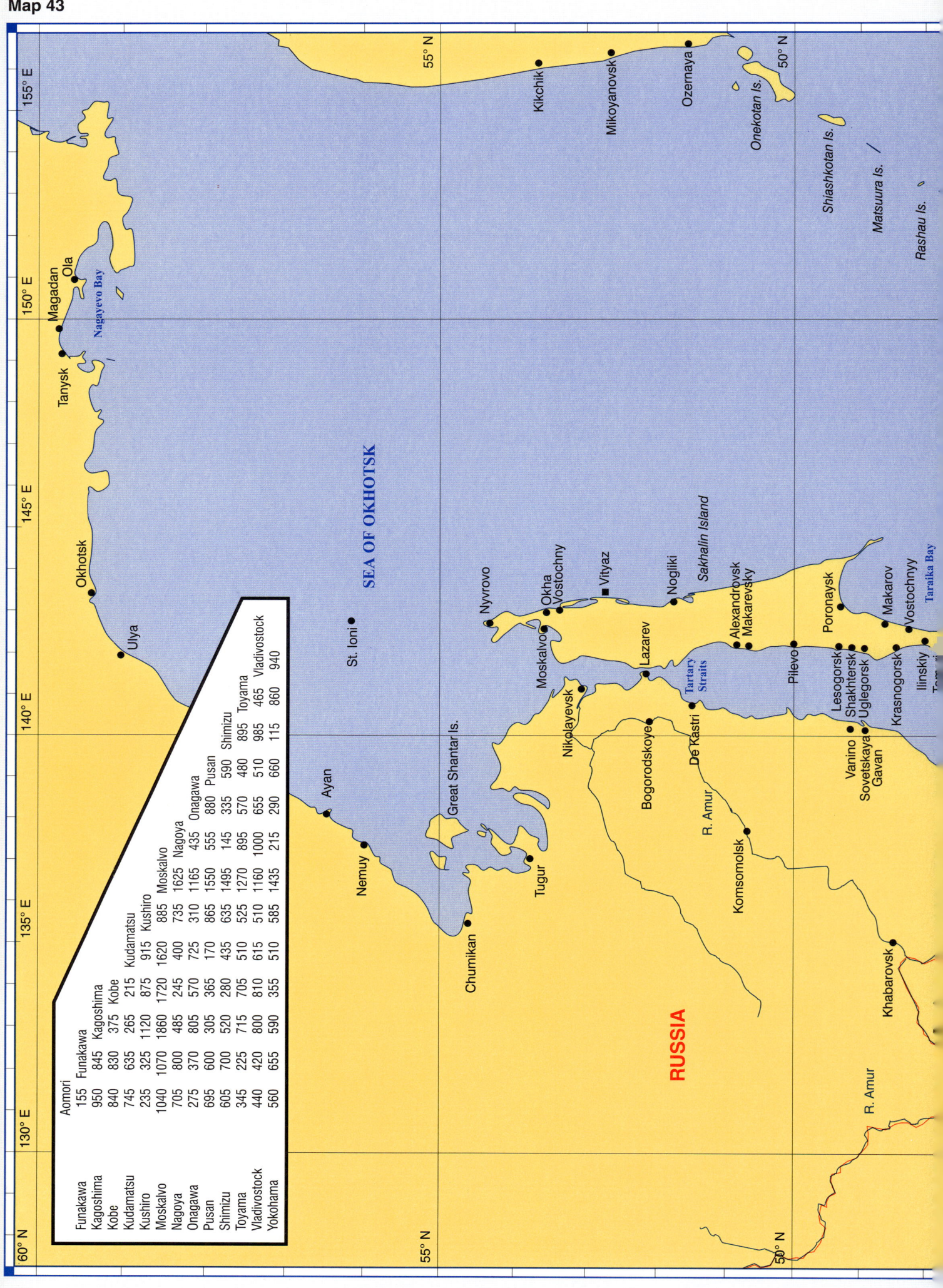

Distance Table

	Aomori	Funakawa	Kagoshima	Kobe	Kudamatsu	Kushiro	Moskalvo	Nagoya	Onagawa	Pusan	Shimizu	Toyama	Vladivostock
Funakawa	155												
Kagoshima	950	845											
Kobe	840	830	375										
Kudamatsu	745	635	265	215									
Kushiro	235	325	1120	875	915								
Moskalvo	1040	1070	1860	1720	1620	885							
Nagoya	705	800	485	245	400	735	1625						
Onagawa	275	370	805	570	725	310	1165	435					
Pusan	695	600	305	365	170	865	1550	435	880				
Shimizu	605	700	520	280	435	635	1495	145	335	590			
Toyama	345	225	715	705	510	525	1270	895	570	895	480		
Vladivostock	440	420	800	810	615	510	1160	1000	655	985	510	465	
Yokohama	560	655	590	355	510	585	1435	215	290	660	115	860	940

SEA OF OKHOTSK

RUSSIA

Locations: Tanysk, Magadan, Ola, Nagayevo Bay, Okhotsk, Ulya, Kikchik, Mikoyanovsk, Ozernaya, Onekotan Is., Shiashkotan Is., Matsuura Is., Rashau Is., St. Ioni, Ayan, Great Shantar Is., Nemuy, Tugur, Chumikan, Nyvrovo, Moskalvo, Okha, Vostochny, Vityaz, Nogliki, Sakhalin Island, Alexandrovsk, Makarevsky, Poronaysk, Makarov, Vostochnyy, Taraika Bay, Nikolayevsk, Bogorodskoye, Lazarev, Tartary Straits, De Kastri, Pilevo, Lesogorsk, Shakhtersk, Uglegorsk, Krasnogorsk, Ilinskiy, Vanino, Sovetskaya Gavan, R. Amur, Komsomolsk, Khabarovsk

© Shipping Guides Ltd., Reigate, United Kingdom

MAP 43 – JAPAN / SEA OF OKHOTSK

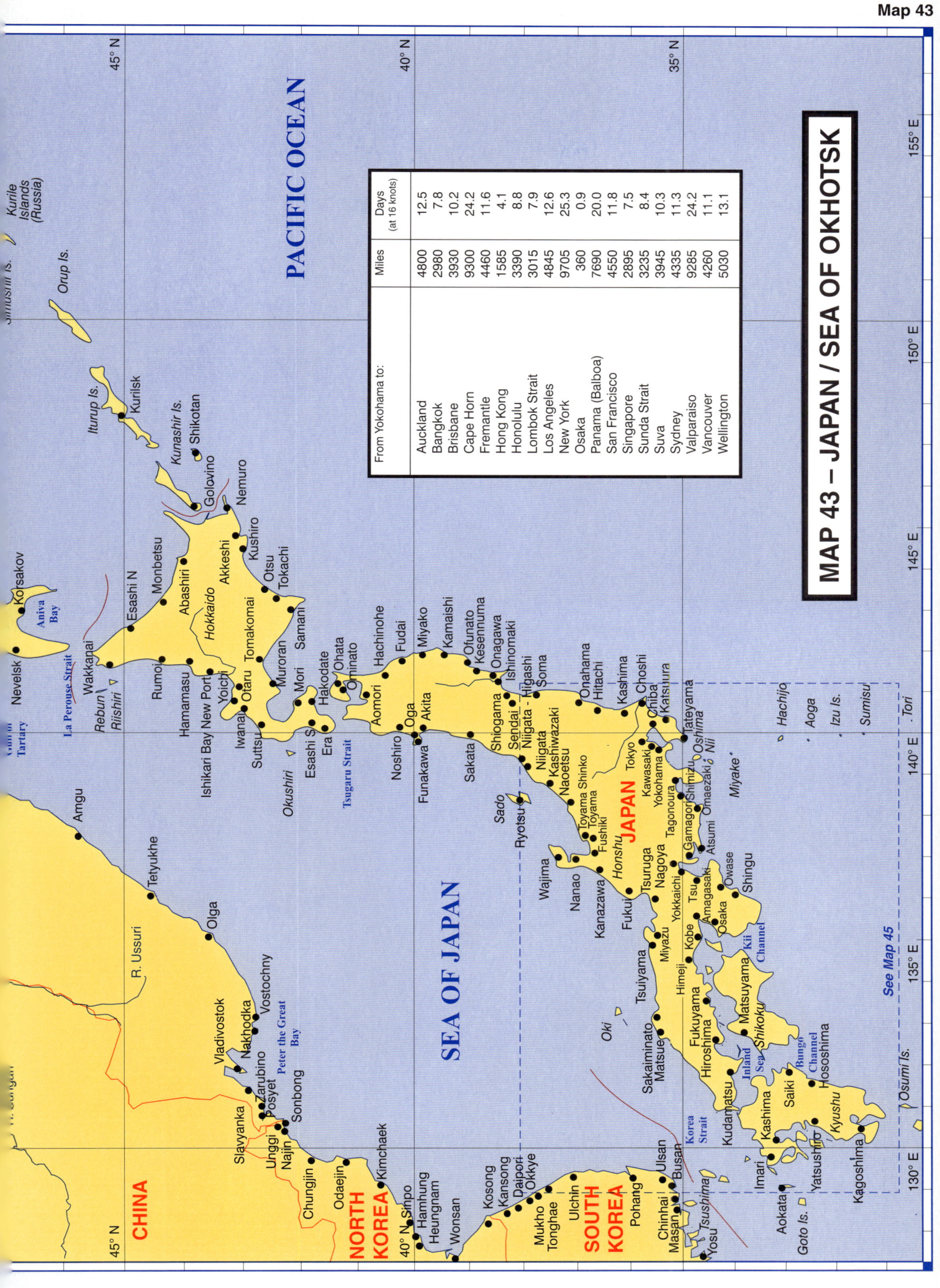

From Yokohama to:	Miles	Days (at 16 knots)
Auckland	4800	12.5
Bangkok	2980	7.8
Brisbane	3930	10.2
Cape Horn	9300	24.2
Fremantle	4460	11.6
Hong Kong	1585	4.1
Honolulu	3390	8.8
Lombok Strait	3015	7.9
Los Angeles	4845	12.6
New York	9705	25.3
Osaka	360	0.9
Panama (Balboa)	7690	20.0
San Francisco	4550	11.8
Singapore	2895	7.5
Sunda Strait	3235	8.4
Suva	3945	10.3
Sydney	4335	11.3
Valparaiso	9285	24.2
Vancouver	4260	11.1
Wellington	5030	13.1

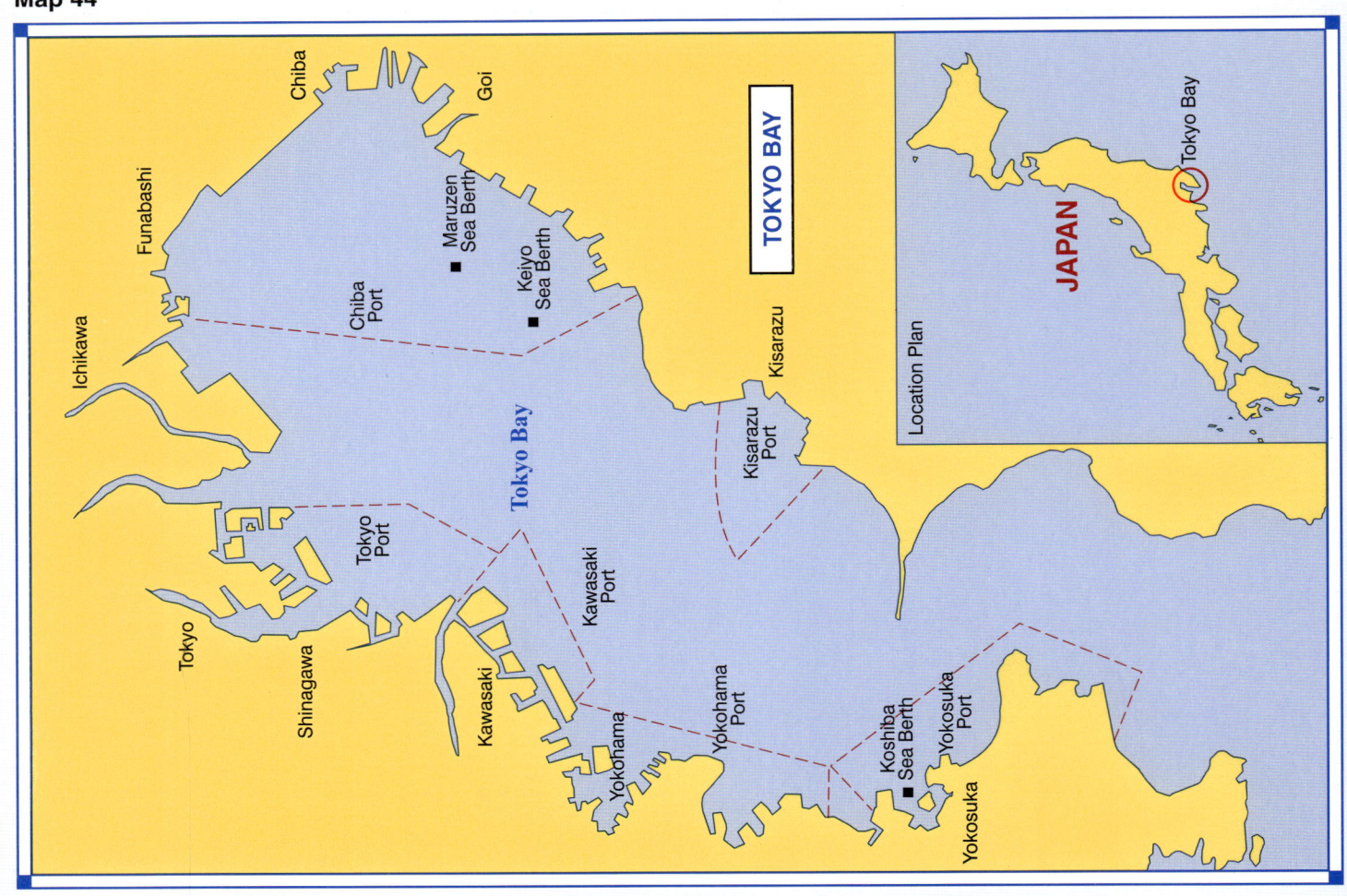

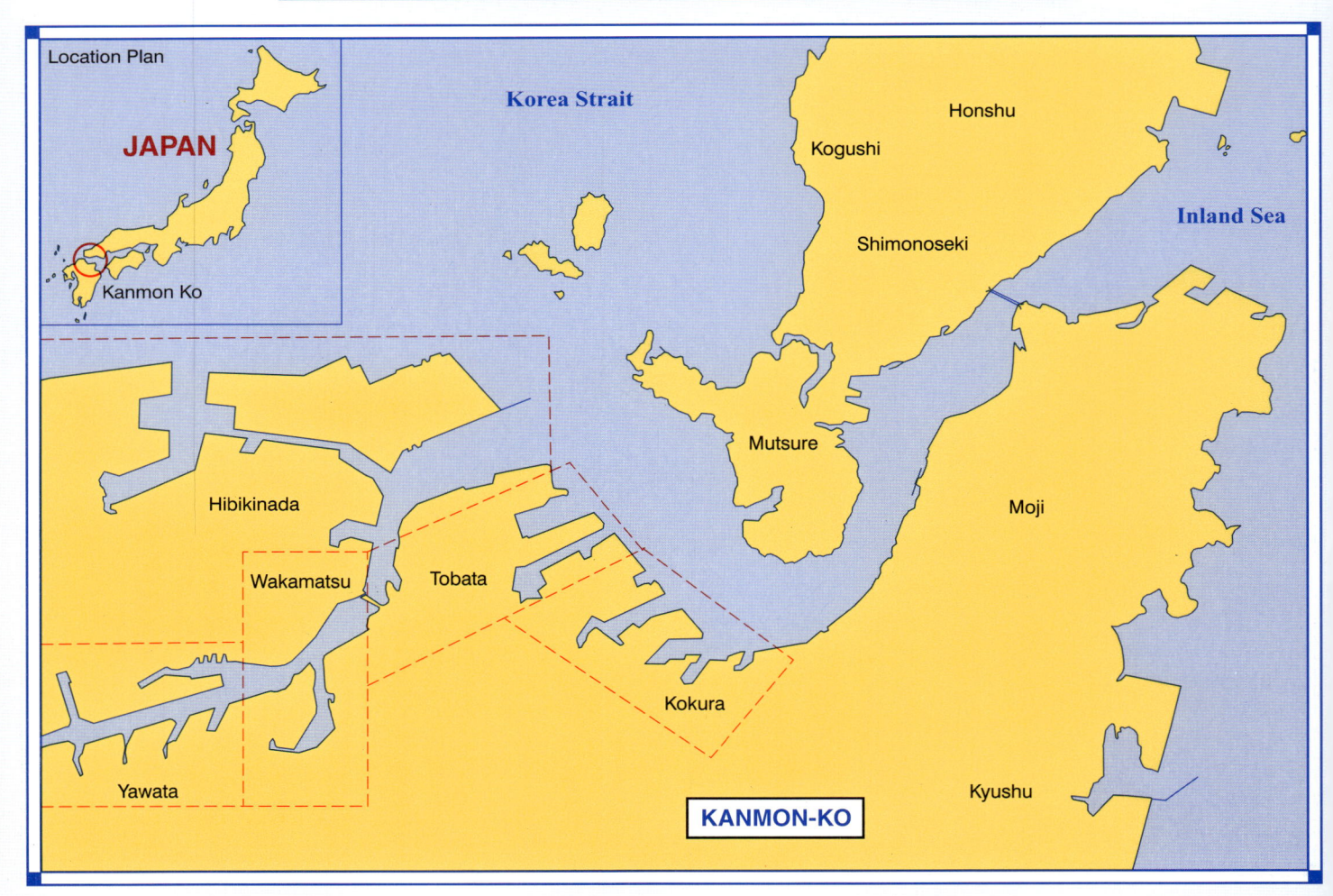

MAP 44 - JAPANESE COASTAL AREAS

Map 44

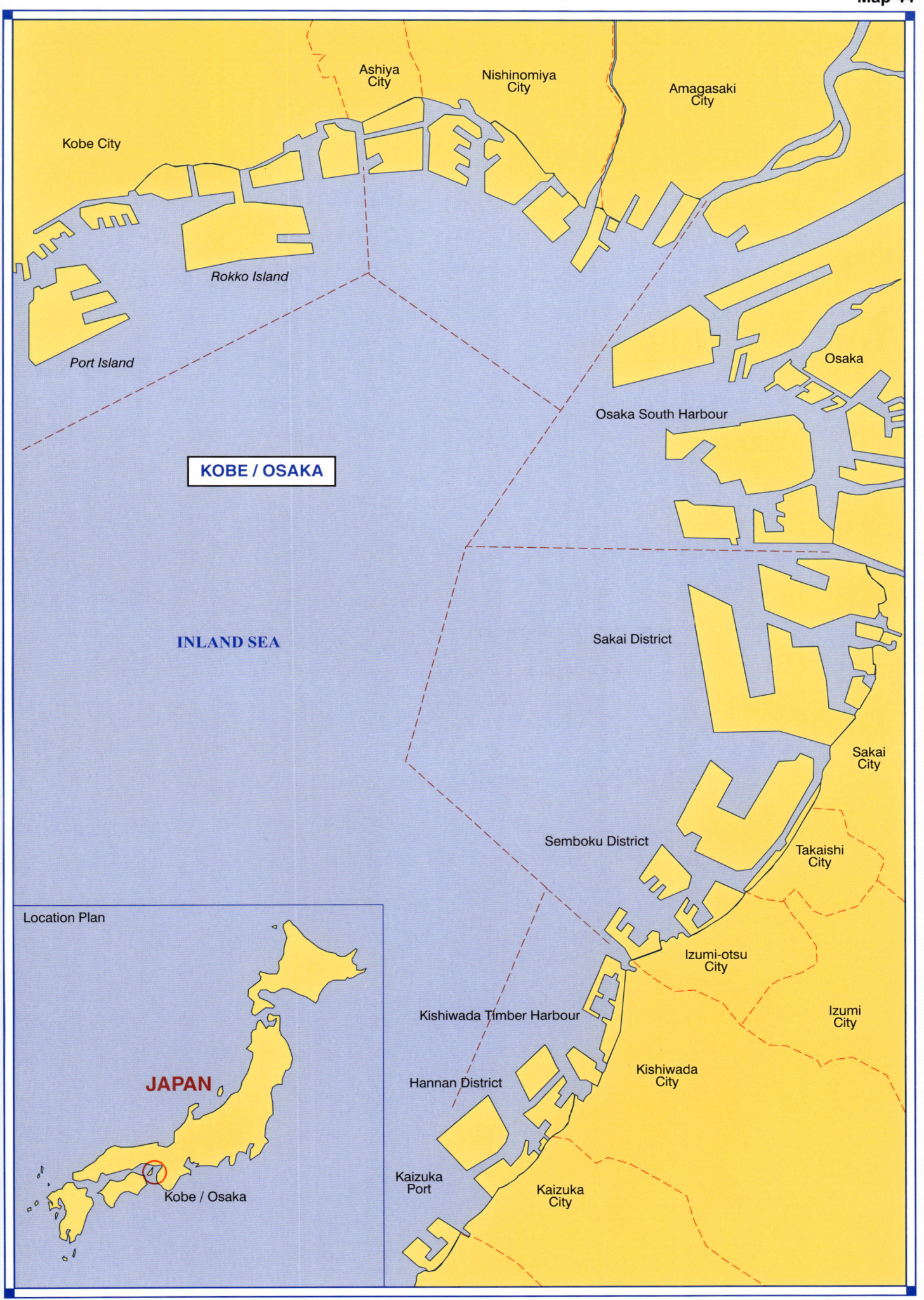

KOBE / OSAKA

INLAND SEA

- Kobe City
- Ashiya City
- Nishinomiya City
- Amagasaki City
- Rokko Island
- Port Island
- Osaka
- Osaka South Harbour
- Sakai District
- Sakai City
- Semboku District
- Takaishi City
- Izumi-otsu City
- Izumi City
- Kishiwada Timber Harbour
- Kishiwada City
- Hannan District
- Kaizuka Port
- Kaizuka City

Location Plan

JAPAN

Kobe / Osaka

MAP 45 – SOUTHERN JAPAN AND INLAND SEA

Map 45

	Hakata															
Hamada	130	Hamada														
Himeji	280	325	Himeji													
Hiroshima	170	210	155	Hiroshima												
Kagoshima	255	365	390	290	Kagoshima											
Kashima	675	955	445	585	665	Kashima										
Kudamatsu	110	155	185	65	265	580	Kudamatsu									
Matsuyama	155	195	130	45	270	560	60	Matsuyama								
Miike	175	280	430	320	180	775	265	305	Miike							
Mutsure	52	95	230	115	285	620	60	100	205	Mutsure						
Nagasaki	115	225	375	265	165	755	205	245	75	145	Nagasaki					
Oita	140	185	195	92	240	565	54	70	295	90	235	Oita				
Osaka	310	355	45	185	380	435	215	160	465	260	405	225	Osaka			
Sakaide	230	275	53	105	345	495	135	80	380	180	325	145	85	Sakaide		
Sasebo	100	205	355	245	190	750	190	230	110	130	50	220	390	305	Sasebo	
Shimizu	530	575	300	440	520	185	435	415	630	480	615	420	290	340	606	Shimizu
Susaki	255	300	175	195	255	455	165	175	360	205	345	145	160	215	330	310	Susaki
Wakayama	320	365	53	195	350	405	220	170	465	270	440	235	42	94	395	255	130

Map 46

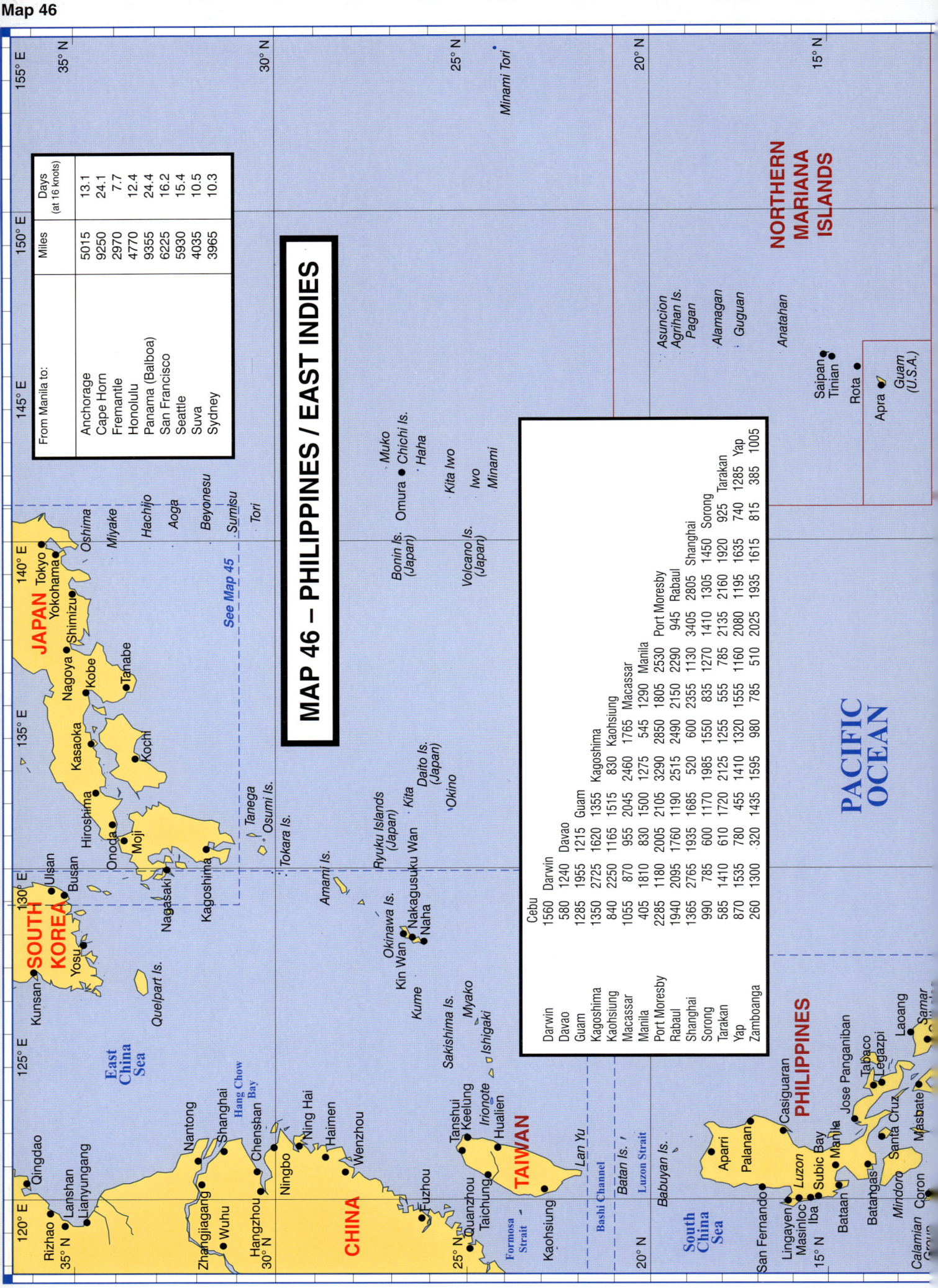

MAP 46 – PHILIPPINES / EAST INDIES

From Manila to:

From Manila to:	Miles	Days (at 16 knots)
Anchorage	5015	13.1
Cape Horn	9250	24.1
Fremantle	2970	7.7
Honolulu	4770	12.4
Panama (Balboa)	9355	24.4
San Francisco	6225	16.2
Seattle	5930	15.4
Suva	4035	10.5
Sydney	3965	10.3

Distance Table

	Cebu	Darwin	Davao	Guam	Kagoshima	Kaohsiung	Macassar	Manila	Port Moresby	Rabaul	Shanghai	Sorong	Tarakan	Yap
Darwin	1560													
Davao	580	1240												
Guam	1285	1955	1215											
Kagoshima	1350	2725	1620	1355										
Kaohsiung	840	2250	1165	1515	830									
Macassar	1055	870	955	2045	2460	1765								
Manila	405	1810	830	1500	1275	545	1290							
Port Moresby	2285	1180	2005	2105	3290	2850	1805	2530						
Rabaul	1940	2095	1760	1190	2515	2490	2150	2290	945					
Shanghai	1365	2765	1935	1685	520	600	2355	1130	3405	2805				
Sorong	990	785	600	1170	1985	1550	835	1270	1410	1305	2160			
Tarakan	585	1410	610	1720	2125	1255	555	785	2135	1920	1450	1195		
Yap	870	1535	780	455	1410	1320	1555	1160	2080	1635	925	740	1285	
Zamboanga	260	1300	320	1435	1595	980	510	785	2025	1935	1615	815	385	1005

Map 46

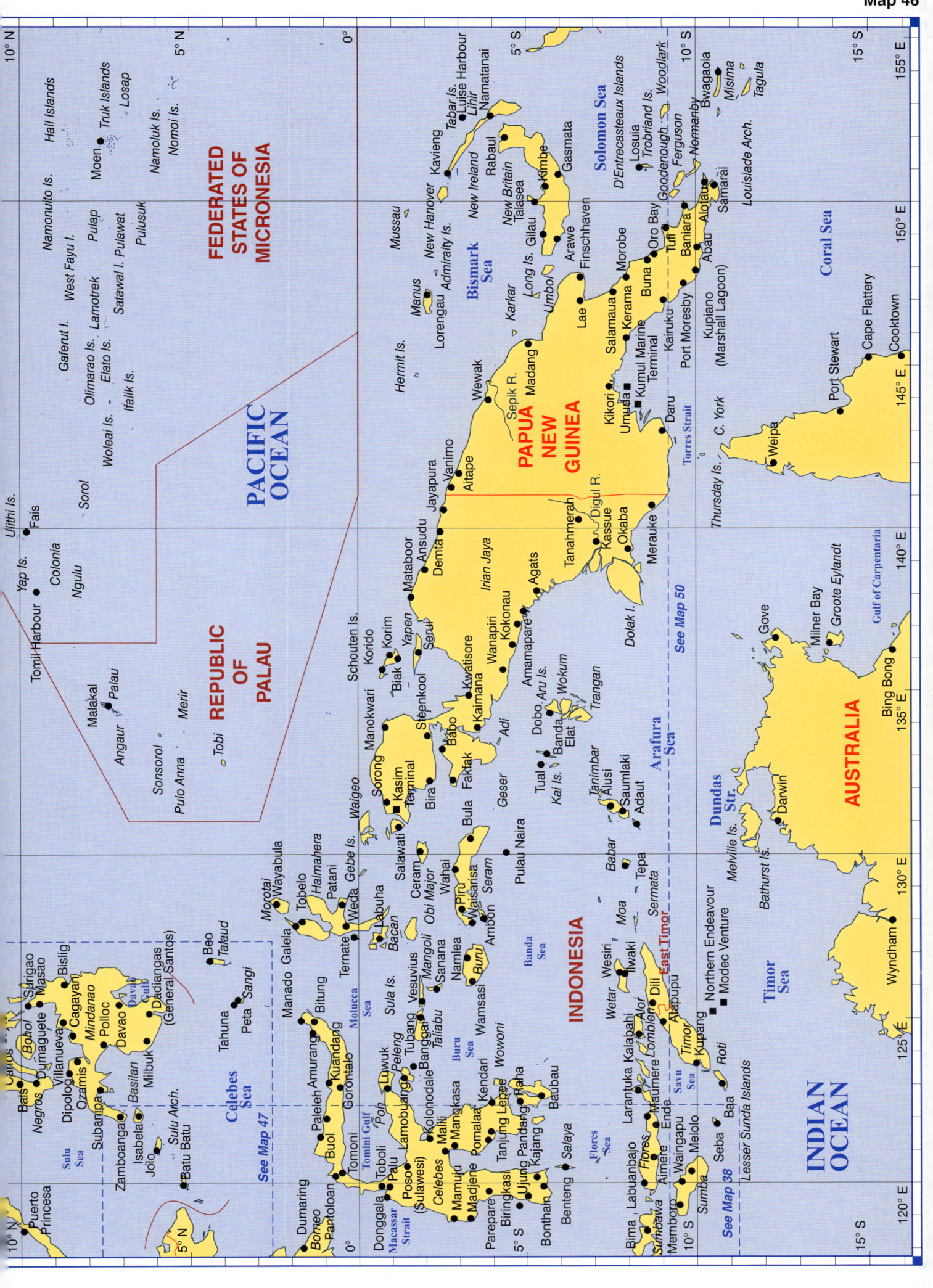

MAP 47 – PHILIPPINE ISLANDS

MAP 48 – GUANGZHOU / HONG KONG / MACAU

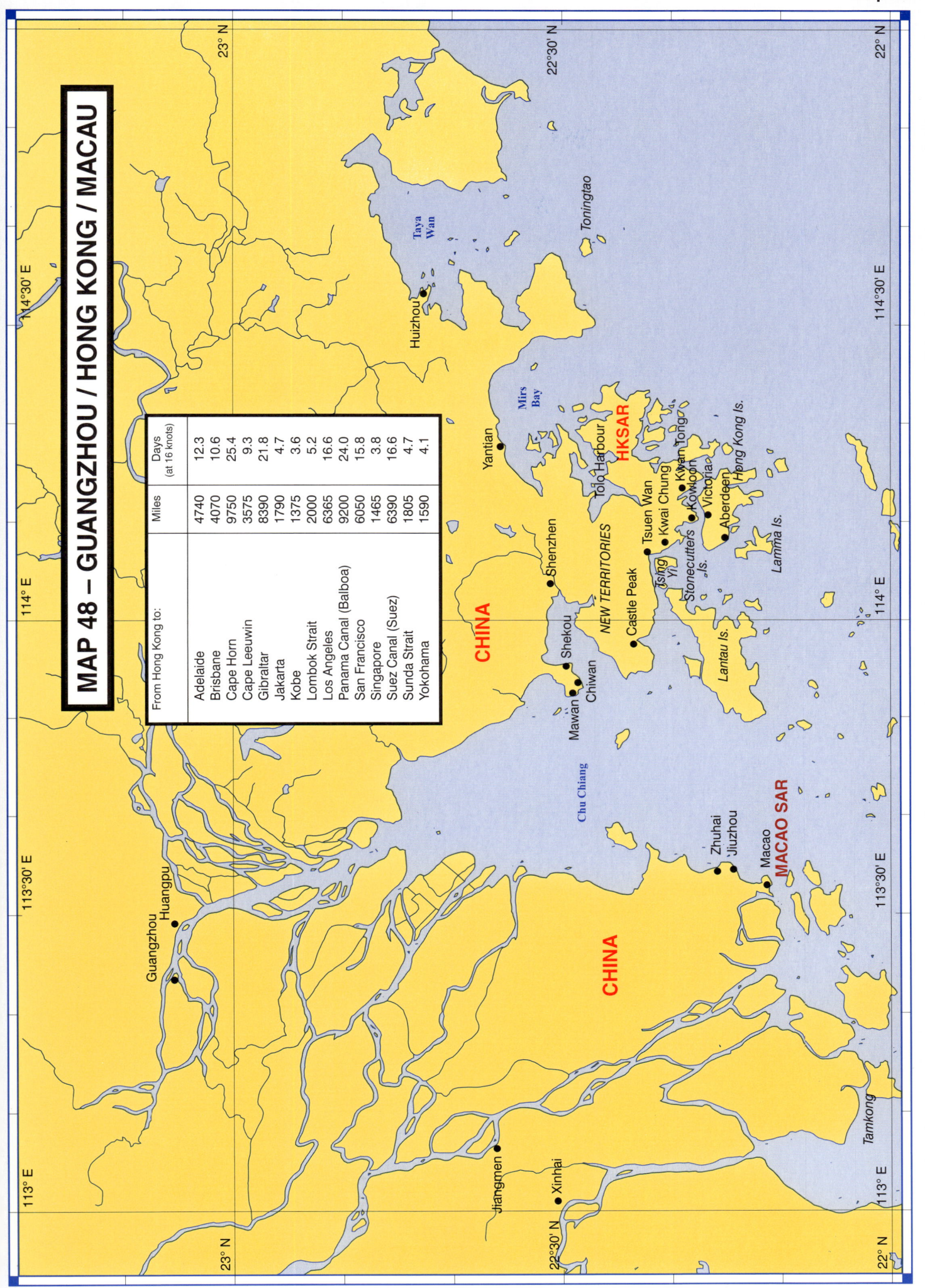

From Hong Kong to:	Miles	Days (at 16 knots)
Adelaide	4740	12.3
Brisbane	4070	10.6
Cape Horn	9750	25.4
Cape Leeuwin	3575	9.3
Gibraltar	8390	21.8
Jakarta	1790	4.7
Kobe	1375	3.6
Lombok Strait	2000	5.2
Los Angeles	6365	16.6
Panama Canal (Balboa)	9200	24.0
San Francisco	6050	15.8
Singapore	1465	3.8
Suez Canal (Suez)	6390	16.6
Sunda Strait	1805	4.7
Yokohama	1590	4.1

Map 49

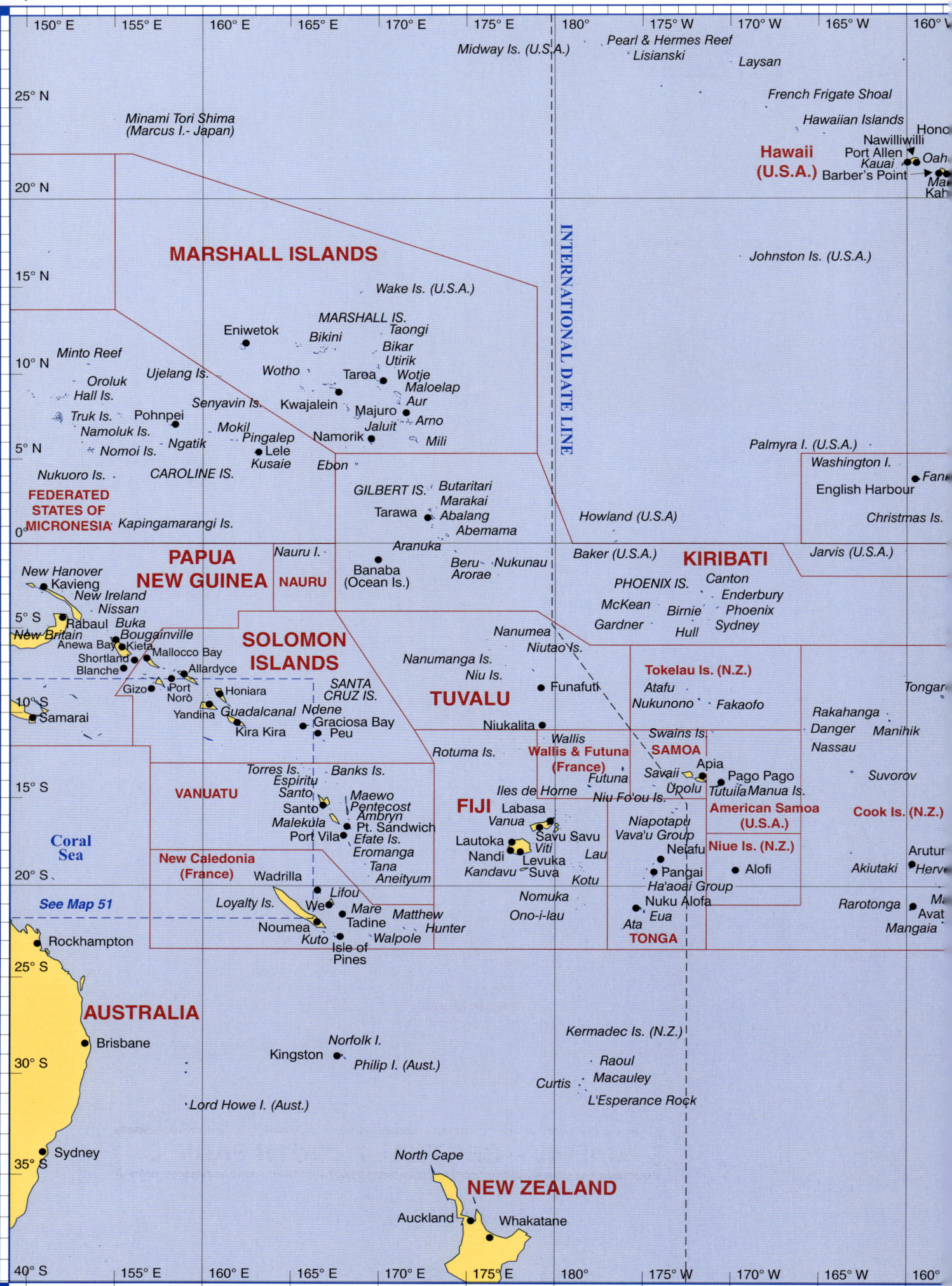

Map 49

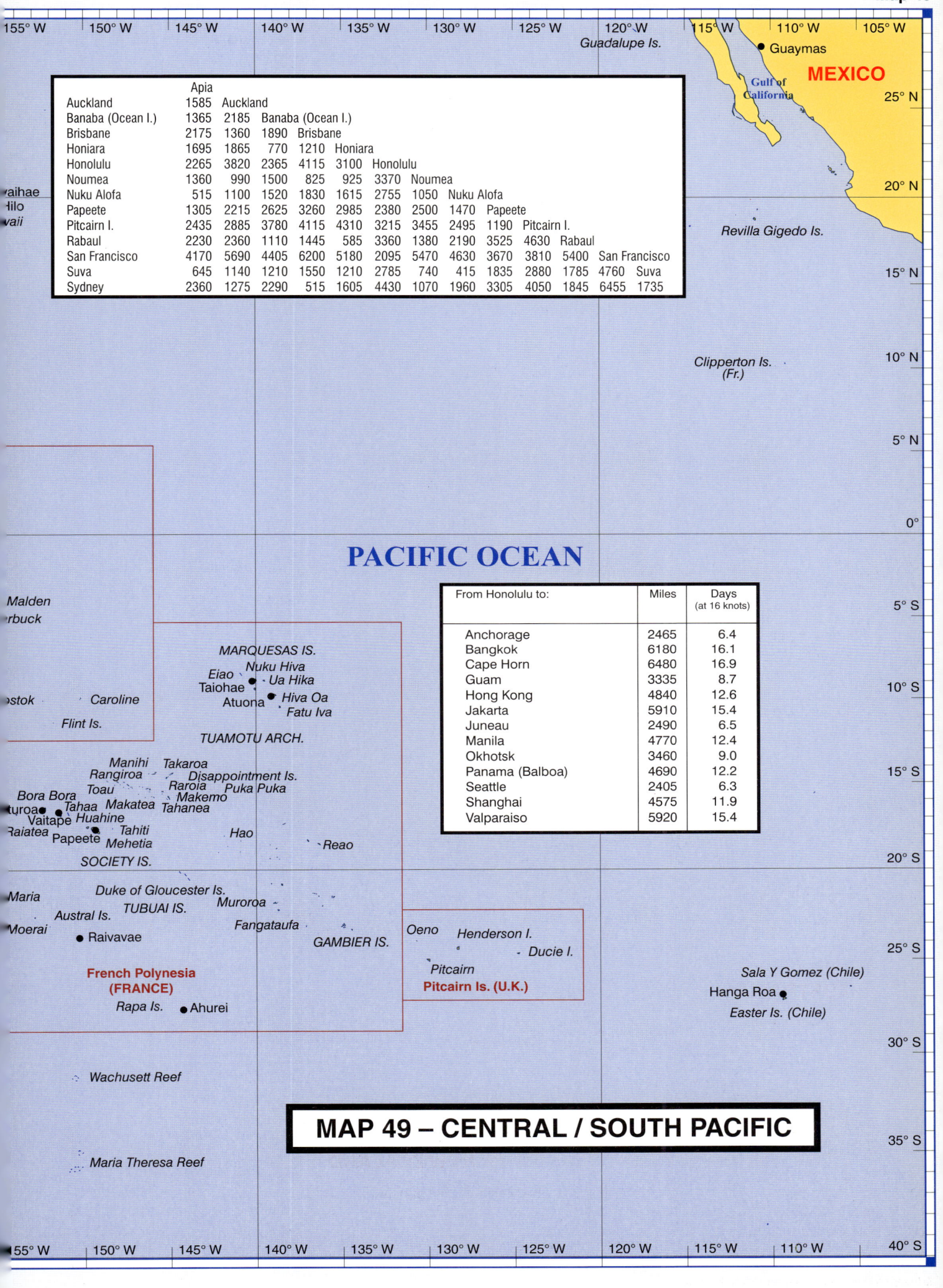

Distance Table

	Apia	Auckland	Banaba (Ocean I.)	Brisbane	Honiara	Honolulu	Noumea	Nuku Alofa	Papeete	Pitcairn I.	Rabaul	San Francisco	Suva	Sydney
Auckland	1585													
Banaba (Ocean I.)	1365	2185												
Brisbane	2175	1360	1890											
Honiara	1695	1865	770	1210										
Honolulu	2265	3820	2365	4115	3100									
Noumea	1360	990	1500	825	925	3370								
Nuku Alofa	515	1100	1520	1830	1615	2755	1050							
Papeete	1305	2215	2625	3260	2985	2380	2500	1470						
Pitcairn I.	2435	2885	3780	4115	4310	3215	3455	2495	1190					
Rabaul	2230	2360	1110	1445	585	3360	1380	2190	3525	4630				
San Francisco	4170	5690	4405	6200	5180	2095	5470	4630	3670	3810	5400			
Suva	645	1140	1210	1550	1210	2785	740	415	1835	2880	1785	4760		
Sydney	2360	1275	2290	515	1605	4430	1070	1960	3305	4050	1845	6455	1735	

From Honolulu to:

From Honolulu to:	Miles	Days (at 16 knots)
Anchorage	2465	6.4
Bangkok	6180	16.1
Cape Horn	6480	16.9
Guam	3335	8.7
Hong Kong	4840	12.6
Jakarta	5910	15.4
Juneau	2490	6.5
Manila	4770	12.4
Okhotsk	3460	9.0
Panama (Balboa)	4690	12.2
Seattle	2405	6.3
Shanghai	4575	11.9
Valparaiso	5920	15.4

MAP 49 – CENTRAL / SOUTH PACIFIC

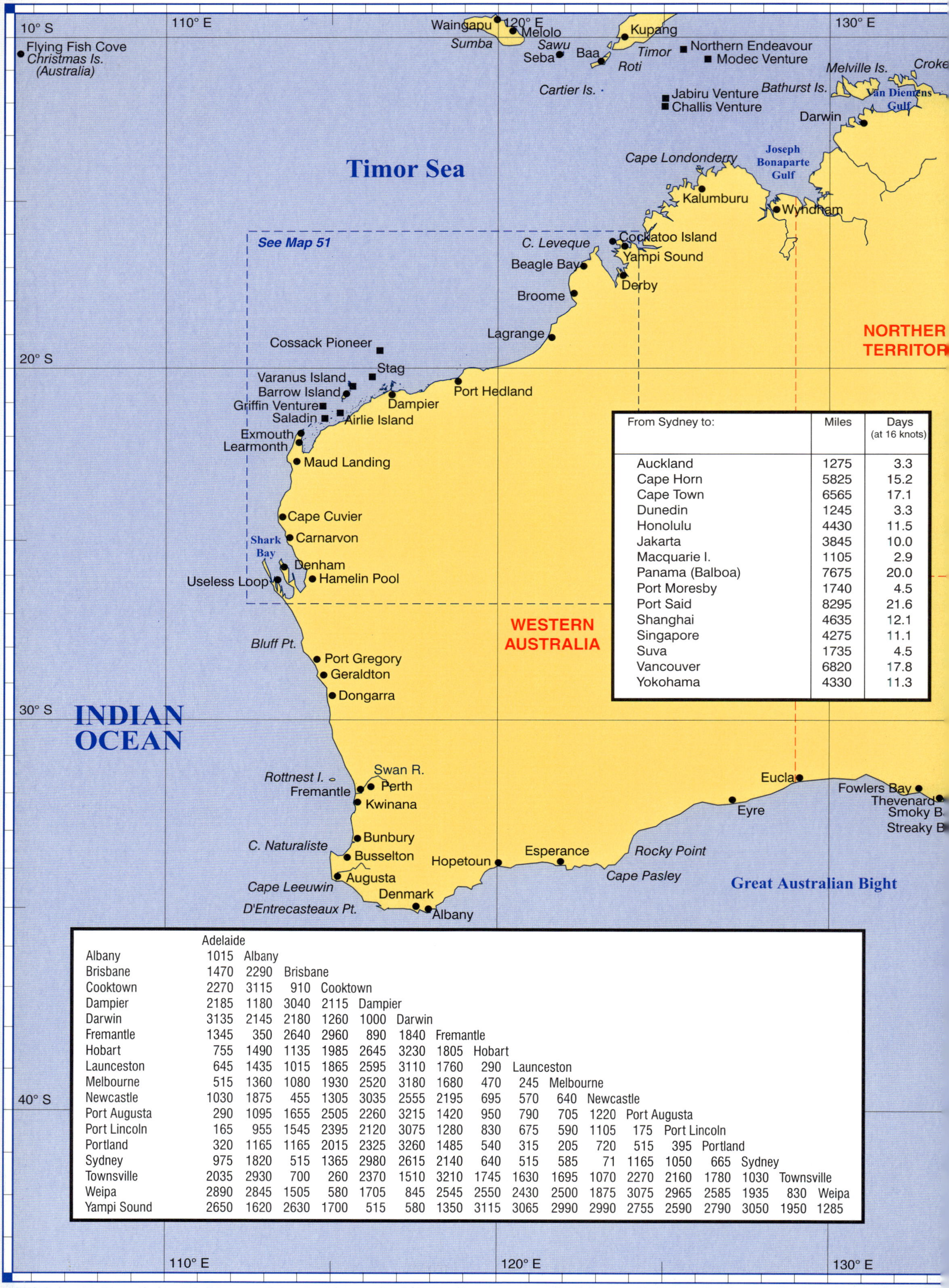

Map 50

Locations on map

- Flying Fish Cove, Christmas Is. (Australia)
- Waingapu, Sumba
- Melolo
- Seba, Sawu, Baa, Roti
- Kupang, Timor
- Northern Endeavour
- Modec Venture
- Cartier Is.
- Jabiru Venture, Bathurst Is.
- Challis Venture
- Melville Is., Croke
- Van Diemens Gulf
- Darwin
- Timor Sea
- Cape Londonderry
- Joseph Bonaparte Gulf
- Kalumburu
- Wyndham
- See Map 51
- C. Leveque, Cockatoo Island
- Beagle Bay, Yampi Sound
- Derby
- Broome
- Lagrange
- NORTHERN TERRITORY
- Cossack Pioneer
- Stag
- Varanus Island
- Barrow Island
- Griffin Venture
- Saladin, Dampier
- Exmouth, Airlie Island
- Learmonth
- Port Hedland
- Maud Landing
- Cape Cuvier
- Carnarvon
- Shark Bay
- Denham
- Useless Loop, Hamelin Pool
- Bluff Pt.
- Port Gregory
- Geraldton
- Dongarra
- WESTERN AUSTRALIA
- Indian Ocean
- Rottnest I., Swan R.
- Fremantle, Perth
- Kwinana
- C. Naturaliste
- Bunbury, Busselton
- Augusta
- Cape Leeuwin, Denmark
- D'Entrecasteaux Pt., Albany
- Hopetoun
- Esperance
- Rocky Point
- Cape Pasley
- Eucla
- Eyre
- Fowlers Bay, Thevenard, Smoky B., Streaky B.
- Great Australian Bight

From Sydney to:

From Sydney to:	Miles	Days (at 16 knots)
Auckland	1275	3.3
Cape Horn	5825	15.2
Cape Town	6565	17.1
Dunedin	1245	3.3
Honolulu	4430	11.5
Jakarta	3845	10.0
Macquarie I.	1105	2.9
Panama (Balboa)	7675	20.0
Port Moresby	1740	4.5
Port Said	8295	21.6
Shanghai	4635	12.1
Singapore	4275	11.1
Suva	1735	4.5
Vancouver	6820	17.8
Yokohama	4330	11.3

Distance table

	Adelaide	Albany	Brisbane	Cooktown	Dampier	Darwin	Fremantle	Hobart	Launceston	Melbourne	Newcastle	Port Augusta	Port Lincoln	Portland	Sydney	Townsville	Weipa
Albany	1015																
Brisbane	1470	2290															
Cooktown	2270	3115	910														
Dampier	2185	1180	3040	2115													
Darwin	3135	2145	2180	1260	1000												
Fremantle	1345	350	2640	2960	890	1840											
Hobart	755	1490	1135	1985	2645	3230	1805										
Launceston	645	1435	1015	1865	2595	3110	1760	290									
Melbourne	515	1360	1080	1930	2520	3180	1680	470	245								
Newcastle	1030	1875	455	1305	3035	2555	2195	695	570	640							
Port Augusta	290	1095	1655	2505	2260	3215	1420	950	790	705	1220						
Port Lincoln	165	955	1545	2395	2120	3075	1280	830	675	590	1105	175					
Portland	320	1165	1165	2015	2325	3260	1485	540	315	205	720	515	395				
Sydney	975	1820	515	1365	2980	2615	2140	640	515	585	71	1165	1050	665			
Townsville	2035	2930	700	260	2370	1510	3210	1745	1630	1695	1070	2270	2160	1780	1030		
Weipa	2890	2845	1505	580	1705	845	2545	2550	2430	2500	1875	3075	2965	2585	1935	830	
Yampi Sound	2650	1620	2630	1700	515	580	1350	3115	3065	2990	2990	2755	2590	2790	3050	1950	1285

© Shipping Guides Ltd., Reigate, United Kingdom

MAP 50 – AUSTRALIA

Map 51

AUSTRALIA – N.W. COAST

- Timor Sea
- 115° E, 120° E, 125° E
- Cockatoo Island
- C. Leveque
- Yampi Sound
- King Sound
- Beagle Bay
- Derby
- Rowley Shoals
- Broome
- Lagrange
- 20° S — Turtle I.
- Cossack Pioneer
- Wandoo
- Stag
- Port Walcott
- Port Hedland
- Varanus Island
- Barrow Island
- Dampier
- Cape Preston
- Griffin Venture
- Saladin
- Airlie Island
- West Cape
- Exmouth
- Onslow
- Learmonth
- Maud Landing
- WESTERN AUSTRALIA
- 25° S
- Cape Cuvier
- Carnarvon
- Shark Bay
- Denham
- Useless Loop
- Hamelin Pool

SPENCER GULF

- 135° E, 140° E
- Port Kenny
- Port Augusta
- AUSTRALIA
- Streaky Bay
- Port Bonython
- Port Germein
- Elliston
- Whyalla
- Port Pirie
- SOUTH AUSTRALIA
- Cowell
- Wallaroo
- Great Australian Bight
- Spencer Gulf
- R. Murray
- Tumby Bay
- Ardrossan
- Port Lincoln
- Port Vincent
- Adelaide
- 35° S
- Cape Catastrophe
- Port Giles
- Gulf of St. Vincent
- Port Stanvac
- Rapid Bay
- Victor Harbour
- Investigator Strait
- Kingscote
- Ballast Head
- Kangaroo Island

© Shipping Guides Ltd., Reigate, England

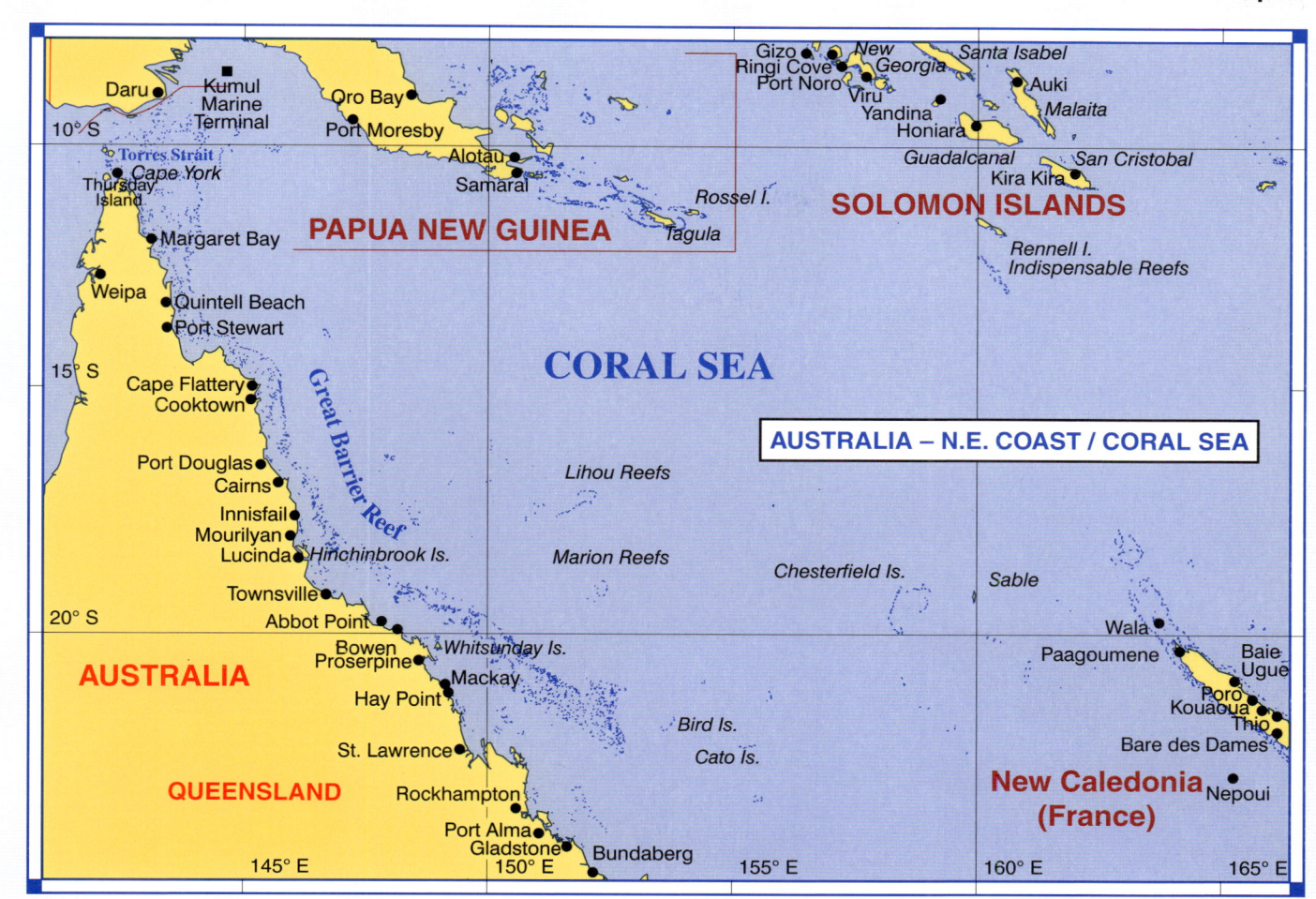

MAP 51 – AUSTRALIAN COASTAL AREAS

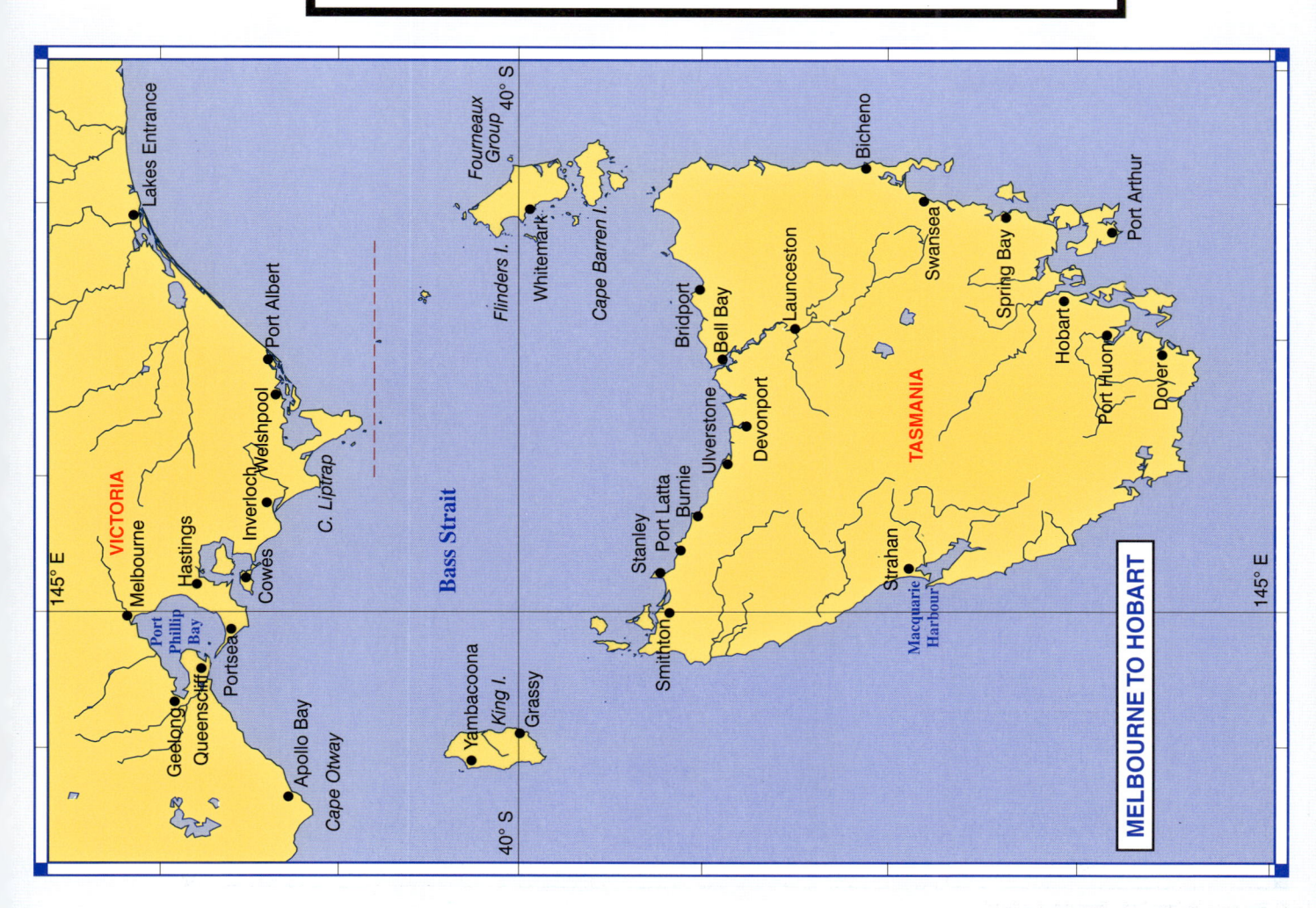

AUSTRALIA – N.E. COAST / CORAL SEA

PAPUA NEW GUINEA
- Daru
- Kumul Marine Terminal
- Oro Bay
- Port Moresby
- Alotau
- Samarai
- Rossel I.
- Tagula

SOLOMON ISLANDS
- Gizo
- Ringi Cove
- New Georgia
- Port Noro
- Santa Isabel
- Viru
- Yandina
- Auki
- Malaita
- Honiara
- Guadalcanal
- San Cristobal
- Kira Kira
- Rennell I.
- Indispensable Reefs

AUSTRALIA / QUEENSLAND
- Thursday Island
- Cape York
- Margaret Bay
- Weipa
- Quintell Beach
- Port Stewart
- Cape Flattery
- Cooktown
- Port Douglas
- Cairns
- Innisfail
- Mourilyan
- Lucinda
- Hinchinbrook Is.
- Townsville
- Abbot Point
- Bowen
- Proserpine
- Whitsunday Is.
- Mackay
- Hay Point
- St. Lawrence
- Rockhampton
- Port Alma
- Gladstone
- Bundaberg

Coral Sea features: Great Barrier Reef, Lihou Reefs, Marion Reefs, Chesterfield Is., Sable, Bird Is., Cato Is., Torres Strait

New Caledonia (France)
- Wala
- Paagoumene
- Baie Ugue
- Poro
- Kouaoua
- Thio
- Bare des Dames
- Nepoui

MELBOURNE TO HOBART

VICTORIA
- Lakes Entrance
- Port Albert
- Welshpool
- Inverloch
- C. Liptrap
- Hastings
- Cowes
- Melbourne
- Port Phillip Bay
- Geelong
- Queenscliff
- Portsea
- Apollo Bay
- Cape Otway

Bass Strait
- Fourneaux Group
- Flinders I.
- Whitemark
- Cape Barren I.
- Yambacoona
- King I.
- Grassy

TASMANIA
- Bicheno
- Bridport
- Bell Bay
- Launceston
- Swansea
- Spring Bay
- Port Arthur
- Ulverstone
- Devonport
- Hobart
- Port Huon
- Dover
- Smithton
- Stanley
- Port Latta
- Burnie
- Strahan
- Macquarie Harbour

Map 52

MAP 52 – NEW ZEALAND

From Wellington to:	Miles	Days (at 16 knots)
Cape Horn	4605	12.0
Cape Town	7470	19.5
Colombo	6065	15.8
Hobart	1295	3.4
Honolulu	4115	10.7
Macquarie I.	455	1.2
Panama (Balboa)	6495	16.9
San Francisco	5910	15.4
Sydney	1235	3.2
Vancouver	6455	16.8

PACIFIC OCEAN
TASMAN SEA
NEW ZEALAND

North Island
North Cape
Houhora
Mangonui
Whangaroa
C. Brett
Russell
Opua
Rawene
Whangarei
Marsden Point
Waipu
Gt. Barrier Is.
Dargaville
Helensville
Devonport
Auckland
Onehunga
Coromandel
Whitianga
Thames
Tauranga
Mount Maunganui
Bay of Plenty
Opotiki
Whakatane
East Cape
Tokomaru
Gisborne
Wairoa
Hawke's Bay
Cape Kidnappers
Napier
Cape Turnagain
Taharoa
Raglan
Waitara
New Plymouth
C. Egmont
Whakaaropai
Opunake
Patea
Waverley Harbour
Wanganui
Tangimoana
Riverdale
Porirua
Petone
Wellington
C. Palliser

Cook Strait
D'Urville I.
C. Farewell
Tasman Bay
Collingwood
Karamea
Motueka
Richmond
Nelson
Picton
C. Campbell
Blenheim
Kaikoura
C. Foulwind
Westport
Runanga
Greymouth
Hokitika
Ross
Westland Bight
Rangiora

180°
175° E
170° E
165° E
35° S
40° S

© Shipping Guides Ltd., Reigate, United Kingdom

Map 52

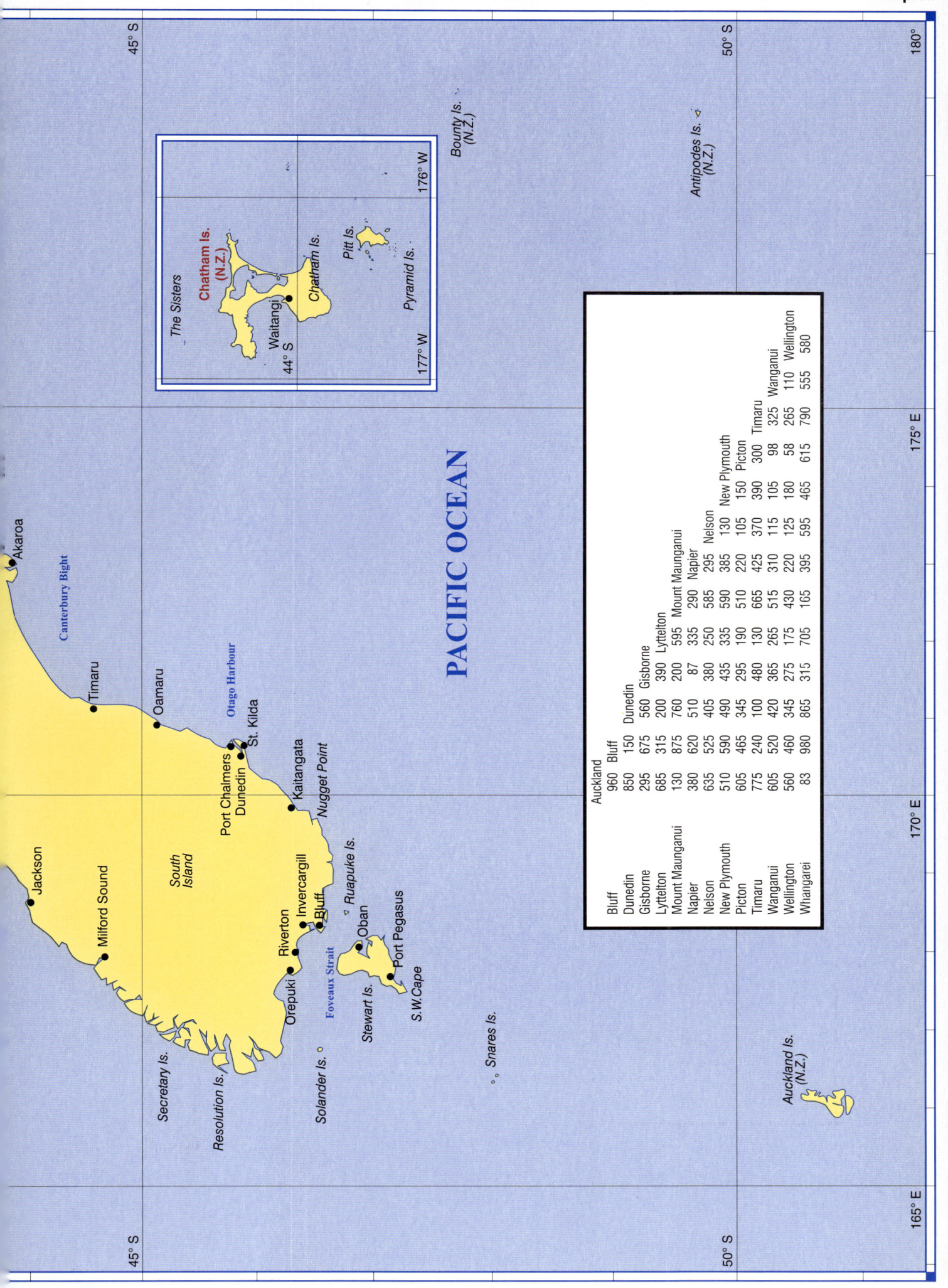

	Auckland	Bluff	Dunedin	Gisborne	Lyttelton	Mount Maunganui	Napier	Nelson	New Plymouth	Picton	Timaru	Wanganui	Wellington
Bluff	960												
Dunedin	850	150											
Gisborne	295	675	560										
Lyttelton	685	315	200	390									
Mount Maunganui	130	875	760	200	595								
Napier	380	620	510	87	335	290							
Nelson	635	525	405	380	250	585	295						
New Plymouth	510	590	490	435	335	590	385	130					
Picton	605	465	345	295	190	510	220	105	150				
Timaru	775	240	100	480	130	665	425	370	390	300			
Wanganui	605	520	420	365	265	515	310	115	105	98	325		
Wellington	560	460	345	275	175	430	220	125	180	58	265	110	
Whangarei	83	980	865	315	705	165	395	595	465	615	790	555	580

PACIFIC OCEAN

Chatham Is. (N.Z.)
The Sisters
Waitangi
Chatham Is.
Pitt Is.
Pyramid Is.
44° S
176° W
177° W

Bounty Is. (N.Z.)
Antipodes Is. (N.Z.)
Auckland Is. (N.Z.)
Snares Is.
Solander Is.
Secretary Is.
Resolution Is.
Jackson
Milford Sound
South Island
Akaroa
Canterbury Bight
Timaru
Oamaru
Port Chalmers
Otago Harbour
Dunedin
St. Kilda
Kaitangata
Nugget Point
Ruapuke Is.
Orepuki
Riverton
Invercargill
Bluff
Foveaux Strait
Oban
Stewart Is.
Port Pegasus
S.W. Cape

Map 53

180°   150° W   120° W

60° N

BERING SEA

ALEUTIAN ISLANDS

INTERNATIONAL DATE LINE

MAP 54
ALASKA/SIBERIA

NORTH
PACIFIC
OCEAN

MAP 56
NORTH AMERICA
NORTH WEST COAST

MAP 57
NORTH AMER
WEST COA

30° N

MAP 49
CENTRAL/SOUTH PACIFIC

HAWAIIAN ISLANDS

MAP 53 – NORTH AMERICA

0°

180°   150° W   120° W

© Shipping Guides Ltd., Reigate, United Kingdom

Map 53

BAFFIN BAY

90° W   60° W   30° W

MAP 59
HUDSON BAY

DAVIS STRAIT

DENMARK STRAIT

HUDSON BAY

60° N

Cape Farewell

MAP 17
GREENLAND/ICELAND

MAP 61
ST. LAWRENCE SEAWAY

MAP 62
NORTH AMERICA
THE GREAT LAKES

MAP 60
GULF OF ST. LAWRENCE/
NEW ENGLAND

NORTH ATLANTIC OCEAN

AZORES

MAP 20
BISCAY TO GIBRALTAR

MAP 65
CHESAPEAKE AND
DELAWARE BAYS

MAP 63
U.S.A. – EAST COAST

MAP 66
USA – GULF COAST

30° N

MAP 69
THE CARIBBEAN

GULF OF MEXICO

MAP 70
NORTHERN CARIBBEAN

MAP 71
EASTERN CARIBBEAN

CARIBBEAN SEA

MAP 74
MARACAIBO LAKE REGION

MAP 72
SOUTH AMERICA
NORTHERN PART

PANAMA CANAL

MAP 75
ORINOCO RIVER

MAP 76
SOUTH AMERICAN COASTAL AREAS

0°

90° W   60° W   30° W

Map 54

From Anchorage to:	Miles	Days (at 16 knots)
Brisbane	6120	15.9
Cape Horn	8175	21.3
Hong Kong	4830	12.6
New Orleans	6573	17.1
New York	7145	18.6
Panama (Balboa)	5130	13.4
San Francisco	1895	4.9
Shanghai	4175	10.9
Singapore	6165	16.1
Vancouver	1350	3.5
Yokohama	3320	8.6

© Shipping Guides Ltd., Reigate, United Kingdom

MAP 54 – ALASKA / SIBERIA

Map 55

CANADA

UNITED STATES OF AMERICA

MEXICO

PACIFIC OCEAN

Ports (north to south):
Ferndale, Bellingham, Anacortes, Everett, Port Angeles, Seattle, Tacoma, Olympia, Grays Harbour, Astoria, Longview, Vancouver, Portland, Coos Bay, Eureka, Sacramento, Benicia, Oakland, San Francisco, Port San Luis, Hueneme, El Segundo, Los Angeles/Long Beach, Huntington Beach, San Diego

Corpus Chr(isti), Browns(ville)

	New York								
Boston	380	Boston							
Baltimore	415	685	Baltimore						
Norfolk	290	560	175	Norfolk					
Charleston	630	875	555	430	Charleston				
Miami	965	1200	890	765	440	Miami			
Mobile	1640	1875	1560	1440	1110	720	Mobile		
New Orleans	1710	1945	1635	1510	1185	765	235	New Orleans	
Houston	1910	2145	1830	1710	1380	975	480	435	Houston
Brownsville	1955	2190	1880	1755	1430	1010	620	580	310 Brownsville
Panama Canal (Cristobal)	1975	2140	1905	1785	1565	1205	1410	1405	1530 1505

	San Francisco			
Portland (Oregon)	650	Portland (Oregon)		
Seattle	800	350	Seattle	
Los Angeles	370	980	1130	Los Angeles
Panama Canal (Balboa)	3250	3860	4010	2915

© Shipping Guides Ltd., Reigate, United Kingdom

MAP 55 – UNITED STATES OF AMERICA

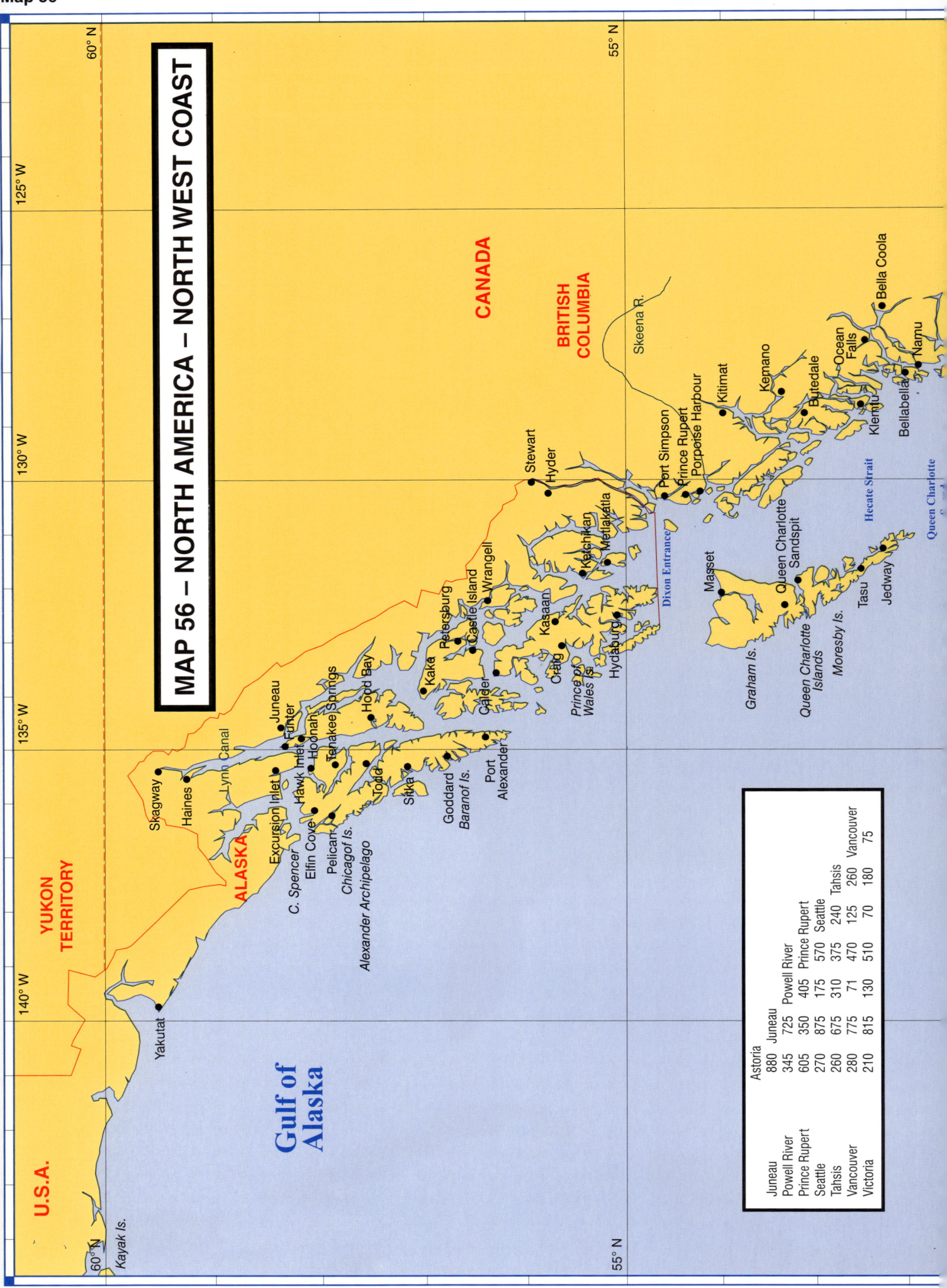

MAP 56 – NORTH AMERICA – NORTH WEST COAST

	Astoria	Juneau	Powell River	Prince Rupert	Seattle	Tahsis	Vancouver
Juneau	880						
Powell River	345	725					
Prince Rupert	605	350	405				
Seattle	270	875	175	570			
Tahsis	260	675	310	375	240		
Vancouver	280	775	71	470	125	260	
Victoria	210	815	130	510	70	180	75

© Shipping Guides Ltd., Reigate, United Kingdom

Map 56

From Vancouver to:	Miles	Days (at 16 knots)
Brisbane	6495	16.9
Cape Horn	7110	18.5
Honolulu	2420	6.3
Manila	5945	15.5
Montreal	7255	18.9
Panama (Balboa)	4020	10.5
Shanghai	5110	13.3
Singapore	7080	18.4
Suva	5185	13.5
Vladivostock	4265	11.1

VANCOUVER / SEATTLE AREA

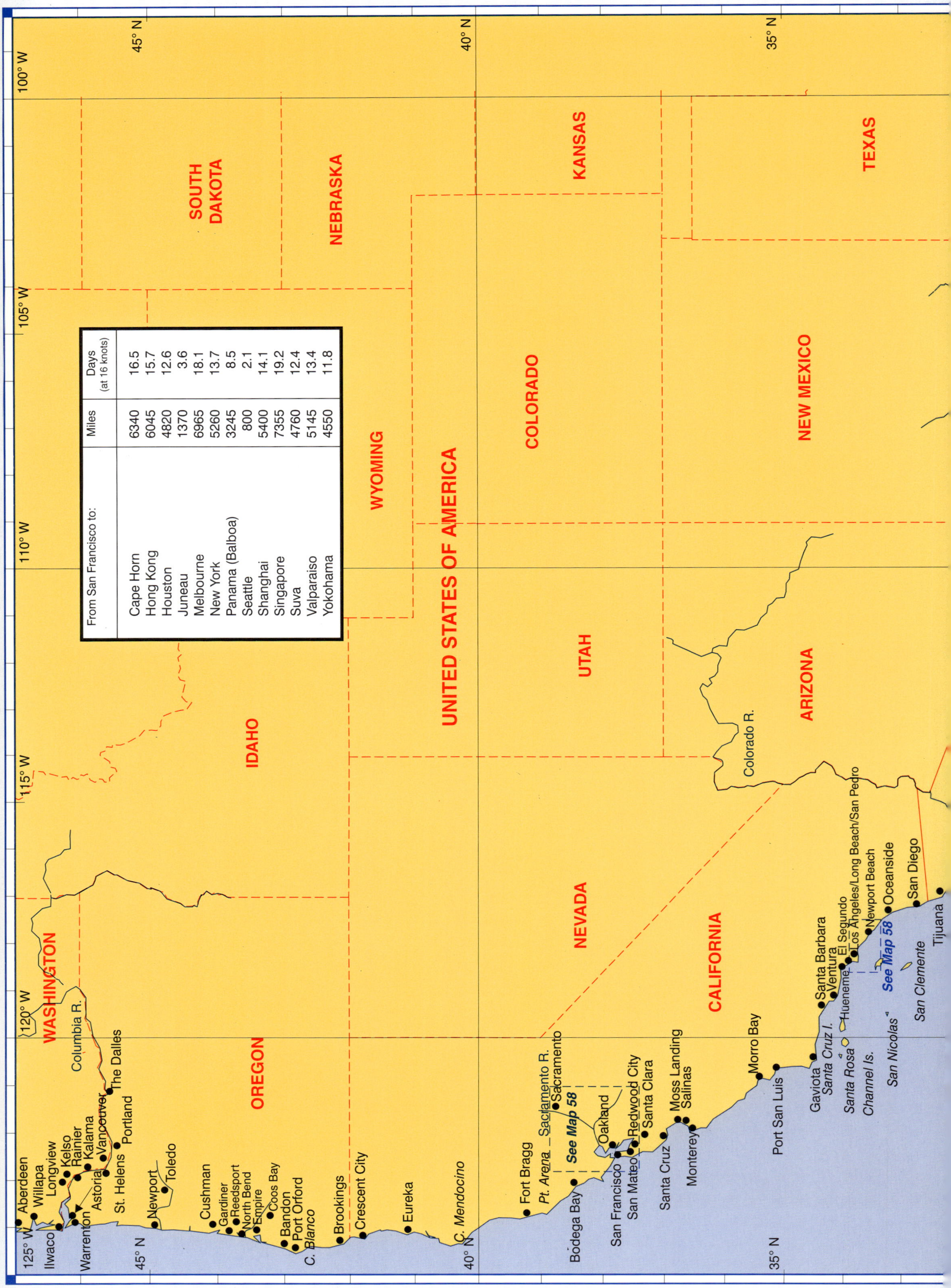

Map 57

From San Francisco to:	Miles	Days (at 16 knots)
Cape Horn	6340	16.5
Hong Kong	6045	15.7
Houston	4820	12.6
Juneau	1370	3.6
Melbourne	6965	18.1
New York	5260	13.7
Panama (Balboa)	3245	8.5
Seattle	800	2.1
Shanghai	5400	14.1
Singapore	7355	19.2
Suva	4760	12.4
Valparaiso	5145	13.4
Yokohama	4550	11.8

© Shipping Guides Ltd., Reigate, United Kingdom

Map 57

MAP 57 – NORTH AMERICA – WEST COAST

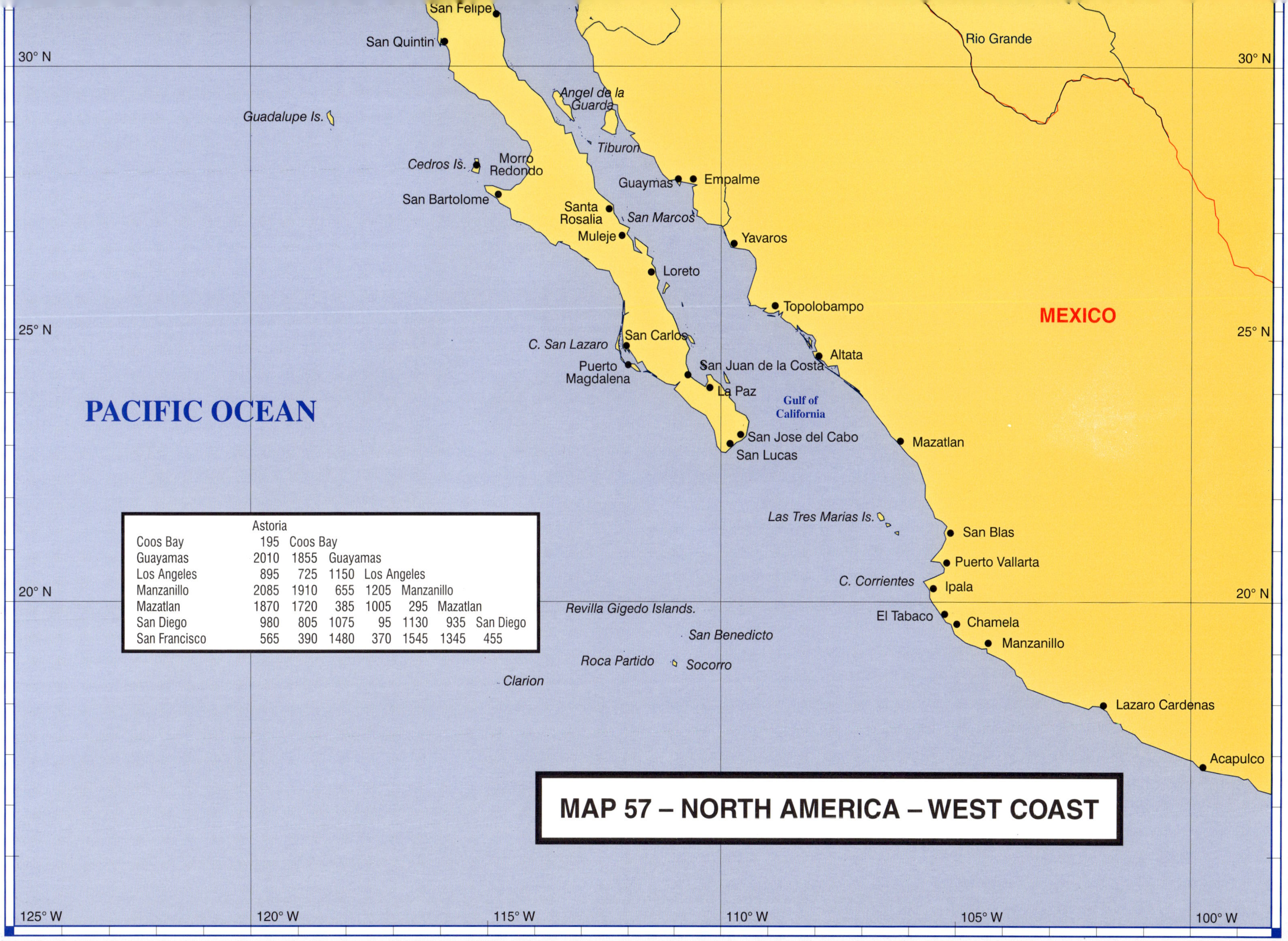

MEXICO

PACIFIC OCEAN

Locations (north to south along coast):
- Rio Grande
- San Felipe
- San Quintin
- Angel de la Guarda
- Tiburon
- Guadalupe Is.
- Empalme
- Guaymas
- San Marcos
- Cedros Is.
- Morro Redondo
- San Bartolome
- Santa Rosalia
- Mulege
- Loreto
- Yavaros
- Topolobampo
- Altata
- C. San Lazaro
- Puerto Magdalena
- San Carlos
- San Juan de la Costa
- La Paz
- Gulf of California
- San Jose del Cabo
- San Lucas
- Mazatlan
- Las Tres Marias Is.
- San Blas
- Puerto Vallarta
- Ipala
- C. Corrientes
- El Tabaco
- Chamela
- Manzanillo
- Revilla Gigedo Islands
- San Benedicto
- Roca Partido
- Socorro
- Clarion
- Lazaro Cardenas
- Acapulco

Distance table:

	Astoria	Coos Bay	Guaymas	Los Angeles	Manzanillo	Mazatlan	San Diego
Coos Bay	195						
Guayamas	2010	1855					
Los Angeles	895	725	1150				
Manzanillo	2085	1910	655	1205			
Mazatlan	1870	1720	385	1005	295		
San Diego	980	805	1075	95	1130	935	
San Francisco	565	390	1480	370	1545	1345	455

Map 58

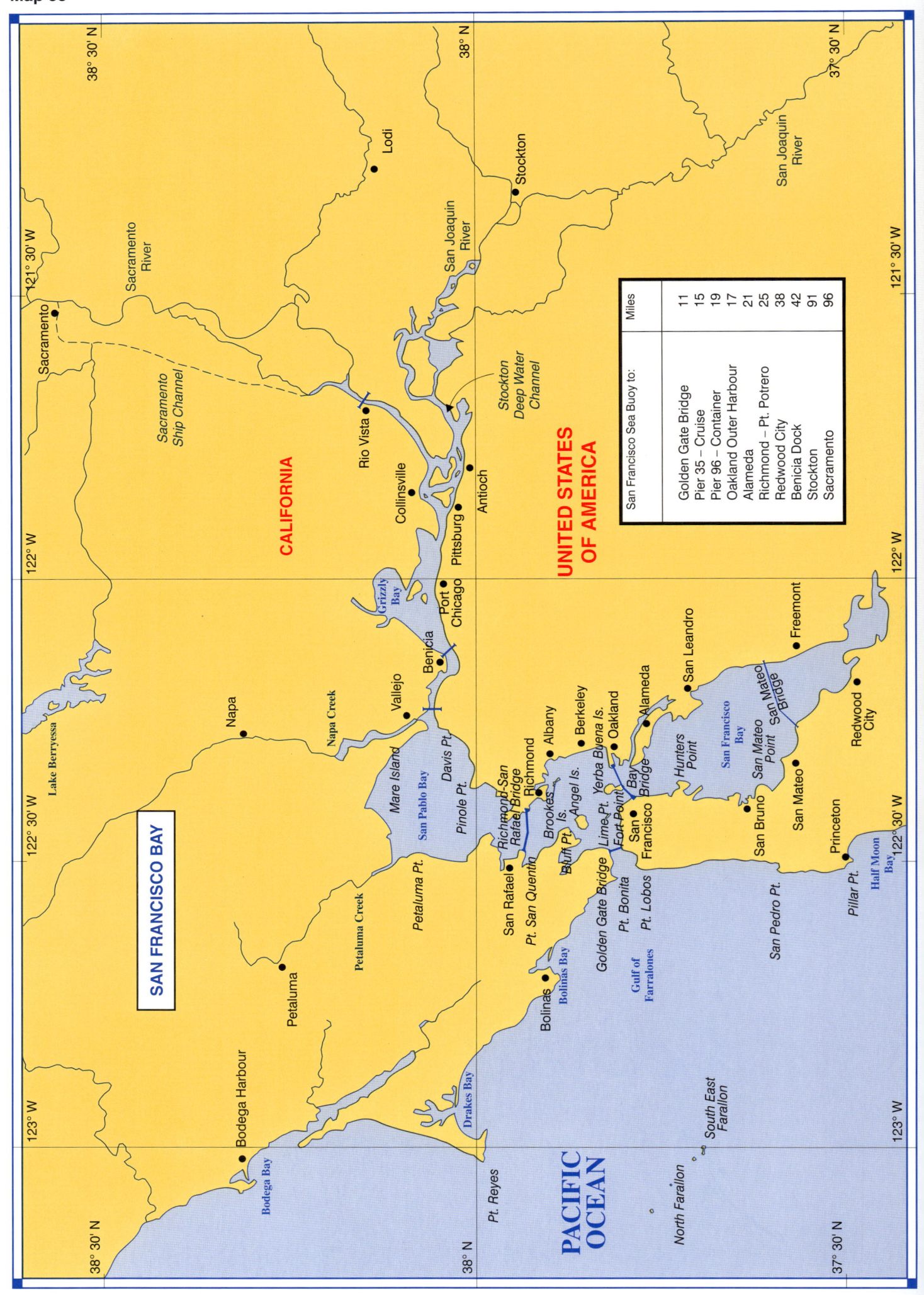

SAN FRANCISCO BAY

San Francisco Sea Buoy to:	Miles
Golden Gate Bridge	11
Pier 35 – Cruise	15
Pier 96 – Container	19
Oakland Outer Harbour	17
Alameda	21
Richmond – Pt. Potrero	25
Redwood City	38
Benicia Dock	42
Stockton	91
Sacramento	96

CALIFORNIA
UNITED STATES OF AMERICA
PACIFIC OCEAN

© Shipping Guides Ltd., Reigate, England

MAP 58 – SAN FRANCISCO / LOS ANGELES AREAS

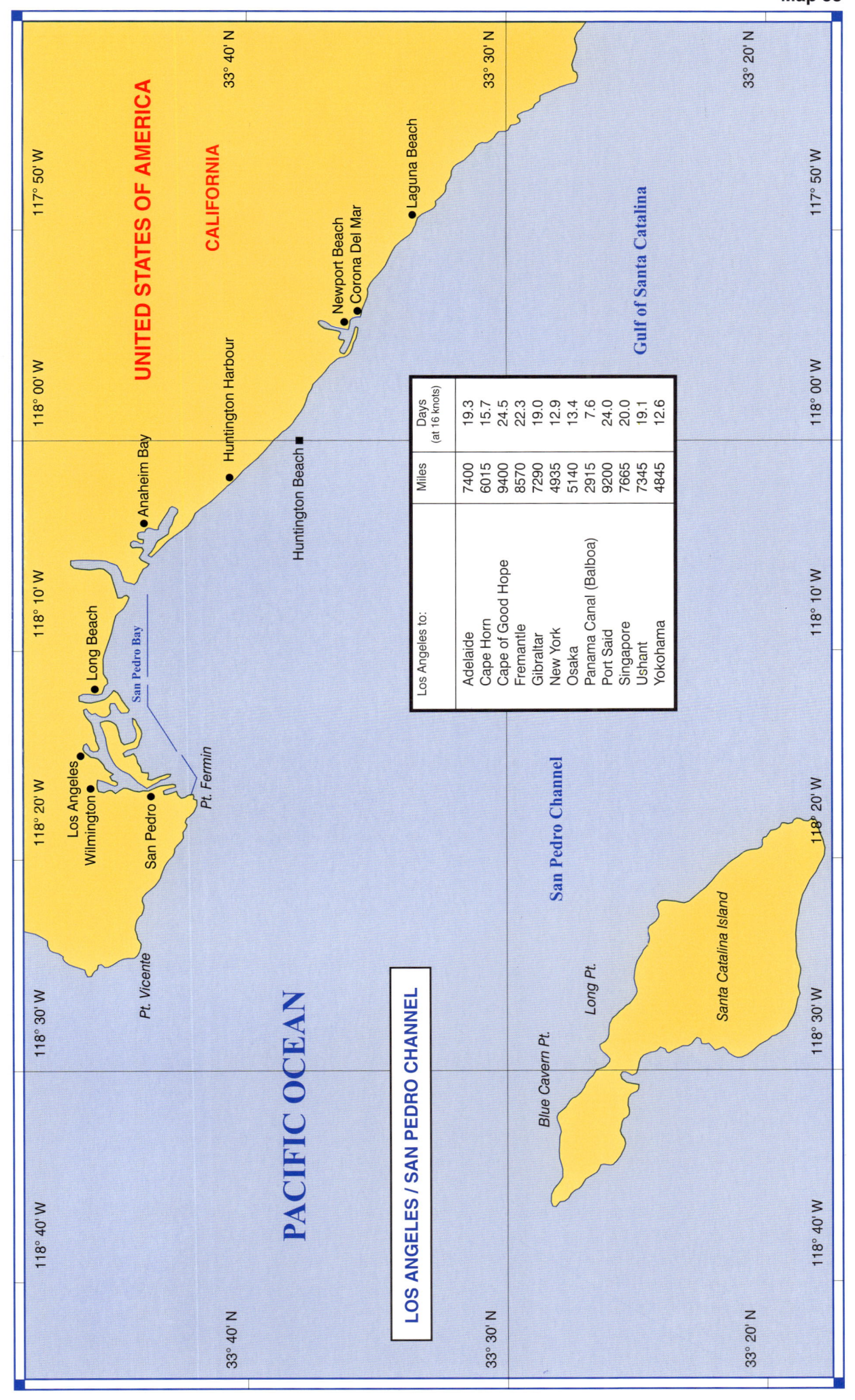

LOS ANGELES / SAN PEDRO CHANNEL

Los Angeles to:	Miles	Days (at 16 knots)
Adelaide	7400	19.3
Cape Horn	6015	15.7
Cape of Good Hope	9400	24.5
Fremantle	8570	22.3
Gibraltar	7290	19.0
New York	4935	12.9
Osaka	5140	13.4
Panama Canal (Balboa)	2915	7.6
Port Said	9200	24.0
Singapore	7665	20.0
Ushant	7345	19.1
Yokohama	4845	12.6

© Shipping Guides Ltd., Reigate, England

Map 59

	Churchill				
Deception	635	Deception			
Fort Chimo	1000	375	Fort Chimo		
Frobisher	1025	405	380	Frobisher	
Godthab	1355	730	590	610	Godthab
Goose Bay	1550	925	785	825	765

© Shipping Guides Ltd., Reigate, United Kingdom

MAP 59 – HUDSON BAY

From Deception to:	Miles	Days (at 16 knots)
Bergen	2535	6.6
Bristol	2475	6.5
Cape Horn	7985	20.8
Cape Town	7340	19.1
Gibraltar	3035	7.9
Montreal	2275	5.9
New York	2330	6.1
Panama (Cristobal)	3930	10.2
St. John's (Newfoundland)	1240	3.2
Thule	1330	3.5

Map 60

MAP 60 – GULF OF ST. LAWRENCE / NEW ENGLAND

From Halifax to:	Miles	Days (at 16 knots)
Belfast	2375	6.2
Bergen	2720	7.1
Bilbao	2585	6.7
Cape Horn	6810	17.7
Cape Town	6490	16.9
Cherbourg	2525	6.6
Dakar	2960	7.7
Deception	1780	4.6
Gibraltar	2720	7.1
Houston	2345	6.1
Panama (Cristobal)	2300	6.0
Rio de Janeiro	4615	12.0
Thule	2400	6.3

Map 60

From Rimouski to:	Miles	Hours (at 16 knots)
Port Sagueney (Chicoutimi)	112	7
Kingston (Ontario)	450	28
Massena	365	23
Montreal	290	18
Port Stanley (Ontario)	705	44
Sorel	250	16
Toronto	585	36

	Baie Verte									
Boston	1140	Boston								
Corner Brook	740	790	Corner Brook							
Halifax	790	385	440	Halifax						
New Richmond	865	885	335	535	New Richmond					
New York	1345	380	995	595	1095	New York				
Norfolk	1525	560	1175	775	1275	285	Norfolk			
Port Hawkesbury	685	515	325	165	415	725	900	Port Hawkesbury		
Portland (Maine)	1100	102	750	345	845	420	600	475	Portland (Maine)	
Rimouski	995	1020	435	670	310	1225	1405	545	980	Rimouski
St. Johns (N.F.)	255	895	495	545	620	1100	1280	435	855	750	St. Johns (N.F.)
Sept Iles	915	940	345	590	235	1150	1330	470	900	140	670	Sept Iles
Sydney (N.S.)	625	600	225	250	310	810	990	135	560	445	380	365

MAP 61 – ST. LAWRENCE SEAWAY

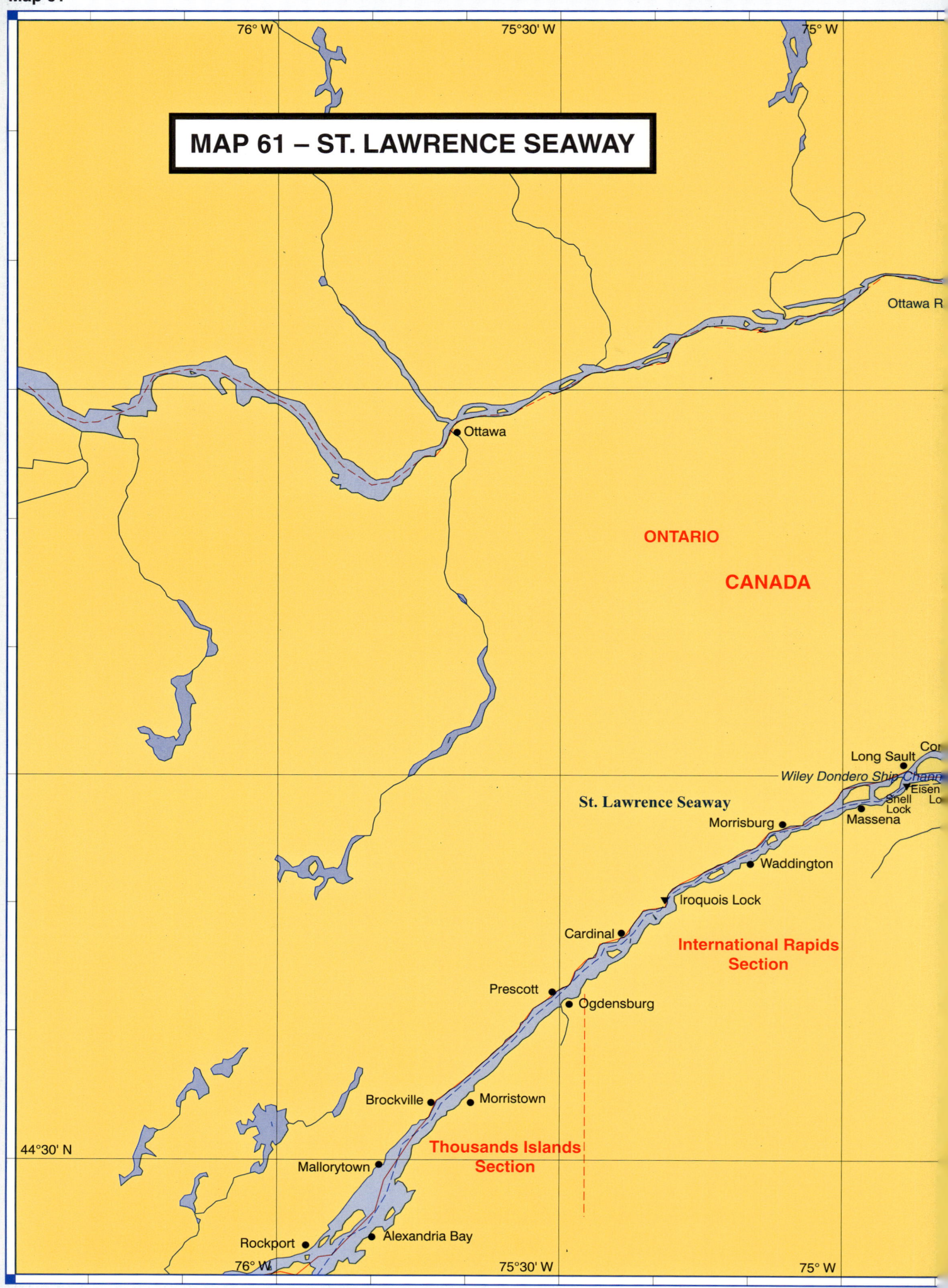

Map 61

74°30' W 74° W 73°30' W

QUEBEC

Contrecoeur

45°30' N

St. Lambert Lock

Montreal
Pointe Claire Lachine
QUEBEC Lake St. Louis
Vaudreuil Caugnawaga Cote St. Catherine Lock

St. Jean

Lachine Section

Coteau Landing
Beauharnois
St. Zotique Beauharnois Lock
Valleyfield
Beauharnois Canal

CANADA

St. Anicet Soulange Section

Lancaster Lake St. Francis

Lake St. Francis Section

45° N

UNITED STATES OF AMERICA

Lake Champlain

NEW YORK

VERMONT

44°30' N

74°30' W 74° W 73°30' W

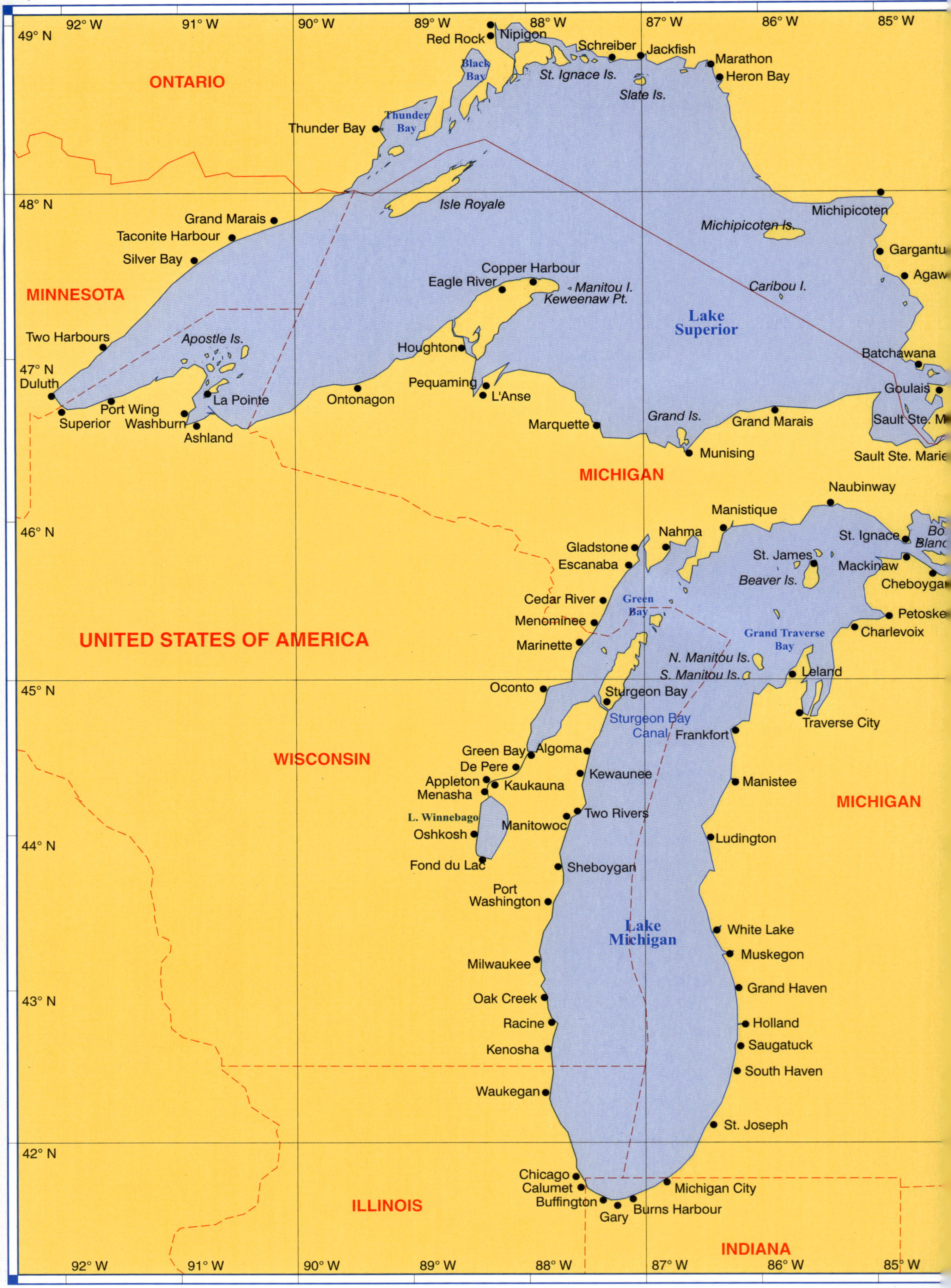
ONTARIO
MINNESOTA
MICHIGAN
WISCONSIN
UNITED STATES OF AMERICA
ILLINOIS
INDIANA
Lake Superior
Lake Michigan
Thunder Bay
Black Bay
Green Bay
Grand Traverse Bay
L. Winnebago
Isle Royale
Apostle Is.
St. Ignace Is.
Slate Is.
Michipicoten Is.
Caribou I.
Manitou I.
Keweenaw Pt.
Grand Is.
Beaver Is.
N. Manitou Is.
S. Manitou Is.
Sturgeon Bay Canal
Red Rock
Nipigon
Schreiber
Jackfish
Marathon
Heron Bay
Thunder Bay
Grand Marais
Taconite Harbour
Silver Bay
Two Harbours
Duluth
Superior
Port Wing
Washburn
Ashland
La Pointe
Ontonagon
Houghton
Eagle River
Copper Harbour
Pequaming
L'Anse
Marquette
Munising
Grand Marais
Michipicoten
Batchawana
Goulais
Sault Ste. Marie
Naubinway
Manistique
Nahma
Gladstone
Escanaba
St. James
St. Ignace
Mackinaw
Cedar River
Menominee
Marinette
Petoskey
Charlevoix
Leland
Traverse City
Oconto
Sturgeon Bay
Frankfort
Green Bay
Algoma
De Pere
Kewaunee
Appleton
Menasha
Kaukauna
Manistee
Two Rivers
Manitowoc
Oshkosh
Ludington
Fond du Lac
Sheboygan
Port Washington
White Lake
Muskegon
Milwaukee
Grand Haven
Oak Creek
Holland
Racine
Saugatuck
Kenosha
South Haven
Waukegan
St. Joseph
Chicago
Calumet
Michigan City
Buffington
Burns Harbour
Gary
49° N
48° N
47° N
46° N
45° N
44° N
43° N
42° N
92° W
91° W
90° W
89° W
88° W
87° W
86° W
85° W

MAP 62 – NORTH AMERICA – THE GREAT LAKES

	Buffalo									
Chicago	775	Chicago								
Collingwood	505	495	Collingwood							
Detroit	230	550	280	Detroit						
Duluth	860	705	570	630	Duluth					
Green Bay	665	220	385	440	595	Green Bay				
Kingston (Ontario)	185	925	650	375	1005	815	Kingston (Ontario)			
Thunder Bay	750	595	460	525	170	485	900	Thunder Bay		
Marquette	665	500	365	425	225	390	800	150	Marquette	
Milwaukee	720	74	440	495	645	155	865	540	440	Milwaukee
Sault Ste.Marie	515	360	225	290	345	250	660	240	140	305	Sault Ste.Marie
Toronto	67	810	540	260	890	700	135	785	685	750	550

Map 63

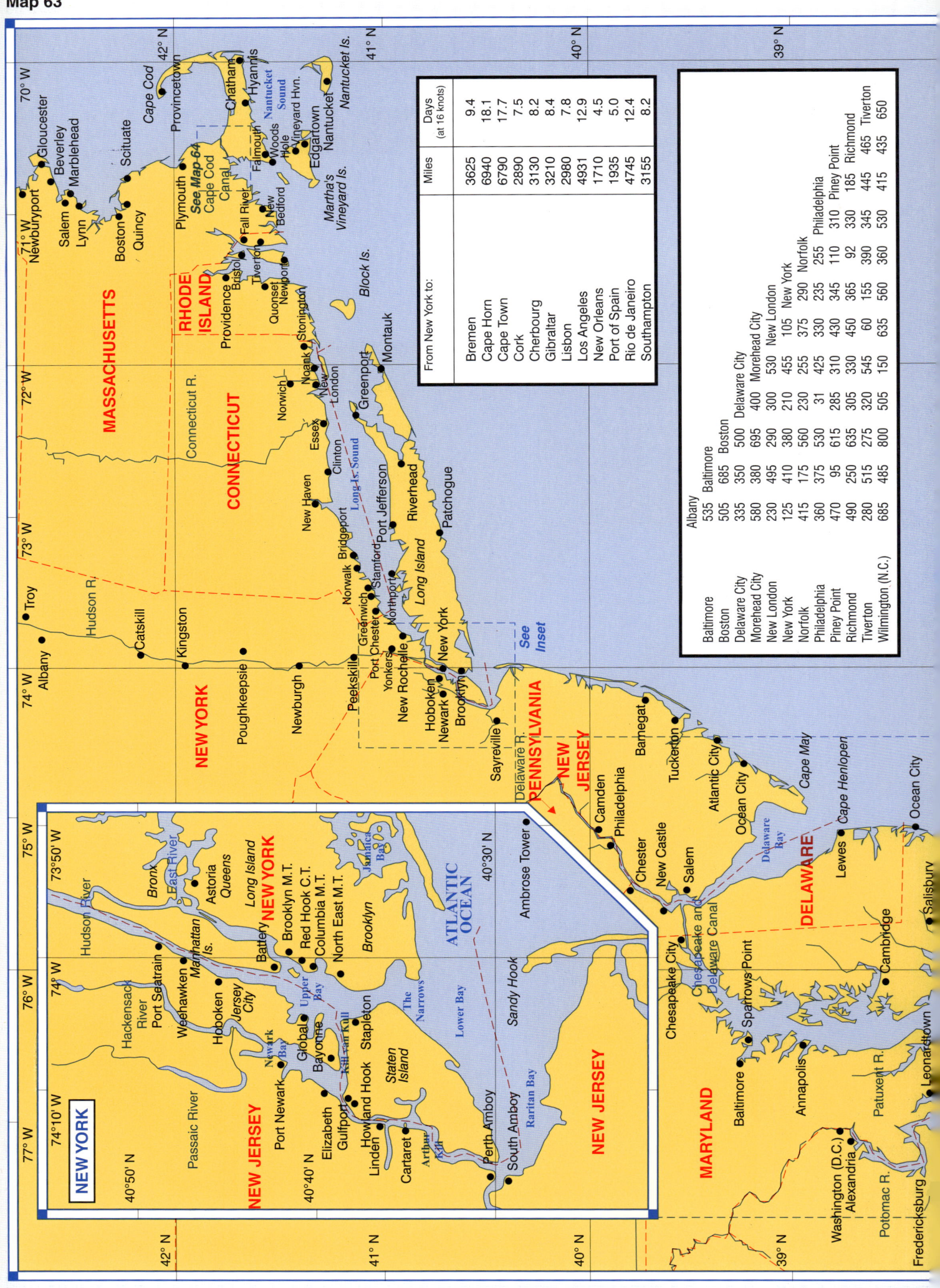

From New York to:	Miles	Days (at 16 knots)
Bremen	3625	9.4
Cape Horn	6940	18.1
Cape Town	6790	17.7
Cherbourg	2890	7.5
Cork	3130	8.2
Gibraltar	3210	8.4
Lisbon	2980	7.8
Los Angeles	4931	12.9
New Orleans	1710	4.5
Port of Spain	1935	5.0
Rio de Janeiro	4745	12.4
Southampton	3155	8.2

	Albany	Baltimore	Boston	Delaware City	Morehead City	New London	New York	Norfolk	Philadelphia	Piney Point	Richmond	Tiverton
Baltimore	535											
Boston	505	685										
Delaware City	335	350	500									
Morehead City	580	380	695	400								
New London	230	495	290	300	530							
New York	125	410	210	455	375	105						
Norfolk	415	175	380	255	330	330	235					
Philadelphia	360	375	560	31	425	430	290	345				
Piney Point	470	95	530	285	310	450	255	110	310			
Richmond	490	250	615	305	330	365	390	92	330	185		
Tiverton	280	515	275	320	545	60	155	255	345	445	465	
Wilmington (N.C.)	685	485	800	505	150	635	560	290	530	360	415	650

© Shipping Guides Ltd., Reigate, United Kingdom

MAP 63 – USA – EAST COAST

BERMUDA (U.K)

Locations shown: St. George's Is., St. George's, St. Davids Is., Hamilton Is., Hamilton, Ireland Is., Freeport, Somerset Is., Somerset

ATLANTIC OCEAN

VIRGINIA
Tappahannock, Piney Point, Richmond, Warwick, West Point, York R., Williamsburg, Hopewell, James R., Newport News, Hampton, Yorktown, Cape Charles, Portsmouth, Norfolk, Hampton Roads, Cape Henry, Chesapeake Bay

NORTH CAROLINA
Kitty Hawk, Elizabeth City, Hertford, Edenton, Columbia, Plymouth, Albemarle Sound, Washington, Pamlico R., Belhaven, Bayboro, Pamlico Sound, Cape Hatteras, New Bern, Neuse R., Morehead City, Beaufort, Cape Lookout, Raleigh Bay, Swansboro, Onslow Bay, Wilmington, Wrightsville

From Hampton Roads to:	Miles	Days (at 16 knots)
Ascension I.	4400	11.5
Belem	2845	7.4
Bordeaux	3405	8.9
Cape Horn	6885	17.9
Cape Town	6795	17.7
Copenhagen	3840	10.0
Dakar	3410	8.9
Havana	965	2.5
Houston	1705	4.4
Lagos	4925	12.8
Liverpool	3275	8.5
Montevideo	5690	14.8
Montreal	1700	4.4
Panama (Cristobal)	1780	4.6
Reykjavik	2890	7.5
San Francisco	5070	13.2

MAP 64 – CAPE COD CANAL

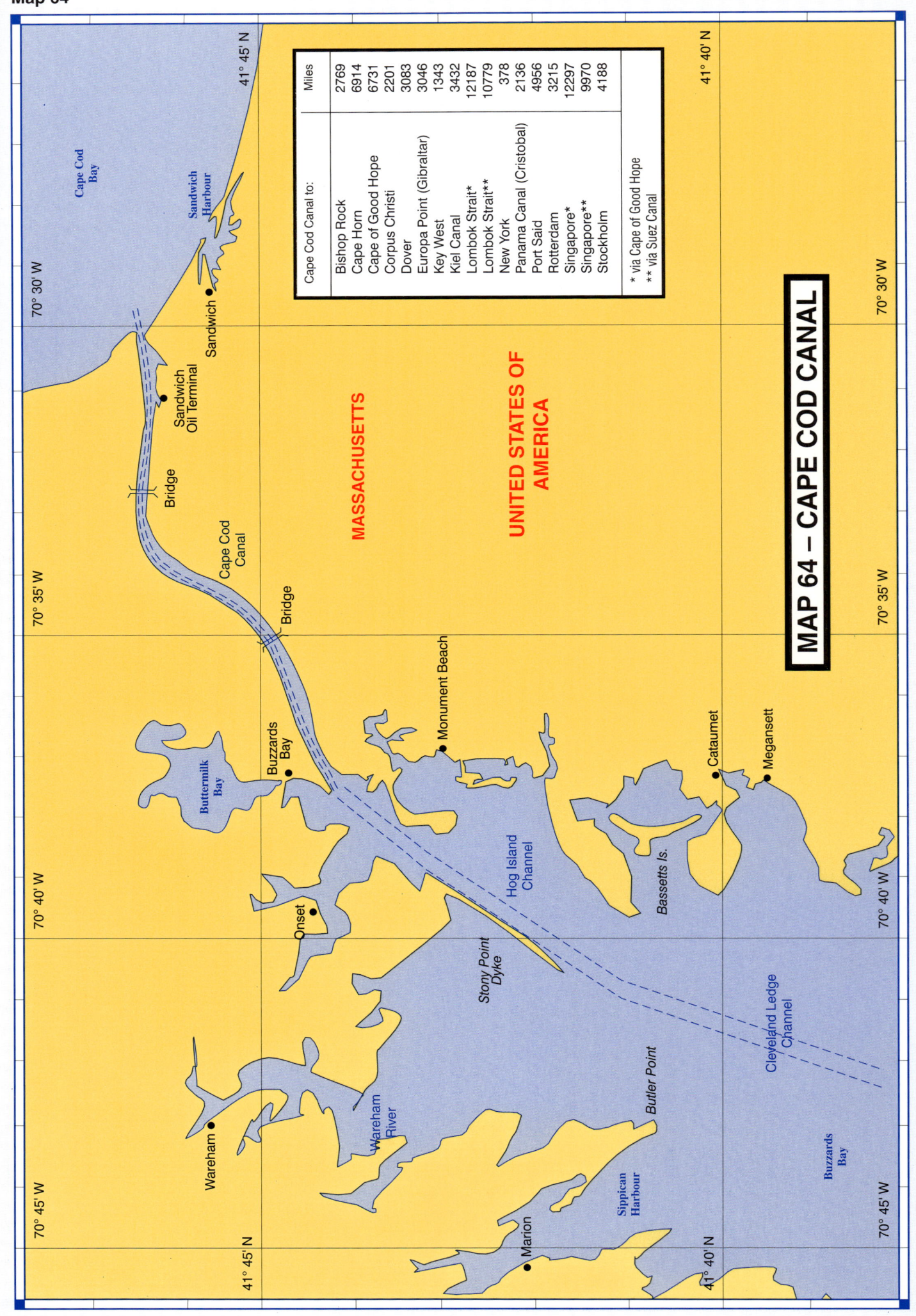

Cape Cod Canal to:	Miles
Bishop Rock	2769
Cape Horn	6914
Cape of Good Hope	6731
Corpus Christi	2201
Dover	3083
Europa Point (Gibraltar)	3046
Key West	1343
Kiel Canal	3432
Lombok Strait*	12187
Lombok Strait**	10779
New York	378
Panama Canal (Cristobal)	2136
Port Said	4956
Rotterdam	3215
Singapore*	12297
Singapore**	9970
Stockholm	4188

* via Cape of Good Hope
** via Suez Canal

MASSACHUSETTS
UNITED STATES OF AMERICA

Features shown: Cape Cod Bay, Sandwich Harbour, Sandwich, Sandwich Oil Terminal, Bridge, Cape Cod Canal, Bridge, Buttermilk Bay, Buzzards Bay, Monument Beach, Onset, Hog Island Channel, Stony Point Dyke, Bassetts Is., Cataumet, Megansett, Wareham, Wareham River, Butler Point, Cleveland Ledge Channel, Marion, Sippican Harbour, Buzzards Bay

© Shipping Guides Ltd., Reigate, United Kingdom

MAP 65
CHESAPEAKE AND DELAWARE BAYS

Map 66

FREEPORT TO LAKE CHARLES

From Houston to:	Miles	Days (at 16 knots)
Cape Horn	7520	19.6
Cape Town	7505	19.5
Copenhagen	5320	13.9
Gibraltar	4775	12.4
Lagos	5955	15.5
London (Gravesend)	5010	13.1
Montreal	3270	8.5
Panama (Cristobal)	1530	4.0
Port of Spain	2255	5.9
Seattle	5580	14.5
Sydney	9250	24.1
Yokohama	9260	24.1

© Shipping Guides Ltd., Reigate, United Kingdom

Map 66 – USA – Gulf Coast

	Brownsville	Charleston	Corpus Christi	Freeport (Bahamas)	Hamilton (Bermuda)	Houston	Jacksonville	Key West	Lake Charles	Miami	Mobile	New Orleans	Panama City	Port Canaveral	Savannah
Charleston	1425														
Corpus Christi	145	1440													
Freeport (Bahamas)	1075	390	1085												
Hamilton (Bermuda)	1935	800	1945	885											
Houston	305	1380	230	1040	1890										
Jacksonville	1315	200	1330	280	910	1270									
Key West	860	580	875	255	1090	815	470								
Lake Charles	345	1315	285	965	1825	155	1205	750							
Miami	1010	435	1020	92	955	970	325	190	900						
Mobile	620	1105	570	785	1620	475	1000	545	395	720					
New Orleans	575	1180	560	830	1690	435	1070	615	380	765	2354				
Panama City	685	1015	635	690	1520	545	905	450	465	625	160	305			
Port Canaveral	1165	280	1180	155	960	1120	175	320	1055	175	850	920	755		
Savannah	1395	100	1410	360	865	1350	150	550	1285	405	1080	1150	985	250	
Tampa	825	850	810	530	1355	725	745	285	640	460	385	495	265	595	825

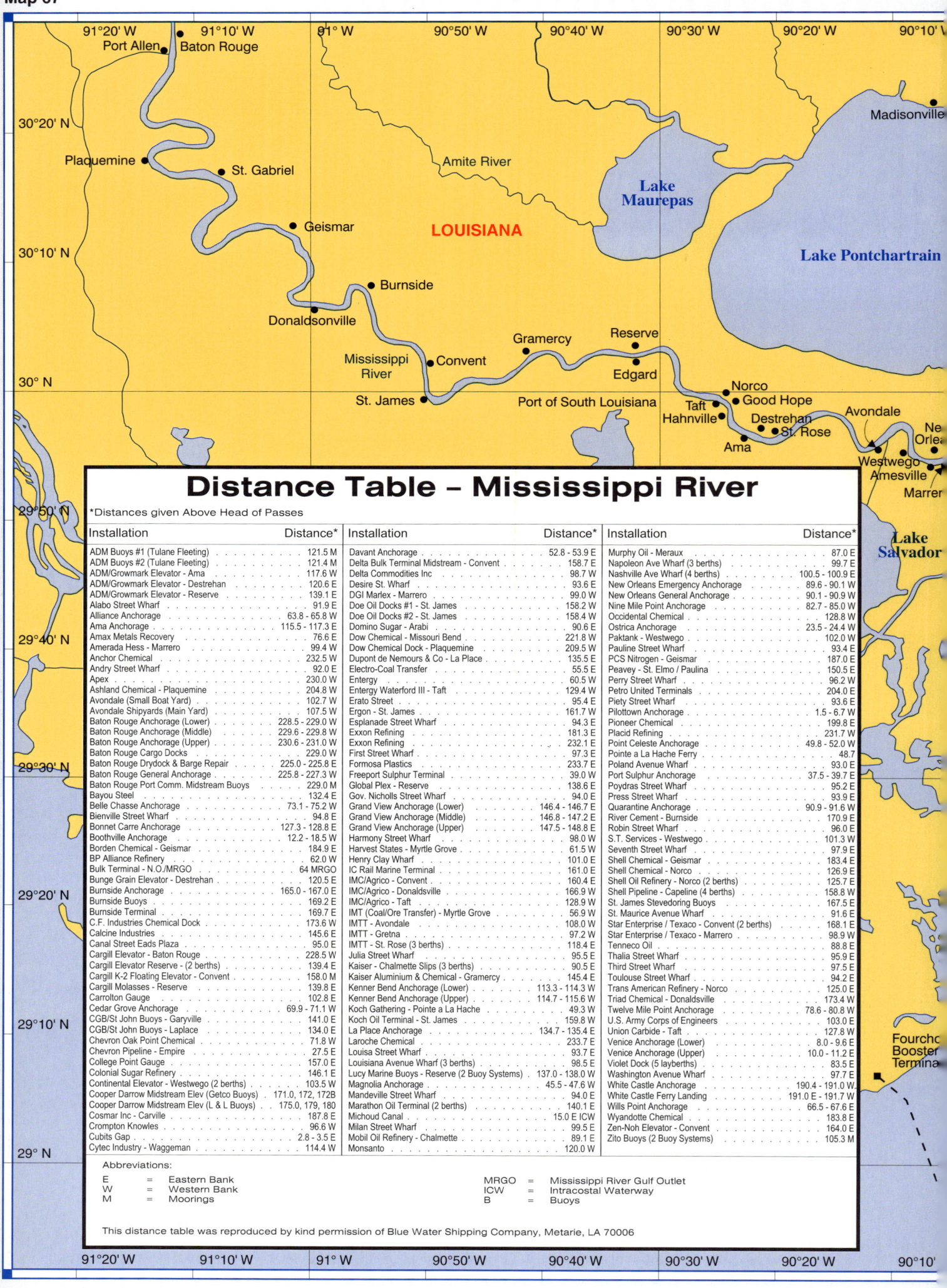

Distance Table – Mississippi River

*Distances given Above Head of Passes

Installation	Distance*	Installation	Distance*	Installation	Distance*
ADM Buoys #1 (Tulane Fleeting)	121.5 M	Davant Anchorage	52.8 - 53.9 E	Murphy Oil - Meraux	87.0 E
ADM Buoys #2 (Tulane Fleeting)	121.4 M	Delta Bulk Terminal Midstream - Convent	158.7 E	Napoleon Ave Wharf (3 berths)	99.7 E
ADM/Growmark Elevator - Ama	117.6 W	Delta Commodities Inc	98.7 W	Nashville Ave Wharf (4 berths)	100.5 - 100.9 E
ADM/Growmark Elevator - Destrehan	120.6 E	Desire St. Wharf	93.6 E	New Orleans Emergency Anchorage	89.6 - 90.1 W
ADM/Growmark Elevator - Reserve	139.1 E	DGI Marlex - Marrero	99.0 E	New Orleans General Anchorage	90.1 - 90.9 W
Alabo Street Wharf	91.9 E	Doe Oil Docks #1 - St. James	158.2 W	Nine Mile Point Anchorage	82.7 - 85.0 W
Alliance Anchorage	63.8 - 65.8 W	Doe Oil Docks #2 - St. James	158.4 W	Occidental Chemical	128.8 W
Ama Anchorage	115.5 - 117.3 E	Domino Sugar - Arabi	90.6 E	Ostrica Anchorage	23.5 - 24.4 W
Amax Metals Recovery	76.6 E	Dow Chemical - Missouri Bend	221.8 W	Paktank - Westwego	102.0 W
Amerada Hess - Marrero	99.4 W	Dow Chemical Dock - Plaquemine	209.5 W	Pauline Street Wharf	93.4 E
Anchor Chemical	232.5 W	Dupont de Nemours & Co - La Place	135.5 E	PCS Nitrogen - Geismar	187.0 E
Andry Street Wharf	92.0 E	Electro-Coal Transfer	55.5 E	Peavey - St. Elmo / Paulina	150.5 E
Apex	230.0 W	Entergy	60.5 W	Perry Street Wharf	96.2 W
Ashland Chemical - Plaquemine	204.8 W	Entergy Waterford III - Taft	129.4 W	Petro United Terminals	204.0 E
Avondale (Small Boat Yard)	102.7 W	Erato Street	95.4 E	Piety Street Wharf	93.6 E
Avondale Shipyards (Main Yard)	107.5 W	Ergon - St. James	161.7 W	Pilottown Anchorage	1.5 - 6.7 W
Baton Rouge Anchorage (Lower)	228.5 - 229.0 W	Esplanade Street Wharf	94.3 E	Pioneer Chemical	199.8 E
Baton Rouge Anchorage (Middle)	229.6 - 229.8 W	Exxon Refining	181.3 E	Placid Refining	231.7 W
Baton Rouge Anchorage (Upper)	230.6 - 231.0 W	Exxon Refining	232.1 E	Point Celeste Anchorage	49.8 - 52.0 W
Baton Rouge Cargo Docks	229.0 W	First Street Wharf	97.3 E	Pointe a La Hache Ferry	48.7
Baton Rouge Drydock & Barge Repair	225.0 - 225.8 E	Formosa Plastics	233.7 E	Poland Avenue Wharf	93.0 E
Baton Rouge General Anchorage	225.8 - 227.3 W	Freeport Sulphur Terminal	39.0 W	Port Sulphur Anchorage	37.5 - 39.7 E
Baton Rouge Port Comm. Midstream Buoys	229.0 M	Global Plex - Reserve	138.6 E	Poydras Street Wharf	95.2 E
Bayou Steel	132.4 E	Gov. Nicholls Street Wharf	94.0 E	Press Street Wharf	93.9 E
Belle Chasse Anchorage	73.1 - 75.2 W	Grand View Anchorage (Lower)	146.4 - 146.7 E	Quarantine Anchorage	90.9 - 91.6 W
Bienville Street Wharf	94.8 E	Grand View Anchorage (Middle)	146.8 - 147.2 E	River Cement - Burnside	170.9 E
Bonnet Carre Anchorage	127.3 - 128.8 E	Grand View Anchorage (Upper)	147.5 - 148.8 E	Robin Street Wharf	96.0 E
Boothville Anchorage	12.2 - 18.5 W	Harmony Street Wharf	98.0 W	S.T. Services - Westwego	101.3 W
Borden Chemical - Geismar	184.9 E	Harvest States - Myrtle Grove	61.5 W	Seventh Street Wharf	97.9 E
BP Alliance Refinery	62.0 W	Henry Clay Wharf	101.0 E	Shell Chemical - Geismar	183.4 E
Bulk Terminal - N.O./MRGO	64 MRGO	IC Rail Marine Terminal	161.0 E	Shell Chemical - Norco	126.9 E
Bunge Grain Elevator - Destrehan	120.5 E	IMC/Agrico - Convent	160.4 E	Shell Oil Refinery - Norco (2 berths)	125.7 E
Burnside Anchorage	165.0 - 167.0 E	IMC/Agrico - Donaldsville	166.9 W	Shell Pipeline - Capeline (4 berths)	158.8 W
Burnside Buoys	169.2 E	IMC/Agrico - Taft	128.9 W	St. James Stevedoring Buoys	167.5 E
Burnside Terminal	169.7 E	IMT (Coal/Ore Transfer) - Myrtle Grove	56.9 W	St. Maurice Avenue Wharf	91.6 E
C.F. Industries Chemical Dock	173.6 W	IMTT - Avondale	108.0 W	Star Enterprise / Texaco - Convent (2 berths)	168.1 E
Calcine Industries	145.6 E	IMTT - Gretna	97.2 W	Star Enterprise / Texaco - Marrero	98.9 W
Canal Street Eads Plaza	95.0 E	IMTT - St. Rose (3 berths)	118.4 E	Tenneco Oil	88.8 E
Cargill Elevator - Baton Rouge	228.5 W	Julia Street Wharf	95.5 E	Thalia Street Wharf	95.9 E
Cargill Elevator Reserve - (2 berths)	139.4 E	Kaiser - Chalmette Slips (3 berths)	90.5 E	Third Street Wharf	97.5 E
Cargill K-2 Floating Elevator - Convent	158.0 M	Kaiser Aluminium & Chemical - Gramercy	145.4 E	Toulouse Street Wharf	94.2 E
Cargill Molasses - Reserve	139.8 E	Kenner Bend Anchorage (Lower)	113.3 - 114.3 W	Trans American Refinery - Norco	125.0 E
Carrolton Gauge	102.8 E	Kenner Bend Anchorage (Upper)	114.7 - 115.6 W	Triad Chemical - Donaldsville	173.4 W
Cedar Grove Anchorage	69.9 - 71.1 W	Koch Gathering - Pointe a La Hache	49.3 W	Twelve Mile Point Anchorage	78.6 - 80.8 W
CGB/St John Buoys - Garyville	141.0 E	Koch Oil Terminal - St. James	159.8 W	U.S. Army Corps of Engineers	103.0 E
CGB/St John Buoys - Laplace	134.0 E	La Place Anchorage	134.7 - 135.4 E	Union Carbide - Taft	127.8 W
Chevron Oak Point Chemical	71.8 W	Laroche Chemical	233.7 E	Venice Anchorage (Lower)	8.0 - 9.6 E
Chevron Pipeline - Empire	27.5 E	Louisa Street Wharf	93.7 E	Venice Anchorage (Upper)	10.0 - 11.2 E
College Point Gauge	157.0 E	Louisiana Avenue Wharf (3 berths)	98.5 E	Violet Dock (5 layberths)	83.5 E
Colonial Sugar Refinery	146.1 E	Lucy Marine Buoys - Reserve (2 Buoy Systems)	137.0 - 138.0 W	Washington Avenue Wharf	97.7 E
Continental Elevator - Westwego (2 berths)	103.5 W	Magnolia Anchorage	45.5 - 47.6 W	White Castle Anchorage	190.4 - 191.0 W
Cooper Darrow Midstream Elev (Getco Buoys)	171.0, 172, 172B	Mandeville Street Wharf	94.0 E	White Castle Ferry Landing	191.0 E - 191.7 W
Cooper Darrow Midstream Elev (L & L Buoys)	175.0, 179, 180	Marathon Oil Terminal (2 berths)	140.1 E	Wills Point Anchorage	66.5 - 67.6 E
Cosmar Inc - Carville	187.8 E	Michoud Canal	15.0 E ICW	Wyandotte Chemical	183.8 E
Crompton Knowles	96.6 W	Milan Street Wharf	99.5 E	Zen-Noh Elevator - Convent	164.0 E
Cubits Gap	2.8 - 3.5 E	Mobil Oil Refinery - Chalmette	89.1 E	Zito Buoys (2 Buoy Systems)	105.3 M
Cytec Industry - Waggeman	114.4 W	Monsanto	120.0 W		

Abbreviations:
- E = Eastern Bank
- W = Western Bank
- M = Moorings
- MRGO = Mississippi River Gulf Outlet
- ICW = Intracoastal Waterway
- B = Buoys

This distance table was reproduced by kind permission of Blue Water Shipping Company, Metarie, LA 70006

MAP 67 – MISSISSIPPI RIVER
90° W
89°50' W
89°40' W
89°30' W
89°20' W
89°10' W
89° W
88°50' W
30°20' N
30°10' N
30° N
29°50' N
29°40' N
29°30' N
29°20' N
29°10' N
29° N
MISSISSIPPI
LOUISIANA
Biloxi
Gulfport
Bay St. Louis
Mississippi Sound
Ship Is.
Cat Is.
Grand Is.
Is. au Pitre
Lake Borgne
Chandeleur Sound
Boudreau Bay
Chalmette
Meraux
etna
Braithwaite
Gulf Outlet Canal
Freemason Is.
Chandeleur Is.
Pt. Chicot Is.
Eloi Bay
Breton Sound
Curlew Is.
liance
Myrtle Grove
Davant
Black Bay
Pointe a La Hache
Errol Is.
Port Sulphur
Breton Is.
Barataria Bay
Empire
Ostrica
Grand Bay
Buras
Main Pass
Mississippi Delta
Grand Terra Is.
Grand Isle
North Pass
Head of Passes
Pilot Town
South East Pass
Garden Island Bay
West Bay
Port Eads
South Pass
East Bay
LOOP Terminal
Southwest Pass

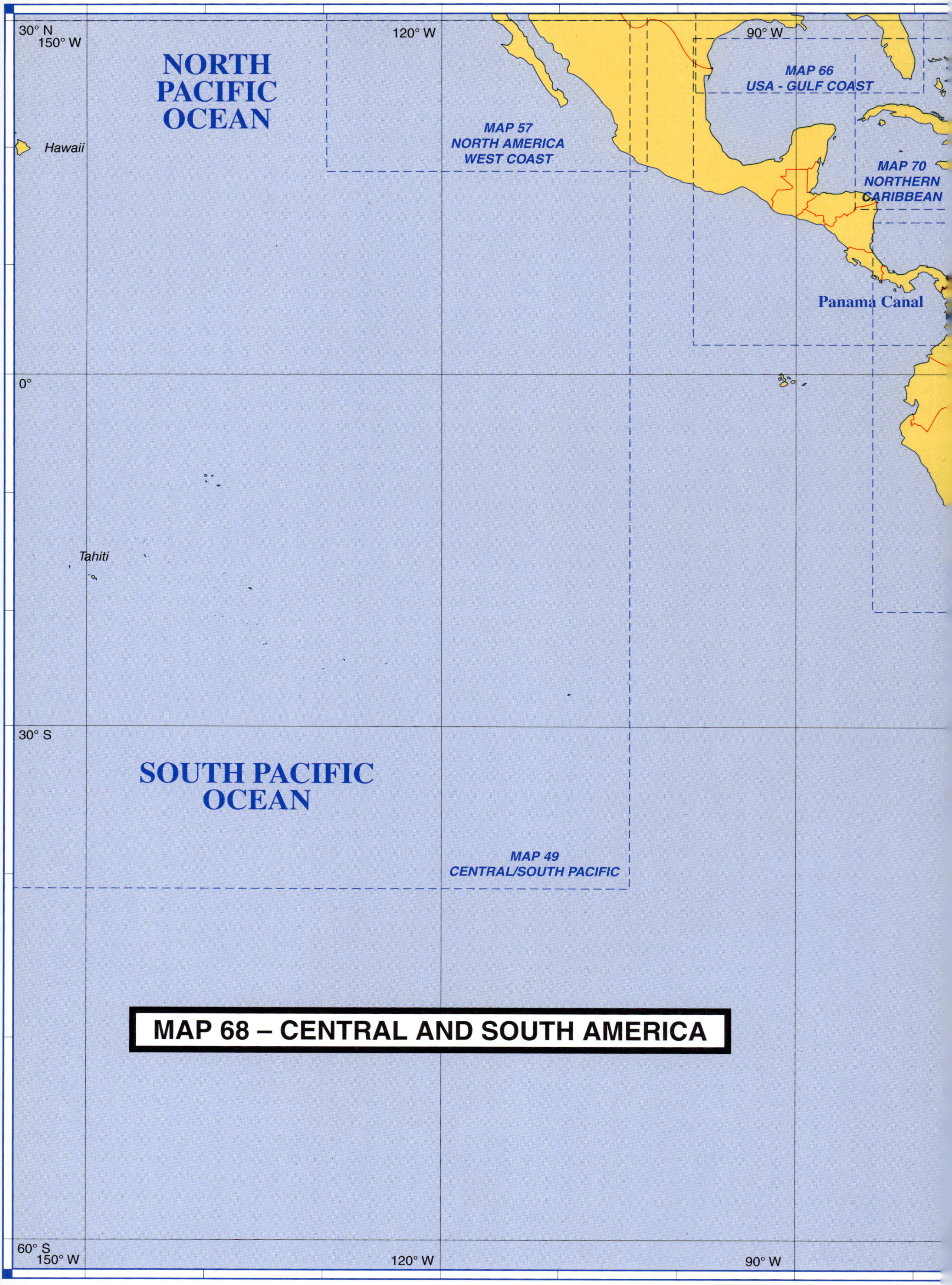

Map 68

30° N
150° W

NORTH PACIFIC OCEAN

120° W

90° W

MAP 66
USA - GULF COAST

Hawaii

MAP 57
NORTH AMERICA
WEST COAST

MAP 70
NORTHERN
CARIBBEAN

Panama Canal

0°

Tahiti

30° S

SOUTH PACIFIC OCEAN

MAP 49
CENTRAL/SOUTH PACIFIC

MAP 68 – CENTRAL AND SOUTH AMERICA

60° S
150° W   120° W   90° W

© Shipping Guides Ltd., Reigate, United Kingdom

Map 68

MAP 69
THE CARIBBEAN

MAP 71
EASTERN CARIBBEAN

NORTH ATLANTIC OCEAN

CARIBBEAN SEA

MAP 74
MARACAIBO
LAKES REGION

MAP 75
ORINOCO RIVER

MAP 76
SOUTH AMERICA
COASTAL AREAS

MAP 72
SOUTH AMERICA
NORTHERN PART

Cape Verde Islands

MAP 27
WEST AFRICA/
CAPE VERDE ISLANDS

MAP 29
GULF OF GUINEA

Fernando de Noronha

Ascension Island

St. Helena

MAP 28
SOUTH WEST AFRICA

MAP 76
SOUTH AMERICA
COASTAL AREAS

Tristan da Cunha

Gough Island

MAP 78
RIVER PLATE

Falkland Islands

SOUTH ATLANTIC OCEAN

South Georgia

MAP 77
SOUTH AMERICA
SOUTHERN PART

South Sandwich Islands

Cape Horn

South Shetland Islands

South Orkneys

Map 69

From Panama (Balboa) to:	Miles	Days (at 16 knots)
Hong Kong	9195	24.0
Melbourne	7915	20.6
Papeete	4580	11.9
Singapore	10495	27.3
Suva	6315	16.5
Vladivostock	7740	20.2

Average transit time of Panama Canal 10-12 hours.

	Barranquilla	Belize	Bridgetown	Cienfuegos	Corpus Christi	Cristobal	Freeport	Georgetown (G.C.)	Georgetown (Guy.)	Havana	Key West	Kingston	La Ceiba	Maracaibo	Miami	Nassau	Port au Prince	Port of Spain	Puerto Ordaz	St. Johns	San Juan	Santiago
Belize	900	Belize																				
Bridgetown	925	1695	Bridgetown																			
Cienfuegos	750	545	1335	Cienfuegos																		
Corpus Christi	1630	995	2300	1050	Corpus Christi																	
Cristobal	340	800	1235	775	1540	Cristobal																
Freeport	1070	805	1355	750	1085	1240	Freeport															
Georgetown (G.C.)	630	410	1310	185	1020	600	745	Georgetown (G.C.)														
Georgetown (Guy.)	1170	1955	395	1630	2600	1475	1700	1595	Georgetown (Guy.)													
Havana	1060	525	1460	475	860	990	305	445	1790	Havana												
Key West	1080	590	1455	535	875	1055	255	500	1785	92	Key West											
Kingston	445	695	1045	390	1320	555	735	300	1330	745	747	Kingston										
La Ceiba	810	135	1610	550	1030	710	835	385	1865	560	625	620	La Ceiba									
Maracaibo	370	1185	750	920	1860	675	1165	850	990	1185	1180	585	1080	Maracaibo								
Miami	1080	735	1420	685	1020	1200	92	680	1770	240	180	750	770	1180	Miami							
Nassau	995	680	1280	840	1180	1155	120	815	1630	380	325	925	1095	190	Nassau							
Port au Prince	595	920	1050	530	1385	765	635	525	1360	660	650	280	865	695	650	1315	Port au Prince					
Port of Spain	835	1625	205	1305	2275	1140	1390	1265	370	1480	1475	1000	1540	665	1455	1315	1035	Port of Spain				
Puerto Ordaz	1165	1950	430	1625	2600	1475	1680	1590	370	1790	1780	1325	1870	1000	1765	1625	1355	365	Puerto Ordaz			
St. Johns	850	1520	290	1145	2065	1155	1100	1130	675	1225	1220	870	1455	695	1175	1025	805	405	680	St. Johns		
San Juan	705	1305	510	890	1810	995	875	895	875	980	965	635	1225	620	930	795	575	875	875	260	San Juan	
Santiago	555	730	1055	330	1300	685	620	320	1340	640	635	180	685	645	635	550	230	1015	1340	830	580	Santiago
Vera Cruz	1500	865	2200	940	540	1410	1080	900	2485	815	865	1200	900	1740	1015	1170	1395	2150	2480	2010	1755	1190

© Shipping Guides Ltd., Reigate, England

MAP 69 – THE CARIBBEAN

From Panama (Cristobal) to:	Miles	Days (at 16 knots)
Avonmouth	4515	11.8
Cape Town	6425	16.7
Dakar	3690	9.6
Lisbon	4155	10.8
London (Gravesend)	4760	12.4
Montreal	3190	8.3
New York	1975	5.1
Oslo	5065	13.2

CUBA — Nuevitas, Puerto Padre, Vita, Banes, Antilla, Moa, Tanamo, Guantanamo, Santiago de Cuba, Guayabal, Manzanillo

JAMAICA — Montego Bay, Port Rhoades, Ocho Rios, Port Antonio, Port Kaiser, Salt River, Kingston

HAITI — Cap Haitien, Port-au-Prince, Miragoane, Gonave I., Windward Passage

DOMINICAN REPUBLIC — Manzanillo, Puerto Plata, Samana, Rio Haina, La Romana, Azua, Palenque, Barahona

PUERTO RICO (U.S.A.) — Aguadilla, San Juan, Mayaguez, Ponce, Guayama; Mona Passage

Bahamas: Grand Bahama, Nassau, New Providence, Eleuthera, Rock Sound, The Bight, Cat Is., San Salvador, Clarence Town, Long Is., Ragged, Crooked, Mayaguana, Caicos Is., Providenciales, Grand Turk, Turks Is. (Turks and Caicos Is. U.K.), Great Inagua, Morton

St. Thomas (U.S.A.), Road Harbour (U.K.), Christianstad, Frederikstad, Limetree Bay

ANTIGUA AND BARBUDA — Basseterre, St. Johns
Guadeloupe (FR.) — Basse Terre, Pointe a Pitre
DOMINICA — Portsmouth, Roseau
Martinique (FR.) — Fort de France
ST. LUCIA — Castries, Vieux Fort
ST. VINCENT — Kingstown
BARBADOS — Bridgetown
GRENADA — St. Georges

See Map 71, See Map 70, See Map 74, See Map 75

CARIBBEAN SEA

COLOMBIA — Puerto Bolivar, Riohacha, Santa Marta, Puerto Colombia, Barranquilla, El Bosque, Mamonal, Cartagena, Tolu, Covenas, Pinos, Pito, La Palma, Turbo, El Real, Jurado, Bahia Solarino, Punta Charambira, Buenaventura, Guapi

Aruba (Neth.) — San Nicolas, Oranjestad
Puerto Lopez, Amuay Bay, Curacao, Willemstad, Brasil, Bonaire, Kralendijk, Coro, Paria, Tucacas, Puerto Cabello, Rio Chico, Pozos Colorados, Maracaibo, Puerto Miranda, La Estacada, Punta de Palmas, Playitas, Solito, San Lorenzo

Blanquilla, Margarita, La Guaira, El Guamache, Porlamar, Tortuga, Carupano, Guiria, Scarborough, Tobago, Port of Spain, Trinidad, Galeota Point, Carenero, Cumana, Pertigalete, Caripito, Puerto la Cruz, Barcelona, Pedernales

VENEZUELA — Ciudad Bolivar, Punta Cuchillo, Palua, Puerto Ordaz, River Orinoco, Puerto Ayacucho

GUYANA

BRAZIL

GALAPOGOS

Isla Isabela, San Salvador, Galapagos Islands (Ecuador), Caleta Tagus, Santa Cruz, San Cristobal, Puerto Villamil, Barqueriza

MAP 70 – NORTHERN CARIBBEAN

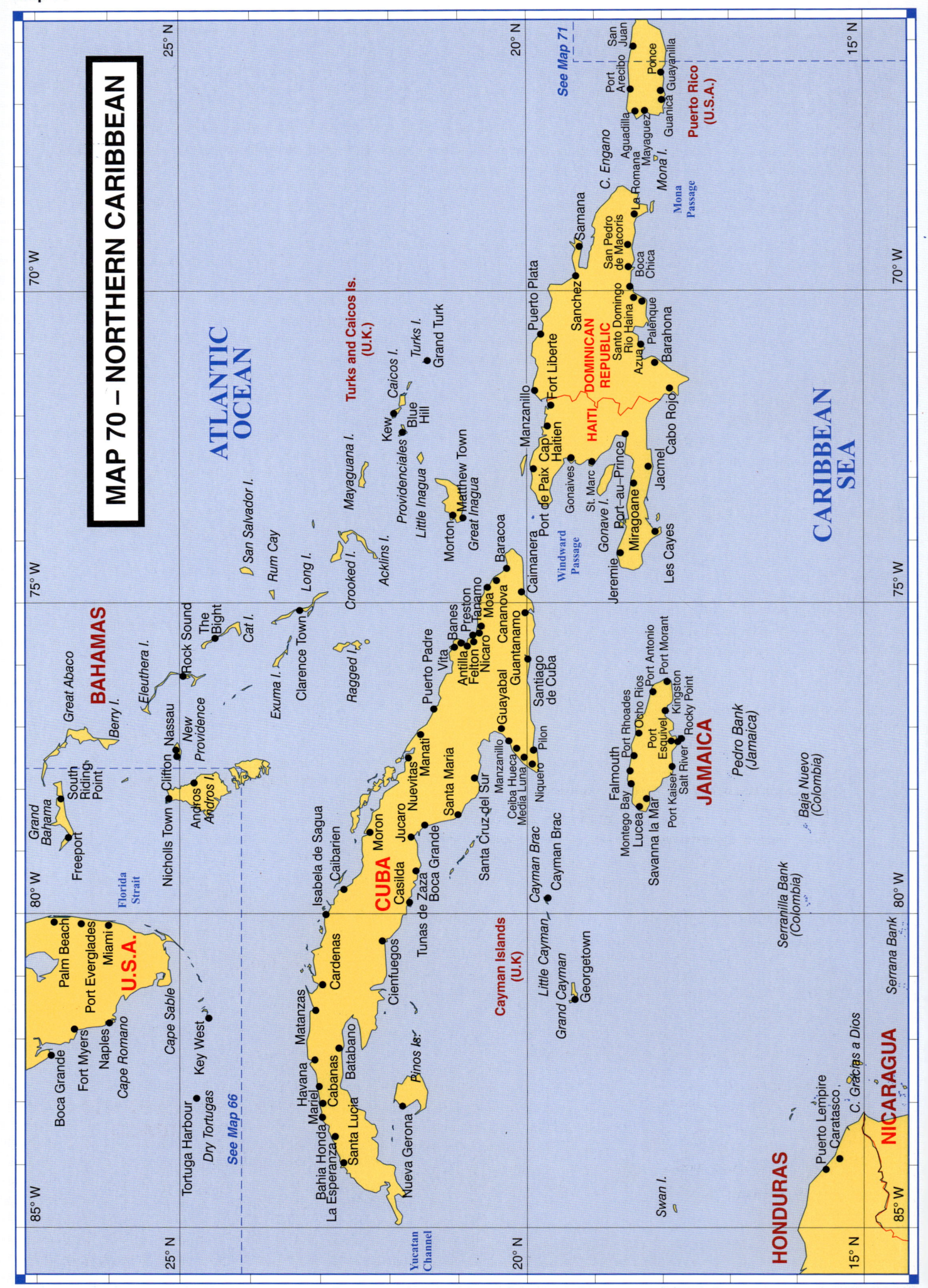

MAP 71 – EASTERN CARIBBEAN

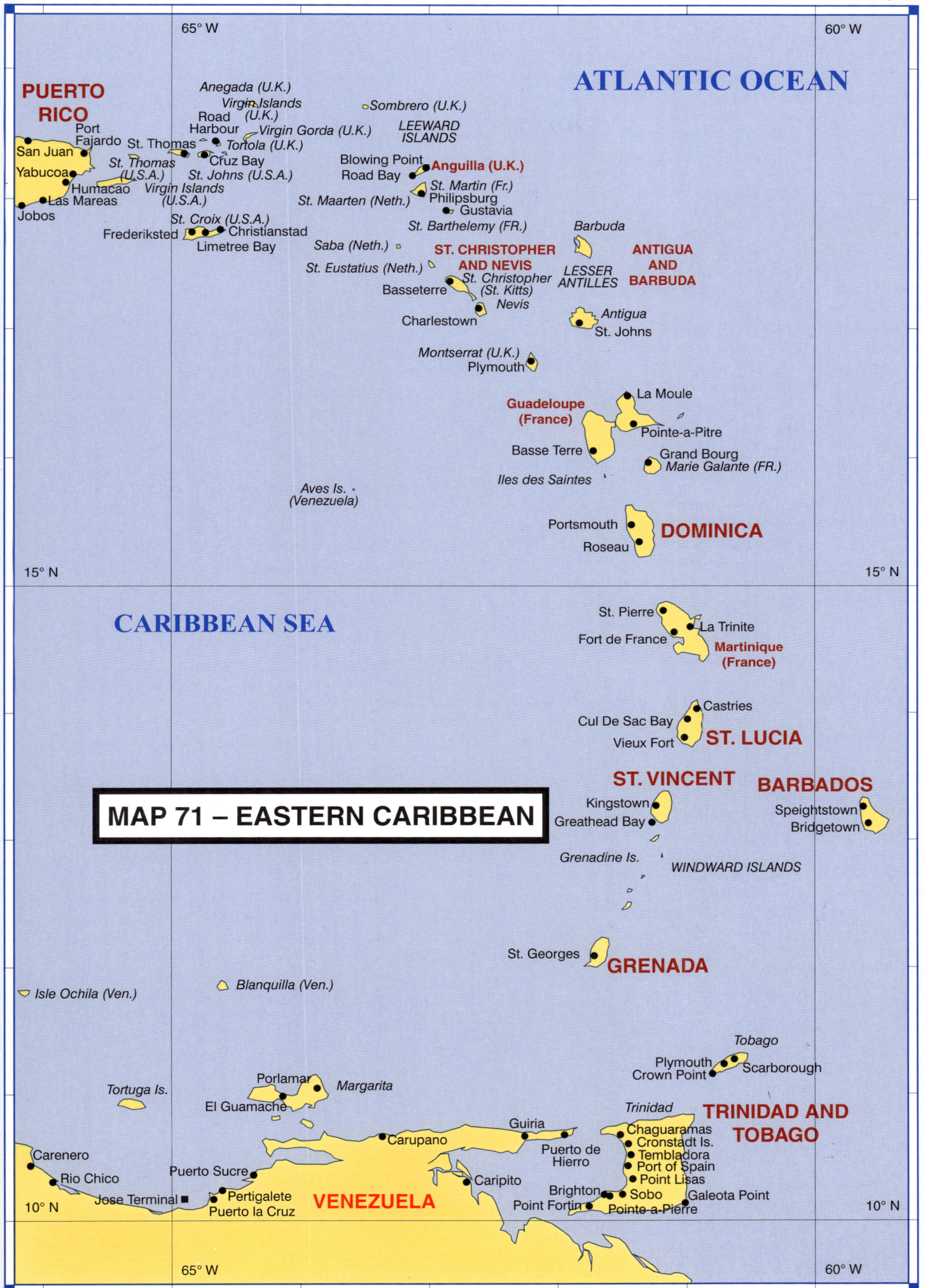

80° W
75° W
70° W
65° W
60° W
ST. LUCIA
ST. VINCENT
Kingstown
BARBAD
Bridgeto
GRENADA
See Map 71
TRINIDAD AND TOBAGO
Aruba (Neth.)
NETHERLANDS ANTILLES
Oranjestad
Puerto Bolivar
San Nicolas
Willemstad
Kralendijk
Amuay Bay
Pozos Colorados
Barranquilla
Santa Marta
El Guamache
Puerto de Hierro
La Guaira
Guanta
Puerto Sucre
Port of Spain
Galeota Point
Caripito
Jose Terminal
Pedernales
10° N
Panama Canal
See Map 73
Cartagena
Maracaibo
La Salina
El Palito
Almirante
Chiriqui Grande
Cristobal
Balboa
Covenas
La Ceiba
See Map 74
PANAMA
Puerto Armuelles
Aguadulce
Gulf of Panama
Turbo
R. Orinoco
Matanzas
Palua
Puerto Ordaz
Jurado
Essequibo Ri
Lind
VENEZUELA
See Map 75
GUYAN
5° N
Atrato R.
COLOMBIA
Malpelo
Buenaventura
Gorgona
See Map 69
Guapi
Tumaco
Balao Terminal
Esmeraldas
San Lorenzo
Rioverde
0°
Bahia de Caraquez
Manta
ECUADOR
R. Negro
R. Napo
Salinas
La Libertad
Guayaquil
Fonte Boa
Manau
Puna
Zorritos
Puerto Bolivar
R. Amazon
Coari
Codajas
Cabo Blanco
Lobitos
Negritos
Talara
Iquitos
Leticia
Sao Paulo
Tabatinga
Paita
5° S
Puerto Bayovar
R. Uguyali
Pimentel
Eten
R. Madeira
Pacasmayo
Puerto Chicama
Humaita
Salaverry
Pucallpa
Chimbote
Porto Velho
Coishco
Samanco
10° S
Huarmey
Paramonga
Supe
Huacho
Chancay
La Pampilla
Callao
PERU
Conchan
Tambo de Mora
Pisco
General San Martin
See Map 77
15° S
San Nicolas
San Juan
Atico
Matarani
Mollendo
BOLIVIA
Ilo
PACIFIC OCEAN
Arica
CHILE
20° S
Pisagua
PARAGUAY

MAP 72 – SOUTH AMERICA – NORTHERN PART

See Map 76

ATLANTIC OCEAN

SURINAME

- Georgetown
- New Amsterdam
- Nickerie
- Paranam
- Paramaribo
- Moengo
- Degrad-des-Cannes

Guyane (Fr.)

BRAZIL

- C. de Norte
- Macapa
- Santana
- Munguba
- Porto Trombetas
- Obidos
- Afua
- *Marajo*
- Breves
- Portel
- Belem
- Miramar
- Salinopolis
- Bragança
- Cameta
- Vila do Conde
- Porto ABC Norte
- Ponta da Madeira
- Itaqui
- Sao Luis
- Alumar
- Tutoia
- Parnaiba
- Acarau
- Camocim
- Fortaleza
- Santarem
- Coatiara
- Itaituba
- Altamira
- Tucurui
- Rio Pacaja
- R. Tocantins
- R. Xingu
- Parintins
- Maraba
- Imperatriz
- Aracati
- Guamare
- Areia Branca
- Natal
- R. Tapajos
- Cabedelo
- Joao Pessoa
- Recife
- Suape
- R. San Francisco
- Maceio
- Penedo
- Aracaju
- Carmopolis
- Madre de Deus
- Aratu
- Salvador

See Map 77

- Ilheus
- Porto Seguro
- Caravelas
- *Abrolhos Is.*
- Puerto Suarez
- Corumba
- Porto Esperanza
- Regencia
- Barra do Riacho
- Aracruz
- Bahia Negra

Map 72

MAP 73 – PANAMA CANAL

MAP 74 – MARACAIBO LAKE REGION

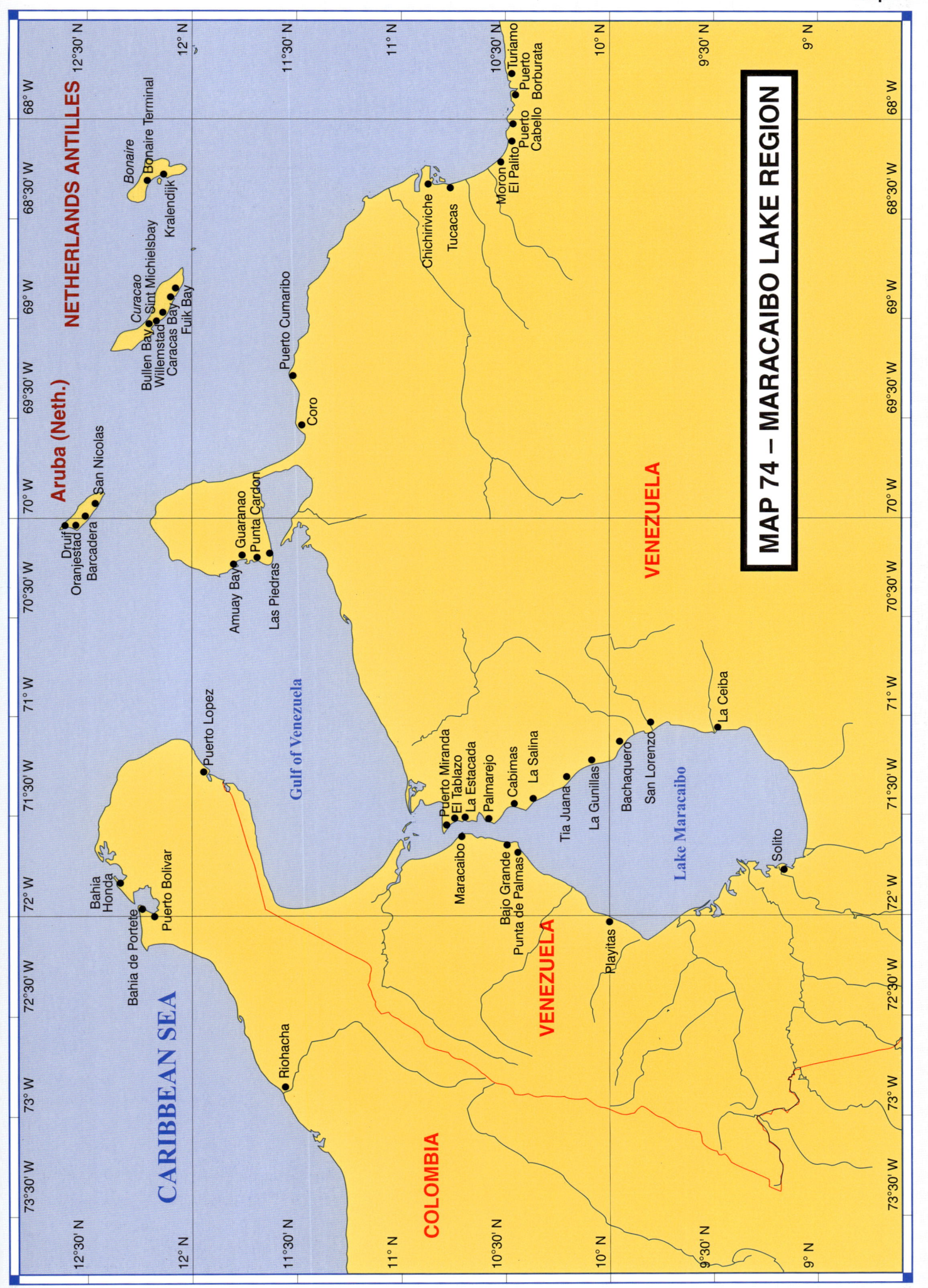

MAP 75 – ORINOCO RIVER

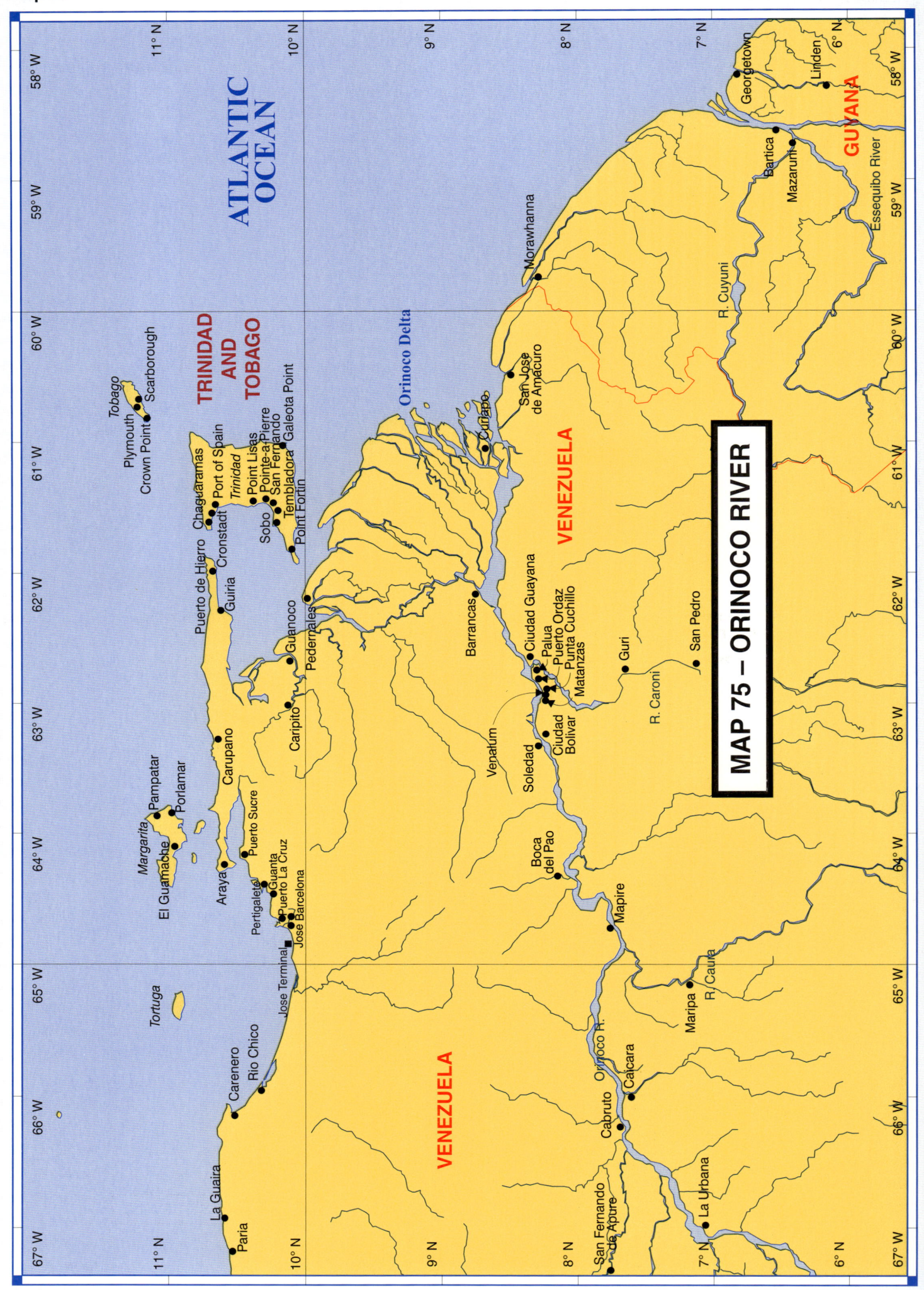

Map 76

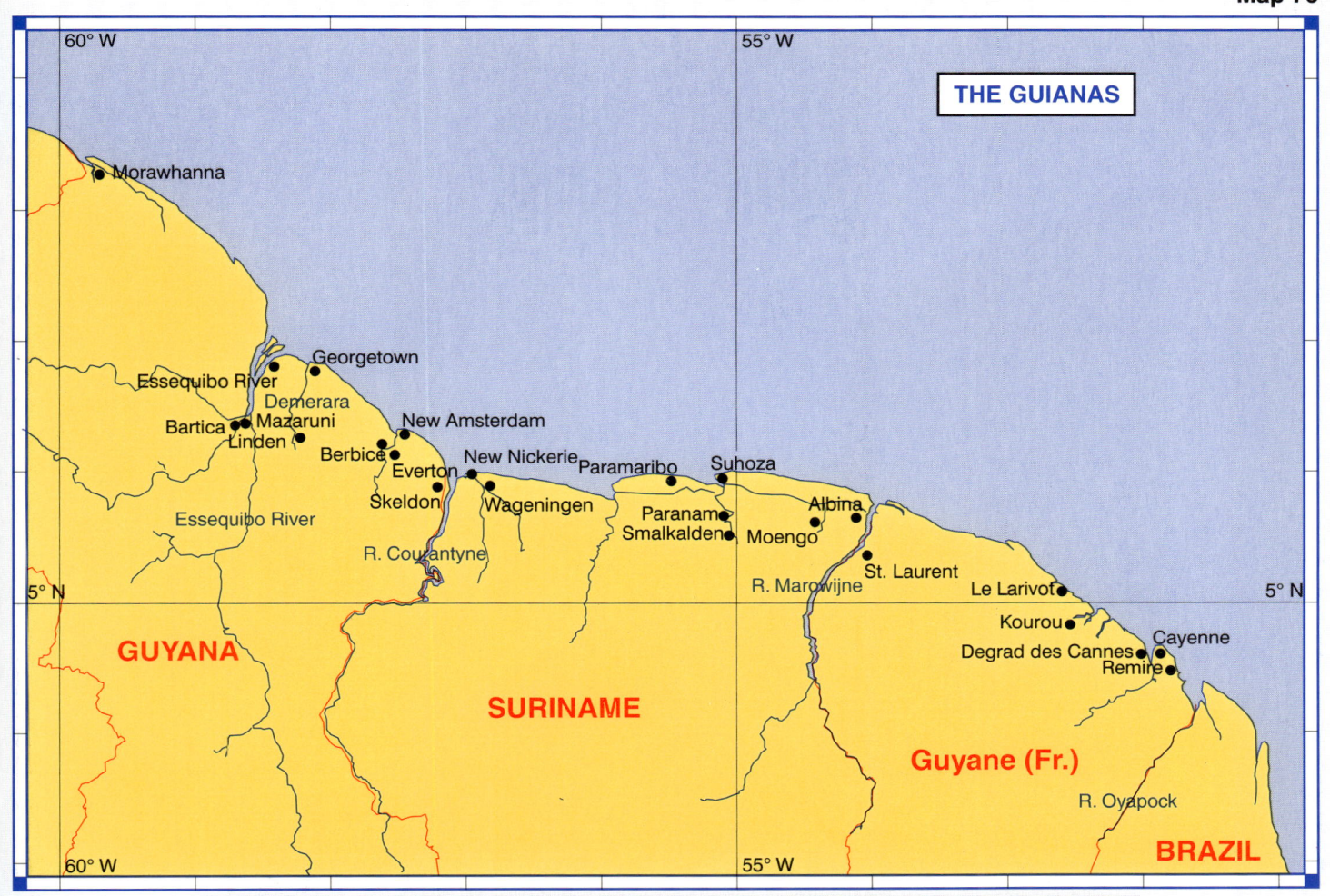

THE GUIANAS

MAP 76 – SOUTH AMERICAN COASTAL AREAS

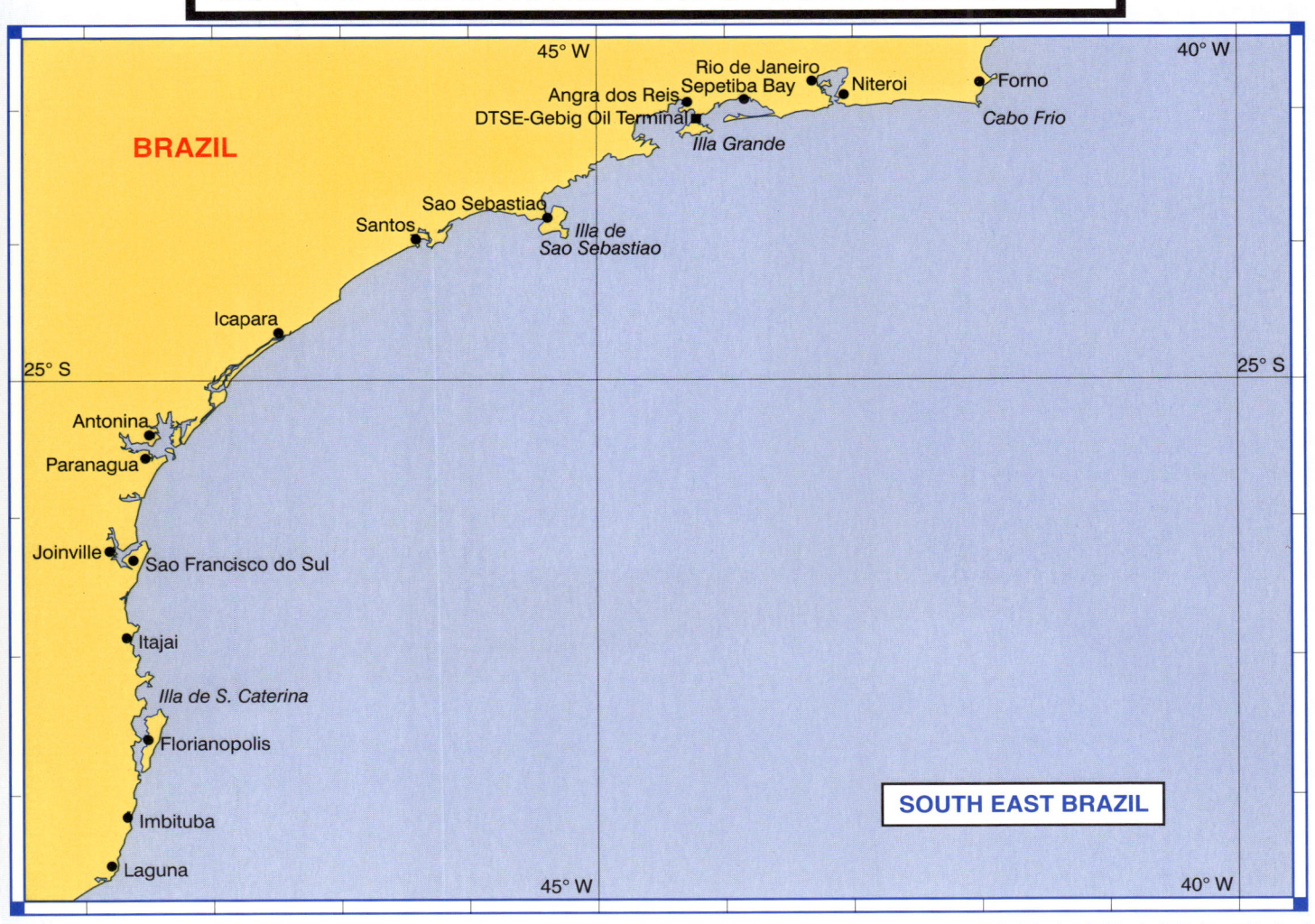

SOUTH EAST BRAZIL

© Shipping Guides Ltd., Reigate, England

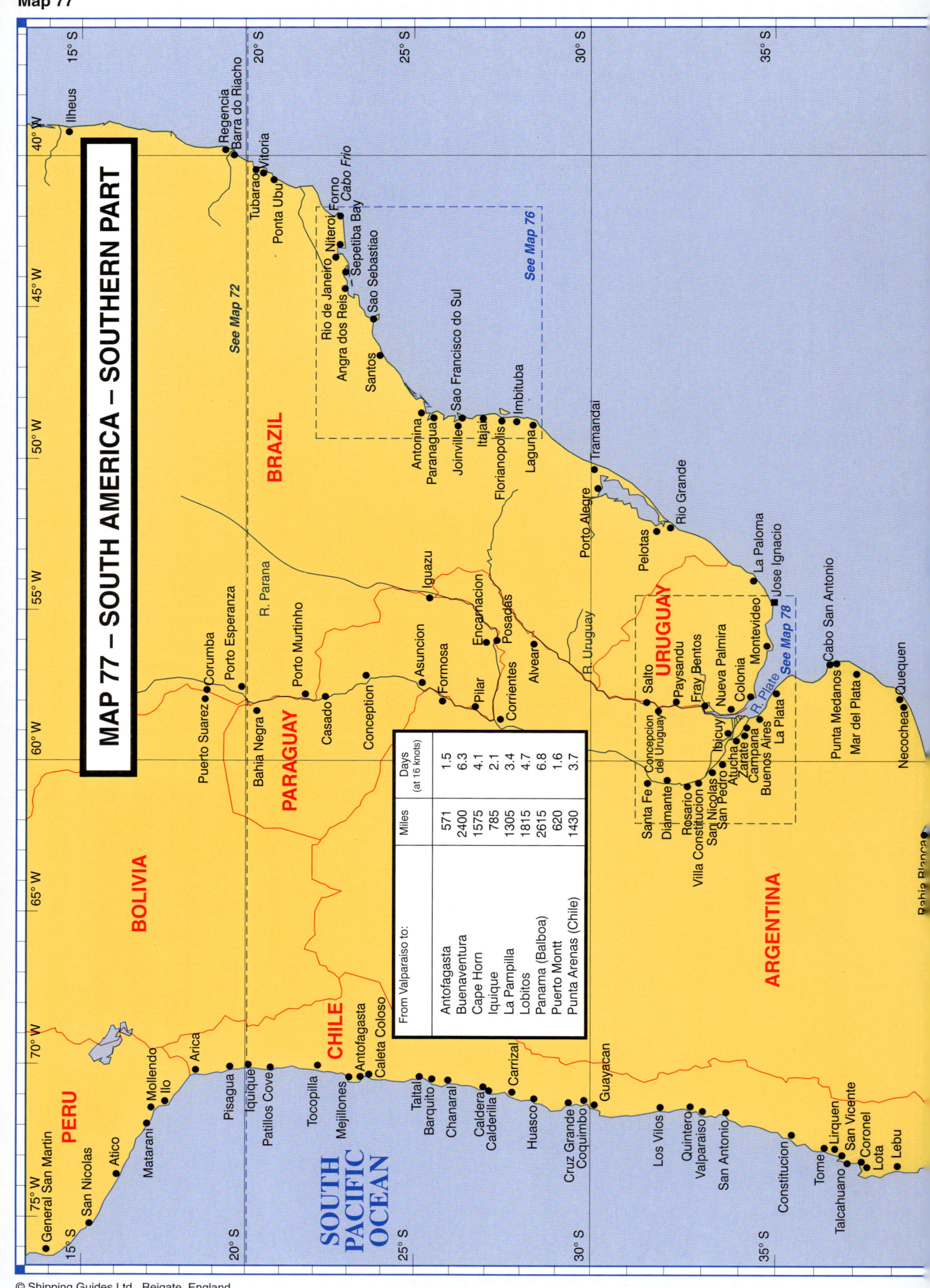

MAP 77 – SOUTH AMERICA – SOUTHERN PART

From Valparaiso to:	Miles	Days (at 16 knots)
Antofagasta	571	1.5
Buenaventura	2400	6.3
Cape Horn	1575	4.1
Iquique	785	2.1
La Pampilla	1305	3.4
Lobitos	1815	4.7
Panama (Balboa)	2615	6.8
Puerto Montt	620	1.6
Punta Arenas (Chile)	1430	3.7

PERU — General San Martin, San Nicolas, Atico, Matarani, Mollendo, Ilo

BOLIVIA

CHILE — Arica, Pisagua, Iquique, Patillos Cove, Tocopilla, Mejillones, Antofagasta, Caleta Coloso, Taltal, Barquito, Chanaral, Caldera, Calderilla, Carrizal, Huasco, Cruz Grande, Coquimbo, Guayacan, Los Vilos, Quintero, Valparaiso, San Antonio, Constitucion, Tome, Talcahuano, Lirquen, San Vicente, Coronel, Lota, Lebu

BRAZIL — Ilheus, Regencia, Barra do Riacho, Tubarao, Vitoria, Ponta Ubu, Forno, Cabo Frio, Rio de Janeiro, Niteroi, Sepetiba Bay, Angra dos Reis, Sao Sebastiao, Santos, Sao Francisco do Sul, Joinville, Itajai, Florianopolis, Imbituba, Laguna, Tramandai, Porto Alegre, Pelotas, Rio Grande

PARAGUAY — Puerto Suarez, Corumba, Porto Esperanza, Bahia Negra, Porto Murtinho, Casado, Conception, Asuncion, Formosa, Pilar, Encarnacion, Posadas

R. Parana, Iguazu, R. Uruguay, Alvear, Corrientes

URUGUAY — Salto, Paysandu, Fray Bentos, Nueva Palmira, Colonia, Montevideo, La Paloma, Jose Ignacio

ARGENTINA — Santa Fe, Concepcion del Uruguay, Diamante, Rosario, Villa Constitucion, San Nicolas, San Pedro, Ibicuy, Atucha, Zarate, Campana, Buenos Aires, La Plata, Punta Medanos, Mar del Plata, Necochea, Quequen, Cabo San Antonio, Bahia Blanca

R. Plate

SOUTH PACIFIC OCEAN

See Map 72
See Map 76
See Map 78

© Shipping Guides Ltd., Reigate, England

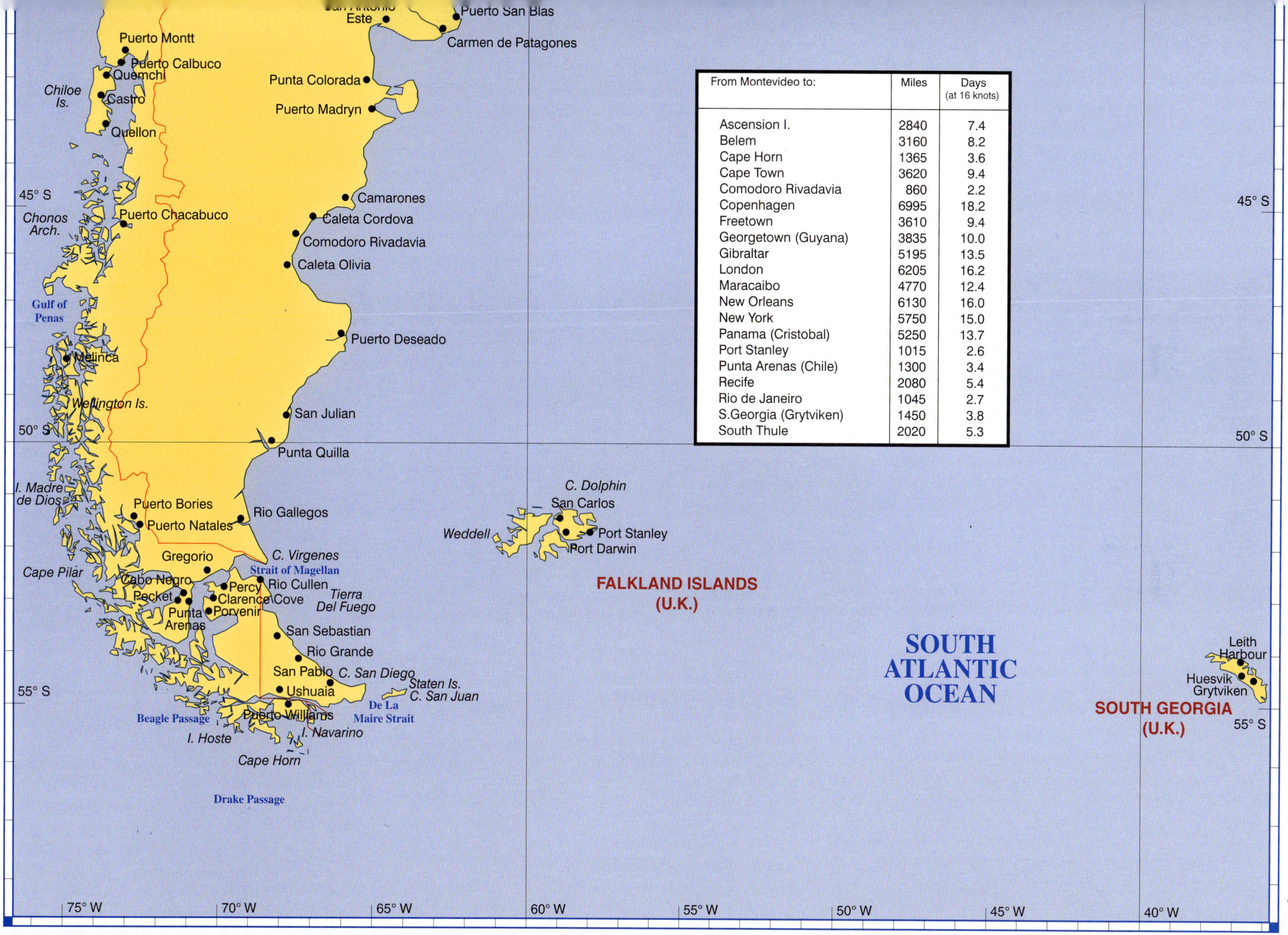
Puerto Montt
Puerto Calbuco
Quemchi
Chiloe Is.
Castro
Quellon
Este
Puerto San Blas
Carmen de Patagones
Punta Colorada
Puerto Madryn
45° S
Chonos Arch.
Puerto Chacabuco
Camarones
Caleta Cordova
Comodoro Rivadavia
Caleta Olivia
Gulf of Penas
Puerto Deseado
Melinca
Wellington Is.
San Julian
50° S
Punta Quilla
I. Madre de Dios
Puerto Bories
Puerto Natales
Rio Gallegos
Cape Pilar
Gregorio
C. Virgenes
Strait of Magellan
Cabo Negro
Pecket
Punta Arenas
Percy
Clarence
Porvenir
Rio Cullen
Cove
Tierra Del Fuego
San Sebastian
Rio Grande
San Pablo
C. San Diego
Staten Is.
C. San Juan
55° S
Ushuaia
Puerto Williams
Beagle Passage
De La Maire Strait
I. Navarino
I. Hoste
Cape Horn
Drake Passage
C. Dolphin
San Carlos
Weddell
Port Stanley
Port Darwin
FALKLAND ISLANDS (U.K.)
SOUTH ATLANTIC OCEAN
Leith Harbour
Huesvik
Grytviken
SOUTH GEORGIA (U.K.)
75° W
70° W
65° W
60° W
55° W
50° W
45° W
40° W

From Montevideo to:	Miles	Days (at 16 knots)
Ascension I.	2840	7.4
Belem	3160	8.2
Cape Horn	1365	3.6
Cape Town	3620	9.4
Comodoro Rivadavia	860	2.2
Copenhagen	6995	18.2
Freetown	3610	9.4
Georgetown (Guyana)	3835	10.0
Gibraltar	5195	13.5
London	6205	16.2
Maracaibo	4770	12.4
New Orleans	6130	16.0
New York	5750	15.0
Panama (Cristobal)	5250	13.7
Port Stanley	1015	2.6
Punta Arenas (Chile)	1300	3.4
Recife	2080	5.4
Rio de Janeiro	1045	2.7
S.Georgia (Grytviken)	1450	3.8
South Thule	2020	5.3

MAP 78 – RIVER PLATE

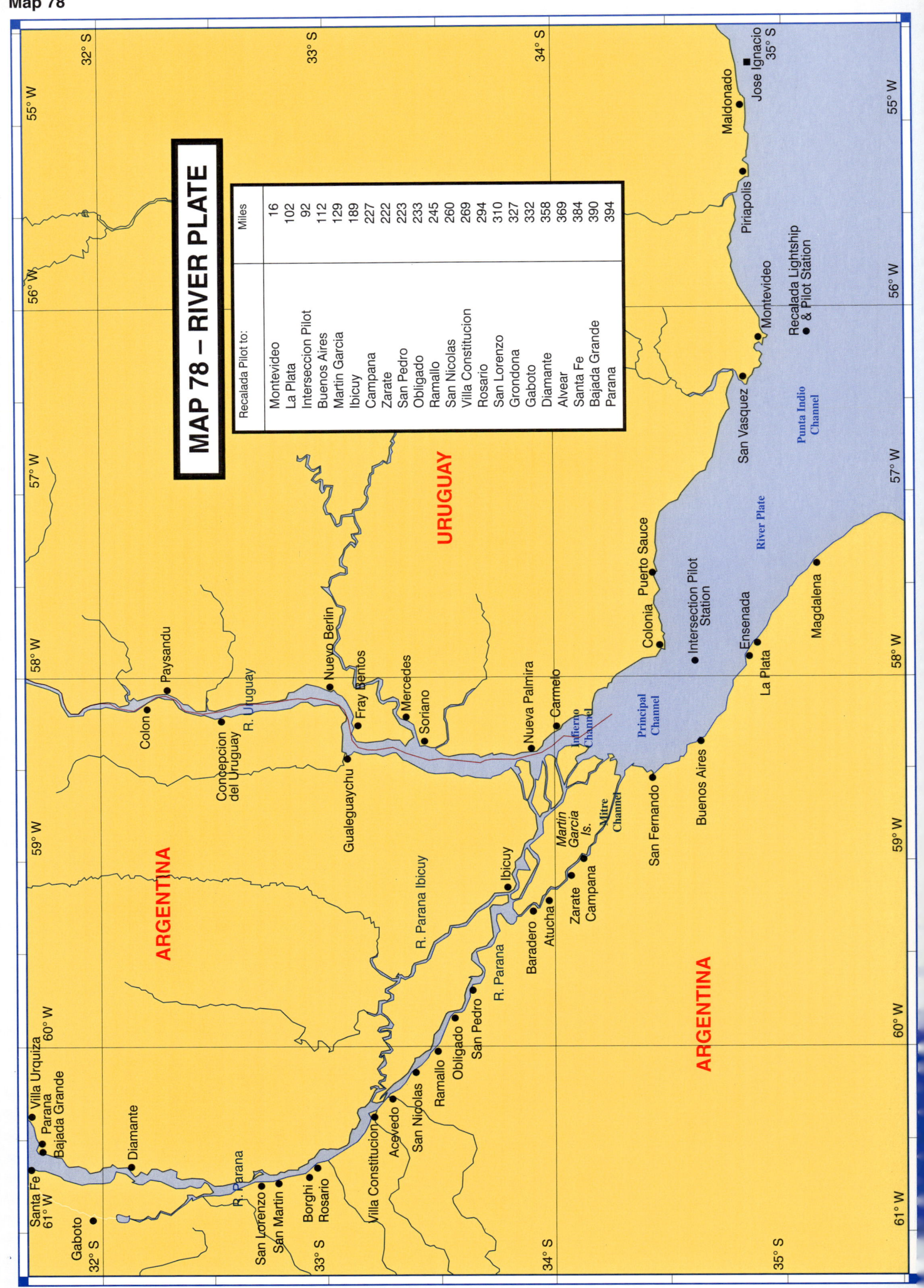

Recalada Pilot to:	Miles
Montevideo	16
La Plata	102
Interseccion Pilot	92
Buenos Aires	112
Martin Garcia	129
Ibicuy	189
Campana	227
Zarate	222
San Pedro	223
Obligado	233
Ramallo	245
San Nicolas	260
Villa Constitucion	269
Rosario	294
San Lorenzo	310
Grondona	327
Gaboto	332
Diamante	358
Alvear	369
Santa Fe	384
Bajada Grande	390
Parana	394

© Shipping Guides Ltd., Reigate, England

MAP 79 – THE ARCTIC

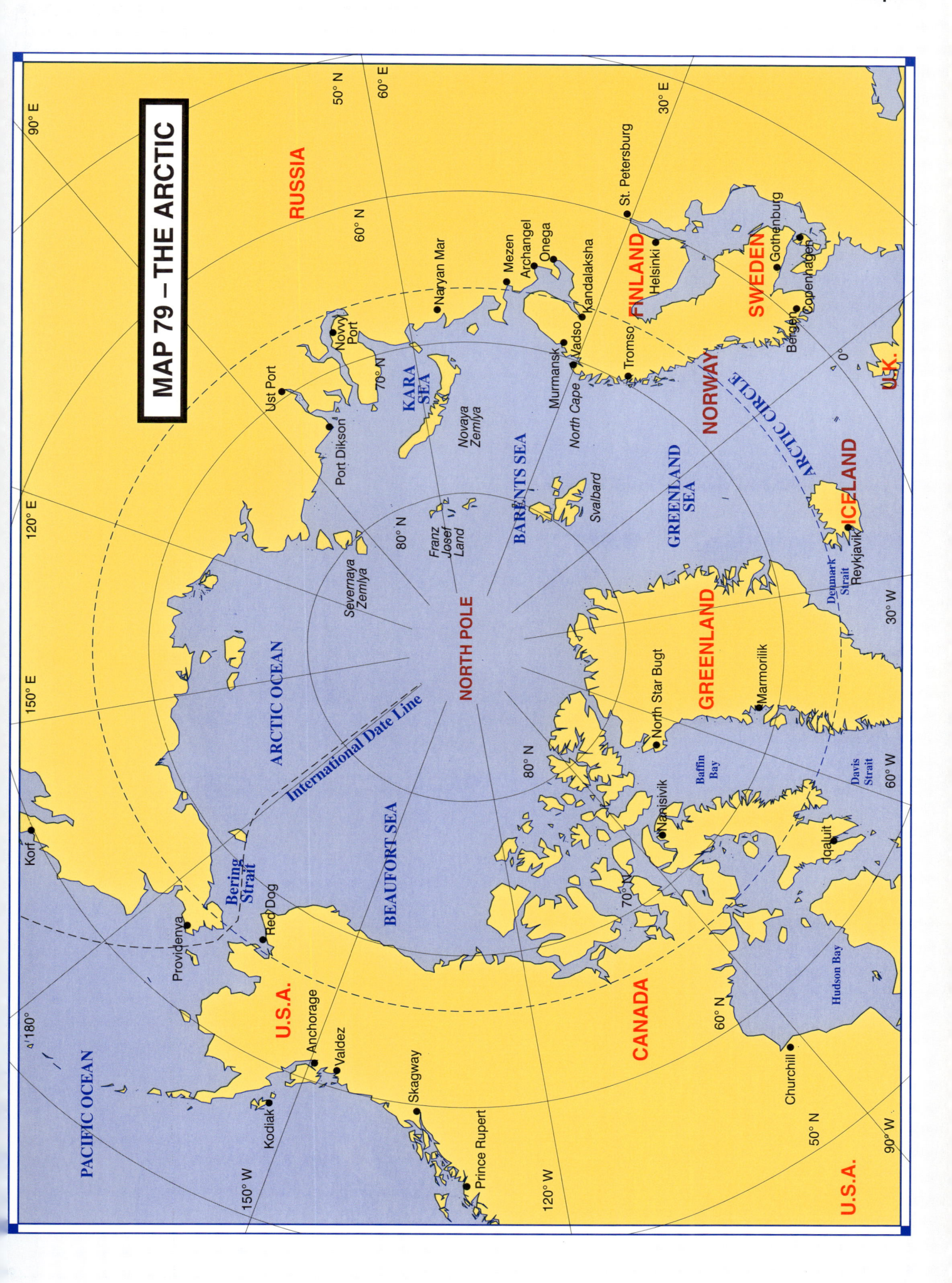

MAP 80 – THE ANTARCTIC

NOTES, ADDITIONS, CORRECTIONS

Please also advise Shipping Guides Ltd.
75 Bell Street, Reigate, RH2 7AN, United Kingdom
Tel: +44 1737 242255   Fax: +44 1737 222449
Email: updates@portinfo.co.uk   Web: www.portinfo.co.uk

NOTES, ADDITIONS, CORRECTIONS

Please also advise Shipping Guides Ltd.
75 Bell Street, Reigate, RH2 7AN, United Kingdom
Tel: +44 1737 242255   Fax: +44 1737 222449
Email: updates@portinfo.co.uk   Web: www.portinfo.co.uk

THE SHIPS ATLAS

INDEX

KEY TO INDEX

The following terms have been used throughout the index:

Ascension Is. (U.K.)	for Ascension Island (U.K.)
A.C.T.	for Australian Capital Territory, Australia
Bosnia	for Bosnia-Herzegovina
B.C.	for British Columbia, Canada
Brunei	for Brunei Darussalam
Cameroon	for Cameroon, Republic of
Canary Is. (Spain)	for Canary Islands (Spain)
Cayman Is. (U.K.)	for Cayman Islands (U.K.)
Chagos Arch. (U.K.)	for Chagos Archipelago (U.K.)
China	for China, People's Republic of
Cocos Is. (Australia)	for Cocos Islands (Australia)
Comoros Is. (France)	for Comoros Islands (France)
Comoros (Rep. of)	for Comoros, Islamic Federal Republic of
Congo (D.R. of)	for Congo, Democratic Republic of
Congo (Rep. of)	for Congo, Republic of
Cook Is. (N.Z.)	for Cook Islands (N.Z.)
D.C.	for District of Columbia, U.S.A.
Falkland Is. (U.K.)	for Falkland Islands (U.K.)
Faroe Is. (Denmark)	for Faroe Islands (Denmark)
Guinea	for Guinea, Republic of
Ireland	for Ireland, Republic of
North Korea	for Korea, Democratic People's Republic of
South Korea	for Korea, Republic of
Marshall Is.	for Marshall Islands
Micronesia	for Micronesia, Federated States of
N.B.	for New Brunswick, Canada
N.S.W.	for New South Wales, Australia
Niue Is. (N.Z.)	for Niue Island (N.Z.)
Norfolk Is. (Australia)	for Norfolk Island (Australia)
Northern Mariana Is. (U.S.A.)	for Northern Mariana Is., Commonwealth of (U.S.A.)
N.T.	for Northern Territory, Australia
N.W.T.	for Northwest Territories, Canada
N.S.	for Nova Scotia, Canada
Oman	for Oman, Sultanate of
Palau	for Palau, Republic of
Panama	for Panama, Republic of
Pitcairn Is. (U.K.)	for Pitcairn Island (U.K.)
P.E.I.	for Prince Edward Island, Canada
Qld.	for Queensland, Australia
Rhode Is.	for Rhode Island, U.S.A.
S.A.	for South Australia, Australia
South Georgia Is. (U.K.)	for South Georgia Island (U.K.)
St. Vincent	for St. Vincent and the Grenadines
Tas.	for Tasmania, Australia
Tokelau Is. (N.Z.)	for Tokelau Islands (N.Z.)
Turks and Caicos Is. (U.K.)	for Turks and Caicos Islands (U.K.)
U.A.E.	for United Arab Emirates
U.K.	for United Kingdom
U.S.A.	for United States of America
Vic.	for Victoria, Australia
Vietnam	for Vietnam, Socialist Republic of
Virgin Is. (U.K.)	for Virgin Islands (U.K.)
Virgin Is. (U.S.A.)	for Virgin Islands (U.S.A.)
Wallis and Futuna (France)	for Wallis and Futuna Islands (France)
W.A.	for Western Australia, Australia
Yemen	for Yemen, Republic of

A

Aabenraa, Denmark: 55.02 N. 9.02 E. **11, 12, 14**
 Max. Size: LOA 250 m., depth 11 m. Tankers: LOA 200 m.,
 depth 11 m. *Fuel:* All grades by barge or truck.
 Dry Docks: Floating dock 600 tons capacity.
 Airport: Skrydstrup, 25 km.
Aaheim, Norway: 62.02 N. 5.32 E. **10, 11, 15**
 Max. Size: Draft 13.5 m. *Fuel:* By road tanker.
Aaiun, see Laayoune.
Aalborg, Denmark: 57.03 N. 9.55 E. **11, 12**
 Max. Size: Draft at Bar 9.3 m. Largest vessel: 102,000 d.w.t.,
 LOA 250 m, draft 9.3 m. *Fuel:* All grades. *Airport:* 3 miles.
Aandalsnes, Norway: 62.34 N. 7.42 E. **15**
Aarhus, Denmark: 56.09 N. 10.13 E. **11, 12**
 Max. Size: Draft: Oil port 10.5 m. General cargo port 9.5 m.
 Container terminal up to 10.5 m. Eastern Division 13 m.
 Bulk/coal terminal 13.0 m. *Fuel:* All grades.
 Dry Docks: 19,000 tons. *Airport:* 32 km.
Aasiaat, Greenland (Denmark): 68.43 N. 52.53 W. **17**
 Max. Size: Largest berthed – LOA 136 m., breadth 20 m.,
 draft 7.5 m. Depth 9.4 m. at medium high tide. *Fuel:* Gas oil.
 Airport: Heliport.
Abadan, Iran: 30.20 N. 48.16 E. **31, 35**
 Max. Size: Length 600 ft. Draft 28 ft. 06 in. *Fuel:* Available.
Abalang Is., Kiribati: 1.50 N. 172.56 E. **49**
Abanto y Ciervana, see Ciervana.
Abashiri, Japan: 44.01 N. 144.17 E. **43**
 Max. Size: 30,000 d.w.t., LOA 199 m., draft 12 m.
 Fuel: Available. *Airport:* Memanbetu.
Abau, Papua New Guinea: 10.11 S. 148.46 E. **46**
Abbeville, France: 50.06 N. 1.50 E. **5, 7**
Abbot Point, Qld., Australia: 19.52 S. 148.05 E. **50, 51**
 Max. Size: LOA 300 m. (or 200,000 d.w.t.). Beam 47.5 m. Depth
 in approaches 17.2 m. Depth alongside 19.4 m. *Fuel:* By barge
 from Townsville. *Airport:* Townsville, 210 km.
Abemama Is., Kiribati: 0.21 N. 173.52 E. **49**
Aberaeron, U.K.: 52.15 N. 4.15 W. **5, 7**
Aberdeen, Hong Kong (SAR), China: 22.14 N. 114.08 E. . . . **48**
Aberdeen, U.K.: 57.09 N. 2.03 W. **4, 5**
 Max. Size: 525 ft. (160 m.) LOA, 80 ft. (24.4 m.) beam and
 draft 30 ft. 6 in. (9.3 m.). A vessel length 166 m. has been
 handled. *Dry Docks:* Capacity 1,000 tons.
 Airport: International at Dyce.
Aberdeen, Washington, U.S.A.: 46.59 N. 123.49 W. **56, 57**
Aberdovey, U.K.: 5.32 S. 137.59 E. **5, 7**
Aberystwyth, U.K.: 52.24 N. 4.05 W. **5, 7**
Abidjan, Ivory Coast: 5.18 N. 4.00 W. **28**
 Max. Size: LOA 243 m., draft 33 ft. Tankers: LOA 200 m.,
 draft 31 ft. MBM – 80,000 d.w.t., LOA 250 m., draft 13.7 m.
 SBM – 250,000 d.w.t., draft 21 m. *Fuel:* 1500 secs. available.
 Airport: Local, international.
Abo, see Turku.
Abonnema, Nigeria: 4.44 N. 6.46 E. **29**
 Also see Degema.
Aboshi, Japan: 34.44 N. 134.34 E. **45**
 Max. Size: Draft 9 m. LOA 180 m.
 Also see Himeji.
Aboukir Bay, see Abu Qir.
Abrolhos Is., Brazil: 17.58 S. 38.42 W. **72**
Abu Al Bukhoosh, U.A.E.: 25.26 N. 53.08 E. **35**
 Max. Size: 280,000 d.w.t. Draft 22.5 m.
Abu Ali, Saudi Arabia: 27.20 N. 49.27 E. **35**
Abu Dhabi, see Mina Zayed.
Abu Flus, Iraq: 30.27 N. 48.01 E. **35**
Abu Kammash, Libya: 33.05 N. 11.50 E. **24**
 Max. Size: LOA 490 ft., draft 25 ft. *Airport:* Tripoli, 140 km.
Abu Musa, U.A.E.: 25.50 N. 55.05 E. **35**
Abu Qir, Egypt: 31.19 N. 30.04 E. **26**
 Max. Size: Draft 5.2 m. *Airport:* Alexandria, 40 km.
Abu Rudeis, Egypt: 28.55 N. 33.12 E. **32**
Abu Zenima, Egypt: 29.02 N. 33.06 E. **32**
Abulog, (Luzon Is.), Philippines: 18.27 N. 121.28 E. **47**
 Also see Aparri.
Aburatsu, Japan: 31.35 N. 131.24 E. **45**
Acajutla, El Salvador: 13.35 N. 89.50 W. **69**
 Max. Size: Draft 12 m. Tankers – CBM: 60,000 d.w.t.,
 draft 12.8 m. *Fuel:* Available.
 Airport: El Salvador International, 134 km.
Acapulco, Mexico: 16.50 N. 99.54 W. **57**
 Max. Size: Draft 28 ft. 6 in. alongside. *Fuel:* Available.
 Airport: International Airport 22 km.
Acarau, Brazil: 3.00 S. 40.05 W. **72**
Accra, Ghana: 5.32 N. 0.12 W. **28**
Acevedo, Argentina: 33.18 S. 60.15 W. **78**
Achladi, Greece: 38.53 N. 22.50 E. **24, 25**
 Max. Size: Draft 15.0 m.
Acindar, see Acevedo.
Acireale, (Sicily), Italy: 37.35 N. 15.10 E. **24**
Acklins Is., Bahamas **70**
Acre, Israel: 32.55 N. 35.05 E. **26**
Adabiyah, Egypt: 29.52 N. 32.28 E. **32, 33, 34**
Adak, Alaska, U.S.A.: 51.52 N. 176.38 W. **54**
Adalia, see Antalya.
Adamas, see Milos Island.
Adams, see Port Adams.
Adaut, Indonesia: 8.08 S. 131.07 E. **46**
Adda, Ghana: 5.44 N. 0.40 E. **28**
Addu Atoll, Maldives **30, 37**
Adelaide, S.A., Australia: 34.51 S. 138.30 E. **50, 51**
 Max. Size: Inner Harbour – LOA 206 m., draft 31 ft. (9.4 m.)
 Neaps, 34 ft. 6 in. (10.5 m.) Springs. Outer Harbour –
 LOA 945 ft. (288 m.), draft 39 ft. (11.9 m.) Springs.
 Tankers: Depth 8.5 m. – 9.8 m. *Fuel:* Available.
 Airport: International, 8 miles.
Aden, Yemen: 12.48 N. 44.54 E. **31, 32**
 Max. Size: Buoys: 50,000 d.w.t., LOA 275 m., draft 11.3 m.
 Container Terminal: Depth 16 m.
 Multi-Purpose Terminal: 40,000 d.w.t., LOA 190 m., draft 10.7 m.
 Tankers: 110,000 d.w.t., LOA 286 m., depth 15.85 m.
 Fuel: Marine fuel, diesel, gas oil.
 Dry Docks: Floating dock capacity 4,500 tons, draft 6 m.
 Airport: International, 5 miles.
Adi Is., Irian Jaya, Indonesia **46**
Adirampattinam, India: 10.22 N. 79.23 E. **37**
Adjim, Tunisia: 33.48 N. 10.48 E. **24**
Admiralty Islands, see Lorengau.
Admiralty Peninsula, (Novaya Zemlya), Russia **16**
Adra, Spain: 36.44 N. 3.02 W. **22**
Adriatic Sea **21, 24**
Advance, see Charlevoix.
Aegean Sea **21, 25, 26**
Aegina I., Greece: 37.45 N. 23.26 E. **23, 25**
Aeolian Is., Italy **24**
Aero Is., Denmark **12, 14**
Aeroskobing, Denmark: 54.54 N. 10.25 E. **11, 12, 14**
 Max. Size: LOA 80 m, beam 17 m., draft 4.5 m.
 Fuel: Available. *Dry Docks:* 1 slipway – 350 tons.
 Airport: Nearest Odense.
Afognak Is., (Aleutian Is.), Alaska, U.S.A. **54**
Afua, Brazil: 0.12 S. 50.21 W. **72**
Agadir, Morocco: 30.25 N. 9.38 W. **21, 27**
 Max. Size: LOA 190 m., draft 29 ft. *Fuel:* Fuel and gas oil.
 Airport: Connects with Casablanca.
Agalaga Is., Mauritius: 10.26 S. 56.40 E. **30**
Agats, Indonesia: 5.32 S. 137.59 E. **46**
Agattu Is., Alaska, U.S.A.: 52.26 N. 173.32 W. **54**
Agawa, Ontario, Canada: 47.25 N. 84.50 W. **62**
Agde, France: 43.14 N. 3.28 E. **22**
Aghios Georgios, see Piraeus.
Aghios Konstandinos, Greece: 38.46 N. 22.52 E. **25**
Aghios Kosmos, see Piraeus.
Aghios Nikolaos, (Crete), Greece: 35.12 N. 25.43 E. **25, 26**
 Max. Size: Up to 100 m. LOA and 9.0 m. draft in the port. At oil
 bunker installation outside port, vessels of any size.
 Fuel: Small quantities by road tankers. *Airport:* Iraklion, 76 km.
Aghios Nikolaos, (Keos Is.), Greece, see Korisia.
Agia Marina, Greece: 38.54 N. 22.36 E. **24, 25**
 Max. Size: Draft 30 ft.
 Also see Stylis.
Agia Trias, see Megara.
Agioi Theodoroi, Greece: 37.55 N. 23.05 E. **25**
 Max. Size: Draft 72 ft. *Fuel:* All grades.
 Also see Piraeus.
Agotnes, Norway: 60.25 N. 5.01 E. **10, 11**
 Max. Size: Depths up to 60 ft. at quayside. *Fuel:* Available.
 Airport: Bergen, 35 km.
 Also see Bergen.
Agria, Greece: 39.20 N. 23.01 E. **25**
Agrihan, Northern Mariana Is. (U.S.A.): 18.45 N. 145.40 E. . . **46**
Agropoli, Italy: 40.22 N. 15.00 E. **23, 24**
Agto, Greenland (Denmark): 67.57 N. 53.44 W. **17**
Agua Amarga, Spain: 36.56 N. 1.57 W. **22**
Aguadilla, Puerto Rico (U.S.A.): 18.26 N. 67.10 W. **69, 70**
 Max. Size: 600 ft. LOA, 36 ft. draft. Tankers: Depth 9 m. (30 ft.).
 Airport: 20 minutes drive.
Aguadulce, Panama: 8.14 N. 80.30 W. **69, 72**
 Max. Size: Depth 3.3 m. (10 ft.) LW. *Airport:* Chitre, 60 km.
Aguanish, Quebec, Canada: 50.16 N. 62.04 W. **60**
Aguilas, Spain: 37.24 N. 1.35 W. **22**
 Max. Size: LOA up to 160 m., draft about 29 ft.
 Airport: Nearest Madrid.
Aguirre, see Jobos.
Ahmed Bin Rashid, Umm Al Qiwain, U.A.E.:
 25.35 N. 55.35 E. **35**
 Max. Size: LOA 210 m. draft 9.8 m. *Fuel:* Available.
 Airport: Dubai and Sharjah within 100 km.

THE SHIPS ATLAS

Ahmedi, see Hodeidah.
Ahurei, (Rapa Is.), French Polynesia (France):
27.36 S. 144.19 W. 49
Ahus, Sweden: 55.56 N. 14.19 E. 11, 12
Max. Size: LOA 160 m., draft 7.7 m. *Fuel:* Available.
Airport: 10 miles.
Also see Solvesborg.
Aidipsos Spas, Greece: 38.51 N. 23.03 E. 25
Aigiali, Greece: 36.54 N. 25.59 E. 25
Ailsa Craig, U.K. 6
Aimere, Indonesia: 8.45 S. 120.41 E. 38, 46
Ain Sukhna, Egypt: 29.32 N. 32.24 E. 26, 32
Max. Size: Up to 500,000 d.w.t., no limit on draft.
Ainazi, Latvia: 57.51 N. 24.24 E. 11
Ainoura, Japan: 33.11 N. 129.38 E. 45
Aioi, Japan: 34.46 N. 134.28 E. 45
Max. Size: LOA 350 m., draft 7.5 m. (LW.) *Fuel:* Lightered from nearest bunker stock ports at max. 7 days prior notice.
Dry Docks: Max. capacity 300,000 d.w.t. *Airport:* Osaka (Itami).
Aion Is., Russia: 69.50 N. 169.00 E. 54
Airbangis, Indonesia: 0.12 N. 99.23 E. 38, 39, 40
Airlie Island, W.A., Australia: 21.20 S. 115.10 E. . . 50, 51
Max. Size: 120,000 d.w.t. tonnes, LOA 300 m., beam 50 m., draft 13.8 m.
Aitape, Papua New Guinea: 3.08 S. 142.21 E. 46
Max. Size: Depth 4.3 m. (14 ft.) LAT. *Fuel:* Small quantities.
Airport: 1 mile, connects Wewak.
Aitutaki Is., see Arutunga.
Aiyina, Greece: 37.45 N. 23.26 E. 25
Aiyion, Greece: 38.15 N. 22.05 E. 25
Ajaccio, (Corsica), France: 41.55 N. 8.44 E. . . . 9, 21, 24
Max. Size: LOA 200 m., draft 8.5 m. Tankers: LOA 110 m., draft 6 m. *Fuel:* Available by truck. *Airport:* 8 km.
Ajman, U.A.E.: 25.25 N. 55.28 E. 35
Max. Size: LOA 190 m., draft 8 m. *Fuel:* By barge or road.
Dry Docks: Capacity 30,000 d.w.t.
Ajos, see Kemi.
Akantias, see Rhodes.
Akaroa, New Zealand: 43.48 S. 172.58 E. 52
Akassa, Nigeria: 4.19 N. 6.04 E. 29
Akcansa, see Ambarli.
Akhtari, see Primorsko-Akhtarsk.
Akhtopol, Bulgaria: 42.05 N. 27.57 E. 26
Aki, Japan: 33.30 N. 133.55 E. 45
Aki Sea, Inland Sea, Japan 45
Akimiski Is., N.W.T., Canada: 52.50 N. 81.30 W. . . . 59
Akita, Japan: 39.45 N. 140.03 E. 43
Max. Size: Draft 11.5 m. *Fuel:* Available. *Airport:* 35 km.
Akkeshi, Japan: 43.03 N. 144.52 E. 43
Akko, see Acre.
Akonniemi, see Saimaa Canal.
Akpatok Is., N.W.T., Canada: 60.30 N. 68.00 W. . . . 59
Akra, Norway: 59.47 N. 6.07 E. 11
Akranes, Iceland: 64.20 N. 22.05 W. 17
Akrotiri, Cyprus: 34.34 N. 33.02 E. 26
Aktau, Kazakhstan: 43.39 N. 51.12 E. 9
Akureyri, Iceland: 65.41 N. 18.03 W. 17
Max. Size: Depth at LW 8.0 m. Tankers: Depth 6 m.
Fuel: Available. *Dry Docks:* Floating dock, capacity 5,000 tons.
Airport: 2 km.
Akutan, Alaska, U.S.A.: 54.08 N. 165.48 W. 54
Akyab, Myanmar: 20.09 N. 92.55 E. 37
Al Bakr, see Albakr Terminal.
Al Bayda, Libya: 32.48 N. 21.38 E. 24
Al Bu Ayrat, Libya: 31.25 N. 15.45 E. 24
Al Hawra, Yemen: 13.50 N. 47.35 E. 31
Al Hoceima, Morocco: 35.15 N. 3.55 W. 22
Max. Size: Depth 6 m. *Airport:* 10 km.
Al Khabura, Oman: 23.59 N. 57.08 E. 35
Al Khaluf, Oman: 20.30 N. 57.50 E. 31, 37
Al Khobar, Saudi Arabia: 26.17 N. 50.13 E. 35
Max. Size: Depth 3.4 m. *Airport:* Dhahran.
Al Khor, Qatar: 25.35 N. 51.32 E. 35
Al Khums, Libya: 32.38 N. 14.15 E. 24
Al Khuraibah, Saudi Arabia: 28.04 N. 35.10 E. 32
Al Laith, Saudi Arabia: 20.09 N. 40.16 E. 32
Al Marj, Libya: 32.23 N. 20.28 E. 24
Al Qadimah, Saudi Arabia: 22.21 N. 39.05 E. 32
Max. Size: Depth 13.0 m. – 14.0 m.
Al Qahmah, Saudi Arabia: 18.01 N. 41.41 E. 32
Al Qatif, Saudi Arabia: 26.33 N. 50.01 E. 32
Al Qunfudah, Saudi Arabia: 19.05 N. 41.04 E. 32
Al Qusayr, see Quseir.
Al Rayyan, Qatar: 26.39 N. 51.33 E. 35
Max. Size: 270,000 tonnes d.w.t., draft 21 m.
Al Shaheen Terminal, Qatar: 26.35 N. 52.00 E. 35
Max. Size: No limit.
Al Udayd, U.A.E.: 24.37 N. 51.25 E. 35
Al Ugayr, Saudi Arabia: 25.39 N. 50.13 E. 35
Al Uqaylah, Libya: 30.12 N. 19.12 E. 24

Al Wajh, Saudi Arabia: 26.12 N. 36.28 E. 32
Ala, see Vallvik.
Alabama, U.S.A. 66
Alacati, Turkey: 38.15 N. 26.20 E. 25, 26
Alamagan, Northern Mariana Is. (U.S.A.): 17.38 N. 145.50 E. . . 46
Alameda, California, U.S.A.: 37.48 N. 122.17 W. . . . 58
Max. Size: Depth 35 ft.
Also see San Francisco.
Aland, Finland: 60.15 N. 20.00 E. 10, 11
Alanya, Turkey: 36.32 N. 32.03 E. 26
Max. Size: Depth 8 m. – 12 m. *Airport:* Antalya, 150 km.
Alaska, U.S.A. 54, 56
Alassio, Italy: 43.59 N. 8.08 E. 23, 24
Alba, Bahrain, see Sitra.
Albakr Terminal, Iraq: 29.41 N. 48.49 E. 35
Max. Size: LOA 366 m., draft 21 m. (1998).
ALBANIA 9, 21, 24, 25
Albany, W.A., Australia: 35.02 S. 117.53 E. 50
Max. Size: Draft 11.5 m., beam 32.0 m., LOA 225 m.
Fuel: Light marine diesel. *Airport:* 11 km., domestic.
Albany, California, U.S.A., see San Francisco.
Albany, New York, U.S.A.: 42.40 N. 73.45 W. . . 55, 58, 60, 63
Max. Size: LOA 750 ft., beam 110 ft., draft 31 ft. *Airport:* 7 miles.
Albatross Bay, see Weipa.
Albemarle Sound, North Carolina, U.S.A. 63
Alberni, see Port Alberni.
Albert, see Port Albert.
Alberton, P.E.I., Canada: 46.48 N. 64.03 W. 60
Albina, Suriname: 5.37 N. 54.15 W. 76
Alboran Is., Spain: 35.58 N. 3.00 W. 22
Albufeira, Portugal: 37.05 N. 8.15 W. 20
Alcanar, Spain: 40.34 N. 0.28 E. 22
Max. Size: Depth 22 ft. – 38 ft. *Fuel:* Available at 24 hours notice. *Airport:* Reus, 97 km.
Alcasa, see Punta Cuchillo.
Alcudia, (Majorca), Spain: 39.51 N. 3.08 E. 22
Max. Size: Depth 5.5 m. – 6.5 m. *Fuel:* Diesel.
Airport: Palma, 60 km.
Aldabra Is., Seychelles: 9.26 S. 46.25 E. 30
Aldeburgh, U.K.: 52.09 N. 1.35 E. 7
Alderney, (Channel Is.), U.K. 19
Alegre, see Porto Alegre.
Aleria, (Corsica), France: 42.06 N. 9.27 E. 24
Alesund, Norway: 62.27 N. 6.09 E. 10, 11, 15
Max. Size: Depth 4 m. – 16 m. *Fuel:* Available at berths.
Dry Docks: Largest 8,000 tons. *Airport:* Alesund Airport, Vigra.
Aleutian Islands, Alaska, U.S.A. 36, 53, 54
Alexander, see Port Alexander.
Alexander Archipelago, Alaska, U.S.A. 56
Alexander Bay, South Africa: 28.35 S. 16.33 E. . . . 28
Alexandre, see Porto Alexandre.
Alexandretta, see Iskenderun.
Alexandria, Egypt: 31.09 N. 29.53 E. 21, 26
Max. Size: Up to 32 ft. draft. Tankers: Depth 38 ft.
El Dekhelia: 160,000 d.w.t., draft 18 m. *Fuel:* By barge.
Dry Docks: Largest 85,000 d.w.t.
Alexandria, Virginia, U.S.A.: 38.48 N. 77.03 W. . . 55, 63, 65
Max. Size: Draft 22 ft. 6 in. *Airport:* 3 miles, Washington National.
Alexandria Bay, New York, U.S.A.: 44.21 N. 75.53 W. . . 61
Alexandroupolis, Greece: 40.51 N. 25.54 E. . . . 9, 25, 26
Max. Size: Draft 19 ft., LOA 200 m. (part loading in good weather). *Fuel:* Diesel by road tanker. *Airport:* 5 km.
Alexandrovsk, Russia: 50.53 N. 142.08 E. 43
Alfaques, see Sant Carles de la Rapita.
Algeciras, Spain: 36.08 N. 5.26 W. 20, 21, 22, 23
Max. Size: Draft 16.0 m. Tankers: LOA 315 m., draft 20 m.
MBM: Depth 60 m., up to 500,000 d.w.t. *Fuel:* Fuel oil and gas oil. *Airport:* Jerez, 110 km. Malaga, 120 km. and Gibraltar.
ALGERIA 21, 22, 24
Alghero, (Sardinia), Italy: 40.35 N. 8.18 E. 24
Algiers, Algeria: 36.50 N. 3.00 E. 21, 22
Max. Size: Draft 38 ft., 25,000 tons. *Fuel:* Available.
Dry Docks: 136 m. long, 18.5 m. wide, 8 m. deep.
Airport: Dar-el-Beida, 20 km.
Algoa Bay, see Port Elizabeth.
Algoma, Wisconsin, U.S.A.: 44.36 N. 87.27 W. 62
Algonac, Michigan, U.S.A.: 42.37 N. 82.31 W. 62
Alholmen, see Jakobstad.
Alhucemas, see Al Hoceima.
Aliaga, Turkey: 38.50 N. 26.57 E. 25, 26
Max. Size: Tankers: 250,000 d.w.t., LOA 360 m., draft 19.2 m.
LPG: 44,000 d.w.t., LOA 230 m., draft 13 m. *Fuel:* Available.
Airport: Adman Menderes International, 70 km.
Alibag, India: 18.38 N. 72.55 E. 37
Alican Point, see Siasi.
Alicante, Spain: 38.23 N. 0.28 W. 21, 22
Max. Size: Up to 225 m. LOA and 38 ft. draft.
Tankers: 36,000 d.w.t., 10.7 m draft. *Fuel:* Available.
Airport: International, 8 km.

Alice, see Port Alice.
Alicia, (Mindanao Is.), Philippines: 7.31 N. 122.57 E. 47
Alicudi Is., Italy: 38.33 N. 14.20 E. 24
Alimnia Is., Greece: 36.16 N. 27.43 E. 25
Aliveri Bay, see Milaki.
Aliverion, Greece: 38.23 N. 24.03 E. 25
  Max. Size: 120,000 d.w.t., LOA 240 m. *Airport:* Athens.
  Also see Milaki.
Alkmaar, Netherlands: 52.38 N. 4.45 E. 8
Allardyce Harbour, Solomon Islands: 7.49 S. 158.39 E. 49
Alleppey, India: 9.29 N. 76.23 E. 37
  Port closed.
Alliance, Louisiana, U.S.A.: 29.40 N. 89.58 W. 67
Allinge, Denmark: 55.17 N. 14.48 E. 12
Alloa, U.K.: 56.08 N. 3.47 W. 6
Alma, Australia, see Port Alma.
Alma, N.B., Canada: 45.36 N. 64.58 W. 60
Almeria, Spain: 36.52 N. 2.30 W. 22, 27
  Max. Size: Draft 39 ft. inner port and 43 ft. outer port.
  Fuel: Diesel and gas oil. *Airport:* 10 km.
Almirante, Panama: 9.18 N. 82.23 W. 69, 72
  Max. Size: Draft 9.2 m. *Airport:* Changuinola 21 km.
Almirante Barrosso Terminal, see Sao Sebastiao.
Almirante Soares Dutra Terminal, see Tramandai.
Alno Is., see Hovid.
Alofi, Niue Is. (N.Z.): 19.02 S. 169.55 W. 49
Alor Is., Indonesia: 8.15 S. 124.30 E. 46
Alor Setar, Malaysia: 6.07 N. 100.21 E. 38, 39
Alotau, Papua New Guinea: 10.19 S. 150.27 E. . . . 46, 50, 51
  Max. Size: LOA 130 m., draft 20 ft. *Fuel:* By road tanker.
  Airport: Domestic, 20 m.
Alpena, Michigan, U.S.A.: 45.05 N. 83.25 W. 62
Alphonse I., Seychelles: 7.15 S. 52.45 E. 30
Als Is., Denmark: 55.00 N. 9.50 E. 12, 14
Alsancak, see Izmir.
Alta, Norway: 69.58 N. 23.15 E. 15
Altagracia, see La Estacada.
Altamira, Brazil: 3.12 S. 52.25 W. 72
Altamira, Mexico: 22.29 N. 97.51 W. 69
  Max. Size: Channel: Max. draft 11.88 m.
  Berth: Max. draft 9.6 m. – 11.58 m. *Fuel:* Available.
  Airport: 25 km.
Altata, Mexico: 24.34 N. 107.58 W. 57
Altea, Spain: 38.34 N. 0.03 W. 22
Altona, Germany: 53.33 N. 9.56 E. 8, 14
  Also see Hamburg.
Alucroix, see Limetree Bay.
Alula, Somalia: 11.57 N. 50.45 E. 31
Alumar, Brazil: 2.40 S. 44.21 W. 72
  Max. Size: Draft 10.5 m. *Fuel:* By barge.
Alushta, Ukraine: 44.40 N. 34.25 E. 26
Alusi, Indonesia: 7.37 S. 131.38 E. 46
Alvarado, Mexico: 18.48 N. 95.45 W. 69
Alvear, Uruguay: 29.04 S. 56.31 W. 77
Alvik, Norway: 60.26 N. 6.24 E. 10, 11
  Max. Size: Depth 7.5 m.
Alvik, Sweden, see Hovid.
Ama, Louisiana, U.S.A.: 29.56 N. 90.18 W. 67
  Max. Size: Berth length about 550 ft. *Fuel:* By barge.
  Also see New Orleans.
Amagasaki, Japan: 34.42 N. 135.24 E. 43, 44, 45
  Max. Size: LOA 230 m., draft 11.70 m. Tankers: LOA 198 m.,
  draft 10.6 m. *Fuel:* Lightered from nearest bunker stock ports.
  Airport: Osaka, 15 miles (International).
Amager Is., Denmark 12
Amakusa Is., Japan 45
Amal, Sweden: 59.05 N. 12.45 E. 12
Amalfi, Italy: 40.38 N. 14.35 E. 23, 24
Amamapare, Indonesia: 4.49 S. 136.58 E. 46
  Max. Size: 38,000 d.w.t., depth 8.0 m. – 9.2 m.
Amami Is., Japan 42, 46
Amapala, Honduras: 13.18 N. 87.39 W. 69
  All cargo operations transferred to San Lorenzo.
Amasra, Turkey: 41.43 N. 32.24 E. 26
Ambalangoda, Sri Lanka: 6.15 N. 80.05 E. 37
Ambarchik, Russia: 69.39 N. 162.18 E. 54
Ambarli, Turkey: 40.58 N. 28.41 E. 23, 25, 26
  Max. Size: Akcansa: Draft 13 m. Anadolu: Draft 3 m. – 9.5 m.
  Armaport: 50,000 d.w.t., depth 11 m. – 12 m.
  Kumport: Depth 4 m. – 13.5 m.
  Mardas: 178,000 d.w.t., depth 6.5 m. – 14.5 m.
  Soyak: Depth 9 m. – 11 m. Tankers: Aygaz: LOA 200 m.,
  draft 7.2 m. BP/Amoco Buoys: 25,000 d.w.t., depth 12 m.
  Cekisan: 40,000 d.w.t., draft 12 m.
  Petrol Ofisi (Buoy): 25,000 d.w.t., depth 31 ft.
  Teas/Petrol Ofisi (Platform): Draft 13 m.
  Total Platform: 40,000 d.w.t., draft 25 m. *Fuel:* Available.
  Airport: 15 km.
Ambes, see Bec d'Ambes.
Amboim, see Porto Amboim.

Ambon, Indonesia: 3.41 S. 128.10 E. 46
  Max. Size: Draft 10.5 m. *Fuel:* Diesel and marine fuel oil.
  Dry Docks: Slipway, capacity 500 d.w.t. *Airport:* 7 miles.
Ambriz, Angola: 7.49 S. 13.07 E. 28
Ambrose Tower, New York, U.S.A.: 40.28 N. 73.50 W. 63
Ambryn Is., Vanuatu: 16.15 S. 168.09 E. 49
Amchitka Is., (Aleutian Is.), Alaska, U.S.A.:
  51.30 N. 179.00 E. 54
Amchitka Passage, (Aleutian Is.), Alaska, U.S.A. 54
Amderma, Russia: 69.45 N. 61.50 E. 16
Amelia, see Pemba.
American Samoa (U.S.A.) 49
Amesville, Louisiana, U.S.A.: 29.54 N. 90.07 W. 67
  Max. Size: Depth 34 ft.
  Also see New Orleans.
Amfilokhia, Greece: 38.52 N. 21.10 E. 25
Amfipolis, Greece: 40.48 N. 23.52 E. 25
Amgu, Russia: 45.44 N. 137.15 E. 43
Amherst, N.S., Canada: 45.50 N. 64.03 W. 60
Amherst, Myanmar, see Kyaikkami.
Amherst Harbour, Quebec, Canada: 47.14 N. 61.50 W. 60
  Max. Size: Depth 5.18 m., Length 183 m. *Fuel:* Diesel
  available. *Airport:* Flights to Charlottetown and Quebec
  Province.
Amherstburg, Ontario, Canada: 42.06 N. 83.08 W. 62
  Max. Size: About 432 ft. LOA and 21 ft. draft.
  Fuel: By road tanker. *Airport:* Windsor, 20 miles.
Amini Is., (Laccadive Is.), India: 11.07 N. 72.45 E. 37
Amirante Is., Seychelles: 5.30 S. 53.20 E. 30
Amlia Is., (Aleutian Is.), Alaska, U.S.A. 54
Ammassalik, see Angmagssalik.
Amolle, see Kongsdal.
Amorgos Is., Greece: 36.50 N. 25.57 E. 25
Amoy, see Xiamen.
Ampenan, Indonesia: 8.34 S. 116.04 E. 38
  Max. Size: Anchorage – no restriction.
  Also see Labuantring Bay.
Amrum Is., Germany: 54.38 N. 8.23 E. 12, 14
Amsterdam, Netherlands: 52.22 N. 4.54 E. 4, 7, 8, 9
  Max. Size: Vessels have to pass locks at Ijmuiden. Dimensions
  of Northern Lock (biggest): 400 m. long, 50 m. wide, 15 m. deep.
  Draft 43 ft. – 45 ft. (SW). Depths at Amsterdam up to 15 m.
  Tankers: Max. draft 45 ft. *Fuel:* All grades.
  Dry Docks: Capacity 85,000 d.w.t. *Airport:* 15 km.
Amuay Bay, Venezuela: 11.46 N. 70.15 W. 69, 72, 74
  Max. Size: LOA 856 ft., draft 42 ft. *Fuel:* All grades.
Amukta Pass, (Aleutian Is.), Alaska, U.S.A. 54
Amurang, Indonesia: 1.13 N. 124.33 E. 46
An-Ping, Taiwan: 22.58 N. 120.09 E. 42
  Max. Size: 6,000 d.w.t., draft 9 m.
Ana Chaves, see Sao Tome.
Anacortes, Washington, U.S.A.: 48.31 N. 122.36 W. . . . 55, 56
  Max. Size: Depth 44 ft. Tankers: Depth 38 ft. – 45 ft.
  Fuel: Available. *Dry Docks:* Largest: Capacity 9,000 tons
  (LOA 400 ft.). *Airport:* Seattle International, 75 miles.
Anadolu, Turkey: 41.05 N. 29.04 E. 23
  Max. Size: Draft 3.0 m. – 9.5 m.
  Also see Ambarli.
Anadyr, Russia: 64.44 N. 177.31 E. 54
Anadyrskiy Bay, Russia 54
Anafi Is., Greece: 36.22 N. 25.48 E. 25
Anaheim Bay, California, U.S.A. 58
Anahuae, see Tampico.
Anakan, see Gingoog.
Analalava, Madagascar: 14.38 S. 47.46 E. 30
Anamba Is., Indonesia 38, 39
Anamur, Turkey: 36.04 N. 32.51 E. 26
Anan, Japan: 33.52 N. 134.40 E. 45
  Max. Size: Draft 10.50 m. Wharf length 200 m. *Fuel:* By barge
  from Hanshin area only. *Airport:* Tokushima.
Anapa, Russia: 44.54 N. 37.20 E. 26
Anatahan, Northern Mariana Is. (U.S.A.): 16.23 N. 145.40 E. . . 46
Anching, see Anqing.
Anchorage, Alaska, U.S.A.: 61.12 N. 150.00 W. 54, 79
  Max. Size: All berths 35 ft. depth MLLW. *Fuel:* All grades.
  Airport: 5 miles.
Ancon, see La Pampilla.
Ancona, Italy: 43.37 N. 13.32 E. 9, 21, 24
  Max. Size: Ancona: Up to 250 m. LOA, depths of water up to
  12.5 m. Tankers: Over 300,000 d.w.t. at Sea Terminal.
  Fuel: All grades. *Dry Docks:* Floating – 1,000 g.r.t.
  Airport: Falconara, 10 km.
Andaman Islands, India 37
Andaman Sea 37
Andenes, Norway: 69.19 N. 16.09 E. 10, 15
Andevoranto, Madagascar: 18.54 S. 49.08 E. 30
Andikithira, Greece: 35.50 N. 23.12 E. 25
Andipsara Is., Greece: 38.30 N. 25.32 E. 25
Andreanof Is., (Aleutian Is.), Alaska, U.S.A. 54
Andres, see Boca Chica.

Androka, Madagascar: 24.55 S. 44.00 E. 30
Andros, (Andros Is.), Bahamas: 24.43 N. 77.48 W. 69, 70
Andros Is., Bahamas 66, 69, 70
Andros Is., Greece: 37.50 N. 24.57 E. 25, 26
Androth Is., (Laccadive Is.), India: 10.45 N. 73.38 E. 37
Anecho, Togo: 6.13 N. 1.34 E. 29
Anegada Is., Virgin Is. (U.K.): 18.45 N. 64.20 W. 71
Aneityum Is., Vanuatu: 20.15 S. 169.45 E. 49
Anewa Bay, Papua New Guinea: 6.11 S. 155.33 E. 49
  Port closed
Angaur Is., (Caroline Is.), Northern Mariana Is. (U.S.A.):
  6.55 N. 134.09 E. 46
Angel, see Puerto Angel.
Angel de La Guarda Is., Mexico: 29.30 N. 113.30 W. . . . 57
Angel Is., California, U.S.A. 58
Angeles, see Port Angeles.
Angelholm, Sweden: 56.16 N. 12.55 E. 12
Angholmen, Sweden: 57.57 N. 11.34 E. 11, 12
Angle Bay, see Milford Haven.
Anglesey, U.K.: 53.15 N. 4.30 W. 5, 7
Angmagssalik, Greenland (Denmark): 65.35 N. 37.25 W. . . . 17
Ango Ango, see Matadi.
Angoche, Mozambique: 16.18 S. 39.54 E. 30
ANGOLA 28
Angra, (Terceira Is.), Azores (Portugal): 38.35 N. 27.10 W. . . . 20
Angra dos Reis, Brazil: 23.01 S. 44.19 W. 76, 77
  Max. Size: Draft 29 ft. Tankers: See DTSE/GEBIG.
  Fuel: No facilities for supplying large vessels.
Anguilla (U.K.) 71
Anholt, Denmark: 56.43 N. 11.32 E. 11, 12
Anholt Is., Denmark 11, 12
Aniva Bay, (Sakhalin Is.), Russia 43
Anjouan Is., see Mutsamuda.
Annaba, Algeria: 36.58 N. 7.47 E. 21, 22
  Max. Size: LOA 656 ft., draft 33 ft. Tankers: Draft 39 ft.
  Fuel: Available.
Annan, U.K.: 54.58 N. 3.16 W. 5
Annapolis, Maryland, U.S.A.: 38.59 N. 76.29 W. 63, 65
Annapolis Royal, N.S., Canada: 44.45 N. 65.31 W. 60
Annobon Is., see Pagalu.
Anoa Marine Terminal, Indonesia: 5.14 N. 105.36 E. . . 38, 39
  Max. Size: 160,000 d.w.t.
Anoraitx, (Majorca), Spain: 39.35 N. 2.28 E. 22
Anqing, China: 30.30 N. 117.02 E. 42
  Max. Size: Draft 4.5 m.
Anstruther, U.K.: 56.13 N. 2.43 W. 6
Ansudu, Indonesia: 2.10 S. 139.20 E. 46
Antalaha, Madagascar: 14.53 S. 50.18 E. 30
Antalya, Turkey: 36.50 N. 30.37 E. 25, 26
  Max. Size: Depth 10 m. Tankers: Depth 17 m. – 18 m.
  Airport: Antalya, 22 km.
Antan Terminal, Nigeria: 4.13 N. 8.20 E. 29
  Max. Size: 60,000 d.w.t. – 150,000 d.w.t. No draft restriction.
ANTARCTICA 80
Antibes, France: 43.35 N. 7.08 E. 9, 22
  Max. Size: Length 50 m., beam 6 m., draft 3.5 m.
  Airport: Nice – Cote d'Azur, 15 km.
Anticosti Is., Quebec, Canada. 60
Antifer, France: 49.40 N. 0.08 E. 7, 8
  Max. Size: Largest vessel – 564,760 d.w.t., LOA 458 m.,
  draft 28.85 m. *Fuel:* All grades. *Airport:* Le Havre, 7 km.
  Also see Le Havre.
Antigonish, N.S., Canada: 45.38 N. 61.59 W. 60
ANTIGUA AND BARBUDA 69, 71
Antilla, Cuba: 20.50 N. 75.44 W. 69, 70
  Max. Size: Draft 6.71 m., LOA 186 m. Tankers: LOA 185.9 m.
  Preston: LOA 146 m., draft 6.1 m.
  Nicaro: LOA 156 m., draft 9.14 m.
  Felton: LOA 170 m., draft 7.92 m. *Fuel:* By road tanker.
Antimonan, (Luzon Is.), Philippines: 14.00 N. 121.55 E. . . 47
  Max. Size: LOA 650 ft., beam 100 ft., draft 44 ft.
Antioch, California, U.S.A.: 38.01 N. 121.46 W. 58
Antipodes Is., New Zealand: 49.42 S. 178.50 E. 52
Antofagasta, Chile: 23.39 S. 70.25 W. 77
  Max. Size: Draft 11.25 m. Tankers: Length 235 m., draft 60 ft.
  La Chimba: LOA 110 m., draft 27 ft. *Fuel:* Fuel and diesel oil.
  Airport: Cerro Moreno, 28 km.
Antongil Bay, Madagascar 30
Antongo, Madagascar: 21.00 N. 43.45 E. 30
Antonina, Brazil: 25.26 S. 48.41 W. 76, 77
  Max. Size: Drafts: Springs: HW 21 ft., Neaps: HW 18 ft.,
  LW: 15 ft. *Fuel:* By road tanker. *Airport:* Curitiba, 65 km.
  Paranagua, 50 km.
Antonio, see Port Antonio.
Antonio Benes, see Angoche.
Antsiranana, Madagascar: 12.14 S. 49.26 E. 30
  Max. Size: Draft 11 m. *Dry Docks:* 199 m. x 28.4 m. x depth at
  sill 10.4 m. (MHWS). *Airport:* 8 miles.

Antwerp, Belgium: 51.14 N. 4.23 E. 4, 7, 8, 9
  Max. Size: Draft 50 ft. 10 in. *Fuel:* All grades.
  Dry Docks: LOA up to 312 m., beam up to 50 m.
  Airport: Zaventem, 50 km.
Anyer, Indonesia: 6.02 S. 105.56 E. 38
  Max. Size: Tankers: Asahimas Chemical: 22,000 tonnes d.w.t.,
  draft 10 m. Chandri Asri Petro-Chemical – 80,000 tonnes,
  draft 13 m. *Fuel:* Available.
Anzio, Italy: 41.25 N. 12.35 E. 24
Ao Shan, see Zhoushan.
Aoga Is., (Izu Is.), Japan: 32.26 N. 139.47 E. 43, 46
Aokata, Japan: 32.59 N. 129.02 E. 43, 45
  Max. Size: Over 200,000 d.w.t.
Aomori, Japan: 40.52 N. 140.45 E. 43
  Max. Size: 50,000 d.w.t., draft 11.7 m. Tankers: LPG
  57,000 d.w.t., draft 11.8 m. – 12.2 m. *Fuel:* By barge from
  nearest stock port (Hakodate).
Apalachicola, Florida, U.S.A.: 29.43 N. 84.59 W. 66
Apapa, see Lagos.
Aparri, (Luzon Is.), Philippines: 18.22 N. 121.38 E. . . . 46, 47
  Max. Size: Depths in anchorages 66 ft. Port Irene 39 ft.
  Maconacon 42 ft. Divilacan 66 ft. *Fuel:* Diesel, gasoline and
  kerosene in drums. *Airport:* Tuguegarao, 110 km.
Api Api, Indonesia: 2.17 S. 104.50 E. 38
Apia, Samoa: 13.50 S. 171.45 W. 49
  Max. Size: Vessels up to 800 ft. LOA, draft 35 ft. Tankers up to
  32,000 d.w.t. *Fuel:* Light diesel. *Airport:* Faleolo, 34 km.
Apollo Bay, Vic., Australia: 38.46 S. 143.40 E. 51
Apollonia, (Sifnos), Greece: 36.57 N. 24.44 E. 25
Apollonia, Libya, see Marsa Susa.
Apostle Is., Wisconsin, U.S.A. 62
Appledore, U.K.: 51.03 N. 4.12 W. 6
Appleton, Wisconsin, U.S.A.: 44.16 N. 88.24 W. 62
Apra, Guam (U.S.A.): 13.26 N. 144.39 E. 46
  Max. Size: LOA 230 m., depth 10.97 m. (HW). Max. beam for
  container vessels 33.55 m. Tankers: Depth 39 ft. – 55 ft.
  Fuel: Available. *Dry Docks:* 2 dry docks available.
Aqaba, Jordan: 29.31 N. 35.01 E. 21, 26, 32
  Max. Size: Up to 20,000 d.w.t., draft 32 ft. cargo berths and
  100,000 d.w.t. and 50 ft. draft for the phosphate loading berth.
  Tankers: 300,000 d.w.t., depth 25 m. *Fuel:* Available.
  Airport: Links with Amman International 355 km. away.
Aqiq, Sudan: 18.14 N. 38.12 E. 32
Arabian Gulf 31, 35
Arabian Sea 31, 37
Aracaju, Brazil: 10.55 S. 37.03 W. 72
  Max. Size: Depth 7 m. alongside. Tankers: See DTBASA/SE.
  Airport: 13 km.
Aracati, Brazil: 4.32 S. 37.46 W. 72
Aracruz, Brazil: 19.40 S. 40.06 W. 72
Arafura Sea 46
Aran Is., Ireland: 53.06 N. 9.40 W. 5
Aransas, see Port Aransas.
Aransas Pass, Texas, U.S.A.: 27.56 N. 97.10 W. 66
Aranuka Is., Kiribati: 0.11 N. 173.30 E. 49
Aratu, Brazil: 12.47 S. 38.30 W. 72
  Max. Size: Bulk: 65,000 d.w.t. Tankers: 45,000 d.w.t.
  Gas: 20,000 d.w.t. *Fuel:* Available. *Dry Docks:* Up to
  45,000 d.w.t. *Airport:* Salvador, 43 km.
Arawak Cay, see Nassau.
Arawe Harbour, Papua New Guinea: 6.11 S. 149.04 E. . . 46
Araya, Venezuela: 10.36 N. 64.16 W. 75
Arbatax, (Sardinia), Italy: 39.57 N. 9.42 E. 24
  Max. Size: LOA 200 m., draft 25 ft. *Fuel:* Available.
Arbroath, U.K.: 56.33 N. 2.35 W. 5
  Max. Size: LOA 65 m., draft 4 m. *Fuel:* Diesel.
  Airport: Dundee, 29 km.
Arcachon, France: 44.40 N. 1.10 W. 8, 19
Archangel, Russia: 64.34 N. 40.30 E. 16, 79
  Max. Size: Depths alongside up to 9.2 m. Tankers: Draft 9 m.
  Dry Docks: Floating docks, capacity up to 7,000 tons.
  Airport: Airport near town, served by regular airlines.
Archer River, see Aurukun.
Arctic Ocean 10, 15, 16, 54, 79
Ardal, see Ardalstangen.
Ardalstangen, Norway: 61.14 N. 7.42 E. 10, 11, 15
  Max. Size: Depths alongside up to 40 ft. *Airport:* Sogndal, 1.5
  hours by ferry.
Ardglass, U.K.: 54.16 N. 5.37 W. 5
Ardjuna, Indonesia: 5.54 S. 107.44 E. 38
  Max. Size: Up to 200,000 d.w.t., draft 30.20 m. *Airport:* Jakarta.
Ardrishaig, U.K.: 56.01 N. 5.27 W. 5, 6
  Max. Size: LOA 80 m., draft 5 m. (H.W.). *Fuel:* By road tanker.
  Airport: Glasgow, 86 miles.
Ardrossan, S.A., Australia: 34.26 S. 137.55 E. 50, 51
  Max. Size: 46,000 d.w.t., LOA 200 m.
Ardrossan, U.K.: 55.38 N. 4.49 W. 6
  Max. Size: Contact General Manager (Marine). *Fuel:* By road
  tanker. *Airport:* Prestwick, 18 miles. Glasgow, 25 miles.
Ardvasar, U.K.: 57.03 N. 5.55 W. 5
Arecibo, see Port Arecibo.

Areia Branca, Brazil: 4.50 S. 37.03 W. 72
Max. Size: Depth 12 m. *Fuel:* Diesel. *Airport:* Mossoro, 50 km.
Arendal, Norway: 58.28 N. 8.46 E. **10, 11, 12**
Max. Size: Depth 15 ft. – 33 ft. *Fuel:* Available.
Airport: Kjevik, 60 km.
Argentia, Newfoundland, Canada: 47.18 N. 53.59 W. 60
Max. Size: Depth 5.5 m. – 12.4 m. *Fuel:* Diesel by road tanker.
Airport: St. John's, 130 km.
ARGENTINA **77, 78, 80**
Argostoli, (Cephalonia), Greece: 38.12 N. 20.29 E. **21, 24, 25**
Max. Size: Up to 19 ft. draft. *Fuel:* Yachts only.
Arguineguin, (Grand Canary), Canary Is. (Spain):
27.45 N. 15.40 W. 27
Max. Size: Depth to 10.5 m. (LW). *Airport:* 40 km.
Arhus, see Aarhus.
Arica, Chile: 18.28 S. 70.20 W. **72, 77**
Max. Size: LOA 213 m., draft 34 ft. Tankers: Draft 43 ft. – 45 ft.
Fuel: Diesel by road tanker. *Airport:* Domestic, 7 miles.
Arichat, N.S., Canada: 45.31 N. 61.02 W. 60
Arild, Sweden: 56.16 N. 12.35 E. 12
Arinagour, U.K.: 56.37 N. 6.32 W. 5
Arios, see Puerto Cortes.
Arisaig, U.K.: 56.54 N. 5.52 W. 5
Arizona, U.S.A. 57
Arkansas, U.S.A. 66
Arklow, Ireland: 52.47 N. 6.08 W. 5
Arkoi Is., Greece: 37.23 N. 26.44 E. 25
Arkosund, Sweden: 58.29 N. 16.57 E. 11
Arkticheski Institut Is., Russia: 75.15 N. 82.00 E. 16
Arles, France: 43.40 N. 4.37 E. **9, 22**
Arlington, Australia, see Queenscliff.
Arlington, Virginia, U.S.A.: 38.51 N. 77.04 W. 65
Armaport, see Ambarli.
ARMENIA 9
Armuelles, see Puerto Armuelles.
Arnhem, Netherlands: 51.58 N. 5.54 E. **7, 8, 9**
Arno, Marshall Is.: 7.07 N. 171.40 E. 49
Arnos Vale, see Kingstown.
Arorae Is., Kiribati: 2.34 S. 176.51 E. 49
Arosund, Denmark: 55.16 N. 9.43 E. 12
Arran Is., U.K. **5, 6**
Arrecife, (Lanzarotte), Canary Is. (Spain): 28.57 N. 13.32 W. . . . 27
Max. Size: LOA 293.5 m., draft 9.94 m. Buoys: 20,000 d.w.t.,
LOA 175 m., draft 14 m. *Fuel:* Available. *Airport:* 5 km.
Arroyo, see Las Mareas.
Ars, France: 46.13 N. 1.31 W. **8, 19**
Art Is., see Wala.
Arta, Greece: 39.10 N. 21.00 E. **24, 25**
Arthur Kill, see New York.
Aru Is., Indonesia 46
Aruba (Netherlands) **69, 72, 74**
Arun Terminal, see Lhokseumawe.
Arutunga, (Aitutaki Is.), Cook Is. (N.Z.): 18.52 S. 159.46 W. . . 49
Arzanah Island, U.A.E.: 24.47 N. 52.33 E. 35
No longer operational.
Arzew, Algeria: 35.50 N. 0.08 W. 22
Max. Size: Depths: Dry cargo 5.0 m. – 8.0 m. LPG, LNG, oil and
crude, 9.8 m. – 26.0 m. Sea Line Tanker
Berth: Up to 100,000 tons. Arzew El Djedid: Depth: 13.5 m. –
26.5 m. 250,000 d.w.t. *Fuel:* Available. *Airport:* Es Senia
(Oran) International, 50 km.
Arzew El-Djedid, see Arzew.
Asa, Denmark: 57.09 N. 10.26 E. 12
Asahan, see Tanjung Balai.
Asaluyeh, see Assaluyeh.
Ascension Island (U.K.) **18, 28, 68**
Ash Shihr Terminal, Yemen: 14.41 N. 49.31 E. 31
Max. Size: 80,000 – 400,000 d.w.t. tonnes. (265,000 S.d.w.t.
part load), depth 45 m.
Ashdod, Israel: 31.49 N. 34.39 E. **26, 32**
Max. Size: Bulk Pier: Draft: Summer, 12.5 m. Winter, 12.0 m.
Draft 9.8 m. at other piers. *Fuel:* By barge or road tanker.
Airport: Ben Gurion, 35 km.
Ashkelon, Israel: 31.38 N. 34.32 E. **26, 32**
Max. Size: 280,000 d.w.t., depth 16 m. – 30 m. *Fuel:* By barge.
Airport: Ben Gurion, 70 km.
Ashland, Wisconsin, U.S.A.: 46.38 N. 90.52 W. 62
Ashtabula, Ohio, U.S.A.: 41.53 N. 80.48 W. **55, 60, 62**
Max. Size: LOA 1,000 ft., beam 105 ft., draft 26 ft.
Fuel: Available. *Airport:* 10 miles.
Ashtart, Tunisia: 34.17 N. 11.23 E. 24
Max. Size: S.B.M.: 150,000 d.w.t. Barge Berth: 100,000 d.w.t.,
depth 66 ft. *Airport:* At Sfax.
Asilah, Morocco: 35.30 N. 6.00 W. **22, 27**
Asinara Is., (Sardinia), Italy: 41.00 N. 8.15 E. 24
Askaig, see Port Askaig.
Askersund, Sweden: 58.50 N. 14.55 E. **11, 12**
Askja, Sweden: 63.01 N. 18.13 E. 15
Asl, Egypt: 29.30 N. 32.40 E. 32

Asnaes, Denmark: 55.40 N. 11.05 E. 12
Max. Size: Depths 7.7 m. – 13.5 m. *Fuel:* By barge or road
tanker. *Airport:* Copenhagen, 100 km.
Aspropyrgos, Greece: 38.02 N. 23.36 E. **23, 25**
Max. Size: 60,000 d.w.t., LOA 220 m., draft 10.89 m. *Fuel:*
All grades. *Airport:* Athens, 35 km.
Asry Dry Dock, see Sitra.
Assab, Eritrea: 13.01 N. 42.44 E. **31, 32**
Max. Size: Commercial Harbour: LOA 200 m., draft 11 m.
Tankers: LOA 185 m., draft 11 m. *Fuel:* All grades. *Airport:*
15 km.
Assaluyeh, Iran: 27.30 N. 52.36 E.
Assens, Denmark: 55.15 N. 9.53 E. **11, 12**
Max. Size: LOA 130 m., beam 20 m., draft 7 m. *Fuel:* Available
with notice. *Dry Docks:* Floating – 1,350 tons, 80 m. length, 15
m. beam. *Airport:* Odense, 50 km.
Assinie, Ivory Coast: 5.08 N. 3.17 W. 28
Assos, Greece: 38.20 N. 20.31 E. 25
Assumption Is., Seychelles: 9.46 S. 46.31 E. 30
Astakos, Greece: 38.32 N. 21.07 E. **24, 25**
Astipalaia Is., Greece: 36.32 N. 26.22 E. 25
Astoria, New York, U.S.A., see New York.
Astoria, Oregon, U.S.A.: 46.11 N. 123.50 W. **55, 56, 57, 63**
Max. Size: Channel width of 500 ft. and project depth at low
water 40 ft. Depths alongside 20 ft. – 40 ft. *Fuel:* Heavy fuel
and diesel.
Astove Is., Seychelles: 10.06 S. 47.45 E. 30
Astrakhan, Russia: 46.20 N. 48.03 E. 9
Astros, see Paralion Astrous.
Asuncion, Paraguay: 25.25 S. 57.38 W. 77
Asuncion Is., Northern Mariana Is. (U.S.A.):
19.40 N. 145.24 E. 46
At Tur, see El Tur.
Ata Is., Tonga: 22.19 S. 176.12 W. 49
Atafu Is., Tokelau Is. (N.Z.): 8.32 S. 172.31 W. 49
Atalandi, Greece 23
Atapupu, (Timor), Indonesia: 9.00 S. 124.52 E. 46
Ataqa, Egypt: 29.54 N. 32.28 E. 34
Athens, see Piraeus.
Atico, Peru: 16.14 S. 73.43 W. **72, 77**
Max. Size: Open roadstead
Atka, Alaska, U.S.A.: 52.13 N. 174.11 W. 54
Atlantic City, New Jersey, U.S.A.: 39.22 N. 74.25 W. . . **60, 63, 65**
Atreco, see Port Arthur.
Atsumi, Japan: 34.40 N. 137.04 E. **43, 45**
Max. Size: Dolphin Pier: 79,900 d.w.t., LOA 354 m.,
draft 12.50 m. SBM: 210,000 d.w.t., draft 13 m. *Fuel:* Available.
Attaka, see Santan Terminal.
Attawapiskat, Ontario, Canada: 52.56 N. 82.26 W. 59
Attu Is., (Aleutian Is.), Alaska, U.S.A. 54
Atucha, Argentina: 33.58 S. 59.16 W. **77, 78**
Max. Size: Depth 44 ft.
Atuona, (Marquesas Is.), French Polynesia (France):
9.48 S. 139.02 W. 49
Atyrau, Kazakhstan: 47.08 N. 51.56 E. 9
Auckland, New Zealand: 36.51 S. 174.45 E. **49, 52**
Max. Size: Depths: Entrance 11.89 m., berths up to 12.20 m.
Tankers: Depth 9 m. – 11 m. *Fuel:* Light fuel oil, diesel, gas oil
and heavy fuel. *Dry Docks:* Max. size: 181.35 m. LOA and
19.8 m. beam. *Airport:* 23 km.
Auckland Is., New Zealand: 51.00 S. 166.00 E. 52
Auderville, France: 49.43 N. 1.57 W. **7, 19**
Audierne, France: 48.01 N. 4.32 W. **7, 19**
Audorf, see Rendsburg.
Aughinish Island Marine Terminal, Ireland: 52.38 N. 9.03 W. . . 5
Max. Size: Outer berth: 75,000 tonnes d.w.t., LOA 235 m.,
draft 12.4 m. Inner berth: 40,000 tonnes d.w.t., LOA 180 m.,
beam 32 m., draft 11.0 m. *Fuel:* By road.
Augusta, S.A., Australia, see Port Augusta.
Augusta, W.A., Australia: 34.18 S. 115.10 E. 50
Augusta, (Sicily), Italy: 37.13 N. 15.14 E. 24
Max. Size: Up to 66 ft. 10 in. draft at Montedison supertanker
jetty, 220,000 g.r.t. (420,000 d.w.t.). *Fuel:* All grades.
Dry Docks: Floating dock: Length 105 m., breadth 17.10 m.,
lifting capacity 3,000 tons. *Airport:* Catania, 40 minutes by car.
Augusta, Maine, U.S.A.: 44.18 N. 69.45 W. 60
Augustenborg, Denmark: 54.58 N. 9.52 E. **12, 14**
Auki, (Malaita Is.), Solomon Islands: 8.45 S. 160.44 E. 51
Aultbea, U.K.: 57.50 N. 5.30 W. 5
Aur, Marshall Is.: 8.15 N. 171.00 E. 49
Aurukun, Australia: 13.25 S. 141.45 E. 50
Austin, see Port Austin.
Austral Islands, French Polynesia (France) 49
AUSTRALIA **46, 49, 50, 51, 80**
Australian Capital Territory, Australia 50
AUSTRIA **9, 21**
Avarua, see Avatiu.
Avatiu, (Rarotonga), Cook Is. (N.Z.): 21.12 S. 159.47 W. . . . 49
Max. Size: LOA 90 m. Depth up to 6.2 m. *Fuel:* Available.
Airport: Rarotonga International, 1 mile.

Aveiro, Portugal: 40.39 N. 8.45 W. **20, 22**
  Max. Size: Draft 5.5 m. – 8.0 m.   *Fuel:* Diesel.   *Dry Docks:* Up to 3,000 d.w.t.   *Airport:* Pedras Rubras, 80 km.
Avernakke, see Nyborg.
Aves Is., Venezuela: 15.41 N. 63.40 W. **71**
Avgo Is., Greece: 35.33 N. 25.37 E. **25**
Avigait, Greenland (Denmark): 62.30 N. 50.20 W. **17**
Aviles, Spain: 43.35 N. 5.56 W. **19, 20, 21, 22**
  Max. Size: LOA 225 m. or draft 10.75 m. Depths: 5.0 m. – 12.0 m. Vessels over 150 m. LOA require 4 ft. keel clearance. Depths alongside 2 m. – 12 m.   *Fuel:* Fuel and gas oil.   *Airport:* Asturias.
Avola, Italy: 36.54 N. 15.09 E. **24**
Avondale, Louisiana, U.S.A.: 29.55 N. 90.11 W. **67**
  Max. Size: Depth 60 ft.
  Also see New Orleans.
Avonmouth, U.K.: 51.30 N. 2.42 W. **5, 6, 7**
  Also see Bristol.
Avranches, France: 48.41 N. 1.21 W. **7, 19**
Awaji Is., Japan **45**
Axelsvik, Sweden: 65.46 N. 23.22 E. **15**
  Max. Size: Draft 8.8 m.   *Airport:* Lulea, 80 km.
  Also see Karlsborgsverken.
Axim, Ghana: 4.52 N. 2.15 W. **28**
Ayacucho, see Puerto Ayacucho.
Ayamonte, Spain: 37.13 N. 7.24 W. **20**
Ayan, Russia: 56.27 N. 138.15 E. **43**
Ayancik, Turkey: 41.55 N. 34.19 E. **26**
Ayia Marina, Greece: 37.07 N. 26.51 E. **25**
Ayia Pelayia, Greece: 36.20 N. 22.59 E. **25**
Ayios Evstratios Is., Greece: 39.34 N. 24.58 E. **25**
Ayios Kirikos, Greece: 37.36 N. 26.17 E. **25**
Aykathonesi Is., Greece: 37.28 N. 26.58 E. **25**
Aynunah, Saudi Arabia: 28.05 N. 35.00 E. **32**
Ayr, U.K.: 55.28 N. 4.38 W. **6**
  Max. Size: Draft 6.0 m.   *Fuel:* All grades.
  Airport: Prestwick, 7 miles, and Glasgow.
  Also see Troon.
Ayvalik, Turkey: 39.19 N. 26.42 E. **25, 26**
AZERBAIJAN **9**
Azhikkal, see Cannanore.
Azores (Portugal) **20, 27, 53**
Azov, Russia: 47.07 N. 39.25 E. **9, 26**
Azovstal, see Mariupol.
Azua, Dominican Republic: 18.30 N. 70.40 W. **69, 70**
  Max. Size: LOA 500 ft., beam 80 ft., draft 30 ft.
  Fuel: By road tanker.   *Airport:* Santo Domingo, 120 km.
Azzawiya, see Zawia.
Azzuro, see Porto Azzurro.

B

Ba Ngoi, Vietnam: 11.54 N. 109.09 E. **39**
  Max. Size: LOA 90 m., depth 11.6 m.   *Fuel:* Available.
  Airport: Nha Trang.
Ba Yu Quan, see Yingkou.
Baa, Indonesia: 10.43 S. 123.03 E. **46, 50**
Babadag, Romania: 44.50 N. 28.45 E. **26**
Babar Is., (Tanimba Is.), Indonesia **46**
Babitonga Bay, see Sao Francisco do Sul.
Babo, Indonesia: 2.33 S. 133.26 E. **46**
Babuyan, (Palawan Is.), Philippines: 10.00 N. 119.02 E. . **47**
Babuyan Is., Philippines **46, 47**
Bacan Is., (Moluccas), Indonesia **46**
Bachaquero, Venezuela: 9.57 N. 71.09 W. **74**
Backfors, Sweden: 64.31 N. 21.25 E. **15**
Bacolod, (Palawan Is.), Philippines: 10.40 N. 122.57 E. . **47**
Badagara, India: 11.36 N. 75.35 E. **37**
Badagri, Nigeria: 6.25 N. 2.53 E. **29**
Badalona, Spain: 41.26 N. 2.15 E. **22**
Badcall, U.K.: 58.17 N. 5.12 W. **5**
Baddeck, N.S., Canada: 46.06 N. 60.44 W. **60**
  Max. Size: LOA 497 ft., beam 66.7 ft., draft 28 ft.
  Fuel: Diesel by road tanker.   *Airport:* 55 miles.
Bado, see Uddevalla.
Baejarbryggjan, see Siglufjord.
Baffin Bay **17, 53, 79**
Baffin Is., N.W.T., Canada **17, 59**
Bagan Datoh, Malaysia: 3.59 N. 100.48 E. **38, 39, 40**
Bagan Datuk, see Bagan Datoh.
Bagansiapi Api, Indonesia: 2.10 N. 100.49 E. . . . **38, 39, 40**
Bagenkop, Denmark: 54.45 N. 10.40 E. **12, 14**
Bagerhat, see Mongla.
Bagfas, see Bandirma.
Bagnoli, Italy: 40.48 N. 14.10 E. **9, 23, 24**
  Max. Size: Ore/Coal discharging: Draft 41 ft. 6 in.
  Loading pier: Draft 10.5 m.   *Fuel:* All grades.
Bagotville, Quebec, Canada: 48.21 N. 70.53 W. **60**
  Max. Size: Depth 28 ft. (LW).
  Also see Port Alfred.
Baguskuning, see Palembang.
BAHAMAS **55, 66, 70**
Bahia, see Salvador.
Bahia Blanca, Argentina: 38.47 S. 62.16 W. **77**
  Max. Size: LOA 250 m. - 270 m., draft about 45 ft. in access channels. Puerto Galvan: LOA 120 m. – 230 m., depth 25 ft. – 38 ft. Tanker Berth: Depth 40 ft. Ingeniero White: Depth 29 ft. – 50 ft.   *Fuel:* All grades.
  Dry Docks: 234 m. x 35 m.   *Airport:* 10 km., domestic.
Bahia de Caraquez, Ecuador: 0.36 S. 80.25 W. **72**
Bahia de Portete, Colombia: 12.15 N. 71.58 W. **74**
Bahia Gregorio, see Gregorio.
Bahia Honda, Colombia: 12.18 N. 71.50 W. **74**
Bahia Honda, Cuba: 22.59 N. 83.10 W. **70**
  Max. Size: Draft (anchorage) 28 ft., (berth) 19 ft., LOA 450 ft.
  Also see Mariel.
Bahia Las Minas, Panama: 9.24 N. 79.49 W. **73**
  Max. Size: LOA 152 m., draft 22 ft. Ro/Ro up to 600 ft. LOA. Tankers: LOA 240 m., draft 39 ft.   *Fuel:* Available.
  Airport: Panama, 90 km.
Bahia Negra, Brazil: 20.05 S. 58.05 W. **72, 77**
Bahia Solarno, Colombia: 6.10 N. 77.30 W. **69**
BAHRAIN **31, 35**
Bahregan, Iran: 29.43 N. 50.10 E. **31, 35**
  Max. Size: Up to 250,000 d.w.t. Depth at SBM is 24 m. (78 ft. 9 in.) LW.
Baia da Ilha Grande Terminal, see DTSE/GEBIG Oil Terminal.
Baie Comeau, Quebec, Canada: 49.14 N. 68.07 W. **60**
  Max. Size: Cargill: Up to 40 ft. draft at LW.   *Fuel:* Available.
  Dry Docks: Les Mechins, 48 miles.   *Airport:* Daily service to Quebec and Montreal.
Baie de la Seine, France **7**
Baie de Mayumba, see M'Bya Terminal.
Baie des Dames, New Caledonia (France): 22.14 S. 166.24 E. . . **51**
  Max. Size: LOA 200 m., draft 10.0 m.
  Also see Noumea.
Baie Johan Beetz, Quebec, Canada: 50.17 N. 62.47 W. **60**
Baie St. Paul, Quebec, Canada: 47.25 N. 70.30 W. **60**
Baie Ugue, New Caledonia (France): 21.09 S. 165.33 E. **51**
  Max. Size: LOA 170 m., draft 11 m.
  Also see Noumea.
Baie Verte, Newfoundland, Canada: 49.57 N. 56.10 W. . . . **60**
Bail, see Port Bail.
Bais, (Negros Is.), Philippines: 9.32 N. 123.08 E. . . . **46, 47**
Baja Nuevo Is., Colombia: 15.48 N. 78.38 W. **69, 70**
Bajada Grande, Argentina: 31.45 S. 60.29 W. **78**

Bajo Grande, Venezuela: 10.29 N. 71.38 W. 74
 Max. Size: 85,000 d.w.t., 39 ft. 6 in. draft. *Fuel:* All grades. *Dry Docks:* Nearest Curacao, up to 30,000 d.w.t.
Bakalskaya, Ukraine: 45.46 N. 33.13 E. 26
Bakapit, Sabah, Malaysia: 4.56 N. 118.34 E. 38
Bakar, Croatia: 45.18 N. 14.32 E. 24
 Max. Size: Bakar: 170,000 d.w.t., LOA 300 m., draft 17.5 m.
 Tankers: 80,000 d.w.t.
 Also see Rijeka.
Baker Is., (U.S.A.): 0.14 N. 176.28 W. 49
Baker Lake, N.W.T., Canada: 64.20 N. 96.05 W. 59
Bakirkoy, Turkey: 40.59 N. 28.53 E. 23
Balabac, (Balabac Is.), Philippines: 8.01 N. 117.04 E. . . . 38, 47
Balabac Strait 38, 47
Balaklava, Ukraine: 44.30 N. 33.35 E. 26
Balancan, (Marinduque Is.), Philippines: 13.32 N. 121.51 E. . . 47
Balao Terminal, Ecuador: 1.02 N. 79.44 W. 72
 Max. Size: Up to 100,000 d.w.t., LOA 274 m., beam 39.6 m.,
 draft 15.2 m. *Fuel:* Limited in emergencies.
Balasore, India: 21.30 N. 87.00 E. 37
Balboa, Panama: 8.58 N. 79.34 W. 69, 72, 73
 Max. Size: Container: Draft 12.9 m. Tankers: LOA 750 ft.,
 draft 32 ft. salt water. *Fuel:* Available. *Dry Docks:* Capacity
 60,000 d.w.t. *Airport:* Tocumen, 32 km.
 Also see Panama Canal.
Balbriggan, Ireland: 53.37 N. 6.11 W. 5
Balchik, Bulgaria: 43.26 N. 28.11 E. 26
 Max. Size: Draft 24 ft.
 Also see Varna.
Balearic Islands, Spain 21, 22
Baler, (Luzon Is.), Philippines: 15.46 N. 121.34 E. 47
Bali Is., Indonesia 38
Baliango, Philippines: 8.39 N. 123.37 E. 47
Balikpapan, Indonesia: 1.16 S. 116.48 E. 38
 Max. Size: Draft: 13.5 m. Tankers: Normally up to LOA 215 m.,
 draft 12 m., 35,000 d.w.t. Sailing drafts up to 33 ft. salt water.
 Depth at cargo berths 9.0 m. – 12.0 m.
 Coal Terminal: 15,000 – 80,000 d.w.t., depth 15 m.
 Fuel: Available. *Airport:* Sepinggan, 12 km.
Baliwasan, see Zamboanga.
Ballah By-Pass, Suez Canal, Egypt 33
Ballangen, Norway: 68.21 N. 16.51 E. 15
Ballast Head, S.A., Australia: 35.45 S. 137.48 E. 50, 51
 Last shipment took place in 1992
Ballast Point, see Sydney.
Ballen, Denmark: 55.49 N. 10.39 E. 12
Ballina, N.S.W., Australia: 28.52 S. 153.35 E. 50
Ballina, Ireland: 54.07 N. 9.10 W. 5
Ballycastle, U.K.: 55.12 N. 6.13 W. 5
Ballyheigue Bay, Ireland 8
Ballyvaughan, Ireland: 53.08 N. 9.09 W. 5
Balmain, see Sydney.
Balongan, Indonesia: 6.21 S. 108.23 E. 38
 Max. Size: SBM: 150,000 d.w.t., LOA 290 m., depth 22 m.
 Airport: Cirebon.
Balsta, Sweden: 59.34 N. 17.32 E. 11
Balstad, Norway: 68.03 N. 13.33 E. 15
Baltasound, U.K.: 60.45 N. 0.50 W. 5
Baltic Sea 4, 10, 11, 12, 14
Baltijeto, Ukraine: 60.37 N. 28.19 E. 11, 13
Baltim, Egypt: 31.34 N. 31.10 E. 26, 32
Baltimore, Ireland: 51.29 N. 9.22 W. 5
Baltimore, Maryland, U.S.A.: 39.17 N. 76.35 W. . . 55, 60, 63, 65
 Max. Size: Depth 28 ft. – 50 ft. Tankers: Depth 20 ft. – 40 ft.
 Fuel: All grades. *Airport:* 8 miles.
Baltiysk, Lithuania: 54.38 N. 19.54 E. 11
Bamburgh, U.K.: 55.30 N. 1.40 W. 5
Bamfield, B.C., Canada: 48.49 N. 125.09 W. 56
Banaba, (Ocean Is.), Kiribati: 0.52 S. 169.35 E. 49
 Port closed.
Banana, Congo (D.R. of): 6.01 S. 12.25 E. 28
 Max. Size: Moanda: Tankers up to 35 ft. draft.
 Banana Wharf: Draft 17 ft. *Fuel:* Gas oil, light and heavy fuel
 oil available.
Banda Elat, (Kai Is.), Indonesia: 5.40 S. 132.59 E. 46
Banda Sea, Indonesia 46
Bandar Abbas, Iran: 27.08 N. 56.12 E. 31, 35, 37
 Max. Size: Old Port (Shadid Bahonar): Cargo vessels –
 LOA 733 ft., draft 34 ft. Tankers – LOA 666 ft., draft 34 ft.
 New Port (Shahid Radjaie): Cargo vessels – LOA 833 ft.,
 draft 40 ft. Tankers – LOA 733 ft., draft 40 ft. Pullad
 Jetty: Max. draft 14.0 m. *Fuel:* Available. *Airport:* 15 km.
Bandar Cassim, see Bosaso.
Bandar e Deylam, Iran: 30.03 N. 50.08 E. 35
Bandar e Rig, Iran: 29.29 N. 50.41 E. 35
Bandar Imam Khomeini, Iran: 30.25 N. 49.05 E. 31, 35
 Max. Size: LOA 780 ft., draft 42 ft. *Fuel:* Available.
 Airport: Mahshahr, 20 km.

Bandar Mahshahr, Iran: 30.27 N. 49.20 E. 31, 35
 Max. Size: 60,000 tonnes d.w.t. or LOA 238 m., draft 12.2 m.
 Fuel: Available.
Bandar Seri Begawan, see Muara.
Bandar Shahid Radjaee, see Bandar Abbas.
Bandar Taheri, Iran: 27.40 N. 52.21 E. 35
 Max. Size: SBM: 40,000 tonnes d.w.t., LOA 200 m.,
 depth 16.0 m. *Airport:* Jam, 65 km.
Bandholm, Denmark: 54.50 N. 11.30 E. 11, 12, 14
 Max. Size: LOA 120 m., depth 5.8 m. *Fuel:* Available by truck.
 Airport: Maribo, 15 km. Copenhagen, 150 km.
Bandirma, Turkey: 40.22 N. 27.58 E. 25, 26
 Max. Size: Draft 12.0 m. Bagfas: Depth 9.3 m. – 16.5 m. *Fuel:*
 By barge or road tanker. *Airport:* Istanbul, 350 km.
Bandon, Oregon, U.S.A.: 43.08 N. 124.25 W. 57
Banes, Cuba: 20.54 N. 75.41 W. 69, 70
 Max. Size: LOA 106 m., draft 5.79 m.
Banff, U.K.: 57.40 N. 2.32 W. 5
Banggai, Indonesia: 1.35 S. 123.30 E. 46
Bangka Is., Indonesia 38
Bangkok, Thailand: 13.26 N. 100.35 E. 37, 39
 Max. Size: 10,000 – 12,000 d.w.t., LOA 172 m., draft 8.2 m.
 Fuel: Available. *Dry Docks:* Up to 360 ft. LOA. *Airport:* 25 km.
BANGLADESH 37
Bangor, Northern Ireland, U.K.: 54.39 N. 5.40 W. 5, 6
 Max. Size: LOA 70 m., draft 4 m. HWOST. *Fuel:* Diesel.
 Airport: Aldergrove or Belfast City Airport, 12 km.
Bangor, Wales, U.K.: 53.14 N. 4.07 W. 5, 7
Bangor, Maine, U.S.A.: 44.49 N. 68.47 W. 55, 60
 Max. Size: LOA 560 ft. Tankers: Depth 22 ft. *Fuel:* Only
 available at oil berth. *Airport:* Bangor, 2 miles.
Bangsaphan, Thailand: 11.11 N. 99.35 E. 37, 39
 Max. Size: 100,000 d.w.t., depth 8 m. – 15 m. *Fuel:* Available.
 Airport: Bangkok, 400 km.
Baniara, Papua New Guinea: 9.44 S. 149.49 E. 46
Banias, Syria: 35.14 N. 35.56 E. 26
 Max. Size: LOA 925 ft. (Loading) and 900 ft. (Unloading),
 draft 53 ft. (Summer) and 51 ft. (Winter). *Fuel:* Diesel.
 Airport: Damascus International, about 300 km.
Banjarmasin, Indonesia: 3.18 S. 114.35 E. 38
 Max. Size: Depth 8.0 m. *Fuel:* Available.
Banjul, Gambia: 13.27 N. 16.34 W. 27
 Max. Size: LOA 182.9 m., draft 8.5 m. *Fuel:* Bunkering
 facilities available. *Dry Docks:* Slipway 500 tons.
 Airport: Yundum, 14 miles.
Bankot, India: 17.59 N. 73.04 E. 37
Banks Is., Vanuatu: 14.00 S. 167.30 E. 49
Bantry Bay, Ireland: 51.41 N. 9.27 W. 5
 Max. Size: Oil Terminal: Not operating. Harbour: Draft 25 ft.
 Pier: LOA 150 ft., draft 12 ft. SPM: 320,000 tonnes d.w.t.,
 LOA 340 m., draft 22 m. *Fuel:* Gas oil and fuel available at
 Bantry Pier in road tenders of 20 tons. *Airport:* Cork, 48 miles.
Banyu, see Bunyu.
Banyuwangi, Indonesia: 8.07 S. 114.23 E. 38
 Max. Size: 40,000 d.w.t., draft 12.5 m. *Fuel:* Available.
 Airport: Ngurah Rai, 60 miles.
Baoshan, see Shanghai.
Bar, Yugoslavia: 42.05 N. 19.03 E. 9, 24
 Max. Size: Up to 12.5 m. draft. Tankers: 80,000 d.w.t.
 Fuel: All grades. *Dry Docks:* Bijela 36 miles from Bar,
 capacity about 130,000 d.w.t.
Bar Harbour, Maine, U.S.A.: 44.23 N. 68.12 W. 60
Barachois, Quebec, Canada: 48.38 N. 64.17 W. 60
Baracoa, Cuba: 20.21 N. 74.30 W. 70
 Max. Size: Up to 100 m. LOA and 6.1 m. draft.
 Also see Moa.
Baradero, Argentina: 34.05 S. 59.15 W. 78
Barahona, Dominican Republic: 18.12 N. 71.04 W. 69, 70
 Max. Size: LOA 600 ft., draft 27 ft. *Fuel:* By road tanker.
 Airport: Santo Domingo, 150 km.
Baram, see Miri.
Baranof Is., Alaska, U.S.A. 56
Barao de Tefe, see Antonina.
Barataria Bay, (Mississippi Delta), Louisiana, U.S.A. 67
BARBADOS 69, 71, 72
Barbate, Spain: 36.12 N. 5.56 W. 23
Barber's Point, Hawaii, U.S.A.: 21.18 N. 158.07 W. 49
 Max. Size: Kalaeloa Barber's Point Harbour: LOA 750 ft.,
 depth 11.28 m. Tankers: Tesoro – LOA 945 ft., draft 65 ft.
 Chevron – LOA 1,000 ft., draft 50 ft. *Fuel:* Available.
 Airport: Honolulu International Airport.
Barbours Cut, Texas, U.S.A.: 29.41 N. 95.01 W. 66
 Also see Houston.
Barbuda Is., Antigua and Barbuda: 17.48 N. 61.55 W. 71
Barcadera, Aruba (Netherlands): 12.29 N. 70.00 W. 74
 Max. Size: LOA 225 m., draft 32 ft. *Fuel:* Available.
Barce, see Al Marj.
Barcelona, Spain: 41.20 N. 2.10 E. 21, 22
 Max. Size: Draft 45 m. Tankers: 60,000 d.w.t., depth 12 m.
 LPG: 125,000 cu.m. *Fuel:* Fuel and Gas Oil.
 Dry Docks: LOA 215 m. for 50,000 d.w.t. *Airport:* 7 km.

THE SHIPS ATLAS

Barcelona, Venezuela: 10.08 N. 64.35 W. **69, 75**
Bardia, Libya: 31.46 N. 25.06 E. **26**
Bardsey Is., U.K.: 52.45 N. 4.48 W. **5**
Barents Is., Norway **17**
Barents Sea **16, 79**
Barentsburg, (Spitsbergen), Norway: 78.04 N. 14.13 E. . . . **17**
Barfleur, France: 49.40 N. 1.16 W. **7, 19**
Barhoft, Germany: 54.26 N. 13.02 E. **12**
Bari, Italy: 41.08 N. 16.51 E. **9, 21, 24**
 Max. Size: Depths up to 10.37 m. Product Tankers: Depth
 12.8 m. – 14.33 m. *Fuel:* By road tanker. *Airport:* 8 km.
Barima Bar, see Orinoco River/Delta.
Barletta, Italy: 41.20 N. 16.17 E. **21, 24**
Barmouth, U.K.: 52.43 N. 4.03 W. **5, 7**
Barnegat, New Jersey, U.S.A.: 39.46 N. 74.06 W. **63**
Barney Point, see Gladstone.
Barnstaple, U.K.: 51.06 N. 4.04 W. **6, 7**
Barqueriza, (Galapagos Is.), Ecuador: 0.54 S. 89.37 W. . . **69**
Barquito, Chile: 26.21 S. 70.38 W. **77**
 Also see Chanaral.
Barra, U.K.: 57.00 N. 7.35 W. **5**
Barra do Riacho, Brazil: 19.50 S. 40.03 W. **72, 77**
 Max. Size: LOA 200 m., beam 35.0 m., draft 10.3 m. – 11.9 m.
 Airport: At Vitoria.
Barrancas, Venezuela: 8.45 N. 62.08 W. **75**
Barrangueras, see Corrientes.
Barranquilla, Colombia: 10.58 N. 74.47 W. **69, 72**
 Max. Size: LOA 600 ft., draft 30 ft. or less due to silting.
 Fuel: Small quantities of gas oil. *Airport:* 6 km.
Barreiro, Portugal: 38.40 N. 9.06 W. **20**
 Max. Size: Depth to 8.5 m.
 Also see Lisbon.
Barrios, see Puerto Barrios.
Barrosso Terminal, see Sao Sebastiao.
Barrow, U.K.: 53.42 N. 0.24 W. **6**
Barrow, Alaska, U.S.A.: 71.17 N. 156.48 W. **54**
Barrow Island, W.A., Australia: 20.49 S. 115.33 E. **50, 51**
 Max. Size: Loaded displacement 105,000 tonnes, beam 47 m.
 Minimum depth 12.0 m.
Barrow-in-Furness, U.K.: 54.07 N. 3.14 W. **5**
 Max. Size: LOA 200 m., beam 35 m., draft 9.15 m. *Fuel:*
 Available. *Airport:* Walney, 4 miles and Manchester.
Barry, U.K.: 51.24 N. 3.16 W. **6, 7**
 Max. Size: LOA 178 m., beam 23.8 m., draft 9.0 m.
 Fuel: By barge. *Airport:* Cardiff, 4 miles.
Barth, Germany: 54.23 N. 12.44 E. **12**
Bartica, Guyana: 6.24 N. 58.37 W. **75, 76**
 Max. Size: Depth 3 ft. less than Demarara Bar prediction.
 Also see Essequibo River.
Bartin, Turkey: 41.41 N. 32.14 E. **26**
 Max. Size: Draft 7.5 m. *Fuel:* Available.
Bartolomeo Diaz, Mozambique: 21.08 S. 35.08 E. **30**
Barton, U.K.: 53.28 N. 2.22 W. **6**
 Also see Manchester.
Baruch, India: 21.48 N. 73.00 E. **37**
Barus, Indonesia: 2.00 N. 98.25 E. **38, 40**
Baruva, India: 18.53 N. 83.46 E. **37**
Basarabi, Romania: 44.10 N. 28.25 E. **26**
Basco, (Batan Is.), Philippines: 20.27 N. 121.58 E. **47**
Bashayer, Sudan: 19.24 N. 37.19 E. **32**
 Max. Size: 300,000 tonnes d.w.t., depth 54 m.
Bashi Channel, Philippines **46**
Basidu, Iran: 26.39 N. 55.16 E. **35**
Basilan Is., Philippines **46, 47**
Basle, Switzerland: 47.33 N. 7.34 E. **9**
 Max. Size: Depth: 3.5 m. *Fuel:* Diesel oil available.
 Airport: Basle-Mulhouse Airport.
Basques Cove, Quebec, Canada: 48.19 N. 69.24 W. **60**
Basrah, see Umm Qasr.
Bass Strait, Victoria/Tasmania, Australia **50, 51**
Bassas de India, Reunion (France): 21.29 S. 39.46 E. . . . **30**
Basse Indre, France: 47.12 N. 1.42 W. **19**
Basse Terre, Guadeloupe (France): 15.59 N. 61.44 W. . . . **69, 71**
 Max. Size: LOA 300 m., beam 30 m., draft approx. 29 ft.
 Depth alongside up to 11.1 m. *Airport:* 60 km.
Bassein, Myanmar: 16.46 N. 94.46 E. **37**
Bassens, France: 44.55 N. 0.32 W. **8, 19**
 Max. Size: Vessels up to 34 ft. draft.
 Also see Bordeaux.
Basseterre, (St. Kitts), St. Christopher and Nevis:
 17.18 N. 62.43 W. **69, 71**
 Max. Size: Passenger – LOA 920 ft., draft 27 ft.
 Cargo – LOA 650 ft., draft 27 ft. Tanker/LPG – LOA 400 ft.,
 draft 17 ft. *Fuel:* Available. *Airport:* 2 miles, connects with
 Antigua and Puerto Rico.
Bassetts Is., (Cape Cod Canal), Massachusetts, U.S.A. . . . **64**
Bastad, Sweden: 56.25 N. 12.50 E. **11, 12**
Bastia, (Corsica), France: 42.42 N. 9.27 E. **21, 23, 24**
 Max. Size: LOA 200 m., draft 9.0 m. *Fuel:* By road tanker.
 Airport: Poretta, 23 km.

Basuanga, (Basuanga Is.), Philippines: 12.09 N. 119.55 E. . **47**
Basuo, China: 19.06 N. 108.37 E. **39**
 Max. Size: LOA 169 m., draft 9.8 m.
Bata, Equatorial Guinea: 1.52 N. 9.46 E. **28, 29**
 Max. Size: SPM. *Airport:* Close to Bata, connects with
 Malabo and Douala.
Bataan, (Luzon Is.), Philippines: 14.30 N. 120.38 E. . . . **46, 47**
 Max. Size: Depth: 3.6 m. – 14.6 m. CBM: LOA 1,000 ft.,
 draft 52 ft. SBM: 310,000 d.w.t., draft 75 ft. and 175 ft. beam.
 Product Pier: 30,000 d.w.t., depth 13 m. LPG: Draft 10 ft.
 Fuel: Fuel oil and diesel.
Batabano, Cuba: 22.41 N. 82.18 W. **69, 70**
Batakan, Indonesia: 4.04 S. 114.39 E. **38**
Batan Is., Philippines **46, 47**
Batang Lupar, see Lingga.
Batangas, (Luzon Is.), Philippines: 13.45 N. 121.03 E. . . **46, 47**
 Max. Size: Draft 45 ft. Tankers: Shell – Tabangao up to 320,000
 d.w.t., draft 23 m. Caltex – Refinery up to 45,000 d.w.t.
 LOA 755 ft., draft 41 ft. *Fuel:* Available at tanker berths.
 Dry Docks: Dry dock with capacity 40,000 d.w.t.
 Airport: Manila, 110 km.
Batchawana, Ontario, Canada: 46.55 N. 84.36 W. **62**
Batemans Bay, N.S.W., Australia: 35.41 S. 150.10 E. . . . **50**
Bath, Ontario, Canada: 44.11 N. 76.46 W. **62**
Bath, Maine, U.S.A.: 43.55 N. 69.49 W. **60**
Bathurst, N.B., Canada: 47.37 N. 65.39 W. **60**
Bathurst, Gambia, see Banjul.
Bathurst Is., N.T., Australia: 11.30 S. 130.10 E. **46, 50**
Batiscan, Quebec, Canada: 46.30 N. 72.14 W. **60**
Baton Rouge, Louisiana, U.S.A.: 30.28 N. 91.12 W. **55, 66, 67**
 Max. Size: Oil Docks can accommodate 1,000 ft. vessels –
 unlimited breadth; draft governed by S.W. pass – project
 depth 45 ft. to 180 AHP. Grain: Draft 40 ft. Bauxite: Draft 40 ft.
 Fuel: All grades. Barging essential. *Airport:* Ryan
 Airport, 6 miles.
Bats, Netherlands: 51.24 N. 4.11 E. **8**
Batsfjord, Norway: 70.38 N. 29.44 E. **10, 15, 16**
 Max. Size: Depth 6 m. – 10 m. (LW). *Fuel:* Available.
 Dry Docks: 70 m. x 25 m. *Airport:* 5 km.
Batskarsnas, Sweden: 65.48 N. 23.26 E. **15**
Battery, see New York.
Batticaloa, Sri Lanka: 7.45 N. 81.40 E. **37**
Battle Harbour, Newfoundland, Canada: 52.15 N. 55.34 W. . **59**
Batu Ampar, Indonesia: 1.10 N. 104.00 E. **39, 40, 41**
 Max. Size: Depth 6.0 m. – 8.0 m.
Batu Batu, (Tawi Tawi Is.), Philippines: 5.04 N. 119.53 E. **46, 47**
Batu Is., Indonesia: 0.25 S. 98.30 E. **38, 40**
Batu Licin, (Borneo), Indonesia: 3.23 S. 116.00 E. **38**
Batu Pahat, Malaya, Malaysia: 1.48 N. 103.00 E. . . . **38, 39, 40**
Batumi, Georgia: 41.39 N. 41.38 E. **26**
 Max. Size: Draft 32.5 ft. Tankers: Berth No. 1, LOA 200 m.,
 draft 10.2 m. Sea Loading Berth: LOA 210 m., draft 12.0 m.
 Fuel: Available. *Airport:* (Internal) Batumi, 5 km.
Bauan, see Batangas.
Baubau, Indonesia: 5.27 S. 122.37 E. **46**
Bawean Is., Indonesia **38**
Bay City, Michigan, U.S.A.: 43.35 N. 83.52 W. **62**
Bay de Chaleurs, Canada **60**
Bay dos Tigres, Angola: 16.28 S. 12.00 E. **28**
Bay Roberts, Newfoundland, Canada: 47.36 N. 53.26 W. . . . **60**
 Max. Size: Depth 20 ft. – 21 ft. (LWOST). *Fuel:* Available.
 Airport: St. John's, 90 km.
Bay St. Louis, Mississippi, U.S.A.: 30.19 N. 89.20 W. . . . **67**
Bayawan, (Palawan Is.), Philippines: 9.22 N. 122.48 W. . . **47**
Baybay, (Leyte Is.), Philippines: 10.41 N. 124.48 E. . . . **47**
Bayboro, North Carolina, U.S.A.: 35.09 N. 76.46 W. **63**
Bayfield, Ontario, Canada: 43.35 N. 81.43 W. **62**
Bayonne, France: 43.30 N. 1.28 W. **19, 21, 22**
 Max. Size: LOA 160 m., draft 8.0 m. (15-20,000 tonnes).
 Tankers: LOA 150 m., draft 24 ft. (7.3 m.) *Fuel:* Available.
 Dry Docks: Usable length 98 m. Length on stocks 94.1 m.
 Width of entry 15 m. *Airport:* Biarritz, 7 km.
Bayonne, U.S.A.: 40.40 N. 74.06 W. **63**
 Max. Size: Tankers: Depth 32 ft. – 38 ft.
 Also see New York.
Bayou Cosotte, see Pascagoula.
Bayovar, see Puerto Bayovar.
Bayport, Texas, U.S.A.: 29.36 N. 95.00 W. **66**
 Also see Houston.
Bays:
 Bay of Bengal **37**
 Bay of Biscay **8, 19, 20, 21, 22**
 Bay of Fundy, Canada **60**
 Bay of Panama, Panama **73**
 Bay of Plenty, (North Is.), New Zealand **52**
Bayside, see St. Andrews.
Baytown, Texas, U.S.A.: 29.44 N. 95.01 W. **55, 66**
 Max. Size: Depth 40 ft. (SW).
Bazaruto Is., Mozambique: 21.40 S. 35.30 E. **30**
Beachport, S.A., Australia: 37.30 S. 140.01 E. **50**

Beagle Bay, W.A., Australia: 17.00 S. 122.33 E. **50, 51**
Beagle Passage, Chile **77**
Beamsville, Ontario, Canada: 43.13 N. 79.29 W. **62**
Bear Is., N.W.T., Canada: 54.20 N. 81.05 W. **59**
Bear Is., Norway: 74.30 N. 19.00 E. **17**
Beaufort, North Carolina, U.S.A.: 34.44 N. 76.40 W. **63**
Beaufort, South Carolina, U.S.A.: 32.25 N. 80.40 W. **66**
Beaufort Sea, Canada **54, 79**
Beauharnois, Quebec, Canada: 45.19 N. 73.53 W. **61**
Beauharnois Canal Locks, see St. Lawrence Seaway.
Beaumaris, U.K.: 53.17 N. 4.05 W. **5**
Beaumont, Texas, U.S.A.: 30.05 N. 94.05 W. **55, 66**
 Max. Size: Cargo Vessels: Depth 30 ft. – 40 ft.
 Tankers: Depth 35 ft. – 36 ft. *Fuel:* Available.
 Dry Docks: 2 side-launching ways over 800 ft. each.
 Floating Dry Dock: Length of 648 ft., length on bottom 576 ft.,
 breadth at entrance 87 ft. and lifting capacity 17,500 tons.
Beauty Point, see Bell Bay.
Beaver Cove, see Englewood.
Beaver Harbour, see St. James.
Beaver Is., Michigan, U.S.A.: 45.35 N. 85.30 W. **62**
Bec d'Ambes, France: 45.02 N. 0.32 W. **8, 19**
 Max. Size: Tankers up to 32 ft. 6 in. draft, LOA 210 m.
 Also see Bordeaux.
Becancour, Quebec, Canada: 46.24 N. 72.23 W. **60**
 Max. Size: Depth 35 ft. LOA about 800 ft. *Fuel:* By road tanker.
 Airport: Trois Rivieres, 30 km.
Bedi Bunder, India: 22.31 N. 70.02 E. **37**
 Max. Size: Lighterage Port: Anchorage 7 fathoms at LW.
 Airport: Jamnagar, 7 miles.
Bedok, see Singapore.
Bee Ness, see Medway Ports.
Beechey Point, Alaska, U.S.A.: 70.00 N. 149.30 W. **54**
Behshahr, Iran: 36.42 N. 53.30 E. **9**
Bei Hai, China: 21.29 N. 109.05 E. **39**
 Max. Size: Anchorage: Draft 12 m. Berths: Depths up to 12 m.
 Fuel: Available.
Beilul, Eritrea: 13.01 N. 42.20 E. **32**
Beilun, China: 29.56 N. 121.53 E. **42**
 Max. Size: 200,000 d.w.t. Draft 20 m. *Fuel:* Available.
 Also see Ningbo.
Beira, Mozambique: 19.46 S. 34.50 E. **30**
 Max. Size: LOA 210 m., draft 10.5 m. (Springs), 7.6 m. (Neaps),
 depths 4.5 m. – 12.0 m. Tankers: Depth 9.5 m. – 13.0 m.
 Fuel: Diesel by truck or direct. *Dry Docks:* Length 115 m., width
 17 m., draft 8.5 m. Up to 5,000 tons. *Airport:* Beira, 7 miles.
Beirut, Lebanon: 33.54 N. 35.30 E. **21, 26**
 Max. Size: Draft 13 m. Tankers: 45,000 d.w.t., max. draft 15 m.
 Fuel: Available. *Airport:* 10 km.
Bejaia, Algeria: 36.45 N. 5.05 E. **21, 22**
 Max. Size: General Cargo: Depths 6.1 m. – 9.3 m.
 Bulk: Draft 9.3 m. Tankers: LOA 260 m., draft 6.5 m. – 12.8 m.
 Fuel: Available. *Dry Docks:* Capacity 15,000 d.w.t.
 (180 m. x 30 m.). *Airport:* Soumam, 5 km.
Bel Air, see Boke.
Bela Vista, Mozambique: 26.10 S. 32.45 E. **30**
BELARUS **9, 10**
Belawan, Indonesia: 3.47 N. 98.41 E. **37, 38, 40**
 Max. Size: Draft 10 m. at HW. *Fuel:* Diesel, marine fuel oil.
Belcher Islands, N.W.T., Canada **59**
Beldeport, Turkey: 40.50 N. 29.31 E. **23**
 Max. Size: Depth 16.5 m.
Belekeri, India: 14.43 N. 74.15 E. **37**
 Max. Size: Anchorage Port: Depths up to 37 ft. *Airport:* Nearest
 Goa or Mumbai.
Belem, Brazil: 1.28 S. 48.29 W. **72**
 Max. Size: Vessels with a draft greater than 26 ft. anchor off
 Icoaraci, 7 miles off the Port. Depth alongside 2.5 m. – 8.5 m.
 Fuel: Available. *Dry Docks:* 727 ft. x 27.5 m. *Airport:* 9 km.
 Also see Miramar.
Belen, Panama: 9.05 N. 80.45 W. **69**
Belfast, U.K.: 54.36 N. 5.56 W. **4, 5, 6**
 Max. Size: Draft 9 m. Tankers: Depth 11.3 m. *Fuel:* Available.
 Dry Docks: Length 1,100 ft., breadth 167 ft. *Airport:* Aldergrove,
 17 miles, or Belfast City Airport.
Belfast, Maine, U.S.A.: 44.25 N. 69.00 W. **60**
Belfast Lough, U.K. **5, 6**
BELGIUM **4, 7, 8, 9**
Belgorod-Dnestrovsky, Ukraine: 46.12 N. 30.21 E. **9, 26**
 Max. Size: Draft up to 4.5 m. *Fuel:* Diesel.
Belgrade, Serbia, Yugoslavia: 44.50 N. 20.30 E. **9**
Belgrano, see Bahia Blanca.
Belhaven, North Carolina, U.S.A.: 35.36 N. 76.36 W. **63**
Belida Marine Terminal, Indonesia: 4.08 N. 105.08 E. . **38, 39, 40**
 Max. Size: 50,000 – 230,000 tonnes d.w.t., depth 250 ft.
Belinyu, Indonesia: 1.38 S. 105.47 E. **38**
Belitung I., see Tanjung Pandan.
Belize, Belize: 17.29 N. 88.11 W. **55, 69**
 Max. Size: Anchorage Port. Tankers: Draft 19 ft. 6 in.
 Fuel: Light diesel. *Airport:* International, 10 miles.
BELIZE **69**

Bell Bay, Tas., Australia: 41.08 S. 146.51 E. **51**
 Max. Size: Depth 12.4 m. Inspection Head, depth 9.9 m.
 Beauty Point, depth 9.7 m. Long Reach, depth 12.3 m.
 Also see Launceston.
Bell Is., Newfoundland, Canada: 50.45 N. 55.34 W. **60**
Bella Coola, B.C., Canada: 52.23 N. 126.48 W. **56**
Bellabella, B.C., Canada: 52.10 N. 128.09 W. **56**
Belle Chase, see Braithwaite.
Belle Fontaine, see Fort de France.
Belle Ile, France: 47.20 N. 3.10 W. **19**
Belle Isle, Newfoundland, Canada: 51.56 N. 55.19 W. . . . **59, 60**
Belle Isle Strait, Newfoundland, Canada **60**
Belledune, N.B., Canada: 47.55 N. 65.50 W. **60**
 Max. Size: 80,000 d.w.t. LOA 289.5 m., beam 32.3 m.,
 draft 12.65 m. *Fuel:* By road tanker. *Airport:* Bathurst, 35 km.
Belleoram, Newfoundland, Canada: 47.31 N. 55.25 W. **60**
Belleville, Ontario, Canada: 44.09 N. 77.24 W. **62**
Bellin, Quebec, Canada: 60.05 N. 70.00 W. **59**
Bellingham, Washington, U.S.A.: 48.45 N. 122.31 W. . . . **55, 56**
 Max. Size: Depth 25 ft. – 31 ft. MLLW. Tankers: See Cherry
 Point. *Fuel:* By barge. *Dry Docks:* Max. 2,800 tons. *Airport:*
 3 miles.
Bellport, see Newport.
Belmullet, Ireland: 54.13 N. 9.59 W. **5**
Belo, see Porto Belo.
Belomorsk, Russia: 64.32 N. 34.48 E. **16**
Belwaarde, see Paramaribo.
Belyy Is., Russia: 73.15 N. 71.00 E. **16**
Ben Nghe, see Ho Chi Minh City.
Ben Thuy, see Nghe Tinh.
Benbecula, U.K.: 57.25 N. 7.20 W. **5**
Benchamas Terminal, Thailand: 10.32 N. 101.16 E. **39**
 Max. Size: 110,000 tonnes d.w.t., depth 70 m.
Bender Beila, Somalia: 9.32 N. 50.47 E. **31**
Benghazi, Libya: 32.06 N. 20.03 E. **21, 24**
 Max. Size: 28 ft. draft (Summer), 27 ft. (Winter).
 Tankers: Ras al Mingar – 10,000 tonnes d.w.t., draft 21 ft.
 (Winter), 22 ft. (Summer), LOA 120 m. *Fuel:* Available.
 Airport: Benina, 29 km.
Bengkalis, Indonesia: 1.28 N. 102.06 E. **38, 39, 40**
Bengkulu, Indonesia: 3.46 N. 102.16 E. **38**
 Max. Size: Draft 9.0 m., 12,000 d.w.t. *Fuel:* Available.
Benguela, Angola: 12.35 S. 13.25 E. **28**
Beni Enzar, see Port Nador.
Beni Saf, Algeria: 35.18 N. 1.24 W. **22**
Benicia, California, U.S.A.: 38.03 N. 122.10 W. **55, 58**
 Max. Size: LOA 1,055 ft., depth 38 ft. *Fuel:* By barge.
Benidorm, Spain: 38.35 N. 0.10 W. **22**
BENIN **28, 29**
Benito, see Rio Benito.
Benoa, Indonesia: 8.45 S. 115.13 E. **38**
 Max. Size: Depth 6.0 m. *Fuel:* High speed diesel.
Benteng, Indonesia: 6.08 S. 120.29 E. **46**
Bentinck Is., Qld., Australia: 17.00 S. 139.35 E. **50**
Beo, (Talaud Is.), Indonesia: 4.14 N. 126.48 E. **46, 47**
Beppu, Japan: 33.16 N. 131.30 E. **45**
Berbera, Somalia: 10.26 N. 45.01 E. **31**
 Max. Size: Draft 28 ft. *Airport:* 5 miles (flights to Djibouti).
Berbice, see New Amsterdam.
Berdyansk, Ukraine: 46.45 N. 36.47 E. **21, 26**
 Max. Size: Draft 7.9 m., LOA 205 m. – 225 m. *Fuel:* Limited
 quantities. *Airport:* Internal, 15 km.
Berenice, Egypt: 23.56 N. 35.29 E. **32**
Bergen, Norway: 60.24 N. 5.19 E. **4, 5, 10, 11, 79**
 Max. Size: Draft 35 m. Up to 100,000 tons.
 Tankers: 30,000 d.w.t., draft 30 ft. *Fuel:* All grades.
 Dry Docks: 1 dry dock, 365 ft. long. Floating dock 20,000 d.w.t.
 Airport: Flesland, 12 miles.
Bergen Op Zoom, Netherlands: 51.30 N. 4.17 E. **8**
Bergkvara, Sweden: 56.23 N. 16.05 E. **11**
 Max. Size: LOA 150 m., draft 5.5 m. *Airport:* Kalmar, 40 km.
Bergs Harbour, see Stockholm.
Bering Is., (Komandorski Is.), Russia: **54**
Bering Sea **36, 53, 54**
Bering Strait, Russia/U.S.A. **54, 79**
Beringovskiy, Russia: 63.02 N. 179.20 E. **54**
Berkeley, see San Francisco.
Berlevag, Norway: 70.51 N. 29.06 E. **15, 16**
Berlin, Germany: 52.32 N. 13.25 E. **9**
Bermagui, N.S.W., Australia: 36.25 S. 150.02 E. **50**
Bermeo, Spain: 43.25 N. 2.43 W. **19**
 Max. Size: LOA 110 m., beam 20.0 m., draft 6.0 m.
 Fuel: Gas oil. *Airport:* Bilbao, 28 km.
Bermuda (U.K.) **63**
Berne, Switzerland: 46.57 N. 7.26 E. **9**
Berner's Bay, see Juneau.
Berre, France: 43.25 N. 5.10 E. **22, 23**
 Max. Size: LOA 160 m., beam 24 m., draft 7.0 m.
 Also see Port de Bouc.
Berry Is., Bahamas: 25.28 N. 77.45 W. **70**

THE SHIPS ATLAS

Berrys Bay, see Sydney.
Beru Is., Kiribati: 1.19 S. 176.01 E. ... 49
Berwick upon Tweed, U.K.: 55.46 N. 1.59 W. ... 5
  Max. Size: LOA 115 m. (if fitted with bow thruster), 70 m. (no bow thruster), draft 4.6 m. *Fuel:* By road tanker. *Airport:* Newcastle or Edinburgh, both 60 miles.
Betanzos, Spain: 43.16 N. 8.13 W. ... 19, 20
Bethel, Alaska, U.S.A.: 60.50 N. 161.45 W. ... 54
Betio, see Tarawa.
Beverley, Massachusetts, U.S.A.: 42.32 N. 70.53 W. ... 63
Beverwijk, Netherlands: 52.29 N. 4.38 E. ... 8
Beykoz, Turkey: 41.08 N. 29.06 E. ... 23
Beyoglu, see Istanbul.
Beyonesu Is., Japan: 31.52 N. 139.55 E. ... 46
Beypore, India: 11.08 N. 75.52 E. ... 37
  Max. Size: LOA 100 m., beam 12.0 m., draft 4.0 m. *Fuel:* HSD by truck.
Beyrouth, see Beirut.
Beziers, France: 43.21 N. 3.13 E. ... 9
Bhatkal, India: 14.00 N. 74.35 E. ... 37
Bhavnagar, India: 21.47 N. 72.08 E. ... 37
  Max. Size: Anchorage: Depth 35 ft. *Fuel:* Available. *Airport:* 7 km., connects with Mumbai.
Bheemunipatnam, India: 17.54 N. 83.30 E. ... 37
Biak, Indonesia: 1.11 S. 136.05 E. ... 46
  Max. Size: 40,000 d.w.t., LOA 205 m., draft 7.2 m. Depth alongside: 8 m. – 13 m. *Fuel:* Limited quantities. *Airport:* 4 km.
Biak Is., Indonesia ... 46
Bianco, Italy: 38.05 N. 16.10 E. ... 24
Biarritz, France: 43.30 N. 1.35 W. ... 19
Bic, Quebec, Canada: 48.22 N. 68.44 W. ... 60
Bicheno, Tas., Australia: 41.50 S. 148.15 E. ... 50, 51
Bideford, U.K.: 51.01 N. 4.13 W. ... 6, 19
  Max. Size: LOA 82 m., beam 12 m., airdraft 24 m., draft – depending on tide. *Fuel:* By road tanker. *Airport:* Exeter, 40 miles.
Big Is., see Lake Harbour.
Bights:
  Bight of Bangkok, Thailand ... 39
  Bight of Benin ... 29
  Bight of Bonny ... 29
Bijagos Archipelago, Guinea-Bissau: 12.00 N. 16.00 W. ... 27
Bikar, Marshall Is.: 12.20 N. 170.10 E. ... 49
Bikini Is., Marshall Is.: 11.30 N. 165.30 E. ... 49
Bilbao, Spain: 43.17 N. 2.55 W. ... 19, 21, 22
  Max. Size: Draft 6.0 m. – 14.5 m. Tankers: Draft up to 32 m. Largest vessel 409,499 d.w.t., LOA 378.01 m. and draft 22.48 m. *Fuel:* Available. *Dry Docks:* 146 m. x 21.8 m. / 170 m. x 19 m. / 130 m. x 23 m. *Airport:* Sondica, 6 km., international.
Bildudalur, Iceland: 65.41 N. 23.36 W. ... 17
Billingham, see Middlesbrough.
Biloxi, Mississippi, U.S.A.: 30.24 N. 88.53 W. ... 66, 67
Bima, Indonesia: 8.25 S. 118.42 E. ... 38, 46
  Max. Size: Anchorage Port. *Airport:* Bima.
Bima Marine Terminal, Indonesia: 5.46 N. 107.04 E. ... 38
  Max. Size: 250,000 d.w.t.
Bimini Is., Bahamas: 25.44 N. 79.17 W. ... 66, 69
Bimlipatam, see Bheemunipatnam.
Bing Bong, N.T., Australia: 15.21 S. 136.30 E. ... 50
  Max. Size: Draft 5 m.
Binh Tri, Vietnam: 10.12 N. 104.35 E. ... 39
  Max. Size: LOA 145 m., draft 7.8 m. *Airport:* Rach Soi, 90 km.
  Also see Hon Chong.
Binic, France: 48.36 N. 2.49 W. ... 7, 19
Binnenhafen, see Kiel.
Bintangor, Sarawak, Malaysia: 2.10 N. 111.38 E. ... 39
  Max. Size: Depth 4.6 m.
  Also see Sibu.
Bintulu, Sarawak, Malaysia: 3.16 N. 112.59 E. ... 38, 39
  Max. Size: Depths: General cargo 10.5 m., Bulk cargo 13.5 m., LNG 15 m. and Tanker berth 13.5 m. *Fuel:* High speed diesel available. *Airport:* 20 km.
Bintulu Terminal, Sarawak, Malaysia: 3.20 N. 113.01 E. ... 38, 39
  Max. Size: 350,000 tonnes (SDWT), draft 52 ft. *Fuel:* Limited supply.
Bioco Is., Equatorial Guinea ... 28
Bioco Macias Ngueme (Fernando Poo), Equatorial Guinea. ... 29
Bir Shalatein, Egypt: 23.05 N. 35.26 E. ... 32
Bira, Indonesia: 2.00 S. 132.00 E. ... 46
Bird Is., N.T., Australia: 22.10 N. 155.28 E. ... 50
Biringkasi, Indonesia: 4.49 S. 119.29 E. ... 38, 46
  Max. Size: Depth 7.0 m.
Birkenhead, U.K.: 53.24 N. 3.01 W. ... 6, 7
  Max. Size: Draft 8.68 m. Tranmere: Draft 12.5 m.
  Also see Liverpool.
Birnie Is., (Phoenix Is.), Kiribati: 3.31 S. 171.40 W. ... 49
Bishop Rock, U.K.: 49.53 N. 6.27 W. ... 19
Bislig, (Mindanao Is.), Philippines: 8.14 N. 126.22 E. ... 46, 47
  Max. Size: Depth 30 ft. *Fuel:* Small quantities. *Airport:* 5 km.

Bismarck Sea, Papua New Guinea ... 46
Bissau, Guinea-Bissau: 11.51 N. 15.34 W. ... 27
  Max. Size: Draft 10 m. *Fuel:* Diesel. *Airport:* 7 km.
Bitter Lakes, Suez Canal, Egypt ... 26, 33
Bitung, Indonesia: 1.26 N. 125.11 E. ... 46
  Max. Size: Draft 12.0 m. *Fuel:* Available. *Airport:* 25 km.
Bizerte, Tunisia: 37.16 N. 9.53 E. ... 21, 24
  Max. Size: Depth 10.67 m. Tankers: Draft 35 ft. *Fuel:* Available. *Dry Docks:* Length 247.50 m., width 40.60 m., draft 12 m. *Airport:* Tunis, 60 km.
Bjorkanas, see Gustavsvik.
Bjorneborg, see Pori.
Black Bay, Ontario, Canada ... 62, 67
Black Cape, Quebec, Canada: 48.08 N. 65.50 W. ... 60
  Also see New Richmond.
Black Sea ... 9, 21, 23, 25, 26
Blacktoft, U.K.: 53.42 N. 0.43 W. ... 6
Blagopoluchiya, Russia: 65.01 N. 35.42 E. ... 16
Blaine, Washington, U.S.A.: 49.00 N. 122.45 W. ... 56
Blair, see Port Blair.
Blanc Sablon, Quebec, Canada: 51.25 N. 57.10 W. ... 59, 60
Blanche Harbour, Solomon Islands: 7.26 S. 155.33 E. ... 49
Blandford, see Port Blandford.
Blanes, Spain: 41.40 N. 2.48 E. ... 22
Blang Lancang, see Lhokseumawe.
Blankaholm, Sweden: 57.35 N. 16.31 E. ... 11
Blankenberge, Belgium: 51.19 N. 3.07 E. ... 7
Blanquilla Is., Venezuela: 11.51 N. 64.37 W. ... 69, 71
Blaye, France: 45.08 N. 0.40 W. ... 8, 19
  Max. Size: Draft 30 ft.
  Also see Bordeaux.
Blenheim, New Zealand: 41.40 S. 174.05 E. ... 52
Blexen, see Bremerhaven.
Blind River, Ontario, Canada: 46.11 N. 82.56 W. ... 62
Block Is., Rhode Is., U.S.A.: 41.15 N. 71.33 W. ... 60, 63
Bloody Foreland, Ireland: 55.09 N. 8.17 W. ... 5
Blount Is., see Jacksonville.
Blowing Point, Anguilla (U.K.): 18.10 N. 63.05 W. ... 71
  Max. Size: 4,000 d.w.t., draft 15 ft. Tankers: Depth 30 ft. *Fuel:* Available. *Airport:* 3 miles.
Blue Cavern Point, California, U.S.A.: 33.27 N. 118.33 W. ... 58
Blue Hill, (Providenciales), Turks and Caicos Is. (U.K.): 21.36 N. 72.22 W. ... 70
Bluefields, Jamaica, see Savanna la Mar.
Bluefields, Nicaragua: 12.00 N. 83.45 W. ... 69
Bluff, New Zealand: 46.37 S. 168.22 E. ... 52
  Max. Size: LOA 200 m., beam 34 m., draft 9.7 m. – 10.0 m. at HW or 225 m. x 33 m. with reduced draft. *Fuel:* Available. *Airport:* 16 miles, connects with Auckland.
Bluff, Alaska, U.S.A.: 64.25 N. 163.50 W. ... 54
Bluff Point, W.A., Australia: 27.50 S. 114.05 E. ... 50, 58
Blyth, U.K.: 55.08 N. 1.30 W. ... 5, 6
  Max. Size: Bulk carriers 22,500 d.w.t., draft 9.8 m., LOA 190 m. Other berths, LOA 190 m., draft 8.5 m. *Airport:* 24 km.
Bo'ness, U.K.: 56.01 N. 3.36 W. ... 6
Boa Vista Is., Cape Verde ... 27
Boca Chica, Dominican Republic: 18.27 N. 69.35 W. ... 70
  Max. Size: LOA 400 ft., draft 25 ft. *Fuel:* By truck from Santo Domingo. *Airport:* Santo Domingo, 5 miles.
Boca del Pao, Venezuela: 8.05 N. 64.25 W. ... 75
Boca Grande, Cuba: 21.33 N. 78.40 W. ... 70
  Max. Size: Anchorage: Depth 24 ft. – 30 ft.
  Also see Jucaro.
Boca Grande, Florida, U.S.A.: 26.43 N. 82.15 W. ... 55, 66, 69, 70
  Max. Size: LOA 700 ft., beam 80 ft., draft 30 ft. *Fuel:* No local facilities.
Bocas del Toro, Panama: 9.21 N. 82.14 W. ... 69
  Max. Size: Draft 8.84 m.
  Also see Almirante.
Boda, Sweden: 57.15 N. 17.05 E. ... 11
Boddam, see Salomon Is..
Bodega Bay, California, U.S.A.: 38.20 N. 123.05 W. ... 57, 58
Bodo, Norway: 67.17 N. 14.24 E. ... 10, 15
  Max. Size: Draft 22 ft. Tankers: 18,000 tons, draft 32 ft. Fish Quay: Depth 3.5 m. – 12.5 m. *Fuel:* All grades. *Airport:* 2 km.
Bodrum, Turkey: 37.02 N. 27.28 E. ... 25, 26
Bogense, Denmark: 55.34 N. 10.05 E. ... 12
Boghaz, see Kalecik.
Bogo, (Cebu Is.), Philippines: 11.03 N. 124.01 E. ... 47
Bogorodskoye, Russia: 52.20 N. 140.30 E. ... 43
Bohavan, see Sandakan.
Bohol I., Philippines ... 46, 47
Bois Blanc I., Michigan, U.S.A.: 45.47 N. 84.27 W. ... 62
Boke, Guinea: 10.56 N. 14.21 W. ... 27
Bokfjord, see Kirkenes.
Bokna Fjord, Norway ... 10
Bolama, Guinea-Bissau: 11.35 N. 15.28 W. ... 27
Bolderaja, Latvia: 57.02 N. 24.03 E. ... 11
Bolinao, (Luzon Is.), Philippines: 16.23 N. 119.55 E. ... 47

Bolinas, California, U.S.A.: 37.50 N. 122.42 W. 58
Bolinas Bay, California, U.S.A. 58
Bolivar, Colombia, see Puerto Bolivar.
Bolivar, U.S.A., see Port Bolivar.
BOLIVIA 72, 77
Bollsta, see Kramfors.
Boma, Congo (D.R. of): 5.51 S. 13.03 E. 28
   Max. Size: Draft 20 ft. to 27 ft. according to local conditions for
   river transit. Depth alongside 24 ft.
Bombay, see Mumbai.
Bonaberi, see Douala.
Bonaire, Netherlands Antilles 69, 74
Bonaire Terminal, Netherlands Antilles: 12.13 N. 68.23 W. . . . 74
   Max. Size: 500,000 d.w.t., depth 110 ft. *Fuel:* Small quantities.
Bonanza, see Sanlucar de Barameda.
Bonavista, Newfoundland, Canada: 48.40 N. 53.07 W. 60
Bone, see Annaba.
Bongabong, (Mindoro Is.), Philippines: 12.45 N. 121.29 E. . . . 47
Bongkot Terminal, Thailand: 8.03 N. 102.20 E. 39
   Max. Size: 40,000 tonnes d.w.t., depth 80 m.
Bonifacio, (Corsica), France: 41.23 N. 9.10 E. 24
Bonin Is., Japan 46
Bonn, Germany: 50.44 N. 7.06 E. 7, 9
Bonny, Nigeria: 4.25 N. 7.08 E. 29
   Max. Size: SPM: 350,000 tonnes d.w.t., length no restriction,
   beam no restriction, draft 22.8 m. (75 ft.). Gas: 85,000 cu.m.
   Condensate: 120,000 d.w.t. *Airport:* Port Harcourt, 30 km.
Bono Bono, (Palawan Is.), Philippines: 8.45 N. 117.20 E. . . . 47
Bonsu Terminal, see Saltpond.
Bontang, Indonesia: 0.11 N. 117.12 E. 38
   Max. Size: 20,000 d.w.t. Depth alongside 13 m.
   LNG: LOA 300 m., 125,000 cu.m., depth 13.5 m.
   Fuel: Available. *Airport:* Samarinda.
Bonthain, Indonesia: 5.33 S. 119.56 E. 46
Bonthe, see Sherbro.
Boom, Belgium: 51.05 N. 4.21 E. 7
Boothby Harbour, Maine, U.S.A.: 43.51 N. 69.39 W. 60
Boqueron, see Caimanera.
Bora Bora, (Society Is.), French Polynesia (France):
   16.31 S. 151.45 W. 49
   Max. Size: LOA 220 m., beam 30 m., draft 9 m.
   Airport: Inter-island, 7 km.
Borbon, (Cebu Is.), Philippines: 10.50 N. 124.02 E. 47
Borburata, see Puerto Cabello.
Bordeaux, France: 44.50 N. 0.34 W. 8, 19, 21
   Max. Size: Verdon: Draft 12.5 m. Tankers: 10 m.
   Fuel: All grades. *Dry Docks:* Length 247 m., width 34 m.,
   depth 13.40 m. *Airport:* 10 km.
Bordighera, Italy: 43.47 N. 7.40 E. 23
Borg, see Fredrikstad.
Borga, see Porvoo.
Borgarnes, Iceland: 64.32 N. 21.55 W. 17
Borghi, Argentina: 32.48 S. 60.37 W. 78
Borgholm, Sweden: 56.53 N. 16.39 E. 11
Bories, see Puerto Natales.
Borj Islam, Syria: 35.40 N. 35.48 E. 26
   Max. Size: Anchorage depth 11 m. – 40 m.
Borkum, Germany: 53.35 N. 6.39 E. 7, 8
Borneo, Indonesia 38, 39, 46
Bornholm, Denmark: 55.05 N. 14.45 E. 10, 11, 12
Borongan, (Samar Is.), Philippines: 11.36 N. 125.26 E. 47
Borsele, Netherlands: 51.25 N. 3.44 E. 8
Borusan, Turkey: 40.25 N. 29.05 E. 25
   Max. Size: LOA 165 m., depth 6 m. – 9 m.
   Fuel: By road tanker. *Airport:* At Bursa, 32 km.
Bosa, (Sardinia), Italy: 40.16 N. 8.32 E. 24
Bosaso, Somalia: 11.16 N. 49.18 E. 31
BOSNIA-HERZEGOVINA 9, 21, 24
Bosporus, Turkey: 41.01 N. 28.58 E. 23, 25, 26
Boston, U.K.: 52.58 N. 0.01 W. 5, 7
   Max. Size: 4,500 d.w.t., LOA 119 m. Depth of lock sill 5.4
   m. – 7.5 m. *Fuel:* By road tanker.
Boston, Massachusetts, U.S.A.: 42.21 N. 71.05 W. . . . 55, 60, 63
   Max. Size: Primary entrance controlling depth is 35 ft. MLW.
   Tankers: Depth 32 ft. – 42 ft. MLW. Chelsea Creek: LOA 661 ft.,
   beam 90 ft., draft 36 ft. HW. *Fuel:* All grades.
   Dry Docks: Length 479 ft., capacity 20,000 tons. Length 622 ft.,
   capacity 18,000 tons. *Airport:* Logan International.
Botany Bay, N.S.W., Australia: 34.00 S. 151.14 E. 50
   Max. Size: Tankers: LOA 254 m., draft 11.6 m. or LOA 256 m.,
   draft 14 m., 90,000 d.w.t. Container: Depth 14.8 m.
   Fuel: Marine fuel and diesel oil. *Airport:* International, 6 km.
Botas, Turkey: 36.53 N. 35.56 E. 26
   Max. Size: 300,000 d.w.t. at outer berths. Toros Gubre:
   100,000 d.w.t. Delta: 40,000 d.w.t. Aygas: 80,000 d.w.t.
   Dortyol: 60,000 d.w.t. *Fuel:* Available at 48 hours notice.
   Airport: Adana Airport 75 km., connects with Istanbul.
Botea, Sweden: 63.05 N. 17.50 E. 15
BOTSWANA 28, 30

Botwood, Newfoundland, Canada: 49.09 N. 55.20 W. 60
   Max. Size: Up to 32 ft. draft. *Fuel:* By road tanker.
   Airport: Gander International, 86 km.
Bouc, see Port de Bouc.
Boucau, France: 43.31 N. 1.29 W. 19
Boudreau Bay, Louisiana, U.S.A. 67
Bouet, see Abidjan.
Bougainville Is., Papua New Guinea 49
Bougie, see Bejaia.
Boulari, see Noumea.
Boulogne-sur-Mer, France: 50.43 N. 1.35 E. 5, 7
   Max. Size: LOA 230 m., draft 11 m. (neaps),
   35,000 d.w.t. (approx.). *Fuel:* Tanker lorry from Dunkirk.
   Airport: Le Touquet, 50 km.
Bounty Is., New Zealand: 47.42 S. 179.03 E. 52
Bourgas, Bulgaria: 42.30 N. 27.29 E. 9, 21, 26
   Max. Size: Draft: General cargo 10 m., bulk 11 m. and tankers
   12.65 m. *Fuel:* Diesel and gas oil. *Airport:* International.
Bouri, Libya: 33.54 N. 12.39 E. 24
   Max. Size: 150,000 d.w.t., LOA 283 m., beam 44 m. and draft
   no limit. *Fuel:* Available in emergency only.
Bovallstrand, Sweden: 58.29 N. 11.19 E. 12
Bowen, Qld., Australia: 20.01 S. 148.15 E. 50, 51
   Port closed.
Bowling, U.K.: 55.56 N. 4.29 W. 6
   Max. Size: Draft 6.5 m.
   Also see Clyde Port.
Bowmore, U.K.: 55.45 N. 6.17 W. 5
Bozca Ada, Turkey: 39.50 N. 26.06 E. 25
Brac Is., Croatia 24
Braefoot Bay, U.K.: 56.02 N. 3.19 W. 6
   Max. Size: Channel depth 8.5 m. Depth alongside
   10 m. – 15 m. *Fuel:* At anchorage. *Airport:* Edinburgh,
   30 miles.
Braganca, Brazil: 1.05 S. 47.02 W. 72
Braganza Bay, (Spitsbergen), Norway 17
Brahestad, see Raahe.
Braila, Romania: 45.15 N. 27.59 E. 9, 26
   Max. Size: 9,000 d.w.t., draft 7.01 m. *Fuel:* By road tanker.
   Airport: Bucharest, 300 km.
Braithwaite, Louisiana, U.S.A.: 29.52 N. 89.57 W. 67
Brake, Germany: 53.20 N. 8.29 E. 8, 12, 14
   Max. Size: LOA 275 m., draft 39 ft. fresh water.
   Tankers: Draft 33 ft. *Fuel:* All grades by barge.
   Dry Docks: Max. LOA 85 m. (279 ft.), breadth 16 m. (52 ft. 6 in.),
   draft 13 ft. 1 in. *Airport:* Bremen, 57 km.
Braniewo, Poland: 54.20 N. 19.50 E. 11
Brannfors, see Byske.
Branolao, see Lisbon.
Brasil, see Bonaire Terminal.
Brass River, Nigeria: 4.19 N. 6.14 E. 29
Brass Terminal, Nigeria: 4.04 N. 6.17 E. 29
   Max. Size: 250,000 d.w.t. – 300,000 d.w.t., depending on
   season.
Bratislava, Slovakia: 48.10 N. 17.10 E. 9
Brava, Somalia: 1.06 N. 44.03 E. 31
Brava Is., Cape Verde: 14.50 N. 24.45 W. 27
Braviken, Sweden: 58.38 N. 16.16 E. 11
   Max. Size: Depth 8.8 m. (MLW).
   Also see Norrkoping.
BRAZIL 69, 72, 76, 77
Brazos Island Harbour, see Brownsville.
Brazzaville, Congo (Rep. of): 4.10 S. 15.10 E. 28
Brega, see Marsa el Brega.
Breiholz, Germany: 54.12 N. 9.32 E. 14
   Also see Kiel.
Brekstad, Norway: 63.30 N. 9.45 E. 15
Bremen, Germany: 53.06 N. 8.46 E. 8, 9, 10, 11, 12, 14
   Max. Size: LOA 230 m., draft 9.45 m., in F.W. *Fuel:* All grades
   by barge. *Airport:* International.
Bremerhaven, Germany: 53.33 N. 8.35 E. 4, 8, 10, 11, 12, 14
   Max. Size: LOA 350 m., draft 42 ft. 8 in. in fresh water. *Fuel:*
   All grades. *Dry Docks:* Capacity 75,000 tons.
   Airport: Bremen, 40 miles.
Bremerton, Washington, U.S.A.: 47.34 N. 122.40 W. 56
Bressay Is., (Shetland Is.), U.K.: 60.08 N. 1.05 W. 5
Brest, France: 48.24 N. 4.30 W. 4, 7, 19
   Max. Size: Inside harbour: LOA 320 m., draft up to 35 ft.
   Fuel: All grades. *Dry Docks:* Dimensions 420 m. by 80 m. Can
   accept 550,000 d.w.t. vessels. *Airport:* Guipavas, 7 km.
Breton Is., Louisiana, U.S.A. 67
Breton Sound, (Mississippi Delta), Louisiana, U.S.A. 67
Breves, Brazil: 1.39 S. 50.30 W. 72
   Max. Size: Depth 5.0 m. – 6.0 m. (LW).
Brevik, Norway: 59.03 N. 9.43 E. 8, 10, 11, 12
   Max. Size: LOA 600 ft., draft 34 ft.Coal: LOA 900 ft., draft 46 ft.
   Tankers: LOA 600 ft., beam 85 ft., draft 34 ft. *Fuel:* All grades.
   Airport: Oslo, 100 miles.
Brewer, see Bangor.

Bridgeport, Connecticut, U.S.A.: 41.07 N. 73.11 W. **55, 63**
Max. Size: 70,000 d.w.t. LOA 825 ft., draft 37 ft. (HW). Tankers: LOA 700 ft., depth 38 ft. MLW. *Fuel:* Available at tanker berth only. *Airport:* 3 miles.

Bridgetown, Barbados: 13.06 N. 59.38 W. **69, 71, 72**
Max. Size: LOA 293 m., draft 9.6 m. Tankers: Draft 11.6 m. *Fuel:* All grades. *Dry Docks:* 73.15 m. x 14.02 m. x 3.96 m. *Airport:* 13 miles.

Bridgewater, N.S., Canada: 44.23 N. 64.31 W. **60**
Max. Size: LOA 325 ft., draft 20 ft. *Fuel:* Diesel and gasoline. *Airport:* Halifax, 90 miles.

Bridgwater, U.K.: 51.10 N. 3.00 W. **6**
Max. Size: LOA 72 m. – 84 m. *Fuel:* By road tanker. *Airport:* Bristol.

Bridlington, U.K.: 54.05 N. 0.12 W. **5**
Max. Size: Fishing vessels only. *Fuel:* All grades. *Airport:* Yeadon, 65 miles. Humberside, 50 miles.

Bridport, Tas., Australia: 41.00 S. 147.24 E. **51**

Bridport, U.K.: 50.43 N. 2.46 W. **5, 7**

Brier Is., see Westport.

Briera, see Port Briera.

Brightlingsea, U.K.: 51.48 N. 1.02 E. **5, 7**
Max. Size: 3,500 tonnes d.w.t., LOA 110 m., draft 5.2 m. *Fuel:* By road tanker. *Airport:* Stansted, 40 miles.

Brighton, Trinidad and Tobago: 10.14 N. 61.37 W. **71**
Max. Size: 15,000 d.w.t., LOA 110 m.

Brighton, U.K.: 50.49 N. 0.07 W. **5, 7**

Brignogan, France: 48.40 N. 4.20 W. **7, 19**

Brindisi, Italy: 40.39 N. 17.56 E. **21, 24**
Max. Size: Inner Harbour: Draft 9.4 m. (30 ft. 10 in.). Offshore Terminal: Draft 11.50 m. (37 ft. 8 in.). *Fuel:* Bunker "C" and gas oil. *Airport:* 5 km.

Brisbane, Qld., Australia: 27.27 S. 153.04 E. **49, 50**
Max. Size: Water line length in river 250 m. at draft 9.7 m. Draft at HWOST for tankers 12.2 m., for cargo vessels 9.7 m. and for bulk carriers 13.2 m. (downstream of Pelican Bank). *Fuel:* Distillate diesel fuel or fuel oil. *Dry Docks:* Capacity 85,000 tonnes. *Airport:* International.

Bristol, U.K.: 51.28 N. 2.35 W. **4, 6, 7**
Max. Size: Avonmouth: LOA 300 m., beam 41.5 m., draft 14.5 m. *Fuel:* Most grades. *Dry Docks:* Length 875 ft., width 100 ft., depth on sill 32 ft. *Airport:* 12 miles, connects with London Heathrow, etc.

Bristol, Pennsylvania, U.S.A.: 40.06 N. 74.51 W. **63, 65**

Bristol, Rhode Is., U.S.A.: 41.40 N. 71.16 W. **63**

Bristol Bay, Alaska, U.S.A. **54**

Bristol Channel, U.K. **5, 6, 7**

Britannia Beach, see Squamish.

British Columbia, Canada **56**

Briton Ferry, U.K.: 51.37 N. 3.49 W. **6**
Also see Neath.

Britt, Ontario, Canada: 45.45 N. 80.35 W. **62**

Brixham, U.K.: 50.24 N. 3.30 W. **5, 7, 19**
Max. Size: LOA 500 ft., draft 26 ft. *Fuel:* Available. *Airport:* Exeter, 35 miles.

Broadford, U.K.: 57.15 N. 5.54 W. **5**

Brockville, Ontario, Canada: 44.36 N. 75.40 W. **61**

Brodick, U.K.: 55.34 N. 5.09 W. **6**

Brofjorden, Sweden: 58.21 N. 11.25 E. **11, 12**
Max. Size: Crude Oil Jetty: 500,000 d.w.t., draft 25 m. Product Jetty: 50,000 d.w.t., draft 14.4 m. *Fuel:* Available. *Airport:* Gothenburg, 100 km. Also see Solvesborg.

Bromarv, Finland: 60.00 N. 23.02 E. **11**

Bromborough Dock, see Manchester.

Bronnoysund, Norway: 65.30 N. 12.13 E. **10, 15**
Max. Size: Inner: Depth 18 ft. – 24 ft. Outer: Depth 60 ft. *Fuel:* Delivered to all berths. *Airport:* 2 km.

Bronx, New York, U.S.A.: 40.50 N. 73.50 W. **63**

Brookes Is., California, U.S.A.: 37.53 N. 122.20 W. **58**

Brookings, Oregon, U.S.A.: 42.04 N. 124.15 W. **56, 57**

Brooklyn, New York, U.S.A.: 40.41 N. 74.01 W. **63**
Also see New York.

Brooklyn Marine Terminal, see New York.

Broome, W.A., Australia: 17.59 S. 122.14 E. **50, 51**
Max. Size: Draft 9.15 m. *Fuel:* Diesel, prior notice required. *Airport:* Connects with Perth.

Brora, U.K.: 58.01 N. 3.45 W. **5**

Brough, U.K.: 53.43 N. 0.35 W. **6**

Brouwershaven, Netherlands: 51.45 N. 3.55 E. **7, 8**

Brownsville, Texas, U.S.A.: 25.54 N. 97.28 W. **55, 66, 69**
Max. Size: LOA 875 ft., beam 135 ft., draft 35 ft. Tankers: Draft 42 ft. *Fuel:* No fuel locally. Must be barged from Corpus Christi. *Airport:* International, 5 miles.

Bruce Mines, Ontario, Canada: 46.17 N. 83.47 W. **62**

Bruges, Belgium: 51.13 N. 3.13 E. **7, 8**
Max. Size: Beam 19 m., draft 6.75 m. *Airport:* Ostend, 30 km. Brussels, 120 km. Also see Zeebrugge.

Bruja Point, Panama: 8.53 N. 79.35 W. **73**

BRUNEI DARUSSALAM **38, 39, 47**

Brunsbuttel, Germany: 53.53 N. 9.09 E. **8, 11, 12, 14**
Max. Size: Dimensions of Lock: Length 310 m., beam 42 m. Canal: Up to 235 m. LOA and 32.5 m. beam. Tankers: LOA 400 m., draft 14.8 m. *Fuel:* All grades. *Airport:* Hamburg, 90 km.

Brunswick, Georgia, U.S.A.: 31.09 N. 81.30 W. **55, 66**
Max. Size: LOA 650 ft., draft 28 ft. – 34 ft. *Fuel:* Bunker "C" at piers, others by barge. *Airport:* 20 minutes drive.

Brusnitchnoe, see Saimaa Canal.

Brussels, Belgium: 50.51 N. 4.22 E. **7, 9**
Max. Size: LOA 393 ft. 8 in., extreme breadth 50 ft. 10 in., draft 19 ft., airdraft 98 ft. *Fuel:* All grades. *Airport:* International.

Bryher Is., (Scilly Is.), U.K.: 49.57 N. 6.21 W. **19**

Buatan, Indonesia: 0.45 N. 101.50 E. **38, 39, 40**
Max. Size: LOA 110 m. 5,000 d.w.t. Depth alongside 6.5 m. *Airport:* At Pekanbaru.

Bubaque, Guinea-Bissau: 11.10 N. 15.55 W. **27**

Bubiyan Is., Kuwait: 29.50 N. 48.15 E. **35**

Buchanan, Liberia: 5.52 N. 10.02 W. **27, 28**
Max. Size: Tankers: Draft 27 ft. Bulk: Depth 14 m. below zero. *Airport:* Roberts International, 1 hour.

Bucharest, Romania: 44.27 N. 25.30 E. **9, 26**

Buchas, see Lisbon.

Buckhaven, see Methil.

Buckie, U.K.: 57.41 N. 2.57 W. **5**
Max. Size: LOA 82 m., beam 12 m., draft 4.5 m. (HW). *Fuel:* Available. *Airport:* Aberdeen 55 miles.

Buckner Bay, see Nishihara.

Bucksport, Maine, U.S.A.: 44.35 N. 68.48 W. **60**
Max. Size: Draft 10.36 m. *Airport:* Bangor International, 30 km.

Buctouche, N.B., Canada: 46.28 N. 64.43 W. **60**

Bud, Norway: 62.54 N. 6.55 E. **15**

Budapest, Hungary: 47.30 N. 19.03 E. **9**

Bude, U.K.: 50.50 N. 4.33 W. **5, 7**
Max. Size: LOA 90 ft., beam 25 ft., draft 8 ft.

Budge Budge, see Kolkata.

Buenaventura, Colombia: 3.53 N. 77.05 W. **69, 72**
Max. Size: Draft 28 ft. *Fuel:* Gas oil and bunker "C" fuel. *Airport:* Internal, 18 km.

Buenos Aires, Argentina: 34.36 S. 58.22 W. **77, 78**
Max. Size: Depth 32.5 ft. *Fuel:* By barge. *Dry Docks:* Syncrolift, capacity 40,000 d.w.t. *Airport:* Available.

Bufadero, see Nuevitas.

Buffalo, New York, U.S.A.: 42.55 N. 78.55 W. **55, 60, 62**
Max. Size: LOA 730 ft. and Seaway draft. (See also St. Lawrence Seaway). Depth alongside 22 ft. – 26 ft. *Fuel:* All grades. *Airport:* 5 miles.

Buffington, Indiana, U.S.A.: 41.38 N. 87.25 W. **62**

Bugama, Nigeria: 4.45 N. 6.53 E. **29**

Bugaz, Romania: 46.05 N. 30.29 E. **26**

Bugo, see Villanueva.

Bugrino, Russia: 69.00 N. 49.50 E. **16**

Buitagro, see Ramallo.

Buka, Papua New Guinea: 5.26 N. 154.40 E. **49**
Max. Size: Depth alongside 12 ft. (3.65 m.) at LAT.

Bukpyung, see Tonghae.

Bula, Indonesia: 3.06 S. 130.30 E. **46**

Buldir Is., Alaska, U.S.A.: 52.25 N. 176.00 E. **54**

Buleleng, Indonesia: 8.06 S. 115.06 E. **38**

BULGARIA **9, 21, 25, 26**

Bulhar, Somalia: 10.25 N. 44.24 E. **31**

Bullen Bay, (Curacao), Netherlands Antilles: 12.11 N. 69.01 W. **74**
Max. Size: 550,000 d.w.t., draft 28.7 m. *Fuel:* All grades.

Bulli, N.S.W., Australia: 34.20 S. 150.56 E. **50**

Bulwer Is., see Brisbane.

Buna, Papua New Guinea: 8.40 S. 148.24 E. **46**

Bunbeg, Ireland: 55.03 N. 8.18 W. **5**

Bunbury, W.A., Australia: 33.19 S. 115.38 E. **50**
Max. Size: Outer Harbour: LOA 225 m., draft 9.0 m. Inner Harbour: LOA 233 m., draft 11.6 m. *Fuel:* Furnace oil, marine and light diesel. *Airport:* Light aircraft only.

Buncrana, Ireland: 55.08 N. 7.28 W. **5**

Bundaberg, Qld., Australia: 24.45 S. 152.24 E. **50, 51**
Max. Size: LOA 182.87 m. Depths: Sugar Berth 9.66 m. Oil Berth 9.66 m. *Fuel:* All grades. *Airport:* Domestic, 2 miles.

Bungo Channel, Japan **43, 45**

Bunguran Is., Indonesia: 4.45 N. 108.00 E. **38, 39**

Bunyu, Indonesia: 3.28 N. 117.50 E. **38, 47**
Max. Size: 30,000 d.w.t. LOA 185 m. Depth 15.3 m. *Airport:* At Tarakan.

Buol, Indonesia: 1.10 N. 121.27 E. **38, 46**

Buras, Louisiana, U.S.A.: 29.22 N. 89.32 W. **67**

Burea, Sweden: 64.37 N. 21.15 E. **15**

Burela, Spain: 43.39 N. 7.20 W. **19, 20, 22**
Max. Size: Draft up to 20 ft.

Burg, Germany: 53.59 N. 9.17 E. **14**
Also see Kiel.

Burgas, see Bourgas.

Burgeo, Newfoundland, Canada: 47.36 N. 57.36 W. 60
Burghead, U.K.: 57.42 N. 3.29 W. 5
  Max. Size: LOA 60 m., draft 3.5 m. *Fuel:* By road tanker.
  Airport: Inverness, 30 miles. Aberdeen, 70 miles.
Burgstaaken, see Puttgarden.
Burgsvik, (Gotland Is.), Sweden: 57.02 N. 18.17 E. 11
Burin, Newfoundland, Canada: 47.03 N. 55.10 W. 60
Burketown, N.T., Australia: 17.44 S. 139.33 E. 50
Burlington, Ontario, Canada: 43.19 N. 79.48 W. 62
Burlington, New Jersey, U.S.A.: 40.05 N. 74.52 W. 65
Burnham, U.K.: 51.37 N. 0.49 E. 6
Burnie, Tas., Australia: 41.03 S. 145.55 E. 50, 51
  Max. Size: Depth 6.5 m. – 11.5 m., LOA 280 m.
  Tankers: Depth 11.0 m. (LW). *Fuel:* Diesel and heavy fuel.
  Airport: 17 km.
Burns Harbour, Indiana, U.S.A.: 41.38 N. 87.11 W. . . . 55, 62
  Max. Size: Draft 8.22 m. *Fuel:* Available.
Burnside, Louisiana, U.S.A.: 30.08 N. 90.55 W. 67
  Max. Size: Bulk Berth: Depth 45 ft. Ormet Berth: LOA 305 m.,
  beam 41 m. and draft 12.19 m.
Burntisland, U.K.: 56.03 N. 3.14 W. 6
  Max. Size: Depth 8.6 m. (MHWS), beam 16.8 m.
Burravoe, U.K.: 60.30 N. 1.15 W. 5
Burriana, Spain: 39.52 N. 0.03 W. 22
Burton upon Stather, U.K.: 53.39 N. 0.41 W. 6
Burtonport, Ireland: 54.59 N. 8.26 W. 5
  Max. Size: LOA 60 m., draft 4.25 m. *Fuel:* Available.
  Airport: 12 km.
Buru Is., Indonesia: 3.33 S. 126.09 E. 46
Buru Sea, Indonesia. 46
Burutu, Nigeria: 5.21 N. 5.31 E. 29
  Port not in use
Burwell, see Port Burwell.
Busan, South Korea: 35.07 N. 129.02 E. 42, 43, 45, 46
  Max. Size: 50,000 d.w.t., LOA 330 m., draft 12.5 m.
  Fuel: Bunker "A", Bunker "C", LRFO, LO and diesel oil. *Dry
  Docks:* 80,000 g.r.t. *Airport:* 28 km.
Bushire, Iran: 28.59 N. 50.50 E. 31, 35
  Max. Size: LOA 600 ft., draft 27 ft. *Airport:* 7 km.
Busselton, W.A., Australia: 33.38 S. 115.20 E. 50
  Port closed
Busuanga, see Basuanga.
Busum, Germany: 54.08 N. 8.51 E. 8, 11, 12, 14
  Max. Size: Draft 6.7 m. (HW), 3.5 m. (LW). Beam 21 m. (inner
  harbour). *Fuel:* Fuel oil available. *Airport:* Hamburg, 150 km.
Butaritari Is., Kiribati: 3.05 N. 172.50 E. 49
Butcher Island, see Mumbai.
Butchers Cove, Newfoundland, Canada: 48.51 N. 54.00 W. . . 60
Bute, U.K.: 55.50 N. 5.10 W. 6
Butedale, B.C., Canada: 53.10 N. 128.41 W. 56
Butinge Marine Terminal, Lithuania: 56.03 N. 20.58 E. . . 11
  Max. Size: 150,000 d.w.t., draft 16 m.
Butler Point, Massachusetts, U.S.A.: 41.41 N. 70.43 W. . . 64
Butt of Lewis, U.K.: 58.31 N. 6.16 W. 5
Buttermilk Bay, Massachusetts, U.S.A. 64
Butterworth, Malaya, Malaysia: 5.24 N. 100.23 E. . . 38, 39, 40
  Also see Penang.
Button Bay, see Churchill.
Button Is., see Port Burwell.
Butuan, (Mindanao Is.), Philippines: 8.57 N. 125.32 E. . . . 47
  Max. Size: Draft 16 ft.
  Also see Nasipit.
Butuku-Lula, see San Carlos.
Butzfleth, Germany: 53.39 N. 9.31 E. 8, 11, 12, 14
  Max. Size: Draft 46 ft. 6 in. FW. *Fuel:* Supplied by barge
  from Brunsbuttel or Hamburg.
Buyukada, Turkey: 40.52 N. 29.08 E. 23, 25
Buyukcekmece, Turkey: 41.01 N. 28.35 E. 23
Buyukdere, Turkey: 41.09 N. 29.02 E. 23
  Also see Istanbul.
Buzzards Bay, Massachusetts, U.S.A.: 41.45 N. 70.37 W. . . 64
Bwagaoia, (Misima Is.), Papua New Guinea:
  10.41 S. 152.51 E. 46
Byng Inlet, see Britt.
Byron Bay, N.S.W., Australia: 28.38 S. 153.37 E. 50
Byske, Sweden: 64.56 N. 21.11 E. 15
BZ 34 Terminal, China: 38.07 N. 119.33 E. 42
  Max. Size: 110,000 d.w.t.

C

Cabanas, Cuba: 23.00 N. 82.59 W. 69, 70
  Max. Size: LOA 574 ft., draft 19 ft.
  Also see Mariel.
Cabedelo, Brazil: 6.58 S. 34.50 W. 72
  Max. Size: LOA 210 m., draft Spring tide 30 ft. Neap 28 ft.
  Fuel: Fuel oil, diesel oil. *Airport:* 9 km. from Joao-Pessoa.
Cabello, see Puerto Cabello.
Cabezas, see Puerto Cabezas.
Cabimas, Venezuela: 10.23 N. 71.29 W. 74
Cabinda, Angola: 5.32 S. 12.11 E. 28
  Max. Size: At anchorage, 32 ft. draft. Tankers: SBM No. 1 –
  150,000 d.w.t., max. draft 55 ft. SBM No. 2 – 325,000 d.w.t.,
  depth 105 ft. LPG: 71,300 cu.m., depth 100 ft. *Airport:* 4 miles,
  connects with Luanda.
Cabo Blanco, Peru: 4.16 S. 81.15 W. 72
Cabo Frio, Brazil: 22.53 S. 42.00 W. 76, 77
Cabo Negro, Chile: 53.01 S. 70.51 W. 77
  Max. Size: LOA 200 m., draft 42 ft., 45,000 d.w.t.
  Also see Punta Arenas.
Cabo Rojo, Dominican Republic: 17.54 N. 71.40 W. 70
  Max. Size: LOA 700 ft., draft 36 ft.
  Airport: Santo Domingo, 360 km.
Cabo Ruivo, see Lisbon.
Cabo San Antonio, Argentina: 36.21 S. 57.33 W. 77
Cabo San Juan, Equatorial Guinea: 1.10 N. 9.21 E. 29
Cabot Strait, Gulf of St. Lawrence, Canada 60
Cabrera Is., (Balearic Is.), Spain: 39.06 N. 2.59 E. 22
Cabruto, Venezuela: 7.50 N. 66.12 W. 75
Cacheu, Guinea: 12.17 N. 16.13 W. 27
Cadiz, (Negros Is.), Philippines: 10.57 N. 123.19 E. 47
Cadiz Bay, Spain: 36.30 N. 6.20 W. 20, 21, 22, 27
  Max. Size: Cargo Vessels: Depth 10 m. – 13 m. (LW).
  Tankers: Depth 9.5 m. – 12.0 m. *Fuel:* Fuel oil, marine diesel
  and gas oil. *Dry Docks:* Largest 380 m. long, 66.65 m. wide.
  Puerto Real Factory Dry Dock 500 m. length, 100 m. width, and
  9.0 m. draft, can accommodate vessels up to 400,000 tons.
  Airport: Jerez, 30 km. Seville, 150 km.
Caen, France: 49.13 N. 0.21 W. 7, 8
  Max. Size: Daytime: LOA 205 m., beam 23.8 m., draft 29.5 ft.
  (F.W.). Tankers: Draft 8.6 m. *Fuel:* By barge or road tanker.
  Airport: 12 km. from the port.
Caernarvon, U.K.: 53.08 N. 4.16 W. 5, 7
Cagayan de Oro, (Mindanao Is.), Philippines:
  8.32 N. 124.40 E. 46, 47
  Max. Size: 40,000 d.w.t., LOA 180 m., beam 30 m.,
  draft 10.5 m. *Fuel:* Fuel oil available. *Airport:* Lumbia
  Airport, 15 km.
Cagliari, (Sardinia), Italy: 39.05 N. 9.01 E. 21, 24
  Max. Size: Draft 26 ft. Tankers: See Sarroch. *Fuel:* All grades.
  Airport: Elmas Airport, 12 km.
Caibarien, Cuba: 22.32 N. 79.28 W. 69, 70
  Max. Size: Anchorage: LOA 200 m., draft 10.67 m.
Caicara, Venezuela: 7.50 N. 66.12 W. 75
Caicos Is., Turks and Caicos Is. (U.K.). 69, 70
Caimanera, Cuba: 19.59 N. 75.09 W. 70
Caimito, see Porto Caimito.
Cairnryan, U.K.: 54.58 N. 5.02 W. 5
Cairns, Qld., Australia: 16.56 S. 145.47 E. 50, 51
  Max. Size: 32,000 d.w.t., draft 8.5 m. Tankers: LOA 200 m.,
  depth alongside 9.3 m. (LAT). *Fuel:* Available.
  Dry Docks: Max. LOA 60 m. *Airport:* Cairns International.
Cajimaya, see Antilla.
Cala Figuera, see Mahon.
Calabar, Nigeria: 5.04 N. 8.17 E. 29
  Max. Size: LOA 170 m., draft 7.6 m. *Airport:* At Calabar.
Calaca, (Luzon Is.), Philippines: 13.55 N. 120.47 E. 47
  Max. Size: Draft 13.5 m. *Fuel:* From Manila.
  Airport: Manila, 2 hours by car.
Calais, France: 50.58 N. 1.50 E. 4, 5, 7
  Max. Size: LOA 245 m., draft 11.5 m. *Fuel:* Available. *Dry
  Docks:* 141 m. x 19.5 m. *Airport:* Calais – Marck
  (international), 8 km.
Calais, Maine, U.S.A.: 45.11 N. 67.17 W. 60
Calamian Group, Philippines 46, 47
Calang, Indonesia: 4.38 N. 95.36 E. 38
Calapan, (Mindoro Is.), Philippines: 13.25 N. 121.08 E. . . 47
Calbayog, (Samar Is.), Philippines: 12.04 N. 124.38 E. . . 47
Calcasieu Pass, Louisiana, U.S.A. 66
Calcutta, see Kolkata.
Calder, Alaska, U.S.A.: 56.10 N. 133.45 W. 56
Caldera, Chile: 27.03 S. 70.53 W. 77
  Max. Size: Ore Quay: LOA 240 m., max. draft 44 ft.
  Tankers: Copec: LOA 200 m., depth 39 ft. *Airport:* At
  Copiapo, 75 km.

Caldera, Costa Rica: 9.54 N. 84.43 W. 69
Max. Size: Draft 10.0 m., LOA 205 m. *Fuel:* By road tanker.
Airport: International, 100 km.
Calderilla, Chile: 27.05 S. 70.52 W. 77
Max. Size: LOA 240 m., draft 40 ft., 60,000 d.w.t.
Caledonian Canal, U.K.: 57.27 N. 4.18 W. 5
Max. Size: LOA 60 ft. (48.77 m.), beam 35 ft. (10.67 m.), draft 9 ft. (2.74 m.) or LOA 150 ft. (45.72 m.), beam 35 ft., draft 13 ft. 6 in. (4.11 m.). *Fuel:* By road tanker.
Airport: Inverness (Dalcross).
Also see Corpach.
Caleta Clarencia, see Punta Arenas.
Caleta Coloso, Chile: 23.45 S. 70.28 W. 77
Max. Size: 45,000 d.w.t., LOA 192 m., beam 31 m., draft 11.25 m.
Caleta Cordova, Argentina: 45.43 S. 67.21 W. 77
Max. Size: SPM 160,000 d.w.t., depth 120 ft.
Also see Comodoro Rivadavia.
Caleta Olivares, see Caleta Cordova.
Caleta Olivia, Argentina: 46.26 S. 67.31 W. 77
Max. Size: SPM 160,000 d.w.t., depth 138 ft.
Caleta Tagus, (Galapagos Is.), Ecuador: 0.16 S. 91.22 W. . 69
Calicut, India: 11.15 N. 75.46 E. 37
Max. Size: (Anchorage) depth 10 m. *Fuel:* Small quantity of 30 tons can be provided. *Airport:* 25 km.
California, U.S.A. 56, 57, 58
Calingapatnam, see Kalingapatnam.
Callao, Peru: 12.03 S. 77.10 W. 72
Max. Size: Length and breadth unlimited, draft 32 ft. plus height of tide, less keel clearance. Tankers: LOA (approx.) 200 m., depth in berth 35 ft., depth in approaches 33 ft. (HW), 31 ft. (LW). *Fuel:* Available.
Dry Docks: Largest: 632 ft. × 82 ft. × 21 ft. *Airport:* Lima/Callao, International.
Caloundra, Qld., Australia: 26.47 S. 153.10 E. 50
Calumet, Illinois, U.S.A.: 41.44 N. 87.31 W. 62
Also see Chicago.
Calvi, (Corsica), France: 42.34 N. 8.46 E. 9, 23, 24
Max. Size: Draft 6.5 m., LOA 140 m. *Fuel:* Diesel.
Cam Pha, Vietnam: 21.02 N. 107.22 E. 39
Max. Size: 50,000 d.w.t., draft 9.5 m. *Fuel:* By barge.
Airport: Noi Bai, 230 km. Catbi, 100 km.
Cam Ranh, Vietnam: 11.53 N. 109.10 E. 39
Camar Marine Terminal, Indonesia: 6.18 N. 113.00 E. . . 38
Max. Size: 106,239 d.w.t., LOA 853 ft.
Camaret, France: 48.17 N. 4.37 W. 7, 19
Camarinas, Spain: 43.08 N. 9.11 W. 20
Camarones, Argentina: 44.48 S. 65.44 W. 77
Cambay, India: 22.19 N. 72.34 E. 37
CAMBODIA 39
Cambridge, Maryland, U.S.A.: 38.34 N. 76.03 W. . . . 63, 65
Camden, Pennsylvania, U.S.A.: 39.57 N. 75.08 W. . . . 63, 65
Max. Size: Depths to 40 ft.
Also see Philadelphia.
Cameron, Louisiana, U.S.A.: 29.50 N. 93.20 W. 66
CAMEROON, REPUBLIC OF 28, 29
Cameta, Brazil: 2.12 S. 49.30 W. 72
Camiguin Is., see Mambajao.
Caminha, Portugal: 41.51 N. 8.50 W. 20, 22
Camocim, Brazil: 2.51 N. 40.52 W. 72
Camogli, Italy: 44.21 N. 9.08 E. 23, 24
Camp Lloyd, see Kangerlussuaq.
Campachuela, see Ceiba Hueca.
Campana, Argentina: 34.15 S. 58.58 W. 77, 78
Max. Size: Draft up to 27 ft. draft, LOA 225 m., dependent on local river conditions. Depth alongside 20 ft. – 35 ft.
Tankers: LOA 100 m. – 230 m., depth 18 ft. – 45 ft.
Fuel: Available.
Campbell, see Port Campbell.
Campbell Is., (New Zealand): 52.32 S. 169.04 E. 80
Campbell River, B.C., Canada: 50.02 N. 125.14 W. . . . 56
Max. Size: Up to 30,000 d.w.t. *Dry Docks:* At Vancouver.
Airport: Frequent flights to Vancouver.
Campbellton, N.B., Canada: 48.00 N. 66.42 W. 60
Campbeltown, U.K.: 55.25 N. 5.36 W. 5
Max. Size: LOA 230 m., draft 12 ft. Tankers: Depth 40 ft.
Fuel: Marine gas oil. *Airport:* Machrihanish, 3 miles.
Campeche, Mexico: 19.50 N. 90.33 W. 69
Campo, Cameroon: 2.21 N. 9.49 E. 28, 29
Max. Size: Anchorage Port: Depth 7 m.
Campoton, Mexico: 19.21 N. 90.45 W. 69
Can Tho, Vietnam: 10.03 N. 105.42 E. 39
Max. Size: Draft 7.0 m. *Airport:* 10 km.
CANADA 17, 55, 56, 59, 60, 61, 62, 79
Canakkale, Turkey: 40.08 N. 26.24 E. 25, 26
Max. Size: Anchorage in 12 – 16 fathoms. *Airport:* Domestic, 2 km.
Canal du Marne, France. 9
Canale di Piombino, Italy. 23
Cananova, Cuba: 20.41 N. 75.05 W. 70

Canaport, N.B., Canada: 45.12 N. 65.59 W. 60
Max. Size: 350,000 d.w.t. – 400,000 d.w.t.
Depth 120 ft. (LW) – 150 ft. (HW).
Canary Islands (Spain) 18, 27
Canaveral, see Port Canaveral.
Cancale, France: 48.40 N. 1.51 W. 7, 19
Max. Size: Depths 0.5 m. – 13 m. at Spring Tide. *Fuel:* Diesel.
Airport: Dinard, 30 km.
Candala, Somalia: 11.30 N. 50.00 E. 31
Candarli, Turkey: 38.56 N. 26.57 E. 25
Canea, (Crete), Greece: 35.30 N. 24.04 E. 25
Cannanore, India: 11.52 N. 75.22 E. 37
Cannes, France: 43.33 N. 7.01 E. 9, 22
Max. Size: Anchorage. *Airport:* Cannes Mandelieu, 5 km.
Canning, see Port Canning.
Canso, N.S., Canada: 45.20 N. 61.00 W. 60
Canso Canal, N.S., Canada: 60
Max. Size: LOA 735 ft., beam 75 ft., draft 28 ft. or 30 ft. by arrangement.
Also see Port Hawkesbury.
Canterbury Bight, New Zealand. 52
Canton, China, see Guangzhou.
Canton, (Phoenix Is.), Kiribati: 2.50 S. 171.40 W. 49
Canvey, U.K.: 51.32 N. 0.35 E. 6
Max. Size: LOA 580 ft., draft 32 ft.
Also see Tilbury.
Cap Chat, Quebec, Canada: 49.06 N. 66.40 W. 60
Cap Couronne, France. 23
Cap d'Antifer, France: 49.41 N. 0.10 E. 7, 8
Cap Gris Nez, France: 50.52 N. 1.35 E. 7
Cap Haitien, Haiti: 19.46 N. 72.12 W. 69, 70
Max. Size: Depth 11 m. *Fuel:* Available in drums.
Capbreton, France: 43.40 N. 1.25 W. 19
Cape Barren Is., (Fourneaux Group), Tas., Australia . . 50, 51
Cape Breton Is., Canada 60
Cape Charles, Virginia, U.S.A.: 37.16 N. 76.01 W. . . 63, 65
Cape Coast, Ghana: 5.07 N. 1.16 W. 28
Cape Cod Bay, U.S.A. 64
Cape Cod Canal, Massachusetts, U.S.A.: 41.46 N. 70.30 W. 60, 63, 64
Max. Size: Canal and alongside: Depth 32 ft. MLW.
Also see Sandwich Oil Terminal.
Cape Cuvier, W.A., Australia: 24.13 S. 113.23 E. . . . 50, 51
Max. Size: 70,000 d.w.t., depth 17.8 m. *Airport:* Connects with Perth.
Also see Carnarvon.
Cape Dorset, N.W.T., Canada: 64.55 N. 76.33 W. 59
Cape Flattery, Qld., Australia: 14.59 S. 145.21 E. . . 46, 50, 51
Max. Size: 70,000 d.w.t., LOA 225 m., beam 32 m. and draft 14 m. *Airport:* Light aircraft only.
Cape Lambert, see Port Walcott.
Cape Limboh, Cameroon: 4.00 N. 9.07 E. 28, 29
Max. Size: Tankers: 80,000 d.w.t.
Also see Limbe.
Cape Lopez, Gabon: 0.38 S. 8.43 E. 28
Max. Size: 250,000 d.w.t., LOA 340 m., draft 20.50 m. (67 ft.).
Max. arrival displacement 160,000 tonnes. *Fuel:* 1,500 sec./3,500 sec. *Airport:* 15 minutes.
Cape Preston, W.A., Australia: 20.50 S. 116.10 E. . . . 51
Cape St. Jacques, see Vung Tau.
Cape Town, South Africa: 33.56 S. 18.26 E. 28
Max. Size: LOA 370 m., beam 87 m., draft 12.0 m. (Duncan Dock) and 12.8 m. (Ben Schoeman Dock).
Tankers: (For discharging) LOA 256 m., draft 13.1 m. (tidal).
Fuel: All grades. *Dry Docks:* Largest: Overall docking length 360.0 m., width at entrance top 45.1 m., depth on entrance sill, HWOST 13.7 m. *Airport:* 20 km., connects with Johannesburg.
CAPE VERDE 18, 27
Cape Verde Is., Cape Verde 27, 68
Capelas, (San Miguel Is.), Azores (Portugal):
37.50 N. 25.45 W. 20
Capes:
   Cape Agulhas, South Africa: 34.50 S. 20.00 E. 28
   Cape Amber, Madagascar: 11.57 S. 49.17 E. 30
   Cape Andreas, Cyprus: 35.42 N. 34.37 E. 26
   Cape Arkona, Germany: 54.41 N. 13.26 E. 11, 12
   Cape Arnhem, N.T., Australia: 12.20 S. 136.55 E. . . . 50
   Cape Bafra, Turkey: 41.44 N. 35.58 E. 26
   Cape Barbas, Morocco: 22.18 N. 16.42 W. 27
   Cape Bastion, (Hainan Island), China: 18.10 N. 110.35 E. . 39
   Cape Blanc, Mauritania: 20.46 N. 17.03 W. 27
   Cape Blanco, Oregon, U.S.A.: 42.50 N. 124.32 W. . . 57
   Cape Bojador, Morocco: 26.15 N. 14.25 W. 27
   Cape Bon, Tunisia: 37.04 N. 11.03 E. 24
   Cape Bougaroni, Algeria: 37.05 N. 6.28 E. 22
   Cape Brett, (North Is.), New Zealand: 35.10 S. 174.19 E. . 52
   Cape Brewster, Greenland (Denmark): 70.10 N. 22.00 W. . 17
   Cape Campbell, (South Is.), New Zealand:
   41.42 S. 174.17 E. 52
   Cape Cantin, Morocco: 32.36 N. 9.20 W. 27
   Cape Carbonara, (Sardinia), Italy: 39.06 N. 9.31 E. . . 24

Entry	Page
Cape Catastrophe, S.A., Australia: 35.00 S. 135.57 E.	51
Cape Charles, Virginia, U.S.A.: 37.08 N. 75.58 W.	63, 65
Cape Chidley, Newfoundland, Canada: 60.25 N. 64.26 W.	59
Cape Chukochi, Russia: 70.10 N. 160.00 E.	54
Cape Cod, Massachusetts, U.S.A.: 42.04 N. 70.10 W.	60, 63
Cape Colonne, Italy: 39.02 N. 17.12 E.	24
Cape Comorin, India: 8.06 N. 77.33 E.	37
Cape Constantine, Alaska, U.S.A.: 58.27 N. 158.50 W.	54
Cape Corrientes, Mexico: 20.25 N. 105.42 W.	57
Cape Corrientes, Mozambique: 24.03 S. 35.31 E.	30
Cape Corse, (Corsica), France: 43.01 N. 9.24 E.	23
Cape Creus, Spain: 42.18 N. 3.19 E.	22
Cape de Fer, Algeria: 37.03 N. 7.10 E.	22
Cape de Gata, Spain: 36.42 N. 2.12 W.	22
Cape de La Hague, France: 49.43 N. 1.57 W.	7, 19
Cape de Nouvelle-France, Quebec, Canada: 62.23 N. 73.40 W.	59
Cape Delgado, Mozambique: 10.40 S. 40.39 E.	30
Cape do Norte, Brazil: 1.42 N. 49.55 W.	72
Cape Dolphin, Falkland Is. (U.K.): 51.14 S. 58.57 W.	77
Cape Dominion, N.W.T., Canada: 66.11 N. 74.23 W.	59
Cape Dorchester, N.W.T., Canada: 65.25 N. 77.25 W.	59
Cape Dyer, N.W.T., Canada: 66.30 N. 61.31 W.	17, 59
Cape Egmont, New Zealand: 39.18 S. 173.45 E.	52
Cape Engano, Dominican Republic: 18.36 N. 68.20 W.	70
Cape Espartel, Morocco: 35.46 N. 5.54 W.	22, 23
Cape Espenberg, Alaska, U.S.A.: 66.32 N. 163.44 W.	54
Cape Espichel, Portugal: 38.25 N. 9.14 W.	20
Cape Falcone, (Sardinia), Italy: 40.55 N. 8.12 E.	24
Cape Farewell, Greenland (Denmark): 59.47 N. 43.54 W.	17, 53
Cape Farewell, (South Is.), New Zealand: 40.30 S. 173.43 E.	52
Cape Fear, North Carolina, U.S.A.: 33.51 N. 77.58 W.	66
Cape Ferret, France: 44.39 N. 1.15 W.	19
Cape Finisterre, Spain: 42.53 N. 9.16 W.	20
Cape Flattery, Qld., Australia: 14.57 S. 145.21 E.	50, 51
Cape Flattery, Washington, U.S.A.: 48.23 N. 124.43 W.	56
Cape Foulwind, (South Is.), New Zealand: 41.47 S. 172.29 E.	52
Cape Frehel, France: 48.41 N. 2.21 W.	19
Cape Frio, Namibia: 18.05 S. 12.00 E.	28
Cape Fullerton, N.W.T., Canada: 63.58 N. 88.46 W.	59
Cape Gata, Cyprus: 34.34 N. 33.03 E.	26
Cape Gracias a Dios, Nicaragua: 15.00 N. 83.10 W.	69, 70
Cape Guardafui, Somalia: 11.50 N. 51.18 E.	31
Cape Harrison, Newfoundland, Canada: 54.56 N. 57.55 W.	59
Cape Hatteras, North Carolina, U.S.A.: 35.15 N. 75.30 W.	63
Cape Henlopen, Delaware, U.S.A.: 38.47 N. 75.05 W.	63, 65
Cape Henrietta Maria, Ontario, Canada: 55.07 N. 82.15 W.	59
Cape Henry, Virginia, U.S.A.: 36.56 N. 76.00 W.	63, 65
Cape Hopes Advance, Quebec, Canada: 61.04 N. 69.32 W.	59
Cape Horn, Chile: 55.59 S. 67.16 W.	68, 77, 80
Cape Huertas, Spain: 38.21 N. 0.24 E.	22
Cape Ince, Turkey: 42.07 N. 34.58 E.	26
Cape Jaffa, S.A., Australia: 36.58 S. 139.40 E.	50
Cape Juby, Morocco: 27.59 N. 12.56 W.	27
Cape Kaliakra, Bulgaria: 43.22 N. 28.30 E.	26
Cape Kanin, Russia: 68.41 N. 43.18 E.	16
Cape Kendal, N.W.T., Canada: 63.36 N. 87.14 W.	59
Cape Kidnappers, (North Is.), New Zealand: 39.38 S. 172.05 E.	52
Cape Leeuwin, W.A., Australia: 34.22 S. 115.09 E.	36, 50
Cape Leveque, W.A., Australia: 16.20 S. 123.00 E.	50, 51
Cape Liptrap, Vic., Australia: 38.55 S. 145.56 E.	51
Cape Lisburn, Alaska, U.S.A.: 68.53 N. 166.08 W.	54
Cape Londonderry, W.A., Australia: 13.45 S. 126.54 E.	50
Cape Lookout, North Carolina, U.S.A.: 34.37 N. 76.30 W.	63
Cape Low, N.W.T., Canada: 63.05 N. 85.25 W.	59
Cape Malea, Greece: 36.27 N. 23.12 E.	25
Cape Matapan, Greece: 36.22 N. 22.29 E.	25
Cape May, New Jersey, U.S.A.: 38.56 N. 74.56 W.	60, 63, 65
Cape Mendocino, California, U.S.A.: 40.26 N. 124.24 W.	57
Cape Mercy, N.W.T., Canada: 65.02 N. 63.32 W.	17, 59
Cape Monze, Pakistan: 24.53 N. 66.40 E.	37
Cape Nao, Spain: 38.44 N. 0.14 E.	22
Cape Nassau, Russia: 76.19 N. 61.40 E.	16
Cape Naturaliste, W.A., Australia: 33.32 S. 115.00 E.	50
Cape Navarin, Russia: 62.14 N. 179.08 E.	54
Cape Newenham, Alaska, U.S.A.: 58.40 N. 162.08 W.	54
Cape North, N.S., Canada: 47.02 N. 60.23 W.	60
Cape of Good Hope, South Africa: 34.22 S. 18.28 E.	18, 28
Cape Otto Schmidta, Russia: 68.56 N. 179.30 E.	54
Cape Otway, Vic., Australia: 38.52 S. 143.31 E.	50, 51
Cape Palliser, (North Is.), New Zealand: 41.37 S. 170.17 E.	52
Cape Palmas, Liberia: 4.22 N. 7.45 E.	28
Cape Palos, Spain: 37.38 N. 0.40 W.	22
Cape Pasley, W.A., Australia: 33.53 S. 123.33 E.	50
Cape Passero, (Sicily), Italy: 36.40 N. 15.09 E.	24
Cape Peloro, (Sicily), Italy: 38.15 N. 15.40 E.	24
Cape Pilar, Chile: 52.43 S. 74.42 W.	77
Cape Race, Newfoundland, Canada: 46.39 N. 53.05 W.	60
Cape Ray, Newfoundland, Canada: 47.36 N. 59.17 W.	60
Cape Recife, South Africa: 34.02 S. 25.42 E.	30
Cape Rhir, Morocco: 30.38 N. 9.52 W.	27
Cape Rizzuto, Italy: 38.56 N. 17.06 E.	24
Cape Roca, Portugal: 38.47 N. 9.28 W.	20
Cape Romano, Florida, U.S.A.: 25.51 N. 81.41 W.	66, 69, 70
Cape Romanzof, Alaska, U.S.A.: 61.47 N. 166.05 W.	54
Cape Rosa, Algeria: 36.57 N. 8.16 E.	24
Cape Sable, N.S., Canada: 43.23 N. 65.37 W.	60
Cape Sable, Florida, U.S.A.: 25.13 N. 81.10 W.	66, 69, 70
Cape St. Andrews, Madagascar: 16.13 S. 44.26 E.	30
Cape St. Maria di Leuca, Italy: 39.48 N. 18.21 E.	24
Cape St. Mary, Madagascar: 25.38 S. 45.06 E.	30
Cape St. Vincent, Portugal: 37.00 N. 8.58 W.	20, 22
Cape San Antonio, Spain: 38.47 N. 0.12 E.	22
Cape San Diego, Argentina: 54.40 S. 65.10 W.	77
Cape San Juan, Argentina: 54.43 S. 63.47 W.	77
Cape San Lazaro, Mexico: 24.49 N. 112.21 W.	57
Cape Sarych, Ukraine: 44.25 N. 33.45 E.	26
Cape Serrat, Tunisia: 37.14 N. 9.14 E.	24
Cape Shelagski, Russia: 70.08 N. 170.06 E.	54
Cape Smith, Quebec, Canada: 60.43 N. 78.40 W.	59
Cape Spartivento, Italy: 37.55 N. 16.04 E.	24
Cape Spartivento, (Sardinia), Italy: 38.52 N. 8.51 E.	24
Cape Spatha, (Crete), Greece: 35.42 N. 23.43 E.	25
Cape Spencer, Alaska, U.S.A.: 58.12 N. 136.40 W.	56
Cape Stilo, Italy: 38.28 N. 16.35 E.	24
Cape Tatnam, Manitoba, Canada: 57.20 N. 91.00 W.	59
Cape Testa, (Sardinia), Italy: 41.13 N. 9.09 E.	24
Cape Tobin, Greenland (Denmark): 70.30 N. 21.50 W.	17
Cape Tortosa, Spain: 40.42 N. 0.52 E.	22
Cape Trafalgar, Spain: 36.10 N. 6.01 W.	20, 22, 23
Cape Tres Forcas, Morocco: 35.27 N. 2.59 W.	22
Cape Turnagain, (North Is.), New Zealand: 40.28 S. 171.38 E.	52
Cape Vaticano, Italy: 38.38 N. 15.48 E.	24
Cape Vert, Senegal: 14.43 N. 17.32 W.	27
Cape Vincent, New York, U.S.A.: 44.08 N. 76.20 W.	60
Cape Virgenes, Argentina: 52.20 S. 68.21 W.	77
Cape Wessel, N.T., Australia: 10.58 S. 136.47 E.	50
Cape Whittle, Quebec, Canada: 50.12 N. 60.07 W.	60
Cape Wolstenholme, Quebec, Canada: 62.34 N. 77.30 W.	59
Cape Wrangell, (Attu Is.), Alaska, U.S.A.: 53.02 N. 172.25 E.	54
Cape Wrath, U.K.: 58.36 N. 5.01 W.	5
Cape York, Qld., Australia: 10.41 S. 142.31 E.	46, 50, 51
Cape Zhelaniya, Russia: 76.55 N. 68.40 E.	16

Capiz, see Roxas.

Capraia, Italy: 43.00 N. 10.00 E. . . . 23, 24

Capri, Italy . . . 23

Car Nicobar, (Nicobar Is.), India: 9.14 N. 92.45 E. . . . 37

Carabane, Senegal: 12.33 N. 16.42 W. . . . 27

Caracas Bay, (Curacao), Netherlands Antilles:
12.04 N. 68.52 W. . . . 74
Max. Size: LOA 1,050 ft., draft 45 ft. *Fuel:* All grades.

Caraga, (Mindanao Is.), Philippines: 7.20 N. 126.34 E. . . . 47

Caraminal, see Puebla del Caraminal.

Caraquet, N.B., Canada: 47.48 N. 64.56 W. . . . 60
Max. Size: LOA 140 m., draft 6.5 m.
Also see Shippegan Harbour.

Caratasco, Honduras: 15.22 N. 83.45 W. . . . 69, 70

Caravelas, Brazil: 17.43 S. 39.15 W. . . . 72

Carbonear, Newfoundland, Canada: 47.43 N. 53.12 W. . . . 60

Carboneras, Spain: 36.58 N. 1.54 W. . . . 22
Max. Size: Draft 11.9 m., LOA 200 m., beam 32 m., airdraft 13 m., 70,000 d.w.t. Pucarsa: LOA 300 m., beam 43 m., draft 17 m. *Fuel:* By road tanker. *Airport:* Almeria.

Cardenas, Cuba: 23.03 N. 81.12 W. . . . 69, 70
Max. Size: LOA 170 m., draft 5.2 m.

Cardiff, U.K.: 51.29 N. 3.10 W. . . . 4, 5, 6, 7
Max. Size: LOA 198 m., beam 26.9 m., draft 10.37 m.
Fuel: Available. *Dry Docks:* Largest 182 m. x 21.7 m. *Airport:* 11 miles.

Cardigan, U.K.: 52.05 N. 4.40 W. . . . 5, 7

Cardigan Bay, U.K. . . . 5

Cardinal, Ontario, Canada: 44.47 N. 75.23 W. . . . 61

Cardon, see Punta Cardon.

Carenero, Venezuela: 10.32 N. 66.00 W. . . . 69, 71, 75

Carentan, France: 49.19 N. 1.15 W. . . . 7

Cargados Carajos Shoals, Mauritius: 16.35 S. 59.40 E. . . . 30

Cargese, (Corsica), France: 42.05 N. 8.35 E. . . . 24

Caribou Is., Ontario, Canada: 47.22 N. 85.48 W. . . . 62

Carino, Spain: 43.44 N. 7.51 W. . . . 19, 20, 22

Caripito, Venezuela: 10.09 N. 63.02 W. . . . 69, 71, 72, 75
Max. Size: LOA 775 ft., 61,000 d.w.t. and draft 33 ft. (FW).
Fuel: Fuel oil, marine diesel and gas oil.

Carleton, Quebec, Canada: 48.06 N. 66.07 W. . . . 60
Max. Size: LOA 140 m., draft 7.2 m. *Fuel:* Diesel. *Dry Docks:* Les Mechins, 245 miles. *Airport:* Local airport.

Carlingford, Ireland: 54.03 N. 6.11 W. . . . 5

Carloforte, (San Pierto Is.), Italy: 39.08 N. 8.19 E. . . . 24

Carlos, (Palawan Is.), Philippines: 10.29 N. 123.25 E. **46, 47**
Carmanville, Newfoundland, Canada: 49.24 N. 54.17 W. **60**
Carmelo, Uruguay: 34.02 S. 58.10 W. **78**
Carmen de Patagone, Argentina: 40.49 S. 62.59 W. **77**
Carmopolis, Brazil: 11.03 S. 37.01 W. **72**
  Max. Size: LOA 300 m. Sea Berth: 115,000 d.w.t., safe
  draft 15 m. Airport: Aracaju.
Carnarvon, W.A., Australia: 24.53 S. 113.40 E. **50, 51**
  Also see Cape Cuvier.
Carnlough, U.K.: 54.59 N. 5.59 W. **5**
Caroline Is., Kiribati: 10.00 S. 151.00 W. **49**
Caroline Islands, Micronesia **49**
Caronte, France: 43.24 N. 5.02 E. **23**
  Max. Size: LOA 200 m., draft 8.23 m.
  Also see Port de Bouc.
Caronte Canal, France. **23**
Carrabelle, Florida, U.S.A.: 29.51 N. 84.40 W. **66**
Carrera, see Marina de Carrera.
Carrickfergus, U.K.: 54.43 N. 5.48 W. **5, 6**
  Also see Belfast.
Carrizal, Chile: 28.04 S. 71.10 W. **77**
Cartagena, Colombia: 10.25 N. 75.32 W. **69, 72**
  Max. Size: LOA 280 m., draft 41 ft. Tankers: See Mamonal.
  Fuel: Fuel oil, bunker "C" and diesel oil available by barge.
  Dry Docks: Synchrolift – 5,000 tons. Airport: International
  airport, 5 km.
Cartagena, Spain: 37.35 N. 0.59 W. **21, 22**
  Max. Size: Cartagena: Draft 11.2 m. Tankers: Draft 21.4 m.,
  250,000 d.w.t. LNG: Draft 11 m. – 14.5 m. Bulk: Draft 14.5 m.
  Fuel: At Cartagena, only gas oil from tank trucks. At
  Escombreras all grades available. Dry Docks: 1 dry dock can
  accept vessels of (35,000 d.w.t.) 566 ft. LOA and 73 ft. beam.
  2 floating docks for vessels up to 333 ft. LOA. Airport: San
  Javier, 27 miles, connects with Madrid, etc.
Carteret, France: 49.22 N. 1.48 W. **7, 19**
Carteret, New York, U.S.A.: 40.35 N. 74.13 W. **63**
Cartier, see Port Cartier.
Cartier Is., W.A., Australia: 12.31 S. 123.31 E. **50**
Cartwright, Newfoundland, Canada: 53.42 N. 57.02 W. . . . **59**
Cartwright, Ontario, Canada, see Mooretown.
Carupano, Venezuela: 10.40 N. 63.15 W. **69, 71, 75**
Casablanca, Morocco: 33.36 N. 7.37 W. **21, 27**
  Max. Size: LOA 884 ft., beam 105 ft., draft 32 ft. (all approx.).
  Containers: Depth 7 m. – 12 m. Bulk: Depth 12 m.
  Tankers: Up to 37 ft. draft. Fuel: All grades. Dry Docks: 152 m.
  long and 22 m. wide (lifting 10,000 tons).
  Airport: International, 30 km.
Casado, Paraguay: 22.16 S. 57.55 W. **77**
Cascais, Portugal: 38.41 N. 9.25 W. **20**
Casiguaran, (Luzon Is.), Philippines: 16.17 N. 122.07 E. . **46, 47**
Casilda, Cuba: 21.45 N. 79.59 W. **69, 70**
  Max. Size: LOA 170 m., draft 7.62 m.
  Also see Cienfuegos.
Caspian Sea **9**
Casquets Lt., (Channel Is.), U.K.: 49.43 N. 2.25 W. **19**
Cassis, France: 43.13 N. 5.32 E. **22**
Castellamare de Stabia, Italy: 40.42 N. 14.29 E. **23, 24**
Castellammare, (Sicily), Italy: 38.02 N. 12.53 E. **24**
Castellon de la Plana, Spain: 39.58 N. 0.01 W. **22**
  Max. Size: LOA 160 m. – 210 m., draft 9.9 m. Tankers (Breasting
  Island): 37,000 d.w.t., 37 ft. (Sea Berth): Draft 22 m.
  Fuel: Available. Airport: Valencia, 70 km.
Castilla, see Puerto Castilla.
Castle Bay, U.K.: 56.57 N. 7.28 W. **5**
Castle Island, Alaska, U.S.A.: 56.39 N. 133.11 W. **56**
  Max. Size: Harbour depth 45 ft. Airport: Charter only.
Castle Peak, see Hong Kong.
Castlemaine Harbour, Ireland: 52.09 N. 9.48 W. **5**
Castletown, (Isle of Man), U.K.: 54.04 N. 4.39 W. **5**
  Max. Size: LOA 49 m., draft 2.8 m. – 3.5 m.
  Fuel: By road tanker. Airport: 2 miles, domestic flights.
Castletownbere, Ireland: 51.41 N. 9.54 W. **5**
  Max. Size: Dinish Island Wharf: Depth 17 ft. (MLWS). Main
  Wharf: Depth 12 ft. Fuel: Diesel. Airport: Cork, 80 miles.
Castries, St. Lucia: 14.01 N. 61.00 W. **69, 71**
  Max. Size: LOA 270 m. (cargo and passenger), draft 9.1 m.
  Pointe Seraphine and Vieux Fort: Depth 32 ft. – 35 ft.
  Tankers: See Cul de Sac Bay. Fuel: Very limited.
  Airport: 2 miles.
Castro, Chile: 42.30 S. 73.45 W. **77**
Castro-Urdiales, Spain: 43.24 N. 3.14 W. **19, 22**
  Max. Size: LOA 105 m., draft 5 m. Airport: Bilbao, 40 km.
Cat Is., Bahamas **69, 70**
Cat Island, Louisiana, U.S.A.: 30.15 N. 89.07 W. **67**
Cat Lo, see Vung Tau.
Catalina, Newfoundland, Canada: 48.30 N. 53.04 W. **60**
Catania, (Sicily), Italy: 37.29 N. 15.06 E. **24**
  Max. Size: Max. depth alongside 30 ft. 6 in. Fuel: Available.
  Airport: International.
Catanuan, (Luzon Is.), Philippines: 13.35 N. 122.19 E. **47**
Catanzaro, Italy: 38.50 N. 16.37 E. **24**

Cataumet, Massachusetts, U.S.A.: 41.40 N. 70.37 W. **64**
Catbalogan, (Leyte Is.), Philippines: 11.46 N. 124.53 E. . **46, 47**
Cato Is., Qld., Australia: 23.15 S. 155.32 E. **50, 51**
Catskill, New York, U.S.A.: 42.13 N. 73.52 W. **63**
Cattolica, Italy: 43.58 N. 12.45 E. **24**
Caudebec, France: 49.32 N. 0.44 E. **7**
Caughnawaga, Quebec, Canada: 45.21 N. 73.41 W. **61**
Cavalla, see Kavalla.
Cavite, (Luzon Is.), Philippines: 14.29 N. 120.55 E. **47**
Cay Frances, see Caibarien.
Cayenne, Guyane (France): 4.56 N. 52.20 W. **76**
  Also see Degrad-des-Cannes.
Cayeux, France: 50.08 N. 1.30 E. **7**
Cayman Brac, Cayman Is. (U.K.): 19.42 N. 79.50 W. . . . **69, 70**
  Max. Size: LOA 200 ft., max. draft 14 ft. Fuel: Available.
  Airport: Gerrad Smith International, 9.5 miles.
Cayman Islands (U.K.) **69, 70**
Cayo Arcas, Mexico: 20.11 N. 91.59 W. **69**
  Max. Size: 350,000 d.w.t.
Cayo Diana, see Cardenas.
Cayo Juan Claro, see Puerto Padre.
Cayos Miskitos, Nicaragua: 14.23 N. 82.48 W. **69**
Ceara, see Fortaleza.
Cebu, (Cebu Is.), Philippines: 10.18 N. 123.53 E. **46, 47**
  Max. Size: Draft 30 ft. Ludo (private port) – draft 40 ft.
  Tankers: Shell – draft 30 ft. Mobil and Texaco – draft 25 ft.
  Fuel: Fuel oil available. Dry Docks: Max. 6,000 d.w.t.
  Airport: 7 miles.
Cedar River, Michigan, U.S.A.: 45.24 N. 87.21 W. **62**
Cedeira, Spain: 43.40 N. 8.02 W. **19, 20**
Cedros Island, (Cedros Is.), Mexico: 28.03 N. 115.10 W. . . **57**
Ceduna, see Thevenard.
Cee, Spain: 42.57 N. 9.11 W. **20, 22**
Cefalu, (Sicily), Italy: 38.05 N. 14.00 E. **24**
Ceiba Hueca, Cuba: 20.13 N. 77.19 W. **70**
  Max. Size: LOA 170 m., draft 9.45 m.
  Also see Manzanillo.
Ceiba Marine Terminal, Equatorial Guinea: 1.24 N. 9.13 E. . **28, 29**
  Max. Size: 155,000 d.w.t., depth 90 m.
Cekisan, see Ambarli.
Celebes, Indonesia **46**
Celebes Sea **38, 46, 47**
Celukan Bawang, Indonesia: 8.11 S. 114.50 E. **38**
Cephalonia Is., Greece: 38.15 N. 20.15 E. **24, 25**
Ceram Sea, Indonesia **46**
Cerigo, see Kithira Is..
Cernavoda, Romania: 44.20 N. 28.03 E. **9, 26**
Cervo, see San Ciprian.
Cesme, Turkey: 38.20 N. 26.19 E. **25, 26**
Cess River, Liberia: 5.32 N. 9.32 W. **27**
Ceuta, Spain: 35.53 N. 5.17 W. **20, 21, 22, 23, 27**
  Max. Size: LOA 220 m., draft 33 ft. 6 in. Fuel: All grades.
  Airport: Tangier International, 100 km.
Ceyhan Terminal, Turkey: 36.53 N. 35.56 E. **26**
  Also see Botas.
Chacabuco, see Puerto Chacabuco.
Chagos Archipelago (U.K.) **30**
Chaguaramas, Trinidad and Tobago: 10.40 N. 61.39 W. . **71, 75**
  Max. Size: Draft 34 ft. 6 in. Fuel: Available.
  Dry Docks: Capacity 25,000 d.w.t. Airport: Piarco, 45 km.
Chah-Bahar, Iran: 25.17 N. 60.37 E. **31, 37**
  Max. Size: 25,000 d.w.t., LOA 180 m., draft 29 ft.
  Fuel: By road tanker. Airport: Konarak, 70 km.
Chake Chake, Tanzania: 5.14 S. 39.46 E. **30**
  Max. Size: LOA 170 ft., draft 15 ft.
Chalivourgiki, see Eleusis.
Chalkis, Greece: 38.27 N. 23.35 E. **25, 26**
  Max. Size: Max. draft 21 ft. in daytime, 19 ft. at night.
  Fuel: Small quantities by road tankers.
  Dry Docks: 2 floating docks, max. 48,000 d.w.t.
  Airport: Athens, 90 km.
Challis Venture, Australia: 12.07 S. 125.00 E. **50**
  Max. Size: 150,000 d.w.t.
Chalmers, see Port Chalmers.
Chalmette, Louisiana, U.S.A.: 29.56 N. 90.00 W. **67**
  Max. Size: Depth 30 ft. – 35 ft.
  Also see New Orleans.
Chalna, see Mongla.
Chamela, Mexico: 19.32 N. 105.05 W. **57**
Champerico, Guatemala: 14.17 N. 91.55 W. **69**
  Max. Size: Varies according to anchorage. Airport: 3 hours
  drive.
Chan Chiang, see Zhanjiang.
Chanaral, Chile: 26.21 S. 70.38 W. **77**
  Max. Size: Draft 40 ft., LOA 250 m. Tankers: Draft 50 ft.
  LOA 250 m. Fuel: Small quantities of diesel. Airport: 150 km.
Chancay, Peru: 11.35 S. 77.16 W. **72**
  Max. Size: Anchorage depth 30 ft. – 48 ft.
Chandeleur Island, U.S.A.: 29.48 N. 88.51 W. **67**
Chandeleur Sound, (Mississippi Delta), Louisiana, U.S.A. . . **67**

Chandler, Quebec, Canada: 48.20 N. 64.39 W. 60
Max. Size: Depth 9.0 m. (LW). *Fuel:* Available.
Dry Docks: Les Mechins, 185 miles. *Airport:* Gaspe Airport.
Chang Chow, see Zhangzhou.
Changhang, South Korea: 36.01 N. 126.45 E. 42
Also see Kunsan.
Changi, see Singapore.
Channel Is., California, U.S.A. 57
Channel Islands, U.K. 19
Chantenay, France: 47.12 N. 1.36 W. 19
Chanthaburi, Thailand: 12.36 N. 102.11 E. 39
Chaparra, see Puerto Padre.
Charleroi, Belgium: 50.25 N. 4.30 E. 7
Charles Is., N.W.T., Canada: 62.41 N. 74.13 W. 59
Charleston, South Carolina, U.S.A.: 32.47 N. 79.56 W. . . 55, 66
Max. Size: LOA 1,043 ft., depth 40 ft. MLW. Coal: Draft 38 ft.
Tankers: Draft 30 ft. – 35 ft. *Fuel:* Bunker "C" and blended
intermediate grades. *Dry Docks:* 1×10,000 ton floating dock.
Airport: 10 miles.
Charlestown, (Nevis Is.), St. Christopher and Nevis:
17.08 N. 62.37 W. 71
Charlestown, U.K.: 50.20 N. 4.45 W. 7
Charlestown, U.S.A., see Boston.
Charlevoix, Michigan, U.S.A.: 45.20 N. 85.15 W. 62
Charlotte Harbour, Florida, U.S.A. 66, 69
Charlotte-Amalie, see St. Thomas.
Charlottetown, P.E.I., Canada: 46.14 N. 63.07 W. 60
Max. Size: Draft 30 ft. Tankers: Depth 28 ft. – 30 ft.
Fuel: By road tanker. *Airport:* 4 miles.
Charlton Is., Hudson Bay, Canada 59
Charny, Quebec, Canada: 46.45 N. 71.15 W. 60
Chatham, Canada, see Miramichi.
Chatham, U.K.: 51.24 N. 0.33 E. 6, 7
Max. Size: Draft 8.0 m., LOA 143 m., beam 25 m.
Fuel: By barge at anchorage.
Also see Medway Ports.
Chatham, Alaska, U.S.A., see Todd.
Chatham, Massachusetts, U.S.A.: 41.41 N. 69.58 W. . . . 63
Chatham Is., New Zealand 52
Chaumont, New York, U.S.A.: 44.04 N. 76.08 W. 62
Cheboygan, Michigan, U.S.A.: 45.39 N. 84.29 W. 62
Cheduba Is., Myanmar 37
Chefoo, see Yantai.
Cheju, South Korea: 33.31 N. 126.32 E. 42
Chekaa, Lebanon: 34.20 N. 35.43 E. 26
Max. Size: 15,000 d.w.t., depth 30 ft. – 31 ft. Tankers: Draft 20 ft.
Chekin Fjord, (Novaya Zemlya), Russia 16
Chelsea, Massachusetts, see Boston.
Chelsea, New York, see New York.
Chemainus, B.C., Canada: 48.55 N. 123.42 W. 56
Max. Size: Depth 19 ft. – 53 ft. (LW). *Fuel:* Diesel.
Chenchiang, see Zhenjiang.
Chennai, India: 13.06 N. 80.18 E. 37
Max. Size: LOA 900 ft., draft 42 ft. Tankers: LOA 900 ft.,
draft 53 ft. Ore: 130,000 d.w.t., draft 53 ft. *Fuel:* Grades
available: Fuel oil, L.D.O., gas oil. *Airport:* 40 km.
Chenshan, China: 30.35 N. 121.05 E. 42, 46
Max. Size: 50,000 d.w.t., depth 14 m.
Cherbourg, France: 49.38 N. 1.38 W. 4, 7, 19
Max. Size: Depth 7 m. – 14 m. No limit on length or beam.
Tankers: Max. draft 9 m. *Fuel:* Available.
Dry Docks: Max. vessel size: LOA 206.4 m., beam 25.70 m.
Airport: Moupertuis, 12 km.
Cherchel, Algeria: 36.35 N. 2.11 E. 22
Cheribon, see Cirebon.
Chernomorsk, Ukraine: 45.30 N. 32.40 E. 26
Max. Size: Draft 6 m. *Fuel:* Not guaranteed.
Cherry Point, Washington, U.S.A.: 48.52 N. 122.30 W. . 56
Max. Size: Depth 36 ft. – 65 ft. (Tankers). Limit
in Puget Sound 125,000 d.w.t.
Also see Bellingham.
Cherskiy, Russia: 68.45 N. 161.20 W. 54
Chesapeake, see Portsmouth.
Chesapeake and Delaware Ship Canal, U.S.A.:
39.16 N. 76.34 W. 63, 65
Max. Size: Draft 35 ft. (FW), LOA 760 ft., beam 170 ft.,
height of mast 133 ft.
Also see Baltimore.
Chesapeake Bay, U.S.A. 60, 63, 65
Chesapeake City, Maryland, U.S.A.: 39.32 N. 75.48 W. . 63, 65
Chester, N.S., Canada: 44.32 N. 64.15 W. 60
Chester, U.K.: 53.12 N. 2.55 W. 6
Chester, New York, U.S.A., see Port Chester.
Chester, Pennsylvania, U.S.A.: 39.51 N. 75.22 W. 63, 65
Also see Marcus Hook.
Chesterfield Inlet, N.W.T., Canada: 63.19 N. 90.45 W. . . 59
Chesterfield Is., Qld., Australia: 19.52 S. 158.15 E. . . . 50, 51
Chetaibi, Algeria: 37.04 N. 7.23 E. 22
Cheticamp, N.S., Canada: 46.38 N. 61.00 W. 60
Chetlat Is., (Laccadive Is.), India: 11.42 N. 72.40 E. 37

Chetumal, Mexico: 18.30 N. 88.17 W. 69
Chi Lung, see Keelung.
Chiang Yin, see Jiangyin.
Chiba, Japan: 35.36 N. 140.07 E. 43, 44, 45
Max. Size: Channel depths 10.5 m. – 18 m. Depth alongside
7.5 m. – 18 m. Tankers: Depth 20.5 m. (Keiyo Sea Berth).
Fuel: Most grades. *Dry Docks:* Largest 500,000 d.w.t.
Airport: 40 km., New Tokyo Airport (Narita).
Chicago, Illinois, U.S.A.: 41.50 N. 87.45 W. 55, 62
Max. Size: Limited at Seaway Locks: Length 740 ft., beam 78 ft.,
draft 26 ft. 3 in. Depth alongside terminals 27 ft. *Fuel:* All grades
available, ex-wharf or by barge. *Airport:* O'Hare.
Chicagof Is., Alaska, U.S.A.: 57.45 N. 136.10 W. 56
Chicama, see Puerto Chicama.
Chichester, U.K.: 50.50 N. 0.48 W. 5
Chichi Is., (Japan): 27.05 N. 142.14 E. 46
Chichiriviche, Venezuela: 10.55 N. 68.16 W. 74
Chicoutimi, see Port Saguenay.
Chignik, Alaska, U.S.A.: 56.20 N. 158.25 W. 54
CHILE 72, 77, 80
Chilka Lake, India 37
Chiloe Is., Chile 77
Chim Wan, see Kin Wan.
Chimbote, Peru: 9.05 S. 78.37 W. 72
Max. Size: Depth 28 ft. – 31 ft. *Dry Docks:* 15,000 ton floating
dock. *Airport:* Domestic.
Chin Men, (Quemoy), Taiwan: 24.30 N. 118.10 E. 42
CHINA, PEOPLE'S REPUBLIC OF 37, 39, 42, 43, 46, 48
Chinde, Mozambique: 18.38 S. 36.28 E. 30
Chinhai, South Korea: 35.07 N. 128.42 E. 42, 43
Max. Size: Harbour draft 17 ft. Chemical Co. Berth: Draft 34 ft.
Fuel: Available ex-barge from Masan.
Chinkiang, see Zhenjiang.
Chinnampo, see Nampo.
Chinwangtao, see Qinhuangdao.
Chioggia, Italy: 45.14 N. 12.19 E. 9, 24
Max. Size: Draft 28 ft. Ro/Ro: Draft 15 ft. *Fuel:* Available.
Chios, see Khios Is..
Chipiona, Spain: 36.45 N. 6.25 W. 20, 22
Chirikof Is., Alaska, U.S.A.: 55.55 N. 155.36 W. 54
Chiriqui, see Puerto Armuelles.
Chiriqui Grande, Panama: 8.56 N. 82.07 W. 69, 72
Max. Size: Pier: Length 600 ft., draft 36 ft. SBM: 150,000 d.w.t.,
draft 72 ft. *Fuel:* Available.
Chisimaio, Somalia: 0.22 S. 42.34 E. 30, 31
Max. Size: Draft 28 ft. (LT). *Airport:* 6 km.
Chittagong, Bangladesh: 22.19 N. 91.48 E. 37
Max. Size: LOA 186 m., depth 7.0 m. – 9.14 m. Anticipated safe
drafts are predicted three months in advance. The depth of water
over the Outer, Inner and Gupta Bars is maintained at 5.2 m. at
low water throughout the year. Tankers: Crude Oil Tankers
(Outer Anchorage) 34 ft. (10.36 m.). Clean tankers – LOA 560 ft.
(170.73 m.). *Fuel:* All grades. *Dry Docks:* Available.
Airport: Patenga, 5 miles.
Chiu Chiang, see Jiujiang.
Chiwan, China: 22.28 N. 113.53 E. 39, 42, 48
Max. Size: Chiwan: 60,000 d.w.t., depth 14.0 m.
Shekou: 76,000 d.w.t., depth 15.1 m. Mawan: 35,000 d.w.t.,
depth 12.4 m. *Fuel:* Available.
Chizha, Russia: 67.08 N. 44.28 E. 16
Chonburi, Thailand: 13.08 N. 100.49 E. 39
Max. Size: Tankers: 100,000 tonnes d.w.t., draft 15.4 m.
Chongiu, North Korea: 39.30 N. 125.10 E. 42
Chongjin, see Chungjin.
Chonos Archipelago, Chile 77
Choshi, Japan: 35.43 N. 140.51 E. 43, 45
Christchurch, New Zealand, see Lyttelton.
Christchurch, U.K.: 50.44 N. 1.46 W. 7
Christian Is., Ontario, Canada: 44.50 N. 80.14 W. 62
Christianshab, Greenland (Denmark): 68.49 N. 51.11 W. . 17
Christianstad, (St. Croix), Virgin Is. (U.S.A.):
17.45 N. 64.42 W. 69, 71
Christmas Island, Pacific Ocean, Kiribati: 1.58 N. 157.27 W. . 49
Christmas Island (Australia) 38, 50
Chuan Chow, see Quanzhou.
Chuginadek Is., see Islands of the Four Mountains.
Chuk Samet Port, see Sattahip.
Chukchi Sea, Russia/U.S.A. 54
Chumikan, Russia: 54.43 N. 135.15 E. 43
Chungjin, North Korea: 41.43 N. 129.42 E. 42, 43
Max. Size: Draft 28 ft. *Fuel:* Available.
Churchill, Manitoba, Canada: 58.47 N. 94.12 W. 59, 79
Max. Size: LOA 735 ft., beam 105 ft. and depth alongside
wharves at zero tide 18 ft. – 36 ft. (depending on cargo
handled). *Fuel:* Bunker fuel requires 30 days notice.
Arctic diesel fuel available all times. *Airport:* 5 miles.
Cide, Turkey: 41.53 N. 33.01 E. 26
Cienfuegos, Cuba: 22.09 N. 80.27 W. 69, 70
Max. Size: LOA 207 m., draft 11.55 m. *Fuel:* Diesel, Fuel oil.
Ciervana, Spain: 43.22 N. 3.06 W. 19

THE SHIPS ATLAS

Cigading, Indonesia: 6.00 S. 105.57 E. 38
  Max. Size: 150,000 d.w.t., draft 18 m.   *Fuel:* Available.
  Airport: Jakarta, 3 hours by road.
Cilacap, Indonesia: 7.44 S. 109.00 E. 38
  Max. Size: (a) Cilacap Port: LOA 190 m., draft 9.5 m. (HW).
  Tankers: LOA 250 m., draft 12 m., 85,000 d.w.t. (b) Iron Sand
  Port: LOA 186 m., draft 10.4 m.   *Fuel:* Available.
  Airport: 14 km.
Cillero, see Vivero.
Cinta Terminal, Indonesia: 5.27 S. 106.15 E. 38
  Max. Size: 175,000 d.w.t. (full cargo). Minimum 20,000 d.w.t.
Ciotat, see La Ciotat.
Cirebon, Indonesia: 6.41 S. 108.33 E. 38
  Max. Size: 8 m. draft at roads, 5 m. draft at wharves.
  Tankers: Up to 300 d.w.t.   *Dry Docks:* 600 d.w.t. graving dock.
  Airport: Kemajoran International, 257 km. Domestic
  airport, 40 km.
Ciro Marina, Italy: 39.24 N. 17.09 E. 24
  Max. Size: Depth 14.5 m.
Ciudad Bolivar, Venezuela: 8.09 N. 63.33 W. 69, 75
Ciudad Del Carmen, Mexico: 18.39 N. 91.50 W. 69
Ciudad Guayana, Venezuela: 8.05 N. 62.40 W. 75
Ciudad Madero, Mexico: 22.20 N. 97.50 W. 69
Ciudad Trujillo, see Santo Domingo.
Ciudadela, (Minorca), Spain: 40.00 N. 3.50 E. 22
Civitavecchia, Italy: 42.05 N. 11.47 E. 9, 21, 24
  Max. Size: Draft 38 ft. Tankers: 100,000 d.w.t., depth 50 m.
  Fuel: Fuel oil and gas oil by barge or tanker lorries.
  Airport: Leonardo da Vinci (Rome), 70 km.
Civitavecchia Port, Italy: 42.05 N. 11.47 E.
Ciwandan, Indonesia: 6.01 S. 105.57 E. 38
  Max. Size: Depth 10 m.   *Airport:* Jakarta, 2 hours by car.
Clacton, U.K.: 51.45 N. 1.10 E. 7
Clarecastle, Ireland: 52.48 N. 8.56 W. 5, 8
Clarence, see Middlesbrough.
Clarence Cove, Chile: 52.55 S. 70.09 W. 77
  Max. Size: LOA 250 m., draft 36 ft. (10.97 m.).
  Also see Punta Arenas.
Clarence River, see Yamba.
Clarence Town, (Long Is.), Bahamas: 23.07 N. 74.57 W. . . . 69, 70
Clarenville, Newfoundland, Canada: 48.08 N. 53.56 W. . . . 60
  Max. Size: Largest vessel: 644 ft. LOA, beam 84 ft., draft 26 ft.
  Fuel: Light fuels only (no bunkers).   *Airport:* Gander
  International, about 2 hours by road.
Clarion Is., (Revilla Gigedo Is.), Mexico: 18.18 N. 114.45 W. . . . 57
Clarks Harbour, N.S., Canada: 43.25 N. 65.38 W. . . . 60
Clarks Point, Alaska, U.S.A.: 58.51 N. 158.33 W. . . . 54
Clarkson, Ontario, Canada: 43.30 N. 79.36 W. 62
Claveria, (Luzon Is.), Philippines: 18.37 N. 121.05 E. . . 47
  Max. Size: Anchorage – depth 90 ft.
  Also see Aparri.
Clayton, New York, U.S.A.: 44.14 N. 76.04 W. 60
Clearwater, Florida, U.S.A.: 27.58 N. 82.48 W. 66
Cleethorpes, see Grimsby.
Cleveland, Ohio, U.S.A.: 41.31 N. 81.43 W. 55, 62
  Max. Size: Limited at Seaway Locks, 730 ft. LOA, 26 ft. draft.
  Tankers: Depth 23 ft.   *Fuel:* Marine diesel and gas oil.
***Cleveland Ledge Channel, (Cape Cod Canal),
  Massachusetts, U.S.A..*** 64
Clew Bay, Ireland 5
Clifden, Ireland: 53.30 N. 10.01 W. 5
Cliffe, see Coryton.
Clifton Point, (New Providence Is.), Bahamas:
  25.00 N. 77.36 W. 70
Clinton, Connecticut, U.S.A.: 41.16 N. 72.31 W. . . . 63
Clinton, Ohio, U.S.A., see Port Clinton.
Clipperton Is., (France): 10.20 N. 109.18 W. 49
Clonakilty, Ireland: 51.38 N. 8.52 W. 5
Clyde Port, U.K.: 55.56 N. 4.46 W. 5, 6
  Max. Size: Greenock: Depth 12.6 m.   *Fuel:* Available.
  Dry Docks: 1,000 ft. x 145 ft.   *Airport:* Glasgow, 12 miles,
  Prestwick, 30 miles.
  Also see Hunterston.
Coari, Brazil: 4.08 S. 63.07 W. 72
Coats Is., N.W.T., Canada 59
Coatzacoalcos, Mexico: 18.08 N. 94.25 W. 69
  Max. Size: Free Zone: LOA 185 m., draft 9.2 m. Pajaritos:
  59,000 d.w.t. LOA 250 m., draft 12 m.
  Fuel: Bunker "C" and diesel.   *Airport:* At Minatitlan, 20 km.
Cobh, Ireland: 51.51 N. 8.18 W. 5
  Max. Size: Draft 6 m.
  Also see Cork.
Cobourg, Ontario, Canada: 43.57 N. 78.10 W. 62
Cobourg, France: 49.17 N. 0.07 W. 8
Cochin, India: 9.58 N. 76.15 E. 37
  Max. Size: LOA 900 ft. (LASH) with draft 32 ft. salt water.
  Tankers: 115,000 d.w.t., draft 38 ft.   *Fuel:* All grades of fuel oils
  available.   *Dry Docks:* Max. LOA 217 ft.   *Airport:* Cochin
  Airport, 2 miles.
Cockatoo Island, W.A., Australia: 16.07 S. 123.35 E. . . 50, 51
  Max. Size: Depth 10.5 m.

Cockburn Harbour, see Grand Turk.
Cockburn Is., Ontario, Canada: 45.56 N. 83.20 W. . . . 62
Cockenzie, U.K.: 55.58 N. 2.58 W. 6
Coco Channel, (Andaman Is.), India 37
Coco Solo North, Panama: 9.22 N. 79.53 W. 73
  Max. Size: LOA 140 m., draft 5 m.   *Fuel:* Available.
Cocobeach, Gabon: 0.59 N. 9.34 E. 29
Coconut Point, see Castries.
Cocos Is., Costa Rica: 5.30 N. 87.00 W. 69
Cocos Islands (Australia) 36
Codajas, Brazil: 3.45 S. 62.00 W. 72
Codroy, Newfoundland, Canada: 47.53 N. 59.23 W. . . 60
Coetivy Is., South Africa: 7.06 S. 56.16 E. 30
Coffs Harbour, N.S.W., Australia: 30.18 S. 153.09 E. . . 50
Coiba Is., Panama: 7.30 N. 81.45 W. 69
Coishco, Peru: 9.01 S. 78.36 W. 72
Colachel, see Kolachel.
Colborne, see Port Colborne.
Colchester, U.K.: 51.54 N. 0.55 E. 5, 7
  Port closed.
Coleraine, U.K.: 55.08 N. 6.40 W. 5
  Max. Size: Recommended LOA 75 m., beam 12.0 m.,
  draft 4.2 m.   *Fuel:* Available at 48 hours notice.   *Airport:*
  Belfast, 40 miles.
Coll Is., U.K. 5
Collingwood, Ontario, Canada: 44.30 N. 80.30 W. . . . 60, 62
  Max. Size: Depths: Channel 6.1 m. – 7.2 m.
  Berths: 3.0 m. – 6.4 m.   *Fuel:* By road tanker.
Collingwood, New Zealand: 40.41 S. 172.40 E. 52
Collinsville, California, U.S.A.: 38.06 N. 121.49 W. . . 58
Collo, Algeria: 37.00 N. 6.35 E. 22
Cologne, Germany: 50.56 N. 6.57 E. 7
COLOMBIA 69, 72, 74
Colombia, see Puerto Colombia.
Colombo, Sri Lanka: 6.56 N. 79.50 E. 37
  Max. Size: Draft 13.2 m., LOA 315 m. Containers: Draft 13.2 m.
  Tankers: LOA 210 m., draft 11.8 m.   *Fuel:* Furnace diesel and
  gas oil.   *Dry Docks:* 263 m. x 44 m. x 89 m.,
  capacity 125,000 d.w.t.   *Airport:* International, 18 miles.
Colon, Argentina: 32.13 S. 58.07 W. 78
Colon, Panama: 9.21 N. 79.55 W. 73
  Max. Size: LOA 100 m., draft 20 ft. (6.1 m.).   *Fuel:* Available.
Colonia, (Yap Is.), Micronesia: 9.31 N. 138.08 E. . . . 46
Colonia, Uruguay: 34.28 S. 57.51 W. 77, 78
  Max. Size: Depth 8 ft. – 10 ft.   *Fuel:* By road tanker.   *Airport:*
  7 km.
Colonsay Is., U.K. 5
Colorado, U.S.A. 57
Colorado Is., Panama: 9.09 N. 79.51 W. 73
Columbia, North Carolina, U.S.A.: 35.55 N. 76.15 W. . . 63
Come-By-Chance, Newfoundland, Canada: 47.48 N.
  54.01 W. 60
  Max. Size: 326,000 d.w.t., LOA 1,500 ft. and draft 85 ft. – 90 ft.
  Fuel: Available.   *Airport:* St. John's, 152 km. and Gander,
  206 km.
Comodoro Rivadavia, Argentina: 45.51 S. 67.27 W. . . 77
  Max. Size: Draft 10.0 m.   *Fuel:* Diesel only.
  Airport: 11 km. from port.
Comoros Islands (France) 30
COMOROS, ISLAMIC FEDERAL REPUBLIC OF 30
Comox, B.C., Canada: 49.40 N. 124.55 W. 56
Con Son Is., Vietnam: 8.40 N. 106.36 E. 39
Conakry, Guinea: 9.31 N. 13.43 W. 27
  Max. Size: LOA 518 ft. – 655 ft., depth 7.0 m. – 11.0 m.
  Bulk: LOA 518 ft. – 655 ft., depth 10.0 m. – 11.0 m.
  Tankers: LOA 518 ft. –655 ft., depth 10.0 m.   *Fuel:* Light diesel.
  Dry Docks: Lifting capacity 700 tons.   *Airport:*
  International, 15 km.
Concarneau, France: 47.52 N. 3.55 W. 7, 19
  Max. Size: Tankers: LOA 105 m. – 106 m., draft 5.7 m.
  Other Vessels: LOA 115 m. – 116 m.   *Fuel:* Available.
  Dry Docks: Synchrolift capacity 2,000 tons; LOA 95 m.,
  keel length 76 m., beam 14 m., draft 5.50 m.
  Airport: Quimper – Pluguffan, 30 km.
Concepcion, Equatorial Guinea: 3.22 N. 8.48 E. 29
Concepcion, Paraguay: 23.22 S. 57.26 W. 77
Concepcion Bay, see Talcahuano.
Concepcion del Uruguay, Argentina: 32.29 S. 58.12 W. . . 77, 78
  Max. Size: Permitted draft in Uruguay River is 19 ft. Fresh water,
  subject to local conditions.   *Fuel:* Available.   *Dry
  Docks:* Length 70 m.   *Airport:* Gualeguaychu 10 km.,
  connects with Buenos Aires.
Conchan, Peru: 12.15 S. 76.56 W. 72
  Max. Size: Pier: 35,000 d.w.t., LOA 185 m., draft 11 m.
  Tanker buoy berth: Depth 60 ft.
  Also see Callao.
Conche, Newfoundland, Canada: 50.53 N. 55.54 W. . . 60
CONGO, DEMOCRATIC REPUBLIC OF 28, 30
CONGO, REPUBLIC OF 28
Connahs Quay, see Flint.
Conneaut, Ohio, U.S.A.: 41.58 N. 80.33 W. 62

Connecticut, U.S.A. **60, 63**
Constable Hook, see New York.
Constantine Harbour, (Aleutian Is.), Alaska, U.S.A.:
 51.24 N. 179.17 E. **54**
Constantza, Romania: 44.10 N. 28.39 E. **9, 21, 26**
 Max. Size: Depth 14 m. Southern Port: Depth 19 m.
 Tankers: 150,000 d.w.t., depth 18.5 m. *Fuel:* Gas oil.
 Dry Docks: Largest has 150,000 d.w.t. capacity. *Airport:* 25 km.
Constitucion, Chile: 35.19 S. 72.29 W. **77**
Contrecoeur, Quebec, Canada: 45.53 N. 73.12 W. **60, 61**
 Max. Size: LOA 350 ft., beam 105 ft., depth alongside 35 ft.
 Fuel: Available.
Convent, Louisiana, U.S.A.: 30.01 N. 90.50 W. **67**
 Also see Burnside.
Conwy, U.K.: 53.18 N. 3.50 W. **5, 7**
Coode Island, see Melbourne.
Cook Inlet, Alaska, U.S.A. **54**
Cook Islands (N.Z.) **49**
Cook Strait, New Zealand **52**
Cooktown, Qld., Australia: 15.20 S. 145.15 E. **46, 50, 51**
Coolangatta, see Tweed Heads.
Coolkeeragh, see Londonderry.
Coondapur, India: 13.37 N. 74.40 E. **37**
 Max. Size: Anchorage: Depth 9 fathoms.
 Airport: Bajpe, 73 miles.
Coos Bay, Oregon, U.S.A.: 43.22 N. 124.22 W. **55, 56, 57**
 Max. Size: LOA 725 ft., beam 110 ft., depth alongside 20 ft. –
 38 ft. (MLW). Tankers: Depth 28 ft. – 30 ft. *Fuel:* Bunker and
 diesel. *Dry Docks:* Largest handles vessels not exceeding
 220 ft. *Airport:* 5 miles.
Copenhagen, Denmark: 55.42 N. 12.37 E. **4, 10, 11, 12, 79**
 Max. Size: Limited by draft only. Depths in the port, 10 m.;
 in the Oil Harbour, 10.5 m.; at the Oil Pier, 12.0 m.
 Fuel: All grades. *Airport:* 6 miles.
Copper Harbour, Michigan, U.S.A.: 47.28 N. 87.52 W. **62**
Coquimbo, Chile: 29.57 S. 71.21 W. **77**
 Max. Size: Draft 10.0 m. *Fuel:* Diesel. *Airport:* 20 km.
Coquitlam, see Port Coquitlam.
Coral Harbour, N.W.T., Canada: 64.07 N. 83.10 W. **59**
Coral Sea **46, 49, 50, 51**
Corcubion, Spain: 42.58 N. 9.11 W. **20**
Cordemais, France: 47.16 N. 1.53 W. **19**
Cordova, Alaska, U.S.A.: 60.33 N. 145.46 W. **54**
 Max. Size: Draft 25 ft. *Fuel:* Fuel oil available.
 Airport: 13 miles.
Corea, Maine, U.S.A.: 44.24 N. 67.58 W. **60**
Corfu, Greece: 39.37 N. 19.56 E. **24, 25**
 Max. Size: Draft 7.0 m. *Fuel:* Diesel by road tanker.
 Airport: La Florida, 20 km.
Coria del Rio, Spain: 37.17 N. 6.03 W. **20, 22**
Corinth, see Isthmia.
Corinth Canal, Greece: 37.55 N. 23.00 E. **25**
 Max. Size: Beam 60 ft., draft 6.2 m. – 7.2 m. (depending on
 beam).
 Also see Isthmia.
Corinto, Nicaragua: 12.30 N. 87.11 W. **69**
 Max. Size: LOA 650 ft., 80 ft. beam. Draft controlled by depth of
 water in approach channel and state of swell, typically 13.5 m.
 Depth alongside 11.2 m. – 13 m. Tankers: Depth 12.2 m.
 Fuel: In emergencies small quantities only.
 Airport: At Managua, 150 km.
Corio Bay, see Geelong.
Corisco Bay **29**
Corisco Is., Equatorial Guinea: 0.56 N. 9.21 E. **29**
Cork, Ireland: 51.50 N. 8.17 W. **4, 5**
 Max. Size: Cork: LOA 152 m. – 158 m. Draft fresh water on
 Spring tides 8.7 m., on Neap tides 7.8 m. Whitegate: Tankers up
 to 275 m. LOA, 11.6 m. draft or 12 m. at highest tides.
 85,000 d.w.t. (100,000 tonnes displacement). Ringaskiddy:
 60,000 d.w.t., LOA 225 m., draft 13 m. *Fuel:* Most grades.
 Dry Docks: Main dry dock can take vessels up to 158.5 m. in
 length. Floating dock of 10,800 tons lifting capacity.
 Airport: 5 miles.
Corn Is., Nicaragua: 12.10 N. 83.05 W. **69**
Corner Brook, Newfoundland, Canada: 48.57 N. 57.57 W. . . . **60**
 Max. Size: LOA 650 ft., draft 30 ft. Wharves: Depth 17 ft. – 34 ft.
 Fuel: Gas oil and marine diesel available by truck.
 Airport: Gander 222 miles. Stephenville, 50 miles.
 Deer Lake, 30 miles.
Corniquel, see Quimper.
Cornwall, Ontario, Canada: 45.01 N. 74.43 W. **61**
 Max. Size: Depth in channel and berth 8.2 m.
 Fuel: By road tanker.
Cornwallis, see Port Cornwallis.
Coro, Venezuela: 11.27 N. 69.36 W. **69, 74**
Coromandel, New Zealand: 36.46 S. 175.32 E. **52**
Coron, (Basuanga Is.), **Philippines:** 12.01 N. 120.12 E. . . **46, 47**
Corona del Mar, California, U.S.A.: 33.37 N. 117.52 W. . . . **58**
Coronation Is., see South Orkney Is..

Coronel, Chile: 37.02 S. 73.10 W. **77**
 Max. Size: LOA 220 m., draft 11 m. – 12.6 m.
 Fuel: By road tanker.
 Airport: Carrel Sur Airport at Concepcion, 25 km.
Corozal, Belize: 18.22 N. 88.26 W. **69**
Corpach, U.K.: 56.50 N. 5.08 W. **5**
 Max. Size: LOA 61.87 m. (203 ft.), beam 10.67 m. (35 ft.),
 draft 4.11 m. (13 ft. 6 in.) FW.
 Also see Caledonian Canal.
Corpus Christi, Texas, U.S.A.: 27.48 N. 97.23 W. **55, 66, 69**
 Max. Size: Cargo vessels: 45 ft. draft. Tankers: 45 ft. draft.
 Fuel: Most grades. *Airport:* 8 miles.
Corral, see Puerto Corral.
Corrientes, Argentina: 27.29 S. 58.50 W. **77**
Corsica, France **21, 23, 24**
Cortes, see Puerto Cortes.
Corumba, Brazil: 19.00 S. 57.37 W. **72, 77**
Corunna, Spain: 43.23 N. 8.22 W. **19, 20, 21, 22**
 Max. Size: Cargo vessels 57 ft. draft. Tankers: LOA 300 m.,
 draft 16.5 m. *Fuel:* Available. *Airport:* Nearest international
 airport at Santiago de Compostella, 60 km. away.
Corvo Is., Azores (Portugal) **20**
Coryton, U.K.: 51.31 N. 0.32 E. **6**
 Max. Size: Coryton: LOA 1,100 ft., draft 14 m. (MLW).
 Shellhaven: LOA 1,200 ft., depth 14.6 m. (MLW).
 Also see London.
Cosmoledo Is., Seychelles: 9.43 S. 47.36 E. **30**
Cossack, see Port Walcott.
Cossack Pioneer, W.A., Australia: 19.35 S. 116.27 E. . . . **50, 51**
 Max. Size: 150,000 d.w.t. (175,000 tonnes displacement).
 Depth 85 m.
COSTA RICA **69**
Cotabato, (Mindanao Is.), **Philippines:** 7.15 N. 124.15 E. . . **47**
Cote St. Catherine Lock, see St. Lawrence Seaway.
Coteau Landing, Quebec, Canada: 45.15 N. 74.13 W. **61**
Cotonou, Benin: 6.20 N. 2.32 E. **28, 29**
 Max. Size: Depth 11 m. Tankers: LOA 215 m., draft 31 ft.
 Fuel: Fuel oil available. *Airport:* International, 5 km.
 Also see Seme Terminal.
Coueron, see Basse Indre.
Country Harbour, see Isaacs Harbour.
Coupeville, Washington, U.S.A.: 48.14 N. 122.41 W. **56**
Courseulles, France: 49.20 N. 0.28 W. **7**
Courtenay Bay, see Saint John, N.B., Canada.
Courtown Cays: 12.24 N. 81.27 W. **69**
Courtright, see Mooretown.
Covenas, Colombia: 9.25 N. 75.42 W. **69, 72**
 Max. Size: 150,000 d.w.t., draft 17.0 m.
 Airport: Cartagena, 3 hours drive. Monteria, 1.5 hours drive.
Covington, see Baltimore.
Cowell, S.A., Australia: 33.41 S. 136.56 E. **51**
Cowes, (Phillip Is.), Vic., **Australia:** 38.27 S. 145.14 E. . . **51**
Cowes, Isle of Wight, U.K.: 50.46 N. 1.18 W. **5, 7, 19**
 Max. Size: LOA 100 m., draft 4.7 m. – 5.4 m. *Fuel:* Fuel oil
 and diesel.
Cowichan Bay, B.C., Canada: 48.45 N. 123.36 W. **56**
 Max. Size: Largest vessel 200.51 m. LOA, beam 30.89 m.
 Depth 8.3 m. – 9.3 m. *Fuel:* Available.
Cox's Bazaar, Bangladesh: 21.27 N. 91.58 E. **37**
Cox's Cove, Newfoundland, Canada: 49.08 N. 58.03 W. **60**
Coxon Hole, (Roatan Is.), **Honduras:** 16.19 N. 86.33 W. . . . **69**
 Max. Size: Draft 9.4 m. *Airport:* National and international
 flights.
Cozumel, Mexico: 20.31 N. 85.57 W. **69**
 Max. Size: Depth 14 m. *Fuel:* By truck.
 Airport: Cozumel International.
Craig, Alaska, U.S.A.: 55.28 N. 133.09 W. **56**
Crail, U.K.: 56.15 N. 2.37 W. **6**
Credit, see Port Credit.
Creeksea, U.K.: 51.37 N. 0.47 E. **6**
 Max. Size: LOA 137 m., draft 6.8 m. – 7.3 m. *Fuel:* Available.
 Airport: Southend, 7 miles.
Cres, Croatia: 44.58 N. 14.25 E. **24**
Crescent City, California, U.S.A.: 41.45 N. 124.12 W. **57**
Crete, Greece **21, 25, 26**
Crib Point, see Hastings.
Crinan Canal, U.K.: 56.05 N. 5.34 W. **5**
Cristobal, Panama: 9.21 N. 79.55 W. **69, 72, 73**
 Max. Size: Harbour limitations generally unrestricted as to length
 and beam. Draft 40 ft. (12.2 m.). *Fuel:* Bunker "C", diesel, light
 fuel and light diesel. *Airport:* Tocument International, 48 miles.
 Also see Panama Canal.
CROATIA **9, 21, 24**
Crofton, B.C., Canada: 48.51 N. 123.38 W. **56**
 Max. Size: LOA 700 ft., depth 40 ft. (LW). *Fuel:* Diesel.
 Also see Chemainus.
Croker Is., N.T., Australia: 11.10 S. 132.32 E. **50**

THE SHIPS ATLAS

Cromarty Firth, U.K.: 57.41 N. 4.06 W. **5**
 Max. Size: Invergordon: Depth 5.5 m. – 13.5 m.
 Ro/Ro: LOA 118 m., draft 6 m. Nigg Bay: 155,000 d.w.t., LOA
 290 m., draft 16.5 m. (H.W.). *Fuel:* Available at Invergordon.
 Airport: Inverness, 30 miles.
Cromer, U.K.: 52.56 N. 1.18 E. **7**
Cronstadt Island, Trinidad and Tobago: 10.39 N. 61.38 W. . . **71, 75**
 Max. Size: LOA 350 ft., depth alongside 13.7 m. *Fuel:* By barge.
Crooked Is., Bahamas: 22.45 N. 74.10 W. **69, 70**
Crotone, Italy: 39.05 N. 17.08 E. **24**
Crown Point, (Tobago), Trinidad and Tobago:
 11.09 N. 60.51 W. **71, 75**
 Airport: Local flights to Port of Spain
Crozet Is., (France): 46.22 S. 51.45 E. **18**
Cruz Bay, (St. John), Virgin Is. (U.S.A.): 18.20 N. 64.48 W. . . **71**
Cruz Grande, Chile: 29.27 S. 71.20 W. **77**
Cua Lo, Vietnam: 18.50 N. 105.45 E. **39**
 Max. Size: LOA 100 m., draft 4.5 m.
CUBA **55, 69, 70**
Cuddalore, India: 11.43 N. 79.46 E. **37**
 Max. Size: Depth in anchorage 42 ft. *Airport:* Chennai 180 km.
Cuio, Angola: 12.58 S. 12.58 E. **28**
Cul de Sac Bay, St. Lucia: 13.59 N. 61.02 W. **71**
 Max. Size: LOA 650 ft., draft 37.5 ft. Tankers: LOA 1,300 ft.,
 draft 82 ft. (Largest vessel – 508,000 d.w.t., draft 84 ft.).
 Also see Castries.
Culebra, Panama Canal, Panama: 9.03 N. 79.39 W. . . . **73**
Culion, (Culion Is.), Philippines: 11.54 N. 120.01 E. . . . **46, 47**
Cullivoe, (Shetland Is.), U.K.: 60.42 N. 1.00 W. **5**
Cumana, Venezuela: 10.28 N. 64.12 W. **69, 71**
Cumaribo, see Puerto Cumaribo.
Cumberland Sound, N.W.T., Canada **17, 59**
Curacao, Netherlands Antilles **69, 74**
Curiapo, Venezuela: 8.30 N. 61.05 W. **75**
Curlew Is., Breton Sound, U.S.A. **67**
Curtis Is., (Kermadec Is.), New Zealand: 30.34 S. 178.34 W. . . **49**
Cushman, Oregon, U.S.A.: 44.00 N. 124.02 W. **57**
Cutler, Ontario, Canada: 46.14 N. 82.30 W. **62**
Cutuco, see La Union.
Cuxhaven, Germany: 53.52 N. 8.42 E. **8, 11, 12, 14**
 Max. Size: Depth 8.5 m. – 12 m. *Fuel:* Bunker and gas oil. *Dry Docks:* Floating dock for vessels up to 140 m. LOA.
 Airport: Hamburg-Fuhlsbuttel, 130 km. Bremen, 110 km.
Cuyahoga, see Cleveland.
Cuyo, Philippines: 10.50 N. 121.01 E. **47**
Cuyo Is., see Cuyo.
Cvetotchnoe, see Saimaa Canal.
Cyclades Is., Greece **25, 26**
CYPRUS **21, 26**
Cyrus Terminal, see Soroosh Terminal.
CZECH REPUBLIC **4, 9**

D

D'Antifer, see Antifer.
D'Entrecasteaux Is., Papua New Guinea **46**
D'Entrecasteaux Point, W.A., Australia: 34.50 S. 116.00 E. . . **50**
D'Urville Is., (South Is.), New Zealand: 40.50 S. 173.52 E. . . **52**
Da Nang, Vietnam: 16.07 N. 108.13 E. **39**
 Max. Size: LOA 190 m., beam 26 m., draft 11 m.
 Fuel: Available. *Dry Docks:* Max. 7,000 d.w.t. *Airport:*
 International, 5 km.
Dabo, Indonesia: 0.30 S. 104.32 E. **38, 40**
Dadiangas, (Mindanao Is.), Philippines: 6.06 N. 125.09 E. . . **46, 47**
 Max. Size: Draft 8.0 m. – 10.0 m. *Fuel:* Available.
 Airport: Buayan, 10.5 km.
Daebul, see Mokpo.
Daepo, see Daipori.
Daesan, South Korea: 37.02 N. 126.21 E. **42**
 Max. Size: 100,000 d.w.t., depth 17 m. at jetty. 300,000 d.w.t.
 at SPM. *Fuel:* By barge from Inchon. *Airport:* Seoul, 4 hours
 by car.
Dagupan, (Luzon Is.), Philippines: 16.05 N. 120.20 E. . . . **47**
Dahab, Egypt: 28.30 N. 34.30 E. **32**
Dahej, India: 21.43 N. 72.32 E. **37**
 Max. Size: Chemical: 50,000 d.w.t., LOA 215 m., draft 14.5 m.
 Copper: 30,000 d.w.t., LOA 200 m., draft 14 m.
 Airport: Vadodara, 90 km.
Dahlak Archipelago, Eritrea **32**
Dahouet, France: 48.35 N. 2.35 W. **7, 19**
Dai Hung, Vietnam: 8.28 N. 108.41 E. **39**
 Max. Size: CALM: Depth 110 m. *Airport:* By helicopter to
 Vung Tau.
Daipori, South Korea: 38.10 N. 128.36 E. **42, 43**
Daito Is., Japan **46**
Dakar, Senegal: 14.40 N. 17.26 W. **27**
 Max. Size: Draft 36 ft. (HW). Containers: Depth 11.6 m.
 Tankers: LOA 300 m., draft 11 m. M'Bao Terminal – Draft 18 m.
 Fuel: All grades. *Dry Docks:* Up to 60,000 d.w.t.
 Airport: International.
Dakhla, see Villa Cisneros.
Dakoank, (Nicobar Is.), India: 7.00 N. 93.50 E. **37**
Dalaro, Sweden: 59.08 N. 18.25 E. **11**
Dalhousie, N.B., Canada: 48.04 N. 66.22 W. **60**
 Max. Size: LOA 750 ft., beam 100 ft., draft 34 ft.
 Fuel: By road tanker. *Airport:* 1 flight daily to Montreal.
Dalhousie, Ontario, Canada, see Port Dalhousie.
Dalian, China: 38.55 N. 121.40 E. **42**
 Max. Size: Draft 8.83 m. – 10.05 m. Tankers: 200,000 d.w.t.,
 max. draft 15 m. *Fuel:* Fuel oil and diesel. *Airport:* Dalian.
Daliao, (Mindanao Is.), Philippines: 7.01 N. 125.31 E. . . . **47**
Dalma Is., U.A.E.: 24.30 N. 52.18 E. **35**
Dalrymple Bay, see Hay Point.
Dalsbruk, Finland: 60.00 N. 22.30 E. **11**
Dam Mon, Vietnam: 12.40 N. 109.24 E. **39**
 Max. Size: Draft 10.6 m. *Fuel:* Available. *Airport:* Nha Trang.
Daman, India: 20.24 N. 72.48 E. **37**
Damietta, Egypt: 31.28 N. 31.46 E. **26, 32**
 Max. Size: Draft 11 m. – 12.5 m., LOA 250 m. *Fuel:* Available.
 Airport: Port Said 60 km. Cairo 180 km.
Dammam, Saudi Arabia: 26.30 N. 50.12 E. **31, 35**
 Max. Size: Berth depths up to 13.4 m. *Fuel:* All grades.
 Airport: Dhahran.
Dampier, W.A., Australia: 20.38 S. 116.45 E. **50, 51**
 Max. Size: Ore loading: Depth 17.2 m. and 21.5 m. (LAT).
 General: Depth 7.19 m. (LAT). Mistaken Is. Salt: Depth 12.0 m.
 (LAT). Withnell Bay: LNG/LPG: Draft (LW) 12.2 m. and 12.5 m.
 Fuel: Available. *Airport:* Karratha 15 km., connects with Perth
 and Darwin.
Damqawt, Yemen: 16.20 N. 52.30 E. **31**
Dandong, China: 39.38 N. 124.09 E. **42**
 Max. Size: Depth at berth 10 m. Depth in channel
 6.3 m. – 8.0 m. *Fuel:* Available.
Danger Is., (New Zealand): 10.45 S. 165.50 W. **49**
Dania, see Hadsund.
Daniel, see Port Daniel.
Daniels Harbour, Newfoundland, Canada: 50.13 N. 57.35 W. . . **60**
Danube – Black Sea Canal, Romania **9**
 Max. Size: 5,000 d.w.t., LOA 138 m., beam 16.5 m. and
 draft 5.5 m.
 Also see Constantza.
Daoulas, France: 48.22 N. 4.16 W. **7, 19**
Dapa, (Siargao Is.), Philippines: 9.45 N. 126.01 E. **47**
Dar-es-Salaam, Tanzania: 6.50 S. 39.17 E. **30**
 Max. Size: Twin-screw: LOA 182.9 m., draft 10.1 m. (HWOST).
 Single-screw: LOA 175 m. Tankers: LOA 182.87 m.,
 36,000 d.w.t., draft 9.8 m. *Fuel:* Available.
 Airport: International.
Dargaville, New Zealand: 35.56 S. 173.52 E. **52**

Darien, Panama Canal, Panama: 9.07 N. 79.47 W. 73
Darien, Georgia, U.S.A.: 31.22 N. 81.25 W. 66
Darin, Saudi Arabia: 26.36 N. 50.04 E. 35
Darius Terminal, see Kharg Island.
Darlowo, Poland: 54.26 N. 16.24 E. 11
Dartford, U.K.: 51.27 N. 0.13 E. 6
Dartmouth, N.S., Canada: 44.40 N. 63.30 W. 60
 Also see Halifax.
Dartmouth, U.K.: 50.21 N. 3.34 W. 5, 7, 19
 Max. Size: LOA 143 m., draft 8.3 m. *Fuel:* Diesel. *Airport:* Exeter, 35 miles.
Daru, Papua New Guinea: 9.04 S. 143.12 E. 46, 51
 Max. Size: Depth at LAT 2.4 m. (8.0 ft.). *Fuel:* Available in drums.
Darvel Bay, see Lahad Datu.
Darwin, N.T., Australia: 12.28 S. 130.50 E. 46, 50
 Max. Size: LOA 246 m., draft 12.83 m. *Fuel:* All grades. *Airport:* International, 10 km.
Darwin, Falkland Is. (U.K.), see Port Darwin.
Das Island, Abu Dhabi, U.A.E.: 25.09 N. 52.52 E. 31, 35
 Max. Size: Loaded draft 79 ft. (24 m.). LNG/LPG: Draft 46 ft. (14 m.). Sulphur Berth: LOA 130 m., draft 10 m. *Fuel:* Small craft only. *Airport:* ADMA private airport.
Datu, see Lahad Datu.
Davant, Louisiana, U.S.A.: 29.36 N. 89.51 W. 67
 Max. Size: Depth at berth 18 m. Depth in channel 12.19 m. Also see Plaquemines.
Davao, (Mindanao Is.), Philippines: 7.04 N. 125.38 E. . . . 46, 47
 Max. Size: Draft to 13 m. *Fuel:* All grades. *Airport:* International, 3 km.
Davao Gulf, Philippines 46, 47
Davis Point, see San Francisco.
Davis Strait, Greenland/Canada 17, 53, 59, 79
Dawas River, see Ramba.
Dayina Is., U.A.E.: 24.57 N. 52.24 E. 35
Dayyer, Iran: 27.50 N. 57.56 E. 35
De Kastri, Russia: 51.29 N. 140.47 E. 43
 Max. Size: Depth 6.7 m. – 7.5 m. Tankers: 30,000 d.w.t., draft 10.0 m. (at anchorage).
De La Maire Strait, Argentina 77
De Panne, Belgium: 51.05 N. 2.35 E. 7
De Pere, Wisconsin, U.S.A.: 44.27 N. 88.04 W. 62
De Tour, Michigan, U.S.A.: 45.50 N. 84.00 W. 62
Dead Sea 26, 32
Deal, U.K.: 51.13 N. 1.25 E. 7
Deauville, France: 49.22 N. 0.06 E. 7, 8
 Max. Size: LOA 210 ft., beam 45 ft. and draft 4.0 m. (Springs). Also see Trouville.
Deception, Quebec, Canada: 62.00 N. 74.45 W. 59
Deer Park, see Houston.
Deering, Alaska, U.S.A.: 66.05 N. 162.44 W. 54
Deganwy, see Nagoya.
Degema, Nigeria: 4.44 N. 6.46 E. 29
 Max. Size: Anchorage 16 ft. draft.
Degerhamn, Sweden: 56.20 N. 16.25 E. 11
Degrad-des-Cannes, Guyane (France): 4.51 N. 52.16 W. . . . 72, 76
 Max. Size: Depth 2.5 m. plus height of tide, LOA 160 m. Tankers: LOA 130 m. *Fuel:* By road tanker.
Dekheila, see Alexandria.
Delair, see Philadelphia.
Delarof Is., (Aleutian Is.), Alaska, U.S.A. 54
Delaware, U.S.A. 60, 63, 65
Delaware Bay, Delaware, U.S.A. 60, 63, 65
Delaware City, Delaware, U.S.A.: 39.35 N. 75.36 W. 65
Delft, Netherlands: 52.01 N. 4.26 E. 7, 8
Delfzijl, Netherlands: 53.20 N. 6.56 E. 7, 8, 9, 11, 12, 14
 Max. Size: Draft up to 9.0 m. (HW). *Fuel:* Available. *Dry Docks:* 20,000 d.w.t. *Airport:* Eelde (Groningen).
Dellys, Algeria: 36.55 N. 3.55 E. 22
 Max. Size: LOA 100 m., draft 18 ft. *Airport:* Algiers, 80 km.
Demerara, see Georgetown.
Demta, Indonesia: 2.21 S. 140.10 E. 46
Den Helder, Netherlands: 52.58 N. 4.47 E. 7, 8, 9
 Max. Size: Draft 9.5 m. *Fuel:* Available. *Airport:* Schiphol, 90 km.
Dendang, Indonesia: 3.06 S. 107.54 E. 38
Denham, W.A., Australia: 25.55 S. 113.31 E. 50, 51
Denia, Spain: 38.50 N. 0.07 E. 22
Denmark, W.A., Australia: 35.00 S. 117.20 E. 50
DENMARK 4, 10, 11, 12, 14
Denofa, see Fredrikstad.
Derby, W.A., Australia: 17.17 S. 123.35 E. 50, 51
 Max. Size: Anchorage – Draft 12 m.
Derince, Turkey: 40.45 N. 29.50 E. 23
 Max. Size: Draft 12.0 m. *Fuel:* Fuel and diesel by truck. *Airport:* Istanbul, 130 km.
Derna, Libya: 32.45 N. 22.40 E. 24
 Max. Size: Depth 9 m. Tankers: 18,000 d.w.t., draft 11.5 m. *Fuel:* Available.

Deseado, see Puerto Deseado.
Deseo, see Caimanera.
Deseronto, Ontario, Canada: 44.12 N. 77.03 W. 62
Destrehan, Louisiana, U.S.A.: 29.56 N. 90.21 W. 67
 Max. Size: Minimum 41 ft. depth. Also see South Louisiana.
Detroit, Michigan, U.S.A.: 42.19 N. 83.05 W. 55, 62
 Max. Size: LOA 730 ft., draft 26 ft. *Fuel:* All grades.
Deventer, Netherlands: 52.15 N. 6.09 E. 8
Deversoir, Egypt: 30.25 N. 32.22 E. 33
Deversoir By-Pass, Suez Canal, Egypt 33
Devonport, Tas., Australia: 41.11 S. 146.22 E. 50, 51
 Max. Size: LOA 235 m., draft 10.5 m. *Fuel:* By road tanker. *Airport:* Internal, 8 km.
Devonport, New Zealand: 36.50 S. 174.50 E. 52
Devonport, U.K.: 50.25 N. 4.10 W. 7
Dhekelia, Cyprus: 34.58 N. 33.45 E. 26
 Max. Size: LOA 735 ft., draft 41 ft.
Dhenousa Is., Greece: 37.08 N. 25.50 E. 25
Dhuba, Saudi Arabia: 27.34 N. 35.33 E. 26, 32
 Max. Size: Draft 9.5 m. Tanker (MBM): 10,500 tonnes d.w.t. *Airport:* Tabuk, 180 km.
Dia Is., Greece: 35.26 N. 25.15 E. 25
Diamante, Argentina: 32.05 S. 60.33 W. 77, 78
 Max. Size: LOA 250 m., depth 9.0 m. *Fuel:* Available.
Diamond Harbour, see Haldia.
Dibba, Oman: 25.38 N. 56.17 E. 35
Dicido, see Castro-Urdiales.
Dickson, see Port Dickson.
Didon Terminal, Tunisia: 33.47 N. 11.54 E. 24
 Max. Size: 50,000 d.w.t., LOA 190 m., depth 70 m.
Diego Alvarez, see Gough Is..
Diego Garcia, Chagos Arch. (U.K.): 6.34 S. 72.24 E. 30
 Max. Size: Depth 13.7 m.
Diego Suarez, see Antsiranana.
Dielette, France: 49.33 N. 1.52 W. 7, 19
Dieppe, France: 49.55 N. 1.04 E. 5, 7, 8
 Max. Size: LOA 160 m. 10,000 – 12,000 d.w.t. Depth 4.5 m. – 9 m. *Fuel:* By road or barge. *Dry Docks:* Can receive ships 129 m. x 17 m. *Airport:* Saint Aubin, 3 km.
Digby, N.S., Canada: 44.38 N. 65.45 W. 60
 Max. Size: LOA 400 ft., 28 ft. depth at LW. *Fuel:* Diesel. *Airport:* Small local. Halifax, 180 miles.
Digges Is., N.W.T., Canada: 62.34 N. 77.55 W. 59
Dijon, France: 47.20 N. 5.02 E. 9
Dikili, Turkey: 39.04 N. 26.54 E. 25, 26
 Max. Size: Depth 7 m. – 9 m. *Fuel:* Available. *Airport:* 100 km.
Dikson, see Port Dikson.
Dikson Is., Russia: 73.40 N. 80.05 E. 16
Dili, East Timor: 8.33 S. 125.31 E. 46
 Max. Size: LOA 120 m., depth 7 m.
Diliskelesi, Turkey: 40.46 N. 29.32 E. 23, 25
 Max. Size: Alemdar – Depth 6 m. – 14 m. Colakoglu – Depth 7.4 m. – 11 m. Solventas – Depth 8.5 m. Sedef – LOA 175 m., draft 11 m. *Fuel:* Available.
Dillingham, Alaska, U.S.A.: 59.00 N. 158.30 W. 54
Dinagat Is., Philippines 47
Dinant, Belgium: 50.15 N. 4.55 E. 7
Dinard, France: 48.38 N. 2.05 W. 7, 19
Dingle, Ireland: 52.08 N. 10.16 W. 5
Dingle, U.K., see Liverpool.
Dingle Bay, Ireland 5
Dingwall, N.S., Canada: 46.54 N. 60.28 W. 60
Diomede Is., Russia: 65.45 N. 169.10 W. 54
Dipilog, (Mindanao Is.), Philippines: 8.35 N. 123.20 E. . . . 46, 47
Disappointment Is., French Polynesia (France): 14.08 S. 141.15 W. 49
Discovery Bay, see Port Rhoades.
Disko Is., Greenland (Denmark) 17
Diu, India: 20.43 N. 71.00 E. 37
Divilacan, see Aparri.
Dixon Entrance, U.S.A./Canada 56
Dixon Island, see Port Walcott.
Djakarta, see Jakarta.
Djen-Djen, Algeria: 36.50 N. 5.54 E. 22
 Max. Size: LOA 189 m., draft 32 ft. *Fuel:* By road tanker. *Airport:* 2 km.
Djeno Terminal, Congo (Rep. of): 4.56 S. 11.54 E. 28
 Max. Size: Draft 16 m. (52 ft. 6 in.). *Fuel:* Available at Pointe Noire. *Airport:* Pointe Noire, 6 km.
Djerba, Tunisia: 33.52 N. 10.51 E. 24
Djibouti, Djibouti: 11.36 N. 43.08 E. 31, 32
 Max. Size: Draft: Cargo vessels 11 m., tankers 12 m., container vessels 11 m. *Fuel:* Fuel and diesel oil. *Airport:* International, 7 km.
DJIBOUTI 31, 32
Djidjelli, see Jijel.
Djupivogur, Iceland: 64.40 N. 14.15 W. 17

THE SHIPS ATLAS

Djuron, Sweden: 58.38 N. 16.20 E. 11
  Max. Size: Depth 12.2 m. (MLW).
  Also see Norrkoping.
Dneprobugsky, Ukraine: 46.35 N. 31.57 E. 26
  Max. Size: LOA 215 m., draft 9.8 m.
Dobo, (Aru Is.), Indonesia: 5.45 S. 134.12 E. 46
Docksta, see Askja.
Dodecanese Is., Greece: 37.00 N. 27.00 E. 25, 26
Doha, Qatar: 25.17 N. 51.32 E. 31, 35
  Max. Size: LOA 625 ft., beam 90 ft., draft 8.3 m. (H.W.). *Fuel:* Available. *Dry Docks:* Capacity 10,000 d.w.t. *Airport:* International, 3 miles.
Dolak Is., Irian Jaya, Indonesia 46
Domburg, Netherlands: 51.35 N. 3.32 E. 7, 8
DOMINICA 69, 71
Dominical, Costa Rica: 9.15 N. 83.50 W. 69
DOMINICAN REPUBLIC 55, 69, 70
Domsjo, see Kopmanholmen.
Donaldsonville, Louisiana, U.S.A.: 30.05 N. 91.00 W. . 67
  Max. Size: CFI: Draft 40 ft. *Fuel:* Available.
Donegal, Ireland: 54.39 N. 8.07 W. 5
Donegal Bay, Ireland 5
Dong Hoi, Vietnam: 17.28 N. 106.38 E. 39
Dong Nai, Vietnam: 10.54 N. 106.50 E. 39
  Max. Size: LOA 120 m., draft 5.2 m. *Fuel:* Available.
  Airport: Tan Son Nhat, 33 km.
Dongarra, W.A., Australia: 29.17 S. 114.56 E. . . . 50
Donges, France: 47.18 N. 2.04 W. 19
  Max. Size: LOA 355 m., draft 16.1 m.
  Airport: Nantes, 1 hour by road.
  Also see Nantes.
Donggala, Indonesia: 0.39 S. 119.44 E. 38, 46
Dongshan, China: 23.45 N. 117.31 E. 42
  Max. Size: 8,000 d.w.t., depth 7.2 m. Tankers: 5,000 d.w.t., depth 5.2 m. *Fuel:* Available.
Donnaconna, Quebec, Canada: 46.40 N. 71.46 W. . . 60
Donnes, Norway: 66.10 N. 12.45 E. 15
Donsol, (Luzon Is.), Philippines: 12.55 N. 123.35 E. . 47
Dordrecht, Netherlands: 51.49 N. 4.40 E. 7, 8
  Max. Size: LOA 175 m., beam 25 m., draft 31 ft.
  Fuel: By barge. *Airport:* Rotterdam, 25 km. Amsterdam, 90 km.
Dornoch, U.K.: 57.50 N. 4.00 W. 5
Dornumersiel, Germany: 53.41 N. 7.22 E. 8, 14
Dorood Terminal, see Kharg Island.
Dortyol Terminal, Turkey: 36.50 N. 36.12 E. 26
  Max. Size: Delta Terminal: LOA 220 m., depth 12.6 m., 40,000 d.w.t. *Airport:* Adana, 100 km.
  Also see Botas.
Dos Bocas, Mexico: 18.37 N. 93.10 W. 69
  Max. Size: 250,000 d.w.t., LOA 345 m.
Douala, Cameroon: 4.03 N. 9.42 E. 28, 29
  Max. Size: LOA 200 m., draft 6.2 m. plus tide.
  Tankers: Depth 9.5 m. at LW (tidal range 2.20 m.).
  Fuel: Available. *Airport:* International, 4 km.
Douarnenez, France: 48.06 N. 4.19 W. 7, 19
Douglas, Australia, see Port Douglas.
Douglas, (Isle of Man), U.K.: 54.09 N. 4.28 W. 5
  Max. Size: Passenger: LOA 130 m., draft 6.0 m. Cargo vessels: LOA 65 m., draft 4.5 m. – 5.25 m. Tankers: LOA 85 m., draft 5.2 m. at LWOST. *Fuel:* By road tanker.
  Airport: Ronaldsway, 9 miles.
Douglastown, Quebec, Canada: 48.46 N. 64.23 W. . . 60
Douro River, see Leixoes.
Dover, Tas., Australia: 43.19 S. 147.02 E. 51
Dover, Canada, see Port Dover.
Dover, U.K.: 51.07 N. 1.18 E. 5, 7
  Max. Size: Cruise Terminal: Depth 10 m. *Fuel:* By barge.
  Airport: London (Heathrow and Gatwick) Airports. Manston nearby for charter flights.
Drag, Norway: 68.02 N. 16.04 E. 15
Dragonera, Spain: 39.35 N. 2.19 E. 22
Dragor, Denmark: 55.36 N. 12.41 E. 12
Drake Passage, Chile. 77, 80
Drakes Bay, California, U.S.A. 58
Drammen, Norway: 59.49 N. 10.13 E. 8, 11, 12
  Max. Size: Draft 30 ft. Tankers: Draft 7.0 m. *Fuel:* All grades.
  Dry Docks: Floating – 20,000 tons. *Airport:* Fornebu (Oslo), 16 miles.
Drapetzona, see Piraeus.
Dreger Harbour, see Finschhaven.
Dreines, Faroe Is. (Denmark): 61.32 N. 6.48 W. 5
Drepano, Greece: 38.19 N. 21.52 E. 24, 25
Drift River Terminal, Alaska, U.S.A.: 60.33 N. 152.08 W. . 54
  Max. Size: Max. displacement 50,000 tons. LOA 850 ft.
Drobak, Norway: 59.40 N. 10.38 E. 8, 11, 12
Drogheda, Ireland: 53.45 N. 6.18 W. 5
Druif, Aruba (Netherlands): 12.32 N. 70.04 W. . . . 74
Drujba, see Bourgas.
Dry Tortugas Is., Florida, U.S.A. 66, 70
DTBASA/SE, see Carmopolis.

DTSE/GEBIG Oil Terminal, Brazil: 23.04 S. 44.13 W. . . 76
  Max. Size: 500,000 d.w.t., max. draft 25 m. *Fuel:* Available.
DTSE/GEGUA, see Rio de Janeiro.
DTSUL, see Sao Francisco do Sul.
DTSUL/GERIG, see Tramandai.
Dubai, U.A.E.: 25.16 N. 55.18 E. 31, 35, 37
  Max. Size: Khor Dubai: Depth 3 m. – 5.5 m. Hamriya Port: Depth 4.5 m. – 6 m. *Airport:* Regular International flights.
  Also see Port Rashid.
Dubandi: 40.26 N. 50.15 E. 9
Dublin, Ireland: 53.21 N. 6.16 W. 4, 5
  Max. Size: Draft 10.2 m. HW Normal Tides, 10.5 m. HW Springs. LOA approx. 220 m. *Fuel:* All grades. *Dry Docks:* Normal length 637 ft. *Airport:* Dublin, 6 miles.
Dublin Bay, Ireland. 5
Dubrovnik, Croatia: 42.38 N. 18.07 E. 9, 21, 24
  Max. Size: See Gruz Harbour. *Fuel:* By coastal tanker from Split. *Airport:* Cilipi, 25 km.
Duc Pho, Vietnam: 14.45 N. 109.05 E. 39
Ducie Is., Pitcairn Is. (U.K.): 24.40 S. 124.48 W. . . . 49
Duckerswich, Germany: 54.03 N. 9.19 E. 14
Dudinka, Russia: 69.25 N. 86.10 E. 16
Due, see Makarevskiy.
Dufferin, see Port Dufferin.
Dugirat, see Omis.
Duisburg-Ruhrort, Germany: 51.25 N. 6.46 E. . . . 7, 8, 9
  Max. Size: LOA 110 m., beam 11.4 m., draft 3.5 m.
  Airport: Dusseldorf, 20 km.
Duke of Gloucester Is., French Polynesia (France):
  20.36 S. 143.16 W. 49
Dukhan, Qatar: 25.28 N. 50.51 E. 35
Dulang Marine Terminal, Malaysia: 5.48 N. 104.10 E. . 38, 39
  Max. Size: Alongside berthing – 85,000 d.w.t. (100,000 tons – full load displacement), LOA 242 m. Tandem mooring – 150,000 d.w.t. (196,000 tons – full load displacement), LOA 281 m.
Duluth-Superior, Minnesota, U.S.A.: 46.49 N. 92.09 W. . 55, 62
  Max. Size: Duluth: Depth 26 ft. Superior: Depth 27 ft.
  Fuel: Available.
  Also see Superior.
Dumaguete, (Negros Is.), Philippines: 9.15 N. 123.18 E. . . 46, 47
  Max. Size: Draft 12 m., 20,000 d.w.t.
Dumai, Indonesia: 1.41 N. 101.27 E. 37, 38, 39, 40
  Max. Size: LOA 315 m. (1,033 ft.), draft 17.7 m.
  Airport: Internal, 10 km.
Dumaring, Indonesia: 1.45 N. 118.10 E. 38, 46
Dumbarton, U.K.: 55.57 N. 4.34 W. 6
Dumfries, U.K.: 55.03 N. 3.36 W. 5
Dun Laoghaire, Ireland: 53.18 N. 6.08 W. 5
  Max. Size: Depth 5.5 m. *Fuel:* Available.
  Airport: Dublin, 20 km.
  Also see Dublin.
Dunbar, U.K.: 56.01 N. 2.31 W. 5, 6
  Max. Size: LOA 50 m., draft 4 m. (HWS). *Fuel:* By road tanker.
  Airport: Edinburgh, 35 miles.
Dunbeath, U.K.: 58.15 N. 3.27 W. 5
Duncan Bay, see Campbell River.
Duncan Passage, (Andaman Is.), India 37
Duncannon, Ireland: 52.13 N. 6.56 W. 5
Dundalk, Ireland: 54.00 N. 6.23 W. 4, 5
  Max. Size: LOA 106 m. Vessels lie aground at LW.
  Fuel: Available. *Airport:* Dublin, 70 km.
Dundalk, U.S.A., see Baltimore.
Dundalk Bay, Ireland 5
Dundas, see North Star Bugt.
Dundas Strait, Australia 46
Dundee, U.K.: 56.28 N. 2.57 W. 6
  Max. Size: LOA 250 m., beam 45 m., draft 9 m.
  Fuel: Available. *Dry Docks:* 500 ft. length, 46 ft. beam, draft 13 ft. 6 in. *Airport:* Dundee.
Dundrum, U.K.: 54.16 N. 5.51 W. 5
Dunedin, New Zealand: 45.53 S. 170.31 E. 52
  Max. Size: Draft 7.92 m. (HW), LOA 190 m. (623 ft.).
  Tankers: Draft 8.0 m. *Fuel:* Available.
  Airport: International, 25 km.
  Also see Otago Harbour.
Dungarvan, Ireland: 52.05 N. 7.35 W. 5
Dungeness, U.K.: 50.55 N. 0.58 E. 5
Dungun, Malaya, Malaysia: 4.47 N. 103.27 E. . . 38, 39, 40
Dungunab, Sudan: 21.10 N. 37.10 E. 32
Dunkirk, France: 51.03 N. 2.24 E. 7
  Max. Size: Eastern Port: Tankers: Draft 14.2 m., LOA 265 m. (Turbine) 289 m. (Motor), width 45.05 m. Grain: Draft 14.50 m. Ore/coal: Draft 14.2 m. Gas: Draft 9.5 m. – 11.7 m.
  Western Port: Tankers: Draft 20.50 m., LOA 380 m.
  Ore/coal: Draft 18 m. *Fuel:* Diesel and gas oil.
  Dry Docks: Max. length of vessel 289 m., beam 45 m., draft 8.5 m. *Airport:* Marck, 35 km.
Dunkirk, New York, U.S.A.: 42.30 N. 79.20 W. . . . 60, 62

Dunmore East, Ireland: 52.09 N. 6.59 W. 5
  Max. Size: Depth 2.9 m. *Fuel:* Diesel.
  Airport: Waterford, 13 km.
Dunoon, U.K.: 55.57 N. 4.55 W. 6
  Max. Size: Depth 4.3 m.
Dunvegan, U.K.: 57.26 N. 6.35 W. 5
Duran, see Guayaquil.
Durazzo, see Durres.
Durban, South Africa: 29.53 S. 31.02 E. 30
  Max. Size: Draft 39 ft., LOA 245 m. Bulk: LOA 255 m., draft 12.5 m. Tankers: SBM up to 300,000 d.w.t.
  Fuel: All grades. *Dry Docks:* Overall docking length 364.44 m. Width at entrance top 33.52 m. Depth on entrance sill MHWS 12.56 m. *Airport:* Louis Botha, 15 miles, connects with Johannesburg.
Durness, U.K.: 58.40 N. 4.30 W. 5
Durres, Albania: 41.19 N. 19.28 E. 9, 21, 24, 25
  Max. Size: Draft 28 ft. 6 in. *Fuel:* Emergency only.
  Airport: Rinas, 35 km.
Dusseldorf, Germany: 51.14 N. 6.46 E. 7, 8, 9
Dutch Harbor, see Unalaska.
Duwwah, (Masirah Is.), Oman: 20.45 N. 59.00 E. . . . 31, 37
Dwarkar, India: 22.15 N. 69.01 E. 37
Dynas, see Kramfors.
Dzaoudzi, (Ile. Mayotte), Comoros Is. (France):
  12.47 S. 45.16 E. 30
  Max. Size: Anchorage. *Airport:* Connects to Reunion Is.
Dzubga, Russia: 44.19 N. 38.42 E. 26

NOTES, ADDITIONS, CORRECTIONS
Please also advise Shipping Guides Ltd.
75 Bell Street, Reigate, RH2 7AN, United Kingdom
Tel: +44 1737 242255   Fax: +44 1737 222449
Email: updates@portinfo.co.uk   Web: www.portinfo.co.uk

E

Eads, see Port Eads.
Eagle Point, see Philadelphia.
Eagle River, Michigan, U.S.A.: 47.25 N. 88.20 W. 62
East Bay, Louisiana, U.S.A.: 67
East Boston, see Boston.
East Cape, (North Is.), New Zealand: 37.42 S. 178.36 E. . . 52, 54
East China Sea 42, 45, 46
East Frisian Islands, Netherlands 8, 14
East London, South Africa: 33.02 S. 27.55 E. 30
  Max. Size: LOA 245 m., draft 10.4 m. Tankers: LOA 204 m., draft 10 m. *Fuel:* Heavy oil and gas oil available.
  Dry Docks: Overall docking length 198.5 m., width at entrance top 27.2 m., depth on sill, HWOST 10.2 m.
  Airport: East London International, 8 km.
East River, New York, U.S.A. 63
East Siberian Sea, Russia 54
EAST TIMOR 46
East Zeit Terminal, Egypt: 27.51 N. 33.36 E. 26, 32
  Max. Size: 85,000 d.w.t., LOA 838 ft., draft 60 ft.
Eastbourne, U.K.: 50.46 N. 0.18 E. 5, 7
Easter Island, Chile: 27.09 S. 109.26 W. 49
  Max. Size: Anchorage. *Fuel:* Available.
  Airport: International, 2 miles.
Eastern Channel, Korea Strait 34, 45
Eastham, U.K.: 53.21 N. 2.58 W. 6
  Also see Manchester.
Eastmain, Quebec, Canada: 52.13 N. 78.30 W. . . . 59
Eastport, Maine, U.S.A.: 44.54 N. 66.59 W. 60
  Max. Size: 50,300 d.w.t., LOA 215 m., draft 12 m.
  Fuel: By road tanker. *Airport:* Eastport, 3 km. Bangor, 190 km.
Ebeltoft, Denmark: 56.12 N. 10.41 E. 11, 12
Ebome Marine Terminal, Cameroon: 2.48 N. 9.49 E. . . . 29
  Max. Size: SBM – 230,000 tonnes d.w.t., depth 30 m.
Ebon, Marshall Is.: 4.35 N. 168.40 E. 49
Eccles, see Manchester.
Eceabat, Turkey: 40.12 N. 26.21 E. 25
Eckernforde, Germany: 54.29 N. 9.51 E. 12, 14
  Max. Size: Outer Harbour: Draft 5 m. Inner Harbour: Draft 3 m.
  Fuel: Diesel.
Ecopetrol, see Mamonal.
ECUADOR 72
Edd, Eritrea: 14.00 N. 41.37 E. 32
Edea, Cameroon: 3.51 N. 10.11 E. 29
Eden, N.S.W., Australia: 37.04 S. 149.55 E. 50
  Max. Size: 50,000 g.r.t., LOA 230 m., draft 11.3 m. Tankers: LOA 183 m., draft 10.3 m. *Fuel:* Distillate and diesel available. *Airport:* Merimbula, 18 km., connects with Sydney.
Edenton, North Carolina, U.S.A.: 36.04 N. 76.37 W. . . . 63
Edgard, Louisiana, U.S.A.: 30.02 N. 90.33 W. 67
Edgartown, Massachusetts, U.S.A.: 41.23 N. 70.29 W. . . 63
Edge Is., Norway: 78.00 N. 23.00 E. 17
Edgell Is., N.W.T., Canada: 61.50 N. 65.00 W. . . . 59
Edgewater, see Hoboken.
Edinburgh, Tristan da Cunha (U.K.): 37.03 S. 12.18 W. . . 28
  Max. Size: Anchorage in 18 fathoms.
Edincik, Turkey: 40.21 N. 27.51 E. 25, 26
  Max. Size: 5,000 d.w.t.
Edithburgh, see Port Giles.
Edmonds, Washington, U.S.A.: 47.48 N. 122.22 W. . . . 56
Eems Canal, Netherlands 8
Eemshaven, Netherlands: 53.27 N. 6.50 E. 7, 8, 9, 12, 14
  Max. Size: Draft 10.5 m. *Fuel:* Available.
  Airport: Eelde (Groningen).
Efate Is., New Caledonia (France) 49
Egadi Is., (Sicily), Italy: 38.00 N. 12.30 E. 24
Ege Gubre, see Nemrut Bay.
Egedesminde, see Aasiaat.
Egegik, Alaska, U.S.A.: 58.12 N. 157.22 W. 54
Egernsund, see Grasten.
Egersund, Norway: 58.27 N. 6.00 E. 10, 11
  Max. Size: 45,000 d.w.t., draft 31 ft. *Fuel:* Gas oil and light marine diesel.
Egmont Is., Chagos Arch. (U.K.): 6.48 S. 71.25 E. . . . 30
Egvekinot, (Falster), Russia: 66.20 N. 179.18 W. . . . 54
EGYPT 21, 26, 32, 33, 34
Eiao, (Marquesas Is.), French Polynesia (France):
  8.00 S. 140.41 W. 49
Eidem, see Elnesvagen.
Eidsvik, see Reykjavik.
Eigg, U.K.: 56.55 N. 6.10 W. 5
Eight Degrees Channel, Maldives 37
Eiketit, Norway: 60.42 N. 5.33 E. 11
Eil, Somalia: 8.01 N. 49.55 E. 31

Eilat, Israel: 29.32 N. 34.57 E. **21, 26, 32**
   Max. Size: Main Cargo Jetty: Draft 11.9 m.
   South Oil Jetty: 500,000 d.w.t., depth 28.6 m. *Fuel:* All grades
   by road tankers. *Dry Docks:* Syncrolift capacity 1,200 tons.
   Airport: Eilat, connects with Tel Aviv.
Eindhoven, Netherlands: 51.26 N. 5.30 E. **9**
Eisenhower Lock, see St. Lawrence Seaway.
Ekenas, Finland: 59.58 N. 23.26 E. **11**
   Max. Size: Draft 15.1 ft. (4.6 m.). *Fuel:* By road tanker.
   Airport: Helsinki, 100 km.
Ekerem: 38.04 N. 53.50 E. **9**
Ekonomiya, Russia: 64.42 N. 40.31 E. **16**
Ekuata, Gabon: 0.16 N. 9.17 E. **29**
El Aaiun, see Laayoune.
El Alamein, see Marsa al Hamra.
El Araich, see Larache.
El Arish, Egypt: 31.10 N. 33.50 E. **26, 32**
El Bahar Tower, see Port Said.
El Ballah, Egypt: 30.45 N. 32.15 E. **33**
El Bluff, Nicaragua: 12.00 N. 83.41 W. **69**
   Max. Size: LOA 102.6 m., draft 4 m. *Fuel:* Available.
   Airport: Bluefields.
El Bosque, Colombia: 10.24 N. 75.32 W. **69**
   Max. Size: Draft 10.4 m. *Fuel:* By barge. *Airport:* Cartagena.
El Cap, Egypt: 30.55 N. 32.18 E. **33**
El Cuyo, Mexico: 21.30 N. 87.40 W. **69**
El Dekheila, see Alexandria.
El Djazair, see Algiers.
El Ferdan, Egypt: 30.40 N. 32.16 E. **33**
El Ferrol, see Ferrol.
El Guamache, Venezuela: 10.52 N. 64.04 W. **69, 71, 72, 75**
   Max. Size: Depth 36 ft. (LW), 42 ft. (HW).
   Airport: Internal, 15 km.
El Jadida, Morocco: 33.15 N. 8.31 W. **27**
   Max. Size: LOA 80 m., draft 5 m. at HW. *Fuel:* Available.
   Airport: Casablanca.
El Kala, see La Calle.
El Kantara, Tunisia: 33.45 N. 11.00 E. **24**
El Nido, (Palawan Is.), Philippines: 11.10 N. 119.25 E. . . . **47**
El Palito, Venezuela: 10.29 N. 68.07 W. **72, 74**
   Max. Size: LOA 210 m. – 250 m., draft 12.2 m. – 14.6 m., max.
   displacement 65,000 tons – 110,000 tonnes. *Fuel:* Available for
   vessels loading or discharging cargo. *Airport:* 4 miles.
   Also see Puerto Cabello.
El Quseir, see Quseir.
El Real, Panama: 8.15 N. 77.50 W. **69**
EL SALVADOR **69**
El Segundo, California, U.S.A.: 33.55 N. 118.27 W. . . . **55, 57**
   Max. Size: Draft 56 ft., LOA 1,000 ft., up to 150,000 d.w.t.
   Airport: Los Angeles International, 2 miles.
El Tabaco, Mexico: 19.20 N. 105.15 W. **57**
El Tablazo, Venezuela: 10.45 N. 71.32 W. **74**
   Max. Size: Draft 29 ft. 6 in., LOA 820 ft., 50,000 d.w.t.
El Tina, Egypt: 31.05 N. 32.18 E. **33**
El Tur, Egypt: 28.14 N. 33.37 E. **32**
Elath, see Eilat.
Elato Is., (Caroline Is.), Micronesia: 7.30 N. 146.10 E. . . . **46**
Elba, Italy: 42.45 N. 10.00 E. **23, 24**
Elbeuf, France: 49.17 N. 1.05 E. **7**
Elblag, Poland: 54.12 N. 19.25 E. **11**
Electrona, see Hobart.
Elephant Pass, Sri Lanka: 9.33 N. 80.25 E. **37**
Elephant Point, Bangladesh: 21.10 N. 92.00 E. **37**
Eleusis, Greece: 38.02 N. 23.33 E. **23, 25, 26**
   Max. Size: Draft entering Eleusis Bay 35 ft., draft at berths 33 ft.
   Tankers: LOA 160 m., beam 30 m., depth at pier 30 ft.
   Fuel: By barge. Tankers: Available ex-wharf.
   Dry Docks: 115,000 d.w.t. *Airport:* Athens.
Eleusis Bay, Greece **23**
Eleuthera Is., Bahamas **69, 70**
Elfin Cove, Alaska, U.S.A.: 58.11 N. 136.20 W. **56**
Elgin, see Port Elgin.
Elim, Alaska, U.S.A.: 64.30 N. 162.37 W. **54**
Elizabeth, South Africa, see Port Elizabeth.
Elizabeth, U.S.A., see New York.
Elizabeth City, North Carolina, U.S.A.: 36.18 N. 76.14 W. . . **63**
Elizabeth River, see Norfolk.
Ellen, see Port Ellen.
Ellesmere Port, U.K.: 53.17 N. 2.54 W. **6**
   Also see Manchester.
Ellington, see Suva.
Ellinoperamaton, see Iraklion.
Elliston, S.A., Australia: 33.39 S. 134.52 E. **51**
Ellsworth, Maine, U.S.A.: 44.30 N. 68.54 W. **60**
Elnesvagen, Norway: 62.51 N. 7.07 E. **15**
   Max. Size: Depth 9.3 m.
Elobey Is., Equatorial Guinea: 1.00 N. 9.34 E. **29**
Eloi Bay, Louisiana, U.S.A. **67**
Eloy Alfaro, see Guayaquil.

Elsfleth, Germany: 53.14 N. 8.28 E. **8, 9, 14**
   Max. Size: LOA 80 m. Depth alongside 4.7 m. *Fuel:* By barge.
   Airport: Bremen, 50 km.
Elsinore, see Helsingor.
Emden, Germany: 53.21 N. 7.12 E. **7, 8, 9, 11, 12, 14**
   Max. Size: Restrictions imposed by locks at
   Emden: 240 m. length and 33 m. width. Draft 10.67 m.
   Fuel: All grades. *Dry Docks:* Largest 218 m. x 30 m.
   Airport: Bremen and Hamburg, about 2 – 3 hours drive.
Emmastad, see Willemstad.
Emmaste, Estonia: 58.50 N. 22.30 E. **11**
Emmerich, Germany: 51.50 N. 6.16 E. **8**
Empalme, Mexico: 28.00 N. 110.50 W. **57**
Empedocle, see Porto Empedocle.
Empire, Panama Canal, Panama: 9.03 N. 79.40 W. **73**
Empire, Louisiana, U.S.A.: 29.24 N. 89.36 W. **67**
   Also see New Orleans.
Empire, Oregon, U.S.A.: 43.25 N. 124.17 W. **57**
Emu Bay, see Burnie.
Encarnacion, Paraguay: 27.15 S. 55.50 W. **77**
Endau, Malaysia: 2.40 N. 103.38 E. **38, 39, 40**
Ende, Indonesia: 8.51 S. 121.39 E. **38, 46**
Enderbury Is., (Phoenix Is.), Kiribati: 3.07 S. 171.03 W. . . . **49**
ENEL Terminal, see Ravenna.
Enggano Is., Indonesia: 5.20 S. 102.10 E. **38**
England, U.K. **7**
Englewood, B.C., Canada: 50.32 N. 126.53 W. **56**
English Bay, Canada, see Vancouver.
English Bay, Alaska, U.S.A.: 59.10 N. 152.00 W. **54**
English Channel **4, 5, 7, 19**
English Harbour, (Fanning Is.), Kiribati: 3.55 N. 159.20 W. . . **49**
Engure, Latvia: 57.10 N. 23.14 E. **11**
   Max. Size: LOA 45 m., beam 8 m., draft 2.7 m.
Eniwetok, Marshall Is.: 11.20 N. 162.20 E. **49**
Enkhuizen, Netherlands: 52.40 N. 5.15 E. **8**
Enkoping, Sweden: 59.38 N. 17.05 E. **11**
Ennore, India: 13.14 N. 80.20 E. **37**
   Max. Size: Draft 13.5 m.
Ensenada, Argentina: 34.50 S. 57.50 W. **78**
Ensenada, Mexico: 31.51 N. 116.38 W. **57**
   Max. Size: LOA 240 m., draft 9.8 m. *Fuel:* Available.
   Dry Docks: For 1,400 tons. *Airport:* Tijuana, International.
Ensenada de Mora, see Pilon.
Ensted, Denmark: 55.01 N. 9.26 E. **12, 14**
   Max. Size: Oil Terminal: LOA 350 m., depth 18 m.
   Coal Terminal: LOA 350 m., depth 18 m. *Fuel:* By barge.
   Airport: Skrydstrup, 25 km.
Enstedvaertkets, see Aabenraa.
Epe, Nigeria: 6.40 N. 3.58 E. **29**
Equatorial Channel, Maldives **37**
EQUATORIAL GUINEA **28, 29**
Era, Japan: 41.41 N. 140.00 E. **43**
Eran, (Palawan Is.), Philippines: 9.00 N. 117.50 E. **47**
Erawan, Thailand: 9.06 N. 101.21 E. **37, 39**
   Max. Size: Alongside: Max. displacement 70,000 tonnes.
   LOA 800 ft. Tandem: 130,000 d.w.t.
Erdek, Turkey: 40.23 N. 27.48 E. **25**
Erdemir, see Eregli.
Eregli, Turkey: 41.18 N. 31.27 E. **21, 25, 26**
   Max. Size: 150,000 d.w.t., draft 62 ft. *Fuel:* Diesel by road
   tanker. *Airport:* Istanbul, 300 km.
Ereglisi, Turkey: 40.58 N. 27.57 E. **25, 26**
Erenkoy, Turkey: 40.58 N. 29.04 E. **23**
Erie, Pennsylvania, U.S.A.: 42.10 N. 80.05 W. **55, 60, 62**
   Max. Size: LOA 730 ft., draft 26 ft. *Fuel:* All grades. *Dry
   Docks:* Available.
Erin, see Port Erin.
ERITREA **31, 32**
Ermioni, Greece: 37.23 N. 23.15 E. **25**
Ermoupolis, see Syros.
Eromanga Is., Vanuatu: 18.42 S. 169.09 E. **49**
Erquy, France: 48.38 N. 2.28 W. **7, 19**
Errol Is., Louisiana, U.S.A. **67**
Es Sider, Libya: 30.38 N. 18.22 E. **24**
   Max. Size: LOA 1,165 ft., beam 184 ft., draft 73 ft., 300,000 d.w.t.
Es Zueitina, see Zueitina.
Esashi N, Japan: 44.58 N. 142.34 E. **43**
Esashi S, Japan: 41.51 N. 140.07 E. **43**
Esbjerg, Denmark: 55.28 N. 8.26 E. **4, 11, 12**
   Max. Size: Draft 10.5 m. Tankers: LOA 225 m. with depth
   up to 40 ft. and LOA 245 m. with depth up to 11.8 m. *Fuel:* By
   road tanker. *Airport:* 8 km., connects with Copenhagen.
Escanaba, Michigan, U.S.A.: 45.45 N. 87.04 W. **62**
Escobal, Panama Canal, Panama: 9.09 N. 79.58 W. . . . **73**
Escombreras, see Cartagena.
Escondida, Mexico: 15.51 N. 97.06 W. **69**
Escravos, Nigeria: 5.30 N. 5.00 E. **29**
   Max. Size: 300,000 d.w.t., draft 51 ft. – 52 ft. *Fuel:* Available by
   barge from Warri.
Eskilstuna, Sweden: 59.22 N. 16.31 E. **11**

Eskimo Point, N.W.T., Canada: 61.07 N. 94.01 W. 59
Eskimonaes, Greenland (Denmark): 75.05 N. 21.15 W. 17
Esmeraldas, Ecuador: 1.00 N. 79.39 W. 72
  Max. Size: LOA 230 m., draft 37.3 ft. *Fuel:* Available.
Esperance, W.A., Australia: 33.52 S. 121.53 E. 50
  Max. Size: Draft 11.5 m. Max. departure displacement 70,000 tons. *Fuel:* By road tanker. *Airport:* 25 km., connects with Perth.
Esperanza, see Porto Esperanza.
Espevaer, Norway: 59.35 N. 5.10 E. 11
Espiritu Santo Is., Vanuatu 49
Esquimalt, B.C., Canada: 48.25 N. 123.25 W. 56
  Dry Docks: Length 1,173 ft., breadth 125.6 ft., depth 49.5 ft. Also see Victoria.
Esquivel, see Port Esquivel.
Essaoira, Morocco: 31.30 N. 9.47 W. 27
Essequibo River, Guyana: 6.24 N. 58.37 W. 72, 75, 76
  Max. Size: Draft 3 ft. less than that predicted for the Demerara Bar.
Essex, Connecticut, U.S.A.: 41.21 N. 72.23 W. 63
Essexville, see Bay City.
Essungo, Angola: 6.20 S. 12.10 E. 28
  Max. Size: Max. displacement 250,000 tonnes. Depth at SPM: 120 ft.
Essvik, see Sundsvall.
Estaque, see Marseilles.
Estepona, Spain: 36.25 N. 5.08 W. 20, 22
ESTONIA 4, 10, 11
Etajima, Japan: 34.11 N. 132.29 E. 45
  Max. Size: C.I. Oil: 127,000 d.w.t. (part load), LOA 273 m., draft 14 m. *Fuel:* Available. *Airport:* Hiroshima.
Etal, see Nomoi Is..
Etang de Berre, see Berre.
Etaples, France: 50.30 N. 1.40 E. 5, 7
Eten, Peru: 6.56 S. 79.52 W. 72
  Port closed
ETHIOPIA 31, 32
Etienne, see Nouadhibou.
Etolin Strait, Alaska, U.S.A. 54
Eu, France: 50.03 N. 1.25 E. 7
Eua Is., Tonga: 21.22 S. 174.56 W. 49
Euboea, Greece: 38.45 N. 23.00 E. 25
Eucla, W.A., Australia: 31.45 S. 128.54 E. 50
Eupatoria, see Evpatoria.
Eureka, California, U.S.A.: 40.48 N. 124.10 W. . . . 55, 56, 57
  Max. Size: LOA 740 ft., beam 115 ft., draft 35 ft. Tankers: Draft 30 ft. *Fuel:* Available. *Airport:* 20 miles, connects with San Francisco and Portland.
Europa Is., Reunion (France): 22.21 S. 40.33 E. 30
Europa Point, Gibraltar (U.K.): 36.06 N. 5.20 W. . . 18, 20, 22, 23
Europoort, Netherlands: 51.58 N. 4.08 E. 7, 8
  Max. Size: Draft 74 ft.
  Also see Rotterdam.
Evanton, see Invergordon.
Everett, Massachusetts, U.S.A., see Boston.
Everett, Washington, U.S.A.: 47.59 N. 122.13 W. 55, 56
  Max. Size: Depth alongside 25 ft. – 45 ft. *Fuel:* Available. *Airport:* Seattle - Tacoma, 45 miles.
Everglades, see Port Everglades.
Everton, see New Amsterdam.
Evpatoria, Ukraine: 45.11 N. 33.23 E. 26
  Max. Size: Dry cargo: LOA 120 m., draft 4.5 m. Passengers: LOA 200 m., draft 5 m. *Airport:* Simpheropol, 60 km.
Evripos Strait, Greece: 38.27 N. 23.34 E. 25
Excursion Inlet, Alaska, U.S.A.: 58.25 N. 135.27 W. 56
Exeter, U.K.: 50.45 N. 3.30 W. 5, 7
Exmouth, W.A., Australia: 22.20 S. 114.10 E. 50, 51
  Max. Size: Depth 12 m. *Airport:* 30 km.
Exmouth, U.K.: 50.37 N. 3.25 W. 7, 19
Exumas Islands, Bahamas 70
Eyemouth, U.K.: 55.53 N. 2.05 W. 5
Eyrarbakki, Iceland: 63.52 N. 21.09 W. 17
Eyre, W.A., Australia: 32.10 S. 126.25 E. 50
Eysturoy, Faroe Is. (Denmark) 5, 15

F

Faborg, Denmark: 55.05 N. 10.15 E. 12, 14
Faddiffolu Atoll, Maldives 37
Faeringehavn, Greenland (Denmark): 63.41 N. 51.34 W. . . . 17
  Max. Size: Oil-carriers 26,000 d.w.t., draft 40 ft. Cargo ships 20 ft. *Fuel:* Available. *Airport:* Nuuk, 35 miles.
Fagerstrand, Norway: 59.44 N. 10.36 E. 8
  Max. Size: Tankers: Draft 38 ft.
  Also see Oslo.
Fagervik, see Sundsvall.
Fagerviken, see Karlholm.
Fahaheel, see Mina Al-Ahmadi.
Faial, see Horta.
Faial Is., Azores (Portugal) 20
Failaka Is., Kuwait: 29.27 N. 48.21 E. 35
Fair Haven, New York, U.S.A.: 43.20 N. 76.42 W. 62
Fair Isle, U.K.: 59.30 N. 1.40 W. 5
Fairless Hills, Pennsylvania, U.S.A.: 40.11 N. 74.51 W. . . . 65
Fairport, Ohio, U.S.A.: 41.45 N. 81.17 W. 62
Fairy, see Port Fairy.
Fais, (Caroline Is.), Micronesia: 9.45 N. 140.31 E. 46
Fajardo, see Port Fajardo.
Fak-Fak, Indonesia: 2.56 S. 132.18 E. 46
  Max. Size: Draft 6.0 m. *Airport:* 11 km.
Fakaofo Is., Tokelau Is. (N.Z.): 9.28 S. 171.03 W. 49
Fakse Ladeplads, Denmark: 55.13 N. 12.10 E. 12
Falconara, Italy: 43.39 N. 13.25 E. 24
  Also see Ancona.
Falkenberg, Sweden: 56.54 N. 12.30 E. 10, 11, 12
Falkland Islands (U.K.) 68, 77
Fall River, Massachusetts, U.S.A.: 41.42 N. 71.10 W. . . 55, 60, 63
  Max. Size: Depth of 35 ft. MLW alongside. Tankers: Depth 35 ft.
Falmouth, Jamaica: 18.29 N. 77.38 W. 70
Falmouth, U.K.: 50.09 N. 5.04 W. 5, 7, 19
  Max. Size: Depth 5.3 m. – 7.8 m. Tankers: Draft 8.4 m. *Fuel:* All grades of fuel oil and diesel oil. *Dry Docks:* Length 850 ft. (259 m.), width 130 ft. (39.6 m.), depth on sill (HWOST) 11 m. *Airport:* London (Heathrow and Gatwick), or Bristol 183 miles.
Falmouth, Massachusetts, U.S.A.: 41.33 N. 70.37 W. 63
Falster Is., Denmark 10, 12
Falsterbo, Sweden: 55.25 N. 12.50 E. 12
Famagusta, Cyprus: 35.07 N. 33.57 E. 21, 26
  Max. Size: LOA 220 m. (722 ft.), draft 9.15 m. (30 ft.). *Fuel:* Limited to lorry delivery. *Airport:* Ercan, 30 miles.
Fangataufa Is., (Tuamotu Arch.), French Polynesia (France): 22.09 S. 138.40 W. 49
Fangcheng, China: 21.31 N. 108.20 E. 39
  Max. Size: LOA 290 m., depth 9 m. – 13.6 m. *Fuel:* Available. *Airport:* Nanning, 180 km.
Fanning Is., Kiribati: 3.51 N. 159.22 W. 49
Fano, Italy: 43.51 N. 13.00 E. 24
Fano I., Denmark 12
Fao, Iraq: 29.58 N. 48.29 E. 35
  Max. Size: Tankers: LOA 675 ft., draft 35 ft. (10.65 m.).
Farafangana, Madagascar: 22.50 S. 47.50 E. 30
Farasan Is., Saudi Arabia: 16.40 N. 41.50 E. 32
Farjsundet, see Mariehamn.
Farmsum, see Groningen.
Farnes, Norway: 61.20 N. 7.45 E. 11, 15
Faro, Portugal: 37.00 N. 7.55 W. 20, 22, 27
  Max. Size: LOA 110 m., draft 6.4 m. *Fuel:* Available. *Airport:* Faro, 8 km.
Faro Is., Sweden 11
Faroe Islands (Denmark) 4, 5, 15
Farosund, (Gotland Is.), Sweden: 57.52 N. 19.04 E. 11
Farrur Is., Iran: 26.18 N. 54.31 E. 35
Farsund, Norway: 58.05 N. 6.49 E. 11
Faslane, U.K.: 56.04 N. 4.49 W. 6
Fastnet Rock, Ireland: 51.22 N. 9.37 W. 5
Fateh Terminal, U.A.E.: 25.35 N. 54.25 E. 35
  Max. Size: 300,000 – 350,000 d.w.t., depending on season. Depth of water 150 ft. *Fuel:* Obtainable at Jebel Ali.
Father Point, Quebec, Canada: 48.31 N. 68.28 W. 60
Fatik, Senegal: 14.20 N. 16.27 W. 27
Fatma, see Mersa Fatma.
Fatsa, Turkey: 41.03 N. 37.30 E. 26
Fatu Iva, (Marquesas Is.), French Polynesia (France): 10.30 S. 138.38 W. 49
Fauske, Norway: 67.15 N. 15.22 E. 15
Faux Cap, Madagascar: 25.30 S. 45.30 E. 30
Faversham, U.K.: 51.19 N. 0.54 E. 6
Favignana Is., Italy: 37.56 N. 12.20 E. 24
Fawley, U.K.: 50.51 N. 1.21 W. 7, 19
  Max. Size: Partly loaded VLCC's up to 14.9 m. draft. *Fuel:* All grades. *Airport:* Southampton.
  Also see Southampton.

Fayal, see Horta.
Fecamp, France: 49.46 N. 0.22 E. **7, 8**
  Max. Size: Spring Tides: LOA 105 m., beam 17 m., draft 7.25 m. *Fuel:* By road tanker. *Airport:* Le Havre, 35 km.
Fedahlah, see Mohammedia.
Fedchem, see Point Lisas.
Fehmarn Belt **12, 14**
Fehmarn Is., Germany **12, 14**
Fehmarnsund, Germany: 54.24 N. 11.08 E. **12, 14**
Felixstowe, U.K.: 51.57 N. 1.21 E. **4, 5, 7**
  Max. Size: Container Terminals: Draft 9.3 m. – 14 m. Roll-on/Roll-off vessels: 250 m. LOA, depth 9.75 m. Tankers: LOA 180 m., draft 9.1 m. LWOST. *Fuel:* Marine diesel and gas oil. *Airport:* Southend, 70 miles. London-Heathrow, 90 miles. Stansted, 65 miles.
Felton, see Antilla.
Fenerive, Madagascar: 17.23 S. 49.25 E. **30**
Fenit, Ireland: 52.17 N. 9.53 W. **5, 8**
  Max. Size: LOA 400 ft., draft 20 ft. Tankers: Draft 18 ft. *Fuel:* Available. *Airport:* Local, 15 miles.
Feodosia, see Theodosia.
Fercom Terminal, Turkey: 40.46 N. 29.33 E. **23**
  Max. Size: LOA 210 m., draft 16.0 m.
Ferguson Is., Papua New Guinea: 9.20 S. 150.40 E. . . **46**
Fernandina Beach, Florida, U.S.A.: 30.42 N. 81.28 W. . **66**
Fernando de Noronha Is., Brazil: 3.48 S. 32.23 W. . . **68**
Fernando Poo, see Bioco Is..
Ferndale, Washington, U.S.A.: 48.49 N. 122.43 W. . . **55, 56**
  Max. Size: Tankers: LOA 1,000 ft., depth alongside 40 ft. MLW.
Ferrol, Spain: 43.28 N. 8.16 W. **19, 20, 21, 22**
  Max. Size: Cargo vessels up to 42 ft. draft. *Fuel:* All grades. *Dry Docks:* Largest 330 m. x 50 m. (230,000 g.r.t.). *Airport:* Connects with Madrid.
Ferryland, Newfoundland, Canada: 47.01 N. 52.52 W. . **60**
Fethiye, Turkey: 36.38 N. 29.10 E. **25, 26**
Fetlar, U.K.: 60.35 N. 0.50 W. **5**
Fiborgtangen, Norway: 63.43 N. 11.10 E. **10, 15**
  Max. Size: LOA 215 m., draft 10.4 m. *Fuel:* Only if ordered from Trondheim. *Airport:* Trondheim.
Fife Ness, U.K.: 56.17 N. 2.36 W. **6**
Figeholm, Sweden: 57.22 N. 16.33 E. **11**
Figueira da Foz, Portugal: 40.09 N. 8.52 W. **20, 22**
  Max. Size: LOA 100 m., draft 22 ft. *Fuel:* Diesel. *Dry Docks:* Slipway – 4,000 tons.
FIJI **36, 49**
Filer City, see Manistee.
Filiatra, Greece: 37.10 N. 21.35 E. **24, 25**
Filicudi Is., Italy: 38.35 N. 14.33 E. **24**
Finike, Turkey: 36.16 N. 30.13 E. **25, 26**
  Max. Size: Depth 4.5 m. – 5.5 m. *Airport:* Antalya, 280 km.
FINLAND **4, 10, 11, 13, 15, 79**
Finnart, U.K.: 56.07 N. 4.50 W. **5**
  Max. Size: Tankers: 300,000 d.w.t., draft 75 ft. *Fuel:* All grades. *Airport:* Glasgow. Also see Clyde Port.
Finnsnes, Norway: 69.14 N. 17.59 E. **10, 15**
Finschhaven, Papua New Guinea: 6.33 S. 147.51 E. . . **46**
Firenze, Italy: 40.56 N. 18.20 E. **24**
  Max. Size: 140,000 d.w.t. FPSO "Firenze" in 817 m. of water.
Firths:
  Firth of Clyde, U.K. **5**
  Firth of Forth, U.K. **5, 6**
  Firth of Lorn, U.K. **5**
  Firth of Tay, U.K. **5**
Fischerhutte, Germany: 54.09 N. 9.22 E. **14**
Fisher Strait, N.W.T., Canada **59**
Fisherman Islands, see Brisbane.
Fishguard, U.K.: 52.01 N. 4.58 W. **5, 6, 7**
  Max. Size: Draft 20 ft. *Fuel:* Available. *Airport:* Cardiff, Swansea and Haverfordwest.
Fiskenaesset, Greenland (Denmark): 63.05 N. 50.41 W. . **17**
Fitzwilliam Is., Ontario, Canada: 45.30 N. 81.45 W. . . **62**
Fiume, see Rijeka.
Fiumicino, Italy: 41.46 N. 12.13 E. **9, 24**
  Max. Size: Up to 290,000 d.w.t., draft 50 ft. *Airport:* International.
Fjallbacka, Sweden: 58.36 N. 11.17 E. **11, 12**
Flateyri, Iceland: 66.03 N. 23.30 W. **17**
Flaxenvik, Sweden: 59.28 N. 18.25 E. **11**
  Max. Size: Draft 10.3 m. Also see Stockholm.
Fleetwood, U.K.: 53.55 N. 3.00 W. **5, 7**
  Max. Size: LOA 58 m., beam 14.1 m. *Fuel:* All grades. *Airport:* Blackpool, 10 miles.
Flekkefjord, Norway: 58.18 N. 6.40 E. **11**
Flemhude, Germany: 54.19 N. 9.58 E. **14**

Flensburg, Germany: 54.48 N. 9.26 E. **10, 12, 14**
  Max. Size: Draft 8.5 m. Tankers: 1,000 g.r.t., depth 5.7 m. *Fuel:* Diesel available in any quantity. Fuel oil subject to 5 hours advance notice. *Dry Docks:* Floating dock: 7,500 tons lifting capacity. *Airport:* Hamburg-Fuhlsbuttel, 175 km.
Fleur de Lys, Newfoundland, Canada: 50.06 N. 56.07 W. . **60**
Flinders, see Hastings.
Flinders Is., Tas., Australia **51**
Flint, U.K.: 53.15 N. 3.07 W. **6, 7**
Flint Is., Kiribati: 11.26 S. 151.48 W. **49**
Flixborough, U.K.: 53.37 N. 0.41 W. **6**
Flores Is., Azores (Portugal) **20**
Flores Is., Indonesia **38, 46**
Flores Sea, Indonesia **38, 46**
Florianapolis, Brazil: 27.36 S. 48.33 W. **76, 77**
Florida, U.S.A. **66**
Florida Keys, U.S.A. **66**
Florida Strait, Florida, U.S.A. **66, 69, 70**
Floro, Norway: 61.38 N. 5.02 E. **10, 11, 15**
  Max. Size: Draft 25 ft. Fugleskjaerskaia: Depth 5 m. – 11 m. Botnaneset: Depth 18 m. *Fuel:* Available. *Airport:* Local, connects Oslo.
Flotta Terminal, (Orkney Is.), U.K.: 58.52 N. 3.04 W. . . **5**
  Max. Size: SPM: Draft 72 ft., 200,000 d.w.t. Jetty: Draft 62 ft., 150,000 d.w.t. *Airport:* Daily service.
Flowers Cove, Newfoundland, Canada: 51.16 N. 56.45 W. . **60**
Flushing, Netherlands: 51.27 N. 3.35 E. **7, 8, 9**
  Max. Size: Total: LOA 280 m., draft 15 m. (S.W.), 100,000 d.w.t. East Harbour: Draft 15.2 m. Outer Harbour: Draft 9.5 m. Inner Docks: Depth 7.3 m. Buoys: Draft 12.5 m. *Fuel:* All grades. *Dry Docks:* 90,000 d.w.t. *Airport:* Rotterdam, 125 km.
Flying Fish Cove, Christmas Island (Australia): 10.25 S. 105.43 E. **50**
  Max. Size: LOA 192 m., beam 28 m., 35,000 d.w.t. *Fuel:* Very limited, only in extreme emergency. *Airport:* Weekly flights to Singapore and Perth.
Foca, Turkey: 38.45 N. 26.55 E. **25, 26**
  Also see Nemrut Bay.
Foglo, Finland: 60.00 N. 20.25 E. **11**
Fogo, Newfoundland, Canada: 49.43 N. 54.16 W. . . . **60**
Fogo Is., Cape Verde **27**
Fohr I., (North Frisian Is.), Germany **12, 14**
Folegandros Island, Greece: 36.40 N. 24.58 E. . . . **25**
Folkestone, U.K.: 51.05 N. 1.10 E. **5, 7**
Follonica, Italy: 42.55 N. 10.45 E. **23, 24**
Fomboni, Comoros Is. (France): 12.15 S. 43.45 E. . . **30**
Fond du Lac, Wisconsin, U.S.A.: 43.45 N. 88.25 W. . . **62**
Fongafale, see Funafuti.
Fonte Boa, Brazil: 2.32 S. 66.00 W. **72**
Foochou, see Fuzhou.
Forcados, Nigeria: 5.22 N. 5.26 E. **29**
Forcados Terminal, Nigeria: 5.10 N. 5.10 E. **29**
  Max. Size: 320,000 tonnes Summer d.w.t. Draft 20 m. – 23 m., depending on berth and weather.
Forestville, Quebec, Canada: 48.45 N. 69.04 W. . . . **60**
Forio, (Ischia Is.), Italy: 40.44 N. 13.52 E. **23, 24**
Formentera Is., (Balearic Is.), Spain: 38.40 N. 1.30 E. . **22**
Formia, Italy: 41.15 N. 13.37 E. **23, 24**
Formigas, Azores (Portugal): 37.17 N. 24.50 W. . . . **20**
Formosa, Argentina: 26.12 S. 58.11 W. **77**
Formosa Strait **42, 46**
Fornells, (Minorca), Spain: 40.05 N. 4.07 E. **22**
Forno, Brazil: 22.58 S. 42.01 W. **76, 77**
  Max. Size: Bar depth 12 m. Depths alongside up to 10 m., 30,000 d.w.t. *Fuel:* By road tanker.
Forsmark, Sweden: 60.23 N. 18.11 E. **11**
Fort Albany, Ontario, Canada: 52.15 N. 81.37 W. . . . **59**
Fort Augustus, U.K.: 57.10 N. 4.40 W. **5**
Fort Bragg, California, U.S.A.: 39.27 N. 123.49 W. . . **57**
Fort Chimo, Quebec, Canada: 58.06 N. 68.22 W. . . . **59**
Fort Dauphin, Madagascar: 25.02 S. 47.02 E. **30**
  Max. Size: Anchorage depth 8 m. *Airport:* 5 km.
Fort de France, Martinique (France): 14.36 N. 61.04 W. . **69, 71**
  Max. Size: LOA 250 m. if vessel has two propellers and bow-thruster, otherwise 180 m. Draft 10 m. Tankers: LOA 300 m., 120,000 tonnes displacement, depth 15.0 m. *Fuel:* All grades. *Dry Docks:* 200 m. length, 21 m. wide. *Airport:* 9.5 miles.
Fort Denison, see Sydney.
Fort George, Quebec, Canada: 53.50 N. 79.00 W. . . . **59**
Fort Lauderdale, Florida, U.S.A.: 26.08 N. 80.08 W. . . **66, 69**
  Also see Port Everglades.
Fort Liberte, Haiti: 19.41 N. 71.51 W. **70**
Fort Mifflin, see Philadelphia.
Fort Myers, Florida, U.S.A.: 26.39 N. 81.51 W. . . . **66, 69, 70**
Fort Pierce, Florida, U.S.A.: 27.27 N. 80.19 W. . . . **55, 66, 69**
  Max. Size: Draft 28 ft. (HW) *Fuel:* By barge. *Airport:* International, 1.5 hours by car.
Fort Point, California, U.S.A.: 37.48 N. 122.26 W. . . **58**

Fort Randal, Alaska, U.S.A.: 55.00 N. 163.00 W. **54**
Fort Rupert, Quebec, Canada: 51.28 N. 78.43 W. **59**
Fort Severn, Ontario, Canada: 56.05 N. 87.45 W. **59**
Fort William, Canada, see Thunder Bay.
Fort William, U.K.: 56.48 N. 5.10 W. **5**
Fortaleza, Brazil: 3.41 S. 38.33 W. **72**
 Max. Size: Up to 27 ft. draft. *Fuel:* Boiler fuel. Diesel oil by
 road tanker. *Airport:* Internal.
Fortune, Newfoundland, Canada: 47.03 N. 55.50 W. **60**
Fortune Harbour, Newfoundland, Canada: 49.33 N. 55.14 W. . **60**
Fos, France: 43.24 N. 4.53 E. **9, 22, 23**
 Max. Size: Draft 22.25 m. (oil jetty), 18.6 m. (Sollac), 17.5 m.
 (mineral quay). *Fuel:* By barge. *Airport:* Marseilles, 60 km.
 Also see Port de Bouc and Marseilles.
Fos/Bouc Canal, France **23**
Fosdyke Bridge, U.K.: 52.52 N. 0.02 W. **7**
 Max. Size: LOA 58 m. (exceptionally 59 m. – 90 m.), draft 5.0 m.
 (Spring tide).
Fosnavag, Norway: 62.21 N. 5.37 E. **15**
Fouad, see Port Fouad.
Foula, see Ham.
Foulpointe, Madagascar: 17.40 S. 49.32 E. **30**
Foundiougne, Senegal: 14.08 N. 16.28 W. **27**
Fouras, France: 46.00 N. 1.05 W. **8, 19**
Fourneaux Group, Australia **51**
Fournoi, (Fournoi Is.), Greece: 37.36 N. 26.31 E. **25**
Foveaux Strait, New Zealand **52**
Fowey, U.K.: 50.20 N. 4.39 W. **5, 7, 19**
 Max. Size: LOA 164 m., draft 8.5 m. (HW) *Fuel:* Gas oil.
Fowlers Bay, S.A., Australia: 32.00 S. 132.30 E. **50**
Fox Is., (Aleutian Is.), Alaska, U.S.A. **54**
Fox River, Quebec, Canada: 49.00 N. 64.23 W. **60**
Foxe Basin, N.W.T., Canada **59**
Foxe Channel, N.W.T., Canada **59**
Foxi, see Sarroch.
Foynes Harbour, Ireland: 52.37 N. 9.06 W. **5**
 Max. Size: LOA 205 m., beam 29 m., draft 10.5 m.
 Fuel: Available. *Airport:* Shannon, 34 miles.
Foynes Island, Ireland: 52.38 N. 9.07 W. **5, 8**
 Max. Size: LOA 950 ft., min. depth 50 ft.
Foz, Spain: 43.34 N. 7.18 W. **19, 20, 22**
Foz do Cunene, Angola: 17.20 S. 11.50 E. **28**
Frafjord, Norway: 58.51 N. 6.17 E. **10, 11**
 Max. Size: LOA 95 m., draft 18 ft.
FRANCE **4, 7, 8, 9, 19, 21, 22, 23**
Francois, Newfoundland, Canada: 47.35 N. 56.44 W. **60**
Frankfort, Michigan, U.S.A.: 44.38 N. 86.14 W. **62**
Frankfurt, Germany: 50.06 N. 8.41 E. **7, 9**
Frano, see Gustavsvik.
Franz Josef Land, Russia **79**
Fraser Is., Qld., Australia: 25.15 S. 153.10 E. **50**
Fraser Mills, see Fraser Port.
Fraser Port, B.C., Canada: 49.12 N. 122.55 W. **56**
 Max. Size: Draft 35 ft. on 13 ft. tide, LOA 750 ft. and
 beam 106 ft. *Fuel:* All grades. *Airport:* Vancouver.
Fraserburgh, U.K.: 57 41 N. 2.00 W. **5**
 Max. Size: LOA 90 m., beam 16 m., draft 6.5 m.
 Fuel: Available. *Dry Docks:* 66 m. x 14 m. *Airport:* Aberdeen,
 64 km.
Fray Bentos, Uruguay: 33.06 S. 58.18 W. **77, 78**
 Max. Size: Draft 26 ft. (FW). *Airport:* Nearest Montevideo.
Fredericia, Denmark: 55.33 N. 9.45 E. **11, 12**
 Max. Size: Draft 14.7 m. Tankers: Draft 13.25 m.
 Fuel: Available. *Dry Docks:* 110 m. x 22 m. x 5.1 m. depth.
 Floating dock 227 m. x 35 m., max. capacity 22,000 tons.
 Airport: Beldringe, 35 miles.
Fredericksburg, Virginia, U.S.A.: 38.17 N. 77.28 W. . . . **63**
Frederiksdal, Greenland (Denmark): 60.00 N. 44.40 W. . . . **17**
Frederikshab, see Paamiut.
Frederikshavn, Denmark: 57.28 N. 10.33 E. **11, 12**
 Max. Size: LOA 200 m., depth 8 m. *Fuel:* All grades.
 Dry Docks: Length 212 m., breadth 32.2 m. and depth 7 m.
 Airport: Aalborg Airport 60 km., connects with Copenhagen.
Frederikssund, Denmark: 55.50 N. 12.05 E. **12**
Frederiksted, (St. Croix), Virgin Is. (U.S.A.):
 17.43 N. 64.53 W. **69, 71**
 Max. Size: LOA 600 ft., forward draft 25 ft. *Airport:* 8.5 miles.
Frederiksvaerk, Denmark: 55.58 N. 12.01 E. **12**
Fredrikshamn, see Hamina.
Fredriksskans, see Gavle.
Fredrikstad, Norway: 59.12 N. 10.57 E. **8, 10, 11, 12**
 Max. Size: Draft 10.5 m. *Fuel:* All grades. *Dry Docks:* 945 ft.
 length, 126 ft. breadth, 25 ft. draft when docking.
 Airport: Fornebo, Oslo, 110 km.
Freemason Is., Louisiana, U.S.A.: 29.49 N. 88.59 W. **67**
Freeport, (Grand Bahama Is.), Bahamas: 26.31 N. 78.46 W. **66, 69, 70**
 Max. Size: Depth 30 ft. Tankers: Up to 500,000 tons.
 Ro-Ro Berth: Depth 28 ft. Container Berth: Depth 51 ft.
 Fuel: All grades. *Airport:* 6 miles.

Freeport, Bermuda (U.K.): 32.19 N. 64.50 W. **63**
 Max. Size: Draft 34 ft., incl. tankers. *Fuel:* Available.
 Also see Hamilton.
Freeport, Maine, U.S.A.: 43.50 N. 70.05 W. **60**
Freeport, Texas, U.S.A.: 28.57 N. 95.21 W. **55, 66**
 Max. Size: LOA 670 ft., draft 43 ft. *Fuel:* All grades by barge
 from Houston. *Airport:* Houston, 80 miles.
Freetown, Sierra Leone: 8.30 N. 13.14 W. **27**
 Max. Size: Draft 48 ft. (HW) *Fuel:* Available.
 Airport: Lungi Airport, 10 minutes by helicopter.
Freiburg, Germany: 53.49 N. 9.18 E. **8, 14**
Fremantle, W.A., Australia: 32.03 S. 115.44 E. **50**
 Max. Size: Outer Harbour: Up to 12.65 m. draft.
 Inner Harbour: Draft 10.5 m. – 12.5 m. Tankers: See Kwinana.
 Fuel: Marine fuel (2 grades); Marine diesel. *Dry
 Docks:* 3 Shiplifters, 7,520, 2,600 and 1,100 tonnes available.
 Airport: 35 km. International, 23 km. Domestic.
French Frigate Shoal, (Hawaiian Is.), U.S.A.:
 23.50 N. 166.10 W. **49**
French Polynesia (France) **49**
Friday Harbour, Washington, U.S.A.: 48.32 N. 123.01 W. . . **56**
Friedrichstadt: 54.22 N. 9.05 E. **14**
Frobisher, see Iqaluit.
Frobisher Bay, N.W.T., Canada: 63.43 N. 68.31 W. **59**
Froland, see Uddevalla.
Frontera, Mexico: 18.35 N. 92.40 W. **69**
Frontignan, see Sete.
Fu Chou, see Fuzhou.
Fudai, Japan: 40.00 N. 142.00 E. **43**
Fuengirola, Spain: 36.32 N. 4.38 W. **20, 22**
Fuerteventura Is., Canary Is. (Spain) **27**
Fuglefjord, Faroe Is. (Denmark): 62.15 N. 6.48 W. . . . **5, 15**
Fuikbay, (Curacao), Netherlands Antilles: 12.03 N. 68.50 W. . **74**
 Max. Size: Draft 24 ft., LOA 360 ft. (exceptionally 380 ft.).
Fujairah, U.A.E.: 25.11 N. 56.21 E. **31, 35, 37**
 Max. Size: LOA 280 m., draft 12.5 m.
 Tankers: 145,000 tonnes d.w.t., LOA 333 m., draft 18 m.
 Fuel: Available. *Airport:* Fujairah, or Dubai or Sharjah –
 1.5 hours by car.
Fukui, Japan: 36.12 N. 136.07 E. **43, 45**
 Max. Size: Channel: Draft 9.0 m. Berth: 15,000 d.w.t.,
 depth 10.0 m.
Fukuma, Japan: 33.42 N. 130.27 E. **45**
Fukuoka, see Hakata.
Fukura, Japan: 34.15 N. 134.42 E. **45**
Fukuyama, Japan: 34.29 N. 133.26 E. **43, 45**
 Max. Size: LOA 350 m., draft 16 m. *Fuel:* Bunkers by lighter
 from Kobe, Mizushima, Tokuyama or Moji area.
 Airport: Okayama, 70 km.
 Also see Innoshima and Onomichi-Itozaki.
Fulford Harbour, B.C., Canada: 48.46 N. 123.26 W. **56**
Funabashi, see Chiba.
Funafuti, Tuvalu: 8.31 S. 179.13 E. **49**
 Max. Size: Te Puapua Passage: Depth 15 m., 250 ft. wide (LW),
 depth alongside 8 m. *Fuel:* Light diesel. *Airport:* Connects Fiji
 and Kiribati.
Funakawa, Japan: 39.52 N. 139.52 E. **43**
 Max. Size: Draft 9.0 m., 15,000 tons. Tankers: 180,000 d.w.t.,
 draft 16.5 m.
Funchal, Madeira (Portugal): 32.38 N. 16.55 W. **27**
 Max. Size: LOA 990 ft., draft 36 ft. Tankers – Praia Formosa:
 LOA 665 ft., draft 36 ft. *Fuel:* All grades. *Airport:* Santa Cruz
 20 km., flights to Lisbon.
Funen Is., Denmark **12**
Funivie, see Savona.
Funter, Alaska, U.S.A.: 58.15 N. 134.54 W. **56**
Furuogrund, Sweden: 64.55 N. 21.14 E. **15**
Furusund, Sweden: 59.04 N. 18.56 E. **11**
Fushiki, Japan: 36.49 N. 137.03 E. **43, 45**
 Max. Size: LOA 175 m., draft 29 ft. *Fuel:* All grades of bonded
 bunkers are stocked in Tokyo Bay, Ise Bay, Osaka Bay and
 Kanmon Port. *Airport:* Toyama, 35 km.
Futila, Angola: 5.27 S. 12.11 E. **28**
 Max. Size: 6,400 d.w.t., draft 15 ft.
Futuna Is., French Polynesia (France): 14.17 S. 176.09 W. . . **49**
Fuzhou, China: 26.03 N. 119.18 E. **42, 46**
 Max. Size: Depth 12 m. – 14 m. Tankers: Hong Shan –
 Depth 11.5 m. Xinmin – Depth 11 m. *Fuel:* All grades.
Fyn, see Funen Is..

G

Gabes, Tunisia: 33.55 N. 10.06 E. 24
   Max. Size: Draft: 35 ft. – 39 ft.   *Fuel:* Available from Sfax.
   Airport: Djerba.
GABON 28, 29
Gaboto, Argentina: 32.22 S. 60.50 W. 78
Gaeta, Italy: 41.13 N. 13.35 E. 9, 23, 24
   Max. Size: Draft 22 ft. Tankers: AGIP – Draft 48 ft. SIOG Sea Berth – 260,000 d.w.t., draft 20.3 m.   *Fuel:* Bunker "C" and gas oil at Oil Jetty; dry cargo only by road tanker. Bunkers not available at Sea Berth.   *Dry Docks:* For vessels 70 m. length.   *Airport:* Naples, 96 km. and Rome, 135 km.
Gaferut Is., (Caroline Is.), Micronesia: 9.14 N. 145.22 E. . . . 46
Gagra, Georgia: 43.20 N. 40.14 E. 26
Gaillard Cut, Panama Canal, Panama 73
Gainsborough, U.K.: 53.24 N. 0.47 W. 6, 7
Gairloch, U.K.: 57.43 N. 5.41 W. 5
Galapagos Islands, Ecuador 69
Galata, see Istanbul.
Galati, see Galatzi.
Galatzi, Romania: 45.25 N. 28.05 E. 9, 21, 26
   Max. Size: Draft 23 ft.   *Fuel:* By barge.
Galaxidhion, Greece: 38.23 N. 22.23 E. 25
Galela, Indonesia: 1.50 N. 127.50 E. 46
Galena Park, see Houston.
Galeota Point, Trinidad and Tobago: 10.05 N. 61.01 W.   69, 71, 72, 75
   Max. Size: 250,000 d.w.t. Depth 95 ft.   *Fuel:* By barge from Port of Spain.
Galite Is., Tunisia: 37.31 N. 8.57 E. 24
Galle, Sri Lanka: 6.01 N. 80.14 E. 37
   Max. Size: LOA 130 m., draft 7.3 m.   *Fuel:* Available.
   Airport: Colombo, 130 m.
Gallipoli, Italy: 40.03 N. 17.59 E. 24
   Max. Size: Draft 10.5 m.   *Fuel:* By road tanker.
   Airport: Brindisi, 75 km.
Gallipoli, Turkey: 40.25 N. 26.39 E. 25, 26
Galvan, see Bahia Blanca.
Galveston, Texas, U.S.A.: 29.17 N. 94.50 W. 55, 66
   Max. Size: Depth alongside 31 ft. – 45 ft.   *Fuel:* Available.
   Dry Docks: Capacity 8,000 tons and 10,000 tons.
Galveston Bay, Texas, U.S.A. 66
Galway, Ireland: 53.16 N. 9.03 W. 5
   Max. Size: Depth on sill of 8.5 m. at springs and 7.3 m. at neaps.   *Fuel:* All grades.   *Airport:* Shannon, 55 miles.
Galway Bay, Ireland 5
Gamagori, Japan: 34.48 N. 137.14 E. 43, 45
   Max. Size: 15,000 d.w.t., LOA 215 m., draft 9.8 m.
Gamba, Gabon: 2.52 S. 9.58 E. 28
   Max. Size: Draft 17.25 m., 150,000 d.w.t.   *Airport:* Local to Port Gentil.
Gambell, Alaska, U.S.A.: 63.44 N. 171.41 W. 54
GAMBIA 27
Gambier Is., French Polynesia (France). 49
Gamble, see Port Gamble.
Gambo, Newfoundland, Canada: 48.46 N. 54.12 W. . . . 60
Gamboa, Panama Canal, Panama: 9.07 N. 79.42 W. . . 73
Gamleby, Sweden: 57.54 N. 16.25 E. 11
Gamvik, Norway: 71.00 N. 28.10 E. 15
Gan Is., (Addu Atoll), Maldives: 0.41 S. 73.10 E. . . 30, 37
Gananoque, Ontario, Canada: 44.20 N. 76.10 W. . . . 62
Ganaveh, Iran: 29.34 N. 50.31 E. 35
Gandia, Spain: 38.59 N. 0.09 W. 22
   Max. Size: Depth 3 m. – 9 m.   *Airport:* Valencia, 70 km.
Ganges, B.C., Canada: 48.51 N. 123.29 W. 56
Ganges Delta 37
Gaogang, see Taizhou.
Garden Is. Bay, U.S.A. 67
Gardiner, Oregon, U.S.A.: 43.43 N. 124.07 W. . . . 57
Gardner Is., (Phoenix Is.) Kiribati: 4.41 S. 174.34 W. . . 49
Garelochead, see Faslane.
Gargantua, Ontario, Canada: 47.34 N. 84.58 W. . . . 62
Garibaldi, see Porto Garibaldi.
Garlieston, U.K.: 54.47 N. 4.21 W. 5
   Max. Size: 1,000 d.w.t., vessel take bottom at L.W.   *Fuel:* By road tanker.   *Airport:* Prestwick, 70 miles. Glasgow, 100 miles.
Garrucha, Spain: 37.10 N. 1.49 W. 22
   Max. Size: LOA 210 m., beam 30 m. – 32 m., air draft 12 m., draft 28 ft.
Garston, U.K.: 53.21 N. 2.54 W. 6
   Max. Size: LOA 152.4 m., beam 19.2 m., draft 8.3 m.
   Airport: Liverpool, 3 km.
Gary, Indiana, U.S.A.: 41.35 N. 87.20 W. 62
Gasan, (Marinduque Is.), Philippines: 13.20 N. 121.51 E. . . 47
Gashaga, see Stockholm.
Gasmata, Papua New Guinea: 6.19 S. 150.18 E. . . . 46

Gaspe, Quebec, Canada: 48.50 N. 64.29 W. 60
   Max. Size: LOA 650 ft., depth 35 ft. (LW).   *Fuel:* Light and medium diesel available. Bunker fuel by truck.   *Airport:* 7 miles, connects with Quebec and Montreal.
Gastgivarchagen, see Norrkoping.
Gastria Bay, see Kalecik.
Gateshead, U.K.: 54.58 N. 1.35 W. 6
Also see Tyne District.
Gatun, Panama Canal, Panama: 9.16 N. 79.55 W. . . . 73
Gatun Dam, Panama 73
Gatun Lake, Panama: 9.00 N. 79.35 W. 73
Gatun Locks, Panama Canal, Panama 73
Gaultois, Newfoundland, Canada: 47.36 N. 55.55 W. . . 60
Gavater, Iran: 25.10 N. 61.28 E. 31, 37
Gavdhos Is., Greece: 34.40 N. 24.10 E. 25, 26
Gavle, Sweden: 60.41 N. 17.11 E. 10, 11
   Max. Size: Draft 8.9 m. Tankers: LOA 220 m., draft 10.4 m.
   Fuel: All grades.   *Airport:* Stockholm, 145 km. Rorberg, 16 km.
Gavopta, California, U.S.A.: 34.28 N. 120.12 W. . . . 57
Gavrilovo, Russia: 69.10 N. 35.51 E. 16
Gavrion, Greece: 37.53 N. 24.44 E. 25
Gaza, Egypt: 31.28 N. 34.28 E. 26, 32
Gazenica, see Zadar.
Gdansk, Poland: 54.25 N. 18.39 E. 4, 10, 11
   Max. Size: Draft 10.2 m., LOA 225 m. Tankers: Draft 15.5 m. Coal: Draft 15 m.   *Fuel:* All grades.   *Dry Docks:* Lifting capacities up to 11,000 tons.   *Airport:* Gdansk, connects with Warsaw.
Gdynia, Poland: 54.32 N. 18.34 E. 4, 10, 11
   Max. Size: 100,000 d.w.t., LOA 300 m., draft 13.5 m.
   Tankers: 35,000 d.w.t., depth 10.7 m.   *Fuel:* All grades.
   Dry Docks: Up to 4,500 tons lifting capacity.
   Airport: Gdansk, 20 km.
Gebe Island, Indonesia: 0.04 S. 129.23 E. 46
   Max. Size: 60,000 d.w.t., draft 20 m.   *Airport:* Flights 2 times weekly between Ternate and Gebe.
Gebze, Turkey: 40.46 N. 29.27 E. 23
Gedser, Denmark: 54.34 N. 11.56 E. 11, 12, 14
   Max. Size: Depth 6.2 m. (20.3 ft.).   *Airport:* Copenhagen.
Geelong, Vic., Australia: 38.09 S. 144.22 E. . . . 50, 51
   Max. Size: Draft 11.6 m. Tankers: LOA 265 m., draft 11.6 m.
   Fuel: All grades by barge and road tanker.   *Dry Docks:* Slipway – 1,000 tons.   *Airport:* Melbourne, 50 miles.
Gefle, see Gavle.
Geismar, Louisiana, U.S.A.: 30.13 N. 91.01 W. . . . 55, 67
   Max. Size: Depth 32 ft.
Gela, (Sicily), Italy: 37.04 N. 14.15 E. 24
   Max. Size: Tankers up to 80,000 g.r.t., with a draft of 42 ft.
   Dry cargo: Draft 31 ft. 6 in.   *Fuel:* Small quantities.
   Airport: Catania and Palermo.
Gelendzhik, Russia: 44.33 N. 38.05 E. 26
Gelibolu, see Gallipoli.
Gellibrand, see Melbourne.
Gelting, Germany: 54.44 N. 9.53 E. 12, 14
Gemikonagi, Cyprus: 35.08 N. 32.50 E. 26
   Max. Size: Karavostassi: Depth 18 m. Xeros: Depth 4.3 m.
   Airport: Ercan, 53 miles.
Gemlik, Turkey: 40.25 N. 29.07 E. 25, 26
   Max. Size: LOA 230 m., draft 12 m.   *Fuel:* Available at 48 hours notice.   *Airport:* Bursa, 36 km.
Gemsah, Egypt: 27.39 N. 33.36 E. 32
General MacArthur, (Samar Is.), Philippines:
   11.14 N. 125.32 E. 47
General San Martin, Peru: 13.48 N. 76.17 W. . . . 72, 77
   Max. Size: Draft: 32 ft. Tankers: Depth 45 ft.
General Santos, see Dadiangas.
Geneva, Switzerland: 46.13 N. 6.09 E. 9
Gennevilliers, France: 48.56 N. 2.17 E. 7
Genoa, Italy: 44.24 N. 8.54 E. 9, 21, 23, 24
   Max. Size: Draft 26 ft. – 44 ft. Tankers: Draft 46 ft.
   Fuel: All grades.   *Dry Docks:* 100,000 d.w.t.   *Airport:* 5 km.
Also see Multedo.
Genteng, Indonesia: 7.23 S. 106.24 E. 38
Gentil, see Port Gentil.
Geographe Bay, see Busselton.
Georgetown, Ascension Is. (U.K.): 7.55 S. 14.20 W. . . . 28
   Max. Size: Anchorage port only, unlimited depth.   *Airport:* No commercial flights. R.A.F. to U.K. and U.S.A.F. to Antigua weekly.
Georgetown, P.E.I., Canada: 46.11 N. 62.32 W. . . . 60
   Max. Size: Depth 3 m. – 6 m.   *Fuel:* Available.
Georgetown, (Grand Cayman), Cayman Is. (U.K.):
   19.18 N. 81.23 W. 69, 70
   Max. Size: Depths to 26 ft.   *Fuel:* Marine diesel.
   Airport: International.
Georgetown, Gambia: 13.30 N. 14.45 W. 27
Georgetown, Guyana: 6.49 N. 58.10 W. 72, 75, 76
   Max. Size: Draft 30 ft. 8 in.   *Fuel:* Bunker "C" and diesel fuel in emergency only.   *Dry Docks:* 210 ft. x 37 ft. 9 in. at entrance.
   Top 46 ft. 4 in., bottom 40 ft. 9 in.   *Airport:* Timehri, 30 miles.
Georgetown, Malaysia, see Penang.

Georgetown, South Carolina, U.S.A.: 33.22 N. 79.17 W. . . . 55, 66
 Max. Size: LOA 700 ft., beam 100 ft., depth 27 ft.
 Fuel: Available. *Airport:* Myrtle Beach, 30 miles.
 Charleston, 80 miles.
GEORGIA 9, 26
Georgia, U.S.A. 66
Georgian Bay, Ontario, Canada 62
Geraldton, W.A., Australia: 28.46 S. 114.36 E. 50
 Max. Size: LOA 213 m., beam 30.4 m. Drafts: 8.7 m. at LW –
 9.3 m. at 1.1 m. tide. *Fuel:* Light diesel. *Airport:* 11 km.,
 connects with Perth (430 km.).
Geras Bay, see Mitilene.
GERMANY 4, 7, 8, 9, 10, 11, 12, 14, 21
Germein, see Port Germein.
Gerona, see Nueva Gerona.
Geser, Indonesia: 3.53 S. 130.54 E. 46
Geta, Finland: 60.25 N. 19.50 E. 11
Geylang, see Singapore.
Geziret Is., see Ras Zabarjad.
GHANA 28
Ghannouche, see Gabes.
Ghazaouet, Algeria: 35.06 N. 1.52 W. 22
 Max. Size: LOA 180 m., draft 28 ft. *Fuel:* Small quantities by
 road tankers and tugs.
Ghenichesk, Ukraine: 46.10 N. 34.49 E. 26
Ghent, Belgium: 51.02 N. 3.44 E. 7, 8, 9
 Max. Size: LOA 256 m., beam 34 m., draft 12.25 m. (FW). *Fuel:*
 All grades. *Dry Docks:* For ships: LOA 120 m., beam 13 m.,
 draft 5 m. *Airport:* Brussels, 70 km. Antwerp, 60 km.
Gibara, see Vita.
Gibbstown, see Philadelphia.
Gibostad, Norway: 69.22 N. 18.06 E. 10, 15
Gibraltar, Gibraltar (U.K.): 36.08 N. 5.21 W. 20, 21, 22, 23, 27
 Max. Size: Draft 31 ft. 6 in. *Fuel:* All grades. *Dry Docks:* 3 dry
 docks. Largest 270 m. x 38 m. *Airport:* Daily flights to London.
Gibraltar (U.K.) 20, 21, 22, 23, 27
Gibsons, B.C., Canada: 49.23 N. 123.34 W. 56
Gifatin Is., Egypt: 27.11 N. 33.56 E. 32
Gigante, Panama Canal, Panama: 9.05 N. 79.50 W. 73
Gijon, Spain: 43.34 N. 5.41 W. 19, 20, 21, 22
 Max. Size: Ore: Draft 17.68 m. General: Depth 12.0 m.
 Tankers: Depth 11.5 m. *Fuel:* Fuel and diesel oil.
 Dry Docks: Largest: 170 m. length, 27.40 m. wide
 (26,000 tons). *Airport:* Asturias 40 km., connects with Madrid.
Gilau, Papua New Guinea: 5.35 S. 149.05 E. 46
Gilbert Islands, Kiribati 49
Gildeskal, Norway: 67.05 N. 14.00 E. 15
Giles, see Port Giles.
Gillam, Manitoba, Canada: 56.25 N. 94.40 W. 59
Gilleleje, Denmark: 56.08 N. 12.19 E. 12
Gillingham, U.K.: 51.23 N. 0.33 E. 6
Gilmanuk, Indonesia: 8.09 S. 114.26 E. 38
Gineifa, Egypt: 30.10 N. 32.31 E. 33
Gingoog, (Mindanao Is.), Philippines: 8.50 N. 125.06 E. 47
 Max. Size: Deep water berth.
Gioia Tauro, Italy: 38.27 N. 15.53 E. 24
 Max. Size: Depth 9 m. – 14 m. *Fuel:* Available.
 Airport: Lamezia, 65 km. Reggio Calabria, 60 km.
Girard Point, see Philadelphia.
Giresun, Turkey: 40.56 N. 38.24 E. 21, 26
 Max. Size: Draft 8 m. *Fuel:* Available. *Airport:*
 Trabzon, 130 km.
Girvan, U.K.: 55.15 N. 4.51 W. 5, 6
 Max. Size: LOA 50 m., beam 9 m., draft 3.5 m. (HW).
 Fuel: Diesel. *Airport:* Prestwick 38 km., Glasgow 91 km.
Gisborne, New Zealand: 38.42 S. 178.02 E. 52
 Max. Size: LOA 200 m., draft 10.2 m. at HW. *Fuel:* By rail
 tanker. *Airport:* 3.5 miles (Internal).
Githion, see Yithior.
Giulianova, Italy: 42.45 N. 13.58 E. 24
Giurgiu, Romania: 43.50 N. 25.55 E. 9, 26
Gizan, Saudi Arabia: 16.54 N. 42.32 E. 31, 32
 Max. Size: LOA 220 m., draft 10.5 m. *Fuel:* Diesel. *Airport:*
 Domestic, 3 km.
Gizhiga, Russia: 62.00 N. 160.30 E. 54
Gizo, Solomon Islands: 8.05 S. 156.52 E. 49, 51
 Max. Size: Depth alongside 9 ft. Anchorage 16 fathoms.
Gjeving, see Risor.
Glace Bay, N.S., Canada: 46.12 N. 59.57 W. 60
Gladstad, Norway: 65.45 N. 12.00 E. 15
Gladstone, Qld., Australia: 23.51 S. 151.15 E. 50, 51
 Max. Size: Draft 17.0 m. Tankers: Depth 11.3 m. (LWOST)
 Fuel: All grades. *Airport:* 3 km., connects with Brisbane.
Gladstone, Michigan, U.S.A.: 45.51 N. 87.01 W. 62
Glan, (Mindanao Is.), Philippines: 5.50 N. 125.12 E. 47
Glasgow, U.K.: 55.51 N. 4.16 W. 4, 5, 6
 Also see Clyde Port.
Glasson Dock, U.K.: 54.00 N. 2.50 W. 5
Glebe Is., see Sydney.
Glenarm, U.K.: 54.58 N. 5.57 W. 5
Glencolumbkille, Ireland: 54.43 N. 8.44 W. 5
Glenelg, Australia, see Adelaide.
Glenelg, U.K.: 57.13 N. 5.37 W. 5
Glensanda, U.K.: 56.34 N. 5.32 W. 5
 Max. Size: 120,000 d.w.t. Depth 12.3 m.
Global Marine Terminal, see New York.
Glomfjord, Norway: 66.50 N. 13.57 E. 10, 15
 Max. Size: Quay: Depth 15.0 m. *Airport:* Bodo, 2.5 hours by car.
Gloucester, U.K.: 51.52 N. 2.14 W. 6
 Also see Sharpness.
Gloucester, Massachusetts, U.S.A.: 42.35 N. 70.40 W. . . . 60, 63
 Max. Size: LOA 475 ft., draft 24 ft. *Fuel:* By barge or road
 tanker. *Airport:* Beverly, 25 km. Boston, 60 km.
Gloucester and Sharpness Ship Canal, U.K. 6
 Max. Size: LOA 205 ft. (62.5 m.), beam 31 ft. (9.45 m.),
 draft 11 ft. 6 in. (3.5 m.) (FW).
 Also see Sharpness.
Gloucester City, Pennsylvania, U.S.A.: 39.54 N. 75.08 W. . . 63, 65
 Max. Size: Depth to 31 ft.
Glovertown, Newfoundland, Canada: 48.40 N. 54.02 W. 60
Gluckstadt, Germany: 53.45 N. 9.25 E. 8, 12, 14
 Max. Size: Outer harbour: LOA 150 m., beam 18 m.,
 draft 5.5 m. – 6.0 m. Inner harbour: LOA 90 m., beam 12.5 m.,
 draft 4.2 m. – 4.5 m. *Fuel:* By road tanker. *Dry Docks:* Slipway
 for waterway vessels up to 500 d.w.t. *Airport:* Hamburg.
Gnarp, Sweden: 62.02 N. 17.25 E. 15
Go Dau, Vietnam: 10.39 N. 107.01 E. 39
 Max. Size: LOA 112 m., draft 7.5 m. *Fuel:* Available.
 Airport: Tan Son Nhat, 75 km.
Go Gia Transshipment Area, see Vung Tau.
Gocek, Turkey: 36.45 N. 28.55 E. 25, 26
 Max. Size: Depth 11.5 m.
Godbout, Quebec, Canada: 49.20 N. 67.36 W. 60
Goddard, Alaska, U.S.A.: 56.50 N. 135.20 W. 56
Goderich, Ontario, Canada: 43.45 N. 81.44 W. 62
 Max. Size: Depth 7.0 m. – 8.2 m. *Fuel:* By road tanker.
Godhavn, see Qeqertarsuaq.
Godovari Delta, India 37
Godthab, see Nuuk.
Gogland Is., Finland: 60.06 N. 26.58 E. 11
Goi, Japan: 35.32 N. 140.10 E. 44
Gokceade, see Imbros Is..
Gokova Iskele, Turkey: 37.03 N. 28.22 E. 25
Golchikha, Russia: 71.45 N. 83.30 E. 16
Golcuk, Turkey: 40.43 N. 29.48 E. 23, 25
Gold River, B.C., Canada: 49.41 N. 126.08 W. 56
 Max. Size: LOA 200 m., draft 10.6 m. *Fuel:* Available in
 emergency only. *Airport:* Campbell River.
Goldboro, see Isaacs Harbour.
Golfito, Costa Rica: 8.37 N. 83.10 W. 69
 Max. Size: LOA 450 ft., depth 35 ft. *Fuel:* Diesel and fuel oil
 available from time to time. *Airport:* One mile.
Golovasi, see Botas.
Golovino, Russia: 43.40 N. 145.30 E. 43
Gomera, Canary Is. (Spain) 27
Gonaives, Haiti: 19.27 N. 72.42 W. 70
 Max. Size: Depth 16 ft. – 21 ft.
 Airport: Port-au-Prince, 3 hours by car.
Gonave Is., Haiti: 18.25 N. 73.00 W. 69, 70
Gonfreville, see Le Havre.
Good Hope, Louisiana, U.S.A.: 29.59 N. 90.24 W. 67
 Max. Size: Depth 40 ft.
 Also see South Louisiana.
Goole, U.K.: 53.42 N. 0.50 W. 6, 7
 Max. Size: LOA 100 m., beam 24 m., draft 6 m., 3,000 d.w.t.
 Fuel: All grades. *Dry Docks:* Largest: 91 m.x15.2 m.x4.75 m.
 Airport: Humberside.
Goose Bay, Newfoundland, Canada: 53.22 N. 60.22 W. 59
 Max. Size: Depth 7.5 m. – 9.0 m. *Fuel:* Light diesel. *Airport:*
 1.5 miles.
Gopalpore, India: 19.15 N. 84.54 E. 37
Gorda, see Moa.
Gore Bay, Ontario, Canada: 45.56 N. 82.28 W. 62
Gorele, Turkey: 41.05 N. 39.07 E. 26
Gorgona, Italy: 43.25 N. 10.00 E. 23
Gorgona Is., Colombia: 3.00 N. 78.10 W. 72
Gorinchem, Netherlands: 51.50 N. 5.00 E. 8
Goritsa Bay, see Corfu.
Gorontalo, Indonesia: 0.30 N. 123.03 E. 46
 Max. Size: Draft 5.0 m. *Airport:* 30 km.
Gosport, U.K.: 50.48 N. 1.07 W. 7
Gota, Sweden: 58.06 N. 12.08 E. 12
Gota Canal, Sweden: 58.30 N. 15.30 E. 11, 12
Goteborg, see Gothenburg.
Gothenburg, Sweden: 57.42 N. 11.57 E. 4, 10, 11, 12, 79
 Max. Size: Tankers: 225,000 d.w.t., draft 18.3 m. with special
 permission. Container ships: Depth up to 12 m. Others: Depth
 10 m. *Fuel:* All grades. *Dry Docks:* Largest 268 m. x 34.8 m. x
 8.0 m. depth. *Airport:* Landvetter, 30 km.
Gotland Is., Sweden: 57.42 N. 18.49 E. 10, 11

THE SHIPS ATLAS

Goto Is., Japan: 32.40 N. 128.45 E. **42, 43, 45**
Gotska Sandon, Sweden: 58.22 N. 19.15 E. **11**
Gough Is., (U.K.): 40.20 S. 9.44 W. **18, 28, 68**
Goulais, Ontario, Canada: 46.44 N. 84.30 W. **62**
Gouraya, Algeria: 36.32 N. 1.55 E. **22**
Gourock, U.K.: 55.51 N. 4.16 W. **6**
  Also see Greenock.
Gove, N.T., Australia: 12.12 S. 136.40 E. **46, 50**
  Max. Size: Max. arrival draft 12.8 m. Tankers: 100,000 d.w.t.
  Airport: Gove, domestic.
Gozo Is., Malta **24**
Graciosa Bay, (Santa Cruz Is.), Solomon Islands:
  10.45 S. 165.50 E. **49**
Graciosa Is., Azores (Portugal) **20**
Grado, Italy: 45.40 N. 13.21 E. **24**
Graham, see English Bay.
Graham Is., B.C., Canada **56**
Gramercy, Louisiana, U.S.A.: 30.03 N. 90.41 W. **67**
  Max. Size: Colonial: Depth 42 ft. Kaiser: Depth 60 ft.
  Riverplex: Depth 50 ft. Peavey Grain at Pauline: Depth 45 ft.
  Tankers: Marathon – Depth 45 ft.
  Also see South Louisiana.
Gran Canaria, Canary Is. (Spain): 28.04 N. 15.27 W. . . **27**
Granaderos, see San Lorenzo.
Grand Bahama Is., Bahamas **66, 69, 70**
Grand Bank, Newfoundland, Canada: 47.06 N. 55.45 W. . . **60**
  Max. Size: Depths 14 ft. – 18 ft. (LWOST) *Fuel:* Limited
  supplies of fuel oil/diesel.
Grand Bassam, Ivory Coast: 5.12 N. 3.43 W. **28**
Grand Bay, Louisiana, U.S.A. **67**
Grand Bereby, Ivory Coast: 4.38 N. 6.54 W. **28**
Grand Bourg, (Marie Galante Is.), Guadeloupe (France):
  15.53 N. 61.19 W. **71**
Grand Canary, see Gran Canaria.
Grand Cayman Is., Cayman Is. (U.K.) **69, 70**
Grand Comore, Comoros (Rep. of): 11.40 S. 43.15 E. . . **30**
Grand Entree, Quebec, Canada: 47.34 N. 61.34 W. **60**
Grand Haven, Michigan, U.S.A.: 43.04 N. 86.15 W. . . . **62**
  Max. Size: Draft 19 ft. *Fuel:* By road tanker.
  Airport: Grand Haven or Muskegon.
Grand Is., Louisiana, U.S.A.: 30.09 N. 89.21 W. **67**
Grand Is., Michigan, U.S.A.: 46.34 N. 86.40 W. **62**
Grand Isle, Louisiana, U.S.A.: 29.14 N. 90.00 W. . . . **67**
Grand Lahou, Ivory Coast: 5.08 N. 5.00 W. **28**
Grand Marais, Michigan, U.S.A.: 46.40 N. 85.58 W. . . . **62**
Grand Marais, Minnesota, U.S.A.: 47.45 N. 90.20 W. . . **62**
Grand Popo, Benin: 6.16 N. 1.51 E. **29**
Grand Terre, Louisiana, U.S.A. **67**
Grand Traverse Bay, Lake Michigan, U.S.A. **62**
Grand Turk, (Turks Is.), Turks and Caicos Is. (U.K.):
  21.28 N. 71.08 W. **69, 70**
  Max. Size: Draft 3.9 m. *Fuel:* Available. *Airport:* 1 mile.
Grande Vallee, Quebec, Canada: 49.13 N. 65.06 W. . . . **60**
Granerudstoen, see Fagerstrand.
Grangemouth, U.K.: 56.01 N. 3.43 W. **5, 6**
  Max. Size: Dry cargo: LOA 600 ft., beam 90 ft., draft 25 ft. 6 in.
  Tankers: LOA 575 ft., beam 90 ft., draft 34 ft. *Fuel:* All grades.
  Dry Docks: Length 350 ft., breadth 50 ft., depth 22 ft. *Airport:*
  1 hour to Glasgow/Edinburgh.
Granna, Sweden: 58.00 N. 14.25 E. **11, 12**
Granton, U.K.: 55.59 N. 3.13 W. **6**
  Port no longer accepts cargo vessels.
Granvik, (Seskaro Is.), Sweden: 65.44 N. 23.45 E. . . . **15**
Granville, France: 48.50 N. 1.37 W. **7, 19**
  Max. Size: LOA 115 m., beam 18 m., draft 7.5 m.
  Fuel: By road tanker. *Airport:* 10 km.
Graso, Sweden: 60.25 N. 18.35 E. **11**
Grassy, Tas., Australia: 40.02 S. 144.06 E. **51**
Grasten, Denmark: 54.55 N. 9.36 E. **12, 14**
Gravelines, France: 51.00 N. 2.08 E. **7**
Gravesend, U.K.: 51.25 N. 0.25 E. **6**
  Also see Tilbury.
Grays, U.K.: 51.27 N. 0.20 E. **6**
Grays Harbor, Washington, U.S.A.: 46.55 N. 124.08 W. . **55, 56**
  Max. Size: Depth 34 ft. – 41 ft. *Fuel:* Available.
Great Abaco Is., Bahamas **70**
Great Australian Bight, Australia **50, 51**
Great Barrier Is., (North Is.), New Zealand: 37.12 S. 175.25 E. . **52**
Great Barrier Reef, Qld., Australia: 10.36 S. 142.05 E. . **50, 51**
Great Belt, Denmark **12**
Great Bitter Lake, Egypt: 30.36 N. 32.17 E. **33**
Great Cumbrae, U.K.: 55.46 N. 4.55 W. **6**
Great Inagua Is., Bahamas **69, 70**
Great Nicobar Is., (Nicobar Is.), India **37**
Great Shantar Is., Russia **43**
Great Sitkin Is., (Aleutian Is.), Alaska, U.S.A. **54**
Great Whale River, see Poste de la Baleine.

Great Yarmouth, U.K.: 52.34 N. 1.44 E. **5, 7**
  Max. Size: LOA 138 m., draft 5.7 m. (HWOST). *Fuel:* Gas oil.
  Dry Docks: Vessels to 85 m. x 12.5 m. Sill depth: 4.45 m. MST.
  Airport: Norwich.
Greater Sunda Islands, Indonesia **38**
Greathead Bay, St. Vincent: 13.09 N. 61.14 W. **71**
Grebbestad, Sweden: 58.41 N. 11.15 E. **11, 12**
GREECE **9, 21, 23, 24, 25, 26**
Green Bay, Wisconsin, U.S.A.: 44.32 N. 88.02 W. . . . **55, 62**
  Max. Size: Depth 26 ft. (HW) *Fuel:* Fuel oil available.
  Dry Docks: Available at Sturgeon Bay, Wisconsin. *Airport:*
  8 miles.
Green Island, Suez Canal, Egypt: 29.55 N. 32.32 E. . . **34**
Greenhithe, see Tilbury.
Greenland (Denmark) **17, 59, 79**
Greenland Sea **17, 79**
Greenock, U.K.: 55.57 N. 4.46 W. **6**
  Max. Size: Container berths: Depth 12.6 m. LWOST.
  Fuel: All grades. *Airport:* Glasgow.
  Also see Clyde Port.
Greenore, Ireland: 54.02 N. 6.08 W. **5**
Greenport, New York, U.S.A.: 41.05 N. 72.22 W. **63**
Greenville, Liberia: 4.59 N. 9.03 W. **28**
  Max. Size: Basin: Up to 156 m. LOA, 7.31 m. draft.
  Fuel: Small quantities of diesel. *Airport:* 5 miles (domestic).
Greenwich, U.K.: 51.29 N. 0.00 E. **6**
Greenwich, Connecticut, U.S.A.: 41.01 N. 73.37 W. . . . **63**
Greenwich Point, see Philadelphia.
Gregorio, Chile: 52.38 S. 70.11 W. **77**
  Max. Size: LOA 250 m., draft 49 ft., 75,000 tons displacement.
  Also see Punta Arenas.
Gregory, see Port Gregory.
Gremikha, Russia: 68.03 N. 39.31 E. **16**
Grenaa, Denmark: 56.25 N. 10.56 E. **11, 12**
  Max. Size: LOA 165 m., beam 23 m., draft 9.0 m.
  Fuel: Available. *Airport:* Tirstrup, 25 km.
GRENADA **69, 71, 72**
Grenadine Is., St. Vincent **71**
Gresik, Indonesia: 7.09 S. 112.40 E. **38**
  Max. Size: Depth 15 m. – 18 m. (LWL), 30,000 d.w.t.
Gretna, Louisiana, U.S.A.: 29.15 N. 90.04 W. **67**
  Max. Size: Depth 30 ft. – 35 ft.
  Also see New Orleans.
Grey Is., Newfoundland, Canada **60**
Greymouth, New Zealand: 42.27 S. 171.12 E. **52**
  Max. Size: 10,000 d.w.t., LOA 109 m., draft 5.5 m.
  Fuel: Diesel oil. *Airport:* Hokitika, 40 km.
Griffin Venture, W.A., Australia: 21.13 S. 114.39 E. . **50, 51**
  Max. Size: 150,000 d.w.t. (Max. displacement 175,000 tonnes).
Grigorevsky, see Yuzhny.
Grimsby, U.K.: 53.34 N. 0.04 W. **5, 6, 7**
  Max. Size: LOA 145 m., beam 20.6 m., draft 5.8 m. *Fuel:* Gas
  and diesel oil. *Airport:* Humberside, 15 miles.
Grimstad, Norway: 58.20 N. 8.35 E. **11, 12**
Grindstone Is., see Magdalen Is..
Grisslehamn, Sweden: 60.06 N. 18.49 E. **11**
Grizzly Bay, California, U.S.A. **58**
Groais Is., Newfoundland, Canada: 50.58 N. 55.32 W. . . **60**
Groningen, Netherlands: 53.15 N. 6.34 E. **7, 8, 9**
  Max. Size: Beam 13 m., draft 4.5 m. *Fuel:* By barge.
  Airport: Eelde, 10 km.
  Also see Delfzijl.
Gronnedal, Greenland (Denmark): 61.15 N. 48.05 W. . . . **17**
Groote Eylandt, N.T., Australia: 13.52 S. 136.25 E. . **46, 50**
  Max. Size: LOA 223 m., beam 32.2 m., draft 12.2 m.
  Airport: Connects with Darwin and Cairns.
Gros Cacouna, Quebec, Canada: 47.55 N. 69.30 W. **60**
  Max. Size: LOA 135 m., draft 10.2 m. *Fuel:* Diesel.
  Dry Docks: Lauzon, 100 km. *Airport:* Riviere-du-Loup and
  Quebec.
Grossenbrode, Germany: 54.21 N. 11.05 E. **12, 14**
Groton, see New London.
Grove Wharf, see Gunness.
Grundartangi, Iceland: 64.21 N. 21.46 W. **17**
  Max. Size: Depth 8 m. – 13 m. *Fuel:* Available from Reykjavik.
  Airport: Keflavik, 80 km.
Grunenthal, see Fischerhutte.
Gruz Harbour, Croatia: 42.39 N. 18.07 E. **24**
  Max. Size: LOA 230 m., draft 11.5 m. *Fuel:* Tankers from Split.
  Airport: Cilipi, 25 km.
  Also see Dubrovnik.
Gryllefjord, Norway: 69.22 N. 17.04 E. **15**
Grytviken, South Georgia Is. (U.K.): 53.45 S. 37.10 W. . **77**
Guacolda, see Huasco.
Guadalcanal Is., Solomon Islands **49, 51**
Guadalupe Is., Mexico: 28.56 N. 118.18 W. **49, 57**
Guadeloupe (France) **69, 71**
Guaiba Is., see Sepetiba Bay.
Gualeguaychu, Argentina: 33.02 S. 58.30 W. **78**
Guam (U.S.A.) **46**

Guamare, Brazil: 4.52 S. 36.21 W. 72
   Max. Size: 116,000 d.w.t., draft 14 m. – 15 m.
Guanaja Is., Honduras: 16.28 N. 85.53 W. 69
Guangzhou, China: 23.05 N. 113.25 E. 39, 48
   Max. Size: LOA 114 m., draft 5.8 m. Tankers: Xiaohudao
   Terminal – 35,000 d.w.t., draft 9.4 m. Fuel: Available.
Guanica, Puerto Rico (U.S.A.): 17.57 N. 66.54 W. 70
   Max. Size: Depth 28 ft. alongside. Fuel: By road tanker.
Guanoco, Venezuela: 10.09 N. 62.56 W. 75
   Also see Caripito.
Guanta, Venezuela: 10.15 N. 64.35 W. 72, 75
   Max. Size: Depth 27 ft. – 34 ft. Fuel: Diesel and gas oil.
   Airport: Barcelona 15 miles, connects with Caracas.
Guantanamo, Cuba: 19.59 N. 75.10 W. 69, 70
   Also see Caimanera.
Guapi, Colombia: 2.35 N. 77.55 W. 69, 72
Guaraguao Terminal, see Puerto La Cruz.
Guaranao, Venezuela: 11.40 N. 70.13 W. 74
   Max. Size: Anchorage: Depth 28 ft. (8.5 m.) – 36 ft. (11 m.).
   Fuel: Available.
Guarello, see Madre de Dios Is..
GUATEMALA 69
Guayabal, Cuba: 20.42 N. 77.36 W. 69, 70
   Max. Size: Draft 9.9 m. (HW – sailing).
Guayacan, Chile: 29.58 S. 71.22 W. 77
   Max. Size: LOA 315 m., beam 50 m., draft 16.2 m.
   Tankers: LOA 190 m., draft 12 m., 41,000 d.w.t. Fuel: Diesel at
   Ore Pier by truck.
Guayama, see Las Mareas.
Guayanilla, Puerto Rico (U.S.A.): 18.00 N. 66.46 W. 70
   Max. Size: 80,000 d.w.t., draft 42 ft. Tallaboa Bay: Depth 38 ft.
   Fuel: Available. Airport: Ponce, connects with San Juan.
   Also see San Juan.
Guayaquil, Ecuador: 2.17 S. 79.54 W. 72
   Max. Size: LOA 855 ft., draft 32 ft. For Guayas River,
   LOA 600 ft., draft 23 ft. 6 in. Dry Docks: Capacity
   3,600 tonnes. Airport: 8 miles.
Guayas River, see Guayaquil.
Guaymas, Mexico: 27.54 N. 110.52 W. 49, 57
   Max. Size: 40,000 d.w.t., LOA 250 m., draft 12 m.
   Fuel: Available. Dry Docks: Slipway, capacity 24,000 tons.
   Airport: 10 km.
Guecho, Spain: 43.21 N. 2.59 W. 19
Guernsey, (Channel Is.), U.K. 7, 19
Guetaria, Spain: 43.19 N. 2.12 W. 19
Guguan, Northern Mariana Is. (U.S.A.): 17.18 N. 145.51 E. . . 46
Guimaras Is., Philippines: 10.35 N. 122.38 E. 46, 47
Guindulman Bay, (Bohol Is.), Philippines: 9.45 N. 124.30 E. . 47
GUINEA, REPUBLIC OF 27
GUINEA-BISSAU 27
Guiria, Venezuela: 10.34 N. 62.17 W. 69, 71, 75
Guiuan, (Samar Is.), Philippines: 11.05 N. 125.45 E. . . . 46, 47
Guldborg, Denmark: 54.52 N. 11.45 E. 12, 14
Gulf of Mexico – Lightering Zones, U.S.A. 66
Gulf of Morresquillo, see Covenas.
Gulf Outlet Canal, (Mississippi Delta), Louisiana, U.S.A. . . . 67
Gulfhavn, Denmark: 55.12 N. 11.16 E. 11, 12
   Max. Size: Draft 15.5 m. Fuel: Available at all berths. Airport:
   Copenhagen, 120 km.
Gulfport, Mississippi, U.S.A.: 30.21 N. 89.05 W. 55, 66, 67
   Max. Size: LOA approximately 900 ft., depth 36 ft.
   Fuel: Bunker service available. Airport: Gulfport, 4 miles.
Gulfport, New York, U.S.A.: 40.38 N. 74.12 W. 63
   Max. Size: Tankers: Depth 32 ft.
Gulfs:
   Gulf of Aden 31, 32
   Gulf of Alaska, Alaska, U.S.A. 54, 56
   Gulf of Antalya, Turkey 26
   Gulf of Aqaba 32
   Gulf of Argolis, Greece 25
   Gulf of Bahrain 35
   Gulf of Bothnia 4, 10, 11, 15
   Gulf of California, Mexico 49, 57
   Gulf of Cambay, India 37
   Gulf of Campeche, Mexico 69
   Gulf of Carpentaria, Australia 46, 50
   Gulf of Cheshskaya, Russia 16
   Gulf of Chihli, China 42
   Gulf of Chiriqui, Panama 69
   Gulf of Corinth, Greece 25
   Gulf of Danzig 11
   Gulf of Dvinskaya, Russia 16
   Gulf of Farralones, California, U.S.A. 58
   Gulf of Finland 11
   Gulf of Follonica, Italy 23
   Gulf of Fos, France 23
   Gulf of Gabes, Tunisia 24
   Gulf of Gaeta, Italy 23
   Gulf of Gascony 19
   Gulf of Genoa, Italy 23, 24
   Gulf of Guinea 28, 29
   Gulf of Hammamet, Tunisia 24
   Gulf of Honduras 69
   Gulf of Iskenderun, Turkey 26
   Gulf of Izmit, Turkey 23
   Gulf of Karkinitsky, Ukraine 26
   Gulf of Kutch, India 37
   Gulf of Lakonia 25
   Gulf of Liaotung, China 42
   Gulf of Lyons, France 22, 23
   Gulf of Manfredonia, Italy 24
   Gulf of Messini, Greece 25
   Gulf of Mexico 53, 55, 66
   Gulf of Naples, Italy 23
   Gulf of Ob, Russia 16
   Gulf of Oman 31, 35, 37
   Gulf of Onezhskaya, Russia 16
   Gulf of Orosei, (Sardinia), Italy 24
   Gulf of Panama, Panama 69, 72, 73
   Gulf of Penas, Chile 77
   Gulf of Riga 11
   Gulf of St. Florent, (Corsica), France 23
   Gulf of St. Lawrence, Canada 60
   Gulf of St. Malo, France 19
   Gulf of Salerno, Italy 23
   Gulf of Sant Eufemia, Italy 24
   Gulf of Santa Catalina, California, U.S.A. 58
   Gulf of Sirte, Libya 24
   Gulf of Squillace, Italy 24
   Gulf of Suez, Egypt 32
   Gulf of Tadjoura, Djibouti 32
   Gulf of Taganrog 26
   Gulf of Taranto, Italy 24
   Gulf of Tartary, Russia 43
   Gulf of Tazovskaya, Russia 16
   Gulf of Tehuantepec, Mexico 69
   Gulf of Thailand, Thailand 38, 39
   Gulf of Thermikos, Greece 25
   Gulf of Tonkin 39
   Gulf of Tunis, Tunisia 24
   Gulf of Valencia, Spain 22
   Gulf of Venezuela, Venezuela 74
   Gulf of Venice 24
   Gulf of Vyborg, Russia 13
Gulluk, Turkey: 37.14 N. 27.38 E. 25, 26
   Max. Size: Depth alongside 39 ft., shelving to 20 ft., 90 m. from
   end.
Gumboda, Sweden: 64.15 N. 21.06 E. 15
Gunness, U.K.: 53.36 N. 0.41 W. 6, 7
Gunsan, see Kunsan.
Gunungsitoli, Indonesia: 1.17 N. 97.36 E. 38, 40
Gunza Kabolo, see Novo Redondo.
Guri, Venezuela: 7.50 N. 62.45 W. 75
Gustavia, (St. Barthelemy), Guadeloupe (France):
17.54 N. 62.51 W. 71
   Max. Size: LOA 60 m., depth 3 m. – 4.5 m. Fuel: Diesel and
   gasoline. Airport: 5 minutes from port.
Gustavsberg, see Stockholm.
Gustavsvik, Sweden: 62.50 N. 17.53 E. 10, 15
GUYANA 72, 75, 76
Guyane (France) 72, 76
Guysborough, N.S., Canada: 45.24 N. 61.30 W. 60
Gwadar, Pakistan: 25.10 N. 62.20 E. 31, 37
Gythion, see Yithion.

H

Ha'apai Group, Tonga 49
Haaften, Netherlands: 51.48 N. 5.11 E. 7, 8
Haapsalu, Estonia: 58.57 N. 23.33 E. 11
Haavik, Norway: 59.19 N. 5.19 E. 5, 11
   Max. Size: LOA 225 m., draft 11.9 m.   *Fuel:* Available.
   Airport: Haugesund.
Habu, see Innoshima.
Hachijo, Japan: 33.05 N. 139.45 E. 43, 46
Hachinoe, see Hachinohe.
Hachinohe, Japan: 40.33 N. 141.33 E. 43
   Max. Size: LOA 230 m., draft 12.0 m. – 12.7 m.   *Fuel:* All grades
   of bonded bunkers.   *Dry Docks:* 8,000 g.r.t. (LOA 140 m.,
   beam 26.5 m.).   *Airport:* Misawa Airport, about 40 km.
Hackensack River, New Jersey, U.S.A. 63
Hadera, Israel: 32.28 N. 34.52 E. 26
   Max. Size: 200,000 d.w.t, LOA 300 m., beam 48 m., draft 17.5 m.
   Tankers: 70,000 d.w.t., depth 18 m.   *Fuel:* Available.
Haderslev, Denmark: 55.15 N. 9.30 E. 12
   Max. Size: LOA 110 m., depth 6.0 m.   *Fuel:* By road tanker.
   Airport: Billund, 70 km.
Hadibu, Yemen: 12.40 N. 54.05 E. 31
Hadsel, Norway: 68.35 N. 14.55 E. 15
Hadsund, Denmark: 56.42 N. 10.06 E. 11, 12
   Max. Size: LOA 130 m., beam 18 m., draft 5.1 m.
   Fuel: Available.
Haeju, North Korea: 37.59 N. 125.42 E. 42
   Max. Size: Depth at low water about 6.8 m.
   Fuel: Restricted quantities.
Hafnarfjordur, Iceland: 64.04 N. 21.58 W. 17
   Max. Size: Draft 8.5 m. Tankers: LOA 190 m., draft 9 m. for
   arriving.   *Fuel:* Available.   *Dry Docks:* 2 dry docks, maximum
   capacity 9,000 tons.   *Airport:* Reykjavik, 10 km. Keflavik, 35 km.
Hagi, Japan: 34.25 N. 131.25 E. 45
Hagu, see Lhokseumawe.
Haha, (Japan): 26.36 N. 142.10 E. 46
Hahnville, Louisiana, U.S.A.: 29.58 N. 90.25 W. 67
Hai Phong, Vietnam: 20.52 N. 106.41 E. 39
   Max. Size: LOA 200 m., beam 26 m., draft 7.0 m.
   Tankers: LOA 70 m., beam 10 m., draft 5.0 m.   *Fuel:* Available.
   Dry Docks: (1) Capacity: 10,000 d.w.t., LOA 150 m.
   (2) 156 m. x 24 m. x 7.0 m. draft at H.W.   *Airport:*
   Catbi, 130 km.
Haifa, Israel: 32.49 N. 35.00 E. 21, 26
   Max. Size: Draft 35 ft. in main port. Kishon Harbour: 9.5 m. draft.
   Tankers: Draft 47.8 ft.   *Fuel:* Heavy fuel oil, light fuel oil, marine
   diesel oil available.   *Dry Docks:* Largest floating dock capacity of
   7,500 tons.   *Airport:* Lod, 105 km.
Haijuube, see Haeju.
Haikou, China: 20.01 N. 110.16 E. 39
   Max. Size: Channel: Depth 6 m. Berth: LOA 150 m., draft 8 m.
   Fuel: Available.
Hailuoto, Finland: 65.00 N. 24.45 E. 15
Haimen, China: 28.41 N. 121.27 E. 42, 46
   Max. Size: 10,000 d.w.t., depth 6.8 m. Tankers: 5,000 d.w.t.,
   depth 7.8 m.
Hainan, China 39
Hainan Straits, China 39
Haines, Alaska, U.S.A.: 59.15 N. 135.25 W. 56
   Max. Size: Depth 36 ft. Lumber Berth: Depth 45 ft.
   Airport: Air taxi service available.
Haiphong, see Hai Phong.
HAITI 55, 69, 70
Hakata, Japan: 33.36 N. 130.24 E. 45
   Max. Size: Draft 11.10 m.   *Fuel:* Bonded bunker oil is lightered
   from another port.   *Airport:* Fukuoka, 20 minutes.
Hakodate, Japan: 41.47 N. 140.42 E. 43
   Max. Size: Cargo: Draft 8.5 m. Tankers: Up to 84,000 d.w.t. at
   S.B.M., draft 14.5 m., LOA 260 m.   *Fuel:* All grades of bonded
   bunkers lightered from Tokyo Bay.   *Dry Docks:* No. 1 capacity
   17,100 g.t., LOA 156 m.   *Airport:* 20 minutes.
Halaib, Sudan: 22.11 N. 36.30 E. 32
Halat al Mubarraz, see Mubarraz Island.
Halden, Norway: 59.08 N. 11.25 E. 11, 12
   Max. Size: LOA 560 ft., beam 70 ft., draft 25 ft.   *Fuel:* Available.
   Airport: Nearest Fornebu – Oslo.
Haldia, India: 22.00 N. 88.05 E. 37
   Max. Size: Draft under constant review, LOA 269.75 m.
   Tankers: LOA 240 m., draft 12.2 m.
Half Assini, Ghana: 5.02 N. 2.50 W. 28
Half Moon Bay, California, U.S.A. 58
Halgenas, Sweden: 58.00 N. 16.32 E. 11
Halifax, N.S., Canada: 44.39 N. 63.34 W. 60
   Max. Size: Depths up to 13.7 m. Tankers: Draft 50 ft.
   Fuel: Available.   *Dry Docks:* Floating dock, capacity
   22,680 tons.   *Airport:* Halifax International.

Hall Is., (Caroline Is.), Micronesia: 8.32 N. 152.07 E. . 46, 49
Hall Is., Alaska, U.S.A.: 60.39 N. 173.05 W. 54
Halle, Belgium: 50.45 N. 4.15 E. 7
Halle, Sweden, see Krokstrand.
Halling, see Rochester.
Hallstanas, see Svano.
Hallstavik, Sweden: 60.03 N. 18.35 E. 11
   Max. Size: LOA 185 m., beam 28 m., draft 6.5 m.
   Fuel: Delivered from Stockholm.   *Airport:* Stockholm, 75 km.
Halmahera Is., Indonesia 46
Halmstad, Sweden: 56.40 N. 12.52 E. 10, 11, 12
   Max. Size: LOA 770 ft., draft 37 ft. Tankers: LOA 700 ft.,
   draft 30 ft.   *Fuel:* Available.   *Dry Docks:* 2 slips.   *Airport:*
   Connects Stockholm.
Hals, Denmark: 57.00 N. 10.15 E. 11, 12
Halul Island, Qatar: 25.40 N. 52.25 E. 35
   Max. Size: SBM No. 2: Up to 29 m. draft (550,000 d.w.t.).
Ham, (Foula Is.), U.K.: 60.07 N. 2.03 W. 5
Ham Ninh, Vietnam: 10.00 N. 104.00 E. 39
Hamada, Japan: 34.52 N. 132.03 E. 45
   Max. Size: 15,000 d.w.t., draft 9.0 m.   *Fuel:* Bonded oil from
   Moji.   *Airport:* Iwami, 40 km.
Hamamasu, Japan: 43.35 N. 141.24 E. 43
Hamamatsu, Japan: 34.45 N. 137.45 E. 45
Hamaroy, Norway: 68.05 N. 15.40 E. 15
Hambantota, Sri Lanka: 6.07 N. 81.07 E. 37
Hamble, U.K.: 50.50 N. 1.19 W. 7
   Max. Size: LOA 260 m., draft 13.1 m.   *Fuel:* All grades.
   Also see Southampton - Port.
Hamburg, Germany: 53.33 N. 9.59 E. 4, 8, 10, 11, 12, 14
   Max. Size: Inward: Draft 12.5 m. – 14.8 m.
   Outward: Draft 13 m. – 13.8 m.   *Fuel:* All grades.
   Dry Docks: Numerous floating docks up to 65,000 tons,
   graving dock capacity 320,000 d.w.t.   *Airport:* 15 km.
Hamelin Pool, W.A., Australia: 26.10 S. 114.30 E. . . . 50, 51
Hamhung, North Korea: 40.05 N. 127.30 E. 43
Hamilton, Australia, see Brisbane.
Hamilton, Bermuda (U.K.): 32.17 N. 64.47 W. 63
   Max. Size: Largest: LOA 703 ft., draft 26.5 ft.   *Fuel:* Grades
   available: Bunker "C" fuel oil, diesel oil.   *Airport:* 10 miles.
Hamilton, Ontario, Canada: 43.14 N. 79.41 W. 60, 62
   Max. Size: LOA 730 ft., draft 26 ft.   *Fuel:* All grades.   *Airport:*
   Hamilton, 10 miles. Toronto, 30 miles.
Hamilton, Alaska, U.S.A.: 62.55 N. 164.00 W. 54
Hamilton Inlet, Newfoundland, Canada 59
Hamilton Is., Bermuda (U.K.) 63
Hamina, Finland: 60.34 N. 27.11 E. 10, 11, 13
   Max. Size: Draft 10.0 m.   *Fuel:* Fuel and diesel oil.
   Airport: Helsinki, 155 km.
Hammamet, Tunisia: 36.25 N. 10.40 E. 24
Hammerfest, Norway: 70.40 N. 23.40 E. 10, 15
   Max. Size: Up to 30,000 g.r.t., draft 30 ft.   *Fuel:* All grades
   except heavy fuel.   *Airport:* Hammerfest.
Hammerhavnen, see Allinge.
Hampden, Newfoundland, Canada: 49.32 N. 56.50 W. . . 60
Hampton, Virginia, U.S.A.: 37.05 N. 76.15 W. 63, 65
Hampton Roads, Virginia, U.S.A. 63
   Also see Newport News, Norfolk and Portsmouth.
Hamra, see Marsa al Hamra.
Hamrawein, Egypt: 26.15 N. 34.12 E. 32
   Max. Size: Draft 33 ft.   *Airport:* Hurghada.
Hamriya, see Dubai.
Hamriyah, Sharjah, U.A.E.: 25.35 N. 55.24 E. 35
   Max. Size: Draft 16.0 m., max. displacement 150,000 tonnes.
   Airport: Sharjah.
Hamriyah LPG Terminal, Sharjah, U.A.E.: 25.28 N. 55.29 E. . 35
   Max. Size: LOA 230 m., 83,000 cu.m., draft 12.6 m.
Handa, Somalia: 10.38 N. 51.07 E. 31
Hang Chow, see Hangzhou.
Hang Chow Bay, China 42, 46
Hanga Roa, (Easter Is.), Chile: 27.07 S. 109.23 W. 49
Hangzhou, China: 30.43 N. 121.20 E. 42, 46
   Max. Size: Draft 6.5 m.
Hanish Is., Yemen: 13.45 N. 42.46 E. 32
Hanko, Finland: 59.49 N. 22.58 E. 10, 11
   Max. Size: LOA 250 m., draft 13 m.   *Fuel:* Delivered by rail
   cars.   *Airport:* Helsinki, 150 km.
Hankou, China: 30.35 N. 114.17 E. 42
Hannan Port, Japan: 34.27 N. 135.22 E. 45
   Max. Size: Depth 6.5 m. – 12 m., 20,000 d.w.t.
   Also see Sakai.
Hannover, Germany: 52.23 N. 9.44 E. 9
Hanoi, Vietnam: 21.05 N. 105.50 E. 39
Hanstholm, Denmark: 57.08 N. 8.36 E. 11, 12
   Max. Size: LOA 135 m., beam 25 m., draft 7.5 m.
   Fuel: By road tanker.
Hansweert, Netherlands: 51.26 N. 4.00 E. 7, 8
Hantsport, N.S., Canada: 45.04 N. 64.10 W. 60
   Max. Size: Draft 25 ft.   *Fuel:* Oil by truck.

Hao Is., (Tuamotu Arch.), French Polynesia (France):
18.10 S. 140.50 W. ... 49
Haparanda, Sweden: 65.50 N. 24.08 E. ... 15
Haql, Saudi Arabia: 29.15 N. 34.56 E. ... 21, 32
Haraholmen, see Pitea.
Haramidere, Turkey: 40.58 N. 28.41 E. ... 23, 25
Also see Ambarli.
Harbor Beach, Michigan, U.S.A.: 43.50 N. 82.40 W. ... 62
Harbor Breton, Newfoundland, Canada: 47.29 N. 55.49 W. ... 60
Harbor Island, see Port Aransas.
Harbor Springs, see Petoskey.
Harbour Buffet, Newfoundland, Canada: 47.32 N. 54.04 W. ... 60
Harbour Grace, Newfoundland, Canada: 47.43 N. 53.08 W. ... 60
Max. Size: LOA 650 ft., draft 24 ft. at low tide. *Fuel:* Available.
Airport: International, 1 hour away.
Harburg, Germany: 53.28 N. 9.59 E. ... 8, 14
Also see Hamburg.
Harcourt, see Port Harcourt.
Harderwijk, Netherlands: 52.20 N. 5.35 E. ... 7, 8
Hardy, see Port Hardy.
Hargshamn, Sweden: 60.10 N. 18.29 E. ... 11
Max. Size: Draft 8.5 m., LOA 185 m., beam 28 m. *Airport:* Stockholm, 100 km.
Harima Sea, Inland Sea, Japan ... 45
Harkness Point, see Philadelphia.
Harlingen, Netherlands: 53.10 N. 5.25 E. ... 7, 8
Harmac, B.C., Canada: 49.08 N. 123.51 W. ... 56
Harmon, see Stephenville.
Harnosand, Sweden: 62.38 N. 17.57 E. ... 10, 15
Max. Size: Up to 32 ft. 5 in. draft. Tankers: Draft 10 m., LOA 200 m., 45,000 d.w.t. *Fuel:* Available.
Dry Docks: At Gustavsvik.
Harper, Liberia: 4.22 N. 7.44 W. ... 28
Max. Size: 3,000 d.w.t., draft 5.2 m.
Harrington Harbour, Quebec, Canada: 50.30 N. 59.30 W. ... 60
Harris Is., (Outer Hebrides), U.K.: 57.50 N. 6.50 W. ... 5
Harrison, see Inoucdjouac.
Harrison Bay, Alaska, U.S.A. ... 54
Harrisville, Michigan, U.S.A.: 44.40 N. 83.20 W. ... 62
Harstad, Norway: 68.48 N. 16.39 E. ... 10, 15
Max. Size: Depths up to 36 ft. *Fuel:* All grades. *Dry Docks:* 1 dry dock, capacity 8,000 d.w.t. *Airport:* Evenes, about 45 km.
Hartlepool, U.K.: 54.42 N. 1.12 W. ... 6
Max. Size: LOA 190 m., beam 33 m., draft 8.0 m. *Fuel:* Available. *Airport:* Teeside.
Harwich, U.K.: 51.56 N. 1.15 E. ... 5, 7
Max. Size: HIP: Cruise: LOA 300 m., draft 9.5 m. Bulk: LOA 180 m., draft 9.5 m. Ro-Ro: LOA 250 m., draft 8.5 m. Navyard: Depth 6.5 m. – 8.2 m. *Fuel:* Available. *Airport:* Stansted, 50 miles.
Hasle, Denmark: 55.11 N. 14.42 E. ... 12
Hastings, Vic., Australia: 38.21 S. 145.14 E. ... 51
Max. Size: Depth 12.1 m. Tankers: 100,000 – 165,000 d.w.t., depth 12.8 m. – 15.8 m. *Fuel:* Fuel oil, diesel oil. *Airport:* Melbourne, 55 miles.
Hastings, U.K.: 50.51 N. 0.35 E. ... 5, 7
Hastings, U.S.A., see New York.
Hasvik, Norway: 70.29 N. 22.10 E. ... 15
Haugesund, Norway: 59.25 N. 5.16 E. ... 5, 10, 11
Max. Size: Depth alongside 6.4 m. – 15 m. *Fuel:* Available. *Dry Docks:* Capacity 155,000 d.w.t. *Airport:* Karmoy, 15 minutes.
Haukipudas, Finland: 65.12 N. 25.21 E. ... 15
Havana, Cuba: 23.09 N. 82.21 W. ... 69, 70
Max. Size: LOA 230 m., draft 11.43 m. Tankers: Draft 11.43 m. *Fuel:* Available. *Dry Docks:* Floating docks up to 22,000 tons lifting capacity. *Airport:* Jose Marti International, 15 km.
Havannah, see Noumea.
Havnso, Denmark: 55.45 N. 11.20 E. ... 12
Havoysund, Norway: 71.00 N. 24.40 E. ... 15
Havre Aubert, see Amherst Harbour.
Havre de Grace, Maryland, U.S.A.: 39.32 N. 76.05 W. ... 65
Havre St. Pierre, Quebec, Canada: 50.14 N. 63.36 W. ... 60
Max. Size: 10,000 d.w.t., draft 28 ft. 6 in. *Fuel:* Available. *Dry Docks:* Les Mechins, 153 miles. *Airport:* Airstrip, 3 km.
Hawaii, U.S.A. ... 49, 68
Hawaiian Islands, U.S.A. ... 49, 53
Hawk Inlet, Alaska, U.S.A.: 58.10 N. 134.03 W. ... 56
Max. Size: 40,000 tonnes d.w.t., LOA 183 m., draft 9.14 m. *Airport:* Juneau, 30 miles.
Hawke Harbour, Newfoundland, Canada: 53.02 N. 55.47 W. ... 59
Hawkes Bay, New Zealand ... 52
Hawkesbury, see Port Hawkesbury.
Hawkins Point, see Baltimore.
Hay Point, Qld., Australia: 21.16 S. 149.19 E. ... 50, 51
Max. Size: Hay Point: 170,000 d.w.t. – 230,000 d.w.t., depth 16.68 m. Dalrymple Bay: 230,000 d.w.t., depth 20.0 m. *Fuel:* Contact BHP in Melbourne. *Airport:* Mackay, 50 km.

Haydarpasa, Turkey: 41.00 N. 29.04 E. ... 23, 25
Max. Size: Depth 6.0 m. – 12 m. *Fuel:* Available. *Airport:* Istanbul, 20 km.
Also see Istanbul.
Hayle, see St. Ives.
Hazira, see Magdalla.
Head of Passes, (Mississippi Delta), Louisiana, U.S.A. ... 67
Hearts Content, Newfoundland, Canada: 47.53 N. 53.23 W. ... 60
Heath Point, (Anticosti Is.), Quebec, Canada:
49.06 N. 61.41 W. ... 60
Hebburn, U.K.: 54.59 N. 1.31 W. ... 6
Hebron, Newfoundland, Canada: 58.12 N. 62.36 W. ... 59
Hecate Strait, B.C., Canada ... 56
Hedland, see Port Hedland.
Heiden, see Port Heiden.
Heiligenhafen, Germany: 54.22 N. 10.59 E. ... 12, 14
Heimaey, Iceland: 63.26 N. 20.17 W. ... 17
Hekkelstrand, Norway: 68.28 N. 16.50 E. ... 15
Max. Size: Depth 7.5 m. – 9. m.
Hel, Poland: 54.35 N. 18.50 E. ... 11
Helensville, New Zealand: 36.40 S. 174.28 E. ... 52
Hellerup, see Copenhagen.
Hellnas, Finland: 63.17 N. 22.14 E. ... 15
Hellville, see Nossi-Be.
Helmi, see Raahe.
Helmsdale, U.K.: 58.07 N. 3.39 W. ... 5
Helsingborg, Sweden: 56.03 N. 12.41 E. ... 10, 11, 12
Max. Size: LOA 220 m., draft 7 m. – 12.3 m. Tankers: Draft 10.5 m. *Fuel:* All grades. *Dry Docks:* Length 354 ft. *Airport:* Kastrup 60 km., Angelholm 30 km.
Helsingor, Denmark: 56.02 N. 12.37 E. ... 10, 11, 12
Max. Size: Up to 6.6 m. draft. *Fuel:* Available. *Airport:* 1 hour by car to Copenhagen.
Helsinki, Finland: 60.10 N. 24.57 E. ... 4, 10, 11, 13, 79
Max. Size: Draft 31 ft. Tankers: Up to 9.6 m. draft. *Fuel:* All grades. *Dry Docks:* Length 208 m., breadth 34 m. Depth on sill 9.6 m. *Airport:* 25 km.
Helville, see Nossi-Be.
Hemiksem, Belgium: 51.09 N. 4.20 E. ... 7, 8
Max. Size: 15,000 d.w.t., LOA 174 m., Draft 31.5 ft. Also see Antwerp.
Hemixem, see Hemiksem.
Hemnesberget, Norway: 66.14 N. 13.37 E. ... 15
Henderson Is., Pitcairn Is. (U.K.): 24.15 S. 128.10 W. ... 49
Henecan, see San Lorenzo.
Hennebont, France: 47.49 N. 3.17 W. ... 7, 19
Henzada, Myanmar: 17.40 N. 95.29 E. ... 37
Hepokari, see Uusikaupunki.
Heraklion, see Iraklion.
Heranza Is., see Kin Wan.
Herbillon, see Chetaibi.
Herceg-Novi, see Zelenika.
Hercules, see San Francisco.
Hercules Port, see Piraeus.
Hereke, Turkey: 40.47 N. 29.37 E. ... 23, 25, 26
Max. Size: Depth 12.3 m. – 17.0 m. *Fuel:* From Istanbul by barge only. *Airport:* Istanbul, 100 km.
Herm Is., (Channel Is.), U.K.: 49.29 N. 2.27 W. ... 7, 19
Hermit Is., Papua New Guinea: 1.33 S. 145.05 E. ... 46
Herne Bay, U.K.: 51.23 N. 1.08 E. ... 6
Hernosund, see Harnosand.
Heron Bay, Ontario, Canada: 48.39 N. 86.20 W. ... 62
Heroya, Norway: 59.07 N. 9.38 E. ... 8, 12
Max. Size: Depth 5 m. – 10.4 m. *Fuel:* All grades. *Dry Docks:* Draft 14 ft., LOA 155 m., breadth 20 m.
Herrang, Sweden: 60.09 N. 18.39 E. ... 11
Herrero Point, Mexico: 19.30 N. 87.25 W. ... 69
Herrttomiemi Harbour, see Helsinki.
Herruda Bay, see Guayacan.
Hertford, North Carolina, U.S.A.: 36.11 N. 76.28 W. ... 63
Hervey Is., Cook Is. (N.Z.): 19.20 S. 158.45 W. ... 49
Heungnam, North Korea: 39.50 N. 127.45 E. ... 42, 43
Max. Size: Draft 25 ft.
Heybeli, Turkey: 40.53 N. 29.06 E. ... 23, 25
Heysham, U.K.: 54.02 N. 2.55 W. ... 4, 5
Max. Size: LOA 549 ft. (167.32 m.), draft 17 ft. *Fuel:* Gas oil by road tanker. *Airport:* Liverpool and Manchester, 60 miles.
Hiakari, see Kokura.
Hibi, Japan: 34.27 N. 133.56 E. ... 45
Max. Size: Draft 12 m., 30,000 d.w.t. *Fuel:* Available. Also see Uno.
Hibikinada, Japan: 33.57 N. 130.50 E. ... 44, 45
Max. Size: LOA 340 m., draft 12.2 m., 150,000 d.w.t. *Fuel:* Available. *Dry Docks:* Available.
Hidakatsu, Japan: 34.39 N. 129.28 E. ... 45
Hierro, Canary Is. (Spain) ... 27
Hierro, Venezuela, see Puerto de Hierro.
Higashi Iwase, see Toyama.

Higashi-Harima, Japan: 34.42 N. 134.51 E. 45
Also see Kakogawa.
Hiiumaa Is., Estonia: 59.00 N. 23.00 E. 10, 11
Hiji, Japan: 33.22 N. 131.31 E. 45
Hikari, Japan: 33.57 N. 131.56 E. 45
Max. Size: 30,000 d.w.t., LOA 200 m., draft 11.20 m.
Fuel: Available.
Hiketa, Japan: 34.15 N. 134.25 E. 45
Hikoshima, see Shimonoseki.
Hillsborough, N.B., Canada: 45.56 N. 64.39 W. 60
Hilo, Hawaii, U.S.A.: 19.46 N. 155.06 W. 49
Max. Size: Draft up to 32 ft. 6 in. *Fuel:* Available.
Airport: Hilo, 1 mile. Kawaihae, 26 miles.
Himanka, Finland: 64.05 N. 23.35 E. 15
Himeji, Japan: 34.47 N. 134.41 E. 43, 45
Max. Size: General Cargo: Draft 13.2 m. – 16.0 m. Sea Buoy Mooring: Draft 19.2 m., 254,000 d.w.t. Oil Jetty: Draft 11.8 m.
Fuel: All grades lightered from nearest bunker stock ports.
Airport: Itami, 60 km.
Also see Aioi.
Himekawa, Japan: 37.02 N. 137.51 E. 45
Max. Size: 10,000 d.w.t., draft 8.2 m.
Hinatuan, (Mindanao Is.), Philippines: 8.21 N. 126.20 E. . . 47
Hinchinbrook Is., see Lucinda.
Hinlopen Strait, (Spitsbergen), Norway 17
Hinnoy, see Lofoten Is..
Hirado Is., Japan 45
Hirao, Japan: 33.55 N. 132.03 E. 45
Hiro Bay, see Kure.
Hirohata, Japan: 34.44 N. 134.37 E. 45
Max. Size: Draft 16 m., LOA 320 m.
Also see Himeji.
Hiroo, see Tokachi.
Hiroshima, Japan: 34.20 N. 132.25 E. 43, 45, 46
Max. Size: Depth 4.0 m. – 12.0 m. *Fuel:* Most grades.
Dry Docks: Largest: Length 154 m., breadth 22 m.
Airport: Hiroshima.
Hirtshals, Denmark: 57.35 N. 9.57 E. 11, 12
Max. Size: LOA 150 m., beam 25 m., draft 7.5 m.
Fuel: Available. *Dry Docks:* 1,500 d.w.t. – 2,300 d.w.t. *Airport:* Alborg, 60 km.
Hitachi, Japan: 36.30 N. 140.37 E. 43, 45
Max. Size: Channel: Draft 8.5 m. Berth: 30,000 d.w.t., draft 10.9 m. *Fuel:* Bonded oil from Yokohama.
Hitra, Norway: 63.28 N. 8.46 E. 15
Hiuchi Sea, Inland Sea, Japan 45
Hiva Oa, (Marquesas Is.), French Polynesia (France) 49
Hiwasi, Japan: 33.42 N. 134.32 E. 45
Ho Chi Minh City, Vietnam: 10.50 N. 106.45 E. 39
Max. Size: LOA 230 m., draft 9.5 m. Tankers: Depth 5.5 m. – 11.0 m. *Fuel:* Available. *Airport:* Tan Son Nhat, 10 km.
Hobart, Tas., Australia: 42.53 S. 147.20 E. 50, 51
Max. Size: Risdon: Depth 10.2 m. – 10.7 m., beam 100 ft. Self's Pt. Oil Wharf: Depth 14 m. Macquarie No. 4: Draft 41 ft. 4 in. *Fuel:* All grades. *Dry Docks:* (Slip): Available for vessels up to 1,200 tons displacement. *Airport:* 11 miles, connects Melbourne/Sydney and New Zealand.
Hoboken, U.S.A.: 40.45 N. 74.01 W. 63
Also see New York.
Hobro, Denmark: 56.38 N. 9.48 E. 12
Hochdonn, Germany: 54.01 N. 9.18 E. 14
Hodeidah, Yemen: 14.47 N. 42.57 E. 31, 32
Max. Size: Draft 32 ft. (Very strict). *Fuel:* Small quantities of diesel. *Airport:* International.
Hofn, see Hornafjord.
Hog Island, see Philadelphia.
Hog Island Channel, (Cape Cod Canal), Massachusetts, U.S.A. . 64
Hoganas, Sweden: 56.12 N. 12.33 E. 11, 12
Max. Size: LOA 130 m., draft 7.4 m. *Fuel:* Available.
Hojer, Denmark: 54.59 N. 8.42 E. 12, 14
Hokitika, New Zealand: 42.42 S. 171.00 E. 52
Hokkaido, Japan 43
Holbaek, Denmark: 55.43 N. 11.43 E. 11, 12
Max. Size: Draft 6.3 m. *Fuel:* Available.
Airport: Copenhagen, 70 km.
Holehaven, see Canvey.
Holland, Philippines, see Port Holland.
Holland, Michigan, U.S.A.: 42.48 N. 86.08 W. 62
Holm, Norway: 65.05 N. 12.20 E. 15
Holmestrand, Norway: 59.29 N. 10.19 E. 8, 12
Holmsund, Sweden: 63.41 N. 20.21 E. 15
Max. Size: Draft 5.5 m.
Also see Umea.
Holsteinsborg, see Sisimiut.
Holtenau, Germany: 54.22 N. 10.09 E. 11, 12, 14
Max. Size: Draft: 9.7 m. – 9.5 m. in Kiel Canal. *Fuel:* Available.
Holy Island, U.K.: 55.40 N. 1.45 W. 5
Holyhead, U.K.: 53.19 N. 4.41 W. 4, 5, 7
Max. Size: Inner Harbour: Draft 4.5 m. Outer Harbour dredged to 13.5 m. at MLWS. *Fuel:* Fuel and diesel oil.
Airport: Manchester, 184 km.

Holyrood, Newfoundland, Canada: 47.23 N. 53.08 W. 60
Max. Size: Depth 34 ft. 6 in. (HW), 32 ft. (LW).
Also see St. John's.
Homer, Alaska, U.S.A.: 59.36 N. 151.25 W. 54
Max. Size: LOA 650 ft., draft 40 ft. *Fuel:* Available.
Airport: Daily air service.
Also see Nikiski.
Hommelvik, Norway: 63.27 N. 10.50 E. 15
Homs, see Al Khums.
Hon Chong, Vietnam: 10.04 N. 104.31 E. 39
Max. Size: Draft 5.0 m.
Hon Gay, Vietnam: 20.57 N. 107.04 E. 39
Max. Size: 10,000 d.w.t., draft 8.6 m. Coal: 12,000 d.w.t., draft 8.5 m. Tankers: 20,000 d.w.t., depth 11.2 m. *Fuel:* By barge. *Dry Docks:* Max. 10,000 d.w.t.
Airport: No Bai, 190 km., Catbi, 70 km.
Hon Khoi, Vietnam: 12.35 N. 109.13 E. 39
Max. Size: Depth 1.4 m. Anchorage – Depth 14 m. – 20 m.
Fuel: By barge. *Airport:* Nha Trang.
Honam, see Yosu.
Honavar, India: 14.16 N. 74.27 E. 37
Max. Size: Vessels up to 34 ft. draft can anchor within 2 to 3 miles from entrance. *Airport:* Belgaum, about 178 miles.
Hondagua, (Luzon Is.), Philippines: 13.56 N. 122.14 E. . . . 47
Max. Size: LOA 500 ft., depth 28 ft. – 39 ft. *Fuel:* Available.
Airport: Manila, 6 hours by train.
Honduras, see Santa Cruz de Tenerife.
HONDURAS 69, 70
Honfleur, France: 49.25 N. 0.14 E. 7, 8
Max. Size: LOA 200 m., draft up to 8.0 m., depending on tide and berth. Tankers: 35,000 tons. *Fuel:* Available.
Airport: Deauville-St. Gatien, 12 km.
Hong Kong, Hong Kong (SAR), China: 22.18 N. 114.10 E. . 39, 42, 48
Max. Size: Container: LOA 305 m., draft 14.6 m.
Tankers: Shell – LOA 245 m., draft 15.5 m.
Fuel: Excellent facilities. *Dry Docks:* Largest floating dock, capacity 45,000 tonnes. *Airport:* 21 miles from city centre.
Honguedo Passage, Gulf of St. Lawrence, Canada 60
Honiara, Solomon Islands: 9.25 S. 159.58 E. 49, 51
Max. Size: Depth 9.14 m. Tankers mooring at buoys: LOA 600 ft., draft 27 ft. 6 in. *Fuel:* Diesel and gas oil.
Airport: 10 miles from the wharf.
Honkalahti, see Saimaa Canal.
Honningsvaag, Norway: 70.59 N. 26.00 E. 10, 15
Honolulu, Hawaii, U.S.A.: 21.19 N. 157.52 W. 49
Max. Size: Harbour: Depth 15 ft. – 40 ft. Tankers: Honolulu, draft 36 ft. Pearl Harbour (U.S. Navy Terminal) LOA 800 ft., draft 38 ft. 6 in. *Fuel:* All U.S. grades available.
Dry Docks: 7,875 long tons lifting capacity, 385 ft. x 56 ft.
Airport: International airport, 5 miles from harbour.
Honshu, Japan 43, 44, 45
Hood, see Port Hood.
Hood Bay, Alaska, U.S.A.: 57.24 N. 134.30 W. 56
Hoodsport, Washington, U.S.A.: 47.25 N. 123.08 W. 56
Hook of Holland, Netherlands: 52.00 N. 4.07 E. 7, 8
Hoonah, Alaska, U.S.A.: 58.07 N. 135.27 W. 56
Hooper Bay, Alaska, U.S.A.: 61.25 N. 165.00 W. 54
Hoorn, Netherlands: 52.40 N. 5.05 E. 8
Hopa, Turkey: 41.23 N. 41.25 E. 26
Max. Size: Draft 10 m. *Fuel:* Available.
Airport: Trabzon, 185 km.
Hope, see Port Hope.
Hope Point, Alaska, U.S.A.: 68.34 N. 166.50 W. 54
Hope Simpson, see Port Hope Simpson.
Hopedale, Newfoundland, Canada: 55.27 N. 60.13 W. 59
Hopen Is., Norway: 76.30 N. 25.30 E. 17
Hopetoun, W.A., Australia: 33.57 S. 120.08 E. 50
Hopewell, Virginia, U.S.A.: 37.17 N. 77.16 W. 63, 65
Hoquiam, Washington, U.S.A.: 46.58 N. 123.55 W. 56
Horie, see Matsuyama.
Hormuz Is., Iran: 27.08 N. 56.28 E. 35
Hornafjord, Iceland: 64.16 N. 15.13 W. 17
Hornefors, Sweden: 63.37 N. 19.54 E. 10, 15
Port not operating.
Hornillo, see Aguilas.
Hornos Ibericos, see Carboneras.
Hornum, Germany: 54.44 N. 8.17 E. 11, 12, 14
Horsens, Denmark: 55.52 N. 9.52 E. 11, 12
Max. Size: LOA approx. 500 ft., beam approx. 70 ft.; draft approx. 22 ft. *Fuel:* All grades. *Airport:* 50 km.
Horseshoe Bay, B.C., Canada: 49.23 N. 123.15 W. 56
Horta, (Faial Is.), Azores (Portugal): 38.32 N. 28.38 W. . . . 20
Max. Size: Berthing: Draft 22 ft. Depth at buoy moorings: 33 ft.
Fuel: Gas oil and gasoline at quay. *Airport:* 10 km.
Horten, Norway: 59.25 N. 10.30 E. 8, 10, 11, 12
Max. Size: LOA 900 ft., draft 28 ft. *Fuel:* All grades by barge.
Dry Docks: Up to about 60,000 d.w.t. *Airport:* Oslo.
Hososhima, Japan: 32.25 N. 131.41 E. 43, 45
Max. Size: LOA 170 m., draft 31 ft. 10 in. (9.7 m.)
Fuel: All grades lightered from nearest bunker stock ports.
Airport: Miyazaki Airport, 2 hours' drive.

Houghton, Michigan, U.S.A.: 47.06 N. 88.34 W. 62
Houhora, New Zealand: 34.49 S. 173.09 E. 52
Houma, Louisiana, U.S.A.: 29.35 N. 90.44 W. 66
Hound Point, U.K.: 56.00 N. 3.22 W. 6
 Max. Size: Draft 21.30 m. (Spring tides), 300,000 d.w.t.
Houston, Texas, U.S.A.: 29.45 N. 95.20 W. 55, 66
 Max. Size: LOA 750 ft. – 950 ft., beam 116 ft. – 135 ft., draft 37 ft. – 39 ft. *Fuel:* All grades. *Dry Docks:* Capacity 2,000 tons – 3,200 tons. *Airport:* 30 minutes by car.
Hov, Denmark: 55.55 N. 10.16 E. 12
Hovic, see Limetree Bay.
Hovid, (Alno Is.), Sweden: 62.28 N. 17.23 E. 15
Howden, U.K.: 53.44 N. 0.51 W. 6
 Max. Size: LOA 88 m., beam 14 m., draft 5 m. *Fuel:* By road tanker. *Airport:* Humberside and Leeds, 40 miles. Manchester, 80 miles.
Howdendyke, see Howden.
Howdon, see Tyne District.
Howland Hook, see New York.
Howland Is., (U.S.A.): 0.48 N. 176.28 W. 49
Howrah, India: 22.35 N. 88.30 E. 37
Howth, Ireland: 53.23 N. 6.04 W. 5
 Max. Size: LOA 38 m., depth 4.0 m. *Fuel:* By road tanker. *Airport:* Dublin, 14 km.
Hoy, U.K.: 58.50 N. 3.13 W. 5
Hoyanger, Norway: 61.10 N. 6.04 E. 10, 11, 15
 Max. Size: Length of quay 600 ft. Depth 36 ft.
Hsia Men, see Xiamen.
Hsingkang, see Xingang.
Hsu Wen, see Xu Wen.
Hu Lu Tao, China: 40.44 N. 121.00 E. 42
Huacho, Peru: 11.07 S. 77.37 W. 72
 Max. Size: Anchorage port.
Huahine Is., (Society Is.), French Polynesia (France):
 16.46 S. 151.00 W. 49
Hualien, Taiwan: 23.59 N. 121.38 E. 42, 46
 Max. Size: Inner Channel: LOA 160 m., draft 9.1 m. Berths: Depth 7.1 m. – 16.5 m. *Fuel:* Available. *Airport:* Domestic connection to Taipei and Kaohsiung, 10 km.
Huang Dao, see Qingdao.
Huang He Delta, China. 42
Huang Kang, China: 23.39 N. 116.58 E. 42
Huangdao, see Qingdao.
Huangpu, China: 23.06 N. 113.26 E. 48
 Max. Size: Draft 8.84 m. – 9.14 m., 10,000 d.w.t.
 Also see Guangzhou.
Huangshi, China: 30.13 N. 115.08 E. 42
 Max. Size: LOA 110 m., draft 4.0 m. *Fuel:* Available.
Huarmey, Peru: 10.06 S. 78.10 W. 72
 Max. Size: Anchorage port.
Huasco, Chile: 28.27 S. 71.14 W. 77
 Max. Size: LOA 315 m., beam 47.5 m., draft 22 m. Tankers: LOA 315 m., draft 25.0 m. *Fuel:* IFO and diesel. *Airport:* Serena, 241 km. and Copiapo, 200 km.
Hudiksvall, Sweden: 61.44 N. 17.07 E. 10, 11, 15
 Max. Size: 16,000 d.w.t., LOA 160 m., draft 8.7 m. Tankers: 45,000 d.w.t., LOA 210 m., draft 9.8 m. *Fuel:* Available. *Airport:* Local airport connects with Stockholm.
Hudson Bay, Canada 53, 59, 79
Hudson River, New York, U.S.A.: 40.43 N. 74.00 W. . . . 63
Hudson Strait, Canada 17, 59
Hue, Vietnam: 16.30 N. 107.32 E. 39
Huelva, Spain: 37.16 N. 6.55 W. 20, 22, 27
 Max. Size: LOA 250 m., draft 39 ft. – 44 ft., depending on tide. Tankers: LOA 240 m., draft 12 m. SBM: LOA 900 ft., draft 70 ft. (SW). *Fuel:* Fuel oil and diesel. *Dry Docks:* Up to 3,500 g.r.t. *Airport:* Seville – San Pablo, 100 km.
Hueneme, California, U.S.A.: 34.09 N. 119.12 W. 55, 57
 Max. Size: Berth length 600 ft., depth 35 ft. MLW. *Fuel:* Diesel oil and bunker fuel. *Airport:* Los Angeles.
Huesvik, South Georgia Is. (U.K.): 53.45 S. 36.50 W. . . . 77
Hugh Town, (Scilly Is.), U.K.: 49.55 N. 6.18 W. 19
Huizhou, China: 22.42 N. 114.34 E. 39, 48
 Max. Size: LOA 150 m., draft 8.5 m. Tankers: LOA 294 m., draft 15.2 m.
Huizhou Terminal, China: 21.22 N. 115.25 E. 39
 Max. Size: 160,000 d.w.t.
 Vessels moor to FPSO "Nan Hai Fa Xian".
Hulaylah Terminal, Ras Al Khaimah, U.A.E.: 25.58 N. 55.56 E. 35
 Max. Size: 300,000 d.w.t. *Fuel:* At anchor only. *Airport:* Ras al Khaimah and Dubai.
Hull, U.K.: 53.44 N. 0.14 W. 4, 5, 6, 7
 Max. Size: LOA 196 m., beam 25.5 m., draft 10.4 m. at springs. Tankers: LOA 214 m., draft 10.4 m. *Fuel:* Fuel oil, gas oil and diesel. *Dry Docks:* Length 139 m., width 17.2 m. *Airport:* Humberside, 40 km.
Hull Is., (Phoenix Is.), Kiribati: 4.30 S. 172.15 W. . . . 49
Humacao, Puerto Rico (U.S.A.): 18.09 N. 65.45 W. 71
Humaita, Brazil: 7.32 S. 63.03 W. 72
Humbermouth, see Corner Brook.

Humbolt Bay, see Eureka.
Hundested, Denmark: 55.58 N. 11.51 E. 12
HUNGARY 4, 9, 21, 24
Hungnam, see Heungnam.
Hunstanton, U.K.: 52.58 N. 0.30 E. 7
Hunter Is., New Caledonia (France): 22.23 S. 172.05 E. . 49
Hunters Point, California, U.S.A.: 37.43 N. 122.22 W. . . 58
Hunterston, U.K.: 55.42 N. 4.54 W. 6
 Max. Size: 350,000 d.w.t., draft 26 m., depth 29 m. *Fuel:* All grades. *Airport:* Glasgow.
 Also see Clyde Port.
Huntington Beach, California, U.S.A.: 33.38 N. 118.00 W. . 55, 58
 Max. Size: (Offshore) LOA 930 ft., beam 145 ft., depth 50 ft.
Huntington Harbour, California, U.S.A.: 33.41 N. 118.03 W. . . 58
Huon, see Port Huon.
Huonville, see Port Huon.
Hurghada, Egypt: 27.14 N. 33.50 E. 32
Huron, Michigan, U.S.A., see Port Huron.
Huron, Ohio, U.S.A.: 41.24 N. 82.35 W. 55, 62
 Max. Size: LOA 716 ft., beam 75 ft., draft 26 ft. *Airport:* Cleveland, 50 miles.
Husavik, Iceland: 66.03 N. 17.21 W. 17
Husevig, Faroe Is. (Denmark): 61.50 N. 6.30 W. 5, 15
Husnes, Norway: 59.52 N. 5.46 E. 10, 11
 Max. Size: 70,000 tons, depth 10.5 m. – 16.5 m. *Airport:* Bergen-Flesland, 2 – 2.5 hours by hydrofoil. Haugesund, 3 hours by car.
Husum, Germany: 54.30 N. 9.05 E. 11, 14
Husum, Sweden: 63.20 N. 19.09 E. 10, 15
 Max. Size: Draft 10.6 m. *Fuel:* All grades. *Airport:* 15 minutes by car.
Hvar, Croatia: 43.08 N. 16.26 E. 24
Hyannis, Massachusetts, U.S.A.: 41.39 N. 70.17 W. . . . 63
Hydaburg, Alaska, U.S.A.: 55.11 N. 132.50 W. 56
Hyder, Alaska, U.S.A.: 55.55 N. 130.01 W. 56
Hydra, see Idhra Is..
Hyeres, France: 43.07 N. 6.10 E. 22
Hyeres Is., France 22

I

Iba, (Luzon Is.), Philippines: 15.20 N. 120.00 E. 46, 47
Ibicuy, Argentina: 33.39 S. 59.15 W. 78
Ibiza, Spain: 38.54 N. 1.28 E. 21, 22
   Max. Size: LOA 135 m., draft 21 ft. Fuel: Available.
   Airport: 10 km.
Ibo, Mozambique: 12.21 S. 40.37 E. 30
Icapara, Brazil: 24.34 S. 47.29 W. 76
ICELAND 17, 79
Ichikawa, Japan: 35.45 N. 139.55 E. 44
Icoarcy, see Belem.
Icy Cape, Alaska, U.S.A.: 70.18 N. 161.45 W. 54
Idaho, U.S.A. 57
Idhra Is., Greece: 37.21 N. 23.28 E. 25
Idi, Indonesia: 5.00 N. 97.46 E. 38, 40
Ierapetra, (Crete), Greece: 35.00 N. 25.45 E. 25, 26
Iersekе, Netherlands: 51.30 N. 4.03 E. 7, 8
Ifalik Is., (Caroline Is.), Micronesia: 7.15 N. 144.26 E. . . 46
Igarka, Russia: 67.27 N. 86.35 E. 16
   Max. Size: LOA 150 m., draft 8 m. Fuel: Not always available.
   Airport: 1.5 km., connects with Krasnogarsk.
Igdlorssuit, Greenland (Denmark): 71.14 N. 53.31 W. . . 17
Iggesund, Sweden: 61.38 N. 17.07 E. 15
   Max. Size: Draft 7.3 m. (MW), LOA 150 m.
   Also see Hudiksvall.
Igneada, Turkey: 41.51 N. 28.00 E. 26
Igoumenitsa, Greece: 39.31 N. 20.17 E. 25
Iguazu, Brazil: 25.33 S. 54.33 W. 77
Iho, Japan: 34.45 N. 134.46 E. 45
   Port closed
Ijmuiden, see Ymuiden.
Ijsselmeer, Netherlands 8
Ikang, Nigeria: 4.49 N. 8.30 E. 29
Ikaria Is., Greece 25, 26
Ikeja, Nigeria: 6.32 N. 3.15 E. 29
Ikerasak, Greenland (Denmark): 70.29 N. 51.19 W. . . . 17
Iki Channel, Japan 45
Iki Is., Japan 45
Ile Amsterdam, (France): 37.51 S. 77.32 E. 36
Ile d'Oleron, France 8, 19
Ile de Groix, France 19
Ile de Kerguelen: 49.21 N. 70.12 E. 36
Ile de Re, France 8, 19
Ile de Yeu, France 19
Ile du Coin, see Peros Banhos Is..
Ile Mayotte, Comoros Is. (France): 12.49 S. 45.10 E. . . 30
Ile Ratonneau, France 23
Ile Rousse, (Corsica), France: 42.39 N. 8.56 E. 9, 23, 24
   Max. Size: Draft 5 m., LOA 160 m.
Ile Tromelin, France: 15.51 S. 54.25 E. 30
Ile Verte, Quebec, Canada: 48.02 N. 69.25 W. 60
Ile. Glorieuses, Reunion (France): 11.30 S. 47.20 E. . . . 30
Iles de Horne, see Futuna Is..
Iles de Los, see Conakry.
Iles des Saintes, (France): 15.52 N. 61.35 W. 71
Iles Gambier, see Gambier Is..
Iles Glenans, France: 47.43 N. 3.58 W. 19
Ilfracombe, U.K.: 51.12 N. 4.07 W. 6
Ilha Barnabe, see Santos.
Ilha de S.Caterina, see Florianapolis.
Ilha de Sao Sebastiao, see Sao Sebastiao.
Ilha Grande, see Angra dos Reis.
Ilha Guaiba, see Sepetiba Bay.
Ilha Madeira, see Sepetiba Bay.
Ilheus, Brazil: 14.47 S. 39.02 W. 72, 77
   Max. Size: Depth 10 m. Fuel: Available. Airport: 3 km.
Ilichevsk, Ukraine: 46.19 N. 30.40 E. 26
   Max. Size: Draft 11.8 m., unless by permission, LOA 280 m.
   Fuel: Available. Dry Docks: Odessa, Floating dock, 250 m.
   length, 18 m. depth. Airport: Odessa, 30 km.
Iligan, (Mindanao Is.), Philippines: 8.14 N. 124.14 E. . . 47
   Max. Size: LOA 240 m., draft 25 ft., 15,000 g.r.t.
   Fuel: Available. Airport: Baloi, 15 km.
Ilinskiy, Russia: 47.59 N. 142.12 E. 43
Iliodhromia Is., Greece: 39.10 N. 23.55 E. 25
Ilistoe, see Saimaa Canal.
Illinois, U.S.A. 62
Ilo, Peru: 17.39 S. 71.21 W. 72, 77
   Max. Size: Depth alongside from 23 ft. – 60 ft.
   Enersur: Draft 16 m. Tankers: Depth 40 ft. Punta
   Tablones: Tankers – LOA 750 ft., depth 40 ft. Airport: Ilo, 8 km.
Iloilo, (Panay Is.), Philippines: 10.41 N. 122.35 E. 46, 47
   Max. Size: Depth 10.6 m. – 11.5 m. Fuel: All viscosities
   available. Dry Docks: Length 587 ft., width 56 ft.
   Airport: 7 km., connects with Manila.

Ilulissat, Greenland (Denmark): 69.13 N. 51.06 W. 17
   Max. Size: Largest vessel to berth, LOA 100 m., draft 6.8 m.,
   depth alongside 8.0 m. Airport: Heliport.
Ilwaco, Washington, U.S.A.: 46.18 N. 124.03 W. 56, 57
Ilwaki, Indonesia: 7.54 S. 126.30 E. 46
Ima Terminal, Nigeria: 4.13 N. 7.24 E. 29
   Max. Size: 270,000 d.w.t., draft 18 m.
Imabari, Japan: 34.04 N. 133.00 E. 45
   Max. Size: Depth 5.5 m. – 12 m. Fuel: All grades of bonded
   bunkers are stocked in Tokyo Bay, Ise Bay, Osaka Bay and
   Kanmon Port. Dry Docks: Largest: 53,000 g.r.t. capacity.
   Airport: Nearest Matsuyama.
Imahuru, see Imabari.
Imam Hasan, Iran: 29.51 N. 50.14 E. 35
Imari, Japan: 33.18 N. 129.49 E. 43, 45
   Max. Size: 88,300 d.w.t., LOA 248 m., beam 43 m., draft 9.0 m.
   Buoy Berth: Draft 11.7 m. LPG: 70,000 d.w.t., draft 14.0 m.
   Fuel: Bonded oil from Moji/Nagasaki.
Imatra, Finland: 61.12 N. 28.47 E. 13
   Also see Saimaa Canal.
Imbituba, Brazil: 28.13 S. 48.38 W. 76, 77
   Max. Size: LOA 200 m., draft 9.5 m. Fuel: Available.
   Airport: Florianopolis, 100 km.
Imbros Is., Greece 25, 26
Immingham, U.K.: 53.37 N. 0.12 W. 5, 6, 7
   Max. Size: Enclosed Docks: Immingham Dock: LOA 198 m.,
   beam 26.2 m., draft 10.36 m. (LOA 233 m. and beam 26.8 m.
   under certain conditions). Humber International
   Terminal: 100,000 d.w.t., depth 14.7 m. Ore: LOA 303 m.,
   beam 47 m., draft 14.5 m. Coal: Depth 12.6 m. Tankers: 284,480
   d.w.tonnes (Max. load displacement 172,000 tonnes),
   LOA 1,100 ft., draft 42 ft. Fuel: All grades. Dry Docks: Length
   225.6 m., width 17.1 m. Airport: Humberside.
Immola, Finland: 61.15 N. 28.52 E. 13
   Also see Saimaa Canal.
Imperatriz, Brazil: 5.30 S. 47.30 W. 72
Imperia, Italy: 43.53 N. 8.02 E. 23, 24
Imrali Is., Turkey: 40.32 N. 28.32 E. 23, 25
Imroz, see Imbros Is..
Ince, U.K.: 53.17 N. 2.51 W. 6
   Also see Manchester.
Inchon, South Korea: 37.28 N. 126.37 E. 42
   Max. Size: 50,000 d.w.t., LOA 302 m., draft 13.0 m.,
   depth 14.5 m. Tankers: Up to 50,000 d.w.t., depth 50 ft. Fuel:
   By barge. Airport: 20 miles (International).
INDIA 37
Indian Bay, Newfoundland, Canada: 49.01 N. 53.44 W. . . 60
Indian Harbour, Newfoundland, Canada: 54.27 N. 57.13 W. . . 59
Indiana, U.S.A. 62
Indiana Harbour, see Buffington.
Indiga, Russia: 67.45 N. 48.50 E. 16
Indispensable Reefs, Solomon Islands 51
INDONESIA 37, 38, 39, 40, 41, 46, 47
Indus Delta, Pakistan 37
Inebolu, Turkey: 41.59 N. 33.45 E. 26
Infierno Channel, River Plate 78
Inga, see Inkoo.
Ingeniero, see La Plata.
Ingeniero White, see Bahia Blanca.
Ingleside, Texas, U.S.A.: 27.51 N. 97.14 W. 66
Inglez, see Porto Inglez.
Ingonish, N.S., Canada: 46.39 N. 60.23 W. 60
Inhambane, Mozambique: 23.53 S. 35.23 E. 30
Inkoo, Finland: 60.01 N. 23.55 E. 11
   Max. Size: Draft 13 m.
Inland Sea, Japan 43, 44
Inner Hebrides, Scotland, U.K. 5
Innisfail, Qld., Australia: 17.32 S. 146.02 E. 50, 51
Innoshima, Japan: 34.17 N. 133.11 E. 45
   Max. Size: Draft for entering port 9 m. For mooring –
   LOA 320 m., beam 50 m., draft 7 m. Fuel: All grades of bonded
   bunkers are stocked in Tokyo Bay, Ise Bay, Osaka Bay and
   Kanmon Port. Dry Docks: Largest 130,000 d.w.t.
   Airport: Osaka for crew joining/leaving.
Inokuchi, see Omishima.
Inoucdjouac, Quebec, Canada: 58.28 N. 78.15 W. 59
Inspection Head, see Bell Bay.
International Rapids Section, see St. Lawrence Seaway.
Intersection Pilot Station, see The River Plate.
Inveraray, U.K.: 56.14 N. 5.05 W. 5
Invercargill, New Zealand: 46.25 S. 168.25 E. 52
Invergordon, U.K.: 57.41 N. 4.10 W. 5
   Max. Size: LOA 1,000 ft., draft 40 ft. Fuel: Available.
   Airport: Dalcross, 30 miles.
   Also see Cromarty Firth.
Inverkeithing, see Rosyth.
Inverloch, Vic., Australia: 38.38 S. 145.45 E. 51
Inverness, U.K.: 57.29 N. 4.14 W. 5
   Max. Size: LOA 125 m., draft 6.25 m. (HWS) Fuel: Marine
   diesel and petroleum. Airport: Dalcross, 7 miles.

Investigator Strait, see Spencer Gulf.
Ioco, B.C., Canada: 49.18 N. 122.53 W. 56
Iokanka, see Gremikha.
Iona, N.S., Canada: 45.58 N. 60.48 W. 60
Ionian Is., Greece 25
Ionian Sea, Greece 21, 24, 25
Ios, (Ios Is.), Greece: 36.43 N. 25.17 E. 25
Ipala, Mexico: 20.05 N. 105.30 W. 57
Ipswich, U.K.: 52.03 N. 1.10 E. 5, 7
  Max. Size: LOA 155 m., draft 8.4 m. *Fuel:* All grades.
  Dry Docks: Slipway for vessels up to 1,000 tons.
  Airport: Stansted, 40 miles.
Iqaluit, N.W.T., Canada: 63.44 N. 68.32 W. . . . 17, 59, 79
  Max. Size: General cargo: Up to 12,000 tons. Tankers: Up to
  9.1 m. draft. *Fuel:* Supplied in emergency. *Airport:* 0.8 km.
  from landing beach, 5 flights weekly to and from Montreal.
Iquique, Chile: 20.12 S. 70.09 W. 77
  Max. Size: Draft 9.3 m. Patillos Cove: LOA 250 m., draft 14.3 m.,
  100,000 d.w.t. Tankers: LOA 228 m., draft 11.34 m.,
  70,000 d.w.t. *Fuel:* Available. *Airport:* Chucumata, 30 minutes
  by car.
Iquitos, Peru: 3.45 S. 73.09 W. 72
Iradier, see Puerto Iradier.
Iraklion, (Crete), Greece: 35.20 N. 25.10 E. . . . 21, 25, 26
  Max. Size: LOA 250 m., draft 29 ft. 6 in. *Airport:* 3 km.
IRAN 9, 31, 35, 37
IRAQ 9, 26, 31, 32, 35
Ireland Is., Bermuda (U.K.): 32.16 N. 64.46 W. 63
IRELAND, REPUBLIC OF 5, 8
Irene, see Aparri.
Irian Jaya, Indonesia 46
Irionote Is., (Ryuku Is.), Japan: 24.20 N. 123.47 E. . . 42, 46
Irish Sea 4, 5, 7
Irlam, see Barton.
Iroquois Lock, see St. Lawrence Seaway.
Irrawaddy Delta, Myanmar 37
Irvine, U.K.: 55.38 N. 4.45 W. 6
Isaac, see Port Isaac.
Isaacs Harbour, N.S., Canada: 45.10 N. 61.40 W. 60
Isabel, Nicaragua, see Prinzapolca.
Isabel, (Leyte Is.), Philippines: 10.54 N. 124.25 E. . . . 47
  Max. Size: Depth 12 m. *Fuel:* Available by barge from Cebu.
  Airport: Tacloban.
Isabel, U.S.A., see Port Isabel.
Isabela, (Basilan Is.), Philippines: 6.43 N. 121.56 E. . . 46, 47
Isabela de Sagua, Cuba: 22.52 N. 80.00 W. 69, 70
  Max. Size: Draft 7.62 m., LOA 180 m. *Fuel:* Small quantities
  by road tankers.
Isabela Is., (Galapagos Is.), Ecuador 69
Isafjord, Iceland: 65.05 N. 23.06 W. 17
  Max. Size: Dry cargo up to 4,000 g.r.t. Tankers up to 30 ft. draft.
  Fuel: All grades. *Dry Docks:* Small. *Airport:* 2 miles.
Ischia Is., Italy: 40.45 N. 13.57 E. 23, 24
Isdemir, Turkey: 36.43 N. 36.11 E. 26
  Max. Size: LOA 300 m., draft 16.5 m.
  Also see Iskenderun.
Ise, Japan: 34.26 N. 136.45 E. 45
Isfjord, (Spitsbergen), Norway 17
Ishigaki Is., (Ryuku Is.), Japan: 24.26 N. 124.10 E. . . . 42, 46
Ishikari Bay New Port, Japan: 43.11 N. 141.17 E. 43
  Max. Size: 15,000 d.w.t., draft 10.0 m. *Fuel:* By barge.
  Airport: Chitose, 60 km.
Ishikariwan-Shinko, see Ishikari Bay New Port.
Ishinomaki, Japan: 38.23 N. 141.19 E. 43
  Max. Size: Channel depth 10 m. LW. Max. draft 9.7 m.
  Fuel: Barge from Tokyo area. *Airport:* Sendai, 60 km.
Isigny, France: 49.19 N. 1.06 W. 7
Iskenderun, Turkey: 36.35 N. 36.10 E. 26
  Max. Size: Depth 4.5 m. – 11 m. Tankers: Draft 12.19 m.
  Fuel: Available. *Airport:* Adana, 147 km., connects with
  Istanbul.
Isla Cristina, Spain: 37.12 N. 7.19 W. 20
Isla d'Agua, see Rio de Janeiro.
Isla de Bioko, see Punta Europa Marine Terminal.
Isla de Pinos, see Nueva Gerona.
Isla di Pantellaria, see Pantellaria Is..
Isla Hoste, Chile 77
Isla Lampedusa, Italy: 35.30 N. 12.36 E. 24
Isla Madre de Dios, Chile 77
Isla Navarino, Chile 77
Islands of the Four Mountains, (Aleutian Is.), Alaska, U.S.A. . . . 54
Islay, U.K.: 55.45 N. 6.10 W. 5
Isle of Grain, see Medway Ports.
Isle of Man, U.K. 5
Isle of May, U.K.: 56.12 N. 2.33 W. 6
Isle of Pines, New Caledonia (France): 22.40 S. 167.26 E. . . . 49
  Max. Size: Depth 4.0 m.
  Also see Noumea.
Isle of Wight, U.K. 5, 7
Isle Royale, Michigan, U.S.A. 62

Isles au Pitre, Louisiana, U.S.A. 67
Isles of Scilly, U.K. 19
Ismailia, Egypt: 30.35 N. 32.17 E. 21, 26, 32, 33
Isnas, Finland: 60.24 N. 26.03 E. 11, 13
ISRAEL 21, 26, 32
Isrecognoseringsstation, see Narssarssuaq.
Istanbul, Turkey: 41.01 N. 28.59 E. 9, 21, 23, 25, 26
  Max. Size: Dry cargo: Istanbul – draft 10 m., Haydarpasa –
  depth 6 m. – 12 m. Tankers: See Ambarli. *Fuel:* Diesel oil, gas
  oil and bunker fuel by barge. *Dry Docks:* 600 ft. length, 63 ft.
  width. *Airport:* Yesikoy, 15 km.
Isthmia, Corinth Canal, Greece: 37.55 N. 23.00 E. . . . 24, 25
  Max. Size: Width 60 ft. (18.3 m.) or draft 7.2 m. *Airport:* 100 km.
Istinye, Turkey: 41.07 N. 29.03 E. 23
Itacoatiara, Brazil: 3.09 S. 58.27 W. 72
Itaituba, Brazil: 4.12 S. 55.53 W. 72
Itajai, Brazil: 26.54 S. 48.39 W. 76, 77
  Max. Size: Draft 33 ft. (HW). Dry cargo: LOA 250 m.
  Airport: 10 km.
ITALY 9, 21, 23, 24
Itaqui, Brazil: 2.35 S. 44.22 W. 72
  Max. Size: Draft 34 ft. (LW), depth 45 ft. – 48 ft. (HW).
  Fuel: Diesel. *Airport:* 18 km.
  Also see Sao Luis.
Itea, Greece: 38.26 N. 22.25 E. 24, 25
  Max. Size: LOA 130 m., draft 6.0 m.
Ithaca, Greece: 38.20 N. 20.45 E. 25
Itozaki, Japan: 34.23 N. 133.07 E. 45
  Max. Size: LOA 200 m., draft 9 m. *Fuel:* Bonded oil brought
  from Kanokawa, Kobe, Iwaki or Moje. *Airport:* Nearest Osaka.
  Also see Onomichi-Itozaki.
Itu, Nigeria: 5.10 N. 7.57 E. 29
Iturup Is., (Kurile Is.), Russia 43
Itzehoe, Germany: 53.56 N. 9.33 E. 8, 11, 12, 14
  Max. Size: LOA 85 m., beam 12 m., draft 3.80 m. – 4.0 m.,
  airdraft 18.50 m. *Fuel:* All grades by road tankers.
  Airport: Hamburg.
Ivigtut, Greenland (Denmark): 61.12 N. 48.10 W. 17
  Mining stopped. Port closed.
IVORY COAST 27, 28
Ivujivic, Quebec, Canada: 62.25 N. 77.55 W. 59
Iwaki, see Onahama.
Iwakuni, Japan: 34.10 N. 132.14 E. 45
  Max. Size: Dry cargo: Up to 11.5 m. draft, 230 m. LOA and
  40,000 d.w.t. Tankers: Up to 150,000 d.w.t., draft 16.5 m.
  Fuel: Available ex-wharf. *Airport:* Hiroshima, 45 km.
Iwanai, Japan: 43.00 N. 140.30 E. 43
Iwo Jima, (Japan): 24.46 N. 141.20 E. 46
Iwopin, Nigeria: 6.32 N. 4.05 E. 29
Iyo, Japan: 33.45 N. 132.40 E. 45
Iyo Sea, Inland Sea, Japan 45
Iyomishima, Japan: 33.58 N. 133.31 E. 45
Izmail, Ukraine: 45.20 N. 28.51 E. 26
  Max. Size: Draft 7 m. *Fuel:* Available. *Airport:* Regular
  connections with internal services.
Izmir, Turkey: 38.25 N. 27.09 E. 21, 25, 26
  Max. Size: Draft 38 ft. Tankers: Draft 33 ft. *Fuel:* All grades.
  Dry Docks: 7,000 d.w.t. *Airport:* 27 km.
Izmit, Turkey: 40.46 N. 29.55 E. 23, 25, 26
  Max. Size: Depth 24 ft. – 27 ft. *Fuel:* Only by barge from
  Istanbul. *Airport:* Istanbul, 130 km.
Izola, Slovenia: 45.32 N. 13.38 E. 24
Izon, France: 44.57 N. 0.22 W. 8, 19
Izu Is., Japan 43
Izuhara, Japan: 34.11 N. 129.17 E. 42, 45
  Max. Size: Draft 5.2 m. *Fuel:* Available. *Airport:*
  Fukuoka, 40 minutes by car.
Izumisano, Japan: 34.23 N. 135.18 E. 45

J

Jabiru Venture, Australia: 11.55 S. 125.00 E. 50
 Max. Size: 150,000 d.w.t.
 Also see Challis Venture.
Jackfish, Ontario, Canada: 48.48 N. 86.58 W. 62
Jackson, New Zealand: 44.00 S. 168.45 E. 52
Jacksonville, Florida, U.S.A.: 30.20 N. 81.40 W. 55, 66
 Max. Size: Draft 37 ft. – 38 ft. *Fuel:* Most grades.
 Dry Docks: Largest 33,000 tons capacity. *Airport:* 20 miles.
Jacmel, Haiti: 18.13 N. 72.32 W. 70
Jacques Cartier Passage, Gulf of St. Lawrence, Canada. . . 60
Jaffa, Israel: 32.05 N. 34.50 E. 26
Jaffna, Sri Lanka: 9.40 N. 80.00 E. 37
Jakarta, Indonesia: 6.10 S. 106.50 E. 38
 Max. Size: Draft 11.0 m. *Fuel:* Available. *Dry Docks:* Floating
 dock with capacity 17,500 tons. *Airport:* Soekarno-Hatta, 26 km.
 Halim, 25 km.
Jakhau, India: 23.15 N. 68.37 E. 37
 Max. Size: Open roadstead, anchorage 6 miles offshore.
Jakobshavn, see Ilulissat.
Jakobstad, Finland: 63.42 N. 22.42 E. 10, 15
 Max. Size: Draft in the inner harbour 9 m. *Fuel:* Available.
 Airport: Kronoby, 30 km.
Jaluit, Marshall Is.: 5.55 N. 169.39 E. 49
JAMAICA 55, 69, 70
Jamaica Bay, New York, U.S.A. 63
Jambi, Indonesia: 1.35 S. 103.38 E. 38
 Max. Size: Depth 2 m.
James Bay, Ontario, Canada 59
Jamestown, St. Helena (U.K.): 15.56 S. 5.40 W. 28
 Max. Size: Anchorage: No restriction. *Fuel:* Limited diesel oil.
Jamnagar, India: 22.30 N. 69.50 E. 37
 Max. Size: SPM: 350,000 d.w.t., LOA 355 m., depth 32 m.
 Jetty: 65,000 d.w.t., LOA 246 m., draft 14 m.
 Fuel: At anchorage.
Jamsah, see Gemsah.
Jan Mayen Island, Norway 4
JAPAN 42, 43, 44, 45, 46
Jarrow, U.K.: 54.59 N. 1.28 W. 6
 Also see Tyne District.
Jarvis Is., (U.S.A.): 0.15 S. 159.55 W. 49
Jask, Iran: 25.38 N. 57.48 E. 31, 35, 37
Java, Indonesia 38
Javea, Spain: 38.48 N. 0.10 E. 22
Jawaharlal Nehru Port, India: 18.57 N. 72.58 E. 37
 Max. Size: Draft 12.0 m. Bulk Terminal: LOA 270 m.,
 displacement 85,000 tons. Container Terminal: LOA 300 m.
 Fuel: Available. *Airport:* 60 km.
 Also see Mumbai.
Jayapura, Indonesia: 2.32 S. 140.43 E. 46
 Max. Size: LOA 160 m., draft 4.5 m. *Airport:* 38 km.
Jazirat Zarakku, see Zirku Island.
Jazirat Zarakku Island, see Zirku Island.
Jebel Ali, Dubai, U.A.E.: 25.00 N. 55.03 E. 31, 35, 37
 Max. Size: Draft 11.5 m. – 14 m. Tankers: 120,000 d.w.t., LOA
 275 m., draft 14 m. *Fuel:* Available with notice. *Airport:*
 Dubai, 30 minutes.
Jebel Dhanna - Ruwais, U.A.E.: 24.11 N. 52.37 E. . . . 31, 35
 Max. Size: Crude Oil Terminal: 330,000 d.w.t., LOA 1,215 ft.,
 depth 55 ft., draft 49 ft. SBM: 450,000 d.w.t. Refinery
 Terminal: LOA 360 m., 330,000 d.w.t. (partially loaded to
 210,000 tons), draft 17 m. GASCO: Gas carriers 125,000 cu.m.,
 depth 15 m. Tankers: LOA 320 m., 95,000 tons
 max. displacement. FERTIL: LOA 200 m., 25,000 d.w.t.,
 max. draft 11 m., depth 12 m. ADNOC (fertiliser): 45,000 d.w.t.
 Fuel: Available. *Airport:* Nearest International is Abu Dhabi.
Jeddah, Saudi Arabia: 21.28 N. 39.10 E. 21, 32
 Max. Size: LOA 250 m. Draft – General 12 m., container 16.4 m.,
 dry bulk 11.5 m. – 13.5 m., Ro-Ro/reefer/livestock 13 m. – 14.2
 m., passenger/pilgrim 10.5 m. Beam – no limit.
 Fuel: All grades. *Dry Docks:* 45,000 d.w.t.
 Airport: International airport 30 km. to the North.
Jeddore, N.S., Canada: 44.43 N. 63.00 W. 60
Jedway, B.C., Canada: 52.18 N. 131.14 W. 56
Jefferson, see Port Jefferson.
Jeju, see Cheju.
Jeremie, Haiti: 18.39 N. 74.07 W. 70
Jerome, see Rouen.
Jersey, (Channel Is.), U.K. 7, 19
Jersey City, U.S.A.: 40.43 N. 74.02 W. 63
 Also see New York.
Jervis Bay, N.S.W., Australia: 35.07 S. 150.47 E. 50
Jesselton, see Kota Kinabalu.
Jiangmen, China: 22.36 N. 113.07 E. 39, 48

Jiangyin, China: 31.55 N. 120.11 E. 42
 Max. Size: Channel draft 15.0 m. (Note: Draft for crossing bar at
 mouth of Chang Jiang River is 9.5 m.).
Jibouti, see Djibouti.
Jijel, Algeria: 36.50 N. 5.47 E. 22
 Max. Size: Draft 10 m.
Jimenez, (Mindanao Is.), Philippines: 8.19 N. 123.52 E. . . 47
 Port closed.
Jiminez, see Puerto Jimenez.
Jinan, China: 36.43 N. 117.00 E. 42
Jinhae, see Chinhai.
Jinzhou, China: 40.48 N. 121.04 E. 42
 Max. Size: 10,000 d.w.t., depth 9.7 m. – 10.4 m. *Fuel:* Available.
Jiujiang, China: 29.38 N. 115.56 E. 42
 Max. Size: Draft 4.5 m. *Fuel:* Available.
Jiuzhou, China: 22.14 N. 113.35 E. 39, 48
 Max. Size: Anchorage 4 m. – 18 m. Berth – 5,000 d.w.t.,
 depth 6 m. *Fuel:* Available.
Jizan, see Gizan.
Joao Pessoa, Brazil: 7.08 S. 34.52 W. 72
Jobos, Puerto Rico (U.S.A.): 17.56 N. 66.13 W. 71
 Max. Size: Anchorage depth 19 ft. – 24 ft.
Joensuu, Finland: 62.36 N. 29.47 E. 13
 Also see Saimaa Canal.
Johannedal, Sweden: 62.25 N. 17.24 E. 11
 Also see Sundsvall.
Johnston Is., (U.S.A.): 16.45 N. 169.31 W. 49
Johor Bahru, Malaya, Malaysia: 1.27 N. 103.45 E. . . 38, 39, 41
Johor Strait, Malaysia/Singapore 41
Joinville, Brazil: 26.18 S. 48.52 W. 76, 77
Joinville, France, see Port Joinville.
Jolo, (Jolo Is.), Philippines: 6.03 N. 121.00 E. . . . 38, 46, 47
 Max. Size: Draft 4 m., LOA 60 m. Tankers: Draft 6 m.
 Fuel: Available. *Airport:* Jolo, connects with Zamboanga.
Jonesport, Maine, U.S.A.: 44.32 N. 67.37 W. 60
Jonkoping, Sweden: 57.45 N. 14.12 E. 11, 12
Jonstorp, Sweden: 56.14 N. 12.41 E. 12
JORDAN 21, 26, 32
Jorf Lasfar, Morocco: 33.08 N. 8.38 W. 27
 Max. Size: Depth 4 m. – 15.6 m. *Fuel:* Available.
 Airport: Casablanca, 120 km.
Jose, Venezuela: 10.06 N. 64.51 W. 71, 72, 75
 Max. Size: Gas – 42,000 d.w.t. (75,000 cu.m.), LOA 800 ft.,
 draft 39 ft. Petroterminal (Offshore Platform) – 250,000 d.w.t.,
 LOA 350 m., draft 75 ft. Bitor SPM – 300,000 d.w.t. Petrozuata
 Jose Marine Terminal – 130,000 d.w.t., depth 25 m.
 Petrochemical Dock: 65,000 d.w.t., LOA 255 m., beam 33.5 m.,
 draft 13 m. Container Berth: 50,000 d.w.t., LOA 292 m., draft
 13 m. Dry Bulk Berth: 65,000 d.w.t., LOA 255 m., draft 13 m.
 Fuel: Available at Puerto La Cruz.
Jose Ignacio, Uruguay: 34.54 S. 54.43 W. 77, 78
 Max. Size: (SBM) 150,000 d.w.t., depth 55 ft.
Jose Panganiban, (Luzon Is.), Philippines:
 14.17 N. 122.42 E. 46, 47
 Max. Size: LOA 230 m., draft 30 ft.
 Fuel: All grades by road tankers. *Airport:* Bagasbas, 48 km.
Joseph Bonaparte Gulf, Australia 50
Jossingfjord, see Rekefjord.
Jounieh, Lebanon: 33.58 N. 35.39 E. 26
Joutseno, Finland: 61.08 N. 28.27 E. 13
 Also see Saimaa Canal.
Ju'aymah, Saudi Arabia: 26.56 N. 50.03 E. 31, 35
 Max. Size: VLCC up to 750,000 d.w.t., arrival draft 21.3 m. Depth
 at SBM No. 34: 35 m. RLPG Terminal: Arrival draft 16.37 m.,
 sailing draft 23.0 m. *Fuel:* Available.
 Also see Dammam.
Juan de Fuca Strait, B.C., Canada 56
Juan de Nova, (France): 17.03 S. 42.46 E. 30
Juan Gallegos Is., Panama Canal, Panama 73
Jubail, Saudi Arabia: 27.01 N. 49.40 E. 31, 35
 Max. Size: Commercial Port: Drafts to 13.3 m.
 Industrial Port: Draft 7.6 m. – 25 m. *Fuel:* Available.
 Airport: Dhahran, 80 km.
Jucaro, Cuba: 21.37 N. 78.51 W. 69, 70
 Max. Size: Draft 29 ft., LOA 800 ft.
Juelsminde, Denmark: 55.43 N. 10.01 E. 12
Jui An, China: 27.47 N. 120.39 E. 42
Julianehab, see Qaqortoq.
Juneau, Alaska, U.S.A.: 58.18 N. 134.24 W. 56
 Max. Size: Depth 36 ft. (LW). *Fuel:* Available. *Airport:* Juneau
 International Airport.
Jura, U.K.: 56.00 N. 5.45 W. 5
Jurado, Colombia: 7.05 N. 77.45 W. 69, 72
Jurmala, Latvia: 57.00 N. 23.45 E. 11
Jurong, see Singapore.
Jutland, Denmark 11, 12

K

Kaarstoe, see Karsto.
Kabret, Egypt: 30.12 N. 32.30 E. ... 33
Kacha, Ukraine: 44.45 N. 33.40 E. ... 26
Kadavu, see Kandavu Is..
Kadikoy, see Haydarpasa.
Kaerbaeksminde, Denmark: 55.10 N. 11.39 E. ... 12
  Max. Size: Draft 5.6 m. *Fuel:* Available.
  Airport: Copenhagen, 80 km.
  Also see Naestved.
Kage, Sweden: 64.50 N. 21.00 E. ... 15
  Max. Size: Depth 20 ft. – 23 ft.
  Also see Skelleftehamn.
Kagoshima, Japan: 31.35 N. 130.33 E. ... 43, 45, 46
  Max. Size: Draft 11.0 m. – 11.5 m.
  Airport: Kagoshima, 50 minutes by car.
Kagowong, Ontario, Canada: 45.55 N. 82.15 W. ... 62
Kahului, Hawaii, U.S.A.: 20.53 N. 156.28 W. ... 49
  Max. Size: LOA 700 ft., draft 34 ft. *Fuel:* By road tanker.
  Airport: 1 mile, connects with Honolulu.
Kai Is., Indonesia ... 46
Kaikoura, New Zealand: 42.25 S. 173.42 E. ... 52
Kaimana, Indonesia: 3.39 S. 133.45 E. ... 46
Kainan, Japan: 34.10 N. 135.12 E. ... 45
  Max. Size: Draft 11.5 m. (Sea berth 21.0 m.), 78,000 d.w.t.
  (Sea berth 245,000 d.w.t.). *Fuel:* Available. *Airport:* Osaka.
  Also see Shimotsu.
Kairuku, Papua New Guinea: 8.51 S. 146.35 E. ... 46
Kaiser, see Port Kaiser.
Kaitangata, New Zealand: 46.15 S. 169.50 E. ... 52
Kaizuka, Japan: 34.25 N. 135.20 E. ... 44
Kajang, Indonesia: 5.19 S. 120.22 E. ... 46
Kakap Natuna Marine Terminal, Indonesia: 5.01 N. 105.57 E. ... 38, 39
  Max. Size: 100,000 d.w.t.
Kake, Alaska, U.S.A.: 56.58 N. 133.56 W. ... 56
Kakinada, India: 16.56 N. 82.15 E. ... 37
  Max. Size: LOA 180 m., beam 31.3 m., draft 8.5 m.
  Fuel: Emergency only, 10/15 tons from Visakhapatnam.
  Airport: Visakhapatnam, 105 miles, Chennai, 350 miles.
Kakogawa, Japan: 34.42 N. 134.50 E. ... 45
  Max. Size: Kobe Steel, Berth No. 4: 165,000 d.w.t. (or 320,000 d.w.t. with part load), draft 16 m., LOA 330 m.
  Fuel: Bunkers lightered from nearest bunker stock port.
Kaktovik, (Barter Is.), Alaska, U.S.A.: 70.08 N. 143.40 W. ... 54
Kalabahi, Indonesia: 7.14 S. 124.32 E. ... 46
Kalaeloa, see Barber's Point.
Kalajoki, Finland: 64.15 N. 23.58 E. ... 15
Kalama, Washington, U.S.A.: 46.01 N. 122.50 W. ... 56, 57
  Max. Size: Depth 23 ft. – 67 ft.
Kalamaki, Greece: 37.52 N. 23.01 E. ... 25
  Max. Size: Draft 12 m. *Fuel:* By road tanker. *Airport:* Athens.
Kalamata, Greece: 37.01 N. 22.07 E. ... 24, 25
  Max. Size: LOA 200 m., beam 50 m. and draft 28 ft. *Fuel:* Supplied by road tankers, or barge from Piraeus.
  Airport: 6 miles.
Kalamos, Greece: 38.38 N. 20.55 E. ... 25
Kalaranta, see Uusikaupunki.
Kalbut STS Terminal, Indonesia: 7.37 S. 113.55 E. ... 38, 39
  Max. Size: 230,000 d.w.t. No draft limit.
Kalecik, Cyprus: 35.19 N. 33.59 E. ... 26
  Max. Size: LOA 100 m., depth 6 m. Tankers: Depth at buoys 8.15 m. and 9 m. *Airport:* Ercan, 50 miles.
Kali Limenes, (Crete), Greece: 34.56 N. 24.49 E. ... 25, 26
  Max. Size: Draft 12.8 m. (280,000 d.w.t. in ballast).
  Fuel: Available. *Airport:* Iraklion, 75 km.
Kaliandak, Indonesia: 5.45 S. 105.36 E. ... 38
Kalianget, see Sumenep.
Kalifoka, see Corfu.
Kalimantan Is., Indonesia ... 38
Kalimnos Is., Greece: 36.57 N. 27.00 E. ... 25
Kalingapatnam, India: 18.20 N. 84.09 E. ... 37
Kaliningrad, Russia: 54.42 N. 20.29 E. ... 4, 10, 11
  Max. Size: LOA 170 m., beam 25 m., draft 8.0 m.
  Tankers: LOA 140 m., beam 25 m., draft 8.0 m.
  Fuel: By barge. *Dry Docks:* 10,000 d.w.t., LOA 170 m.
  Airport: Kaliningrad.
Kalivia, see Yerakini.
Kalix, Sweden: 65.50 N. 23.10 E. ... 15
  Max. Size: Draft 5.4 m.
  Also see Karlsborgsverken.
Kallero, Sweden: 60.21 N. 18.15 E. ... 11
Kallvken, see Lovanger.
Kalmar, Sweden: 56.40 N. 16.22 E. ... 10, 11
  Max. Size: Largest vessel: 25,000 d.w.t., LOA 560 ft., draft 24 ft.
  Channel and harbour depth 26 ft. Tankers: 30,000 d.w.t., depth 8 m. *Fuel:* Available. *Airport:* 5 km.

Kalmar Sound, Sweden ... 11
Kalpeni Is., (Laccadive Is.), India: 10.04 N. 73.35 E. ... 37
Kalumburu, W.A., Australia: 14.30 S. 126.00 E. ... 50
Kalundborg, Denmark: 55.41 N. 11.06 E. ... 10, 11, 12
  Max. Size: Depth 6 m. – 12 m. Tankers: 130,000 d.w.t., LOA 870 ft., draft 41 ft. (70,000 d.w.t.). *Fuel:* All grades.
  Airport: Copenhagen, 80 miles.
Kalutara, Sri Lanka: 6.35 N. 80.00 E. ... 37
Kalvehave, Denmark: 54.59 N. 12.10 E. ... 12, 14
Kamaishi, Japan: 39.16 N. 141.55 E. ... 43
  Max. Size: Draft 14 m. and LOA 300 m. (915 ft.) Beam no restriction. *Fuel:* Domestic diesel oil (Bunker A) is available. Bonded oil will be brought from Sendai, Yokohama and Kashima. *Airport:* Hanamaki, 100 km.
Kamaran Is., Yemen: 15.25 N. 42.35 E. ... 32
Kamares, (Sifnos), Greece: 36.59 N. 24.41 E. ... 25
Kamariotissa, (Samothraki), Greece: 40.28 N. 25.28 E. ... 25
Kamchatka Peninsula, Russia ... 54
Kamenka, Russia: 65.51 N. 44.01 E. ... 16
Kamien, Poland: 53.58 N. 14.46 E. ... 11
Kamigoto, see Aokata.
Kampen, Netherlands: 52.32 N. 5.53 E. ... 7, 8
Kampot, Cambodia: 10.36 N. 104.12 E. ... 39
Kampung Echah, Malaya, Malaysia: 3.57 N. 100.43 E. ... 39
Kamsar, see Port Kamsar.
Kanaga Is., (Aleutian Is.), Alaska, U.S.A. ... 54
Kanakanak, Alaska, U.S.A.: 59.00 N. 158.45 W. ... 54
Kanatak, Alaska, U.S.A.: 57.34 N. 156.02 W. ... 54
Kanazawa, Japan: 36.37 N. 136.35 E. ... 43, 45
  Max. Size: 15,000 d.w.t., draft 8.7 m.
Kanda, Japan: 33.49 N. 131.00 E. ... 45
  Max. Size: LOA 210 m., draft 10.0 m. *Fuel:* Available from Moji or Shimonoseki.
Kandalaksha, Russia: 67.08 N. 32.25 E. ... 16, 79
  Max. Size: LOA 200 m., draft 9 m. *Airport:* 100 km.
Kandavu Is., Fiji: 19.00 S. 178.15 E. ... 49
Kandilli, see Anadolu.
Kandla, India: 23.00 N. 70.12 E. ... 37
  Max. Size: Cargo Vessels: LOA 225 m., draft 9.75 m.
  Tankers: LOA 225 m., draft 10.36 m. *Fuel:* Furnace oil and light diesel oil. *Dry Docks:* Floating dock – Max. size: LOA 100 m., draft 5 m. *Airport:* 20 km.
Kangamiut, Greenland (Denmark): 65.49 N. 53.18 W. ... 17, 59
Kangan, Iran: 27.49 N. 52.04 E. ... 35
  Also see Bandar Taheri.
Kangaroo Is., S.A., Australia: 35.45 S. 137.48 E. ... 50, 51
  Also see Ballast Head.
Kangatsiaq, Greenland (Denmark): 68.20 N. 53.30 W. ... 17
Kangean Is., Indonesia ... 38
Kangerlussuaq, Greenland (Denmark): 66.58 N. 50.57 W. ... 17
  Max. Size: Depth 3 m. Tankers: Depth 24 m. – 26 m.
  Airport: 8 miles.
Kango, Gabon: 0.10 N. 10.05 E. ... 29
Kankesanturai, Sri Lanka: 9.49 N. 80.03 E. ... 37
  Max. Size: (Anchorage) Depth about 31 ft.
Kanmon-Ko, Japan: 33.53 N. 130.55 E. ... 44
  Also see Kokura, Moji, Shimonoseki, Tobata, Wakamatsu and Yawata.
Kanokawa, Japan: 34.11 N. 132.26 E. ... 45
  Max. Size: LOA 270 m., beam 40 m., draft 14 m., 125,000. d.w.t. *Fuel:* Most grades of domestic and bonded oil obtainable by barge. *Airport:* Kure.
Kanonji, Japan: 34.10 N. 133.38 E. ... 45
Kansas, U.S.A. ... 57
Kansola, see Saimaa Canal.
Kansong, South Korea: 38.10 N. 128.30 E. ... 42, 43
Kantang, Thailand: 7.25 N. 99.31 E. ... 37, 38, 39
  Max. Size: Depth 10 ft. – 16 ft. *Fuel:* High Speed Diesel only.
Kantara, Egypt: 30.50 N. 32.16 E. ... 33
Kantvik, Finland: 60.05 N. 24.23 E. ... 11
  Also see Porkkala
Kaohsiung, Taiwan: 22.37 N. 120.16 E. ... 42, 46
  Max. Size: Length and breadth no restriction (largest to date 950 ft. LOA and 106 ft. beam). Draft Inner Harbour 52 ft. (H.W.). Tankers with draft over 50 ft. discharge at SBM's outside where depth is 105 ft. (300,000 d.w.t.) *Fuel:* All grades.
  Dry Docks: 950 m. long, breadth 92 m., depth 14 m. *Airport:* International, 7 miles.
Kaolack, Senegal: 14.09 N. 16.06 W. ... 27
  Max. Size: LOA 105 m. Depth in river 3.0 m.
Kapingamarangi Is., Micronesia: 1.08 N. 154.45 E. ... 49
Kapiskau, Ontario, Canada: 52.50 N. 82.10 W. ... 59
Kapitana Varzugina, Russia: 72.35 N. 80.50 E. ... 16
Kappeln, Germany: 54.40 N. 9.56 E. ... 12, 14
  Max. Size: LOA 90 m., draft 4.5 m. *Fuel:* Available.
Kapsali, (Kithira), Greece: 36.08 N. 23.00 E. ... 25
Kara, Russia: 69.10 N. 65.20 E. ... 16
Kara Sea, Russia ... 16, 79
Kara Strait, Russia ... 16
Karabiga, Turkey: 40.24 N. 27.18 E. ... 25

THE SHIPS ATLAS

Karachi, Pakistan: 24.49 N. 66.59 E. 37
  Max. Size: Draft 32 ft. Tankers, White Oil: LOA 750 ft., draft 35 ft.
  Black Oils: LOA 750 ft., draft 35 ft. Oil Pier No. 4: LOA 850 ft.,
  draft 39 ft. *Fuel:* Available.
  Dry Docks: Largest 609 ft. x 90 ft. x 18 ft. for 25,000 d.w.t.
  Airport: 7 miles.
Karadeniz Eregli, see Eregli.
Karadzha, Ukraine: 45.15 N. 32.50 E. 26
Karajinski Is., Russia 54
Karambu, Indonesia: 3.50 S. 116.05 E. 38
Karamea, New Zealand: 41.18 S. 172.08 E. 52
Karatas, Turkey: 36.35 N. 35.25 E. 26
Karathuri, Myanmar: 10.50 N. 98.35 E. 37
Karatsu, Japan: 33.27 N. 129.58 E. 42, 45
Karaul, Russia: 69.55 N. 83.50 E. 16
Karavostasis, (Folegrandos), Greece: 36.37 N. 24.57 E. . . 25
Karavostassi, see Gemikonagi.
Kardamyla, Greece: 38.32 N. 26.05 E. 25
Kardeljevo, see Ploce.
Kardla, Estonia: 58.45 N. 22.40 E. 11
Karen, (Andaman Is.), India: 12.50 N. 92.55 E. 37
Karikal, India: 10.55 N. 79.51 E. 37
Karimata Is., Indonesia: 1.40 S. 109.00 E. 38
Karimun Besar, Indonesia: 1.05 N. 103.30 E. 40
  Max. Size: Anchorage for S-T-S operations.
Karimuntung, see Sandakan.
Karin, Somalia: 10.50 N. 45.50 E. 31
Karistos, Greece: 38.01 N. 24.25 E. 25
Karkar Is., Papua New Guinea: 4.40 S. 146.00 E. 46
Karlholm, Sweden: 60.31 N. 17.39 E. 11
Karlobag, Croatia: 44.32 N. 15.04 E. 24
Karlovasi, (Samos), Greece: 37.48 N. 26.41 E. 25
Karlsborgsverken, Sweden: 65.48 N. 23.17 E. 10, 15
  Max. Size: Draft 6 m. Tankers: Draft 8.8 m.
  Airport: Lulea, 85 km.
Karlshamn, Sweden: 56.10 N. 14.52 E. 11, 12
  Max. Size: 40,000 d.w.t., depth 11.0 m. Tankers: LOA 260 m.,
  draft 13.5 m. *Fuel:* All grades. *Airport:* 30 km.
Karlskrona, Sweden: 56.10 N. 15.36 E. 10, 11
  Max. Size: Draft 9 m. Tankers: Draft 8.5 m. *Fuel:* All grades.
  Dry Docks: Largest: Length 185 m., breadth 20.76 m.,
  depth 8.80 m. *Airport:* 30 km.
Karlsruhe, Germany: 49.00 N. 8.24 E. 9
Karlstad, Sweden: 59.23 N. 13.31 E. 11, 12
  Max. Size: Vessel's length, breadth and draft controlled by locks
  of Trollhatte Canal (88 m. x 13.2 m. x 5.4 m.). *Fuel:* Available.
  Airport: Domestic.
Karlsvik, see Hovid.
Karluk, Alaska, U.S.A.: 57.20 N. 154.50 W. 54
Karpathos Is., Greece: 35.30 N. 27.13 E. 25, 26
Karpathos Strait, Greece 25, 26
Karrebaeksminde, see Naestved.
Karskar, Sweden: 60.40 N. 17.18 E. 11
  Max. Size: Draft 7.8 m.
  Also see Gavle.
Karsto, Norway: 59.16 N. 5.30 E. 10, 11
  Max. Size: LOA 210 m., draft 11.3 m. *Fuel:* By road or barge.
  Airport: Haugesund, 45 km.
Kartal, Turkey: 40.53 N. 29.11 E. 23
Karumba, Qld., Australia: 17.30 S. 140.50 E. 50
  Max. Size: Depth 3.4 m. (LAT). *Fuel:* Available with notice.
  Airport: Light aircraft only.
Karwar, India: 14.48 N. 74.06 E. 37
  Max. Size: Depth 8 m. *Fuel:* No bunkering facilities for
  ocean-going vessels. *Airport:* Goa, 60 miles.
Kas, Turkey: 36.15 N. 29.45 E. 25, 26
Kasaan, Alaska, U.S.A.: 55.32 N. 132.24 W. 56
Kasaoka, Japan: 34.23 N. 133.26 E. 45, 46
  Max. Size: LOA 220 m., draft 11.0 m. *Fuel:* Bonded oil
  from Kobe, etc.
  Also see Fukuyama.
Kasaragod, India: 12.30 N. 74.59 E. 37
Kashima, Japan: 35.54 N. 140.42 E. 43, 45
  Max. Size: Tankers: 250,000 d.w.t., LOA 340 m., safe draft 19 m.
  Bulk carriers: Draft up to 44 ft. LPG: 100,000 c.w.t.,
  draft 13.43 m., LOA 258 m. *Fuel:* Bonded bunkers are stocked
  in Tokyo Bay, Ise Bay, Osaka Bay and Kanmon Port. Bunkers
  are also available. *Airport:* Narita Airport, Tokyo.
Kashiwazaki, Japan: 37.21 N. 138.32 E. 43, 45
  Max. Size: 15,000 d.w.t., draft 9.0 m.
Kasim, see Port Muhammad Bin Qasim.
Kasim Marine Terminal, Indonesia: 1.18 S. 131.01 E. . . . 46
  Max. Size: Draft 50 ft., LOA 1,000 ft., beam 150 ft. Dry Cargo
  Berth: Depth 15 ft. (MLWS).
Kaskinen, Finland: 62.23 N. 21.13 E. 10, 11, 15
  Max. Size: Draft 9 m. *Fuel:* By road tanker. *Airport:* Vasa,
  90 km.
Kasko, see Kaskinen.
Kaskoy, see Istanbul.
Kasos Is., Greece: 35.20 N. 26.55 E. 25

Kasos Strait, Greece 25, 26
Kassa Is., see Conakry.
Kassue, Indonesia: 6.58 S. 139.21 E. 46
Kastelli, (Crete), Greece: 35.30 N. 23.35 E. 25
Kastellorizon, Greece: 36.09 N. 29.37 E. 25, 26
Kastet, see Karskar.
Kastrades, see Corfu.
Kastrup, (Amager), Denmark: 55.38 N. 12.39 E. 12
Katakolon, Greece: 37.39 N. 21.20 E. 24, 25
  Max. Size: Draft 23 ft. *Fuel:* Available by tank truck from
  Patras or Kalamata. *Airport:* Andravis, 26 km.
Katalla, Alaska, U.S.A.: 60.12 N. 144.32 W. 54
Katapola, (Amorgos Is.), Greece: 36.50 N. 25.52 E. 25
Katchall Is., (Nicobar Is.), India: 9.55 N. 93.20 E. . . . 37
Kato Akhaia, Greece: 38.08 N. 21.34 E. 25
Katsini Bay, see Aghios Nikolaos.
Katsunan, Japan: 35.40 N. 139.58 E. 45
  Also see Chiba.
Katsuura, Japan: 35.09 N. 140.20 E. 43, 45
Kattegat. 10, 11, 12
Katwijk, Netherlands: 52.12 N. 4.24 E. 7, 8
Kauai Is., Hawaii, U.S.A. 49
Kaukas, see Lappeenranta.
Kaukauna, Wisconsin, U.S.A.: 44.18 N. 88.15 W. 62
Kaukopaa Harbour, see Saimaa Canal.
Kaunissaari, Finland: 61.15 N. 21.32 E. 15
Kavalla, Greece: 40.55 N. 24.25 E. 21, 25, 26
  Max. Size: LOA 200 m., draft 27 ft. 6 in. *Fuel:* Small quantities
  by road tankers. *Airport:* 30 km.
Kavaratti Is., (Laccadive Is.), India: 10.34 N. 72.46 E. . 37
Kavieng, Papua New Guinea: 2.35 S. 150.48 E. 46, 49
  Max. Size: Depth 7 m. at LAT. *Fuel:* Diesel.
  Airport: 3 km. (internal).
Kavkaz, Russia: 45.20 N. 36.39 E. 26
  Max. Size: 5,000 d.w.t., LOA 130 m., draft 4 m.
Kavonisi-Kissamos, (Crete), Greece: 35.31 N. 23.38 E. . 25, 26
  Max. Size: LOA 120 m., depth 5.0 m. – 8.0 m. *Fuel:* MDO by
  truck. *Airport:* Heraklion, 56 km.
Kawaihae, Hawaii, U.S.A.: 20.02 N. 155.50 W. 49
  Max. Size: Draft up to 33 ft. *Fuel:* Available. *Airport:* At Hilo.
  Also see Hilo.
Kawanoe, see Mishima-Kawanoe.
Kawanoishi, Japan: 33.30 N. 132.20 E. 45
Kawasaki, Japan: 35.32 N. 139.46 E. 43, 44, 45
  Max. Size: Depth alongside 12.0 m. Bulk: 200,000 d.w.t.
  LOA 360 m., draft 19.0 m. Container: Depth 14 m. Tanker
  (Sea Berth): 250,000 d.w.t., LOA 300 m., draft 30 m.
  Fuel: All grades. *Dry Docks:* Largest: 60,000 d.w.t.,
  LOA 228 m. *Airport:* Haneda, 20 minutes.
Kawthaung, Myanmar: 10.00 N. 98.34 E. 37
Kayak Is., Alaska, U.S.A.: 59.55 N. 144.26 W. 54, 56
Kayts, Sri Lanka: 9.42 N. 79.50 E. 37
KAZAKHSTAN 9
Keadby, U.K.: 53.35 N. 0.42 W. 6
  Max. Size: 3,500 tonnes d.w.t.
Keelung, Taiwan: 25.09 N. 121.44 E. 42, 46
  Max. Size: LOA 900 ft., depth 5.2 m. – 13.5 m.
  Tankers: Depth 11.5 m. Shen-Ao: 36,000 d.w.t., LOA 225 m.,
  draft 10.8 m. Shalung: 350,000 d.w.t., draft 35 m.
  Fuel: Available. *Dry Docks:* Depth 12 m., for vessels
  100,000 tons. *Airport:* C.K.S. International, 65 km.
Kefalo, Greece: 40.09 N. 25.59 E. 25
Kefalomandouko, see Corfu.
Keflavik-Njarovik, Iceland: 64.00 N. 22.33 W. 17
  Max. Size: Depth of water 20 ft. – 45 ft. *Fuel:* Available.
  Airport: 4 km.
Kehl, see Strasbourg.
Kelang, see Port Klang.
Kelibia, Tunisia: 36.50 N. 11.05 E. 24
Kelloniemi, see Kuopio.
Kelso, Washington, U.S.A.: 46.10 N. 122.55 W. 56, 57
Kem, Russia: 65.00 N. 34.37 E. 16
Kemaman, Malaya, Malaysia: 4.16 N. 103.29 E. 38, 39, 40
  Max. Size: 150,000 d.w.t., LOA 260 m., beam 35 m.,
  draft 16.4 m. *Fuel:* Available. *Airport:* Kerteh, 40 km.
  Kuantan, 75 km.
Kemano, B.C., Canada: 53.29 N. 128.07 W. 56
Kembla, see Port Kembla.
Kemi, Finland: 65.40 N. 24.31 E. 10, 15
  Max. Size: Draft 10 m. Tankers: Draft 10.0 m. *Fuel:* Available.
  Airport: Lautiosaari.
Kenai, Alaska, U.S.A.: 60.33 N. 151.16 W. 54
  Also see Nikiski.
Kendari, Indonesia: 3.58 S. 122.36 E. 46, 47
  Max. Size: LOA 120 m., draft 9.0 m. *Fuel:* Available.
  Airport: 25 km.
Kenitra, Morocco: 34.17 N. 6.30 W. 21, 27
  Max. Size: Depth 4.20 m. – 5.40 m. *Fuel:* Diesel, gas oil
  and petrol. *Airport:* Rabat-Sale.
Kenje, Gabon: 0.31 N. 9.36 E. 29

40

Kenmare, Ireland: 51.52 N. 9.35 W. 5
Kennedy, see Thursday Island.
Kenny, see Port Kenny.
Kenosha, Wisconsin, U.S.A.: 42.35 N. 87.50 W. 62
Kent Terminal, U.K.: 51.26 N. 0.43 E. 6
  Max. Size: LOA 200 m., 45,000 tonnes displacement,
  depth of channel 11.0 m.
  Also see Medway Ports.
KENYA 30
Keos Is., Greece 25
Keppel Harbour, see Singapore.
Keppel Terminal, see Singapore.
Kerain, see Norrkoping.
Kerama, Papua New Guinea: 7.58 S. 145.47 E. 46
Keramotis, Greece: 40.52 N. 24.42 E. 25
Kerasunda, see Giresun.
Keratsini, see Piraeus.
Kerawalapitiya Terminal, Sri Lanka: 7.01 N. 79.50 E. 37
  Max. Size: 20,000 cu.m., LOA 165 m., draft 7 m.
Kerch, Ukraine: 45.21 N. 36.29 E. 21, 26
  Max. Size: Draft 7.8 m. *Dry Docks:* Floating docks (2),
  8,500 tonnes maximum lifting capacity. *Airport:* Local 6 km.,
  international 300 km.
Kerchensky Strait, Russia 26
Keret, Russia: 66.17 N. 33.34 E. 16
Keri, (Zante Is.), Greece: 37.39 N. 20.49 E. 25
Kerkenna Is., Tunisia: 34.45 N. 11.15 E. 24
Kerkira, Greece: 39.37 N. 19.56 E. 21, 24, 25
  Max. Size: Draft 7.5 m. *Fuel:* Diesel. *Airport:* 2 km.
  Also see Corfu.
Kermadec Islands, New Zealand 49
Kertapati, see Palembang.
Kerteh Port, Malaya, Malaysia: 4.36 N. 103.28 E. 40
  Max. Size: 40,000 d.w.t., LOA 210 m., draft 10.5 m.
  Airport: 10 km.
Kerteh Terminal, Malaya, Malaysia: 4.31 N. 103.33 E. ... 38, 39, 40
  Max. Size: Tankers: Petronas – 85,000 d.w.t. (part load),
  draft 11 m., LOA 265 m., beam 38 m. Esso – 140,000 d.w.t. –
  250,000 d.w.t. (Max. 140,000 d.w.t. from November to March),
  draft 57 ft. – 67 ft., depth 85 ft. – 92 ft.
Kerteminde, Denmark: 55.27 N. 10.40 E. 12
Kesennuma, Japan: 38.53 N. 141.35 E. 43
  Max. Size: 5,000 d.w.t. Depth 6.0 m. – 7.5 m.
Kesklinna, see Vanasadam.
Keta, Ghana: 5.53 N. 1.00 E. 28
Ketapang, Indonesia: 1.50 S. 109.58 E. 38
Ketchikan, Alaska, U.S.A.: 55.20 N. 131.38 W. 56
  Max. Size: Largest vessel 26,000 tons. Depths up to 45 ft. (LW).
  Fuel: No. 2 diesel and gasoline available. *Dry Docks:* Floating
  dock with length 434 ft. *Airport:* Daily flights to and from Seattle.
Keti Bandar, Pakistan: 24.10 N. 67.25 E. 37
Kew, (Caicos), Turks and Caicos Is. (U.K.): 21.55 N. 71.55 W. ... 70
Kewaunee, Wisconsin, U.S.A.: 44.28 N. 87.30 W. 62
Keweenaw Point, Michigan, U.S.A.: 47.26 N. 87.40 W. 62
Key Harbour, Ontario, Canada: 45.53 N. 80.45 W. 62
Key West, Florida, U.S.A.: 24.33 N. 81.48 W. 55, 66, 69, 70
Khaabarovsk, Russia: 48.31 N. 135.10 E. 43
Khabarovo, Russia: 69.35 N. 60.28 E. 16
Khalf, see Mukalla.
Khalid, see Sharjah.
Khalki Is., Greece: 36.15 N. 27.35 E. 25
Khamili Is., Greece: 35.52 N. 26.14 E. 25
Khamir, Iran: 26.58 N. 55.35 E. 35
Khanom, Thailand: 9.12 N. 99.54 E. 37, 39
  Max. Size: 25,000 d.w.t., draft up to 9.76 m.
Kharg Island, Iran: 29.14 N. 50.19 E. 31, 35
  Max. Size: Kharg Terminal: 500,000 d.w.tonnes, depth 32 m.
  Khemco Terminal: Depth 39 ft. Dorood Terminal: Depth 65 ft.
  Fuel: Available at Dorood Terminal.
Khatyrka, Russia: 62.05 N. 175.15 E. 54
Khemco Terminal, see Kharg Island.
Kherson, Ukraine: 46.37 N. 32.37 E. 21, 26
  Max. Size: LOA 200 m., draft in Channel 7.6 m. Depth at berths
  8.25 m. Tankers: Draft 7.5 m.
Khios Is., Greece: 38.22 N. 26.09 E. 25, 26
Khiri Khan, Thailand: 11.50 N. 99.40 E. 39
Kholmsk, Russia: 47.03 N. 142.03 E. 43
  Max. Size: Draft 6 m. LOA 105 m.
Khor al Zubair, Iraq: 30.12 N. 47.53 E. 35
  Max. Size: Draft 10.0 m. *Fuel:* Available.
Khor Dubai, see Dubai.
Khor el Mufatta, Kuwait: 28.39 N. 48.23 E. 35
Khor Fakkan, Sharjah, U.A.E.: 25.22 N. 56.22 E. 31, 35, 37
  Max. Size: Draft 15 m. *Fuel:* Available. *Airport:* Sharjah and
  Dubai International.
Khor Khuwair, see Mina Saqr.
Khor Musa, Iran: 30.27 N. 49.19 E. 35
Khor Musa Lightship, Iran: 29.37 N. 49.34 E. 35

Khor-al-Amaya, Iraq: 29.47 N. 48.49 E. 35
  Max. Size: 330,000 d.w.t. loading part cargo, LOA 1,200 ft.,
  draft 69 ft.
Khorly, see Port Khorly.
Khorramshahr, Iran: 30.26 N. 48.10 E. 31, 35
  Max. Size: 2,000 d.w.t.
Khulna, see Mongla.
Kiabo Marine Terminal, Angola: 7.20 S. 12.35 E. 28
  Max. Size: 150,000 d.w.t., depth 250 ft.
Kiame, Angola: 7.20 S. 12.23 E. 28
  Max. Size: Depth 142 m.
Kichiga, Russia: 59.50 N. 163.08 E. 54
Kiel, Germany: 54.19 N. 10.10 E. 10, 11, 12, 14
  Max. Size: For Nordhafen and ships passing Canal, 235 m. LOA,
  32.5 m. beam, 7.0 m. draft; (FW) Max. LOA in Kiel Port 245 m.
  Depth in Harbour: Scheerhafen 10.0 m. *Fuel:* All grades.
  Dry Docks: Floating Dock No. 2: 164 m. x 35 m.
  Airport: Kiel. Hamburg approx. 90 km.
Kiel Bay, Germany 12, 14
Kiel Canal, Germany: 54.19 N. 10.10 E. 8, 10, 11, 12, 14
  Also see Kiel.
Kieta, Papua New Guinea: 6.13 S. 155.38 E. 49
  Max. Size: Depth at LAT 8.5 m. *Fuel:* Diesel by road tanker.
  Airport: Aropa Airport, 19 km. (international).
Kihnu Is., Estonia: 58.07 N. 23.58 E. 11
Kii Channel, Japan 43, 45
Kiire, Japan: 31.23 N. 130.32 E. 45
  Max. Size: LOA 450 m., draft 30.6 m., 500,000 d.w.t.
  Fuel: Domestic oil from Kagoshima, bonded oil from Moji.
  Airport: 2 hours by car, domestic.
Kijang, Indonesia: 0.51 N. 104.37 E. 38, 39, 40
  Max. Size: LOA 185 m., draft 11 m., beam 28 m.
  Airport: 9 miles from Kijang.
Kikchik, Russia: 53.35 N. 156.00 E. 43, 54
Kikori, Papua New Guinea: 7.45 S. 144.15 E. 46
Kikuma, Japan: 34.03 N. 132.51 E. 45
  Max. Size: Dolphin: 88,500 d.w.t., LOA 250 m., draft 14.5 m.
  Sea Berth: 132,700 d.w.t., LOA 280 m., draft 20 m.
  Fuel: By barge from Hanshin and Kanmon area.
  Airport: Nearest Matsuyama, 50 km.
Kilchoan, U.K.: 56.40 N. 6.10 W. 5
Kildonan, U.K.: 55.27 N. 5.07 W. 6
Kilia, Ukraine: 45.26 N. 29.17 E. 9, 26
  Max. Size: Draft 7.0 m. *Fuel:* Available with notice.
Kilifi, Kenya: 3.40 S. 39.50 E. 30
Kilindini, see Mombasa.
Kilkee, Ireland: 52.41 N. 9.40 W. 5, 8
Kilkeel, U.K.: 54.03 N. 6.00 W. 5
Kill van Kull, see New York.
Killala, Ireland: 54.14 N. 9.13 W. 5
Killarney, Ontario, Canada: 45.57 N. 81.31 W. 62
Killary Harbour, Ireland: 53.37 N. 9.51 W. 5
Killingholme, U.K.: 53.39 N. 0.13 W. 6, 7
  Max. Size: LOA 800 ft. *Fuel:* Available.
  Also see Immingham.
Killini, Greece: 37.56 N. 21.09 E. 24, 25
Killorglin, see Castlemaine Harbour.
Killybegs, Ireland: 54.38 N. 8.26 W. 5
  Max. Size: Depth 7.5 m. *Fuel:* Fuel oil available.
Kilmore Quay, Ireland: 52.11 N. 6.35 W. 5
Kilondoni, Tanzania: 7.56 S. 39.50 E. 30
Kilronan, (Aran Is.), Ireland: 53.07 N. 9.07 W. 5
  Max. Size: Depth 5.5 m. (Springs).
Kilroot, see Belfast.
Kilrush, Ireland: 52.37 N. 9.30 W. 5, 8
  Max. Size: LOA 75 m. *Fuel:* Available.
  Airport: Shannon, 40 km.
Kiltan Is., (Laccadive Is.), India: 11.24 N. 73.00 E. 37
Kilwa Kisiwani, Tanzania: 8.57 S. 39.33 E. 30
Kilwa Kivinje, Tanzania: 8.45 S. 39.25 E. 30
Kilwa Masoko, Tanzania: 8.55 S. 39.32 E. 30
Kimbe, Papua New Guinea: 5.33 S. 150.09 E. 46
  Max. Size: Depth at LAT 15.0 m. *Fuel:* Diesel by road tanker.
  Airport: Hoskins, 50 km.
Kimchaek, North Korea: 40.37 N. 129.12 E. 43
Kimi, Greece: 38.38 N. 24.05 E. 25
Kimitsu, see Kisarazu.
Kimolos Is., Greece: 36.46 N. 24.35 E. 25
Kin Wan, (Okinawa), Japan: 26.22 N. 127.58 E. 42, 46
  Max. Size: Tankers: 500,000 d.w.t., depth 102 ft.
  Fuel: All grades. *Airport:* 2 hours by car to Naha Airport.
Kinaros Is., Greece: 36.58 N. 26.20 E. 25
Kincardine, Ontario, Canada: 44.10 N. 81.39 W. 62
King Abdul Aziz Port, see Dammam.
King Cove, Alaska, U.S.A.: 55.03 N. 162.19 W. 54
King Fahd Industrial Port, see Jubail.
King George Is., N.W.T., Canada: 57.20 N. 80.30 W. 59
King Is., Tas., Australia 50, 51
King Is., Alaska, U.S.A.: 64.58 N. 168.05 W. 54
King Sound, W.A., Australia 51

King's Lynn, U.K.: 52.45 N. 0.24 E. 5, 7
  Max. Size: LOA 96 m., beam 13.8 m., draft 5.5 m. on highest
  Spring tides. *Fuel:* Light-grade fuel oil, gas oil, petrol and
  paraffin. *Airport:* Heathrow, 100 miles. Norwich, 45 miles.
Kingisepp, see Roomassaare.
Kings Bay, (Spitsbergen), Norway 17
Kings Bay, Georgia, U.S.A.: 30.49 N. 81.31 W. 55, 66
Kingscote, S.A., Australia: 35.39 S. 137.38 E. 51
Kingsnorth, U.K.: 51.25 N. 0.36 E. 6
  Max. Size: LOA 229 m., depth 10 m. – 15.5 m.
  Also see Medway Ports.
Kingston, S.A., Australia: 36.50 S. 139.52 E. 50
Kingston, Ontario, Canada: 44.12 N. 76.30 W. 60, 62
  Max. Size: Max. depth alongside 17 ft. – 25 ft. *Fuel:* Bunker "C"
  and diesel. *Dry Docks:* Will take ships of LOA 210 ft.,
  beam 44 ft., depth on sill 13 ft.
Kingston, Jamaica: 17.59 N. 76.50 W. 69, 70
  Max. Size: Max. draft into Port Royal 40 ft.
  Main ship channel: Max. draft 39 ft. 6 in.
  Newport West: Max. draft 32 ft. 6 in.
  Esso Terminals: Max. draft 32 ft. 6 in.
  Newport East: Max. draft 27 ft. 6 in. *Fuel:* All grades.
  Dry Docks: Available. *Airport:* 10 miles.
Kingston, Norfolk Is. (Australia): 29.00 S. 168.00 E. 49
Kingston, New York, U.S.A.: 41.54 N. 73.58 W. 63
Kingstown, Ireland, see Dun Laoghaire.
Kingstown, St. Vincent: 13.09 N. 61.14 W. 69, 71, 72
  Max. Size: LOA 550 ft., draft 30 ft. *Fuel:* Available.
  Airport: 2 miles.
Kingsville, Ontario, Canada: 42.02 N. 82.44 W. 62
  Max. Size: Depth 4.6 m. – 5.5 m.
Kinlochbervie, U.K.: 58.26 N. 5.06 W. 5
Kinsale, Ireland: 51.42 N. 8.31 W. 5
  Max. Size: LOA 90 m., draft 5.0 m. (HW) and 3,000 d.w.t.
  Airport: Cork, 19 km.
Kinshasa, Congo (D.R. of): 4.22 S. 15.15 E. 28
Kintyre, U.K.: 55.15 N. 5.05 W. 5
Kinuura, Japan: 34.50 N. 136.56 E. 45
  Max. Size: Depth alongside 12.0 m. Bulk: Draft 11.4 m. – 11.8 m.
  Chemicals: Draft 10.5 m. *Fuel:* All grades of bonded bunkers
  are stocked in Tokyo Bay.
Kiparissia, Greece: 37.16 N. 21.40 E. 24, 25
Kipevu, see Mombasa.
Kira Kira, (San Cristobal Is.), Solomon Islands:
  10.27 S. 161.54 E. 49, 51
KIRIBATI 49
Kirillovka, Ukraine: 46.25 N. 35.00 E. 26
Kiriwina Is., see Trobriand Is..
Kirkcaldy, U.K.: 56.07 N. 3.09 W. 6
Kirkcudbright, U.K.: 54.50 N. 4.03 W. 5
Kirkenes, Norway: 69.43 N. 30.03 E. 10, 16
  Max. Size: Oil carriers: 20,000 d.w.t., draft 33 ft. Iron ore
  carriers: 120,000 d.w.t., sailing draft 51 ft. under optimal
  conditions. *Fuel:* Heavy fuel, 7 days notice.
  Dry Docks: Floating dock, capacity 8,500 tons. *Airport:* 16 km.
Kirkwall, (Orkney Is.), U.K.: 58.59 N. 2.58 W. 4, 5
  Max. Size: Depth 5 m. *Fuel:* By road tanker.
  Airport: Domestic, 4 miles.
Kisarazu, Japan: 35.22 N. 139.52 E. 44, 45
  Max. Size: 310,000 d.w.t., draft 7.5 m. – 18.0 m., depending on
  berth. *Fuel:* All grades of bonded bunkers are stocked in Tokyo
  Bay. *Airport:* Narita (Toyko) is about 2 hours by car.
  Also see Chiba.
Kishinev, Moldova: 47.00 N. 28.50 E. 9
Kishiwada, see Hannan Port.
Kishon, see Haifa.
Kisiju, Tanzania: 7.20 S. 39.20 E. 30
Kiska Is., Alaska, U.S.A.: 51.58 N. 177.33 E. 54
Kismayu, see Chisimaio.
Kistrand, Norway: 70.24 N. 25.13 E. 15
Kita Is., (Daito Is.), Japan: 25.56 N. 131.18 E. 46
Kita Iwo, (Japan): 25.45 N. 141.19 E. 46
Kitakyushu, see Moji.
Kitee, see Saimaa Canal.
Kithira Is., Greece 25
Kithnos Is., (Cyclades), Greece 25
Kitimat, B.C., Canada: 53.59 N. 128.46 W. 56
  Max. Size: LOA 680 ft. (207 m.), beam 90 ft. (27.4 m.), draft 36 ft.
  (11 m.) *Fuel:* Available. *Airport:* Eight flights daily from Terrace
  (40 miles distant) to Vancouver.
Kitsuki, Japan: 33.28 N. 131.35 E. 45
Kitty Hawk, North Carolina, U.S.A.: 36.20 N. 75.50 W. . . 63
Kivalina, Alaska, U.S.A.: 67.48 N. 164.45 W. 54
  Also see Red Dog.
Kivik, Sweden: 55.40 N. 14.15 E. 11, 12
Kjerringoy, Norway: 67.31 N. 14.46 E. 15
Kjollefjord, Norway: 70.58 N. 27.20 E. 15
Kjopsvik, Norway: 68.06 N. 16.21 E. 15
Klagshamn, Sweden: 55.31 N. 12.54 E. 12

Klaipeda, Lithuania: 55.43 N. 21.07 E. 4, 10, 11
  Max. Size: LOA 200 m., draft 10.6 m. Tankers: Draft 10.5 m.
  Fuel: By barge. *Dry Docks:* 3 floating docks, lifting capacity
  up to 27,000 tons. *Airport:* At Palanga, 25 km.
Klakksvik, Faroe Is. (Denmark): 62.14 N. 6.35 W. 5, 15
  Max. Size: Up to 560 ft. LOA, draft 25 ft. *Fuel:* Diesel. *Airport:*
  Nearest airport on Vagoy, about 6 hours travelling.
Klang, see Port Klang.
Klang Baram, see Miri.
Klang Niah, see Miri.
Klang Suai, see Miri.
Klemtu, B.C., Canada: 52.36 N. 128.31 W. 56
Kleven, see Mandal.
Klintehamn, Sweden: 57.23 N. 18.11 E. 11
  Max. Size: Depth 5.0 m. *Fuel:* Available.
Knebel, Denmark: 56.13 N. 10.30 E. 12
Knysna, South Africa: 34.02 S. 23.03 E. 30
Ko Si Chang, Thailand: 13.08 N. 100.50 E. 39
  Max. Size: 100,000 d.w.t., LOA 280 m., draft 14.8 m.
Koartac, Quebec, Canada: 61.00 N. 69.39 W. 59
Kobe, Japan: 34.40 N. 135.12 E. 43, 44, 45, 46
  Max. Size: Draft 11.50 m. for cargo vessels.
  Container: Depth 15.0 m. Tankers: 70,000 d.w.t., LOA 250 m.,
  draft 12.73 m. *Fuel:* All grades supplied by barge.
  Dry Docks: Largest: Length 290 m., width 41.2 m., depth 13.0 m.
  Capacity 150,000 d.w.t. *Airport:* Osaka.
Kobenhavn, see Copenhagen.
Koblenz, Germany: 50.21 N. 7.36 E. 7, 9
Kochi, Japan: 33.31 N. 133.34 E. 45, 46
  Max. Size: LOA 140 m., draft 7.0 m. *Fuel:* Bonded oil from
  Kobe, etc. *Airport:* Kochi, 30 km.
Kodgubi Is., see Tobi.
Kodiak, Alaska, U.S.A.: 57.47 N. 152.24 W. 54, 79
  Max. Size: Depth 38 ft. (MLLW). *Fuel:* Light fuels only.
  Airport: Local, 5 miles.
Koge, Denmark: 55.27 N. 12.12 E. 11, 12
  Max. Size: LOA 180 m., beam 25 m., draft 6.7 m.
  Fuel: Available. *Airport:* Copenhagen, about 40 km.
Kogo, see Puerto Iradier.
Kogushi, Japan: 34.08 N. 130.50 E. 44
Kohani, see Mkoani.
Koja, see Botea.
Koje Is., South Korea 42
Kojiro, Japan: 32.25 N. 130.24 E. 45
Kokkola, Finland: 63.50 N. 23.08 E. 10, 15
  Max. Size: Draft 13 m. *Fuel:* Available.
  Airport: Kokkola, 19 km.
Koko, Nigeria: 6.01 N. 5.29 E. 29
  Max. Size: Wharf length, 137 m., draft at Escravos River Bar
  6.4 m. (10 m. planned). Draft at berth 7.32 m. *Fuel:* By barge.
Kokonau, Indonesia: 4.43 S. 136.26 E. 46
Kokopo, see Rabaul.
Kokura, Japan: 33.54 N. 130.53 E. 44, 45
  Max. Size: Draft 11.0 m. Tankers: Draft 6.5 m. *Fuel:* All grades
  of bonded bunkers. *Dry Docks:* Max. size: LOA 160 m., beam
  22.5 m., draft 5.5 m. *Airport:* Fukuoka or Kitakyushu.
Kola, Russia: 68.52 N. 33.01 E. 16
Kola Inlet, Russia 16
Kolachel, India: 8.10 N. 77.15 E. 37
Kolberg, see Kolobrzeg.
Kolby Kas, Denmark: 55.49 N. 10.31 E. 12
Kolding, Denmark: 55.29 N. 9.30 E. 11, 12
  Max. Size: LOA 180 m., depth 7.0 m. *Fuel:* Available.
  Airport: Billund Airport, 40 km.
Kole, Cameroon: 4.13 N. 8.33 E. 29
  Max. Size: Draft 22 m. (72 ft.).
Kolguyev Is., Russia: 69.20 N. 48.30 E. 16
Koliuchin Bay, Russia 54
Kolkata, India: 22.32 N. 88.22 E. 37
  Max. Size: Max. LOA 565 ft., beam 80 ft., draft 8.70 m.
  Tankers: Budge Budge: LOA 620 ft., draft 9.0 m.
  Fuel: Redwood 600/700 sec. supplied at Kolkata. Fuel also
  supplied at Budge Budge Terminal. *Dry Docks:* 5 dry docks.
  Largest 596 ft. x 80 ft. x 22 ft. (Length/beam of vessel
  allowed: 565 ft. x 75 ft.). *Airport:* 12 miles.
Kollefjord, Faroe Is. (Denmark): 62.06 N. 6.55 W. 5, 15
Kolo, Sweden: 56.09 N. 14.43 E. 12
  Max. Size: LOA 260 m., draft 13.5 m., depth 14.0 m.
  Fuel: Available.
  Also see Karlshamn.
Kolobrzeg, Poland: 54.11 N. 15.35 E. 11
Kolonodale, Indonesia: 1.59 S. 121.20 E. 46
Kolpos Kallonis, (Lesbos), Greece: 39.05 N. 26.05 E. . . . 25
Kolskiy Peninsula, Russia 16
Komandorski Islands, Russia 54
Komatsushima, see Tokushima-Komatsushima.
Kompongsom, see Sihanoukville.
Komsomolsk, Russia: 50.32 N. 136.59 E. 43
Konakri, see Conakry.
Konertino, see Rene.

Kongmoon, see Jiangmen.
Kongsdal, Denmark: 56.40 N. 10.04 E. 12
Kongshavn, Faroe Is. (Denmark): 62.07 N. 6.44 W. 5, 15
Kongsmoen, Norway: 67.54 N. 12.25 E. 15
Konigsberg, see Kaliningrad.
Koolan Island, see Yampi Sound.
Koper, Slovenia: 45.31 N. 13.44 E. 9, 24
  Max. Size: Draft: General cargo 12 m., coal/ore 17.2 m.,
  grain 14.5 m., containers 11.2 m., tankers 12 m., fertiliser 14 m.
  Fuel: Fuel oil, gas oil and diesel oil. *Dry Docks:* 20,000 d.w.t.
  Airport: Ljubljana 120 km., Trieste 80 km., Venice 140 km.,
  Portoroz 20 km. and Pula (Croatia) 100 km.
Kopervik, Norway: 59.17 N. 5.19 E. 10, 11
  Max. Size: Depth 5 m. – 8 m. *Fuel:* Available.
  Airport: Haugesund and Karmoy.
  Also see Haugesund and Skudeneshavn.
Koping, Sweden: 59.30 N. 16.01 E. 11
  Max. Size: Draft 7.0 m. via Sodertalje, 5.65 m. via Stockholm.
  Fuel: Available.
Kopli, see Tallinn.
Kopmanholmen, Sweden: 63.10 N. 18.37 E. 15
Kopparverket, see Helsingborg.
Korea Bay 42
Korea Strait 42, 43, 44, 45
KOREA, DEMOCRATIC PEOPLE'S REPUBLIC OF . . 42, 43
KOREA, REPUBLIC OF 42, 43
Korf, Russia: 60.18 N. 165.22 E. 54, 79
Korido, Indonesia: 0.50 S. 135.35 E. 46
Korim, Indonesia: 0.55 S. 136.04 E. 46
Korisia, (Keos Is.), Greece: 37.39 N. 24.20 E. 25
Korkula, Croatia: 42.58 N. 17.09 E. 24
Koroni, Greece: 36.48 N. 21.57 E. 25
Koror, see Malakal.
Korpo, Finland: 60.15 N. 21.45 E. 11
Korsakov, Russia: 46.37 N. 142.45 E. 43
  Max. Size: Depth 5 m. – 8.5 m.
  Also see Vladivostok.
Korsnes, Norway: 68.15 N. 16.05 E. 15
Korsor, Denmark: 55.20 N. 11.08 E. 11, 12
  Max. Size: LOA 225 m., draft 7.5 m. *Fuel:* By road tanker.
  Dry Docks: Slipway 600 tons.
  Airport: Nearest Copenhagen, 40 miles.
Kos, (Kos Is.), Greece: 36.54 N. 27.16 E. 25, 26
Koshiki Is., Japan 45
Kosichang, see Ko Si Chang.
Kosong, North Korea: 39.00 N. 127.50 E. 42, 43
Kosseir, see Quseir.
Kosulanniemi, see Saimaa Canal.
Kota Bahru, Malaya, Malaysia: 6.08 N. 102.15 E. . . . 38, 39
Kota Baru, Indonesia: 3.14 S. 116.13 E. 38
Kota Kinabalu, Sabah, Malaysia: 5.59 N. 116.00 E. . 38, 39, 47
  Max. Size: 20,000 d.w.t. Depth alongside 9.10 m.
  Tankers: Draft 22 ft. Sapangar Bay: 30,000 d.w.t., LOA 815 ft.,
  draft 36 ft. *Airport:* 4 km. – 10 km.
Kotadabok, see Dabo.
Kotka, Finland: 60.28 N. 26.57 E. 10, 11, 13
  Max. Size: Draft 15.3 m. *Fuel:* All grades.
  Dry Docks: Largest accepts vessels, LOA 165 m., beam 28 m.,
  draft 7.8 m./12,000 tons. *Airport:* Helsinki-Vantaa, 140 km.
Kotlik, Alaska, U.S.A.: 63.02 N. 163.35 W. 54
Kotor, Yugoslavia: 42.27 N. 18.36 E. 24
  Max. Size: Draft 7.5 m. *Fuel:* By road tanker.
  Dry Docks: Lifting capacity 10,000 tonnes – 33,000 tonnes.
  Airport: Tivat, 5 km.
Kotzebue, Alaska, U.S.A.: 66.54 N. 162.36 W. 54
Kotzebue Sound, Alaska, U.S.A. 54
Kouaoua, New Caledonia (France): 21.24 S. 165.50 E. . . 51
  Max. Size: LOA 150 m., draft 8.5 m.
  Also see Noumea.
Kouilou, Congo (Rep. of): 4.28 S. 11.39 E. 28
Kourou, Guyane (France): 5.09 N. 52.40 W. 76
  Also see Degrad-des-Cannes.
Koutalas, (Serifos Is.), Greece: 37.08 N. 24.27 E. 25
Kovda, Russia: 66.41 N. 32.52 E. 16
Koverhar, Finland: 59.52 N. 23.13 E. 11
  Max. Size: Draft 30 ft., LOA 200 m., beam 30 m.
Kowloon, see Hong Kong.
Kozlu, see Zonguldak.
Kozu Is., Japan: 34.14 N. 139.14 E. 45
Kpeme, Togo: 6.12 N. 1.30 E. 29
  Max. Size: Tankers: Draft 27 ft. Bulk carriers: Draft 38 ft. (sailing),
  LOA up to 225 m. *Airport:* Lome.
Krabi, Thailand: 8.04 N. 98.44 E. 37, 38
  Max. Size: Depth 13 m. – 14 m. *Airport:* Phuket.
Kragenaes, Denmark: 54.55 N. 11.22 E. 12, 14
Kragero, Norway: 58.52 N. 9.25 E. 11, 12
  Max. Size: Draft 30 ft. *Fuel:* May be available. *Airport:*
  Kristiansand 170 km. Oslo 200 km.
Krakow, Poland: 50.03 N. 19.55 E. 9

Kralendijk, (Bonaire), Netherlands Antilles:
  12.09 N. 68.17 W. 69, 72, 74
  Max. Size: LOA 1,050 ft. Depth alongside 40 ft.
  Salina: 70,000 d.w.t., depth 45 ft. *Fuel:* Gas oil.
  Airport: Flights from Bonaire to Curacao.
Kraljevica, see Krikvenica.
Kramfors, Sweden: 62.55 N. 17.45 E. 15
Krasino, Russia: 70.50 N. 54.55 E. 16
Krasnogorsk, Russia: 48.05 N. 141.25 E. 43
Krefeld, Germany: 51.20 N. 6.34 E. 7, 8
  Max. Size: Depth 4 m. *Fuel:* Available.
  Airport: Dusseldorf, 26 km.
Kribi, Cameroon: 2.56 N. 9.54 E. 28, 29
  Max. Size: Anchorage – no restrictions.
  Also see Douala.
Krikvenica, Croatia: 45.15 N. 14.35 E. 24
Krionerion, Greece: 38.21 N. 21.36 E. 25
Krishnapatnam, India: 14.17 N. 80.06 E. 37
Kristiansand S., Norway: 58.09 N. 8.00 E. 10, 11, 12
  Max. Size: Depths alongside up to 39 ft. (MLW).
  Fuel: All grades. *Dry Docks:* Length 689 ft., entrance width 95.9
  ft., depth 25 ft., up to 13,000 d.w.t. *Airport:* 17 km.
Kristiansund N., Norway: 63.07 N. 7.45 E. 4, 10, 15
  Max. Size: Draft 4.5 m. – 15 m. *Fuel:* All grades. *Airport:*
  Connects with Oslo and Bergen.
Kristinehamn, Sweden: 59.19 N. 14.07 E. 11, 12
  Max. Size: As for Trollhatte Canal: LOA 88 m., beam 13.1 m.,
  draft 5.3 m. *Fuel:* By road tanker. *Airport:* Karlstad, 45 km.
Kristinestad, Finland: 62.16 N. 21.23 E. 10, 11, 15
  Max. Size: General cargo and timber: 20 ft. depth in old port.
  Tankers: Depth 33 ft. Coal harbour: Depth 12.0 m.
  Fuel: Available. *Airport:* Vaasa and Pori, 100 km.
Krk, Croatia: 45.05 N. 14.38 E. 24
Krokstrand, Sweden: 59.00 N. 11.27 E. 11, 12
Kronshtadt, Russia: 60.00 N. 29.45 E. 10, 11
Krueng Geukeuh, see Lhokseumawe.
Krueng Raya, see Malahayati.
Krui, Indonesia: 5.11 S. 103.56 E. 38
Kuala Baram, see Miri.
Kuala Belait, Brunei: 4.38 N. 114.11 E. 39
  Also see Seria.
Kuala Beukah, Indonesia: 4.53 N. 97.57 E. 37, 38, 40
  Max. Size: 90,000 d.w.t., LOA 220 m., depth 25 m.
Kuala Enok, Indonesia: 0.31 S. 103.23 E. 40
  Max. Size: 50,000 tonnes d.w.t., LOA 225 m., draft 8.5 m.
Kuala Kapuas, Indonesia: 3.00 S. 114.23 E. 38
Kuala Niah, see Niah.
Kuala Pahang, see Pahang.
Kuala Rompin, see Rompin.
Kuala Suai, see Suai.
Kuala Tanjung, Indonesia: 3.22 N. 99.28 E. 37, 38, 39, 40
  Max. Size: Depth 9 m.
Kuala Terengganu, Malaysia: 5.21 N. 103.08 E. . . . 38, 39, 40
Kualalangsa, Indonesia: 4.31 N. 98.00 E. 38, 40
Kuandang, Indonesia: 0.51 N. 122.55 E. 46
Kuang Chou, see Guangzhou.
Kuantan, Malaya, Malaysia: 3.58 N. 103.26 E. . . . 38, 39, 40
  Max. Size: LOA 200 m., draft 11.2 m.
  Tankers: (Palm, minerals and oil) LOA 250 m., draft 11.5 m.
  Fuel: Diesel. *Airport:* Domestic, 25 miles (41 km.).
Kubikenborg, Sweden: 62.23 N. 17.22 E. 11
  Max. Size: LOA 192 m., draft 10.5 m.
  Also see Sundsvall.
Kuching, Sarawak, Malaysia: 1.34 N. 110.21 E. 38, 39
  Max. Size: Senari: LOA 200 m., draft 9.3 m. Baiwak Wharf,
  Pending Point: LOA 110 m., draft 6.4 m. Pelabuhan Datuk Sim
  Kheng Hong (Pending): LOA 175 m., draft 7.62 m.
  Sejingkat Terminal: LOA 115 m., draft 5.0 m.
  Fuel: High-speed diesel fuel oil.
  Airport: 10 km. from Pending Terminal.
Kuchinotsu, Japan: 32.36 N. 130.11 E. 45
Kudamatsu, Japan: 34.00 N. 131.52 E. 43, 45
  Max. Size: Draft 9.5 m. Tankers: Draft 19 m., 178,000 d.w.t.
  Fuel: All grades of marine oil. *Dry Docks:* Largest – Length
  243.8 m., breadth 44.8 m., draft 6.4 m., capacity 90,000 d.w.t.
  Airport: Ube and Hiroshima.
Kudat, Sabah, Malaysia: 6.53 N. 117.51 E. 38
  Max. Size: Depth 6.4 m., 3,000 d.w.t.
Kuito Marine Terminal, Angola: 5.27 S. 11.22 E. 28
  Max. Size: 320,000 tonnes d.w.t., LOA 1,150 ft., depth 400 m.
Kumai, Indonesia: 2.45 S. 111.43 E. 38
Kume Is., Japan: 26.24 N. 126.45 E. 42, 46
Kumkale, Turkey: 40.03 N. 26.15 E. 25, 26
Kumlinge, Finland: 60.15 N. 20.45 E. 11
Kumnyong, (Quelpart Is.), South Korea: 33.30 N. 126.45 E. . . 42
Kumport, see Ambarli.
Kumpusalmi, see Saimaa Canal.
Kumta, India: 14.26 N. 74.24 E. 37
Kumul Marine Terminal, Papua New Guinea:
  8.06 S. 144.34 E. 46, 51
  Max. Size: 150,000 d.w.t., draft 17.1 m.

Kunak, Sabah, Malaysia: 4.41 N. 118.15 E. **38, 47**
   Max. Size: 28,000 d.w.t., depth 35 ft.
Kunashir Is., (Kurile Is.), Russia **43**
Kunda, Estonia: 59.31 N. 26.33 E. **11**
Kundapura, see Coondapur.
Kungsbacka, Sweden: 57.29 N. 12.05 E. **12**
Kungshamn, see Smogen.
Kungsor, Sweden: 59.26 N. 16.06 E. **11**
Kunsan, South Korea: 36.00 N. 126.42 E. **42, 46**
   Max. Size: Depth 7 m. – 10 m. *Fuel:* HFO and DO.
   Airport: 5 km.
Kuntaur, Gambia: 13.40 N. 14.52 W. **27**
   Max. Size: Loaded draft 17 ft. 6 in.
   Also see Banjul.
Kuop Is., see Truk Is..
Kuopio, Finland: 62.52 N. 27.31 E. **13**
   Also see Saimaa Canal.
Kupang, Indonesia: 10.10 S. 123.35 E. **46, 50**
Kupiano, Papua New Guinea: 10.06 S. 148.05 E. . . . **46**
Kure, Japan: 34.14 N. 132.32 E. **45**
   Max. Size: 276,000 d.w.t., LOA 360 m., draft 17.4 m. with tide.
   Fuel: Most grades of domestic oil are available.
   Dry Docks: Repair dock: 69,000 g.r.t.
   Building dock: 251,000 g.r.t. *Airport:* Hiroshima, 35 km.
Kuressaare, see Roomassaare.
Kurgan, Russia: 64.45 N. 173.00 E. **54**
Kuria Muria Is., Oman: 17.30 N. 56.00 E. **31, 37**
Kurihama, see Uraga.
Kuril Strait, Russia **54**
Kurile Islands, Russia **43**
Kurilsk, Russia: 45.15 N. 147.50 E. **43**
Kurkurah, Libya: 31.30 N. 20.00 E. **24**
Kurnell, see Botany Bay.
Kusadasi, Turkey: 37.52 N. 27.16 E. **25, 26**
Kusaie Is., (Caroline Is.), Micronesia: 5.20 N. 162.58 E. . **49**
Kusanartoq, Greenland (Denmark): 61.45 N. 42.15 W. . **17**
Kushan, China: 39.50 N. 123.32 E. **42**
Kushikino, Japan: 31.42 N. 130.16 E. **45**
Kushiro, Japan: 42.58 N. 144.21 E. **43**
   Max. Size: 40,000 d.w.t., depth 12 m.
   Fuel: Domestic oil available. Bonded oil from Hakodate, etc.
   Airport: 40 minutes by road.
   Also see Hakodate.
Kushunnai, see Ilinskiy.
Kuskokwim Bay, see Kwigillingok.
Kutdlek, Greenland (Denmark): 62.30 N. 42.12 W. . . **17**
Kuto, see Isle of Pines.
Kutubidia, see Chittagong.
Kutubu, see Kumul Marine Terminal.
KUWAIT **31, 35**
Kuwait Harbour, see Shuwaikh.
Kuzkin Is., Russia: 72.50 N. 78.45 E. **16**
Kuzomen, Russia: 66.20 N. 36.50 E. **16**
Kvalsund, Norway: 70.30 N. 24.00 E. **15**
Kvarnholmen, see Stockholm.
Kvinesdal, Norway: 58.17 N. 6.58 E. **11, 12**
Kwa Iboe, see Qua Iboe.
Kwai Chung, Hong Kong (SAR), China: 22.21 N. 114.08 E. . **48**
Kwajalein, Marshall Is.: 8.43 N. 167.44 E. **49**
Kwan Tong, Hong Kong (SAR), China: 22.19 N. 114.13 E. . **48**
Kwangchow, see Guangzhou.
Kwangyang, South Korea: 34.54 N. 127.45 E. **42**
   Max. Size: 250,000 d.w.t., depth 20.0 m.
   Also see Yosu.
Kwatisore, Indonesia: 3.10 S. 134.59 E. **46**
Kwethluk, Alaska, U.S.A.: 60.30 N. 161.10 W. **54**
Kwigillingok, Alaska, U.S.A.: 59.45 N. 163.00 W. . . . **54**
Kwiguk, Alaska, U.S.A.: 62.44 N. 164.30 W. **54**
Kwinana, W.A., Australia: 32.15 S. 115.47 E. **50**
   Max. Size: Tankers: LOA 275 m., depth 14.7 m. (LWOST).
   Alumina: LOA 200 m., draft 11.0 m. Caustic: LOA 200 m.,
   draft 11.2 m. *Fuel:* Available.
   Also see Fremantle.
Kyaikkami, Myanmar: 16.02 N. 97.55 E. **37**
Kyaukpyu, Myanmar: 19.26 N. 93.34 E. **37**
Kyle of Lochalsh, U.K.: 57.17 N. 5.44 W. **5**
Kyleakin, see Kyle of Lochalsh.
Kymassi, Greece: 38.49 N. 23.32 E. **25**
   Max. Size: Draft 26 ft. 6 in.
Kyndby, Denmark: 55.49 N. 11.53 E. **11, 12**
   Max. Size: Oil Berth: Depth 21 ft. 6 in., LOA 570 ft.
   Coal Berth: Depth 23 ft. *Fuel:* Available by trucks or barge
   from Copenhagen. *Airport:* 40 miles to Copenhagen.
Kyomipo, North Korea: 38.44 N. 125.38 E. **42**
Kyrenia, Cyprus: 35.20 N. 33.19 E. **26**
   Max. Size: LOA 110 m., draft 7 m. *Fuel:* By road tanker.
   Airport: Ercan, 25 miles.
KYRGYZSTAN **9**
Kyushu Is., Japan **43, 44, 45**

L

L'Aberwrach, France: 48.36 N. 4.33 W. **7, 19**
L'Anse, Michigan, U.S.A.: 46.45 N. 88.28 W. **62**
L'Esperance Rock, (Kermadec Is.), New Zealand:
   31.30 S. 178.36 W. **49**
L'Estaque, see Marseilles.
L.O.O.P. Terminal, Louisiana, U.S.A.: 28.53 N. 90.01 W. . **55, 66, 67**
   Max. Size: Draft 96.3 ft. *Fuel:* Can be arranged privately.
   Airport: New Orleans, 90 miles.
La Albufera, Spain: 39.20 N. 0.16 W. **22**
La Calle, Algeria: 36.55 N. 8.27 E. **24**
La Callera, see Mazarron.
La Ceiba, Honduras: 15.47 N. 86.47 W. **69**
   Max. Size: Draft 6.7 m. *Airport:* Local airport, or San Pedro
   Sula, 200 km.
La Ceiba, Venezuela: 9.28 N. 71.04 W. **72, 74**
   Max. Size: Approach channel dredged to 9 m. LOA 120 m.
   Airport: Maracaibo.
La Chimba Cove, see Antofagasta.
La Chiva, see Antilla.
La Ciotat, France: 43.10 N. 5.36 E. **9**
   Max. Size: Largest vessel: LOA 380 m., beam 60 m.,
   draft 7.5 m. *Fuel:* Available. *Airport:* Marseilles, 55 km.
La Coruna, see Corunna.
La Cruz, see Puerto La Cruz.
La Esperanza, Cuba: 22.50 N. 83.45 W. **69, 70**
La Estacada, Venezuela: 10.42 N. 71.32 W. **69, 74**
   Terminal not in use. Buoys have been removed
La Flotte, see St. Martin.
La Goulette, Tunisia: 36.49 N. 10.18 E. **24**
   Max. Size: Draft 29 ft., LOA 220 m. Rades: LOA 190 m.,
   draft 9 m. Tankers: Up to 27 ft. 6 in. draft.
   Fuel: By road tanker. *Dry Docks:* Menzel Bourguiba: 253 m.
   long, 41 m. wide, 10.5 m. depth. *Airport:* Tunis – Carthage,
   15 km. from La Goulette and 5 km. from Tunis.
La Guaira, Venezuela: 10.36 N. 66.56 W. **69, 72, 75**
   Max. Size: Depths to 10.95 m. *Airport:* 10 km.
   Also see Puerto Cabello.
La Gunillas, Venezuela: 10.08 N. 71.17 W. **74**
La Have, N.S., Canada: 44.17 N. 64.20 W. **60**
La Libertad, Ecuador: 2.12 S. 80.55 W. **72**
   Max. Size: Anchorage: Depth 36 ft. Tankers: LOA 650 ft.,
   beam 84 ft., loaded draft 34 ft. 6 in. *Fuel:* Available with
   72 hours' prior notice. *Airport:* Guayaquil, 130 km.
La Libertad, El Salvador: 13.29 N. 89.19 W. **69**
   Port closed
La Linea, Spain: 36.10 N. 5.21 W. **20, 23**
La Louviere, Belgium: 50.25 N. 4.20 E. **7**
La Maddalena, (Sardinia), Italy: 41.13 N. 9.25 E. . . **21, 24**
La Mede, France: 43.24 N. 5.07 E. **23**
   Max. Size: Draft 5.18 m.
   Also see Port de Bouc.
La Mondah, Gabon: 0.34 N. 9.32 E. **29**
La Moule, (Grand Terre), Guadeloupe (France):
   16.20 N. 61.21 W. **71**
La Nouvelle, France: 43.01 N. 3.04 E. **9, 22**
   Max. Size: LOA 145 m., beam 22 m., draft 8.0 m.
   Tanker sea line: LOA 200 m. Draft 12 m. *Fuel:* Available.
   Airport: Marseilles International.
La Pallice, France: 46.10 N. 1.14 W. **8, 19**
   Max. Size: Oil Pier: 130,000 d.w.t., LOA 280 m., draft 16 m.
   Cargo vessels: Depth 12 m. *Fuel:* By road tanker.
   Dry Docks: Largest: 170 m. x 21.8 m.
   Also see La Rochelle.
La Palma, Panama: 8.13 N. 78.00 W. **69**
La Paloma, Uruguay: 34.37 S. 54.09 W. **77**
La Pampilla, Peru: 11.55 N. 77.09 W. **72**
   Max. Size: 250,000 tonnes d.w.t., LOA 283 m., draft 16.1 m.
La Paz, Mexico: 24.12 N. 110.20 W. **57**
La Perouse Strait, Japan/Russia **43**
La Plata, Argentina: 34.54 S. 57.55 W. **77, 78**
   Max. Size: LOA 215 m., beam 33 m., draft 23 ft. – 25 ft.
   Fuel: Available. *Dry Docks:* 170 m. x 26.0 m., capacity
   12,000 tons.
La Pointe, Wisconsin, U.S.A.: 46.47 N. 90.47 W. . . . **62**
La Push, Washington, U.S.A.: 47.54 N. 124.38 W. . . . **56**
La Rochelle, France: 46.10 N. 1.14 W. **8, 19**
   Max. Size: Tidal harbour: LOA 560 ft., draft 29 ft.
   Also see La Pallice.
La Romana, Dominican Republic: 18.26 N. 68.57 W. . **69, 70**
   Max. Size: LOA: 600 ft., draft 28 ft. (Sailing) and 26 ft. (Arriving).
   Fuel: Limited quantities by road.
   Airport: Santo Domingo, 45 miles.
La Salina, Venezuela: 10.22 N. 71.28 W. **72, 74**
   Max. Size: 112,000 d.w.t. LOA 900 ft., draft 39 ft.
   Fuel: Bunker "C", marine diesel and intermediate.

La Salinetas, (Grand Canary), Canary Is. (Spain):
27.58 N. 15.22 W. 27
Max. Size: LOA 150 m., draft 8.5 m. *Airport:* 5 km.
Also see Las Palmas.
La Seyne, see Toulon.
La Skhirra, Tunisia: 34.18 N. 10.09 E. 24
Max. Size: LOA 300 m. Draft 47 ft. 6 in. or 50 ft. (HW). Acid: 15,000 d.w.t., draft 9.0 m. *Airport:* Tunis, 350 km. Sfax, 80 km.
La Spezia, Italy: 44.01 N. 9.51 E **9, 21, 23, 24**
Max. Size: Draft: 33 ft. for the Commercial Port and grain silos, and 30 ft. 4 in. for Coal berth. Containers: Depth 13 m. – 14 m. Tankers: Draft 42 ft. *Fuel:* Available. *Dry Docks:* Floating dock 110,000 d.w.t. *Airport:* Pisa, 75 km.
La Teja, see Montevideo.
La Tremblade, France: 45.46 N. 1.08 W. 19
La Trinite, Martinique (France): 14.45 N. 60.58 W. . . . 71
La Union, El Salvador: 13.20 N. 87.50 W. 69
Max. Size: Depth 25 ft., LOA 550 ft. At anchor 43 ft. least depth. *Fuel:* Bunkers and diesel at berths. *Airport:* El Salvador, 102 miles.
La Urbana, Venezuela: 7.10 N. 66.55 W. 75
La Vela de Coro, see Coro.
Laajasalo Harbour, see Helsinki.
Laayoune, Morocco: 27.04 N. 13.28 W. 27
Max. Size: Depth 17 m. at LWL at phosphate berth, and 8 m. LWS at general cargo berth. *Airport:* Aaiun, 30 km.
Labasa, Fiji: 16.26 S. 179.22 E. 49
Max. Size: LOA 174 m., draft 10.5 m. *Airport:* Suva.
Also see Suva.
Laboe, Germany: 54.25 N. 10.13 E. 12, 14
Labrador, Newfoundland, Canada 59
Labrador Sea 17, 59
Labuan, Sabah, Malaysia: 5.17 N. 115.15 E. . . . 38, 39, 47
Max. Size: Depth 28 ft. 6 in. at Liberty Wharf, 31 ft. at Shell Wharf. *Fuel:* Bulk furnace oil and high speed diesel usually available.
Labuan Terminal, Sabah, Malaysia: 5.16 N. 115.07 E. . . . 38, 39
Max. Size: 350,000 s.d.w.t., draft 62 ft. (67 ft. over tide occasionally).
Also see Labuan.
Labuanbajo, Indonesia: 8.33 S. 119.55 E. 38, 46
Labuantring Bay, Indonesia: 8.44 S. 116.04 E. 38
Max. Size: Depth 6.5 m. – 7.5 m.
Anchorage (Ampenan): No restrictions.
Fuel: Limited availability. *Airport:* Services to Bali and Java.
Labuha, Indonesia: 0.38 S. 127.28 E. 46
Labuhanbilik, Indonesia: 2.31 N. 100.10 E. 38, 39, 40
Labutta, Myanmar: 16.05 N. 94.30 E. 37
Labytnangi, Russia: 66.38 N. 66.20 E. 16
Laccadive Is., India 37
Lachine, Quebec, Canada: 45.28 N. 73.39 W. 61
Lachine Section, see St. Lawrence Seaway.
Lackawanna, New York, U.S.A.: 42.50 N. 78.52 W. 62
Lacustre, see La Salina.
Ladario, see Corumba.
Ladner, B.C., Canada: 49.05 N. 123.05 W. 56
Ladysmith, B.C., Canada: 48.59 N. 123.47 W. 56
Lae, Papua New Guinea: 6.44 S. 146.59 E. 46
Max. Size: Depth 11.00 m. at LAT. Tankers: 40,000 d.w.t., depth 14 m. *Fuel:* Diesel and fuel oil. *Airport:* 40 km.
Laem Chabang, Thailand: 13.05 N. 100.53 E. 37, 39
Max. Size: Bulk Terminal: 70,000 d.w.t., depth 15.0 m. Container Terminal: 33,000 d.w.t., depth 15 m.
Multi-Purpose Terminal: 25,000 d.w.t., depth 15 m.
Fuel: Available. *Dry Docks:* Capacity 40,000 tons, length 283 m., width 47 m.
Airport: U-Tapao, 50 km. Bangkok, 150 km.
Laeso Is., Denmark 11, 12
Lagarterito, Panama Canal, Panama: 9.05 N. 79.55 W. . . . 73
Lage, Spain: 43.13 N. 9.00 W. 19, 20
Lagos, Greece: 41.00 N. 25.08 E. 25
Lagos, Nigeria: 6.27 N. 3.24 E. 28, 29
Max. Size: Draft 10.5 m. Tankers: 50,000 d.w.t., draft 16.9 m. at SBM. *Fuel:* By barge. *Dry Docks:* Largest has draft 18 ft. *Airport:* International, 14.4 km.
Lagos, Portugal: 37.06 N. 8.40 W. 20, 22
Lagrange, W.A., Australia: 18.45 S. 121.45 E. 50, 51
Laguna, Brazil: 28.30 S. 48.46 W. 76, 77
Max. Size: Depth 5 m. *Fuel:* Diesel. *Airport:* Nearest, Florianopolis, 130 km.
Laguna Beach, California, U.S.A.: 33.32 N. 117.45 W. . . . 58
Lahad Datu, Sabah, Malaysia: 5.02 N. 118.20 E. . . . 38, 47
Max. Size: 25,000 d.w.t., depth 9.3 m.
Also see Kudat.
Lahinch, Ireland: 52.58 N. 9.21 W. 5, 8
Lajes, (Flores Is.), Azores (Portugal): 39.23 N. 31.11 W. . . 20
Lake Charles, Louisiana, U.S.A.: 30.13 N. 93.15 W. . . 55, 66
Max. Size: LOA 1,000 ft., draft 40 ft.
Tankers: Depth 28 ft. – 40 ft. *Fuel:* Bunker "C" and diesel.
Airport: 7 miles.
Lake Dimun: 61.38 N. 6.42 W. 15

THE SHIPS ATLAS

Lake Harbour, N.W.T., Canada: 62.49 N. 69.50 W. 59
Lake River, Ontario, Canada: 53.35 N. 82.19 W. 59
Lakehead Harbour, see Thunder Bay.
Lakeport, Michigan, U.S.A.: 43.05 N. 82.35 W. 62
Lakes Entrance, Vic., Australia: 37.48 S. 148.00 E. . . . 50, 51
Lakes:
Lake Berryessa, California, U.S.A. 58
Lake Borgne, (Mississippi Delta), Louisiana, U.S.A. . . . 67
Lake Champlain, U.S.A. 60, 61
Lake Erie, Canada/U.S.A. 55, 60, 62
Lake Huron, Canada/U.S.A. 55, 60, 62
Lake Iliamna, Alaska, U.S.A. 54
Lake Inari, Finland 15
Lake Kivu, Congo (D.R. of) 30
Lake Madden, Panama 73
Lake Malar, Sweden 11
Lake Manzala, Egypt 33
Lake Maracaibo, Venezuela 74
Lake Maurepas, (Mississippi Delta), Louisiana, U.S.A. . . 67
Lake Melville, Newfoundland, Canada 59
Lake Michigan, U.S.A. 55, 62
Lake Nyasa, Malawi 30
Lake Ontario, Canada/U.S.A. 55, 60, 62
Lake Pontchartrain, (Mississippi Delta), Louisiana, U.S.A. . 67
Lake St. Clair, Canada/U.S.A. 62
Lake St. Francis 61
Lake St. Louis 61
Lake Salvador, (Mississippi Delta), Louisiana, U.S.A. . . 67
Lake Superior, Canada/U.S.A. 55, 62
Lake Tanganyika, Congo, D.R. of/Tanzania 30
Lake Tiberias, Israel 26
Lake Timsah, Suez Canal, Egypt 33
Lake Vanern, Sweden 10, 11, 12
Lake Vattern, Sweden 11, 12
Lake Victoria, Kenya/Tanzania/Uganda 30
Lake Winnebago, Wisconsin, U.S.A. 62
Lakewood, Ohio, U.S.A.: 41.30 N. 81.50 W. 62
Lakhpat, India: 23.45 N. 68.45 E. 37
Lakki, Greece: 37.07 N. 26.51 E. 25
Lakselv, Norway: 70.00 N. 24.55 E. 15
Lakshadweep Is., see Laccadive Is..
Lalang Marine Terminal, Indonesia: 1.11 N. 102.13 E. . . 38, 39, 40
Max. Size: 140,000 d.w.t., draft 55 ft.
Lamaline, Newfoundland, Canada: 46.51 N. 55.48 W. . . . 60
Lamao, see Bataan.
Lambasa, see Labasa.
Lamberts Bay, South Africa: 32.05 S. 18.18 E. 28
Lameque, Ontario, Canada: 47.47 N. 64.40 W. 60
Lamlash, U.K.: 55.32 N. 5.08 W. 6
Lamma Is., see Hong Kong.
Lamobuang, (Peleng Is.), Indonesia: 1.19 S. 123.20 E. . . 46
Lamoliaur Ulu Is., see Ngulu Is..
Lamotrek, (Caroline Is.), Micronesia: 7.28 N. 146.22 E. . . 46
Lampione, Italy: 35.30 N. 12.30 E. 24
Lampung, see Panjang.
Lamu, Kenya: 2.15 N. 40.54 E. 30
Lan Shui Terminal, China: 20.50 N. 115.42 E. 39, 47
Lan Yu Is., Taiwan: 22.03 N. 121.33 E. 42, 46
Lancaster, Ontario, Canada: 75.09 N. 74.30 W. 61
Lancaster, U.K.: 54.03 N. 2.47 W. 5
Landana, see Cabinda.
Landernau, France: 48.27 N. 4.15 W. 7, 19
Lands End, U.K.: 50.05 N. 5.45 W. 5, 19
Landskrona, Sweden: 55.52 N. 12.48 E. 10, 11, 12
Max. Size: Draft 10 m, LOA 190 m. *Fuel:* Small quantities of fuel oil can be obtained. *Dry Docks:* 25,000 d.w.t. *Airport:* Sturup, 60 km. Angelholm, 50 km. Kastrup (Copenhagen), 35 km.
Landwehr, see Flemhude.
Langeland Belt, Denmark 12, 14
Langeland Is., Denmark 12
Langemak Bay, see Finschhaven.
Langesand, see Kollefjord.
Langkawi, Malaya, Malaysia: 6.26 N. 99.46 E. . . . 37, 38, 39
Max. Size: Draft 9.0 m.
Langoya, (Lofoten Is.), Norway: 68.45 N. 15.00 E. 15
Langror, Sweden: 61.16 N. 17.11 E. 15
Max. Size: Depth 8.3 m. at quay. LOA 170 m. *Fuel:* Available.
Airport: Nearest Stockholm.
Also see Soderhamn.
Langshan, see Nantong.
Lankaran, Azerbaijan: 38.45 N. 48.51 E. 9
Lannion, France: 48.44 N. 3.28 W. 7, 19
Lanshan, China: 35.06 N. 119.22 E. 42, 46
Max. Size: LOA 210 m., draft 10.2 m. *Fuel:* Available.
Lantau Is., see Hong Kong.
Lanzarote Is., Canary Is. (Spain) 27
Laoag, (Luzon Is.), Philippines: 18.10 N. 120.35 E. . . . 47
Laoang, (Samar Is.), Philippines: 12.30 N. 125.10 E. . . 46, 47
LAOS 39

Lapaluoto, see Raahe.
Lappeenranta, Finland: 61.05 N. 28.09 E. **13**
  Also see Saimaa Canal.
Lappohja, Finland: 59.55 N. 23.18 E. **11**
Larache, Morocco: 35.12 N. 6.09 W. **22, 27**
Larak Is., Iran: 26.53 N. 56.21 E. **35**
Larantuka, Indonesia: 8.20 S. 122.59 E. **46**
Largs, U.K.: 55.48 N. 4.52 W. **6**
Larimna, Greece: 38.34 N. 23.16 E. **25**
Larivot, see Le Larivot.
Lark Harbour, Newfoundland, Canada: 49.06 N. 58.20 W. . . . **60**
Larnaca, Cyprus: 34.55 N. 33.39 E. **26**
  Max. Size: LOA 272 m., draft 11.4 m. Tankers: LOA 730 ft.,
  draft 41 ft. *Fuel:* Available. *Airport:* 3 miles (International).
Larne, U.K.: 54.51 N. 5.48 W. **5, 6**
  Max. Size: LOA 175 m., beam 30 m., depth 7.5 m.
  Tankers: LOA 260 ft., channel depth 9.1 m. (MLWS), berth
  depth 10.5 m. *Fuel:* By road tanker. *Airport:* Belfast, 20 miles.
Larsen Bay, Alaska, U.S.A.: 57.32 N. 153.59 W. **54**
Larvik, Norway: 59.03 N. 10.02 E. **8, 12**
  Max. Size: LOA 644 ft. 8 in., beam 83 ft. 3 in., draft 32 ft. 6 in.
  Fuel: Fuel oil, gas oil and diesel. *Airport:* Sandefjord, 25 km.
  Oslo (Gardermoen), 460 km.
Las Cascadas, Panama Canal, Panama: 9.05 N. 79.41 W. . . . **73**
Las Mareas, Puerto Rico (U.S.A.): 17.55 N. 66.10 W. **71**
  Max. Size: Draft 37 ft.
  Also see San Juan.
Las Minas, see Bahia Las Minas.
Las Minas Bay, Panama **73**
Las Palmas, (Grand Canary), Canary Is. (Spain):
  28.05 N. 15.27 W. **27**
  Max. Size: Depth 10 m. – 16 m. Tankers: Draft 66 ft. Largest
  vessel 550,000 d.w.t. *Fuel:* Fuel oil, gas oil and diesel.
  Dry Docks: Vessels up to 212 m. LOA, 30 m. beam and
  30,000 d.w.t. *Airport:* International, 25 km.
Las Piedras, Venezuela: 11.30 N. 70.10 W. **74**
Las Piedras Paraguana, see Amuay Bay.
Las Salinetas, see Las Palmas.
Las Tres Marias Is., Mexico: 21.20 N. 106.40 W. **57**
Lastovo, Croatia: 42.46 N. 16.54 E. **24**
Latchford, see Warrington.
Latchi, Cyprus: 35.03 N. 32.27 E. **26**
  Max. Size: No restrictions, loading by barge.
  Airport: Larnaca, 112 km. or Paphos, 50 km.
Latouche, Alaska, U.S.A.: 60.03 N. 148.04 W. **54**
Latta, see Port Latta.
Lattakia, Syria: 35.31 N. 35.46 E. **21, 26**
  Max. Size: Draft 13.5 m. *Fuel:* Available.
  Airport: Damascus, 360 km.
LATVIA **4, 10, 11**
Launceston, Tas., Australia: 41.27 S. 147.07 E. **50, 51**
  Max. Size: Depth 8.4 m. – 12.4 m. *Fuel:* Available.
  Dry Docks: 62.5 m. length and 3.66 m. (12 ft.) draft. Width of
  entrance 12.80 m. *Airport:* 15 km., connects with Melbourne
  and Sydney.
Lauritsala, Finland: 61.05 N. 28.17 E. **13**
  Also see Saimaa Canal.
Laurium, see Lavrion.
Lausanne, Switzerland: 46.32 N. 6.39 E. **9**
Lauterbach, Germany: 54.20 N. 13.30 E. **11, 12**
Lautoka, (Viti Levu Is.), Fiji: 17.36 S. 177.26 E. **49**
  Max. Size: Up to 32 ft. draft. Tankers (Vuda Pt.): Available
  depth about 36 ft., 18,000 – 24,000 d.w.t. *Fuel:* Diesel.
  Airport: Nandi, 16 miles.
Lauzon, Quebec, Canada: 46.48 N. 71.09 W. **60**
Lavaca, see Port Lavaca.
Lavan Island, Iran: 26.47 N. 53.20 E. **31, 35**
  Max. Size: 225,000 d.w.t., depth 69 ft.
  Max. departure draft 64 ft. *Airport:* Charter only.
Lavera, France: 43.23 N. 5.00 E. **23**
  Max. Size: LOA 275 m., draft 12.8 m.
  Also see Port de Bouc.
Lavola, see Vyborg.
Lavrentiya, Russia: 65.35 N. 171.05 W. **54**
Lavrion, Greece: 37.42 N. 24.04 E. **25, 26**
  Max. Size: LOA 130 m. (approx.), draft 21 ft. *Fuel:* By barge
  or road tanker. *Airport:* Athens, 45 km.
Lawas, see Limbang.
Lawi Lawi, Indonesia: 1.27 S. 116.46 E. **38**
  Max. Size: 135,000 d.w.t., LOA 290 m., depth 22 m. *Airport:*
  Sepinggan, 8 km.
Laxey, U.K.: 54.13 N. 4.23 W. **5**
Laysan Is., Hawaii, U.S.A.: 25.25 N. 171.45 W. **49**
Lazaret, see Toulon.
Lazareta, see Syros.
Lazarev, Russia: 52.12 N. 141.33 E. **43**
Lazaro Cardenas, Mexico: 17.55 N. 102.10 W. **57**
  Max. Size: 125,000 d.w.t., LOA 269 m., draft 13.0 m.
  Depth 9.4 m. – 16.5 m. *Fuel:* Available. *Airport:* 5 km.,
  connects with Mexico City.

Lazi Bay, (Siquijor Is.), Philippines: 9.07 N. 123.40 E. . . . **47**
  Max. Size: LOA 245 m., draft 14.5 m. *Fuel:* By barge.
Le Carnet, France: 47.17 N. 2.00 W. **19**
Le Chateau d'Oleron, France: 45.53 N. 1.11 W. **8, 19**
  Max. Size: Tidal Harbour – depth 4.9 m. HW.
Le Conquet, France: 48.21 N. 4.47 W. **7, 19**
Le Croisic, France: 47.18 N. 2.31 W. **19**
Le Guildo, France: 48.37 N. 2.13 W. **7, 19**
Le Havre, France: 49.30 N. 0.07 W. **4, 7, 8**
  Max. Size: Depth 12.0 m. Tankers: LOA 292 m., draft 20 m.
  Bulk Carriers: Up to 195,000 d.w.t., draft 17.16 m.
  Fuel: All grades available,
  viscosities from 200 sec. to 3,000 sec. Redwood.
  Dry Docks: Large dry docks and floating docks.
  Airport: 7 km. from town, connects to Paris and Gatwick (U.K.).
  Also see Antifer.
Le Larivot, Guyane (France): 4.54 N. 52.22 W. **76**
  Max. Size: LOA 100 m., depth 4.9 m.
  Also see Degrad-des-Cannes.
Le Mon, see Thanh Hoa.
Le Palais, France: 47.21 N. 3.09 W. **19**
Le Treport, France: 50.04 N. 1.22 E. **7**
Le Verdon, see Verdon.
Leamington, Ontario, Canada: 42.02 N. 82.36 W. **62**
Learmonth, W.A., Australia: 22.12 S. 114.06 E. **50, 51**
LEBANON **21, 26**
Lebu, Chile: 37.38 S. 73.41 W. **77**
Leer, Germany: 53.14 N. 7.27 E. **7, 8, 14**
Leeuwarden, Netherlands: 53.15 N. 5.47 E. **7, 8**
Leeward Islands, South China Sea **71**
Lefkandion, Greece: 38.24 N. 23.41 E. **25**
Legazpi, (Luzon Is.), Philippines: 13.10 N. 123.45 E. . . . **46, 47**
  Max. Size: LOA 120 m.; draft 25 ft. Tankers: LOA 230 m.,
  draft 35 ft. *Fuel:* All grades. *Airport:* 5 km.
Leghorn, see Livorno.
Lei Zhou, China: 20.50 N. 110.12 E. **39**
Leiden, Netherlands: 52.09 N. 4.29 E. **7, 8**
Leirvik, see Lervik.
Leith, U.K.: 55.59 N. 3.10 W. **4, 5, 6**
  Max. Size: Entrance lock: 259 m. x 31.6 m. wide x depth on sill
  12.2 m. (Max. LOA 210 m.). Imperial Dock: Draft 9.15 m.
  Western Harbour: Draft 9.5 m. Tankers: Draft 9.5 m.
  Fuel: All grades. *Dry Docks:* Length 167.6 m.,
  width of entrance 21.3 m., depth over blocks 7.7 m. *Airport:*
  Edinburgh, 9 miles.
Leith Harbour, South Georgia Is. (U.K.): 53.44 S. 36.48 W. . . **77**
Leixoes, Portugal: 41.11 N. 8.42 W. **20, 21, 22**
  Max. Size: Draft 31 ft. Tankers: Draft 36 ft. – 44.5 ft.,
  120,000 d.w.t. *Fuel:* Available. *Airport:* 7 km., connects
  with Lisbon.
Leksvik, Norway: 63.45 N. 10.50 E. **15**
Leland, Michigan, U.S.A.: 45.01 N. 85.46 W. **62**
Lembar, see Labuantring Bay.
Lemieux Is., N.W.T., Canada: 63.50 N. 64.15 W. **59**
Lemmer, Netherlands: 52.52 N. 5.43 E. **7, 8**
Lemnos Is., Greece **25, 26**
Lemvig, Denmark: 56.33 N. 8.19 E. **11, 12**
  Max. Size: LOA 90 m., draft 4 m. *Fuel:* Available.
Lenadura, see Punta Arenas.
Lengua de Pajaro, see Antilla.
Leningrad, see St. Petersburg.
Leonardtown, Maryland, U.S.A.: 38.18 N. 76.39 W. **63, 65**
Leonidhion, Greece: 37.09 N. 22.53 E. **25**
Lepu, Indonesia: 1.00 N. 107.34 E. **38, 39**
Lequeitio, Spain: 43.22 N. 2.32 W. **19**
Leros Is., Greece **25**
Lervik, Norway: 59.49 N. 5.31 E. **11**
Lerwick, U.K.: 60.09 N. 1.08 W. **5**
  Max. Size: Normally 9 m. draft and 169 m. LOA. *Fuel:* Gas oil.
  Dry Docks: Floating Dock, 2,750 tons. *Airport:* 25 miles.
Les Cayes, Haiti: 18.11 N. 73.44 W. **70**
Les Escoumins, Quebec, Canada: 48.20 N. 69.20 W. **60**
Les Falaises, Algeria: 36.38 N. 5.25 E. **22**
Les Minquiers, France: 48.58 N. 2.04 W. **19**
Les Sables d'Olonne, France: 46.29 N. 1.47 W. **19**
  Max. Size: LOA 110 m., beam 16 m., draft 6.2 m. *Fuel:* By road
  tanker. *Airport:* Nantes, 87 km.
Lesbos Is., Greece **25, 26**
Lesnoy, Russia: 66.35 N. 34.20 E. **16**
Lesogorsk, Russia: 49.27 N. 142.08 E. **43**
LESOTHO **30**
Lesser Antilles, U.K. **71**
Lesser Sunda Islands, Indonesia **46**
Letangi Harbour, N.B., Canada: 45.03 N. 66.50 W. **60**
Leticia, Colombia: 4.08 S. 70.00 W. **72**
Leuchars, U.K.: 56.23 N. 2.53 W. **6**
Levadhia, Greece: 38.25 N. 22.55 E. **25**
Levanger, Norway: 63.45 N. 11.18 E. **15**
Leven, see Methil.
Levis, Quebec, Canada: 46.47 N. 71.10 W. **60**

Levisa Bay, see Antilla.
Levitha Is., Greece: 37.00 N. 26.30 E. 25
Levkas, Greece: 38.48 N. 20.45 E. 24, 25
Levuka, (Ovalau Is.), Fiji: 17.41 S. 178.51 E. 49
Max. Size: LOA 560 ft., draft 25 ft. *Fuel:* Light marine diesel.
Airport: 12 miles from port, connects to Nandi International.
Lewes, Delaware, U.S.A.: 38.47 N. 75.08 W. 63, 65
Lewis, U.K.: 58.15 N. 6.45 W. 5
Lewisporte, Newfoundland, Canada: 49.15 N. 55.03 W. . . 60
Lewiston, New York, U.S.A.: 43.10 N. 79.03 W. 62
Leyte Is., Philippines 46, 47
Lezardrieux, France: 48.47 N. 3.06 W. 7, 19
Lhoknga, Indonesia: 5.27 N. 95.14 E. 37, 38, 40
Max. Size: LOA 150 m., draft 9.1 m.
Airport: Blang Bintang, 32 km.
Lhokseumawe, Indonesia: 5.15 N. 97.07 E. 37, 38, 40
Max. Size: Lhokseumawe: Old port – depth 2.4 m.
New port – LOA 150 m. Hagu: Draft 6 m.
Blang Lancang: LNG – LOA 290 m., draft 12.5 m.
General – draft 7 m. CBM – LOA 275 m., 100,000 d.w.t.
SBM – 280,000 d.w.t. Krueng Geukueh: LOA 175 m.,
draft 7.5 m. *Airport:* 30 km.
Lhotuan, see Bontang.
Lianyungang, China: 34.45 N. 119.27 E. 42, 46
Max. Size: 35,000 d.w.t., depth 11 m. *Fuel:* Available.
LIBERIA 27, 28
Libertador, see Manzanillo.
Libourne, France: 44.55 N. 0.15 W. 8
Max. Size: LOA 120 m., depth 4.5 m.
Also see Bordeaux.
Libreville, Gabon: 0.23 N. 9.26 E. 28, 29
Max. Size: Draft 7.4 m. anchorage port. *Fuel:* By barge.
Airport: 9 km.
LIBYA 21, 24, 26
Licata, (Sicily), Italy: 37.06 N. 13.57 E. 24
Max. Size: Draft 6.1 m. *Fuel:* By road tanker. *Airport:*
Catania, 190 km.
Lidkoping, Sweden: 58.30 N. 13.10 E. 11, 12
Max. Size: As for Trollhatte Canal: LOA 87 m., beam 13 m.,
draft 5.3 m. Airdraft 27 m. *Fuel:* Gas oil.
Airport: Gothenburg, 130 km.
Lido, Italy: 45.25 N. 12.26 E. 24
Liege, Belgium: 50.38 N. 5.34 E. 7, 9
Max. Size: Largest LOA 134 m., beam 12.5 m., draft 3.4 m.
Airport: Bierset, 20 km.
Lielupe, Latvia: 57.00 N. 23.56 E. 11
Max. Size: LOA 80 m., beam 12 m., draft 4.5 m.
Airport: Riga, 10 km.
Lien Yun Chiang, see Lianyungang.
Lienyunkang, see Lianyungang.
Liepaja, Latvia: 56.32 N. 20.59 E. 10, 11
Max. Size: LOA 200 m., depths up to 10.5 m.
Tankers: Draft 6 m. *Fuel:* By barge. *Dry Docks:* Length
200 m., width 21 m. Floating Dock: Capacity 2,200 tons.
Airport: 7 km.
Lifou Is., see We.
Lifuka Is., see Pangai.
Lightering Zones – Gulf of Mexico, U.S.A. 66
Ligurian Sea, Italy 23, 24
Lihir Is., Papua New Guinea: 3.05 S. 152.38 E. 46
Lihou Reefs, Australia 51
Lille, France: 50.36 N. 3.04 E. 7
Lillebonne, see Quillebeuf.
Lilleborg, see Fredrikstad.
Lillesand, Norway: 58.15 N. 8.23 E. 11, 12
Max. Size: Depth 10 m. *Airport:* 30 km.
Lim Chu Kang, see Singapore.
Limas, Indonesia: 0.30 N. 104.20 E. 39, 40
Limassol, Cyprus: 34.39 N. 33.01 E. 21, 26
Max. Size: New Breakwater Port: Draft 10.5 m. – 13.5 m.
Fuel: Available. *Dry Docks:* Floating dock, capacity 1,200 tons.
Airport: Larnaca, 70 km. Paphos, 63 km.
Limay, see Bataan.
Limbang, Sarawak, Malaysia: 4.48 N. 115.05 E. 38, 39
Max. Size: Depth 26 ft. at anchorage.
Limbe, Cameroon: 4.01 N. 9.13 E. 28, 29
Max. Size: Anchorage – no restrictions. *Airport:* Douala, 100
km.
Also see Douala.
Lime Island, see Sault Ste. Marie, Canada.
Lime Point, California, U.S.A. 58
Limenaria, Greece: 40.32 N. 24.31 E. 25, 26
Limerick, Ireland: 52.40 N. 8.38 W. 4, 5, 8
Max. Size: 5,000 tonnes d.w.t., LOA 150 m., beam 19.8 m.,
draft 6.0 m. *Fuel:* All grades. *Dry Docks:* In emergency only.
Airport: Shannon, 15 miles.
Limetree Bay, (St. Croix), Virgin Is. (U.S.A.):
17.41 N. 64.44 W. 69, 71
Max. Size: LOA 650 ft., draft 34 ft. – 38 ft. 6 in., 45,000 d.w.t.
Tankers: LOA 1,200 ft., draft 55 ft., 300,000 d.w.t.
Fuel: Bunker C and light marine diesel. *Airport:* 5 miles.

Limfjord, see Aalborg.
Limhamn, Sweden: 55.35 N. 12.56 E. 12
Max. Size: Depth 8.6 m. Tankers: Depth 10.5 m.
Fuel: Available. *Airport:* Sturup.
Also see Malmo.
Limni, Greece: 38.45 N. 23.20 E. 25
Limni Mines, see Latchi.
Limon, see Puerto Limon.
Limon Bay, Panama 73
Limon Patron, see Patras.
Lin Kao, China: 19.55 N. 109.40 E. 39
Lincoln, see Port Lincoln.
Lincoln Is., (Paracel Is.), South China Sea:
16.35 N. 112.48 E. 39
Linden, Guyana: 6.00 N. 58.17 W. 72, 75, 76
Max. Size: Draft 21 ft. 6 in. *Fuel:* Available.
Linden, U.S.A., see Carteret.
Lindesnes, Norway: 57.59 N. 7.03 E. 10
Lindi, Tanzania: 10.00 S. 39.43 E. 30
Lindoe, Denmark: 55.37 N. 10.12 E. 12
Lindos, Greece: 36.02 N. 28.05 E. 25
Lindsey, see Immingham.
Lingah, Iran: 26.35 N. 54.53 E. 35
Lingayen, (Luzon Is.), Philippines: 16.00 N. 120.05 E. . . . 46, 47
Lingga, Sarawak, Malaysia: 1.20 N. 111.11 E. 38, 39, 40
Lingkas, see Tarakan.
Linosa, Italy: 35.45 N. 12.45 E. 24
Linz, Austria: 48.19 N. 14.18 E. 9
Lion Terminal, Ivory Coast: 5.02 N. 4.48 W. 28
Max. Size: Depth 64 m. – 71 m.
Lionas, (Naxos Is.), Greece: 37.08 N. 25.35 E. 25
Lipari, (Aeolian Is.), Italy: 38.30 N. 14.57 E. 24
Lipsoi Is., Greece: 37.19 N. 26.50 E. 25
Lirquen, Chile: 36.42 S. 72.59 W. 77
Max. Size: LOA 220 m., draft 50 ft. 10 in. *Fuel:* Diesel.
Airport: 16 km.
Lisbon, Portugal: 38.42 N. 9.11 W. 20, 21, 22
Max. Size: Depth alongside to 13.0 m. Cereals: Depth up to
18.0 m. Tankers: Depth alongside to 16 m. *Fuel:* Available.
Dry Docks: Up to 1,000,000 tons. *Airport:* International.
Liscomb, N.S., Canada: 45.01 N. 61.59 W. 60
Max. Size: Channel depths to 9.1 m. Wharves closed.
Airport: Halifax, 225 km.
Lisianski Is., Hawaii, U.S.A.: 25.50 N. 173.50 W. 49
List, Germany: 55.01 N. 8.27 E. 11, 12, 14
LITHUANIA 4, 10, 11
Little Aden, see Aden.
Little Andaman Is., (Andaman Is.), India: 10.42 N. 92.30 E. . . 37
Little Batanga, Cameroon: 3.15 N. 9.55 E. 29
Little Belt, Denmark 12, 14
Little Bitter Lake, Suez Canal, Egypt 33
Little Cayman Is., Cayman Is. (U.K.): 19.40 N. 79.59 W. . . 69, 70
Also see Cayman Brac.
Little Current, Ontario, Canada: 45.58 N. 81.57 W. 62
Little Inagua Is., Bahamas: 21.30 N. 73.00 W. 70
Little Narrows, see Iona.
Little Nicobar Is., (Nicobar Is.), India: 7.20 N. 93.37 E. . . . 37
Littlehampton, U.K.: 50.48 N. 0.33 W. 7
Max. Size: LOA 70 m., beam 15 m., draft 4.5 m. *Fuel:*
By road tanker. *Airport:* Gatwick, 35 miles.
Liuhua Terminal, China: 20.50 N. 115.42 E. 39, 47
Max. Size: 140,000 d.w.t., LOA 265 m., beam 50 m.
Livardi, (Serifos Is.), Greece: 37.08 N. 24.31 E. 25
Liverpool, N.S., Canada: 44.03 N. 64.42 W. 60
Max. Size: LOA 650 ft., draft 26 ft. *Fuel:* Diesel. *Airport:* Halifax
International, 170 km.
Liverpool, U.K.: 53.28 N. 3.02 W. 4, 5, 6, 7
Max. Size: Liverpool Docks: Up to 12.8 m. draft.
Seaforth Dock: LOA 292 m., beam 36 m., draft 12.8 m. *Fuel:*
Range of fuels of various viscosities.
Dry Docks: 5 small dry docks. *Airport:* 7 miles.
Liverpool Bay, U.K.: 53.41 N. 3.33 W. 5
Max. Size: 150,000 d.w.t., depth over 30 m.
Livingston, Guatemala: 15.50 N. 88.45 W. 69
Livorno, Italy: 43.33 N. 10.20 E. 9, 21, 23, 24
Max. Size: Commercial Port: Depth 37 ft. Tankers: Draft
37 ft. 6 in., LOA 984 ft. *Fuel:* All grades. *Dry Docks:* Graving
dock 290 m. x 56 m. (300,000 d.w.t.). *Airport:* 20 km.
Also see Vada.
Lixuri, Greece: 38.14 N. 20.24 E. 25
Lizard Point, U.K.: 49.56 N. 5.13 W. 5, 19
Ljusne, Sweden: 61.12 N. 17.09 E. 15
Also see Vallvik.
Llandulas, U.K.: 53.17 N. 3.39 W. 5, 7
Llanelli, U.K.: 51.40 N. 4.10 W. 6, 7
Llanes, Spain: 43.25 N. 4.48 W. 19, 20

Lobito, Angola: 12.20 S. 13.34 E. **28**
  Max. Size: LOA 900 ft., draft 33 ft.
  Tankers: Depth 10 m. – 11 m. *Fuel:* Fuel oil (Ordinary), gas oil available. *Dry Docks:* Floating dock up to 2,000 tons.
  Airport: Lobito (Catumbela), 13 km. Lobito (Benguela), 33 km.
Lobitos, Peru: 4.27 S. 81.18 W. **72**
Local, see Gijon.
Lochaline, U.K.: 56.32 N. 5.46 W. **5**
Lochboisdale, U.K.: 57.09 N. 7.18 W. **5**
Lochinver, U.K.: 58.09 N. 5.14 W. **5**
Lochmaddy, U.K.: 57.36 N. 7.11 W. **5**
  Max. Size: Berth length 370 ft., depth 4 m. – 6 m. (LWS).
  Fuel: Gas oil. *Airport:* Benbecula, 20 miles.
Lochranza, (Arran), U.K.: 55.42 N. 5.18 W. **6**
Lockeport, N.S., Canada: 43.43 N. 65.06 W. **60**
Loctudy, France: 47.50 N. 4.10 W. **7, 19**
Locust Point, see Baltimore.
Lodi, California, U.S.A.: 38.07 N. 121.18 W. **58**
Lodingen, Norway: 68.25 N. 16.00 E. **15**
Lofang, see Shortland Harbour.
Lofoten Is., Norway **10, 15**
Logstor, Denmark: 56.58 N. 9.15 E. **12**
Lohals, Denmark: 55.08 N. 10.54 E. **12**
Loheiya, Yemen: 15.42 N. 42.42 E. **32**
Lokken, Denmark: 57.20 N. 9.40 E. **11, 12**
Lokoja, Nigeria: 7.49 N. 6.44 E. **28**
Loks Land, N.W.T., Canada: 62.25 N. 64.30 W. **59**
Loksa, Estonia: 59.35 N. 25.45 E. **11**
Loktuan, see Bontang.
Lolland Is., Denmark **12, 14**
Lomblen Is., Indonesia: 8.30 S. 123.30 E. **46**
Lombo, Angola: 6.50 S. 12.22 E. **28**
  Max. Size: SPM – Max. displacement 155,000 tons, depth 120 ft.
Lombok Is., Indonesia **38**
Lombok Strait, Indonesia **36, 38**
Lombrum, see Lorengau.
Lome, Togo: 6.08 N. 1.17 E. **28, 29**
  Max. Size: LOA 270 m., draft 31 ft. Tankers: LOA 250 m., draft 45 ft. Bulk carriers: Draft 38 ft. Containers: Depth 11 m.
  Fuel: Diesel fuel for small craft. Gas oil. *Airport:* Lome.
Lomma, Sweden: 55.41 N. 13.04 E. **12**
Lomond, Newfoundland, Canada: 49.28 N. 57.46 W. **60**
Lomonosov, Russia: 59.55 N. 29.46 E. **11**
London, U.K.: 51.30 N. 0.05 W. **4, 5, 6, 7**
  Max. Size: See Tilbury. Tankers: Contact Terminal.
  Fuel: All grades. *Airport:* London (Heathrow), London (Gatwick), London (Stansted) and London (City).
Londonderry, U.K.: 55.02 N. 7.16 W. **5**
  Max. Size: LOA 190 m., draft (SW) 9.3 m., airdraft 39 m. (HWOST), beam 60 ft. Oil Jetty, Coolkeeragh: LOA 190 m., draft (SW) 7.2 m. *Fuel:* Gas oil, light marine diesel and light, medium and heavy oil. *Airport:* Eglington Airport, 9 miles.
Londunarbryggia, see Siglufjord.
Long Bay, see Georgetown.
Long Beach, California, U.S.A.: 33.45 N. 118.13 W. . . **57, 58**
  Max. Size: Depth at general cargo berths 30 ft. – 42 ft. (MLLW).
  Dry bulk: Depth 36 ft. – 50 ft. (MLLW).
  Tankers: Depth 37 ft. – 76 ft. (MLLW). *Fuel:* All grades.
  Dry Docks: Large dock yards and large floating docks.
  Airport: 18 miles.
Long Harbour, Newfoundland, Canada: 47.27 N. 53.49 W. . . **60**
  Max. Size: Depth 10.98 m. *Airport:* 130 km.
Long Is., Bahamas **69, 70**
Long Is., Ontario, Canada **59**
Long Is., Papua New Guinea: 5.20 S. 147.05 E. **46**
Long Is., New York, U.S.A. **60, 63**
Long Island Sound, U.S.A. **63**
Long Point, (Santa Catalina Is.), California, U.S.A. . . . **58**
Long Point Bay, Ontario, Canada **62**
Long Pond, Newfoundland, Canada: 47.31 N. 52.58 W. . . . **60**
  Max. Size: Channel depth 7.9 m.
  Alongside depth 6.9 m. – 8.2 m. *Fuel:* Available.
  Airport: 25 km.
Long Reach, see Bell Bay.
Long Sault, Ontario, Canada: 45.05 N. 74.55 W. **61**
Long Strait, Russia **54**
Long Thanh, Vietnam: 10.39 N. 107.01 E. **39**
  Max. Size: LOA 50 m., draft 6.0 m. *Fuel:* Available.
  Airport: Tan Son Nhat, 80 km.
  Also see Phuoc Thai.
Longkou, China: 37.29 N. 120.20 E. **42**
  Max. Size: Depth 6.5 m. – 10.5 m. *Fuel:* Available. *Airport:* 120 km.
Longoni, (Ile. Mayotte), Comoros Is. (France):
  12.43 S. 45.10 E. **30**
  Max. Size: LOA 185 m., draft 11.5 m. *Fuel:* Small quantities by road tankers. *Airport:* 20 km.
Longuy, Cameroon: 3.05 N. 9.58 E. **29**

Longview, Washington, U.S.A.: 46.10 N. 122.55 W. . . **55, 56, 57**
  Max. Size: Depth up to 40 ft. *Fuel:* By road tanker.
  Airport: Portland.
Longyear, (Spitsbergen), Norway: 78.14 N. 15.35 E. . . . **17**
Lonholmen, see Pitea.
Looe, U.K.: 50.21 N. 4.27 W. **5, 7**
Lopez, see Puerto Lopez.
Lopez I., Panama Canal, Panama **73**
Lorain, Ohio, U.S.A.: 41.28 N. 82.12 W. **62**
Lord Howe Island, N.S.W., Australia: 31.30 S. 159.08 E. **49, 50**
Lorengau, Papua New Guinea: 2.01 S. 147.16 E. **46**
  Max. Size: Min. depth 1.4 m. at LAT. *Fuel:* Diesel by road tanker. *Airport:* Momote, 45 km.
Loreto, Mexico: 26.01 N. 111.21 W. **57**
Loreto, (Dinagat Is.), Philippines: 10.22 N. 125.36 E. . . **47**
  Max. Size: Anchorage port.
Lorient, France: 47.45 N. 3.21 W. **4, 7, 19**
  Max. Size: LOA 260 m., depth of water 10 m.
  Tankers: LOA 180 m., depth 9.0 m.
  Dry Docks: 186.2 m. long x 26.33 m. wide.
Los Angeles, California, U.S.A.: 33.43 N. 118.16 W. . **55, 57, 58**
  Max. Size: Depth 45 ft. Containers: Depth 40 ft. – 45 ft.
  Bulk: Depth 72 ft. Tankers: Depth 32 ft. – 51 ft.
  Fuel: Available. *Dry Docks:* 559 ft. by 110 ft., 22,000 displacement tons. *Airport:* 20 miles.
Los Barrios, Spain: 36.11 N. 5.30 W. **23**
Los Hermanos Is., see Blanquilla Is..
Los Marmoles, see Arrecife.
Los Vilos, Chile: 31.55 S. 71.31 W. **77**
Losap Is., (Caroline Is.), Micronesia: 6.54 N. 152.41 E. . **46**
Lossiemouth, U.K.: 57.43 N. 3.17 W. **5**
Losuia, (Trobriand Is.), Papua New Guinea: 8.27 S. 151.05 E. **46**
Lota, Chile: 37.06 S. 73.10 W. **77**
  Max. Size: LOA 160 m., draft 27 ft. (8.2 m.).
Loudden, see Stockholm.
Lough Swilly, Ireland **5**
Louisbourg, N.S., Canada: 45.55 N. 59.58 W. **60**
  Max. Size: Largest vessel: 8,000 g.r.t., draft 30 ft. 6 in. *Fuel:* Available.
Louisiade Archipelago, Papua New Guinea **46**
Louisiana, U.S.A. **66, 67**
Louisiana Offshore Oil Port, see L.O.O.P. Terminal.
Louvain, Belgium: 50.53 N. 4.42 E. **7**
Lovanger, Sweden: 64.20 N. 21.10 E. **15**
Lovisa, Finland: 60.25 N. 26.16 E. **11, 13**
  Max. Size: Depth 8.5 m. *Airport:* Helsinki, 90 km.
Lower Bay, New York, U.S.A. **63**
Lower Beauharnois Lock, see St. Lawrence Seaway.
Lowestoft, U.K.: 52.29 N. 1.45 E. **5, 7**
  Max. Size: LOA approx. 125 m., draft 6 m. (MHWS).
  Fuel: Marine diesel by road or at bunker berth.
  Dry Docks: Length 76 m. Width at entrance 14.6 m. Depth of water on sill 4.6 m. (MHWS). *Airport:* London (Heathrow), Norwich, 27 miles.
Loyalty Islands, New Caledonia (France) **49**
Loyang Offshore Base, see Singapore.
Lu Shun, China: 38.48 N. 121.15 E. **42**
Lu Ta, see Dalian.
Luanda, Angola: 8.48 S. 13.15 E. **28**
  Max. Size: LOA 1,000 ft. (alongside), draft 34 ft. (alongside).
  Tankers: 55 ft. draft at the refinery buoys. *Fuel:* Limited number of grades. *Airport:* 4.5 miles.
Luarca, Spain: 43.32 N. 6.32 W. **19, 20**
Luba, see San Carlos.
Lubang Is., Philippines: 13.45 N. 120.10 E. **47**
Lubeck, Germany: 53.52 N. 10.40 E. **10, 11, 12, 14**
  Max. Size: Depths up to 9.5 m. alongside. Vessels of 15,000 d.w.t., can reach Stadhafen. *Fuel:* Available.
  Dry Docks: Floating docks up to 13,500 tons (45,000 tonnes d.w.t.). *Airport:* 1 hour by bus or train to Hamburg.
Lubljana, Slovenia: 46.04 N. 14.30 E. **9**
Lucea, Jamaica: 18.28 N. 78.11 W. **70**
Lucina Marine Terminal, Gabon: 3.40 S. 10.46 E. **28**
  Max. Size: 120,000 tonnes d.w.t. – 140,000 tonnes d.w.t., depth 114 ft.
Lucinda, Qld., Australia: 18.32 S. 146.20 E. **50, 51**
  Max. Size: LOA 222 m., beam 31.0 m., draft 12.3 m., 52,000 d.w.t.
Luconia Shoals, Malaysia **39**
Luda, see Dalian.
Luderitz, Namibia: 26.39 S. 15.09 E. **28**
  Max. Size: LOA 150 m., draft 8 m. *Fuel:* Available.
  Airport: 12 km., connects with Cape Town.
Ludington, Michigan, U.S.A.: 43.57 N. 86.27 W. **62**
Lufeng 13-1 Terminal, China: 21.36 N. 116.09 E. . . . **39, 42**
  Max. Size: 35,000 – 100,000 d.w.t. tonnes, depth 141 m.
Lufeng 22-1 Terminal, China: 21.29 N. 116.28 E. **39**
  Max. Size: 150,000 d.w.t.
Luganville Bay, see Santo.
Lugnvik, see Svano.

Luhuashan Anchorage, see Shanghai.
Luise Harbour, Papua New Guinea: 3.07 S. 152.39 E. **46**
 Max. Size: LOA 140 m., depth 12 m.
Lukumor, see Nomoi Is..
Lulea, Sweden: 65.35 N. 22.09 E. **4, 10, 15**
 Max. Size: Draft 11.2 m. (MW). Tankers: LOA 250 m.,
 draft 11.1 m. *Fuel:* All grades. *Airport:* 15 km.
Lumbovka, Russia: 67.45 N. 40.30 E. **16**
Lumut, Brunei: 4.43 N. 114.26 E. **38, 39, 40**
 Max. Size: Draft 10.0 m. (arrival), 11.3 m. (departure).
Lumut, Malaya, Malaysia: 4.14 N. 100.38 E. **37, 38, 39, 40**
 Max. Size: Grain: LOA 575 ft., draft 30 ft. 6 in. salt water on
 Spring tides. Marine Terminal: LOA 230 m., draft 9.3 m.
 Fuel: By road tanker. *Airport:* Ipoh, 90 km.
Lundu, Sarawak, Malaysia: 1.40 N. 109.52 E. **38, 39**
Lundy Is., U.K.: 51.10 N. 4.40 W. **5, 6, 7**
Lunenburg, N.S., Canada: 44.23 N. 64.19 W. **60**
Lutong, see Miri.
Luwuk, Indonesia: 0.57 S. 122.47 E. **46**
LUXEMBOURG **7, 9**
Luzon Is., Philippines **46, 47**
Luzon Strait, Philippines **46, 47**
Lybster, U.K.: 58.18 N. 3.18 W. **5**
Lydney, U.K.: 51.43 N. 2.33 W. **6, 7**
 Max. Size: Basin 82.3 m. x 22.8 m., depth 7.3 m. (HWST).
 Inner dock: 237.7 m. x 32 m. Entrance: Width
 7 m., depth 3.6 m. *Airport:* Gloucester (Domestic) 24 miles.
 Bristol, 24 miles. Cardiff, 30 miles.
Lyme Bay, U.K. **7, 19**
Lyme Regis, U.K.: 50.43 N. 2.56 W. **7**
Lymington, U.K.: 50.45 N. 1.32 W. **7**
Lynaes, Denmark: 55.56 N. 11.52 E. **12**
Lyndiane, see Kaolack.
Lyngdal, Norway: 58.09 N. 7.08 E. **11, 12**
Lyngor, Norway: 58.38 N. 9.09 E. **11, 12**
Lyngsodde, Denmark: 55.31 N. 9.44 E. **12**
 Max. Size: Draft 11.0 m. *Fuel:* Available. *Dry Docks:* Floating
 dock, max. 8,000 tonnes *Airport:* Odense, 44 miles.
Lynmouth, U.K.: 51.15 N. 3.52 W. **6, 7**
Lynn, Massachusetts, U.S.A.: 42.27 N. 70.57 W. **63**
Lynn Canal, Alaska, U.S.A. **56**
Lyon, France: 45.46 N. 4.50 E. **9**
Lysekil, Sweden: 58.17 N. 11.26 E. **11, 12**
 Max. Size: Draft 18 ft. – 33 ft. *Fuel:* Diesel and gas oil.
Lyttelton, New Zealand: 43.35 S. 172.42 E. **52**
 Max. Size: Draft 12.2 m. (HW). LOA 294 m. at Cashin Quay,
 230 m. at Inner Harbour. Tankers: Draft 12 m. *Fuel:* Available.
 Dry Docks: A graving dock for vessels up to 6,500 g.r.t.,
 draft 5 m. *Airport:* 6 miles.
Lytton, see Brisbane.

M

M'Bao Terminal, see Dakar.
M'Bya Terminal, Gabon: 3.53 S. 10.56 E. **28**
 Max. Size: Draft 18.0 m., 150,000 d.w.t.
Ma Kung, Taiwan: 23.34 N. 119.33 E. **42**
 Max. Size: Depth 2.5 m. – 8 m.
Ma'anshan, China: 31.48 N. 118.32 E. **42**
Maaloy, Norway: 61.55 N. 5.07 E. **10, 11, 15**
 Max. Size: Depth 7 m. – 15 m. *Fuel:* Available. *Airport:* Floro,
 1 hour by boat.
Maarup, Denmark: 55.56 N. 10.33 E. **12**
Maasluis, Netherlands: 51.55 N. 4.15 E. **8**
 Also see Europoort and Rotterdam.
Maastricht, Netherlands: 50.47 N. 5.40 E. **7**
Mabou, N.S., Canada: 46.06 N. 61.27 W. **60**
Macao (SAR), China **39, 48**
Macapa, Brazil: 0.02 N. 51.03 W. **72**
 Max. Size: Depth 8.8 m. *Airport:* Nearby, connects with Belem.
 Also see Santana.
Macassar, see Ujung Pandang.
Macassar Strait, Indonesia **46**
Macau, see Areia Branca.
Macauley Is., (Kermadec Is.), New Zealand:
 30.15 S. 178.30 W. **49**
MacDonnell, see Port MacDonnell.
Macduff, U.K.: 57.40 N. 2.30 W. **5**
 Max. Size: LOA 61 m., beam 11 m., draft 4 m. *Fuel:* Available.
 Airport: Aberdeen, 45 miles.
Maceio, Brazil: 9.40 S. 35.44 W. **72**
 Max. Size: Draft 33 ft. *Fuel:* Diesel and fuel oil.
 Airport: Palmares, 30 km.
Machevna, Russia: 61.15 N. 172.25 E. **54**
Machilipatnam, see Masuilipatnam.
Macias, see Bata.
Macias Ngueme, see Bioco Is..
Mackay, Qld., Australia: 21.06 S. 149.14 E. **50, 51**
 Max. Size: Depths at berths 10.4 m. – 12.0 m. *Fuel:* Available.
 Airport: Connects with Brisbane.
Mackenzie, see Linden.
Mackinaw City, Michigan, U.S.A.: 45.47 N. 84.44 W. **62**
Maconacon, see Aparri.
Macoris, see San Pedro de Macoris.
Macquarie, see Port Macquarie.
Macquarie Harbour, Tas., Australia: 42.10 S. 145.19 E. **51**
Mactan, see Cebu.
Macun, see Haikou.
Macuse, see Porto Belo.
MADAGASCAR. **30**
Madagho, see Escravos.
Madang, Papua New Guinea: 5.13 S. 145.49 E. **46**
 Max. Size: Depth 10.1 m. at LAT. *Fuel:* Diesel and Distillate.
 Airport: Madang, 6 km.
Madden Dam, Panama Canal, Panama: 9.15 N. 79.37 W. **73**
Madeira (Portugal) **27**
Madisonville, Louisiana, U.S.A.: 30.24 N. 90.09 W. **67**
Madjene, Indonesia: 3.33 S. 118.57 E. **38, 46**
Madras, see Chennai.
Madre de Deus, Brazil: 12.45 S. 38.38 W. **77**
 Max. Size: LOA 240 m., draft 37 ft. – 41 ft. *Fuel:* Fuel oil
 available.
 Also see Salvador.
Madre de Dios Is., Chile: 50.20 S. 75.00 W. **72**
Madryn, see Puerto Madryn.
Madura, Indonesia: 6.51 S. 112.57 E. **38**
 Max. Size: LOA 250 m., 105,000 d.w.t., depth 21.3 m.
 Airport: Surabaya.
Madura Is., Indonesia **38**
Maewo Is., Vanuatu: 15.10 S. 168.10 E. **49**
Mafia Is., Tanzania **30**
Magadan, Russia: 59.36 N. 150.45 E. **43**
 Max. Size: Depth 9.75 m. – 11.5 m.
Magallanes Bay, (Luzon Is.), Philippines: 12.50 N. 123.50 E. . . . **47**
Magazine Point, see Mobile.
Magdalen Is., Quebec, Canada **60**
Magdalena, Argentina: 35.03 S. 57.29 W. **78**
Magdalena Bay, (Spitsbergen), Norway **17**
Magdalla, India: 21.08 N. 72.44 E. **37**
 Max. Size: Anchorage: Depth 12 m. – 30 m. SPM: 50,000 d.w.t.,
 LOA 170 m. – 250 m., max. arrival draft 13.0 m.
Magdeburg, Germany: 52.08 N. 11.37 E. **9**
Magellan Straits, Chile: 53.10 N. 70.54 W. **77**
 Max. Size: Normally 70 ft. draft, unless by arrangement.
 Also see Punta Arenas.
Magnisi, see Priolo.
Magpetco, Texas, U.S.A.: 30.02 N. 93.59 W. **66**
Maguilllin, see Constitucion.

Mahajunga, Madagascar: 15.44 S. 46.20 E. 30
  Max. Size: Draft 10 m. *Airport:* 7 km.
Mahanoro, Madagascar: 19.55 S. 48.50 E. 30
Mahares, Tunisia: 34.30 N. 10.30 E. 24
Mahdia, Tunisia: 35.30 N. 11.04 E. 24
Mahe, see Port Victoria.
Mahebourg, Mauritius: 20.25 S. 57.41 E. 30
Mahon, (Minorca), Spain: 39.52 N. 4.18 E. 21, 22
  Max. Size: Draft: Commercial port 25 ft., anchorage 43 ft. *Fuel:*
  Available. *Dry Docks:* Military dry dock of 2,000 tonnes.
  Airport: International, 4 km.
Mahone Bay, N.S., Canada: 44.27 N. 64.22 W. 60
Mailiao, Taiwan: 23.47 N. 120.07 E. 42
  Max. Size: LOA 310 m., draft 19.54 m. *Fuel:* Available.
Main Brook, Newfoundland, Canada: 5.10 N. 56.00 W. . . 60
Main Pass, (Mississippi Delta), Louisiana, U.S.A. . . . 67
Maine, U.S.A. 60
Mainland, (Orkney Is.), U.K. 5
Mainland, (Shetland Is.), U.K. 5
Maintirano, Madagascar: 18.04 S. 44.01 E. 30
Mainz, Germany: 50.00 N. 8.16 E. 7, 9
Maio Is., Cape Verde 27
Maitland, see Port Maitland.
Maizuru, Japan: 35.27 N. 135.19 E. 45
  Max. Size: Draft 9.5 m. – 12 m. Depth at buoys 14 m.
  Fuel: Bonded oil will be brought from Moji.
  Dry Docks: Largest: 246 m. x 33.5 m. x 12.5 m.
Majorca, (Balearic Is.), Spain 21, 22
Majunga, see Mahajunga.
Majuro, Marshall Is.: 7.07 N. 171.10 E. 49
  Max. Size: Depth 43 ft.
Makarevskiy, Russia: 50.50 N. 142.05 E. 43
Makarov, Russia: 48.37 N. 142.47 E. 43
Makarska, Croatia: 43.18 N. 17.01 E. 24
Makassar, see Ujung Pandang.
Makatea, (Society Is.), French Polynesia (France):
  15.50 S. 148.15 W. 49
Makemo, (Tuamotu Arch.), French Polynesia (France):
  16.35 S. 143.40 W. 49
Makhachkala, Russia: 42.59 N. 47.30 E. 9
Makin, see Butaritari Is..
Makiyama, see Wakamatsu.
Makkaur, Norway: 70.35 N. 30.00 E. 16
Makronisi Is., Greece: 37.42 N. 24.06 E. 25
Makurazaki, Japan: 31.16 N. 130.19 E. 45
Malabang, (Mindanao Is.), Philippines: 7.36 N. 124.04 E. . 47
Malabar Coast, India 37
Malabo, Equatorial Guinea: 3.46 N. 8.48 E. 29
  Max. Size: Draft 24 ft.
Malacca, Malaya, Malaysia: 2.13 N. 102.09 E. . . . 38, 39, 40
  Max. Size: Depth 9.0 m., LOA 125 m. *Fuel:* Available.
  Airport: Batu Berendam, 15 km.
  Also see Sungai Udang.
Malacca/Singapore Straits 36, 40
  Max. Size: To transit: Draft 20.5 m.
Malaga, Spain: 36.43 N. 4.25 W. 20, 21, 22, 27
  Max. Size: LOA 220 m. – 240 m., draft 40 ft. – 42 ft.
  Fuel: By road tanker. *Dry Docks:* Floating dock for vessels up to
  4,000 tons. *Airport:* 8 km.
Malahayati, Indonesia: 5.35 N. 95.31 E. 37, 38, 40
  Max. Size: Depth 4 m. – 5 m. Krueng Raya: Depth 4 m. – 10 m.
  Fuel: Available. *Airport:* Blang Bintang.
Malaita Is., Solomon Islands 51
Malakal, (Palau Is.) Palau: 7.20 N. 134.28 E. 46
Malamocco, Italy: 45.20 N. 12.19 E. 24
  Max. Size: Depth 12 m.
  Also see Venice.
MALAWI 30
Malaya, Malaysia 38, 39, 40
MALAYSIA 37, 38, 39, 40, 41, 47
Malden Is., Kiribati: 4.10 S. 154.50 W. 49
MALDIVES 37
Maldon, U.K.: 51.43 N. 0.42 E. 5, 7
Maldonado, Uruguay: 34.55 S. 54.58 W. 78
Male, (Hulule Is.), Maldives: 4.10 N. 73.30 E. 37
  Max. Size: 15,000 d.w.t., draft 9.5 m. *Fuel:* Available.
  Airport: 2.5 km.
Malekula Is., see Port Sandwich.
Malhado, see Ilheus.
MALI 27
Mali Losinj, Croatia: 44.32 N. 14.28 E. 24
Malili, Indonesia: 2.39 S. 120.59 E. 38, 46
  Max. Size: Anchorage: Depth over 20 m. (LWS). *Airport:*
  Daily flight to Ujung Pandang.
Malimba, Cameroon: 3.36 N. 9.39 E. 29
Malindi, Kenya: 3.10 N. 40.05 E. 30
Malingping, Indonesia: 6.45 S. 106.05 E. 38
Malitbog, (Leyte Is.), Philippines: 10.10 N. 125.00 E. . 47
Mallacoota, Vic., Australia: 37.40 S. 139.40 E. 50

Mallaig, U.K.: 57.01 N. 5.50 W. 5
  Max. Size: Depth 5 m. *Fuel:* Diesel by road tanker. *Airport:*
  Inverness, 180 km.
Malloco Bay, Solomon Islands: 7.36 S. 156.37 E. 49
  Max. Size: LOA 115 m., draft 7.2 m. *Airport:* 2 flights by light
  plane a week to Honiara.
Mallorytown, Ontario, Canada: 44.30 N. 75.55 W. 61
Malm, Norway: 64.04 N. 11.14 E. 15
Malmo, Sweden: 55.37 N. 13.00 E. 10, 11, 12
  Max. Size: Depth 9.2 m. Bulk: LOA 260 m., draft 12.5 m.
  Tankers: Draft 11.4 m. *Fuel:* All normal grades.
  Airport: Sturup, 25 km.
Maloelap, Marshall Is.: 8.43 N. 171.43 E. 49
Malong Marine Terminal, Malaysia: 4.38 N. 104.49 E. . 38, 39, 40
  Max. Size: 150,000 d.w.t., LOA 281 m.
Malongo LPG Terminal, Angola: 5.31 S. 12.10 E. 28
  Also see Cabinda.
Malongo Terminal, Angola: 5.26 S. 12.05 E. 28
  Max. Size: 325,000 d.w.t., LOA 1,150 ft.
  Also see Cabinda.
Malpe, India: 13.21 N. 74.42 E. 37
  Max. Size: Anchorage: Depth 4.5 fathoms. *Airport:* Nearest
  Mangalore.
Malpelo Is., Colombia: 4.03 N. 81.36 W. 69, 72
MALTA 21, 24
Malta Channel 24
Maltepe, Turkey: 40.54 N. 29.09 E. 23, 25
Malus Is., see Dampier.
Malygin Strait, Russia 16
Malyye Karmakuly, Russia: 72.25 N. 52.43 E. 16
Mambajao, (Camiguin Is.), Philippines: 9.15 N. 124.42 E. . 47
Mamburao, (Mindoro Is.), Philippines: 13.13 N. 120.38 E. . 47
Mamonal, Colombia: 10.19 N. 75.31 W. 69
  Max. Size: LOA 853 ft., beam 125 ft., draft 37 ft. 6 in.
  Also see Cartagena.
Mamoutsou, see Mamutza.
Mamuju, Indonesia: 2.41 S. 118.53 E. 38, 46
Mamutza, (Ile. Mayotte), Comoros Is. (France):
  12.47 S. 45.15 E. 30
Manado, Indonesia: 1.30 N. 124.50 E. 46
Manakara, Madagascar: 22.08 S. 48.05 E. 30
Manama, Bahrain: 26.13 N. 50.35 E. 35
Mananara, Madagascar: 16.12 S. 49.45 E. 30
Mananjary, Madagascar: 21.14 S. 48.20 E. 30
Manantenina, Madagascar: 24.15 S. 47.20 E. 30
Manatee, see Port Manatee.
Manati, Cuba: 21.24 N. 76.48 W. 70
  Max. Size: LOA 560 ft., draft 26 ft.
  Also see Puerto Padre.
Manaus, Brazil: 3.08 S. 60.00 W. 72
  Max. Size: Via the North Channel: Max. draft 30 ft.
  Via Belem: Draft 29 ft. with LOA up to 175 m. and
  draft 24 ft. with LOA up to 210 m. *Fuel:* Bunker "C" and diesel.
  Airport: Manaus.
Manchester, U.K.: 53.29 N. 2.14 W. 6, 7
  Max. Size: Depths: Eastham to Ince 8.78 m. Ince to Runcorn,
  Manchester 8.07 m. Manchester Docks 4.27 m. – 4.88 m.
  Max. LOA 170.6 m., beam 21.9 m. Height above water 21.5 m.
  Tankers for Queen Elizabeth II Dock: Lock: LOA 208.8 m.,
  beam 28.35 m., draft 10 m. *Fuel:* Available.
  Dry Docks: 163 m. x 19.8 m.
Manchester, Washington, U.S.A.: 47.32 N. 122.32 W. . . . 56
Mandal, Norway: 58.02 N. 7.29 E. 10, 11, 12
  Max. Size: Approx. 20,000 g.r.t. Tankers: 50,000 tons.
  Fuel: Available. *Airport:* Kjevik, 64 km.
Mandoukion, see Corfu.
Mandvi, India: 22.49 N. 69.24 E. 37
  Max. Size: Anchorage: Depth 3 – 5 fathoms. Drafts up to 9 ft. can
  reach wharves at HW.
Manfredonia, Italy: 41.37 N. 15.55 E. 9, 24
  Max. Size: Draft 32 ft. 6 in. (MHWS). *Fuel:* Available.
  Airport: Foggia, 36 km.
Mangaia Is., Cook Is. (N.Z.): 21.55 S. 157.58 W. 49
Mangalia, Romania: 43.49 N. 28.35 E. 9, 26
  Max. Size: Depth 9.0 m. – 10.0 m. *Fuel:* By road tanker.
  Dry Docks: Max. 150,000 d.w.t. *Airport:* Constantza, 70 km.
Mangalore, India: 12.50 N. 74.50 E. 37
  Max. Size: LOA 80 m., draft 4.5 m. *Fuel:* Available.
  Dry Docks: 110 ft. x 30 ft. Sill 8 ft. (MHWS). Capacity 450 d.w.t.
  Airport: Bajpe, 12 miles (20 km.).
  Also see New Mangalore.
Mangarin, see Tacloban.
Manggar, Indonesia: 2.52 S. 108.18 E. 38
Mangkasa, Indonesia: 2.44 S. 121.04 E. 38, 46
  Max. Size: LOA 600 ft., draft 31 ft., 20,000 d.w.t.
  Also see Malili.
Mangoli Is., Indonesia 46
Mangonui, New Zealand: 35.00 S. 173.32 E. 52
Mangrol, India: 21.06 N. 70.07 E. 37
Manguinhos, see Rio de Janeiro.
Manhattan, see New York.

Manifah, Saudi Arabia: 27.36 N. 48.56 E. 35
Manihi, (Society Is.), French Polynesia (France):
   14.24 S. 145.56 W. 49
Manihiki Is., Cook Is. (N.Z.): 10.18 S. 161.00 W. 49
Maniitsoq, Greenland (Denmark): 65.25 N. 52.54 W. 17, 59
   Max. Size: LOA 100 m., draft 6 m. Largest 4,000 tons.
   Airport: Heliport.
Manila, (Luzon Is.), Philippines: 14.35 N. 120.58 E. 46, 47
   Max. Size: Draft 9.75 m. Containers: Depth 12.0 m. – 14.5 m.
   Tankers: Sea Berth – Depth 45 ft. – 50 ft. *Fuel:* Only sufficient
   to reach next port of call. *Dry Docks:* Graving dock,
   16,000 d.w.t. *Airport:* Nimoy Aquino International, 8 km.
   Also see Subic Bay.
Manistee, Michigan, U.S.A.: 44.15 N. 86.19 W. 62
Manistique, Michigan, U.S.A.: 45.58 N. 86.16 W. 62
Manitoba, Canada 59
Manitou Is., Michigan, U.S.A.: 47.25 N. 87.36 W. 62
Manitoulin Is., Ontario, Canada 62
Manitowaning, Ontario, Canada: 45.44 N. 81.49 W. 62
Manitowoc, Wisconsin, U.S.A.: 44.06 N. 87.38 W. 55, 62
   Max. Size: LOA 600 ft., draft 21 ft. *Fuel:* Available.
   Dry Docks: Floating dock: 604 ft. x 70 ft. x 15 ft. over keel
   blocks, LOA 640 ft. *Airport:* Manitowoc.
Manna, Indonesia: 4.25 S. 102.53 E. 38
Mannar, Sri Lanka: 9.00 N. 79.55 E. 37
Mannheim, Germany: 49.30 N. 8.28 E. 9
Manoka, Cameroon: 3.51 N. 9.37 E. 29
Manokwari, Indonesia: 0.51 S. 134.05 E. 46
   Max. Size: Draft 12.0 m. *Airport:* Rendani, 9 km.
Manombo, Madagascar: 22.55 S. 43.30 E. 30
Manopla, see Santa Cruz del Sur.
Mansel Is., N.W.T., Canada 59
Manta, Ecuador: 0.56 S. 80.43 W. 72
   Max. Size: LOA 600 ft., beam 60 ft., draft 33 ft. *Fuel:* Diesel oil
   in small quantities. *Airport:* Flights to Quito.
Mantyluoto, see Pori.
Manua Is., American Samoa (U.S.A.): 14.14 S. 169.30 W. . . . 49
Manukau Harbour, see Onehunga.
Manus Is., (Admiralty Is.), Papua New Guinea 46
Manzanillo, Cuba: 20.20 N. 77.12 W. 69, 70
   Max. Size: Anchorage: LOA 180 m., draft 9.14 m.
   Tankers: LOA 147 m., draft 8.53 m.
Manzanillo, Dominican Republic: 19.43 N. 71.45 W. . . . 69, 70
   Max. Size: LOA 700 ft., beam 120 ft., draft 30 ft.
   Fuel: By road tanker. *Airport:* La Union, 130 km.
Manzanillo, Mexico: 19.03 N. 104.20 W. 57
   Max. Size: Interior Port: Draft 46 ft.
   Container Terminal: LOA 250 m., draft 46 ft.
   San Pedrito: Draft 36 ft. – 39 ft. Tankers: LOA 650 ft.,
   draft 31 ft. – 38 ft. New Pemex Jetty: Depth 52 ft. – 64 ft.
   Fuel: All grades. *Airport:* Domestic only.
Manzanillo, Panama: 9.22 N. 79.40 W. 73
   Max. Size: Depth 13 m.
   Also see Cristobal.
Map Ta Phut, Thailand: 12.39 N. 101.09 E. 37, 39
   Max. Size: Thai Tank Terminal: 45,000 d.w.t., LOA 200 m.,
   draft 11.9 m. Rayong Refining: LOA 260 m., draft 11.5 m. Star
   Petroleum: Tankers: LOA 125 m. LPG: Draft 7.5 m.
   SBM: 280,000 d.w.t., LOA 345 m., draft 20.4 m. National
   Petrochemical: 35,000 d.w.t., LOA 200 m., draft 12 m.
   MTT: LOA 260 m., beam 46 m., draft 12 m. *Fuel:* Available
   at some berths. *Airport:* Bangkok, 170 km.
Mapire, Venezuela: 7.58 N. 64.58 W. 75
Maputo, Mozambique: 25.59 S. 32.34 E. 30
   Max. Size: Draft 11.3 m., LOA up to 820 ft.
   Tankers: Depth 33 ft. – 35 ft. *Fuel:* Available. *Airport:* 4 km.
Maqal, see Umm Qasr.
Maqna, Saudi Arabia: 28.23 N. 34.48 E. 32
Mar del Plata, Argentina: 38.00 S. 57.32 W. 77
   Max. Size: Keel clearance of 2 ft. required. Normal
   draft 27 ft. 6 in., greater in best possible conditions.
   Tankers: Depth 22 ft. – 22 ft. 6 in. *Fuel:* Fuel oil and diesel.
   Airport: 6 miles, Domestic.
Maraba, Brazil: 5.22 S. 49.06 W. 72
Maracaibo, Venezuela: 10.42 N. 71.39 W. 69, 72, 74
   Max. Size: Depth 33 ft. *Fuel:* Heavy and medium marine diesel,
   intermediate fuel, and bunker "C". *Airport:* International.
Maracaibo Lake, Venezuela: 10.42 N. 71.39 W. 69, 72, 74
   Max. Size: Channel: Draft 34 ft. – 38 ft., depending on tide.
Marajo Is., Brazil: 1.00 S. 49.30 W. 72
Marakai, Kiribati: 2.03 N. 173.17 E. 49
Marans, France: 46.18 N. 1.00 W. 8, 19
Marathon, Ontario, Canada: 48.45 N. 86.23 W. 62
Marbella, Spain: 36.30 N. 4.55 W. 20, 22
Marblehead, Massachusetts, U.S.A.: 42.30 N. 70.51 W. . . . 63
Marcus Hook, Pennsylvania, U.S.A.: 39.49 N. 75.25 W. . . . 65
   Max. Size: Depth 35 ft. – 40 ft. *Fuel:* Available.
   Also see Philadelphia.
Marcus Is., see Minami Tori.
Mardas, see Ambarli.
Mare Is., see Tadine.

Marennes, France: 45.49 N. 1.07 W. 8, 19
Margaret Bay, Qld., Australia: 11.58 S. 143.12 E. 51
Margarita Is., Venezuela: 10.52 N. 64.04 W. 69, 71, 75
Margate, U.K.: 51.23 N. 1.23 E. 6
Marghera, see Venice.
Margosatubig, (Mindanao Is.), Philippines: 7.35 N. 123.10 E. . . 47
Maria Is., French Polynesia (France) 49
Maria Theresa Reef: 37.08 S. 151.10 W. 49
Mariager, Denmark: 56.39 N. 9.59 E. 11, 12
Maribyrnong, see Melbourne.
Maricourt, Quebec, Canada: 61.35 N. 71.59 W. 59
Marie Byrd Land, Antarctica 80
Marie Galante Is., Guadeloupe (France) 71
Marieberg, see Botea.
Mariehamn, Finland: 60.06 N. 19.56 E. 10, 11
   Max. Size: LOA 220 m. and draft 8.2 m., but require twin screw
   and bow thruster for safe manoeuvring. Tankers: LOA 100 m.,
   depth alongside 6 m. *Fuel:* Diesel. *Dry Docks:*
   Slipway 300 d.w.t. – 400 d.w.t. *Airport:* 5 km.
Mariel, Cuba: 23.01 N. 82.46 W. 70
   Max. Size: Draft through channel 30 ft., LOA 610 ft.
Mariestad, Sweden: 58.45 N. 13.50 E. 11, 12
Marin, Spain: 42.24 N. 8.42 W. 20, 22
   Max. Size: Draft 12 m. Tankers: LOA 100 m., draft 21 ft.
   Fuel: Available. *Dry Docks:* Up to 3,000 tons.
   Airport: Vigo, 25 km.
Marina de Carrera, Italy: 44.02 N. 10.02 E. 23, 24
Marina Grande, (Capri Is.), Italy: 40.33 N. 14.15 E. . . . 23, 24
Marinduque Is., see Santa Cruz.
Mariners Harbour, see Stapleton.
Marinette, Wisconsin, U.S.A.: 45.05 N. 87.37 W. 62
Marion, Massachusetts, U.S.A.: 41.42 N. 70.46 W. 64
Marion Reefs, Australia 51
Maripa, Venezuela: 7.25 N. 65.10 W. 75
Maritime, see Guayaquil.
Mariupol, Ukraine: 47.06 N. 37.35 E. 21, 26
   Max. Size: LOA 240 m., draft 8 m. *Fuel:* Available.
   Dry Docks: 15,000 tons. *Airport:* 15 km.
Mariveles, see Bataan.
Marmagoa, see Mormugao.
Marmara Is., Turkey: 40.37 N. 27.35 E. 25
Marmaris, Turkey: 36.51 N. 28.18 E. 25, 26
Marmaron, Greece: 38.33 N. 26.06 E. 25
Marmorilik, Greenland (Denmark): 71.07 N. 51.17 W. . . 17, 79
   Mining operations ceased
Maroantsetra, Madagascar: 15.17 S. 49.46 E. 30
Maromandia, Madagascar: 14.15 S. 48.05 E. 30
Marquesas Islands, French Polynesia (France) 49
Marquesas Keys, Florida, U.S.A.: 24.34 N. 82.07 W. . . 66, 69
Marquette, Michigan, U.S.A.: 46.32 N. 87.25 W. 62
Marrero, Louisiana, U.S.A.: 29.54 N. 90.06 W. 67
   Max. Size: Depth 35 ft. – 38 ft.
   Also see New Orleans.
Marsa al Hamra, Egypt: 30.59 N. 28.52 E. 26
   Max. Size: 100,000 d.w.t., draft 38 ft.
Marsa al Hariga, Libya: 32.04 N. 24.00 E. 26
   Max. Size: Max. Summer deadweight 150,000 long tons.,
   draft 56 ft.
Marsa Alam, Egypt: 25.05 N. 34.48 E. 32
Marsa Bashayer, see Bashayer.
Marsa el Brega, Libya: 30.25 N. 19.34 E. 24
   Max. Size: Cargo vessels: LOA 500 ft., draft 10.0 m.
   Tankers: 300,000 d.w.t., depth 140 ft. Naphtha: Depth 44 ft.,
   65,000 d.w.t. LOA 800 ft., draft 42 ft. Product: LOA 500 ft.,
   draft 26 ft. Gas: Depth 37 ft.
Marsa Susa, Libya: 32.54 N. 21.58 E. 24
Marsala, Italy: 37.47 N. 12.26 E. 24
Marsaxlokk, Malta: 35.49 N. 14.33 E. 24
   Max. Size: Depth 9.5 m. – 15.5 m. Tankers: 120,000 d.w.t.,
   LOA 300 m., draft 16 m. *Fuel:* By barge or road tanker.
   Airport: Malta International, 6 km.
   Also see Valletta.
Marsden Point, New Zealand: 35.51 S. 174.30 E. 52
   Max. Size: LOA 304 m., draft 15.24 m. *Fuel:* Available.
   Airport: Auckland.
Marseilles, France: 43.18 N. 5.25 E. 9, 21, 22, 23
   Max. Size: Draft 14.5 m. *Fuel:* Available. *Dry Docks:*
   Largest: 465 m. x 84 m. x 10 m. *Airport:* Marseilles.
   Also see Fos and Port de Bouc.
Marsh Is., Louisiana, U.S.A.: 29.30 N. 91.48 W. 66
Marshall, Liberia: 6.08 N. 10.22 W. 27
MARSHALL ISLANDS 49
Marshall Lagoon, see Kupiano.
Marstal, Denmark: 54.51 N. 10.31 E. 12, 14
   Max. Size: LOA 115 m., beam 32 m., draft 4.5 m.
   Fuel: By road tanker.
Marstrand, Sweden: 57.53 N. 11.34 E. 11, 12
Martas, Turkey: 40.57 N. 27.55 E. 25, 26
   Max. Size: 45,000 d.w.t., LOA 250 m., draft 13 m.
   Fuel: Available. *Airport:* Tekirdag, 40 km.

Marthas Vineyard Is., Massachusetts, U.S.A. 63
Martigues, see Port de Bouc.
Martin Garcia, Argentina: 34.11 S. 58.17 W. 78
Martinez, see Benicia.
Martinique (France) 69, 71
Martinniemi, see Haukipudas.
Marugame, Japan: 34.18 N. 133.47 E. 45
  Max. Size: 15,000 d.w.t., draft 8.6 m. *Fuel:* From Sakaide.
Maryborough, Qld., Australia: 25.30 S. 152.49 E. 50
Maryland, U.S.A. 60, 63, 65
Maryport, U.K.: 54.43 N. 3.30 W. 5
Marystown, Newfoundland, Canada: 47.10 N. 55.09 W. . . . 60
  Max. Size: Depth alongside 5.5 m. – 15 m. *Fuel:* Available.
  Dry Docks: Syncrolift, capacity 3,000 tonnes. *Airport:* St. John's, 300 km.
Marysville, see St. Clair.
Masan, South Korea: 35.11 N. 128.35 E. 42, 43
  Max. Size: 20,000 d.w.t., LOA 210 m. draft 11 m.
  Fuel: Available. *Dry Docks:* 3 minor dry docks.
  Airport: Kimhae, 70 km.
Masao, (Mindanao Is.), Philippines: 9.06 N. 125.22 E. . . 46, 47
  Max. Size: Depth 7 m. alongside. Deep water anchorage berths available.
  Also see Nasipit.
Masbate, (Masbate Is.), Philippines: 12.23 N. 123.37 E. . 46, 47
  Max. Size: LOA 300 m., draft 40 ft. *Fuel:* All grades.
  Airport: 1 km., connects with Manila.
Mashabih Is., Saudi Arabia: 25.35 N. 36.30 E. 32
Masinloc, (Luzon Is.), Philippines: 15.33 N. 119.58 E. . 46, 47
  Port closed
Masirah Is., Oman 31
Maslenica, Croatia: 43.24 N. 16.13 E. 24
Masnedoevaerket, Denmark: 55.00 N. 11.53 E. 12, 14
  Max. Size: LOA 100 m., beam 17 m., draft 6.7 m.,
  bridge height: 21 m. *Fuel:* Available.
  Airport: Copenhagen, 60 miles.
Masnedsund, see Vordingborg.
Massachusetts, U.S.A. 60, 63, 64
Massacre Bay, (Attu Is.), Alaska, U.S.A.: 52.40 N. 173.14 W. . 54
Massawa, Eritrea: 15.37 N. 39.28 E. 32
  Max. Size: LOA 175 m., draft 8.8 m. *Fuel:* By road tanker.
  Dry Docks: Slipway for vessel up to 600 g.r.t. *Airport:* 7 km., connects with Asmara International.
Massawa Channel, Eritrea 32
Massena, New York, U.S.A.: 44.50 N. 74.55 W. 61
Masset, B.C., Canada: 54.02 N. 132.09 W. 56
Mastaba, Saudi Arabia: 20.52 N. 39.29 E. 32
Mastura, Saudi Arabia: 23.10 N. 38.50 E. 32
Masuda, Japan: 34.40 N. 131.42 E. 45
Masuilipatnam, India: 16.10 N. 81.15 E. 37
Mataboor, Indonesia: 1.40 S. 138.05 E. 46
Matadi, Congo (D.R. of): 5.49 S. 13.27 E. 28
  Max. Size: Controlled by draft in river, 19 ft. Max. draft at berth 23 ft. – 24 ft. *Fuel:* Gas oil, light and heavy fuel in small quantities.
Matagorda Is., Texas, U.S.A. 66
Matala, (Crete), Greece: 34.59 N. 24.44 E. 25
Matamoros, Mexico: 25.53 N. 97.30 W. 66, 69
Matane, Quebec, Canada: 48.51 N. 67.34 W. 60
  Max. Size: 30,000 d.w.t., LOA 175 m., draft 8.5 m. *Fuel:* Light fuel and diesel oil. *Dry Docks:* Les Mechins, 30 miles.
  Airport: Daily flight to Montreal.
Matanzas, Cuba: 23.03 N. 81.34 W. 69, 70
  Max. Size: Draft 32 ft.
Matanzas, Venezuela: 8.17 N. 62.52 W. 72, 75
  Max. Size: LOA 600 ft., beam 74 ft., draft 41 ft. in rainy season (May-Nov.), 28 ft. in dry season. *Fuel:* Available.
  Airport: 10 miles, connects with Caracas.
Matara, Sri Lanka: 5.57 N. 80.31 E. 37
Matarani, Peru: 17.00 S. 72.07 W. 72, 77
  Max. Size: LOA 570 ft., depth 30 ft.
  Tankers: Mollendo: Draft 16 m.
Mataro, Spain: 41.32 N. 2.30 E. 22
Mategata, Japan: 34.06 N. 132.55 E. 45
  Max. Size: Anchorage: Depth 12.0 m. – 20.0 m.
  Also see Imabari.
Mati, (Mindanao Is.), Philippines: 6.56 N. 126.14 E. . . . 47
  Max. Size: 18,000 g.r.t. *Airport:* Davao.
Matias de Galvez, see Santo Tomas de Castilla.
Matochkin Strait, (Novaya Zemlya), Russia 16
Matola, see Maputo.
Matsu Is., Taiwan: 26.10 N. 119.55 E. 42
Matsue, Japan: 35.27 N. 133.08 E. 43, 45
Matsunaga, Japan: 34.26 N. 133.15 E. 45
  Max. Size: Draft 8.5 m. *Fuel:* Available.
  Also see Onomichi-Itozaki.
Matsushima, Japan: 32.56 N. 129.36 E. 42, 45
  Max. Size: 87,000 d.w.t., LOA 235 m., draft 14 m.
  Fuel: Available. *Airport:* Nagasaki, 70 km.

Matsuura, Japan: 33.21 N. 129.41 E. 42, 45
  Max. Size: 130,000 d.w.t., LOA 270 m., draft 16.3 m.
  Fuel: By barge. *Airport:* Fukuoka or Nagasaki.
Matsuura Is., (Kurile Is.), Russia: 48.00 N. 153.10 E. . . 43
Matsuyama, Japan: 33.52 N. 132.42 E. 43, 45
  Max. Size: Tankers: 50,000 d.w.t., LOA 240 m., draft 12 m.
  Umaiso Bay: LOA 160 m., draft 15 m. Yura Bay: LOA 110 m., draft 10 m. *Fuel:* All grades lightered from nearest bunker stock ports. *Airport:* Matsuyama.
  Also see Sakaide.
Matsuzaka, Japan: 34.37 N. 136.34 E. 45
  Max. Size: 5,000 d.w.t., depth 7.5 m. *Airport:* Nagoya, 3.5 hours.
Matthew Is., New Caledonia (France): 22.20 S. 171.23 E. . . 49
Matthew Town, (Great Inagua Is.), Bahamas: 20.57 N. 73.40 W. 70
Matua, Indonesia: 2.55 S. 110.50 E. 38
Maturin Bar, see Caripito.
Maubau, Philippines: 14.38 N. 120.18 E. 47
Maud Landing, W.A., Australia: 23.07 S. 113.47 E. . . 50, 51
Maui Is., Hawaii, U.S.A. 49
Mauke Is., Cook Is. (N.Z.): 20.12 S. 157.30 W. 49
Maumere, Indonesia: 8.37 S. 122.13 E. 38, 46
  Max. Size: LOA 130 m., draft 11.0 m. *Fuel:* By road tanker.
Maungdaw, Myanmar: 20.50 N. 92.21 E. 37
MAURITANIA 27
MAURITIUS 30
Mawan, see Chiwan.
Mayaguana, Bahamas: 22.25 N. 73.00 W. 69, 70
Mayaguez, Puerto Rico (U.S.A.): 18.13 N. 67.12 W. . . 69, 70
  Max. Size: Safe draft is 27 ft. *Fuel:* All grades.
  Airport: Mani, 15 minutes from pier, connects with San Juan.
Maydi, Yemen: 16.18 N. 42.48 E. 32
Mayne, B.C., Canada: 48.51 N. 123.18 W. 56
Mayport, Florida, U.S.A.: 30.24 N. 81.26 W. 66
Mayumba, see M'Bya Terminal.
Mazagan, see El Jadida.
Mazara del Vallo, (Sicily), Italy: 37.40 N. 12.35 E. . . . 24
Mazarron, Spain: 37.33 N. 1.15 W. 22
Mazaruni, Guyana: 6.24 N. 58.40 W. 75, 76
  Dry Docks: 160 ft. x 35 ft.
  Also see Georgetown.
Mazatlan, Mexico: 23.11 N. 106.26 W. 57
  Max. Size: Cargo vessels: LOA 190 m., draft 27 ft. or LOA 180 m., draft 33 ft. Cruise vessels: LOA 240 ft., draft 30 ft. (if vessel is fitted with bow thruster, has 2 engines and uses 2 tugs). Tankers: Draft 30 ft. *Fuel:* Available.
  Airport: International, 12.5 miles.
Mazirbe, Latvia: 57.45 N. 22.25 E. 11
McKean Is., (Phoenix Is.), Kiribati: 4.28 S. 174.10 W. . . 49
McNeil, see Port McNeil.
McNicoll, see Port McNicoll.
Me Tho, see My Thoi.
Meadows, see Port Meadows.
Meaford, Ontario, Canada: 44.37 N. 80.35 W. 62
Mechigmen, Russia: 65.20 N. 172.00 W. 54
Mecklenburg Bay, Germany 12, 14
Mede, see Port de Bouc.
Medgidia, Romania: 44.15 N. 28.16 E. 26
  Max. Size: 5,000 d.w.t., LOA 138 m., beam 16.5 m. and draft 5.5 m.
Media Luna, Cuba: 20.10 N. 77.26 W. 70
  Max. Size: (Anchorage) LOA 170 m., draft 9.45 m.
  Also see Manzanillo.
Mediterranean Sea 21, 22, 23, 24, 25, 26, 32, 33, 34
Medway, Canada, see Port Medway.
Medway Ports, U.K.: 51.27 N. 0.44 E. 6
  Max. Size: Draft 13.5 m. *Fuel:* Available.
  Dry Docks: Slipway up to 42.67 m.
  Airport: Gatwick and Stansted.
  Also see Kent Terminal, Ridham Dock, Rochester, Sheerness, Thamesport, Chatham and Kingsnorth.
Mega, Japan: 34.44 N. 134.42 E. 45
  Max. Size: Draft 11.8 m. Sea Berth: Depth 19 m.
  Also see Himeji.
Megalo Khorio, (Tilos), Greece: 36.27 N. 27.24 E. 25
Meganisi, Greece: 38.39 N. 20.47 E. 25
Meganssett, Massachusetts, U.S.A.: 41.39 N. 70.37 W. . . 64
Megara, Greece: 37.58 N. 23.24 E. 23
  Max. Size: 75,000 d.w.t., draft 12.19 m. *Airport:* Athens, 60 km.
Mehamn, Norway: 71.00 N. 27.45 E. 15
Mehdia, Morocco: 34.16 N. 6.41 W. 27
Mehetia Is., (Society Is.), French Polynesia (France): 17.52 S. 148.03 W. 49
Meizhou, China: 25.10 N. 118.58 E. 42
  Max. Size: Tankers: 100,000 d.w.t., draft 12 m.
  Also see Xiuyu.
Mejillones, Chile: 23.06 S. 70.28 W. 77
  Max. Size: Anchorage port: No restrictions. Ammonia: (Buoys) LOA 180 m., 15,000 d.w.t. *Airport:* Cerro Moreno, 25 km.

Mekar Putih, Indonesia: 4.01 S. 116.02 E. 38
  Max. Size: South Pulau Laut Coal Terminal: 80,000 d.w.t.,
  depth 13.5 m. – 16 m. *Airport:* Banjarmasin, 8 hours by car.
Mekong Delta, Vietnam 39
Mekoryuk, Alaska, U.S.A.: 60.24 N. 166.10 W. 54
Melaka, see Malacca.
Melbourne, Vic., Australia: 37.50 S. 144.58 E. 50, 51
  Max. Size: Dry Cargo: Webb Dock: LOA 250 m., draft 11.9 m.
  Port Melbourne: LOA 305 m., draft 10 m.
  Containers: LOA 290 m., draft 11.9 m.
  Tankers: Yarraville: LOA 190 m., draft 9.6 m. *Fuel:* All grades.
  Dry Docks: Floating dock: 156 m. × 24 m. *Airport:* 10 miles.
Meldrum Bay, Ontario, Canada: 45.56 N. 83.07 W. 62
Melilla, Spain: 35.18 N. 2.57 W. 22
  Max. Size: Up to 30 ft. draft. *Fuel:* Available. *Airport:* 1 km.,
  connects with Malaga and Almeria.
  Also see Port Nador.
Melilli, (Sicily), Italy: 37.07 N. 15.16 E. 24
  Also see Augusta and Santa Panagia.
Melina, Greece: 39.10 N. 23.13 E. 25
Melinca, Chile: 43.54 S. 73.45 W. 77
Melito, Italy: 37.45 N. 15.50 E. 24
Mellerud, Sweden: 58.40 N. 12.30 E. 12
Mellon, see Port Mellon.
Melolo, Indonesia: 9.53 S. 120.40 E. 38, 46, 50
Melville Bay, see Gove.
Melville Is., N.T., Australia 46, 50
Mem, Sweden: 58.29 N. 16.25 E. 11
Memba, Mozambique: 14.10 S. 40.30 E. 30
Memboro, Indonesia: 9.28 S. 119.30 E. 38, 46
Mena Saud, see Mina Saud.
Menai Strait, U.K. 5
Menasha, Wisconsin, U.S.A.: 44.12 N. 88.27 W. 62
Meneng, see Banyuwangi.
Menier, see Port Menier.
Menominee, Michigan, U.S.A.: 45.07 N. 87.37 W. 62
Menstad, see Skien.
Menton, France: 43.47 N. 7.31 E. 22, 23
Menzies Bay, B.C., Canada: 50.07 N. 125.23 W. 56
Merak, Indonesia: 5.55 S. 106.00 E. 38
Merauke, Indonesia: 8.28 S. 140.23 E. 46
  Max. Size: Draft 6.0 m. *Airport:* Mopah, 6 km.
Meraux, Louisiana, U.S.A.: 29.55 N. 89.56 W. 67
  Also see New Orleans.
Merca, Somalia: 1.43 N. 44.47 E. 31
Mercedes, (Luzon Is.), Philippines: 14.07 N. 123.01 E. 47
Mercedes, Uruguay: 33.10 S. 58.10 W. 78
Meregh, Somalia: 3.46 N. 47.15 E. 31
Mergui, Myanmar: 12.29 N. 98.36 E. 37
Mergui Archipelago, Myanmar 37
Merikhas, (Kithnos), Greece: 37.24 N. 24.24 E. 25
Merir Is., (Caroline Is.), Micronesia: 4.19 N. 132.19 E. . . . 46
Mers-el-Kebir, Algeria: 35.44 N. 0.42 W. 21, 22
Mersa Fatma, Eritrea: 14.55 N. 40.17 E. 32
Mersa Matruh, Egypt: 31.22 N. 27.14 E. 26
Mersin, Turkey: 36.47 N. 34.38 E. 21, 26
  Max. Size: Depth 14 m. Tankers: 100,000 d.w.t., draft 12.5 m.
  Fuel: Available. *Airport:* Adana, 60 km.
Mersing, Malaya, Malaysia: 2.23 N. 103.48 E. 38, 39, 40
Mersrags, Latvia: 57.20 N. 23.08 E. 11
  Max. Size: LOA 80 m., beam 12 m., draft 4.5 m.
Mesaieed, Qatar: 24.54 N. 51.34 E. 31, 35
  Max. Size: Draft 37 ft. (HW), LOA 850 ft. LNG: LOA 950 ft.,
  depth 42 ft. Tankers: 320,000 d.w.t., LOA 340 m., beam 60 m.,
  depth 65 ft. Products: LOA 780 ft., depth 13 m.
  Fuel: Available at Berth No. 6.
Meschers, France: 45.34 N. 0.57 W. 8
Mesolongion, Greece: 38.22 N. 21.26 E. 25
Messina, (Sicily), Italy: 38.11 N. 15.34 E. 21, 24
  Max. Size: Draft 33 ft. at passenger quay. Other berths 27 ft.,
  LOA 200 m. – 300 m. Tankers: LOA 100 m., draft 27 ft.
  Dry Docks: Length 853 ft. (260 m.), breadth 118 ft. (36 m.).
  Airport: Reggio Calabria, 10 km.
Messini, Greece: 37.05 N. 22.00 E. 24, 25
Mesta, Greece: 38.15 N. 25.52 E. 25
Mestghanem, see Mostaganem.
Metas, see Nemrut Bay.
Meteghan, N.S., Canada: 44.13 N. 66.09 W. 60
Methil, U.K.: 56.11 N. 3.01 W. 6
  Max. Size: Depth 7.9 m. (MHWS), beam 14.4 m.
Methoni, Greece: 36.49 N. 21.42 E. 25
Methonis, Greece: 40.27 N. 22.36 E. 24, 25
Metkovic, Croatia: 43.05 N. 17.40 E. 24
Metlakatla, Alaska, U.S.A.: 55.08 N. 131.35 W. 56
  Max. Size: Depth 23 ft. – 35 ft. *Airport:* Small charter plane only,
  connects Ketchikan.
Metz, France: 49.07 N. 6.11 E. 9
Meulaboh, Indonesia: 4.09 N. 96.08 E. 38, 40
Mevagissey, U.K.: 50.16 N. 4.47 W. 7
MEXICO 49, 55, 57, 66, 69

Mezen, Russia: 65.50 N. 44.04 E. 16, 79
  Max. Size: Draft 3.9 m. – 4.2 m., LOA 70 m.
  Fuel: Not guaranteed.
Mezhdusharski Is., Russia: 71.10 N. 53.00 E. 16
Miami, Florida, U.S.A.: 25.46 N. 80.10 W. 55, 66, 69, 70
  Max. Size: Depth 25 ft. – 42 ft. Tankers: Draft 34 ft. (MLW).
  Fuel: All grades. *Airport:* 8 miles.
Miao Tao Is., China 42
Michigan, U.S.A. 62
Michigan City, Michigan, U.S.A.: 41.43 N. 86.55 W. 62
Michipicoten, Ontario, Canada: 47.57 N. 84.54 W. 62
Michipicoten Is., Ontario, Canada 62
Michurin, Bulgaria: 42.10 N. 27.54 E. 26
MICRONESIA, FEDERATED STATES OF 46, 49
Middelburg, Netherlands: 51.30 N. 3.37 E. 8
Middelfart, Denmark: 55.30 N. 9.44 E. 12
  Max. Size: 5,000 d.w.t. – 6,000 d.w.t., 6.5 m. draft.
  Fuel: All grades. *Airport:* Billund, Beldringe – both 45 km.
Middelharnis, Netherlands: 51.47 N. 4.12 E. 8
Middle Andaman Is., (Andaman Is.), India: 12.30 N. 92.57 E. . . 37
Middlesbrough, U.K.: 54.35 N. 1.14 W. 4, 5, 6
  Max. Size: LAT Nominal depth 4.8 m., 7,000 d.w.t.
  Also see Teesport.
Mideye, Turkey: 41.45 N. 27.55 E. 26
Midia, Romania: 44.20 N. 28.41 E. 26
  Max. Size: 7,000 d.w.t., draft 7.5 m. *Fuel:* Available.
  Dry Docks: 2 × 10,000 d.w.t. and 1 × 20,000 d.w.t.
  Airport: Constantza.
Midland, Ontario, Canada: 44.44 N. 79.44 W. 62
Midvaag, Faroe Is. (Denmark): 62.03 N. 7.11 W. 5, 15
Midway Is., (U.S.A.): 28.11 N. 177.20 W. 49
Mihara, see Itozaki.
Miike, Japan: 33.00 N. 130.23 E. 45
  Max. Size: Drafts 29 ft. 6 in. up to 20,000 d.w.t.; 26 ft. 4 in. up to
  25,000 d.w.t., 24 ft. 6 in. up to 30,000 d.w.t. *Fuel:* By barge.
  Airport: Fukuoka.
  Also see Shimonoseki.
Mikoyanovsk, Russia: 52.40 N. 156.00 E. 43, 54
Milaki, Greece: 38.22 N. 24.04 E. 25
  Max. Size: Discharge: LOA 280 m., beam 43.5 m., draft 16.0 m.
  (forward), 17.5 m. (aft). Loading: LOA 220 m., beam 32 m.,
  draft 12.5 m. *Fuel:* Small quantities by truck. *Airport:* Athens.
Milazzo, (Sicily), Italy: 38.13 N. 15.16 E. 24
  Max. Size: Depth at quay to 9 m. Tankers: 420,000 d.w.t.,
  depth 83 ft. *Fuel:* All grades. *Airport:* Reggio Calabria, 2 hours.
Milbuk, (Mindanao Is.), Philippines: 6.10 N. 124.16 E. . . . 46, 47
Milford Haven, U.K.: 51.42 N. 5.10 W. 4, 5, 6, 7
  Max. Size: Depth 2.5 m. – 20.3 m. Tankers: Draft 68 ft. in
  favourable conditions. *Fuel:* All grades. *Dry*
  Docks: 600 ft. × 63 ft. × 18 ft. *Airport:* Cardiff, 100 miles.
Milford Sound, New Zealand: 44.41 S. 167.53 E. 52
Milgravis, Latvia: 57.02 N. 24.07 E. 11
Milhaud, see Toulon.
Mili, Marshall Is.: 6.08 N. 171.49 E. 49
Mill Is., N.W.T., Canada 59
Millbank, see Miramichi.
Milner Bay, see Groote Eylandt.
Milos Island, Greece: 36.43 N. 24.27 E. 25, 26
  Max. Size: Draft 36 ft. *Fuel:* Small quantities of lubricants.
Milton Regis, U.K.: 51.22 N. 0.46 E. 6
Milwaukee, Wisconsin, U.S.A.: 43.01 N. 87.53 W. 55, 62
  Max. Size: LOA 730 ft., beam 78 ft., draft 26 ft. (F.W.).
  Fuel: All grades. *Airport:* 5 miles.
Mina Abdulla, Kuwait: 29.02 N. 48.11 E. 35
  Max. Size: 276,000 d.w.t., LOA 350 m., draft 16.92 m.
  Fuel: Fuel oil available. *Airport:* Kuwait.
Mina Al Bakir, see Albakr Terminal.
Mina Al Zoor, see Mina Saud.
Mina Al-Ahmadi, Kuwait: 29.04 N. 48.09 E. 35
  Max. Size: South Pier: Displacement 120,000 tonnes,
  LOA 292 m., draft 13.72 m. (crude) – 14.02 m. (LPG).
  North Pier: Displacement 315,000 tonnes (part load), LOA 454
  m., draft 16.92 m. SPM: Displacement 550,000 tonnes,
  draft 27.43 m. SBM: Draft 27.43 m. *Fuel:* Available.
Mina Jebel Ali, see Jebel Ali.
Mina Khalid, see Sharjah.
Mina Qaboos, see Port Sultan Qaboos.
Mina Raysut, see Port Salalah.
Mina Saqr, Ras Al Khaimah, U.A.E.: 25.59 N. 56.03 E. 35
  Max. Size: LOA 244 m. Draft 11.5 m.
  Fuel: Fuel oil, marine diesel oil, gas oil and marine lubricants.
  Airport: Ras al Khaimah, 45 km.
Mina Saud, Kuwait: 28.45 N. 48.23 E. 35
  Max. Size: Draft up to 56 ft. 10 in. *Fuel:* By barge.
  Airport: Kuwait, 85 km.
Mina Sulman, Bahrain: 26.12 N. 50.37 E. 31, 35
  Max. Size: LOA 300 m., depth to 10.9 m. *Fuel:* Available.
  Dry Docks: 375 m. × 75 m. *Airport:* International.
Mina Zayed, Abu Dhabi, U.A.E.: 24.32 N. 54.23 E. 31, 35, 37
  Max. Size: Draft 12 m. – 12.5 m. *Fuel:* Diesel oil and gas oil by
  barge. *Airport:* Dubai, 40 km.

Mina-al-Fahal, Oman: 23.40 N. 58.30 E. **31, 35, 37**
  Max. Size: Tankers: 554,000 d.w.t. *Fuel:* By barge.
  Airport: Muscat.
Minamata, Japan: 32.11 N. 130.21 E. **45**
  Max. Size: 10,000 d.w.t., depth 6.5 m.
  Airport: Kumamoto, 100 km.
Minami Io, (Japan): 24.14 N. 141.29 E. **46**
Minami Tori, (Japan): 24.17 N. 153.58 E. **46, 49**
Minatitlan, Mexico: 17.54 N. 94.35 W. **69**
  Max. Size: Tankers: LOA 475 ft., depth 9.4 m.
  Dry cargo (fertiliser): LOA 440 ft., draft 21 ft. (FW).
  Fuel: Marine diesel oil and Bunker "C" obtainable at Tanker
  berths. Diesel oil only by tank truck. *Airport:*
  15 minute car drive, connects with Mexico City.
Mindanao, Philippines **46, 47**
Minden, Germany: 52.18 N. 8.55 E. **9**
Mindoro, Philippines **46, 47**
Mingan, Quebec, Canada: 50.17 N. 64.01 W. **60**
Minicoy, (Laccadive Is.), India: 8.22 N. 73.07 E. . . . **37**
Minimata, see Minamata.
Minnesota, U.S.A. **62**
Mino, Japan: 34.46 N. 131.09 E. **45**
Minorca, (Balearic Is.), Spain **21, 22**
Minto Reef, (Caroline Is.), Micronesia: 8.10 N. 154.17 E. **49**
Miquelon, St. Pierre and Miquelon (France):
  47.06 N. 56.22 W. **60**
Miraflores Lake, Panama Canal, Panama **73**
Miraflores Lock, Panama Canal, Panama: 9.00 N. 79.36 W. . . **73**
Miragoane, Haiti: 18.25 N. 73.04 W. **69, 70**
  Max. Size: Depth: 10 ft. at general cargo wharf; 34 ft. at
  Bauxite wharf.
Miramar, Brazil: 1.24 S. 48.29 W. **72**
  Max. Size: 23,000 d.w.t., LOA 210 m., draft 7.9 m.
  Fuel: Available. *Airport:* 1 km.
Miramar, New Zealand, see Wellington.
Miramichi, N.B., Canada: 47.07 N. 64.47 W. **60**
  Max. Size: Draft 7 m. *Fuel:* By road tanker. *Airport:* Miramichi
  East (Chatham), private traffic only.
Miranda, see Puerto Miranda.
Mirbat, Oman: 17.02 N. 54.35 E. **31, 37**
Miri, Sarawak, Malaysia: 4.26 N. 113.55 E. **38, 39**
  Max. Size: Anchorage: No limit. Kuala Baram: 5,000 g.r.t.,
  depth 5 m. Tankers: Lutong (S.B.M.'s) 30,000 d.w.t. –
  150,000 d.w.t., draft 37 ft. – 56 ft. *Fuel:* Available.
  Airport: 47 km.
Mirina, Greece: 39.51 N. 25.04 E. **25**
Mirs Bay, Hong Kong (SAR), China **48**
Mirtoan Sea, Greece **25**
Misaki, Japan: 33.23 N. 132.08 E. **45**
Mishima-Kawanoe, Japan: 34.00 N. 133.30 E. **45**
  Max. Size: LOA 290 m., draft 13.5 m. *Fuel:* By barge with
  advance notice. *Airport:* Takamatsu, 80 km.
  Matsuyama, 100 km.
Misima Is., Papua New Guinea: 10.35 S. 152.50 E. **46**
Mispec Point, see Saint John, N.B., Canada.
Mission City, B.C., Canada: 49.17 N. 122.21 W. **56**
Mission Port, see Aparri.
Mississippi, U.S.A. **66, 67**
Mississippi Delta, Louisiana, U.S.A. **66, 67**
  Also see Southwest Pass.
Mississippi Sound, Louisiana, U.S.A. **67**
Mistaken Is., see Dampier.
Mistley, U.K.: 51.57 N. 1.05 E. **7**
  Max. Size: Draft 5.3 m. Springs. *Fuel:* Available.
Misumi, Japan: 32.38 N. 130.27 E. **45**
  Max. Size: 27,000 d.w.t. from South entrance. Depth
  alongside: 8.0 m. – 9.0 m. *Dry Docks:* Small docks for less than
  1,000 tons. *Airport:* Kumamoto, 60 km.
Misurata, Libya: 32.22 N. 15.13 E. **24**
  Max. Size: Depth 11 m. *Fuel:* Available.
  Airport: Tripoli, 220 km.
Mitajiri, see Nakanoseki.
Mithimna, Greece: 39.22 N. 26.10 E. **25**
Mitilene, Greece: 39.06 N. 26.35 E. **21, 25, 26**
  Max. Size: Inner Port: LOA 120 m., draft 5.6 m.
  Outer Port: LOA 264 m., draft 9 m. *Fuel:* Supplies to Mitylene
  port by tanker trucks only. *Airport:* 8 km.
Mitkof Is., see Petersburg.
Mitre Canal, see The River Plate.
Mitre Channel, see The River Plate.
Mitsukojima, Japan: 34.11 N. 132.31 E. **45**
  Max. Size: 156,000 d.w.t., LOA 303 m., draft 17.40 m.
  Fuel: Available by barge with 3 days notice. *Airport:* Hiroshima.
Miyake, Japan: 34.04 N. 139.30 E. **43, 45, 46**
Miyako, Japan: 39.39 N. 141.58 E. **43**
  Max. Size: LOA 240 m., draft 12.0 m. (LOA 270 m., draft 13.0 m.
  under construction). *Fuel:* Bonded oil will be brought from
  Tokyo or Sendai. *Airport:* Hanamaki, 150 km. Flights to Tokyo.
Miyazaki, Japan: 31.56 N. 131.26 E. **45**

Miyazu, Japan: 35.32 N. 135.12 E. **43, 45**
  Max. Size: LOA 100 m., draft 5.0 m. Anchorage: Depth 14.0 m.
  Fuel: Available from Moji.
Mizushima, Japan: 34.31 N. 133.45 E. **45**
  Max. Size: Draft up to 16.5 m., depending on cargo.
  Fuel: Most grades. *Dry Docks:* Length 630 m., width 63 m.,
  depth 13 m. *Airport:* Okayama, 50 km. Flights to Tokyo.
Mjimwema Terminal, Tanzania: 6.49 S. 39.22 E. **30**
  Max. Size: Tankers up to 120,000 d.w.t. Min. length 200 m.,
  max. draft 16.75 m. *Fuel:* Fuel oil by barge.
Mkoani, Tanzania: 5.21 S. 39.38 E. **30**
  Max. Size: LOA 250 ft., depth 6 fathoms.
Mljet Is., Croatia **24**
Mo-I-Rana, Norway: 66.19 N. 14.08 E. **10, 15**
  Max. Size: Depths 23 ft. – 37 ft. *Fuel:* All grades.
  Airport: Rana, 12 km.
Moa, Cuba: 20.41 N. 74.52 W. **46, 69, 70**
  Max. Size: Moa: LOA 500 ft., draft up to 30 ft. (HW).
  Punta Gorda: LOA 442 ft., draft 28 ft.
Moa Is., Indonesia: 8.10 S. 127.55 E. **46**
Moana, Spain: 42.18 N. 8.44 W. **20, 22**
Moanda, see Banana.
Mobile, Alabama, U.S.A.: 30.40 N. 88.02 W. **55, 66**
  Max. Size: Depths 30 ft. – 41 ft. MLW. Tankers: LOA 950 ft.,
  depth at jetty 38 ft. Magazine Point: Depth 43 ft. *Fuel:* Most
  grades fuel/diesel. *Dry Docks:* To 18,000 tons displacement.
Mocambique, see Mozambique.
Mocamedes, see Namibe.
Mocimboa, Mozambique: 11.23 S. 40.20 E. **30**
Mocka, Yemen: 13.17 N. 43.10 E. **31, 32**
  Max. Size: Depth 8.5 m.
Modec Venture, Australia: 10.53 S. 126.34 E. **50**
  Max. Size: 175,000 tonnes displacement, 150,000 d.w.t.
Modewheel, see Manchester.
Moelfre, U.K.: 53.21 N. 4.14 W. **5, 7**
Moen, (Caroline Is.), Micronesia: 7.26 N. 151.52 E. . . **46**
Moengo, Suriname: 5.38 N. 54.25 W. **72, 76**
  Max. Size: LOA 525 ft., draft depends on bar.
  Fuel: Small quantities. *Airport:* 5 km.
Moerai, (Austral Is.), French Polynesia (France):
  22.27 S. 151.22 W. **49**
Moerdijk, Netherlands: 51.42 N. 4.38 E. **7, 8**
  Max. Size: LOA 175 m., draft 7.5 m. *Fuel:* Available.
  Also see Rotterdam.
Mogadiscio, Somalia: 2.02 N. 45.20 E. **31**
  Max. Size: Depth 8.53 m. – 10.36 m. Tankers: Draft 32 ft.
  Fuel: Available. *Airport:* 5 km.
Mogador, see Essaoira.
Mogi, Japan: 32.42 N. 129.55 E. **45**
Mogpo, see Mokpo.
Mohammedia, Morocco: 33.45 N. 7.22 W. **27**
  Max. Size: Tankers: LOA 290 m., draft 17 m., 150,000 d.w.t.
  Basin: LOA 120 m., draft 6.7 m. (22 ft.). *Fuel:* Available.
  Airport: Casablanca.
Moheli, Comoros (Rep. of) **30**
Moin Bay, see Puerto Moin.
Moji, Japan: 33.57 N. 130.58 E. **44, 45, 46**
  Max. Size: Draft to 10.8 m. Tankers: 33,000 d.w.t., LOA 200 m.,
  draft 9.1 m. *Fuel:* All grades by lighter. *Airport:* Fukuoka.
  Also see Shimonoseki.
Mokil Is., (Caroline Is.), Micronesia: 6.40 N. 159.47 E. **49**
Mokpo, South Korea: 34.46 N. 126.24 E. **42**
  Max. Size: 30,000 d.w.t., depth 10.5 m. Daebul: 35,000 d.w.t.,
  depth 12 m. *Fuel:* Available from Yosu.
  Airport: Kwangji, 1 hour by car.
Mola di Bari, Italy: 41.03 N. 17.05 E. **24**
Molde, Norway: 62.44 N. 7.10 E. **10, 15**
  Max. Size: Depths to 32 ft. LW, 39 ft. in New port.
  Airport: Aaro, 4 km.
MOLDOVA **9, 21, 26**
Molfetta, Italy: 41.12 N. 16.35 E. **24**
Molle, Sweden: 56.17 N. 12.30 E. **12**
Mollendo, Peru: 17.02 S. 72.00 W. **72, 77**
  Also see Matarani.
Moller, see Port Moller.
Moller Bay, Russia: 72.20 N. 53.00 E. **16**
Molos, Greece: 38.45 N. 22.35 E. **24, 25**
Molucca Sea, Indonesia **46**
Mombasa, Kenya: 4.04 S. 39.40 E. **30**
  Max. Size: LOA 850 ft., draft 43 ft. 06 in. *Fuel:* All grades.
  Dry Docks: Dimensions: 590 ft. (180 m.) x 80 ft. (24.75 m.).
  Airport: 7 miles.
Mommark, Denmark: 54.56 N. 10.03 E. **12, 14**
Mon Is., Denmark **12, 14**
Mona Is., (U.S.A.): 18.05 N. 67.53 W. **70**
Mona Passage, South China Sea **69, 70**
MONACO **9**
Monastir, Tunisia: 35.45 N. 10.50 E. **24**
Monbetsu, Japan: 44.21 N. 143.22 E. **43**
  Max. Size: Depth 7.5 m., 5,000 d.w.t. *Fuel:* Available.
Moncton, N.B., Canada: 46.05 N. 64.45 W. **60**

Monemvasia, Greece: 36.41 N. 23.03 E. ... 25
Money Point, Ireland: 52.36 N. 9.25 W. ... 5, 8
  Max. Size: 180,000 tonnes d.w.t., LOA 282 m., beam 43 m., draft 17.2 m. *Fuel:* Available.
Monfalcone, Italy: 45.48 N. 13.32 E. ... 9, 24
  Max. Size: LOA 180 m. at the ENEL berth. Draft 10.5 m. *Fuel:* By barge. *Dry Docks:* 300,000 d.w.t. *Airport:* 5 km.
Mongla, Bangladesh: 22.29 N. 89.36 E. ... 37
  Max. Size: Draft 7 m. in all seasons. In S.W. monsoons up to 8 m. on Spring tide. *Fuel:* Limited fuel oil. *Airport:* Jessore, 70 miles. Also see Chittagong.
Mongstad, Norway: 60.49 N. 5.02 E. ... 10, 11
  Max. Size: 380,000 d.w.t., draft 23 m. *Fuel:* All grades. *Airport:* Flesland, 86 km.
Moni, Cyprus: 34.42 N. 33.11 E. ... 26
  Max. Size: LOA 750 ft., draft 40 ft.
Monifieth, U.K.: 56.29 N. 2.50 W. ... 6
Monopoli, Italy: 40.57 N. 17.18 E. ... 24
Monroe, Michigan, U.S.A.: 41.54 N. 83.26 W. ... 62
Monrovia, Liberia: 6.20 N. 10.50 W. ... 27, 28
  Max. Size: Draft 30 ft. *Fuel:* Light diesel oil and heavy fuel oil. *Dry Docks:* Floating dock capable of lifting 300 tons. *Airport:* Roberts, 45 miles.
Mons, Belgium: 50.25 N. 3.59 E. ... 7
Monsteras, Sweden: 57.04 N. 16.28 E. ... 11
Mont St. Michel, France: 48.40 N. 1.30 W. ... 19
Mont-Louis, Quebec, Canada: 49.14 N. 65.44 W. ... 60
  Port being demolished.
Montague, P.E.I., Canada: 46.10 N. 62.38 W. ... 60
Montague Is., Alaska, U.S.A. ... 54
Montauk, New York, U.S.A.: 41.03 N. 71.57 W. ... 63
Monte Carlo, Monaco: 43.44 N. 7.26 E. ... 21, 22, 23
  Max. Size: LOA 135 m., draft 8 m. *Fuel:* No heavy fuel. *Airport:* Nice, 25 km.
Monte Lirio, Panama Canal, Panama: 9.15 N. 79.51 W. ... 73
Montecristo Is., Italy: 42.18 N. 10.16 E. ... 24
Montedison, see Brindisi.
Montego Bay, Jamaica: 18.30 N. 77.56 W. ... 69, 70
  Max. Size: Depth 34 ft. *Fuel:* All grades. *Airport:* 5 miles.
Monterey, California, U.S.A.: 36.36 N. 121.54 W. ... 57
Montevideo, Uruguay: 34.55 S. 56.13 W. ... 77, 78
  Max. Size: Depth 33 ft. Tankers: LOA 241.5 m., beam 32.33 m., draft 28 ft. *Fuel:* All grades. *Dry Docks:* Floating dock, lifting capacity 12,000 tons, 545 ft. (165.99 m.) long and 93 ft. (28.51 m.) wide. *Airport:* 30 minutes by car.
Montijo, see Lisbon.
Montmagny, Quebec, Canada: 46.59 N. 70.34 W. ... 60
Montoir, France: 47.18 N. 2.08 W. ... 19
  Max. Size: LOA 300 m., draft 16.1 m. *Fuel:* Available. Also see Nantes.
Montreal, Quebec, Canada: 45.30 N. 73.33 W. ... 60, 61
  Max. Size: Entry restricted by draft. Main channel depth 11.30 m. Depths alongside up to 10.7 m. *Fuel:* All grades. *Airport:* International.
Montreuil, France: 50.28 N. 1.45 E. ... 7
Montrose, U.K.: 56.42 N. 2.27 W. ... 5
  Max. Size: LOA 165 m., 16,700 d.w.t., draft 7.5 m. *Fuel:* Available. *Airport:* Aberdeen, 36 miles.
Montserrat (U.K.) ... 71
Montserrat Is., Montserrat (U.K.) ... 71
Montt, see Puerto Montt.
Monument Beach, Massachusetts, U.S.A.: 41.43 N. 70.37 W. ... 64
Moody, see Port Moody.
Mooretown, Ontario, Canada: 42.50 N. 82.28 W. ... 62
Moose Factory, Ontario, Canada: 51.18 N. 80.39 W. ... 59
Moosonee, Ontario, Canada: 51.17 N. 80.35 W. ... 59
Morant, see Port Morant.
Morant Bay, see Port Morant.
Moratuwa, Sri Lanka: 6.43 N. 79.54 E. ... 37
Morawhanna, Guyana: 8.10 N. 59.40 W. ... 75, 76
Moray Firth, U.K. ... 5
Morbylanga, Sweden: 56.32 N. 16.23 E. ... 11
Morecambe, U.K.: 54.05 N. 2.50 W. ... 5
Morehead City, North Carolina, U.S.A.: 34.43 N. 76.42 W. ... 55, 63
  Max. Size: Depth 35 ft. – 45 ft. *Fuel:* Available. *Airport:* 1 hour's drive.
Morelas, see Puerto Morelas.
Moresby, see Port Moresby.
Moresby Is., B.C., Canada ... 56
Moreton Bay, see Brisbane.
Morgan City, Louisiana, U.S.A.: 29.42 N. 91.12 W. ... 66
Mori, Japan: 42.06 N. 140.34 E. ... 43
Morlaix, France: 48.35 N. 3.50 W. ... 7, 19
Mormugao, India: 15.25 N. 73.47 E. ... 37
  Max. Size: Draft 13.0 m., LOA 335 m. Vessels loading West of breakwater in fair weather – no restriction. Tankers: LOA 260 m., draft 12.5 m. *Fuel:* High speed diesel oil, light diesel oil and furnace oil. *Airport:* 7 km.
Mornington Is., Qld., Australia: 16.30 N. 139.30 E. ... 50

Moro Gulf, Philippines ... 47
Morobe, Papua New Guinea: 7.47 S. 147.38 E. ... 46
MOROCCO ... 20, 21, 22, 23, 27
Morombe, Madagascar: 21.45 S. 43.20 E. ... 30
Moron, Cuba: 22.02 N. 78.29 W. ... 70
Moron, Venezuela: 10.32 N. 68.11 W. ... 74
  Terminal closed. Operations now at El Palito
Morondava, Madagascar: 20.17 S. 44.18 E. ... 30
Moroni, (Grand Comore Is.), Comoros (Rep. of): 11.42 S. 43.14 E. ... 30
  Max. Size: Anchorage: LOA 130 m.
Morotai Is., Indonesia ... 46
Morphou Bay, see Gemikonagi.
Morrisburg, Ontario, Canada: 44.55 N. 75.09 W. ... 61
Morristown, New York, U.S.A.: 44.35 N. 75.39 W. ... 61
Morro Bay, California, U.S.A.: 35.22 N. 120.51 W. ... 57
Morro Redondo, (Cedros Is.), Mexico: 28.02 N. 115.11 W. ... 57
  Max. Size: 160,000 d.w.t., depth 18.5 m. *Airport:* 3 flights to mainland each week.
Mors, Denmark: 56.47 N. 8.45 E. ... 12
Mort Bay, see Sydney.
Mortagne, France: 45.29 N. 0.48 W. ... 8, 19
Morton, (Great Inagua Is.), Bahamas: 21.03 N. 73.39 W. ... 69, 70
  Max. Size: Length of berth 650 ft., depth 40 ft. – 42 ft.
Moruya, N.S.W., Australia: 35.56 S. 150.04 E. ... 50
Mosjoen, Norway: 65.51 N. 13.11 E. ... 10, 15
  Max. Size: Draft above 33 ft. only at HW and immediate discharge. *Fuel:* Gas oil by road tanker.
Moskalvo, Russia: 53.35 N. 142.30 E. ... 43
Moskenesoya, (Lofoten Is.), Norway: 68.00 N. 13.10 E. ... 15
Moss, Norway: 59.26 N. 10.40 E. ... 8, 11, 12
  Max. Size: Depth 7 m. – 11 m.
Moss Landing, California, U.S.A.: 36.48 N. 121.47 W. ... 57
Mossbank, see Sullom Voe.
Mossel Bay, South Africa: 34.10 S. 22.09 E. ... 28, 30
  Max. Size: LOA 130 m., draft 6.5 m., displacement 5,000 tons. Tankers: CBM – 32,000 d.w.t., draft 12 m. SBM – 50,000 tonnes d.w.t. (min. LOA 130 m.). Depth 21 m. *Fuel:* Limited supplies of gas oil. *Airport:* George Airport, 40 km.
Mostaganem, Algeria: 35.56 N. 0.04 E. ... 22
  Max. Size: LOA 180 m., depth 13.3 ft. – 27 ft. *Airport:* Oran, 80 km.
Mostyn, U.K.: 53.19 N. 3.16 W. ... 6, 7
  Max. Size: LOA 120 m., beam 20 m., draft 6.5 m. *Fuel:* By road tanker. *Airport:* Manchester, 40 miles.
Motala, Sweden: 58.30 N. 15.00 E. ... 11, 12
Motril, Spain: 36.43 N. 3.30 W. ... 20, 22, 27
  Max. Size: Draft 34 ft. *Fuel:* Available. *Airport:* Malaga, 105 km. Granada, 70 km.
Motueka, New Zealand: 41.05 S. 173.00 E. ... 52
Moudhros, Greece: 39.51 N. 25.17 E. ... 25, 26
Moudi Marine Terminal, Cameroon: 4.07 N. 8.29 E. ... 29
  Max. Size: 280,000 d.w.t., depth 57 m.
Moulmein, Myanmar: 16.29 N. 97.37 E. ... 37
Mount Maunganui, New Zealand: 37.39 S. 176.11 E. ... 52
  Max. Size: LOA 228 m., depth 13.0 m., draft 120 m. (HW). Also see Tauranga.
Mountain Village, Alaska, U.S.A.: 62.05 N. 163.20 W. ... 54
Mourilyan, Qld., Australia: 17.36 S. 146.08 E. ... 50, 51
  Max. Size: LOA 183 m., beam 30.0 m. or LOA 175 m., beam 32.2 m., departure draft 7.62 m. *Fuel:* Limited supplies of fuel oil/diesel. *Airport:* Nearest Cairns, 110 km.
Moutsouna, (Naxos Is.), Greece: 37.05 N. 25.35 E. ... 25
Moville, Ireland: 55.11 N. 7.03 W. ... 5
  Also see Londonderry.
MOZAMBIQUE ... 30
Mozambique, Mozambique: 14.58 S. 40.45 E. ... 30
  Max. Size: Draft less than 30 ft. cross the bar. *Fuel:* Small quantities. *Airport:* 7 km., connects with Maputo.
Mozambique Channel ... 30
Mtwara, Tanzania: 10.16 S. 40.12 E. ... 30
  Max. Size: LOA 175 m., draft 9.76 m. *Airport:* Internal, 7 miles.
Muar, Malaya, Malaysia: 2.03 N. 102.35 E. ... 38, 39, 40
Muara, Brunei: 5.01 N. 115.04 E. ... 38, 39
  Max. Size: LOA 180 m., draft 8.5 m. *Fuel:* High speed diesel in small quantities. *Airport:* International, 12 miles.
Mubarek Terminal, Sharjah, U.A.E.: 25.49 N. 55.11 E. ... 35
  Max. Size: Max. berthing deadweight 275,000 tons.
Mubarraz Island, Abu Dhabi, U.A.E.: 24.26 N. 53.32 E. ... 35
  Max. Size: Depth at buoy 15.5 m.
Mucuripe, see Fortaleza.
Mudanya, Turkey: 40.24 N. 28.52 E. ... 25, 26
Muelle de Hierro, see Bahia Blanca.
Muftiyah, see Umm Qasr.
Muhammed Bin Qasim, see Port Muhammad Bin Qasim.
Muhammed Qol, Sudan: 20.53 N. 37.09 E. ... 32
Muhu, Estonia: 58.34 N. 23.20 E. ... 11
Mukaishima, see Onomichi-Itozaki.
Mukalla, Yemen: 14.31 N. 49.09 E. ... 31
  Max. Size: LOA 145 m., draft 8.5 m. *Airport:* Rayan, 29 km.

Mukawwar Is., Sudan: 20.45 N. 37.16 E. **32**
Mukho, South Korea: 37.33 N. 129.07 E. **42, 43, 45**
Max. Size: LOA 180 m., beam 25 m., draft 8.5 m.
Fuel: Most grades. *Airport:* Nearest Seoul.
Mukilteo, Washington, U.S.A.: 47.57 N. 122.18 W. **56**
Muko, (Japan): 27.40 N. 142.08 E. **46**
Muldwarka, India: 20.45 N. 70.40 E. **37**
Max. Size: Depth 9 m. *Airport:* Rajkot, 250 km.
Muleje, Mexico: 26.54 N. 112.00 W. **57**
Mulgrave, N.S., Canada: 45.37 N. 61.27 W. **60**
Also see Port Hawkesbury.
Mull, U.K.: 56.25 N. 6.00 W. **5**
Mullaittivu, Sri Lanka: 9.15 N. 80.49 E. **37**
Mullerup, see Reerso.
Multedo, Italy: 44.25 N. 8.50 E. **23, 24**
Max. Size: 500,000 d.w.t., depth 50 m.
Also see Genoa.
Mumbai, India: 18.56 N. 72.49 E. **37**
Max. Size: Draft 10.5 m. Tankers: Draft 14.3 m.
Fuel: Available. *Dry Docks:* Largest 1,000 ft. long, 100 ft. wide.
Airport: Sahar, 25 km.
Mundra, India: 22.44 N. 69.47 E. **37**
Max. Size: LOA 250 m., draft 15 m. *Fuel:* Available.
Airport: Bhuj, 65 km.
Munguba, Brazil: 0.55 S. 52.25 W. **72**
Max. Size: Draft 10.0 m., LOA 200 m. *Airport:* 15 miles.
Munising, Michigan, U.S.A.: 46.25 N. 86.40 W. **62**
Munkedal, Sweden: 58.26 N. 11.41 E. **12**
Munksund, Sweden: 65.17 N. 21.32 E. **15**
Muntok, Indonesia: 2.04 S. 105.10 E. **38**
Max. Size: Depth 2 m.
Muqam, Iran: 26.58 N. 53.29 E. **35**
Murilo Is., see Hall Is..
Murmansk, Russia: 69.00 N. 33.03 E. **16, 79**
Max. Size: LOA 280 m., draft 12.5 m. *Fuel:* All grades by
barge. *Dry Docks:* Largest: Length 225 m., width 45 m.
Muroran, Japan: 42.20 N. 140.58 E. **43**
Max. Size: Tankers: 59,000 d.w.t., LOA 240 m., draft 9.9 m.
Sea Berth: 260,000 d.w.t., LOA 321 m., draft 15 m.
Ore Carriers: 160,000 d.w.t. LOA 313 m., draft 16 m.
Fuel: Available. *Airport:* Sapporo, 100 km.
Muroroa Is., (Tuamotu Arch.), French Polynesia (France):
21.52 S. 138.55 W. **49**
Muros, Spain: 42.47 N. 9.03 W. **20**
Muroto, Japan: 33.13 N. 134.09 E. **45**
Murray, P.E.I., Canada: 46.00 N. 62.32 W. **60**
Murtinho, see Porto Murtinho.
Murud, India: 18.26 N. 73.00 E. **37**
Muruvik, see Stjordalshalsen.
Murwik, see Flensburg.
Muscat, Oman: 23.37 N. 58.37 E. **31, 35, 37**
Also see Port Sultan Qaboos.
Musel, Spain: 43.34 N. 5.42 W. **19, 20, 22**
Also see Gijon.
Musi Bar, Indonesia: 2.09 S. 104.58 E. **38**
Muskegon, Michigan, U.S.A.: 43.15 N. 86.16 W. **62**
Musko Is., Sweden: 59.01 N. 18.06 E. **11**
Mussau Is., Papua New Guinea: 1.25 S. 149.40 E. . . . **46**
Musselburgh, U.K.: 55.57 N. 3.04 W. **6**
Mustola, Finland: 61.04 N. 28.18 E. **13**
Also see Saimaa Canal.
Mutrah, see Port Sultan Qaboos.
Mutsamuda, (Anjouan Is.), Comoros (Rep. of):
12.09 S. 44.25 E. **30**
Max. Size: Depth at buoy 12 m.
Mutsure, Japan: 33.58 N. 130.54 E. **44**
Also see Shimonoseki.
Muuga, see Tallinn.
My Tho, Vietnam: 10.20 N. 106.19 E. **39**
Max. Size: LOA 100 m., draft 6.5 m. *Fuel:* Available.
Airport: Tan Son Nhat.
My Thoi, Vietnam: 10.20 N. 105.29 E. **39**
Max. Size: LOA 90 m., draft 5.7 m. *Fuel:* Available.
Airport: Tan Son Nhat, 70 km.
Myako Is., (Ryuku Is.), Japan: 24.46 N. 125.25 E. . . **42, 46**
MYANMAR **37, 39**
Myedhi Is., (Komandorski Is.), Russia: 54.40 N. 167.32 E. . **54**
Mykonos, Greece: 37.26 N. 25.25 E. **25, 26**
Max. Size: Vessels in excess of 22,000 d.w.t. have been
accommodated at Ormos Ayias Annas.
Mylaki, see Milaki.
Myre, Norway: 69.00 N. 15.10 E. **15**
Myrnas, see Hovid.
Myrtle Grove, Louisiana, U.S.A.: 29.38 N. 89.57 W. . . . **67**
Mystic, see Noank.

N

N'Kossa Terminal, Congo (Rep. of): 5.16 S. 11.36 E. . . . **28**
Max. Size: 280,000 d.w.t., depth 126 m.
N. Manitou Is., Michigan, U.S.A.: 45.07 N. 86.01 W. . . **62**
Naandendaal, see Turku.
Naantali, Finland: 60.28 N. 22.01 E. **11**
Max. Size: Depth 13 m. *Fuel:* All grades. *Dry Docks:* Dry dock
220 m. x 70 m. Floating dock 100 m. x 30 m. *Airport:* 20 km.
Naband, Iran: 27.24 N. 52.38 E. **35**
Nabq, Egypt: 28.05 N. 34.10 E. **26, 32**
Nacala, Mozambique: 14.32 S. 40.40 E. **30**
Max. Size: Anchorage: Draft 18.0 m., 130,000 d.w.t.
Container Terminal: Depth 14.0 m. *Fuel:* Available.
Airport: 190 km.
Nador, see Port Nador.
Nadym, Russia: 65.30 N. 72.52 E. **16**
Naersnes, see Slemmestad.
Naestved, Denmark: 55.14 N. 11.45 E. **12**
Max. Size: LOA 118 m., draft 5.6 m. with breadth 12.2 m. or
draft 4.8 m. with breadth 14.4 m. *Fuel:*
All grades by road tankers. *Airport:* Copenhagen, 100 km.
Naga Is., (Kyushu), Japan: 32.10 N. 130.08 E. **45**
Nagahama, Japan: 33.35 N. 132.28 E. **45**
Nagapattinam, India: 10.45 N. 79.50 E. **37**
Max. Size: Anchorage: No restrictions. *Fuel:* Limited diesel oil.
Airport: Chennai.
Nagasaki, Japan: 32.45 N. 129.52 E. **45, 46**
Max. Size: LOA 1,200 ft., beam 120 ft., draft 15 m.
Tankers: 8,000 d.w.t., LOA 100 m., draft 7 m. *Fuel:* By barge.
Dry Docks: Largest – length 400 m., width 100 m., depth
14.5 m., capacity 250,000 g.r.t. *Airport:* 54 km., flights to Tokyo
and Osaka.
Nagayeva, see Magadan.
Nagayevo Bay, Russia. **43**
Nagercoil, India: 8.11 N. 77.25 E. **37**
Nagoya, Japan: 35.02 N. 136.51 E. **43, 45, 46**
Max. Size: Depth 12 m. Ore: Depth 14 m.
Container: Depth 14 m. Tankers: 280,000 d.w.t., LOA 345 m.,
draft 20 m., depth 25.5 m. *Fuel:* Most grades.
Dry Docks: Length 810 m., width 92 m., capacity 161,000 g.r.t.
Airport: Nagoya, 20 km.
Nagu, Finland: 60.15 N. 22.00 E. **11**
Naguabo, see Humacao.
Naha, (Okinawa), Japan: 26.12 N. 127.40 E. **42, 46**
Max. Size: Draft 11 m. *Fuel:* All grades.
Nahma, Michigan, U.S.A.: 45.50 N. 86.40 W. **62**
Nain, Newfoundland, Canada: 56.33 N. 61.41 W. **59**
Naira, see Pulau Naira.
Nairn, U.K.: 57.35 N. 3.55 W. **5**
Najin, North Korea: 42.15 N. 130.18 E. **43**
Nakagusuku Wan, see Nishihara.
Nakanoseki, Japan: 34.00 N. 131.34 E. **45**
Max. Size: Channel: 30,000 d.w.t., draft 9.5 m. *Fuel:* All grades
from Tokyo Bay. *Airport:* Ube.
Nakatsu, Japan: 33.35 N. 131.15 E. **45**
Nakhodka, Russia: 42.48 N. 132.53 E. **43**
Max. Size: Draft for Commercial port 9.10 m.,
Passenger Terminal 8.6 m. Tankers: Draft 12 m.
Fuel: Available. *Airport:* 1,000 km.
Naknek, Alaska, U.S.A.: 58.42 N. 157.01 W. **54**
Nakskov, Denmark: 54.50 N. 11.08 E. **10, 12, 14**
Max. Size: Draft 19 ft., LOA 660 ft., beam 70 ft. (Approx.
3,500 d.w.t.). *Fuel:* Available. *Dry Docks:* Up to 32,000 d.w.t.
Airport: International, 160 km.
Nam Can, Vietnam: 8.47 N. 104.59 E. **39**
Max. Size: Draft 5.0 m. (Depth at berth 13 m.).
Namatanai, Papua New Guinea: 3.38 S. 152.30 E. . . . **46**
Nambucca, N.S.W., Australia: 30.38 S. 153.00 E. . . . **50**
Namibe, Angola: 15.11 S. 12.07 E. **28**
Max. Size: Mocamedes: Depth 33 ft. Tankers: Draft 54 ft.
Porto Saco: Draft 14 m. *Fuel:* Available. *Airport:* Small airstrip.
NAMIBIA **28**
Namikata, Japan: 34.07 N. 132.55 E. **45**
Max. Size: Tankers: 125,000 d.w.t. Gas tankers: 67,000 d.w.t.
Airport: Nearest at Matsuyama.
Namlea, Indonesia: 3.17 S. 127.05 E. **46**
Namoluk Is., (Caroline Is.), Micronesia: 5.55 N. 153.08 E. . **46, 49**
Namonuito, (Caroline Is.), Micronesia: 8.42 N. 150.00 E. . **46**
Namorik, Marshall Is.: 5.35 N. 168.10 E. **49**
Nampo, North Korea: 38.43 N. 125.25 E. **42**
Max. Size: Coal berth: 20,000 d.w.t., depth 6 m. – 12 m.
Dry Docks: Vessel about 180 m.
Namsos, Norway: 64.28 N. 11.30 E. **4, 10, 15**
Max. Size: Largest: 15,000 d.w.t., depth 9 m.
Tankers: Depth 5 m. at LW alongside. *Fuel:* All grades.
Airport: 4 km.

Namu, B.C., Canada: 51.52 N. 127.51 W. 56
Namur, Belgium: 50.26 N. 4.51 E. 7
Nan Tung, see Nantong.
Nanaimo, B.C., Canada: 49.10 N. 123.57 W. 56
  Max. Size: Controlling depths: Harbour entrance, 17.37 m. HW.
  Inner Harbour: 8.0 m. – 9.0 m. Deep Sea Terminal: 13.5 m.
  Cruise Ship: Depth 8.5 m.
  Private Facilities: Depths 4.88 m. – 10.4 m. *Fuel:* Available.
  Dry Docks: Max. 200 ft. and 600 tons. *Airport:* Nanaimo, 16 km.
  Also see Vancouver.
Nanao, Japan: 37.02 N. 136.58 E. 43, 45
  Max. Size: 60,000 d.w.t., LOA 232 m., draft 12.5 m.
  Fuel: Available from Fushiki. *Airport:* Komatsu, 100 km.
Nanchital, Mexico: 18.00 N. 94.27 W. 69
  Max. Size: LOA 580 ft., draft 27 ft. 6 in. *Fuel:* Available.
  Airport: Minatitlan – 1 hour car drive, connects with Mexico City.
Nancowry, (Nicobar Is.), India: 8.02 N. 93.32 E. 37
Nancy, France: 48.42 N. 6.12 E. 9
Nandi, Fiji: 17.45 S. 176.25 E. 49
Nanisivik, N.W.T., Canada: 73.04 N. 84.32 W. 79
  Max. Size: Draft must not exceed approx. 40 ft. alongside.
  Airport: Approx. 8 miles.
Nanjing, China: 32.03 N. 118.47 E. 42
  Max. Size: LOA 200 m., draft 9.5 m. (F.W.), 30,000 d.w.t.
  Fuel: Available. *Airport:* 26 km.
Nanking, see Nanjing.
Nanok, Greenland (Denmark): 75.10 N. 19.48 W. 17
Nanoose Harbour, B.C., Canada: 49.16 N. 124.09 W. 56
Nanortalik, Greenland (Denmark): 60.08 N. 45.13 W. 17
Nanterre, see Paris.
Nantes, France: 47.14 N. 1.34 W. 4, 19
  Max. Size: LOA 225 m., max. draft 10.05 m. *Fuel:* Available.
  Dry Docks: Careening unit 1,700 tons, max. length 100 m.
  Airport: Nantes.
Nanticoke, Ontario, Canada: 42.49 N. 80.04 W. 62
Nantong, China: 32.01 N. 120.49 E. 42, 46
  Max. Size: Nantong: LOA 70 m., draft 5 m.
  Langshan: LOA 180 m., draft 9.5 m. *Fuel:* Available.
  Dry Docks: 150,000 d.w.t. and 85,000 d.w.t.
Nantucket, Massachusetts, U.S.A.: 41.17 N. 70.06 W. 63
Nantucket Is., Massachusetts, U.S.A.: 41.16 N. 70.03 W. . . . 60, 63
Nantucket Sound, Massachusetts, U.S.A.: 63
Nanumanga Is., Tuvalu: 6.18 S. 176.18 E. 49
Nanumea, Tuvalu: 5.40 S. 176.08 E. 49
Naoetsu, Japan: 37.11 N. 138.14 E. 43, 45
  Max. Size: 50,000 d.w.t., draft 11.7 m. *Fuel:* Bonded oil will be
  brought from Moji or Hakodate. *Airport:* Niigata, 2 hours by
  train. Tokyo, 4 hours by train.
Naos, see Arrecife.
Naos Is., Panama: 8.55 N. 79.32 W. 73
Naoshima, Japan: 34.28 N. 133.58 E. 45
  Max. Size: 20,000 g.r.t., LOA 180 m., draft 9.70 m.
  Fuel: Bonded oil will be brought from Kobe.
Napa, California, U.S.A.: 38.19 N. 122.18 W. 58
Napa Creek, California, U.S.A. 58
Napanee, Ontario, Canada: 44.15 N. 76.58 W. 62
Napassoq, Greenland (Denmark): 65.03 N. 52.24 W. 17, 59
Napier, New Zealand: 39.29 S. 176.54 E. 52
  Max. Size: LOA 260 m., draft 11.0 m. *Fuel:* 220 sec. and
  1,000 sec. Most grades available. *Airport:* Hawke's Bay,
  3 miles.
Naples, Italy: 40.50 N. 14.17 E. 9, 21, 23, 24
  Max. Size: Containers: Depth 13 m. Tankers: Up to 45 ft. draft.
  Fuel: All grades. *Dry Docks:* Largest: 349 m. length, 45 m.
  width. *Airport:* 8 km.
Naples, Florida, U.S.A.: 26.09 N. 81.46 W. 66, 70
Narooma, N.S.W., Australia: 36.13 S. 150.07 E. 50
Narovik, see Keflavik-Njarovik.
Narssalik, Greenland (Denmark): 61.40 N. 49.10 W. 17
Narssaq, Greenland (Denmark): 60.54 N. 46.01 W. 17
Narssarssuaq, Greenland (Denmark): 61.08 N. 45.26 W. . . . 17
  Max. Size: Largest vessel to berth at quay was LOA 130 m.,
  draft 8 m. *Airport:* Landing-strip for aircraft.
Naruto, Japan: 34.11 N. 134.37 E. 45
Narva Joessu, Estonia: 59.28 N. 28.03 E. 11
Narvik, Norway: 68.25 N. 17.25 E. 4, 10, 15
  Max. Size: Depths 13.5 m. to 26.5 m. alongside. *Fuel:* Only
  clean oil (diesel) and lubricating oil. *Airport:* Narvik, 5 minutes
  by taxi. Connects with major airports.
Naryan-Mar, Russia: 67.38 N. 53.00 E. 16, 79
  Max. Size: Draft declared by Port Authorities after being
  checked in the beginning of the season, and is about 15 ft.
  Fuel: Not guaranteed. *Airport:* Situated near town.
Nas, see Botea.
Nash Harbour, Alaska, U.S.A.: 60.12 N. 166.57 W. 54
Nasipit, (Mindanao Is.), Philippines: 9.06 N. 125.22 E. 47
  Max. Size: LOA 550 ft., beam 65 ft., mean draft 23 ft.
  Fuel: Available. *Airport:* Boncasi, 29 km.

Nassau, (New Providence Is.), Bahamas: 25.05 N. 77.20 W. . . 69, 70
  Max. Size: Safe draft 35 ft. Safe draft at cargo pier 25 ft. Depth
  at cruise berths 30 ft. – 40 ft. Tankers at Clifton Pier 36 ft. draft.
  Fuel: Small quantities diesel only. *Airport:* International.
Nassau Is., Cook Is. (N.Z.): 11.25 S. 165.25 W. 49
Nastapoka Is., N.S., Canada 59
Nasugbu, Philippines: 14.05 N. 120.38 E. 47
Nasva, Estonia: 58.12 N. 22.27 E. 11
Natal, Brazil: 5.47 S. 35.12 W. 72
  Max. Size: LOA 520 ft., draft up to 23 ft. 6 in. (Spring tide.) *Fuel:*
  Available. *Dry Docks:* Up to 2,800 tonnes, 5.8 m. draft.
  Airport: Internal, 20 km.
Natal, South Africa, see Durban.
Natales, see Puerto Natales.
Natashquan, Quebec, Canada: 50.11 N. 61.48 W. 60
Naubinway, Michigan, U.S.A.: 46.08 N. 85.28 W. 62
NAURU 49
Nauru, Nauru: 0.32 S. 166.56 E. 49
  Max. Size: LOA 192 m., beam 28.34 m., 50,000 tons sailing
  displacement, depth at buoys 30 m. *Fuel:* Limited quantities
  of heavy fuel or diesel oil. *Airport:* 1 km.
Navarino Bay, see Pylos.
Navia, Spain: 43.33 N. 6.43 W. 19
Navlakhi, India: 22.57 N. 70.27 E. 37
  Max. Size: Open roadstead port – LOA 190 m., draft 11.35 m.
Navpaktos, Greece: 38.24 N. 21.50 E. 25
Navplion, Greece: 37.34 N. 22.48 E. 25
Navyard Wharf, see Harwich.
Nawiliwili, Hawaii, U.S.A.: 21.57 N. 159.21 W. 49
  Max. Size: LOA 800 ft., beam 90 ft., draft 32 ft. 6 in.
  Fuel: Diesel. *Airport:* Lihue, 3 miles.
Naxos Is., Greece: 37.07 N. 25.24 E. 25, 26
Nayakhan, Russia: 61.55 N. 159.00 E. 54
Nazare, Portugal: 39.36 N. 9.05 W. 20, 22
Ndene Is., (Santa Cruz Is.), Solomon Islands 49
Nea Moudhania, Greece: 40.14 N. 23.17 E. 25
Nea Peramos, Greece: 40.50 N. 24.18 E. 25
Nea Rodha, Greece: 40.23 N. 23.55 E. 25
Neah Bay, Washington, U.S.A.: 48.23 N. 124.38 W. 56
Neap House, U.K.: 53.37 N. 0.40 W. 6
Neapolis, Greece: 36.30 N. 23.05 E. 25
Near Is., (Aleutian Is.), Alaska, U.S.A. 54
Neath, U.K.: 51.40 N. 3.48 W. 6
  Max. Size: Draft 6.0 m. *Airport:* Cardiff, 35 miles.
Nebraska, U.S.A. 57
Neches, U.S.A., see Port Neches.
Necochea, Argentina: 38.35 S. 58.43 W. 77
  Also see Quequen.
Needles, U.K.: 50.40 N. 1.35 W. 5
Neendakara, India: 8.53 N. 76.34 E. 37
  Max. Size: Anchorage port.
Negishi, see Yokohama.
Negombo, Sri Lanka: 7.12 N. 79.50 E. 37
Negritos, Peru: 4.41 S. 81.19 W. 72
Negros Is., Philippines 46, 47
Neiafu, (Vavau Is.), Tonga: 18.39 S. 173.59 W. 49
Neka: 36.37 N. 54.00 E. 9
Nekso, Denmark: 55.04 N. 15.08 E. 12
Nelma, Russia: 47.38 N. 139.00 E. 43
Nelson, Manitoba, Canada, see York Factory.
Nelson, New Zealand: 41.16 S. 173.17 E. 52
  Max. Size: LOA 200 m., draft 9.2 m., beam 32.5 m.
  Tankers: Draft 7.9 m. *Fuel:* Marine fuel oil, gas oil.
  Dry Docks: Slipway for up to 1,500 ton vessels. *Airport:* 3 miles.
Nelson Is., Alaska, U.S.A. 54
Nemours, see Ghazaouet.
Nemrut Bay, Turkey: 38.46 N. 26.55 E. 25, 26
  Max. Size: Depths up to 21 m. *Fuel:* Available at Petro Ofisi.
  Airport: Izmir, 75 km.
Nemuro, Japan: 43.22 N. 145.34 E. 43
Nemuy, Russia: 55.38 N. 135.05 E. 43
Nepoui, New Caledonia (France): 21.20 S. 164.26 E. 51
  Max. Size: LOA 163 m., draft 8.7 m.
  Also see Noumea.
Neringa, Lithuania: 55.30 N. 21.05 E. 11
Nes, Russia: 66.40 N. 44.45 E. 16
Neskaupstadur, Iceland: 65.09 N. 13.41 W. 17
  Max. Size: Depth close to jetty 7 m. *Fuel:* Diesel.
  Dry Docks: None. Slipway – 450 tons. *Airport:* 0.5 km.
Nessabar, see Bourgas.
Nesseby, Norway: 70.10 N. 28.50 E. 15
NETHERLANDS 4, 7, 8, 9, 11, 14
NETHERLANDS ANTILLES 72, 74
Neuss, Germany: 51.12 N. 6.41 E. 8, 9
  Max. Size: Rhine dimensions. *Fuel:* Available.
  Airport: Dusseldorf, 10 km.
Neustadt, Germany: 54.06 N. 10.50 E. 11, 12, 14
Nevada, U.S.A. 57
Nevelsk, Russia: 46.40 N. 141.51 E. 43
  Max. Size: Depth to 6.5 m. *Fuel:* Diesel.

THE SHIPS ATLAS

Nevis Island, St. Christopher and Nevis 71
New Amsterdam, Guyana: 6.14 N. 57.31 W. 72, 76
Max. Size: 2 ft. less than Demerara Bar draft predictions.
Fuel: Available.
New Bedford, Massachusetts, U.S.A.: 41.38 N. 70.55 W. . . . 55, 63
Max. Size: LOA 700 ft. Vessels over 30 ft. draft restricted by tides. *Fuel:* All grades. *Airport:* 3 international airports within 1 hour's drive.
New Bern, North Carolina, U.S.A.: 35.07 N. 77.03 W. 63
New Brighton, U.K.: 53.27 N. 3.03 W. 6
New Britain, Papua New Guinea 46, 49
New Brunswick, Canada 60
New Caledonia (France) 36, 49, 51
New Castle, Delaware, U.S.A.: 39.39 N. 75.33 W. 63, 65
Also see Wilmington.
New Georgia Is., see Viru Harbour.
New Glasgow, N.S., Canada: 45.36 N. 62.38 W. 60
New Hampshire, U.S.A. 60
New Hanover, Papua New Guinea 46, 49
New Haven, Connecticut, U.S.A.: 41.14 N. 72.55 W. . . 55, 60, 63
Max. Size: Draft up to 36 ft. Tankers: 50,000 d.w.t., draft 36 ft. *Fuel:* Available. *Airport:* New Haven, 1 mile. New York, 70 miles.
New Holland, U.K.: 53.42 N. 0.21 W. 6, 7
Max. Size: 5,000 d.w.t., LOA 110 m., draft 6.5 m. – 7 m.
Fuel: Available by barge from Hull.
Airport: Humberside, 15 minutes by road.
New Hythe, see Rochester.
New Ireland, Papua New Guinea 46, 49
New Jersey, U.S.A.: 40.43 N. 74.00 W. 60, 63, 65
New London, Connecticut, U.S.A.: 41.21 N. 72.06 W. . . 55, 60, 63
Max. Size: Vessels 650 ft. LOA use the harbour. Depths to 36 ft. MLW. Tankers: Draft 36 ft. *Fuel:* Available with notice.
Airport: Groton-New London, 3 miles.
New Mangalore, India: 12.57 N. 74.48 E. 37
Max. Size: Draft 6.5 m. – 12.5 m. Tankers: 120,000 tonnes d.w.t., LOA 275 m., draft 14 m. *Fuel:* By road tanker. *Airport:* 15 km.
New Mexico, U.S.A. 57
New Nickerie, Suriname: 5.57 N. 56.59 W. 72, 76
Max. Size: Draft 14 ft. – 17 ft., LOA 130 m. (426 ft.).
Tankers: Draft 12 ft. 1 in. *Fuel:* Small quantities of fuel available. *Airport:* 16 km., connects with Paramaibo.
New Orleans, Louisiana, U.S.A.: 29.56 N. 90.04 W. . . 55, 66, 67
Max. Size: Draft governed by S.W. Pass, project depth 45 ft. Depth at berths 40 ft. *Fuel:* Available by barge or Bunker "C" at Amesville/Marrero. *Airport:* New Orleans.
New Plymouth, New Zealand: 39.03 S. 174.02 E. 52
Max. Size: LOA 225 m., draft 10 m. *Fuel:* Available.
Airport: 10 miles.
New Providence Is., Bahamas 69, 70
New Richmond, Quebec, Canada: 48.08 N. 65.50 W. 60
Max. Size: Depth 17 ft.
New Rochelle, New York, U.S.A.: 40.55 N. 73.46 W. 63
New Ross, Ireland: 52.23 N. 6.56 W. 5
Max. Size: Draft 19 ft. at Neap tides, 22 ft. at Spring tides, LOA 360 ft., beam 60 ft. *Fuel:* By road tanker. *Airport:* Dublin, 95 miles. Cork, 90 miles.
New South Wales, Australia 50
New Territories, see Hong Kong.
New Tuticorin, India: 8.42 N. 78.20 E. 37
New Westminster, see Fraser Port.
New York, U.S.A. 60, 61, 62, 63
New York, New York, U.S.A.: 40.43 N. 74.00 W. . . . 55, 60, 63
Max. Size: Depths to 40 ft. Tankers: Depth 37 ft. Kill van Kull: Tankers: Depth 38 ft. *Fuel:* All grades.
Dry Docks: LOA 1,100 ft., beam 140 ft. and 120,000 d.w.t.
Airport: J.F. Kennedy, Newark and La Guardia.
NEW ZEALAND 49, 52, 80
Newark, U.S.A.: 40.42 N. 74.10 W. 63
Max. Size: Depth 32 ft.
Also see New York.
Newark Bay, New Jersey, U.S.A. 63
Newburgh, Fife, U.K.: 56.21 N. 3.14 W. 6
Newburgh, Grampian, U.K.: 57.19 N. 2.00 W. 5
Newburgh, New York, U.S.A.: 41.30 N. 74.02 W. 63
Newburyport, Massachusetts, U.S.A.: 42.49 N. 70.52 W. . . . 63
Newcastle, N.S.W., Australia: 32.55 S. 151.48 E. 50
Max. Size: Kooragang: 232,000 tonnes d.w.t., LOA 300 m., draft 15.2 m. plus tide. Carrington: 180,000 tonnes d.w.t., LOA 300 m., draft 15.2 m. plus tidal factor.
Tankers: Depth 11.6 m. (38 ft.). *Fuel:* Available.
Dry Docks: Floating dock: 195 m. length, 33.5 m. clear width. Capacity 15,000 tonnes. *Airport:* 7 miles, connects with Sydney.
Newcastle, Canada, see Miramichi.
Newcastle, U.K.: 54.58 N. 1.35 W. 4, 5, 6
Max. Size: Depth 6.0 m.
Also see Tyne District.
Newfoundland, Canada 59, 60

Newhaven, U.K.: 50.47 N. 0.04 E. 5, 7
Max. Size: LOA 160 m., draft 8 m. taking bottom on soft mud at LW. North Quay: LOA 88 m., beam 14.25 m., draft 6 m.
Fuel: Available. *Airport:* London-Gatwick, 30 miles.
Newlyn, U.K.: 50.06 N. 5.33 W. 7, 19
Max. Size: LOA 90 m., draft 6.0 m. *Fuel:* By road tanker.
Newport, Ireland: 53.53 N. 9.33 W. 5
Newport, Isle of Wight, U.K.: 50.42 N. 1.17 W. 7
Max. Size: LOA 150 ft., draft 9 ft. 6 in. (MHWS).
Also see Cowes.
Newport, Wales, U.K.: 51.35 N. 2.59 W. 4, 6, 7
Max. Size: LOA 244 m., beam 30.1 m., draft 10.5 m. *Fuel:* All grades. *Dry Docks:* 454 ft. x 64 ft. *Airport:* Rhoose Airport, 28 miles.
Newport, Oregon, U.S.A.: 44.38 N. 124.03 W. 56, 57
Max. Size: Depth 30 ft.
Newport, Rhode Is., U.S.A.: 41.30 N. 71.20 W. 63
Newport Beach, California, U.S.A.: 33.38 N. 117.53 W. . . 57, 58
Newport Rock Lt., see Suez.
Newport Rocks, see Suez.
Newport News, Virginia, U.S.A.: 36.59 N. 76.26 W. 63, 65
Max. Size: Depths up to 40 ft. Tankers: Depth 34 ft.
Fuel: Available. *Dry Docks:* 2,173 ft. x 250 ft. x 32 ft. 7 in. (MHW). *Airport:* Patrick Henry International.
Newquay, U.K.: 50.25 N. 5.05 W. 5, 7
Newry, U.K.: 54.11 N. 6.20 W. 5
Ngatik Is., (Caroline Is.), Micronesia: 5.50 N. 157.17 E. . . . 49
Nghe Tinh, Vietnam: 18.39 N. 105.42 E. 39
Max. Size: LOA 127 m., draft 6 m. *Fuel:* Available.
Airport: Noi Bai, 340 km. Vihn, 7 km.
Ngulu Is., (Caroline Is.), Micronesia: 8.25 N. 137.30 E. . . . 46
Nha Be, Vietnam: 10.49 N. 106.45 E. 39
Nha Trang, Vietnam: 12.12 N. 109.13 E. 39
Max. Size: LOA 160 m., depth 8.5 m. *Fuel:* Available. *Dry Docks:* 400,000 d.w.t. and 80,000 d.w.t. capacity. *Airport:* Local airport connects with Hanoi and Ho Chi Minh City.
Nha-Be, Vietnam: 10.41 N. 106.47 E. 39
Also see Ho Chi Minh City.
Nhava Sheva, see Jawaharlal Nehru Port.
Niagara Falls, Ontario, Canada: 43.05 N. 79.04 W. 62
Niagara Falls, New York, U.S.A.: 43.05 N. 79.02 W. 62
Niagara River, Canada/U.S.A. 62
Niagara-on-the-Lake, Ontario, Canada: 43.15 N. 79.04 W. . . 62
Niah, Sarawak, Malaysia: 3.54 N. 113.46 E. 38, 39
Max. Size: Anchorage: Depth 30 ft., 3.5 miles offshore.
Also see Miri.
Niapotapu Is., Tonga: 15.50 S. 173.50 W. 49
Nias Is., Indonesia 38, 40
Nibe, Denmark: 56.59 N. 9.38 E. 12
NICARAGUA 69, 70
Nicaro, see Antilla.
Nice, France: 43.42 N. 7.17 E. 9, 21, 22
Max. Size: LOA 160 m., draft 7 m. *Fuel:* All grades.
Airport: 7 km.
Nicholls Town, (Andros Is.), Bahamas: 25.10 N. 78.12 W. . 66, 69, 70
Nicholson, see Wellington.
Nicobar Islands, India 37
Niedersachsenbruke, see Wilhelmshaven.
Nieuwpoort, Belgium: 51.09 N. 2.43 E. 7
Max. Size: LOA 82 m., draft 5 m. *Fuel:* Available.
Airport: Middelkerke, 10 km.
Niger Delta, Nigeria 29
NIGERIA 28, 29
Nigg Oil Terminal, see Cromarty Firth.
Nightingale Is., (U.K.): 37.30 S. 12.30 W. 28
Nii, Japan: 34.23 N. 139.20 E. 43, 45
Niigata-Higashi, Japan: 38.01 N. 139.13 E. 43
Max. Size: LNG: 65,000 d.w.t., draft 12.5 m.
Tankers: 50,000 d.w.t., draft 11.60 m. *Fuel:* Available.
Airport: 20 km.
Niigata-Nishi, Japan: 37.54 N. 139.04 E. 43
Max. Size: LOA 210 m., draft 10 m. Tankers: 130,000 d.w.t., draft 17.0 m. *Fuel:* Bonded oil will be brought from Hakodate or Moji. *Airport:* 5 km.
Niihama, Japan: 33.58 N. 133.16 E. 45
Max. Size: LOA 250 m., draft 13 m. *Fuel:* Bunkers in bond available from main ports. *Airport:* Matsuyama and Takamatsu.
Also see Imabari.
Nijmegan, Netherlands: 51.50 N. 5.51 E. 8, 9
Nikiski, Alaska, U.S.A.: 60.41 N. 151.24 W. 54
Max. Size: 80,000 d.w.t. Depth in excess of 40 ft. Kenai (LPG): LOA 261 m., beam 40 m., draft 10.1 m. Unocal: Depth 40 ft.
Fuel: Available. *Airport:* Air transport available.
Nikitas, Greece: 40.17 N. 23.35 E. 25
Nikolaev, Ukraine: 46.56 N. 31.57 E. 26
Max. Size: LOA 215 m., draft 9.8 m. *Fuel:* Available.
Nikolayev, see Nikolaev.
Nikolayevsk, Russia: 53.08 N. 140.44 E. 43
Nikolskoye, Russia: 55.11 N. 166.00 E. 54
Nile Delta, Egypt 21, 26
Nine Degrees Channel, (Laccadive Is.), India 37

Ning Hai, China: 29.15 N. 121.25 E. **42, 46**
Ning Te, China: 26.43 N. 120.00 E. **42**
Ningbo, China: 29.52 N. 121.31 E. **42, 46**
  Max. Size: Draft 5.5 m. in channel, 4.5 m. – 7 m. in berths.
  Fuel: Available.
Ningpo, see Ningbo.
Ninilchik, Alaska, U.S.A.: 60.03 N. 151.40 W. **54**
Nipigon, Ontario, Canada: 49.00 N. 88.15 W. **62**
Niquero, Cuba: 20.03 N. 77.35 W. **70**
  Max. Size: LOA 147 m., draft 6.83 m.
  Also see Manzanillo.
Nishihara, (Okinawa), Japan: 26.14 N. 127.50 E. **42**
  Max. Size: S.A.L.M. for crude vessels: 270,000 d.w.t.
  Product vessels: Up to 97,000 d.w.t. at Pier.
Nishinomiya, Japan: 34.44 N. 135.20 E. **44, 45**
Nishtun, Yemen: 15.50 N. 52.12 E. **31**
  Max. Size: 3,000 d.w.t., LOA 90 m., draft 5 m.
  Airport: Al-Gaidah, 40 km.
Nisiros Is., Greece: 36.36 N. 27.12 E. **25**
Nissan Is., Papua New Guinea: 4.37 S. 154.12 E. **49**
Nissyros, see Nisiros Is..
Niteroi, Brazil: 22.53 S. 42.08 W. **76, 77**
  Max. Size: Depth 6 m., 20,000 d.w.t. *Fuel:* Available. *Airport:* Rio de Janeiro.
Niu Fo'ou Is., Tonga: 15.36 S. 175.38 E. **49**
Niu Is., Tuvalu: 7.12 S. 177.12 E. **49**
Niue Is., see Alofi.
Niue Island (N.Z.) **49**
Niukalita Is., Tuvalu: 10.40 S. 179.20 E. **49**
Niutao Is., Tuvalu: 6.04 S. 177.12 E. **49**
Niva, Denmark: 55.55 N. 12.31 E. **12**
Nizhne Kolymsk, Russia: 68.37 N. 160.55 E. **54**
Njarovik, see Keflavik-Njarovik.
Noank, Connecticut, U.S.A.: 41.19 N. 71.59 W. **63**
Noatak, Alaska, U.S.A.: 67.34 N. 163.00 W. **54**
Nobeoka, Japan: 32.36 N. 131.41 E. **45**
Nogliki, Russia: 51.48 N. 143.12 E. **43**
Noirmoutier Is., France: 47.00 N. 2.15 W. **19**
Nolloth, see Port Nolloth.
Nome, Alaska, U.S.A.: 64.30 N. 165.28 W. **54**
Nomoi Is., (Caroline Is.), Micronesia: 5.24 N. 153.35 E. . . . **46, 49**
Nomwin Is., see Hall Is..
None, Japan: 33.30 N. 134.15 E. **45**
Nootka, see Gold River.
Norco, Louisiana, U.S.A.: 29.59 N. 90.24 W. **67**
Nord Ostsee Canal, see Kiel Canal.
Nordagota, see Fuglefjord.
Nordby, Denmark: 55.27 N. 8.24 E. **12**
Norddeich, Germany: 53.38 N. 7.10 E. **7, 8, 14**
Nordenham, Germany: 53.29 N. 8.29 E. **8, 12, 14**
  Max. Size: LOA 270 m., draft 44 ft. (FW). Tankers: Draft 32 ft. – 42 ft. 8 in. *Fuel:* All grades. *Airport:* Bremen, 70 km.
  Also see Bremen and Bremerhaven.
Norderney, Germany: 53.42 N. 7.10 E. **7, 8, 14**
Nordfjordeid, Norway: 61.50 N. 6.00 E. **15**
Nordfjordur, see Neskaupstadur.
Nordhafen, see Kiel.
Nordmaling, Sweden: 63.35 N. 19.30 E. **15**
Norfolk, Virginia, U.S.A.: 36.51 N. 76.19 W. **55, 63, 65**
  Max. Size: Depths up to 40 ft. Tankers: Depth 27 ft. – 40 ft.
  Fuel: All grades. *Dry Docks:* Floating dock: Length 950 ft., capacity 54,250 ton. *Airport:* Norfolk.
Norfolk Island, (Australia) **49**
Norheimsund, Norway: 60.22 N. 6.10 E. **11**
Normanby Is., Papua New Guinea: 9.55 S. 151.00 E. . . **46**
Normanton, Qld., Australia: 17.40 S. 141.05 E. **50**
Norresundby, Denmark: 57.05 N. 9.53 E. **12**
Norris Arm, Newfoundland, Canada: 49.05 N. 55.16 W. . . **60**
Norrkoping, Sweden: 58.36 N. 16.12 E. **10, 11**
  Max. Size: About 45,000 d.w.t. with draft of 11.4 m. (MLW).
  Largest tanker: 66,875 d.w.t., LOA 236.46 m. *Fuel:* All grades.
  Airport: Kungsangen, 4 miles.
Norrsundet, Sweden: 60.56 N. 17.09 E. **11**
  Max. Size: Draft 6.6 m., LOA 135 m. *Fuel:* By road tanker.
Norrtalje, Sweden: 59.46 N. 18.43 E. **10, 11**
Norsholm, Sweden: 58.30 N. 16.00 E. **11**
Norsminde, Denmark: 56.02 N. 10.16 E. **12**
North Andaman Island, (Andaman Is.), India. **37**
North Bend, Oregon, U.S.A.: 43.26 N. 124.10 W. **57**
North Berwick, U.K.: 56.04 N. 2.43 W. **6**
North Cape, (North Is.), New Zealand: 34.22 S. 173.03 E. . . **49, 52**
North Cape, Norway: 71.10 N. 25.46 E. **10, 15, 79**
North Carolina, U.S.A. **63, 66**
North Channel, U.K. **5**
North East Land, (Spitsbergen), Norway **17**
North East Marine Terminal, see New York.
North Farallon, California, U.S.A. **58**
North Foreland, U.K.: 51.23 N. 1.27 E. **6, 7**
North Frisian Islands, Germany **12, 14**
North Island, New Zealand **52**

North Keeling Is., Cocos Is. (Australia) **36**
North Pagai, Indonesia: 2.45 S. 100.05 E. **38**
North Pass, (Mississippi Delta), Louisiana, U.S.A. **66, 67**
North Pulau Laut Coal Terminal, see Tanjung Pemancingan.
North Ronaldsay, U.K.: 59.18 N. 2.30 W. **5**
North Sea **4, 5, 6, 7, 8, 10, 11, 14**
North Sea Canal, Netherlands: 52.22 N. 4.54 E. **7**
  Max. Size: Northern Lock: LOA 325 m., beam 42 m.
  Also see Amsterdam.
North Shields, U.K.: 55.02 N. 1.27 W. **5, 6**
  Also see Tyne District.
North Star Bugt, Greenland (Denmark): 76.36 N. 68.52 W. . . **17, 79**
  Max. Size: Largest vessel to berth alongside quay was LOA 130 m., and draft 7 m. *Airport:* Two rescue helicopters stationed at this base.
North Sydney, N.S., Canada: 46.16 N. 60.13 W. **60**
  Max. Size: Depth alongside 7.3 m. – 7.9 m. *Fuel:* Fuel and diesel oil. *Dry Docks:* Small vessels only, LOA 125 ft.
  Airport: Sydney, connects with Halifax and Montreal.
North Uist, U.K.: 57.35 N. 7.17 W. **5**
North West Cape, W.A., Australia: 21.47 S. 114.09 E. . . **51**
Northern Endeavour, Australia: 10.37 S. 125.59 E. . . . **46, 50**
  Max. Size: 150,000 d.w.t., depth 385 m.
Northern Ireland, U.K. **4, 5**
Northern Mariana Is., Commonwealth of (U.S.A.) **46**
Northern Sporades Is., Greece **25, 26**
Northern Territory, Australia **50**
Northfleet Hope, see Tilbury.
Northport, (Long Is.), New York, U.S.A.: 40.57 N. 73.20 W. . . **55, 63**
  Max. Size: LOA 825 ft., beam 144 ft., draft 40 ft. at HW.
Northumberland Strait, Canada **60**
Northville, see Riverhead.
Northwest Territories, Canada **59**
Norton Sound, see Nome.
Norwalk, Connecticut, U.S.A.: 41.05 N. 73.25 W. **63**
NORWAY **4, 8, 10, 11, 12, 15, 16, 79**
Norwegian Sea, Norway **4, 10, 15**
Norwich, U.K.: 52.38 N. 1.18 E. **5**
Norwich, Connecticut, U.S.A.: 41.32 N. 72.05 W. **63**
Norwuz Terminal, see Bahregan.
Noshiro, Japan: 40.13 N. 140.00 E. **43**
  Max. Size: LOA 130 m., draft 9.4 m.
Nosok, Russia: 70.08 N. 82.21 E. **16**
Nossi-Be, Madagascar: 13.24 S. 48.16 E. **30**
Notre Dame Bay, Newfoundland, Canada **60**
Notre Dame de Koartac, see Koartac.
Nottingham Is., N.W.T., Canada: 63.10 N. 78.10 W. . . . **59**
Nouadhibou, Mauritania: 20.49 N. 17.03 W. **27**
  Max. Size: Point Central – LOA 310 m., beam 47 m., draft 16.15 m. *Fuel:* Available in small quantities by barge.
Nouakchott, Mauritania: 18.02 N. 16.02 W. **27**
  Max. Size: Draft 10.3 m.
Noumea, New Caledonia (France): 22.16 S. 166.26 E. . . **49**
  Max. Size: Draft 10.30 m. Tankers: SLN: LOA 260 m., draft 9.7 m. Mobil: Draft 10.7 m. *Fuel:* Several grades available. *Airport:* International, 50 km.
Nouveau Comptoir, Quebec, Canada: 53.03 N. 78.55 W. . . **59**
Nova Mambone, Mozambique: 21.00 S. 35.05 E. **30**
Nova Scotia, Canada **60**
Novaya Tarya, Russia: 52.55 N. 158.31 E. **54**
Novaya Zemlya, Russia **16, 79**
Novigrad, Croatia: 45.19 N. 13.33 E. **24**
Novo Redondo, Angola: 11.11 S. 13.49 E. **28**
Novorossiysk, Russia: 44.43 N. 37.47 E. **21, 26**
  Max. Size: LOA 250 m., draft 11 m. for dry cargo vessel.
  Tankers: 250,000 d.w.t., draft 19.5 m. *Fuel:* Most grades. *Dry Docks:* 100,000 ton range. *Airport:* Anapa, 50 km.
Novvy Port, Russia: 67.40 N. 72.54 E. **16, 79**
Nowy Port, Poland: 54.24 N. 18.40 E. **11**
Noyelles, France: 50.12 N. 1.42 E. **7**
Nueva Gerona, (Isla de Pinos), Cuba: 21.58 N. 82.56 W. . . **69, 70**
  Max. Size: Draft 19 ft.
Nueva Palmira, Uruguay: 33.53 S. 58.25 W. **77, 78**
  Max. Size: Old Port: Draft 23 ft. New Port: Draft 26 ft. 6 in.
  Fuel: By road tanker. *Airport:* Zagarzazu, 15 km.
Nuevitas, Cuba: 21.33 N. 77.16 W. **69, 70**
  Max. Size: Pastellilo: Up to 575 ft. LOA, 33 ft. draft; up to 610 ft. LOA, 31 ft. draft. Puerto Tarafa: Draft 27 ft. Bufadero: LOA 600 ft., draft 25 ft. 6 in. *Fuel:* Regular fuel oil in Pastellilo.
Nuevo Berlin, Uruguay: 33.05 S. 58.05 W. **78**
Nugget Point, New Zealand: 46.27 S. 169.52 E. **52**
Nuijamaa, Russia: 60.59 N. 28.31 E. **13**
  Also see Saimaa Canal.
Nuku Hiva, (Marquesas Is.), French Polynesia (France) . . **49**
Nuku'alofa, (Tongatapu Is.), Tonga: 21.08 N. 175.12 W. . . **49**
  Max. Size: Draft 10 m. *Fuel:* Light diesel fuel to reach Suva only. *Airport:* 14 miles, flights to Suva, New Zealand, Samoa and Hawaii.
Nukunau, Kiribati: 1.26 S. 176.25 E. **49**

Nukunono Is., Tokelau Is. (N.Z.): 9.02 S. 171.42 W. **49**
Nukuoro Is., (Caroline Is.), Micronesia: 3.49 N. 155.00 E. **49**
Numancia, (Siargao Is.), Philippines: 9.52 N. 125.58 E. **47**
Numazu, Japan: 35.05 N. 138.51 E. **45**
   Max. Size: 5,000 d.w.t., depth 7.5 m. *Fuel:* Bonded fuel from Yokohama or Tokyo.
Nunivak Is., Alaska, U.S.A. **54**
Nunukan, Indonesia: 4.05 N. 117.37 E. **38, 47**
   Max. Size: Depth 3.5 m. *Airport:* Flights to Tarakan.
Nuottasaari, see Oulu.
Nurnberg, Germany: 49.27 N. 11.05 E. **9**
Nuuk, Greenland (Denmark): 64.10 N. 51.44 W. **17**
   Max. Size: Largest to berth: LOA 135 m., beam 17 m., draft 7 m. Tankers: To 30,000 d.w.t. *Fuel:* Small quantities of gas oil available. *Airport:* Airstrip.
Ny Alesund, (Spitsbergen), Norway: 78.55 N. 11.56 E. **17**
Nyborg, Denmark: 55.19 N. 10.49 E. **12**
   Max. Size: Depth 16 ft. – 36 ft. Tankers: Draft 32 ft. *Fuel:* All grades. Tankers: 1,000 d.w.t. *Airport:* Beldringe and Odense, 50 km. Copenhagen, 130 km.
Nyborg, Norway: 70.05 N. 28.30 E. **15, 16**
Nyda, Russia: 66.38 N. 73.02 E. **16**
Nyhamn, Finland: 62.10 N. 21.20 E. **15**
Nyhamn, Sweden, see Gavle.
Nykarleby, Finland: 63.32 N. 22.28 E. **15**
Nykobing, (Falster), Denmark: 54.46 N. 11.52 E. **11, 12**
   Max. Size: Draft 19 ft. 6 in., beam 25 m. *Fuel:* All grades. *Airport:* 2 hours by train Copenhagen.
Nykobing, (Mors), Denmark: 56.48 N. 8.52 E. **11, 12, 14**
   Max. Size: LOA 120 m., beam 25 m., draft 4.3 m. (SW). *Fuel:* By road tanker. *Airport:* Thisted, 45 km. Karup, 70 km.
Nykobing, (Zeeland), Denmark: 55.55 N. 11.41 E. **12**
Nykoping, Sweden: 58.45 N. 17.02 E. **11**
   Max. Size: Draft 5.4 m. *Fuel:* All grades. *Airport:* Norrkoping, 80 km.
Nyland, see Botea.
Nymindegab, (Falster), Denmark: 55.50 N. 8.10 E. **11, 12**
Nynashamn, Sweden: 58.55 N. 17.58 E. **11**
   Max. Size: LOA 300 m., depth 17 m. *Fuel:* All grades. *Airport:* Nearest is Stockholm.
Nystad, see Uusikaupunki.
Nysted, Denmark: 54.40 N. 11.44 E. **12, 14**
Nyvik, see Hovid.
Nyvrovo, Russia: 54.18 N. 142.36 E. **43**

O

O'Connor, see Port O'Connor.
Oahu Is., Hawaii, U.S.A. **49**
Oak Creek, Wisconsin, U.S.A.: 42.53 N. 87.51 W. **62**
Oak Harbour, Washington, U.S.A.: 48.17 N. 122.39 W. . . . **56**
Oak Pt., see New Orleans.
Oakland, California, U.S.A.: 37.50 N. 122.18 W. . . . **55, 57, 58**
   Max. Size: Depths 10.7 m. – 12.8 m. *Fuel:* Available. *Airport:* Oakland.
   Also see San Francisco.
Oakville, Ontario, Canada: 43.26 N. 79.40 W. **62**
Oamaru, New Zealand: 45.05 S. 171.00 E. **52**
Oaxen, Sweden: 58.58 N. 17.43 E. **11**
Oban, New Zealand: 46.54 S. 168.06 E. **52**
Oban, U.K.: 56.25 N. 5.28 W. **5**
Obbia, Somalia: 5.23 N. 48.31 E. **31**
Obbola, Sweden: 63.42 N. 20.20 E. **15**
   Also see Umea.
Obi Major Is., Indonesia **46**
Obidos, Brazil: 1.51 S. 55.35 W. **72**
   Max. Size: 7,000 d.w.t., depth 10 m.
Obligato, Argentina: 33.38 S. 59.48 W. **78**
Obock, Djibouti: 12.01 N. 43.19 E. **31, 32**
Obubra, Nigeria: 6.05 N. 8.28 E. **29**
Ocean City, Maryland, U.S.A.: 38.20 N. 75.05 W. **63, 65**
Ocean City, New Jersey, U.S.A.: 39.18 N. 74.34 W. . . . **63, 65**
Ocean Falls, B.C., Canada: 52.21 N. 127.41 W. **56**
   Max. Size: LOA 600 ft., draft 30 ft. *Airport:* Daily seaplane service to Vancouver.
Ocean Island, see Banaba.
Oceanside, California, U.S.A.: 33.13 N. 117.25 W. **57**
Ochakov, Ukraine: 46.36 N. 31.33 E. **26**
Ochamchire, Georgia: 42.45 N. 41.25 E. **26**
Ocho Rios, Jamaica: 18.25 N. 77.07 W. **69, 70**
   Max. Size: LOA 900 ft., draft 40 ft. Cruise Ship: LOA 900 ft., draft 32 ft. *Fuel:* Bunker "C" and diesel.
Oconto, Wisconsin, U.S.A.: 44.53 N. 87.51 W. **62**
Odaejin, North Korea: 41.23 N. 129.47 E. **43**
Odda, Norway: 60.05 N. 6.33 E. **11**
Odense, Denmark: 55.25 N. 10.23 E. **11, 12**
   Max. Size: Inner Port: Draft 7.0 m. (FW), 6,000 d.w.t., LOA 160 m. Lindoe Terminal: 35,000 d.w.t., draft 9.9 m. *Fuel:* All grades. *Dry Docks:* 500,000 d.w.t. at Lindoe. *Airport:* 9 km., connects with Copenhagen.
Odessa, Ukraine: 46.32 N. 30.54 E. **21, 26**
   Max. Size: Inner Harbour: LOA 240 m., beam 40 m., draft 12 m. Tankers: LOA 240 m., draft 11.5 m. or LOA 195 m., draft 12 m. *Fuel:* By barge. *Dry Docks:* Available. *Airport:* 10 miles.
Odudu Terminal, Nigeria: 4.00 N. 7.45 E. **28, 29**
   Max. Size: 80,000 – 280,000 d.w.t. tonnes. Depth 64 m.
Oeno Is., Pitcairn Is. (U.K.): 23.56 S. 130.45 W. **49**
Ofunato, Japan: 39.03 N. 141.44 E. **43**
   Max. Size: Channel: LOA 190 m., draft 14.0 m. Berth: Max. draft 12.0 m. Tankers: 35,000 d.w.t., draft 9.0 m. *Fuel:* Bonded oil will be brought from Yokohama or Hakodate. *Airport:* Hanamaki (Domestic), 97 km.
Oga, Japan: 39.59 N. 139.55 E. **43**
Ogdensburg, New York, U.S.A.: 44.42 N. 75.30 W. . . . **55, 60, 61**
   Max. Size: Largest vessel to enter: LOA 730 ft., draft 27 ft. *Fuel:* One day's notice, all grades. *Airport:* 0.5 mile from city, connects with New York.
Ogidigbe, Nigeria: 5.31 N. 5.04 E. **29**
Ogorode, see Sapele.
Oguendjo Terminal, Gabon: 1.27 S. 8.55 E. **28**
   Max. Size: 170,000 d.w.t., max. displacement 200,000 tons, draft 60 ft.
Ohata, Japan: 41.30 N. 141.10 E. **43**
Ohio, U.S.A. **60, 62**
Ohita, see Oita.
Ohmishima, see Omishima.
Oil Fields, North Sea:
   Alba: 58.00 N. 1.06 E. **5**
   Albuskjell: 56.38 N. 3.03 E. **5**
   Amethyst: 58.38 N. 0.41 E. **5**
   Andrew: 58.02 N. 1.27 E. **5**
   Anglia: 53.21 N. 1.38 E. **5**
   Anne: 53.44 N. 2.06 E. **5**
   Arbroath: 57.23 N. 1.23 E. **5**
   Audrey: 53.34 N. 1.58 E. **5**
   Balder: 59.14 N. 2.26 E. **5**
   Balmoral: 58.14 N. 1.07 E. **5**
   Barque: 53.36 N. 1.32 E. **5**
   Beatrice: 58.07 N. 2.55 W. **5**
   Beryl: 59.36 N. 1.28 E. **5**
   Birch: 58.38 N. 1.15 E. **5**
   Brae: 58.47 N. 1.22 E. **5**

Brage: 60.33 N. 3.02 E. 5
Brent: 61.04 N. 1.36 E. 5
Bruce: 59.44 N. 1.32 E. 5
Brule: 59.45 N. 1.49 E. 5
Buchan: 57.54 N. 0.02 E. 5
Caister: 54.13 N. 2.27 E. 5
Camelot: 52.59 N. 2.16 E. 5
Chanter: 58.25 N. 0.20 E. 5
Claymore: 58.26 N. 0.26 W. 5
Cleeton: 54.02 N. 0.45 E. 5
Clipper: 53.27 N. 1.42 E. 5
Clyde: 56.28 N. 2.17 E. 5
Cod: 57.04 N. 2.26 E. 5
Cormorant: 61.05 N. 1.04 E. 5
Cyrus: 58.07 N. 1.27 E. 5
Dagmer: 55.34 N. 4.37 E. 5
Dan: 55.30 N. 5.10 E. 5
Don: 61.31 N. 1.30 E. 5
Donan: 58.23 N. 0.58 E. 5
Dunbar: 60.32 N. 1.40 E. 5
Edda: 56.28 N. 3.05 E. 5
Ekofisk: 56.32 N. 3.16 E. 5
Elder: 61.21 N. 1.09 E. 5
Eldfisk: 56.24 N. 3.19 E. 5
Embla: 56.28 N. 3.15 E. 5
Emerald: 60.39 N. 1.00 E. 5
Esmond: 54.36 N. 1.25 E. 5
Everest: 57.46 N. 1.47 E. 5
Forties: 57.44 N. 0.56 E. 5
Frigg: 59.56 N. 2.06 E. 5
Fulmar: 56.29 N. 2.07 E. 5
Galleon: 53.23 N. 2.00 E. 5
Gannet: 57.11 N. 1.00 E. 5
Glamis: 58.10 N. 1.00 E. 5
Gordon: 54.29 N. 1.56 E. 5
Gorn: 55.35 N. 4.45 E. 5
Gryphon: 59.21 N. 1.34 E. 5
Gullfaks: 61.10 N. 2.13 E. 5
Gyda: 56.55 N. 3.05 E. 5
Heather: 60.57 N. 0.57 E. 5
Heimdal: 59.36 N. 2.18 E. 5
Helder: 53.02 N. 4.13 E. 5
Helm: 52.52 N. 4.09 E. 5
Hewett: 53.02 N. 1.44 E. 5
Hod: 56.10 N. 3.28 E. 5
Hudson: 61.16 N. 0.40 E. 5
Huldra: 60.53 N. 2.40 E. 5
Hutton: 61.08 N. 1.24 E. 5
Hyde: 53.48 N. 1.02 E. 5
Indefatigable: 53.21 N. 2.32 E. 5
Ivanhoe & Rob Roy: 58.11 N. 0.07 E. 5
Kinsale: 51.20 N. 8.20 W. 5
Kittiwake: 57.27 N. 0.31 E. 5
Kraka: 55.24 N. 5.05 E. 5
Leman: 53.01 N. 2.14 E. 5
Linnhe: 59.40 N. 1.34 E. 5
Loke: 58.26 N. 1.54 E. 5
Lomond: 57.18 N. 2.08 E. 5
Magnus: 61.43 N. 1.15 E. 5
Maureen: 58.06 N. 1.45 E. 5
Miller: 58.44 N. 1.25 E. 5
Moira: 58.02 N. 1.41 E. 5
Montrose: 57.26 N. 1.24 E. 5
Murchison: 61.24 N. 1.44 E. 5
Murdoch: 54.16 N. 2.19 E. 5
Nelson: 57.39 N. 1.09 E. 5
Ness: 59.34 N. 1.24 E. 5
Ninian: 60.52 N. 1.24 E. 5
Noordwinning: 53.12 N. 3.14 E. 5
Odin: 60.05 N. 2.08 E. 5
Oseberg: 60.29 N. 2.52 E. 5
Osprey: 61.18 N. 0.35 E. 5
Petroland: 53.34 N. 4.10 E. 5
Petronella: 58.20 N. 0.05 E. 5
Pickerill: 53.32 N. 1.07 E. 5
Piper: 58.29 N. 0.27 E. 5
Placid: 53.26 N. 4.17 E. 5
Ravenspurn: 54.01 N. 1.06 E. 5
Regnar: 55.20 N. 5.10 E. 5
Rolf: 55.37 N. 4.29 E. 5
Rough: 53.50 N. 0.23 E. 5
Saltire: 58.25 N. 0.15 E. 5
Scapa: 58.24 N. 0.21 E. 5
Scott: 58.17 N. 0.12 E. 5
Sean: 53.16 N. 2.51 E. 5
Skjold: 55.33 N. 4.54 E. 5
Sleipner: 58.22 N. 1.54 E. 5
Snorre: 61.27 N. 2.08 E. 5
Statfjord: 61.15 N. 1.52 E. 5
Strathspey: 60.56 N. 1.42 E. 5
Tartan: 58.22 N. 0.04 E. 5
Thelma: 58.26 N. 1.14 E. 5
Thistle: 61.25 N. 1.40 E. 5
Tiffany: 58.29 N. 1.18 E. 5
Tommeliten: 56.29 N. 2.55 E. 5
Toni: 58.26 N. 1.18 E. 5
Tor: 56.39 N. 3.19 E. 5
Troll: 60.49 N. 3.30 E. 5
Tyra: 55.42 N. 4.46 E. 5
Ula: 57.07 N. 2.51 E. 5
Valdemar: 55.49 N. 4.34 E. 5
Valhall: 56.17 N. 3.23 E. 5
Veslefrikk: 60.47 N. 2.53 E. 5
Viking: 53.30 N. 2.18 E. 5
Welland: 52.58 N. 2.44 E. 5
West Sole: 53.46 N. 1.08 E. 5

Oinousai Is., Greece: 38.31 N. 26.13 E. **25**
Oistins Bay, see Bridgetown.
Oita, Japan: 33.17 N. 131.40 E. **45**
Max. Size: 30,000 d.w.t., depth 12.0 m. LPG: Depth 13.1 m. LNG: Depth 11.4 m. Tankers: 270,000 d.w.t., draft 21.3 m. Coal: 300,000 d.w.t., draft 25 m. *Fuel:* Bonded bunkers supplied by oil barges. *Airport:* 56 km. by road.
Okaba, Indonesia: 8.03 S. 139.42 E. **46**
Okanda, Sri Lanka: 6.40 N. 81.50 E. **37**
Okarito, New Zealand: 43.16 S. 170.09 E. **52**
Okawa, Japan: 33.12 N. 130.22 E. **45**
Okayama, Japan: 34.39 N. 133.54 E. **45**
Okha, India: 22.28 N. 69.05 E. **37**
Max. Size: LOA 525 ft. during N.E. monsoon and LOA 540 ft. during S.W. monsoon. Draft 22 ft. – 27 ft. *Fuel:* Available. *Airport:* Jamnagar, 110 miles.
Okha, Russia: 53.34 N. 143.00 E. **43**
Okhotsk, Russia: 59.21 N. 143.11 E. **43**
Oki Is., Japan: 36.15 N. 133.15 E. **43, 45**
Okimura, see Haha.
Okinawa Is., Japan **42, 46**
Okino Is., (Daito Is.), Japan: 24.28 N. 131.11 E. **46**
Okino Is., (Shikoku), Japan: 32.44 N. 132.33 E. **45**
Okkye, South Korea: 37.37 N. 129.03 E. **42, 43, 45**
Max. Size: Depth is reported to be 15.0 m. *Airport:* Seoul.
Oklahoma, U.S.A. **66**
Okrika, Nigeria: 4.44 N. 7.05 E. **29**
Max. Size: Sailing draft reported as 31 ft. 9 in. Also see Port Harcourt.
Oksfjiord, Norway: 70.14 N. 22.22 E. **15**
Oku, Japan: 26.35 N. 127.50 E. **42**
Okubo, see Moji.
Okushiri Is., (Hokkaido), Japan: 42.15 N. 139.30 E. **43**
Ola, Russia: 59.35 N. 151.16 E. **43**
Olafsfjordur, see Siglufjord.
Olafsvik, Iceland: 64.54 N. 23.34 W. **17**
Oland, Sweden **10, 11**
Olbia, (Sardinia), Italy: 40.55 N. 9.31 E. **9, 21, 24**
Max. Size: Inner Port: Draft 20 ft. *Fuel:* By road tanker. *Airport:* 3 km.
Olcott, New York, U.S.A.: 43.20 N. 78.43 W. **62**
Old Harbour, Alaska, U.S.A.: 57.05 N. 153.30 W. **54**
Oldenburg, Germany: 53.09 N. 8.14 E. **8, 9, 14**
Max. Size: LOA 85 m., beam 10 m., draft 4 m. *Airport:* Bremen, 50 km.
Olga, Russia: 43.44 N. 135.17 E. **43**
Olga Strait, (Spitsbergen), Norway **17**
Olhao, Portugal: 37.03 N. 7.50 W. **20, 22**
Olimarao, (Caroline Is.), Micronesia: 7.41 N. 145.52 E. **46**
Olimbos, Greece: 35.45 N. 27.10 E. **25, 26**
Oljysatama, see Turku.
Olongapo, see Subic Bay.
Olympia, Washington, U.S.A.: 47.00 N. 122.53 W. **55, 56**
Max. Size: Turning Basin: LOA 800 ft., draft 30 ft. (MLW). Berth: Depth 40 ft. *Fuel:* Most grades from Seattle. *Dry Docks:* Nearest Seattle (60 miles). *Airport:* Local airport, connects with Seattle.
Olyutorskiy, Russia: 60.12 N. 169.52 E. **54**
Omaezaki, Japan: 34.36 N. 138.13 E. **43, 45**
Max. Size: 30,000 d.w.t., LOA 220 m., draft 11.3 m. *Fuel:* Bonded oil from Yokohama.
OMAN, SULTANATE OF **31, 35, 37**
Ominato, Japan: 41.15 N. 141.10 E. **43**
Omis, Croatia: 43.27 N. 16.42 E. **24**
Omisalj, (Krk Is.), Croatia: 45.13 N. 14.32 E. **24**
Max. Size: Draft 27 m., 350,000 d.w.t. *Fuel:* Available. Also see Rijeka.
Omishima, Japan: 34.16 N. 133.00 E. **45**
Refinery closed
OML 100, see Odudu Terminal.
Omura, see Chichi Is..
Omuta, Japan: 33.02 N. 130.26 E. **45**
Onagawa, Japan: 38.27 N. 141.27 E. **43**

Onahama, Japan: 36.56 N. 140.55 E. **43, 45**
Max. Size: Tankers: Sea Berth 99,000 d.w.t., draft 13.50 m. Other Vessels: Draft 11.3 m. *Fuel:* Bonded oil will be brought from Yokohama.

Ondarroa, Spain: 43.20 N. 2.25 W. **19**

One and a Half Degree Channel, Maldives **37**

One Fathom Bank, (Malacca Strait), Malaysia **40**

Onega, Russia: 63.54 N. 38.06 E. **16, 79**
Max. Size: Draft is usually announced at the beginning of the navigation season (4.0 m. – 5.8 m.), LOA 125 m. *Fuel:* Availability not guaranteed. *Airport:* Archangel.

Onehunga, New Zealand: 36.56 S. 174.47 E. **52**
Max. Size: LOA 95 m., draft 4.7 m. *Fuel:* Available. *Airport:* Auckland, 8 km.

Onekotan Is., (Kurile Is.), Russia **43**

Onich, U.K.: 56.41 N. 5.14 W. **5**

Onitsha, Nigeria: 6.05 N. 6.45 E. **29**

Ono-i-lau, Fiji: 20.40 S. 178.30 W. **49**

Onoda, Japan: 33.58 N. 131.10 E. **45, 46**
Max. Size: Depth 5.7 m. – 7.6 m.

Onomichi-Itozaki, Japan: 34.20 N. 133.16 E. **45**
Max. Size: Depth 5.0 m. – 10.0 m. *Fuel:* Bonded oil will be brought from Kobe, Kanokawa, Hirohata or Moji. *Dry Docks:* Mukaishima – largest 25,000 d.w.t., 175 m. x 9 m. x 9 m. *Airport:* Hiroshima or Osaka.

Onon Is., see Namonuito.

Onsala, Sweden: 57.25 N. 12.00 E. **11, 12**

Onsan, see Ulsan.

Onset, Massachusetts, U.S.A.: 41.45 N. 70.40 W. . . . **64**

Onslow, W.A., Australia: 21.40 S. 115.08 E. **51**

Onslow Bay, North Carolina, U.S.A. **63**

Ontario, Canada **59, 60, 61, 62**

Onton, see Castro-Urdiales.

Ontonagon, Michigan, U.S.A.: 46.53 N. 89.19 W. . . . **62**

Oosterhout, Netherlands: 51.38 N. 4.51 E. **8**

Opatija, Croatia: 45.20 N. 14.18 E. **24**

Opobo, Nigeria: 4.35 N. 7.32 E. **29**

Oporto, Portugal: 41.09 N. 8.37 W. **20, 22**
Max. Size: Douro River: Draft 19 ft. (HWST). *Fuel:* Available. *Airport:* 17 km., connects with Lisbon. Also see Leixoes.

Opotiki, New Zealand: 38.00 S. 177.20 E. **52**

Opua, New Zealand: 35.19 S. 174.07 E. **52**
Max. Size: Draft 7 m. *Fuel:* By road tanker. *Airport:* At Whangarei.

Opunake, New Zealand: 39.27 S. 173.51 E. **52**

Oran, Algeria: 35.43 N. 0.39 W. **21, 22**
Max. Size: LOA 800 ft., draft 38 ft. *Fuel:* All grades. *Airport:* La Senia, 7 km.

Orand Is., U.S.A.: 42.57 N. 78.50 W. **62**

Orange, France: 44.08 N. 4.48 E. **9**

Orange, Texas, U.S.A.: 30.06 N. 93.44 W. **55, 66**
Max. Size: Draft 30 ft. *Fuel:* All grades. *Dry Docks:* 388 ft x 142 ft., 10,000 tons, 10 ft. 6 in. draft over blocks. *Airport:* 30 miles.

Oranjemund, Namibia: 28.34 S. 16.28 E. **28**

Oranjestad, Aruba (Netherlands): 12.31 N. 70.02 W. . . **69, 72, 74**
Max. Size: Safe salt water draft 28 ft. – 30 ft. *Fuel:* Available by barge at 48 hours notice. *Airport:* 5 miles.

Orchard, see Port Orchard.

Ordu, Turkey: 41.00 N. 37.53 E. **26**

Orebro, Sweden: 59.18 N. 15.12 E. **11**

Oregon, U.S.A. **56, 57**

Oregrund, Sweden: 60.21 N. 18.28 E. **11**

Orehoved, Denmark: 54.57 N. 11.51 E. **12, 14**
Max. Size: LOA 150 m., draft 6.5 m.

Orepuki, New Zealand: 46.20 S. 167.45 E. **52**

Orinoco River/Delta, Venezuela **75**
Max. Size: Draft about 44 ft.

Oristano, (Sardinia), Italy: 39.45 N. 8.30 E. **24**
Max. Size: Martini Silo Quay: Draft 8.5 m. *Airport:* 1 hour's drive.

Oritkari, see Oulu.

Orkanger, Norway: 63.20 N. 9.52 E. **10, 15**
Max. Size: LOA 200 m., draft 11 m. *Fuel:* By road tanker. *Airport:* Vaernes, 80 km.

Orkney Isles, U.K. **4, 5**

Ormara, Pakistan: 25.15 N. 64.35 E. **31, 37**

Orno Is., Sweden: 59.03 N. 18.26 E. **11**

Ornskoldsvik, Sweden: 63.17 N. 18.43 E. **10, 15**
Max. Size: LOA 700 ft., beam 100 ft., draft 34 ft. Tankers: LOA 200 m., draft 10 m., 40,000 d.w.t. *Fuel:* Gas oil, light fuel, heavy fuel. *Airport:* 10 miles.

Oro Bay, Papua New Guinea: 8.54 S. 148.29 E. **46, 51**
Max. Size: Depth at ISLW 11.4 m. *Fuel:* Diesel by road tanker. *Airport:* Popondetta, 40 km.

Oroluk, (Caroline Is.), Micronesia **49**

Oron, Nigeria: 4.50 N. 8.14 E. **29**

Oropos, Greece: 38.19 N. 23.48 E. **25**

Orrington, see Bangor.

Orrskar, see Soderhamn.

Orth, Germany: 54.27 N. 11.03 E. **12, 14**

Ortigueira, Spain: 43.40 N. 7.51 W. **19, 20**

Ortona, Italy: 42.20 N. 14.25 E. **24**

Ortviken, Sweden: 62.24 N. 17.22 E. **15**
Max. Size: Draft 10.8 m., LOA 200 m. Also see Sundsvall.

Orup Is., (Kurile Is.), Russia **43**

Orust Is., Sweden: 58.10 N. 11.40 E. **10**

Osaka, Japan: 34.39 N. 135.26 E. **43, 44, 45**
Max. Size: Depth 12 m. Containers: Depth 13.0 m. Tankers: LOA 250 m., draft 11.6 m. *Fuel:* All grades of bonded bunkers lightered from nearest stock ports. *Dry Docks:* Largest 355 m. x 62.7 m. x 11 m. depth. *Airport:* 25 km.

Oscoda, Michigan, U.S.A.: 44.25 N. 83.20 W. **62**

Oshawa, Ontario, Canada: 43.52 N. 78.50 W. **60, 62**
Max. Size: Depth 22 ft. – 27 ft. *Fuel:* Available. *Airport:* Toronto, 45 miles.

Oshima, Japan: 34.45 N. 139.22 E. **43, 45, 46**

Oshkosh, Wisconsin, U.S.A.: 44.02 N. 88.33 W. **62**

Oshmarino Point, Russia: 71.43 N. 83.00 E. **16**

Oskarshamn, Sweden: 57.15 N. 16.27 E. **10, 11**
Max. Size: Draft 34 ft. 6 in. *Fuel:* Available. *Dry Docks:* Length 81 m., capacity 4,000 d.w.t. *Airport:* 3 km.

Oslo, Norway: 59.54 N. 10.43 E. **4, 8, 10, 11, 12**
Max. Size: Draft 31 ft. Tankers: Draft 36 ft. – 38 ft. *Fuel:* All grades. *Airport:* Fornebu, 8 km. New international airport at Gardermoen, 50 km.

Oslo Fjord, Norway **10, 11**

Osman Digna, see Sawakin.

Osmussaar, Estonia: 59.18 N. 23.23 E. **11**

Osor, Croatia: 44.42 N. 14.24 E. **24**

Ossora, Russia: 59.20 N. 163.15 E. **54**

Ostend, Belgium: 51.14 N. 2.55 E. **7**
Max. Size: Entrance lock to Commercial Docks: Length 125 m., draft 6.1 m. *Fuel:* All grades. *Dry Docks:* Shiplift with 1,750 tons capacity. *Airport:* 3 miles.

Osterby, Denmark: 57.19 N. 11.08 E. **12**

Ostermoor, Germany: 53.55 N. 9.11 E. **14**
Max. Size: LOA 235 m., draft 10.4 m. Also see Brunsbuttel.

Osthammar, Sweden: 60.16 N. 18.23 E. **11**

Ostia, Italy: 41.43 N. 12.17 E. **24**

Ostrand, see Sundsvall.

Ostrava, Czech Republic: 49.50 N. 18.15 E. **9**

Ostrica, Louisiana, U.S.A.: 29.22 N. 89.32 W. **55, 66, 67**
Port closed.

Osumi Is., Japan **43, 46**

Osumi Strait, Japan **45**

Oswego, New York, U.S.A.: 43.28 N. 76.30 W. **55, 60, 62**
Max. Size: Depths to 25 ft. (LW). *Fuel:* Available.

Otago Harbour, New Zealand: 45.49 S. 170.37 E. . . . **52**
Also see Dunedin and Port Chalmers.

Otaru, Japan: 43.12 N. 141.01 E. **43**
Max. Size: Depths to 13 m. Tankers: Draft 7.2 m. *Fuel:* All grades of bonded bunkers lightered from nearest stock ports. *Airport:* Sin-Chitose, 80 km.

Otranto, Italy: 40.09 N. 18.30 E. **24**

Otsu, Japan: 42.36 N. 143.38 E. **43**

Ottawa, Ontario, Canada: 45.26 N. 75.42 W. **60, 61**

Ottawa Is., N.W.T., Canada **59**

Ottenby, Sweden: 56.15 N. 16.25 E. **11**

Otterbacken, Sweden: 58.57 N. 14.02 E. **11, 12**
Max. Size: All ships able to pass through the Trollhatte Canal with draft of 16.9 ft. at MLW. *Fuel:* Available. *Airport:* Karlstad, 90 km.

Otterham Quay, U.K.: 51.22 N. 0.38 E. **6**
Max. Size: LOA 73 m., depth 3.3 m. – 4.6 m. Also see Medway Ports.

Ouddorp, Netherlands: 51.49 N. 3.57 E. **7, 8**

Ouidah, Benin: 6.20 N. 2.02 E. **29**

Ouistreham, France: 49.17 N. 0.15 W. **7**

Oulu, Finland: 65.00 N. 25.25 E. **4, 10, 15**
Max. Size: Vihreasaari Harbour, Oil Quay: Depth 10 m. Bulk Quay: Depth 10 m. Toppila: Depth 6.1 m. Oritkari: 10 m. Nuottasaari: Depth 6.4 m. *Fuel:* Small quantities of all grades. *Dry Docks:* One small slipway. *Airport:* 15 km.

Outer Hebrides, Scotland, U.K. **5**

Ouvea, see Wadrilla.

Ouzinkie, Alaska, U.S.A.: 57.55 N. 152.30 W. **54**

Ovacik, Turkey: 36.10 N. 33.42 E. **26**

Ovendo, Gabon: 0.17 N. 9.30 E. **28, 29**
Max. Size: Draft 12.5 m. *Airport:* 12 miles.

Owase, Japan: 34.04 N. 136.15 E. **43, 45**
Max. Size: Sea Berth: LOA 350 m., draft 19 m., 210,000 d.w.t. *Fuel:* Bonded oil will be brought from Nagoya, Yokohama, Chiba or Kobe.

Owen Sound, Ontario, Canada: 44.35 N. 80.55 W. . . . **60, 62**

Owendo, see Ovendo.

Oxelosund, Sweden: 58.40 N. 17.08 E. 11
  Max. Size: LOA 265 m., beam 38 m., draft 50 ft.
  Bulk (discharging): 130,000 d.w.t., depth up to 45 ft.
  Tankers: Depth 45 ft., 95,000 d.w.t. *Fuel:* Available.
  Airport: Stockholm-Skafsta, 20 km.
Oxhaga, see Karlshamn.
Oxnard, see Hueneme.
Oya, Sarawak, Malaysia: 2.58 N. 111.56 E. **38, 39**
Ozamis, (Mindanao Is.), Philippines: 8.08 N. 123.51 E. **46, 47**
Ozernaya, Russia: 51.30 N. 156.30 E. **43, 54**
Ozol, see San Francisco.

NOTES, ADDITIONS, CORRECTIONS
Please also advise Shipping Guides Ltd.
75 Bell Street, Reigate, RH2 7AN, United Kingdom
Tel: +44 1737 242255   Fax: +44 1737 222449
Email: updates@portinfo.co.uk   Web: www.portinfo.co.uk

P

Paagoumene, New Caledonia (France): 20.29 S. 164.11 E. . . . 51
  Also see Noumea.
Paamiut, Greenland (Denmark): 62.00 N. 49.41 W. 17
  Max. Size: LOA 100 m., draft about 6 m. *Fuel:* Diesel and
  gas oil. *Airport:* Heliport.
Paarden Bay, see Oranjestad.
Pacasmayo, Peru: 7.24 S. 79.35 W. 72
  Max. Size: Anchorage port: Recommended draft 24 ft., but 36 ft.
  possible *Airport:* 2 km. (Emergency only).
  Also see Callao.
Pachi, Greece: 37.58 N. 23.23 E. **23, 25**
  Max. Size: 600,000 d.w.t., draft 29 m. *Airport:* Athens, 60 km.
  Also see Eleusis.
Padang, see Teluk Bayur.
Padloping Is., N.W.T., Canada: 67.00 N. 62.50 W. 17
Padre, see Puerto Padre.
Padre Is., Texas, U.S.A. **66, 69**
Padstow, U.K.: 50.35 N. 4.55 W. **5, 7, 19**
  Max. Size: Draft 15 ft. (Spring), LOA 350 ft.
  Fuel: Marine gas oil. *Dry Docks:* One, 70 ft. x 32 ft. x 12 ft.
Pag, Croatia: 44.27 N. 15.03 E. 24
Pagadian, (Mindanao Is.), Philippines: 7.50 N. 123.26 E. . . . 47
Pagalu, Equatorial Guinea: 1.26 S. 5.36 E. 28
Pagan Is., Northern Mariana Is. (U.S.A.): 18.08 N. 145.47 E. . . . 46
Pagbilao, (Luzon Is.), Philippines: 13.51 N. 121.45 E. 47
  Max. Size: Depth 16 m.
Pagerungan, Indonesia: 6.58 S. 115.57 E. 38
  Max. Size: SBM: 125,000 d.w.t.
Pago Pago, American Samoa (U.S.A.): 14.17 S. 170.41 W. . . . 49
  Max. Size: Largest vessel: 43,000 g.r.t., draft 11.4 m.
  Tankers: LOA 195 m., draft 10.1 m. *Fuel:* Available.
  Airport: Tafuna, 11 km.
Pahang, Malaysia: 3.32 N. 103.27 E. **38, 39**
  Also see Rompin.
Paimboeuf, France: 47.17 N. 2.02 W. 19
Paimpol, France: 48.45 N. 3.05 W. **7, 19**
Paita, Peru: 5.05 S. 81.07 W. 72
  Max. Size: Draft 31 ft. (LW). *Airport:* Piura, 55 km., connects
  with Lima.
Pajaritos, see Coatzacoalcos.
Pakan Baru, see Pekanbaru.
PAKISTAN **31, 37**
Palacois, Texas, U.S.A.: 28.42 N. 96.13 W. 66
Palairos, Greece: 38.46 N. 20.52 E. **24, 25**
Palamos, Spain: 41.50 N. 3.08 E. **9, 22**
  Max. Size: Draft 14 m. *Fuel:* Available at 24 hours notice.
  Airport: Gerona, 42 km.
Palana, Russia: 59.12 N. 160.08 E. 54
Palanan, (Luzon Is.), Philippines: 17.07 N. 122.28 E. **46, 47**
Palanca, Angola: 6.58 S. 12.24 E. 28
  Max. Size: 150,000 d.w.t. (bow-to-bow), 300,000 d.w.t. at SPM.
  Depth 42 m. – 44 m. *Airport:* Luanda.
Palanga, Lithuania: 55.55 N. 21.03 E. 11
Palaskas Bay, Greece 23
Palau Is., see Malakal.
PALAU, REPUBLIC OF 46
Palawan Island, Philippines **46, 47**
Paldiski, Estonia: 59.24 N. 24.05 E. 11
  Max. Size: LOA 140 m., draft 8.4 m. *Fuel:* Limited supply.
  Airport: Tallinn, 50 km.
Paleleh, Indonesia: 1.08 N. 121.48 E. **38, 46**
Palembang, Indonesia: 2.59 S. 104.45 E. 38
  Max. Size: LOA 185 m., draft 7.5 m. *Fuel:* Available. *Airport:*
  Talang Betutu, 12 km.
Palenque, Dominican Republic: 18.12 N. 70.11 W. **69, 70**
  Max. Size: LOA 1,000 ft., draft 45 ft.
  Airport: Santo Domingo, 100 km.
Palermo, (Sicily), Italy: 38.08 N. 13.22 E. **21, 24**
  Max. Size: Draft to 44 ft. Tankers: Up to 15 m. draft. *Fuel:* Fuel
  oil, gas oil and marine diesel available. *Dry Docks:* Largest has
  length 370 m., breadth 68 m. for vessels up to 400,000 d.w.t.
  Airport: Punta Raisi, 30 km.
Palk Strait, India/Sri Lanka 37
Palli, see Saimaa Canal.
Palm Beach, Florida, U.S.A.: 26.46 N. 80.03 W. **55, 66, 69, 70**
  Max. Size: Up to 680 ft. LOA with draft of 33 ft.
  Tankers: Up to 18,000 g.r.t. *Fuel:* Available. *Airport:* Miami.
Palma, (Majorca), Spain: 39.34 N. 2.38 E. **21, 22**
  Max. Size: LOA 294 m., draft 14.56 m. *Fuel:* Available.
  Airport: Palma, 14 km.
Palma Is., Canary Is. (Spain) 27
Palmeira Bay, (Sal Is.), Cape Verde: 16.45 N. 22.59 W. 27
  Max. Size: Depth 2 m. – 4 m. Tankers: Max. draft 40 ft.
  Also see Porto Grande.
Palmer, Alaska, U.S.A.: 61.33 N. 149.07 W. 54

THE SHIPS ATLAS

Palmi, Italy: 38.20 N. 15.50 E. **24**
Palmyra Is., Kiribati: 5.52 N. 162.06 W. **49**
Palo Alto, see Jucaro.
Palourion, Greece: 39.58 N. 23.40 E. **25**
Palu, Indonesia: 0.53 S. 119.51 E. **38, 46**
Palua, Venezuela: 8.21 N. 62.41 W. **69, 72, 75**
 Max. Size: 100,000 d.w.t., LOA 274 m. beam 33.53 m.
 Fuel: All grades by barge.
Paluan, (Mindoro Is.), Philippines: 13.26 N. 120.29 E. **47**
Palupandan, see Iloilo.
Pamatacualito, see Pertigalete.
Pamfyllon, see Mitilene.
Pamlico Sound, North Carolina, U.S.A. **63**
Pampatar, Venezuela: 11.00 N. 63.48 W. **75**
Pampushamnen, see Norrkoping.
PANAMA, REPUBLIC OF **69, 72, 73**
Panama Canal, Panama: 9.00 N. 79.35 W. . . **53, 55, 68, 69, 72, 73**
 Max. Size: LOA 950 ft., beam up to 107 ft., draft up to 39 ft. 6 in.
 TFW (dependent on height of Gatun Lake and other limitations).
 Average transit time 10-12 hours. *Fuel:* Bunker C, diesel, light
 fuel and light diesel available. *Dry Docks:* Balboa:
 Length 318 m., max. draft 12.77 m.
 Airport: 18 miles from Balboa; 48 miles from Cristobal.
Panama City, Panama: 8.57 N. 79.32 W. **73**
Panama City, Florida, U.S.A.: 30.10 N. 85.40 W. . . **55, 66**
 Max. Size: Depths to 32 ft. *Fuel:* Limited diesel oil.
 Airport: 4 miles.
Panambur, see New Mangalore.
Panarea Is., Italy: 38.36 N. 15.03 E. **24**
Panarukan, Indonesia: 7.42 S. 113.56 E. **38**
 Max. Size: Anchorage: Draft up to 15 m.
Panay Is., Philippines **46, 47**
Pandan, (Panay Is.), Philippines: 11.43 N. 122.08 E. . . **46, 47**
Pangai, Tonga: 19.48 S. 174.21 W. **49**
 Max. Size: Unlimited (Anchorage port).
 Also see Nuku'alofa.
Pangani, Tanzania: 5.25 S. 38.58 E. **30**
Pangkalan Susu, Indonesia: 4.07 N. 98.12 E. . . **37, 38, 40**
 Max. Size: Wharf: LOA 95 m., depth 6 m.
 Tankers: SBM: 100,000 d.w.t., LOA 275 m., depth 22 m.
Pangkalanberandan, see Pangkalan Susu.
Pangkalbalam, Indonesia: 2.06 S. 106.08 E. **38**
 Max. Size: LOA 140 m., beam 30 m., 8 ft. draft alongside.
 Airport: 14 km.
Pangnirtung, N.W.T., Canada: 66.09 N. 65.45 W. . . . **59**
Panjang, Indonesia: 5.28 S. 105.19 E. **38**
 Max. Size: Draft 9.5 m. Tarahan Terminal; LOA 179 m.,
 beam 27 m., draft 8.0 m. *Fuel:* Available at Wharf B.
 Airport: Branti, 34 km.
Panjim, India: 15.28 N. 73.48 E. **37**
Pantalan of Assesa, see Tarragona.
Pantellaria Is., Italy: 36.50 N. 11.57 E. **24**
Pantoloan, Indonesia: 0.42 S. 119.51 E. **38, 46**
 Max. Size: Draft 9.5 m. *Fuel:* Available. *Airport:* 25 km.
Paola, Italy: 39.20 N. 16.03 E. **24**
Papa Westray Is., (Orkney Is.), U.K.: 59.27 N. 2.53 W. . . **5**
Papeete, (Society Is.), French Polynesia (France):
 17.33 S. 149.34 W. **49**
 Max. Size: LOA 250 m., beam 32 m., draft 34 ft. The Q.E.2,
 LOA 294 m. has docked. *Fuel:* Available.
 Dry Docks: Vessels up to 3,800 tons. *Airport:*
 Tahiti – Faaa, 6 km.
Papenburg, Germany: 53.06 N. 7.23 E. **7, 8, 9, 14**
 Max. Size: Draft 5.5 m. *Fuel:* Available.
 Dry Docks: 250 m x 36 m.
Paphos, Cyprus: 34.45 N. 32.25 E. **26**
PAPUA NEW GUINEA **46, 49, 50, 51**
Par, U.K.: 50.21 N. 4.42 W. **5, 7**
Para, see Belem.
Paracale, (Luzon Is.), Philippines: 14.10 N. 122.50 E. . . **47**
Paracel Is., South China Sea **39**
Paradero, see Palua.
Paradip, India: 20.14 N. 86.42 E. **37**
 Max. Size: LOA 260 m. (larger subject to weather) and
 draft 12.0 m. (12.8 m. for ore carriers on sailing in fair weather).
 Fuel: Available with notice. *Dry Docks:* 500 ton slipway.
 Airport: Bhubaneswar, 120 km.
PARAGUAY **72, 77**
Parainen, see Pargas.
Paraiso, Panama Canal, Panama: 9.02 N. 79.38 W. . . **73**
Paralion Astrous, Greece: 37.25 N. 22.46 E. **25**
Paramaribo, Suriname: 5.50 N. 55.09 W. **72, 76**
 Max. Size: Bar depth 15 ft., tidal rise between 6 ft. 7 in. and 8
 ft. 10 in. Draft limit is 22 ft. – 23 ft. Tankers: Depth 18 ft.
 Fuel: Available in small quantities. *Dry Docks:* Capacities
 400 tons – 650 tons. *Airport:* Zanderij, 46 km.
Paramashiru Is., Russia: 50.20 N. 155.45 E. **54**
Paramonga, Peru: 10.42 S. 77.48 W. **72**
 Max. Size: Depth 36 ft.
 Also see Supe.
Parana, Argentina: 31.43 S. 60.30 W. **78**

Paranagua, Brazil: 25.30 S. 48.30 W. **76, 77**
 Max. Size: Depths to 37 ft. (HW). Tankers: Draft to 31 ft.
 Fuel: Available. *Airport:* Curitiba, 80 km.
Paranam, Suriname: 5.38 N. 55.05 W. **72, 76**
 Max. Size: Up to 47,500 d.w.t. load to outer bar draft (see
 Paramaribo). LOA 700 ft. Depths alongside: 25 ft. – 30 ft. *Fuel:*
 Small quantities of light diesel No. 2 only in emergency.
 Airport: Zanderij, 30 km.
Parang, see Polloc.
Parapola Is., Greece: 36.54 N. 23.28 E. **25**
Pare-Pare, Indonesia: 4.01 S. 119.37 E. **38, 46**
 Max. Size: Depth in Channel 12 m. – 18 m.
 Depth alongside 5 m. – 14 m. *Airport:* Hasanuddin, 155 km.
Parga, Greece: 39.13 N. 20.24 E. **24, 25**
Pargas, Finland: 60.18 N. 22.18 E. **11**
 Max. Size: Depth 7.5 m. *Fuel:* No local supply. If needed,
 by truck from Abo. *Airport:* Abo, 25 km.
 Also see Turku.
Parham Harbour, see St. John's, Antigua and Barbuda.
Paria, Venezuela: 10.35 N. 67.17 W. **75**
 Max. Size: Draft 19 ft. *Fuel:* Available.
 Dry Docks: 1,200 tonnes d.w.t., LOA 65 m., draft 18 ft.
Parida Is., Panama: 8.07 N. 82.22 W. **69**
Parintins, Brazil: 2.41 S. 56.49 W. **72**
Paris, France: 48.51 N. 2.20 E. **7**
 Max. Size: LOA 120 m., beam 15.5 m., draft 3.5 m. up to Paris,
 draft 2.8 beyond. *Fuel:* By barge. *Airport:* Charles de Gaulle
 and Orly.
Parkeston Quay, see Harwich.
Parnaiba, Brazil: 2.54 S. 41.47 W. **72**
Parnu, see Pyarnu.
Paros, (Paros Is.), Greece: 37.05 N. 25.09 E. **25**
Parrsboro, N.S., Canada: 45.24 N. 64.20 W. **60**
Parry Sound, Ontario, Canada: 45.20 N. 80.02 W. . . **60, 62**
 Max. Size: Depth 6.4 m. *Fuel:* By road tanker.
Partington, see Barton.
Pasadena, Texas, U.S.A.: 29.43 N. 95.13 W. **66**
 Also see Houston.
Pasajes, Spain: 43.20 N. 1.56 W. **19, 21, 22**
 Max. Size: LOA 185 m. and draft 29 ft. *Fuel:* Available.
 Dry Docks: Largest floating dock: 76.5 m. long, 23.25 m. wide,
 and 10.4 m. depth of water. *Airport:* 10 km., connects with
 Madrid.
Pascagoula, Mississippi, U.S.A.: 30.21 N. 88.34 W. **55, 66**
 Max. Size: River: LOA approx. 900 ft., draft 38 ft. at MLW.
 Bayou Casotte: LOA 785 ft., beam 125 m., draft 38 ft. at MLW.
 Fuel: All grades. *Dry Docks:* 38,000 ton capacity.
 Airport: 35 miles.
Pasir Gudang, Malaya, Malaysia: 1.26 N. 103.54 E. . . . **39, 40, 41**
 Max. Size: Depth 5 m. – 15 m. Tankers: Depth 10 m. – 13 m.
 Fuel: All grades. *Dry Docks:* Length 395 m., width 80 m.,
 depth 14 m., 400,000 d.w.t. *Airport:* Singapore or Kuala
 Lumpur.
Pasir Panjang, see Singapore.
Paskallavik, Sweden: 57.10 N. 16.30 E. **11**
Pasni, Pakistan: 25.15 N. 63.25 E. **31, 37**
Paspebiac, Quebec, Canada: 48.01 N. 65.15 W. **60**
 Max. Size: Depth 6.0 m. *Fuel:* Available.
 Airport: Gaspe, 150 km.
Passage West, see Cobh.
Passaic River, New Jersey, U.S.A. **63**
Pastelillo, see Nuevitas.
Pasuruan, Indonesia: 7.38 S. 112.54 E. **38**
Pataholm, Sweden: 56.55 N. 16.27 E. **11**
Patani, Indonesia: 0.17 N. 128.46 E. **46**
Patchogue, New York, U.S.A.: 40.45 N. 73.01 W. . . . **63**
Patea, New Zealand: 39.46 S. 174.30 E. **52**
Pateniemi, Finland: 65.06 N. 25.23 E. **10, 15**
 Port closed
Patillos Cove, Chile: 20.45 S. 70.12 W. **77**
 Max. Size: LOA 200 m., draft 12 m.
 Also see Iquique.
Patmos Is., Greece: 37.18 N. 26.35 E. **25**
Patras, Greece: 38.14 N. 21.45 E. **21, 24, 25**
 Max. Size: Less than 34 ft. draft. Tankers (Rio): Draft 18 ft. and
 2,500 tons. *Fuel:* Deliveries by tank trucks at Patras. Available
 at Texaco-Restis Berth at Rio.
Patreksfjordur, Iceland: 65.35 N. 23.59 W. **17**
 Max. Size: Depth 18 ft. – 19 ft. *Fuel:* Available. *Airport:* 26 km.
Pattani, Thailand: 6.57 N. 101.21 E. **38, 39**
 Max. Size: 1,000 g.t.
Pauillac, France: 45.12 N. 0.45 W. **8, 19**
 Max. Size: Tankers up to 34 ft. draft, LOA 240 m.
 Also see Bordeaux.
Paulina, see Gramercy.
Paulsboro, Pennsylvania, U.S.A.: 39.51 N. 75.15 W. . . . **65**
 Max. Size: Depth 38 ft.
 Also see Philadelphia.
Pavilosta, Latvia: 56.53 N. 21.11 E. **11**
 Max. Size: LOA 60 m., beam 12 m., draft 3.5 m. – 4.5 m.
 Airport: Liepaja, 50 km.

Pavitt Point, see Sandakan.
Paxos Is., Greece: 39.14 N. 20.12 E. 25
Payardi, see Bahia Las Minas.
Paysandu, Uruguay: 32.18 S. 58.06 W. 77, 78
  Max. Size: Draft 15 ft. (FW). *Fuel:* Available.
Peanut Is., see Palm Beach.
Pearl & Hermes Reef, Hawaii, U.S.A.: 27.50 N. 175.58 W. 49
Pearl Harbour, see Honolulu.
Peathoura Is., Greece: 39.30 N. 24.11 E. 25
Pebane, Mozambique: 17.10 S. 38.05 E. 30
Pechenga, Russia: 69.30 N. 31.23 E. 16
Pecket, Chile: 52.56 S. 71.13 W. 77
  Max. Size: LOA 220 m., draft 14 m.
  Also see Punta Arenas.
Pedasi, Panama: 7.45 N. 80.05 W. 69
Pedernales, Venezuela: 9.58 N. 62.15 W. 69, 72, 75
Pedregal, Panama: 8.23 N. 82.26 W. 69
  Max. Size: Draft 15 ft. *Fuel:* By road tanker.
  Airport: David, 5 km.
Pedro Miguel Locks, Panama Canal, Panama:
  9.01 N. 79.37 W. 73
Peekskill, New York, U.S.A.: 41.16 N. 73.56 W. 63
Peel, (Isle of Man), U.K.: 54.14 N. 4.40 W. 5
  Max. Size: LOA 49 m., draft 2.6 m. – 3.7 m. (dries).
  Tankers: LOA 76 m., draft 4.3 m.
Peenemunde, Germany: 54.10 N. 13.55 E. 12
Pegasus, see Port Pegasus.
Pegasus Bay, New Zealand 52
Pei Chieh, see Jiangmen.
Pekalongan, Indonesia: 6.51 S. 109.42 E. 38
Pekan, Malaysia: 3.30 N. 103.25 E. 38, 39, 40
Pekanbaru, Indonesia: 0.34 N. 101.31 E. 38, 39, 40
Pelabuhan Dutuk, see Kuching.
Pelabuhanratu, Indonesia: 7.00 S. 106.32 E. 38
Pelagie Is., Italy 24
Pelagos Is., Greece: 39.17 N. 24.05 E. 25
Pelee Is., Ontario, Canada: 41.49 N. 82.40 W. 62
Peleng Is., Indonesia 46
Pelican, Alaska, U.S.A.: 57.58 N. 136.14 W. 56
Pelotas, Brazil: 31.47 S. 52.20 W. 77
  Max. Size: Depth 2.5 m. *Fuel:* Available. *Airport:* 10 km.
Pemangkat, Indonesia: 1.05 N. 108.56 E. 38, 39
Pemba, Mozambique: 13.00 S. 40.28 E. 30
  Max. Size: Draft 27 ft. 6 in. *Fuel:* Available. *Airport:* 7 km.,
  flights to Maputo and Beira.
Pemba, Tanzania, see Wete.
Pemba Is., Tanzania 30
Pembroke Dock, U.K.: 51.40 N. 4.56 W. 6, 7
Penang, Malaya, Malaysia: 5.25 N. 100.21 E. . . . 37, 38, 39, 40
  Max. Size: Depth 10.0 m. Containers: Depth 9 m. – 12 m.
  Tankers: Depths up to 10.7 m. *Fuel:* Available. *Airport:* 18 km.
Penang Is., Malaya, Malaysia 38, 39, 40
Penarth, U.K.: 51.26 N. 3.10 W. 6
  Max. Size: Berth length 500 ft.
  Also see Cardiff.
Penco, see Talcahuano.
Pending Point, see Kuching.
Penedo, Brazil: 10.15 S. 36.35 W. 72
Penetanguishene, Ontario, Canada: 44.46 N. 79.55 W. 62
Peng Hu, Taiwan: 23.34 N. 119.31 E. 42
Peng Lai, China: 37.47 N. 120.49 E. 42
Penguin, see Burnie.
Peniche, Portugal: 39.22 N. 9.22 W. 20, 22
Peninsular Harbour, see Marathon.
Penmaenmawr, see Nagoya.
Pennington, Nigeria: 4.15 N. 5.36 E. 29
  Max. Size: 250,000 tons displacement, depth 88 ft.
Pennsauken, see Philadelphia.
Pennsylvania, U.S.A. 60, 62, 63, 65
Penrhyn, see Port Penrhyn.
Penrhyn Is., see Tongareva Is..
Penryn, see Falmouth.
Pensacola, Florida, U.S.A.: 30.25 N. 87.13 W. 55, 66
  Max. Size: Depth 35 ft. (LW). *Airport:* Pensacola.
Pentecost Is., Vanuatu: 15.45 S. 168.12 E. 49
Pentland Firth, U.K. 5
Penuba, Indonesia: 0.19 S. 104.27 E. 38, 40
Penzance, U.K.: 50.07 N. 5.32 W. 5, 7, 19
  Max. Size: LOA 300 ft., depth 5.49 m. *Fuel:* Available.
  Dry Docks: LOA 74.7 m., breadth 11.9 m., draft 3.35 m.
  Airport: Newquay.
Pepel, Sierra Leone: 8.34 N. 13.04 W. 27
  Max. Size: LOA 840 ft., beam 128 ft., water depth 38 ft. plus
  height of tide (7 ft. – 11 ft.). The channel has not been
  maintained since 1975. Depth alongside 45 ft. *Fuel:* Limited
  quantities.
Pequaming, Michigan, U.S.A.: 46.51 N. 88.24 W. 62
Perama, Greece: 37.58 N. 23.35 E. 23
  Dry Docks: Length 202 m., depth 40 m., capacity 15,000 tons.
  Also see Piraeus.

Perce, Quebec, Canada: 48.30 N. 64.13 W. 60
Percy, see Punta Arenas.
Perim Is., Yemen: 12.30 N. 43.30 E. 32
Perlis, Malaya, Malaysia: 6.24 N. 100.08 E. 38, 39
Pernambuco, see Recife.
Pernis, see Schiedam.
Peros Banhos Is., (U.K.): 5.22 S. 71.45 E. 30
Perros Guirec, France: 48.48 N. 3.27 W. 7, 19
Perryville, Alaska, U.S.A.: 55.58 N. 159.03 W. 54
Persian Gulf 31, 35
Perth, W.A., Australia: 31.57 S. 115.52 E. 50
Perth, U.K.: 56.23 N. 3.26 W. 5, 6
  Max. Size: LOA 90 m., draft 4.2 m. *Fuel:* By road tanker.
  Airport: Edinburgh, 70 km. Glasgow, 115 km.
Perth Amboy, U.S.A.: 40.30 N. 74.16 W. 63
  Max. Size: Tankers: Depth 26 ft. – 34 ft.
  Also see New York.
Pertigalete, Venezuela: 10.15 N. 64.34 W. 69, 71, 75
  Max. Size: Depth of water alongside the pier is 20 ft. (shore side)
  to 40 ft. (sea side). Tankers (Pamatacualito): Depth 10 m.
Pertuis d'Antioche, France: 46.06 N. 1.20 W. 19
PERU 72, 77
Pesaro, Italy: 43.56 N. 12.55 E. 24
  Max. Size: LOA 114 m., draft 13 ft. *Fuel:* Gasoline and
  benzene only.
Pescara, Italy: 42.28 N. 14.14 E. 24
Peschici, Italy: 41.55 N. 16.00 E. 24
Peta, Indonesia: 3.39 N. 125.34 E. 46
Petaluma, California, U.S.A.: 38.13 N. 122.39 W. 58
Petaluma Creek, California, U.S.A. 58
Petaluma Point, California, U.S.A. 58
Peter the Great Bay, Russia 43
Peterhead Bay Harbour, U.K.: 57.30 N. 1.47 W. 5
  Max. Size: Depth 7.0 m. – 14.0 m. Tankers: 50,000 d.w.t.,
  LOA 250 m., draft 11.5 m. *Fuel:* Available.
  Airport: Aberdeen, 30 miles.
Petersburg, Alaska, U.S.A.: 56.49 N. 132.57 W. 56
  Max. Size: Depth 24 ft. (MLLW). *Fuel:* Diesel and gasoline.
Petit Couronne, see Rouen.
Petit Metis, Quebec, Canada: 48.40 N. 68.00 W. 60
Petkim, see Nemrut Bay.
Petone, New Zealand: 41.14 S. 174.53 E. 52
Petoskey, Michigan, U.S.A.: 45.22 N. 84.58 W. 62
Petrodvorets, Russia: 59.50 N. 29.57 E. 11
Petrolimex K2 Port, see Vung Tau.
Petropavlovsk, Russia: 53.01 N. 158.40 E. 54
  Max. Size: Depth 9.2 m. – 10.5 m.
Petrovac, Yugoslavia: 42.13 N. 18.55 E. 24
Peu, (Santa Cruz Is.), Solomon Islands: 11.41 S. 166.52 E. . . 49
Pevek, Russia: 69.43 N. 170.18 E. 54
Phangnga, Thailand: 8.25 N. 98.30 E. 37
Philadelphia, Pennsylvania, U.S.A.: 39.57 N. 75.10 W. . 55, 60, 63, 65
  Max. Size: Draft 55 ft. for lightering. Depths alongside to 40 ft.
  Tankers: Depth 30 ft. – 40 ft. *Fuel:* Bunker "C" and diesel.
  Dry Docks: Capacity 70,000 tons. *Airport:* 6 miles.
Philip Is., Australia: 29.06 S. 167.57 E. 49
Philip Is., Vic., Australia, see Cowes.
Philippeville, see Skikda.
Philippine Sea, Philippines 47
PHILIPPINES 38, 46, 47
Philipsburg, (St. Maarten), Netherlands Antilles: 18.01 N.
  63.03 W. 71
  Max. Size: Depth 6 m. *Airport:* International.
Phnom Penh, Cambodia: 11.35 N. 104.55 E. 39
Phoenix Islands, Kiribati 49
Phu My, Vietnam: 10.35 N. 107.01 E. 39
  Max. Size: 60,000 d.w.t., LOA 250 m., depth 12 m.
  Fuel: Available. *Airport:* Ho Chi Minh City, 71 km.
Phuket, Thailand: 7.49 N. 98.25 E. 37, 38
  Max. Size: Depth 10.0 m. *Fuel:* Limited supply.
Phuoc Thai, Vietnam: 10.40 N. 107.01 E. 39
  Max. Size: Draft 6.2 m. – 6.5 m.
Pianosa Is., Italy: 42.30 N. 10.06 E. 23, 24
Pico Is., Azores (Portugal): 38.28 N. 28.18 W. 20
Picton, Ontario, Canada: 44.01 N. 77.09 W. 62
Picton, New Zealand: 41.17 S. 174.00 E. 52
  Max. Size: LOA 213 m., draft 11 m. aft, 8 m. – 10 m. forward.
  Fuel: By tank wagon only. *Airport:* Woodbourne, 22 miles.
Pictou, N.S., Canada: 45.41 N. 62.43 W. 60
  Max. Size: Depth alongside 6.4 m. – 11.3 m. *Fuel:* By truck.
  Dry Docks: 2,000 ton capacity. *Airport:* Halifax, 80 miles.
Pierowall, U.K.: 59.18 N. 2.59 W. 5
Pietarsaari, see Jakobstad.
Pigadia, see Karpathos Is..
Pilar, Paraguay: 26.51 S. 58.21 W. 77
Pilevo, Russia: 50.00 N. 142.08 E. 43
Pilion, Greece: 38.46 N. 23.36 E. 25
Pillar Point, California, U.S.A. 58

THE SHIPS ATLAS

Pilon, Cuba: 19.54 N. 77.19 W. 70
  Max. Size: LOA 143 m., draft 6.1 m. Tankers: LOA 152 m.
  Also see Manzanillo.
Pilos, see Pylos.
Pilot Point, Alaska, U.S.A.: 57.30 N. 157.35 W. 54
Pilottown, Louisiana, U.S.A.: 29.11 N. 89.15 W. 66, 67
  Also see New Orleans.
Pimentel, Peru: 6.50 S. 79.56 W. 72
  Max. Size: Anchorage: Depth 40 ft. – 48 ft. Tankers: Draft 18 ft.
Pinamalayan, (Mindoro Is.), Philippines: 13.02 N. 121.29 E. . . . 47
Pinang, see Penang.
Pindo, see Tumaco.
Pine Is., Florida, U.S.A.: 26.36 N. 82.06 W. 66
Piney Point, Maryland, U.S.A.: 38.08 N. 76.32 W. . . . 55, 60, 63, 65
  Max. Size: LOA 850 ft., beam 120 ft., draft 35 ft. 6 in.
  Airport: Washington National, 80 miles.
Pingalep Is., (Caroline Is.), Micronesia: 6.14 N. 160.42 E. . . . 49
Pini Is., Indonesia: 0.10 N. 98.40 E. 38, 40
Pinkenba, see Brisbane.
Pinole Point, California, U.S.A. 58
Pinos, Panama: 9.05 N. 77.58 W. 69
Pinos Island, see Nueva Gerona.
Piombino, Italy: 42.56 N. 10.33 E. 9, 23, 24
  Max. Size: Draft 39 ft., LOA 260 m. (80,000 d.w.t.).
  Tankers: Draft 14 ft. *Fuel:* Available by barge from Livorno.
Pipavav, India: 20.54 N. 71.31 E. 37
  Max. Size: LOA 225 m., draft 11.5 m. LPG: 35,000 d.w.t., LOA
  305 m., draft 9.5 m. *Airport:* Diu, 90 km.
Piperi Is., Greece: 39.20 N. 24.19 E. 25
Pir Pau, see Mumbai.
Piraeus, Greece: 37.57 N. 23.38 E. 21, 23, 25, 26
  Max. Size: Aghios Georgios: Draft 32 ft. Drapetzona: Draft 38 ft.
  Piraeus: Draft 36 ft. Tankers: Draft 26 ft – 48 ft. *Fuel:* Gas oil,
  fuel oil and mixtures of both to a certain viscosity available.
  Dry Docks: Length 136.4 m., depth 9.2 m.
  Airport: Athens, 10 km.
Piran, Slovenia: 45.32 N. 13.34 E. 24
Pirgos, Greece: 36.32 N. 22.20 E. 25
Piriac, France: 47.23 N. 2.33 W. 19
Piriapolis, Uruguay: 34.50 S. 55.15 W. 78
Pirie, see Port Pirie.
Piru, Indonesia: 3.04 S. 128.11 E. 46
Pisa, Italy: 43.43 N. 10.23 E. 23, 24
Pisagua, Chile: 19.38 S. 70.14 W. 72, 77
Pisciotta, Italy: 40.05 N. 15.10 E. 24
Pisco, Peru: 13.44 S. 76.15 W. 72
  Also see General San Martin.
Piscopi, see Tilos Is..
Pitcairn Is., (U.K.) 49
Pitcairn Island (U.K.) 49
Pitch Point, see Sobo.
Pitea, Sweden: 65.14 N. 21.38 E. 10, 15
  Pitea town closed to navigation.
Pithagorion, Greece: 37.42 N. 26.57 E. 25
Pito, Panama: 8.40 N. 77.30 W. 69
Pitsundet, see Pitea.
Pitt Is., see Chatham Is..
Pittsburg, California, U.S.A.: 38.01 N. 122.55 W. 58
Pizzo, Italy: 38.44 N. 16.10 E. 24
Placentia, Newfoundland, Canada: 47.15 N. 53.58 W. . . . 60
Placentia Bay, Newfoundland, Canada 60
Plaju, Indonesia: 2.59 S. 104.50 E. 38
  Max. Size: Plaju: 18,000 d.w.t., LOA 160 m., depth 13.2 m.
  Sungai Gerong: 18,000 d.w.t., LOA 160 m., depth 9.7 m.
  Fuel: Available. *Airport:* Palembang, 20 km.
Plaquemine, Louisiana, U.S.A.: 30.20 N. 91.14 W. 67
  Max. Size: Dow: LOA 825 ft., beam 130 ft., draft 39 ft.
  Fuel: Bunkering not permitted. *Airport:* Ryan Airport, 25 miles.
Plaquemines, Louisiana, U.S.A.: 29.40 N. 89.55 W. 67
  Max. Size: Depth 35 ft. – 80 ft.
Platinum, Alaska, U.S.A.: 59.00 N. 161.50 W. 54
Playa Grande, Guatemala: 14.05 N. 91.30 W. 69
Playitas, Venezuela: 10.00 N. 72.10 W. 69, 74
Plitra, Greece: 36.41 N. 22.50 E. 25
Ploce, Croatia: 43.03 N. 17.26 E. 9, 24
  Max. Size: LOA 220 m., draft 34 ft. 6 in., beam 30 m.,
  air draft 10 m. *Airport:* Split or Dubrovnik, 110 km.
Plomarion, Greece: 38.58 N. 26.23 E. 25
Plominj, see Rabac.
Plymouth, Montserrat (U.K.): 16.42 N. 62.13 W. 71
Plymouth, (Tobago), Trinidad and Tobago:
  11.11 N. 60.48 W. 71, 75
Plymouth, U.K.: 50.22 N. 4.09 W. 5, 7, 19
  Max. Size: Draft 5 m. – 8.5 m. Tankers: Draft 8.5 m.
  Fuel: Available. *Airport:* Domestic, 6 miles.
Plymouth, Massachusetts, U.S.A.: 41.58 N. 70.40 W. 63
Plymouth, North Carolina, U.S.A.: 35.53 N. 76.45 W. . . . 63
Poh, Indonesia: 0.45 N. 122.50 E. 46

Pohang, South Korea: 36.01 N. 129.24 E. 42, 43, 45
  Max. Size: 150,000 d.w.t., LOA 350 m. beam 50 m.,
  draft 16.5 m. *Fuel:* All grades. *Airport:* Kimhae, 150 km.
Pohnpei, Micronesia: 6.55 N. 158.10 E. 49
  Max. Size: 10,000 g.r.t., draft 8 m. *Fuel:* Available.
  Airport: Nearby.
Point Alice, Italy: 39.23 N. 17.12 E. 24
Point Arena, California, U.S.A.: 38.56 N. 123.44 W. 57
Point Barrow, Alaska, U.S.A.: 71.17 N. 156.40 W. 54
Point Bonita, California, U.S.A.: 37.48 N. 122.31 W. . . . 58
Point Breeze, see Philadelphia.
Point Central, Mauritania: 20.49 N. 17.03 W. 27
  Max. Size: LOA 310 m., beam 47 m., draft 12 m. (arrival),
  16.15 m. (departure).
  Also see Nouadhibou.
Point Chicot Is., Louisiana, U.S.A.: 29.48 N. 89.16 W. . . . 67
Point Comfort, Texas, U.S.A.: 28.40 N. 96.35 W. 66
  Also see Port Lavaca.
Point de Grave, France: 45.33 N. 1.04 W. 19
Point de la Coubre, France: 45.42 N. 1.16 W. 19
Point de Penmarch, France: 47.48 N. 4.22 W. 7, 19
Point du Raz, France: 48.02 N. 4.43 W. 7, 19
Point Edward, see Sarnia.
Point Fermin, California, U.S.A.: 33.42 N. 118.17 W. . . . 58
Point Fortin, Trinidad and Tobago: 10.12 N. 61.42 W. . . 71, 75
  Max. Size: Conventional buoy mooring: Depth 53 ft.
  Jetty: Depth 38 ft. *Fuel:* Not available at CBM.
  Airport: Port of Spain.
  Also see Chaguaramas.
Point Henry, see Geelong.
Point Konkhi, Greece 23
Point Lay, Alaska, U.S.A.: 69.52 N. 162.40 W. 54
Point Licosa, Italy: 40.14 N. 14.55 E. 24
Point Limbo, see Limbe.
Point Lisas, Trinidad and Tobago: 10.22 N. 61.29 W. . . . 71, 75
  Max. Size: HATL No. 2: LOA 560 ft., draft 29.5 ft.
  HATL No. 1: LOA 560 ft., draft 28.5 ft. Industrial Port: LOA
  170 m., draft 7.8 m. Savonetta Pier: LOA 245 m., draft 12.8 m.
  ISPAT: LOA 245 m., draft 12.8 m. *Fuel:* All grades. *Airport:* 48
  km.
  Also see Chaguaramas.
Point Lobos, California, U.S.A.: 37.45 N. 122.29 W. 58
Point Reyes, California, U.S.A.: 37.59 N. 123.04 W. . . . 58
Point Samson, see Port Walcott.
Point Tupper, see Port Hawkesbury.
Point Vicente, California, U.S.A.: 33.46 N. 118.24 W. . . . 58
Point Wilson, see Geelong.
Pointe a la Hache, Louisiana, U.S.A.: 29.35 N. 89.53 W. . . 67
Pointe au Pere, see Father Point.
Pointe au Pic, Quebec, Canada: 47.37 N. 70.08 W. 60
  Max. Size: LOA 120 m., depth 7.9 m. *Fuel:* Diesel.
  Dry Docks: Lauzon, 70 miles. *Airport:* Quebec, 130 km.
Pointe Claire, Quebec, Canada: 45.25 N. 73.50 W. 61
Pointe Clairette, see Cape Lopez.
Pointe de Ca Mau, Vietnam: 8.34 N. 104.44 E. 39
Pointe de la Gracieuse, France 23
Pointe des Galets, see Reunion Port.
Pointe Noire, Quebec, Canada: 50.10 N. 66.30 W. 60
Pointe Noire, Congo (Rep. of): 4.47 S. 11.49 E. 28
  Max. Size: Draft 31 ft. Ore: Draft 34 ft. 4 in.
  Tankers: LOA 230 m., draft 33 ft. 6 in. *Fuel:* Available.
  Dry Docks: Slipway up to 800 tons. *Airport:* 6 km.
Pointe-a-Pierre, Trinidad and Tobago: 10.19 N. 61.29 W. . . 71, 75
  Max. Size: No. 6 Sea Berth: Draft 51 ft., LOA 950 ft.
  Fuel: All grades. *Airport:* 28 miles.
  Also see Chaguaramas.
Pointe-a-Pitre, (Grand Terre), Guadeloupe (France):
  16.13 N. 61.32 W. 69, 71
  Max. Size: LOA 260 m., depth 8.0 m. – 10.5 m.
  Tankers: LOA 125 m. – 180 m., depth 6.3 m. – 7.2 m.
  Fuel: By barge or road tanker. *Airport:* Pole Caraibe, 5 km.
Pola, see Pula.
Polambato, see Bogo.
POLAND 4, 9, 10, 11, 12
Poleng, Indonesia: 6.39 S. 112.55 E. 38
  Max. Size: Depth 180 ft.
Police, Poland: 53.34 N. 14.34 E. 11, 12
  Max. Size: LOA 200 m., beam 26 m., draft 9.15 m.
  Airport: Goleniow, 50 km.
Polillo Is., Philippines: 14.44 N. 121.56 E. 47
Pollensa, Spain: 39.54 N. 3.05 E. 22
Polloc, (Mindanao Is.), Philippines: 7.21 N. 124.13 E. . . 46, 47
  Max. Size: Depth 10.5 m. *Fuel:* Diesel by road tanker.
  Airport: Connects with Manila.
Polnochny, see Gdansk.
Poloi, Russia: 66.42 N. 86.35 E. 16
Polyarnyy, Russia: 69.12 N. 33.28 E. 16
Pomalaa, Indonesia: 4.14 S. 121.32 E. 38, 46
  Max. Size: LOA 135 m., draft 7 m. Tankers: LOA 110 m.,
  draft 7 m. Ore Carriers: Draft 11 m. *Airport:* Pomalaa.
Pomarao, Spain: 37.34 N. 7.30 W. 20, 22

Pomona, Namibia: 26.50 S. 15.20 E. 28
Ponape Harbour, see Pohnpei.
Ponce, Puerto Rico (U.S.A.): 17.58 N. 66.37 W. 69, 70
Max. Size: Draft 40 ft. *Fuel:* Available.
Pondicherry, India: 11.56 N. 79.50 E. 37
Max. Size: Anchorage is 7 fathoms within 1 mile from New Pier.
Airport: Chennai, 160 km.
Ponnani, India: 10.47 N. 75.55 E. 37
Ponoi, Russia: 67.02 N. 41.10 E. 16
Pont Audemer, France: 49.20 N. 0.25 E. 7
Pont L'Abbe, France: 47.52 N. 4.13 W. 7, 19
Ponta da Madeira, Brazil: 2.34 S. 44.23 W. 72
Max. Size: 420,000 d.w.t., depth 23 m. *Fuel:* Available.
Airport: Tirical, 26 km.
Ponta Delgada, (San Miguel Is.), Azores (Portugal):
37.44 N. 25.40 W. 20
Max. Size: Up to 38 ft. draft. *Fuel:* Available. *Airport:* 3 km.
Ponta Ubu, Brazil: 20.47 S. 40.35 W. 77
Max. Size: Depth of channel 18 m. (59 ft.). Departure draft: 16 m.
plus height of tide. Max. LOA 308 m. *Airport:* Vitoria, 70 km.
(Internal). Guarapari, 20 km. (Air taxi).
Pontaubault, France: 48.39 N. 1.21 W. 7, 19
Pontevedra, Spain: 42.26 N. 8.39 W. 20
Pontianak, Indonesia: 0.01 S. 109.19 E. 38, 39
Max. Size: LOA 110 m., draft 5 m.
Pontrieux, France: 48.42 N. 3.09 W. 7, 19
Ponza, (Ponziane Is.), Italy: 40.54 N. 12.58 E. 23, 24
Ponziane Is., Italy 23, 24
Poole, U.K.: 50.43 N. 1.59 W. 5, 7, 19
Max. Size: LOA 160 m., draft 5.2 m. – 5.5 m. *Fuel:* Gas oil.
Dry Docks: 2 Slipways, max. 220 ft. x 40 ft.
Airport: Bournemouth International, 9 miles.
Popof Is., see Sand Point.
Porbandar, India: 21.38 N. 69.36 E. 37
Max. Size: LOA 177 m., draft 8 m. Anchorage – No restriction.
Fuel: By road tanker. *Dry Docks:* 150 ft. x 55 ft.
Airport: 3 miles.
Porec, Croatia: 45.14 N. 13.35 E. 24
Pori, Finland: 61.36 N. 21.29 E. 10, 11, 15
Max. Size: Draft 10 m. – 15.3 m. *Fuel:* Available.
Airport: 22 km.
Porirua, New Zealand: 41.00 S. 174.55 E. 52
Porkkala, Finland: 60.05 N. 24.23 E. 11
Max. Size: Draft 9.2 m. *Airport:* Helsinki, 45 km.
Porlamar, Venezuela: 10.57 N. 63.51 W. 69, 71, 75
Pornic, France: 47.07 N. 2.06 W. 19
Poro, New Caledonia (France): 21.19 S. 165.44 E. 51
Max. Size: LOA 169 m., draft 9 m.
Also see Noumea.
Poro, Philippines, see San Fernando.
Poronaysk, Russia: 49.13 N. 143.08 E. 43
Poros, Greece: 37.30 N. 23.28 E. 25
Porpoise Harbour, B.C., Canada: 54.13 N. 130.17 W. 56
Porquerolles Is., see Hyeres.
Porsgrunn, see Heroya.
Port Adams, Texas, U.S.A.: 29.45 N. 95.11 W. 66
Max. Size: See Houston.
Port Adelaide, see Adelaide.
Port Alberni, B.C., Canada: 49.14 N. 124.50 W. 56
Max. Size: Depths up to 50 ft. alongside. *Fuel:* By barge or
road tanker.
Port Albert, Vic., Australia: 38.41 S. 146.41 E. 50, 51
Port Alexander, Alaska, U.S.A.: 56.15 N. 134.39 W. 56
Port Alfred, Quebec, Canada: 48.20 N. 70.52 W. 60
Max. Size: Up to 39 ft. draft. *Fuel:* By road tanker.
Airport: 6 miles, connects with Montreal.
Port Alfred, South Africa: 33.35 S. 26.58 E. 30
Port Alice, B.C., Canada: 50.22 N. 127.28 W. 56
Max. Size: LOA 565 ft., draft 25 ft. Tankers: LOA 580 ft.,
draft 35 ft. *Fuel:* Limited diesel oil. Fuel oil only in emergency.
Airport: 35 miles.
Port Allen, Hawaii, U.S.A.: 21.54 N. 159.35 W. 49
Max. Size: LOA 687 ft., draft 32 ft. *Airport:* 20 miles.
Also see Nawiliwili.
Port Allen, Louisiana, U.S.A.: 30.28 N. 91.13 W. 67
Also see Baton Rouge.
Port Alma, Qld., Australia: 23.36 S. 150.53 E. 50, 51
Also see Rockhampton.
Port Alucroix, see Limetree Bay.
Port Angeles, Washington, U.S.A.: 48.08 N. 123.25 W. 55, 56
Max. Size: Depths to 44 ft. MLW. *Fuel:* By barge.
Airport: 3.5 miles.
Port Antonio, Jamaica: 18.11 N. 76.27 W. 69, 70
Max. Size: LOA 550 ft., draft 26 ft. *Airport:* Kingston.
Port Aransas, Texas, U.S.A.: 27.50 N. 97.03 W. 66
Port Arecibo, Puerto Rico (U.S.A.): 18.29 N. 66.42 W. . . . 69, 70
Max. Size: Depth 20 ft.
Port Arlington, see Queenscliff.
Port Arthur, Tas., Australia: 43.08 S. 147.52 E. 51
Port Arthur, Canada, see Thunder Bay.
Port Arthur, China, see Lu Shun.

Port Arthur, Texas, U.S.A.: 29.52 N. 93.56 W. 55, 66
Max. Size: Authorised channel depth 40 ft. Depths alongside up
to 40 ft. *Fuel:* Almost any grade. *Dry Docks:* 825 ft. x 121 ft. or
362 ft. x 310 ft. Lifting capacity 56,000 long tons.
Airport: 10 miles.
Port Askaig, U.K.: 55.51 N. 6.07 W. 5
Max. Size: Quay length 60 m., depth 4.06 m.
Port Augusta, S.A., Australia: 32.29 S. 137.46 E. 50, 51
No longer used by commercial shipping
Port Austin, Michigan, U.S.A.: 44.05 N. 83.00 W. 62
Port aux Basques, Newfoundland, Canada:
47.35 N. 59.08 W. 60
Airport: 160 km.
Port Bail, France: 49.20 N. 1.43 W. 7, 19
Port Balchik, see Balchik.
Port Blair, (Andaman Is.), India: 11.40 N. 92.44 E. 37
Port Blandford, Newfoundland, Canada: 48.22 N. 54.10 W. 60
Port Bolivar, Texas, U.S.A.: 29.21 N. 94.47 W. 66
Port Bonython, S.A., Australia: 33.01 S. 137.46 E. 50, 51
Max. Size: Tankers: LOA 265 m., draft 15.8 m., 110,000 d.w.t.,
depth 20 m. LPG: 75,000 cu.m. *Airport:* Whyalla, connects with
Adelaide.
Port Botany, see Botany Bay.
Port Bou, Spain: 42.25 N. 3.09 E. 22
Port Bouet, see Abidjan.
Port Briera, Algeria: 36.32 N. 1.35 E. 22
Port Burwell, (Labrador), Newfoundland, Canada: 60.25 N.
64.51 W. 59
Port Burwell, Ontario, Canada: 42.38 N. 80.48 W. 60, 62
Port Campbell, Vic., Australia: 38.37 S. 142.59 E. 50
Port Canaveral, Florida, U.S.A.: 28.25 N. 80.35 W. 55, 66
Max. Size: Depth 39 ft. Tankers: LOA 650 ft., depth 39 ft.
Fuel: Available. *Airport:* Orlando, 54 miles.
Melbourne, 22 miles.
Port Canning, India: 22.15 N. 88.45 E. 37
Port Cartier, Quebec, Canada: 50.02 N. 66.47 W. 60
Max. Size: Vessels of 100,000 d.w.t. and over, draft 33 ft.
forward, 38 ft. aft on arrival. Ore: Loaded draft 54 ft. (MHW),
airdraft 42 ft. (MHW). Grain: Loaded draft 47 ft., airdraft 45 ft.
(MHW). *Fuel:* Available. *Airport:* 40 miles, connects with
Montreal, etc.
Port Chalmers, New Zealand: 45.49 S. 170.31 E. 52
Max. Size: LOA 850 ft., draft 12.5 m. *Fuel:* Available.
Airport: Dunedin.
Also see Otago Harbour.
Port Chester, New York, U.S.A.: 41.00 N. 73.40 W. 63
Port Chicago, California, U.S.A.: 38.03 N. 122.01 W. 58
Port Clinton, Ohio, U.S.A.: 41.31 N. 82.57 W. 62
Port Colborne, Ontario, Canada: 42.52 N. 79.15 W. 62
Max. Size: LOA 730 ft., beam 76 ft., draft 26 ft. 3 in.
Fuel: Bunker and diesel.
Also see Port Weller.
Port Coquitlam, B.C., Canada: 49.16 N. 122.46 W. 56
Port Cornwallis, (Andaman Is.), India: 13.20 N. 92.55 E. . . . 37
Port Covington, see Baltimore.
Port Credit, Ontario, Canada: 43.33 N. 79.35 W. 62
Port Curtis, see Gladstone.
Port Dalhousie, Ontario, Canada: 43.12 N. 79.16 W. 62
Max. Size: Channel depth 21 ft. – 23 ft. *Fuel:* Gasoline only.
Port Daniel, Quebec, Canada: 48.10 N. 64.55 W. 60
Port Darwin, Falkland Is. (U.K.): 51.50 S. 58.55 W. 77
Port de Berre, see Berre.
Port de Bouc, France: 43.24 N. 4.59 E. 9, 22, 23
Max. Size: LOA 250 m., draft 12.8 m. *Fuel:* Available.
Airport: Marseilles.
Also see Fos and Marseilles.
Port de l'Amitie, Mauritania: 17.59 N. 16.02 W. 27
Max. Size: Depth 10.3 m.
Also see Nouakchott.
Port de la Coribierre, see Marseilles.
Port de la Mede, see La Mede.
Port de Lave, see Marseilles.
Port de Lavera, see Lavera.
Port de Paix, Haiti: 19.57 N. 72.50 W. 70
Port Dickson, Malaya, Malaysia: 2.31 N. 101.47 E. 38, 39, 40
Max. Size: Up to 49 ft. draft at S.B.M. terminal.
Fuel: Bunker fuel oil available, no diesel.
Port Dikson, Russia: 73.31 N. 80.15 E. 16, 79
Port Douglas, Qld., Australia: 16.29 N. 145.29 E. 50, 51
Port Dover, Ontario, Canada: 42.47 N. 80.12 W. 62
Port Dufferin, N.S., Canada: 44.55 N. 62.25 W. 60
Port Dzaoudzi, see Dzaoudzi.
Port Eads, Louisiana, U.S.A.: 29.01 N. 89.10 W. 67
Port Edward, B.C., Canada, see Porpoise Harbour.
Port Edward, Ontario, Canada, see Sarnia.
Port Elgin, Ontario, Canada: 44.26 N. 81.24 W. 62
Port Elizabeth, South Africa: 33.57 S. 25.39 E. 30
Max. Size: Passenger, dry cargo and container
vessels: Draft 11.6 m. Tankers: LOA 203.3 m., draft 9.7 m.
Ore Carriers: LOA 251.5 m., draft 12.0 m. *Fuel:* Bunker
fuel and gas oil. *Airport:* 4 km.

67

Port Ellen, U.K.: 55.37 N. 6.13 W. **5**
  Max. Size: Depth at pier 12 ft. (LWOST).
Port en Bessin, France: 49.21 N. 0.45 W. **7, 19**
Port Erin, U.K.: 54.05 N. 4.46 W. **5**
Port Esquivel, Jamaica: 17.53 N. 77.08 W. **70**
  Max. Size: LOA 198 m., draft 11.0 m. *Fuel:* Bunker "C".
  Airport: Norman Manley, 40 miles.
Port Etienne, see Nouadhibou.
Port Everglades, Florida, U.S.A.: 26.05 N. 80.05 W. **55, 66, 69, 70**
  Max. Size: Depth 7 m. – 13.5 m. Tankers: Depth 38 ft. – 43 ft.
  Fuel: Fuel oil and diesel. *Dry Docks:* Capacity 4,200 tons.
Port Fairy, Vic., Australia: 38.23 S. 142.15 E. **50**
Port Fajardo, Puerto Rico (U.S.A.): 18.20 N. 65.38 W. **71**
Port Fouad, Egypt: 31.14 N. 32.21 E. **33, 34**
Port Gamble, Washington, U.S.A.: 47.51 N. 122.35 W. **56**
Port Gentil, Gabon: 0.43 S. 8.48 E. **28**
  Max. Size: Depth 11 m. Tankers: LOA 70 m., draft 5 m. *Airport:* 4 km.
Port Germein, S.A., Australia: 33.01 S. 138.01 E. **51**
Port Giles, S.A., Australia: 35.02 S. 137.46 E. **50, 51**
  Max. Size: LOA 206 m., beam 40 m., 40,000 d.w.t.
  Fuel: By road tanker. *Airport:* Adelaide.
Port Glasgow, U.K.: 55.51 N. 4.16 W. **6**
  Also see Greenock.
Port Graham, see English Bay.
Port Gregory, W.A., Australia: 28.12 S. 114.15 E. **50**
Port Harcourt, Nigeria: 4.46 N. 7.00 E. **28, 29**
  Max. Size: Draft 7.32 m. – 8.23 m. at HW, LOA 600 ft.
  Tankers: Arrival 7.32 m., sailing 9.67 m. *Fuel:* By barge
  or road tanker. *Airport:* 30 km.
Port Hardy, B.C., Canada: 50.42 N. 127.30 W. **56**
Port Harmon, see Stephenville.
Port Harrison, see Inoucdjouac.
Port Harvey, see Oro Bay.
Port Hastings, see Port Hawkesbury.
Port Hawkesbury, N.S., Canada: 45.36 N. 61.22 W. **60**
  Max. Size: Port Hawkesbury: Up to 350,000 d.w.t. Max.
  draft 84 ft. *Fuel:* Available. *Airport:* Halifax, 150 miles.
  Sydney, 90 miles.
Port Hedland, W.A., Australia: 20.18 S. 118.35 E. **50, 51**
  Max. Size: LOA 330 m., subject to restrictions. Departure draft
  determined by computer. Depths: BHP Finucane Island: 17 m.
  Berth No. 1: 11.2 m. Berth No. 3: 13.2 m. BHP Nelson Point
  Wharf: 19 m. *Fuel:* Available. *Airport:* 12 km., connects with
  Perth and Darwin.
Port Heiden, Alaska, U.S.A.: 56.55 N. 158.40 W. **54**
Port Holland, (Basilan Is.), Philippines: 6.33 N. 121.52 E. **47**
Port Hood, N.S., Canada: 46.00 N. 61.32 W. **60**
Port Hope, Ontario, Canada: 43.56 N. 78.17 W. **62**
  Max. Size: Depth 7 ft. – 9 ft. alongside. *Fuel:* Available.
Port Hope Simpson, Newfoundland, Canada:
  52.31 N. 56.17 W. **59**
Port Huon, Tas., Australia: 43.10 S. 146.59 E. **50, 51**
  Max. Size: LOA 190 m., draft 9 m. *Fuel:* Limited supplies by
  road from Hobart. *Airport:* Hobart, 40 miles.
Port Huron, Michigan, U.S.A.: 42.59 N. 82.26 W. **55, 62**
  Max. Size: LOA 730 m., draft 26 ft. *Fuel:* All grades.
Port Ibrahim, see Suez.
Port Irene, see Aparri.
Port Isaac, U.K.: 50.35 N. 4.50 W. **7**
Port Isabel, Texas, U.S.A.: 26.05 N. 97.13 W. **66, 69**
Port Jackson, see Sydney.
Port Jefferson, (Long Is.), New York, U.S.A.:
  40.59 N. 73.06 W. **55, 63**
  Fuel: Not readily available.
Port Jerome, see Quillebeuf.
Port Joinville, France: 46.44 N. 2.21 W. **19**
Port Kaiser, Jamaica: 17.52 N. 77.37 W. **69, 70**
  Max. Size: Tankers: Draft 40 ft. Bulk Carriers: LOA 650 ft.,
  beam 90 ft., draft 36 ft.
Port Kamsar, Guinea: 10.39 N. 14.37 W. **27**
  Max. Size: LOA 229 m., draft 10.0 m. (For entering) and 11.9 m.
  – 13.8 m. (Leaving). *Airport:* Conakry, 280 km.
Port Kasim, see Port Muhammad Bin Qasim.
Port Kelang, see Port Klang.
Port Kembla, N.S.W., Australia: 34.28 S. 150.54 E. **50**
  Max. Size: 150,000 d.w.t., channel depth 15.25 m. (ISLW).
  Coal: LOA 315 m., beam 55 m., depth 16.25 m. (LW).
  Grain: LOA 315 m., beam 45 m., draft 15.20 m. – 15.88 m.
  Iron ore: Depth 12.8 m. – 15.75 m. (ISLW).
  Tankers: LOA 183 m., draft 10.7 m. or LOA 233 m., draft 9.0 m.
  Fuel: Available. *Airport:* Sydney.
Port Kennedy, see Thursday Island.
Port Kenny, S.A., Australia: 33.11 S. 134.41 E. **51**
Port Khalid, see Sharjah.
Port Khorly, Ukraine: 46.05 N. 33.18 E. **26**
Port Klang, Malaya, Malaysia: 3.00 N. 101.24 E. . . . **37, 38, 39, 40**
  Max. Size: South Port: LOA 192 m., draft 10.5 m.
  Tankers: LOA 178 m., draft 10.5 m. North Port: Container ships
  – LOA 300 m., depth 13.2 m. West Port: Depth 10 m. – 15 m.
  Fuel: Available. *Airport:* Subang, 35 km. Kuala Lumpur, 80 km.

Port Kopli, see Tallinn.
Port la Vie, France: 46.39 N. 1.54 W. **19**
Port Latta, Tas., Australia: 40.51 S. 145.23 E. **50, 51**
  Max. Size: LOA 245 m. (804 ft.), beam 38.5 m. (126 ft.),
  draft 16 m. (52.5 ft.). *Airport:* Wynyard, 25 miles.
Port Lavaca, Texas, U.S.A.: 28.40 N. 96.35 W. **55, 66**
  Max. Size: LOA 1,000 ft., draft controlled by channel
  depth 36 ft. *Fuel:* Available. *Airport:* Victoria, 30 miles.
Port Lincoln, S.A., Australia: 34.42 S. 135.50 E. **50, 51**
  Max. Size: LOA: Tankers 178 m., grain 263 m., Phosphate
  196 m. Draft: 14.7 m. *Fuel:* Limited fuel oil/diesel, by road
  tanker. *Airport:* Connects to Adelaide.
Port Louis, France: 47.42 N. 3.21 W. **7, 19**
Port Louis, Mauritius: 20.09 S. 57.30 E. **30**
  Max. Size: LOA: Tankers 178 m., draft 11 m. Sugar: LOA 198 m., draft 11 m.
  Containers: LOA 220 m., draft 11 m. *Fuel:* Available.
  Dry Docks: 100 m. × 15 m., with max. draft of 5 m.
Port Lyantey, see Kenitra.
Port MacDonnell, S.A., Australia: 38.03 S. 140.42 E. **50**
Port Macquarie, N.S.W., Australia: 31.25 S. 152.55 E. **50**
Port Maitland, Ontario, Canada: 42.51 N. 79.35 W. **62**
Port Manatee, Florida, U.S.A.: 27.30 N. 82.35 W. **66**
  Max. Size: Draft 34 ft.
  Also see Tampa.
Port Manati, see Manati.
Port Maubert, France: 45.26 N. 0.46 W. **8**
Port McNeil, B.C., Canada: 50.36 N. 127.04 W. **56**
Port McNicoll, Ontario, Canada: 44.45 N. 79.48 W. **62**
Port Meadows, (Andaman Is.), India: 12.00 N. 92.47 E. **37**
Port Medway, N.S., Canada: 44.09 N. 64.34 W. **60**
Port Melbourne, see Melbourne.
Port Mellon, B.C., Canada: 49.31 N. 123.29 W. **56**
Port Meneng, see Banyuwangi.
Port Menier, Quebec, Canada: 49.49 N. 64.21 W. **60**
Port Moller, Alaska, U.S.A.: 56.00 N. 160.35 W. **54**
Port Moody, B.C., Canada: 49.17 N. 122.53 W. **56**
Port Morant, Jamaica: 17.52 N. 76.20 W. **70**
Port Moresby, Papua New Guinea: 9.29 S. 147.09 E. . . . **46, 50, 51**
  Max. Size: Depth 10 m. at LAT alongside. Tankers: Draft 13 m.
  at buoys. *Fuel:* Diesel and distillate. *Airport:* 13 km.
Port Muhammad Bin Qasim, Pakistan: 24.46 N. 67.21 E. **37**
  Max. Size: Draft 10.0 m. – 10.5 m. (Seasonal – amended every
  3 months.), LOA 185 m. – 250 m. Tankers: 75,000 d.w.t. LOA
  245 m., beam 40 m., draft 10.5 m. (Marginal Wharf: LOA 183 m.,
  draft 10 m., 25,000 d.w.t.). *Fuel:* Available.
  Airport: Karachi, 30 km.
  Also see Karachi.
Port Nador, Morocco: 35.17 N. 2.56 W. **22, 27**
  Max. Size: 60,000 d.w.t., depth 5 m. – 13 m. Tankers:
  Depth 13 m. *Fuel:* Available. *Airport:* Oujda, 140 km. Melilla
  (Spain) nearby.
  Also see Melilla.
Port Natal, see Durban.
Port Neches, Texas, U.S.A.: 30.00 N. 93.57 W. **66**
  Max. Size: Depth 38 ft., LOA 810 ft. *Fuel:* Bunker "C" by barge
  from Port Arthur or Beaumont. *Airport:* Connects Houston.
  Also see Port Arthur.
Port Nelson, Canada, see York Factory.
Port Nelson, New Zealand, see Nelson.
Port Nessabar, see Bourgas.
Port Newark, see Newark.
Port Nicholson, see Wellington.
Port Nolloth, South Africa: 29.15 S. 16.50 E. **28**
  Max. Size: LOA 200 m., draft 3.5 m. *Fuel:* Diesel.
  Airport: Alexander Bay, 80 km.
Port Noro, Solomon Islands: 8.13 S. 157.12 E. **49, 51**
  Max. Size: Depth over 20 m.
Port Nouveau, Quebec, Canada: 58.42 N. 65.58 W. **59**
Port O'Connor, Texas, U.S.A.: 28.27 N. 96.24 W. **66**
Port of Spain, Trinidad and Tobago: 10.39 N. 61.32 W. **69, 71, 72, 75**
  Max. Size: Depth 4 m. – 9.75 m. *Fuel:* All grades.
  Airport: 17 miles.
  Also see Chaguaramas.
Port Orchard, Washington, U.S.A.: 47.32 N. 122.38 W. **56**
Port Orford, Oregon, U.S.A.: 42.45 N. 124.30 W. **57**
Port Pegasus, New Zealand: 47.10 S. 167.40 E. **52**
Port Penrhyn, U.K.: 53.14 N. 4.07 W. **5**
  Max. Size: LOA 76 m., beam 18 m., 2,500 d.w.t., berths dry
  at L.W. *Fuel:* Available. *Airport:* Manchester or Liverpool.
Port Phillip Bay, Vic., Australia: 37.50 S. 144.58 E. **51**
Port Pirie, S.A., Australia: 33.10 S. 138.08 E. **50, 51**
  Max. Size: LOA 185 m., beam 30.0 m., depth in channel 6.4 m.
  (LWOST). Max. sailing draft 8.23 m. *Fuel:* Limited supply of
  diesel oil, by road tanker.
Port Polnochny, see Gdansk.
Port Purcell, see Road Harbour.
Port Qaboos, see Port Sultan Qaboos.
Port Qasim, see Port Muhammad Bin Qasim.

Port Rashid, Dubai, U.A.E.: 25.16 N. 55.16 E. 35
 Max. Size: Draft 9.3 m. – 11.5 m.
 Container Terminal: Draft 12.8 m. Tankers: Draft 11.3 m.
 Fuel: Available. *Dry Docks:* 1,000,000 d.w.t. *Airport:* 3.2 km.
Port Raysut, see Port Salalah.
Port Redi, India: 15.44 N. 73.39 E. 37
 Max. Size: Up to 34 ft. draft at anchorage.
 Airport: Belgaum, 90 miles.
Port Renfrew, B.C., Canada: 48.34 N. 124.25 W. 56
Port Rhoades, Jamaica: 18.29 N. 77.24 W. 69, 70
 Max. Size: LOA 700 ft., beam 92 ft. – 104 ft., draft 37 ft. 6 in.
 Airport: Montego Bay, 40 miles.
Port Richmond, New York, see Stapleton.
Port Richmond, Pennsylvania, see Philadelphia.
Port Rowan, Ontario, Canada: 42.38 N. 80.28 W. 62
Port Royal, Jamaica, see Kingston.
Port Royal, South Carolina, U.S.A.: 32.23 N. 80.42 W. . . . 66
 Max. Size: LOA 182.9 m., draft 8.23 m. *Fuel:* Available.
 Airport: Beaufort County (9.6 km.), Savannah or Charleston.
Port Saguenay, Quebec, Canada: 48.24 N. 70.50 W. 60
 Max. Size: Depth 13.8 m., 100,000 d.w.t. Tankers: LOA 137 m.,
 draft 7.8 m. *Fuel:* By road tanker. *Airport:* 25 miles.
Port Said, Egypt: 31.15 N. 32.18 E. 21, 26, 32, 33, 34
 Max. Size: Anchorage: Depth 38 ft. Alongside: Draft 27 ft.
 Containers: Draft 42 ft. Tankers: Draft 38 ft. Grain:
 Draft 38 ft. – 42 ft. *Fuel:* Available. *Dry Docks:* 50,000 d.w.t.
 Airport: Cairo, 2.5 hours.
 Also see Suez Canal.
Port Said By-Pass, Suez Canal, Egypt. 33, 34
Port St. Joe, Florida, U.S.A.: 29.49 N. 85.19 W. 55, 66
 Max. Size: Draft 32 ft. *Airport:* 40 miles.
Port St. Johns, South Africa: 31.37 S. 29.32 E. 30
Port St. Louis, Madagascar: 13.05 S. 48.50 E. 30
 Max. Size: No information available. *Airport:* Local, Sirana
 7 km., Antsiranana 134 km.
Port St. Mary, (Isle of Man), U.K.: 54.04 N. 4.44 W. 5
 Max. Size: LOA 170 m., draft 10 ft. 6 in. (LWOST).
Port Salalah, Oman: 16.56 N. 54.00 E. 31, 37
 Max. Size: Draft 15.5 m. Tankers: 10 m. *Fuel:* Available at
 berth. *Airport:* Salalah, 25 km.
Port Salazar, see Namibe.
Port San Carlos, see San Carlos.
Port San Juan, see Port Renfrew.
Port San Luis, California, U.S.A.: 35.10 N. 120.45 W. . . . 55, 57
 Max. Size: Tankers: LOA 750 ft., draft 26 ft. *Fuel:* Diesel.
 Airport: 12 miles.
Port Sandwich, Vanuatu: 16.27 S. 167.47 E. 49
Port Sanilac, Michigan, U.S.A.: 43.25 N. 82.35 W. 62
Port Saunders, Newfoundland, Canada: 50.39 N. 57.18 W. . . 60
Port Seatrain, see New York.
Port Severn, see Waubaushene.
Port Shepstone, South Africa: 30.45 S. 30.28 E. 30
Port Simpson, B.C., Canada: 54.33 N. 130.25 W. 56
Port Socony, see Carteret.
Port Stanley, Ontario, Canada: 42.39 N. 81.13 W. 62
 Max. Size: Depth in channel 7.0 m. Depth alongside 4.6 m. –
 6.4 m. *Fuel:* By road tanker.
Port Stanley, Falkland Is. (U.K.): 51.42 S. 57.51 W. 77
 Max. Size: LOA 130 m. *Fuel:* Available. *Airport:* 32 miles.
Port Stanvac, S.A., Australia: 35.06 S. 138.28 E. 50, 51
 Max. Size: Product Berth: LOA 183 m., draft 10.7 m.,
 displacement 42,000 tonnes. SBM: LOA 345 m., draft 17.1 m.,
 300,000 d.w.t. *Fuel:* Fuel and diesel oil available at Product
 Berth.
Port Stephens, N.S.W., Australia: 32.43 S. 152.12 E. 50
Port Stewart, Qld., Australia: 14.05 S. 143.41 E. . . . 46, 50, 51
Port Sucre, see Cumana.
Port Sudan, Sudan: 19.37 N. 37.14 E. 32
 Max. Size: LOA 850 ft. Draft at Oil Terminal 39 ft., other berths
 between 28 ft. and 34 ft. 6 in. *Fuel:* Marine fuel oil, marine
 diesel oil and gas oil. *Airport:* 16 miles, connects with Cairo
 and Khartoum.
Port Sulphur, Louisiana, U.S.A.: 29.28 N. 89.41 W. 67
 Max. Size: LOA 750 ft., draft 35 ft. – 40 ft. *Fuel:* By barge.
 Airport: New Orleans International, 55 miles.
Port Sultan Qaboos, Oman: 23.37 N. 58.34 E. 31, 35, 37
 Max. Size: LOA 850 m., draft 12.5 m. *Fuel:* Available.
 Airport: Seeb International Airport, 45 km.
Port Sunlight, U.K.: 53.22 N. 3.00 W. 6
Port Sutton, see Tampa.
Port Swettenham, see Port Klang.
Port Talbot, U.K.: 51.35 N. 3.49 W. 6, 7
 Max. Size: Ore terminal: 160,000 d.w.t., draft 16.7 m.
 Fuel: All grades. *Airport:* Rhoose, 25 miles.
Port Tampa, see Tampa.
Port Taranaki, see New Plymouth.
Port Taufiq, Egypt: 29.58 N. 32.34 E. 26, 33, 34
 Also see Suez Canal.
Port Tewfik, see Port Taufiq.
Port Topolly, see Varna.
Port Townsend, Washington, U.S.A.: 48.06 N. 122.45 W. . . . 56

Port Trinidad, see Casilda.
Port Tudy, France: 47.39 N. 3.27 W. 19
Port Union, see Catalina.
Port Vauban, see Antibes.
Port Vendres, France: 42.31 N. 3.07 E. 9, 22
 Max. Size: LOA 150 m., draft 25 ft. – 26 ft. *Fuel:* Small craft
 only. *Airport:* Perpignan, 30 km.
Port Victoria, (Mahe), Seychelles: 4.37 S. 55.28 E. 30
 Max. Size: Draft 11.5 m. Tankers: LOA 180 m., beam 34 m.,
 draft 11.5 m. *Fuel:* Available. *Airport:* International.
Port Vila, Vanuatu: 17.45 S. 168.18 E. 49
 Max. Size: LOA 250 m. Depth 10.7 m. Tankers: Draft 7 ft., plus
 height of tide (HW). *Fuel:* By road tanker. *Airport:* Connects
 with Noumea.
Port Vincent, S.A., Australia: 34.47 S. 137.51 E. 51
Port Vladimir, Russia: 69.25 N. 33.08 E. 16
Port Walcott, W.A., Australia: 20.37 S. 117.11 E. 51
 Max. Size: Cape Lambert Ore Jetty: 225,000 – 323,000 d.w.t.,
 LOA 355 m., beam 50 m. – 55 m., depth 18.5 m. – 19.5 m. Cape
 Lambert Service Jetty: LOA 625 ft., depth 10 m. (LW).
 Airport: Karratha, connects with Perth daily.
Port Waratah, see Newcastle.
Port Washington, Washington, U.S.A.: 43.24 N. 87.52 W. . . . 62
Port Weld, Malaya, Malaysia: 4.50 N. 100.38 E. 38, 39, 40
Port Weller, Ontario, Canada: 43.14 N. 79.13 W. 60, 62
 Max. Size: LOA 730 ft. (222.5 m.), beam 76 ft. (23.16 m.),
 draft 8.0 m. *Dry Docks:* 228.6 m. (750 ft.), graving dock gate
 width 24.38 m. (80 ft.)
Port Wentworth, Georgia, U.S.A.: 32.09 N. 81.08 W. 55, 66
 Max. Size: LOA 700 ft., least depth in Channel 28 ft., depth in
 berth 40 ft. *Fuel:* Fuel oil, diesel oil and lubricating oils.
 Also see Savannah.
Port Whangarei, see Whangarei.
Port William, see Port Stanley.
Port Williams, N.S., Canada: 45.05 N. 64.25 W. 60
Port Williams, Chile, see Puerto Williams.
Port Wing, Wisconsin, U.S.A.: 46.45 N. 91.25 W. 62
Port Wreck, see Barqueriza.
Port Xili, see Plitra.
Port Zayed, see Mina Zayed.
Port-au-Port, Newfoundland, Canada: 48.35 N. 58.45 W. . . . 60
Port-au-Prince, Haiti: 18.33 N. 72.21 W. 69, 70
 Max. Size: Depth alongside 32 ft. (MLW).
 Fuel: Fuel oil by tanker truck. *Airport:* International.
Port-aux-Francais, Ile de Kerguelen (France):
 49.21 S. 70.14 E. 36
Portaferry, U.K.: 54.23 N. 5.33 W. 5
Portavogie, U.K.: 54.27 N. 5.26 W. 5, 6
Portbury, see Avonmouth.
Portel, Brazil: 1.56 S. 50.49 W. 72
 Max. Size: Depth 4.9 m. – 5.1 m. (LW).
Porthcawl, U.K.: 51.32 N. 3.39 W. 6
Porthleven, U.K.: 50.05 N. 5.19 W. 7
Porthmadog, U.K.: 52.55 N. 4.08 W. 5, 7
Portici, see Naples.
Portiglione, see Follonica.
Portimao, Portugal: 37.08 N. 8.33 W. 20, 22
Portishead, U.K.: 51.29 N. 2.45 W. 6
 Max. Size: LOA 415 ft., beam 60 ft., draft 24 ft.
 Also see Bristol.
Portland, Vic., Australia: 38.20 S. 141.36 E. 50
 Max. Size: Largest to date – LOA 263 m., departure
 draft 12.70 m. Tankers: 38,000 tonnes d.w.t., draft 10.5 m.
 Fuel: By road tanker. *Airport:* Daily flights to Melbourne.
Portland, U.K.: 50.34 N. 2.26 W. 7, 19
 Max. Size: Draft 12.5 m. – 20 m. *Fuel:* Gas oil.
 Airport: Bournemouth International, 50 miles.
Portland, Maine, U.S.A.: 43.39 N. 70.14 W. 55, 60
 Max. Size: Draft 45 ft. *Fuel:* No. 6 diesel oil and blended
 intermediate fuel oils. *Dry Docks:* Length 257 m., width 40.7 m.,
 depth overblocks 14.0 m., 80,000 ton lift floating dock. *Airport:* 4
 miles.
Portland, Oregon, U.S.A.: 45.30 N. 122.40 W. 55, 56, 57
 Max. Size: River Channel to Portland/Vancouver maintained at
 40 ft. by 600 ft., draft 36 ft. – 39 ft. Tankers: Depth 27 ft. – 42 ft.
 Fuel: Viscosity grades of B and lower.
 Dry Docks: Capacity 81,000 long tons. *Airport:* 10 miles.
Portland Bill, U.K.: 50.31 N. 2.27 W. 5, 7
Portmahomack, U.K.: 57.49 N. 3.50 W. 5
Portneuf, Quebec, Canada: 46.40 N. 71.52 W. 60
 Max. Size: Depth 2 m. – 10.7 m. *Fuel:* By road tanker.
 Airport: Quebec, 65 km.
Portnockie, see Buckie.
Porto ABC Norte, Brazil: 2.48 S. 50.30 W. 72
 Max. Size: Depth 7 m. *Airport:* Private.
Porto Alegre, Brazil: 30.05 S. 51.15 W. 77
 Max. Size: LOA 235 m., beam 35 m. Safe draft 17 ft. to Porto
 Alegre. Tankers: Draft 17 ft., see Tramandai. *Fuel:* Available.
 Dry Docks: LOA 300 ft. *Airport:* International.
Porto Alexandre, Angola: 15.47 S. 11.50 E. 28
Porto Amboim, Angola: 10.45 S. 13.45 E. 28

Porto Amelia, see Pemba.
Porto Antonio Benes, see Angoche.
Porto Azzurro, Italy: 42.46 N. 10.24 E. 23
Porto Belo, Mozambique: 17.46 S. 37.12 E. 30
Porto Branolao, see Lisbon.
Porto Caimito, Panama: 8.53 N. 79.43 W. 73
Porto dos Buchos, see Lisbon.
Porto Empedocle, (Sicily), Italy: 37.17 N. 13.32 E. . . . 24
  Max. Size: East Pier (2nd arm): Max. draft 28 ft.
  Fuel: Small quantities. *Airport:* Palermo, 170 km.
Porto Esperanza, Brazil: 19.37 S. 57.29 W. 72, 77
Porto Foxi, see Sarroch.
Porto Garibaldi, Italy: 44.40 N. 12.15 E. 24
Porto Grande, (St. Vincent), Cape Verde: 16.53 N. 25.00 W. . . 27
  Max. Size: Pier: Depth 11.5 m. Tankers: LOA 775 ft., draft 36 ft.,
  53,000 d.w.t. *Fuel:* Available. *Airport:* Inter-island service only.
Porto Inglez, (Maio), Cape Verde: 15.08 N. 23.15 W. . . 27
Porto Lavante, Italy: 45.10 N. 12.26 E. 24
  Max. Size: SBM: LOA 159 m., draft 7.8 m.
Porto Marghera, see Venice.
Porto Megarese, see Augusta.
Porto Murtinho, Brazil: 21.45 S. 57.52 W. 77
Porto Nogaro, Italy: 45.59 N. 13.13 E. 24
  Max. Size: LOA 180 m., beam 22 m., draft 7 m.
  Airport: Ronchi dei Legionari, 30 km.
Porto Novo, Benin: 6.25 N. 2.40 E. 29
Porto Novo, India: 11.30 N. 79.46 E. 37
Porto Praia, Cape Verde: 14.54 N. 23.31 W. 27
  Max. Size: Depth 7.0 m. – 9.5 m. *Fuel:* Limited supply.
Porto Rafti, Greece: 37.53 N. 24.02 E. 25
Porto Recanati, Italy: 43.25 N. 13.40 E. 24
Porto Saco, see Namibe.
Porto Santo Is., Madeira (Portugal): 33.08 N. 16.22 W. . . 27
Porto Santo Stefano, Italy: 42.26 N. 11.07 E. 24
Porto Seguro, Brazil: 16.27 S. 39.04 W. 72
Porto Tolle, Italy: 44.55 N. 12.20 E. 24
Porto Torres, (Sardinia), Italy: 40.51 N. 8.24 E. . . 9, 21, 24
  Max. Size: West Mole: LOA 150 m., draft 8 m. – 10 m.
  ANIC: Draft 15 m. *Fuel:* All grades. *Airport:* 34 km.
Porto Trinidad, Panama Canal, Panama: 8.58 N. 79.57 W. . . 73
Porto Trombetas, Brazil: 1.28 S. 56.23 W. 72
  Max. Size: Amazon River bar: Draft 38 ft. FW at HW.
  Trombetas River: Draft 38 ft. FW.
  Berth: Panamax (LOA 245 m.) *Airport:* Internal to Manaus.
Porto Vecchio, (Corsica), France: 41.35 N. 9.17 E. . . . 24
Porto Velho, Brazil: 8.48 S. 63.54 W. 72
Porto Vesme, (Sardinia), Italy: 39.11 N. 8.23 E. 24
  Max. Size: Draft 12 m. *Airport:* 90 km.
Portocel, see Barra do Riacho.
Portoferraio, Italy: 42.49 N. 10.21 E. 23, 24
Portofino, Italy: 44.18 N. 9.12 E. 23, 24
Portreath, U.K.: 50.16 N. 5.18 W. 7
Portree, U.K.: 57.24 N. 6.07 W. 5
  Max. Size: LOA 65.5 m., draft 4.08 m. *Fuel:* Gas oil.
  Airport: Broadford, 50 km.
Portrieux, France: 48.39 N. 2.49 W. 7, 19
Portrush, U.K.: 55.13 N. 6.40 W. 5
Portsea, Vic., Australia: 38.19 S. 144.43 E. 51
Portsmouth, Dominica: 15.32 N. 61.29 W. 69, 71
  Max. Size: Anchorage: Depth 70 ft.
  Pier at Cabrits: Depth 35 ft. – 49 ft. *Airport:* At Portsmouth.
Portsmouth, U.K.: 50.48 N. 1.07 W. 5, 7, 19
  Max. Size: Depth 3.5 m. – 7 m. *Fuel:* Fuel and diesel oil.
  Airport: London – Gatwick and London – Heathrow.
  Also see Southampton.
Portsmouth, New Hampshire, U.S.A.: 43.03 N. 70.45 W. . . 55, 60
  Max. Size: Depth 32.6 ft. – 40 ft. *Fuel:* Available.
Portsmouth, Virginia, U.S.A.: 36.50 N. 76.17 W. . . . 63, 65
  Max. Size: Depth 40 ft. *Fuel:* Available. *Airport:* Norfolk
  and Newport News.
  Also see Newport News and Norfolk.
Portsoy, U.K.: 57.41 N. 2.41 W. 5
PORTUGAL 20, 21, 22
Portugaleta, Spain: 43.19 N. 3.01 W. 19
  Also see Bilbao.
Porvenir, Chile: 53.19 S. 70.21 W. 77
Porvoo, Finland: 60.18 N. 25.33 E. 11, 13
  Max. Size: Draft 15.3 m., 260,000 d.w.t. *Fuel:* Available.
  Airport: Helsinki, 50 km.
Posadas, Argentina: 27.28 S. 55.52 W. 77
Poso, Indonesia: 1.23 S. 120.45 E. 38, 46
Poste de la Baleine, Quebec, Canada: 55.18 N. 77.41 W. . . 59
Posyet, Russia: 42.39 N. 130.48 E. 43
  Max. Size: LOA 185 m., draft 9 m. *Airport:* Vladivostok, 220 km.
Potamos, Greece: 35.53 N. 23.14 E. 25
Potapovo, Russia: 68.35 N. 86.28 E. 16
Poti, Georgia: 42.09 N. 41.39 E. 26
  Max. Size: Draft 9.4 m., LOA 190 m. *Fuel:* Small quantities or
  over 500 tons if ordered 5 days in advance. *Airport:* Sukhumi or
  Batumi.

Poughkeepsie, New York, U.S.A.: 41.41 N. 73.56 W. . . . 60, 63
Poulsbo, Washington, U.S.A.: 47.44 N. 122.39 W. 56
Povena, see Ciervana.
Povungnituk, Quebec, Canada: 60.00 N. 77.20 W. 59
Powell River, B.C., Canada: 49.52 N. 124.33 W. 56
  Max. Size: LOA 660 ft., draft 32 ft. Tankers: LOA 615 ft.
  Fuel: Available. *Airport:* 4 miles, connects with Vancouver.
Pozos Colorados, Colombia: 11.09 N. 74.15 W. 69, 72
  Max. Size: Up to 69,000 d.w.t., LOA 300 m., beam 33 m.,
  draft 15 m.
Pozzallo, (Sicily), Italy: 36.44 N. 14.51 E. 24
  Max. Size: Depth: 7 m. – 12 m. *Fuel:* By road tanker.
Pozzuoli, Italy: 40.49 N. 14.07 E. 23, 24
Prachuap, Thailand: 11.52 N. 99.38 E. 39
  Also see Bangsaphan.
Praesto, Denmark: 55.10 N. 12.03 E. 12, 14
Prague, Czech Republic: 50.05 N. 14.28 E. 9
Prai, see Penang.
Praia, see Porto Praia.
Praia de Vitoria, see Vitoria.
Praia Formosa, see Funchal.
Praia Mole, see Tubarao.
Preko, Croatia: 44.05 N. 15.12 E. 24
Prescott, Ontario, Canada: 44.44 N. 75.31 W. 60, 61
  Max. Size: Draft 7.92 m. *Fuel:* By road tanker.
  Airport: Ottawa, 45 miles.
Presque Isk Point, see Marquette.
Preston, Cuba, see Antilla.
Preston, U.K.: 53.45 N. 2.40 W. 5, 7
Prestwick, U.K.: 55.29 N. 4.37 W. 6
Prevesa, Greece: 38.57 N. 20.46 E. 24, 25
Pribilof Islands, Alaska, U.S.A. 54
Primorsk, Russia: 60.22 N. 28.38 E. 11, 13
Primorsko-Akhtarsk, Russia: 46.01 N. 38.10 E. 26
Prince Edward Is., Canada 60
Prince Edward Is., South Africa 18
Prince of Wales Is., Alaska, U.S.A. 56
Prince Rupert, B.C., Canada: 54.19 N. 130.20 W. . . . 56, 79
  Max. Size: Grain: Max. LOA 285 m., depth 14.5 m.
  Coal: LOA 325 m., beam 50 m., draft 20 m.
  Fairview Terminal: Depth 13.7 m. *Fuel:* Available.
  Dry Docks: Slipway for 150 ft. vessels.
  Airport: 1 hour, connects with Vancouver.
Princesa, see Puerto Princesa.
Princeton, California, U.S.A.: 37.30 N. 122.29 W. . . . 58
Principal Channel, River Plate 78
Principe Is., Sao Tome and Principe 29
Prinos, Greece: 40.56 N. 24.31 E. 9, 25
Prins Karls Foreland, (Spitsbergen), Norway 17
Prinzapolca, Nicaragua: 13.20 N. 83.35 W. 69
Priolo, (Sicily), Italy: 37.09 N. 15.12 E. 24
  Also see Augusta.
Probolinggo, Indonesia: 7.43 S. 113.13 E. 38
Procida Is., Italy: 40.46 N. 14.02 E. 23, 24
Progreso, Mexico: 21.17 N. 89.39 W. 69
  Max. Size: LOA 190 m., draft 23 ft. *Fuel:* Diesel. *Dry Docks:*
  3 available. *Airport:* Merida, 37 km.
Prome, Myanmar: 18.46 N. 95.18 E. 37
Proper Bay, see Port Lincoln.
Propriano, (Corsica), France: 41.40 N. 8.54 E. 9, 24
  Max. Size: Draft 5 m., LOA 160 m. *Fuel:* Available.
  Airport: 6 km.
Proserpine, Qld., Australia: 20.20 S. 148.35 E. . . . 50, 51
Proti Is., Greece: 37.05 N. 21.32 E. 25
Proven, Greenland (Denmark): 72.21 N. 55.34 W. 17
Provesten, see Copenhagen.
Providence, Rhode Is., U.S.A.: 41.48 N. 71.23 W. . . 55, 60, 63
  Max. Size: Draft 38 ft. *Fuel:* Bunker fuel oil, lubricating oils.
  Airport: Rhode Island Green Airport.
Providence Bay, Ontario, Canada: 45.40 N. 82.15 W. . . . 62
Providence I., Seychelles: 9.14 S. 51.02 E. 30
Providencia Is., Colombia: 13.20 N. 81.25 W. 69
Providenciales, Turks and Caicos Is. (U.K.):
  21.44 N. 72.17 W. 69, 70
Provideniya, Russia: 64.23 N. 173.18 W. 54, 79
Provincetown, Massachusetts, U.S.A.: 42.03 N. 70.11 W. . . 63
Prudhoe Bay, Alaska, U.S.A.: 70.20 N. 148.25 W. 54
Psara, (Psara Is.), Greece: 38.35 N. 25.36 E. 25
Psittalia, Greece 23
Pu Tai, Taiwan: 23.22 N. 120.04 E. 42
Pucallpa, Peru: 8.23 S. 74.30 W. 72
Pucarsa, see Carboneras.
Pucisce, Croatia: 43.22 N. 16.44 E. 24
Puck, Poland: 54.45 N. 18.25 E. 11
Puebla del Caraminal, Spain: 42.36 N. 8.56 W. 20
Puerto Acevedo, see Acevedo.
Puerto Aisen, see Puerto Chacabuco.
Puerto Angel, Mexico: 15.39 N. 96.31 W. 69
Puerto Arios, see Puerto Cortes.

Puerto Armuelles, Panama: 8.17 N. 82.52 W. **69, 72**
Max. Size: Depth 40 ft. (12.2 m.). Oil Terminal: 265,000 d.w.t., depth 50 ft. – 80 ft. *Airport:* David, 100 km.

Puerto Ayacucho, Venezuela: 5.37 N. 67.40 W. **69**

Puerto Barrios, Guatemala: 15.44 N. 88.36 W. **69**
Max. Size: LOA 600 ft., draft 28 ft.

Puerto Bayovar, Peru: 5.47 S. 81.03 W. **72**
Max. Size: 250,000 d.w.t., LOA 400 m., draft 21.95 m.
Airport: Piura, 125 km.

Puerto Belgrano, Argentina: 38.53 S. 62.06 W. **77**

Puerto Bolivar, Colombia: 12.16 N. 71.57 W. **69, 72, 74**
Max. Size: 150,000 d.w.t., LOA 300 m., beam 45 m., draft 17 m.
Airport: Nearest at Barranquilla, 326 km.

Puerto Bolivar, Ecuador: 3.14 S. 80.01 W. **72**
Max. Size: Depths alongside 30 ft. inner end to 36 ft. at quay head. *Fuel:* Limited supply available from Guayaquil.
Airport: 6 km., connects with Guayaquil.

Puerto Borburata, Venezuela: 10.29 N. 67.59 W. **74**

Puerto Borghi, see Borghi.

Puerto Bories, Chile: 51.43 S. 72.33 W. **77**

Puerto Buitagro, see Ramallo.

Puerto Cabello, Venezuela: 10.29 N. 68.01 W. **69, 74**
Max. Size: Draft 34 ft. 6 in. Tankers: Draft 20 ft. – 34 ft.
Chemicals: Depth 45 ft. *Fuel:* Available.
Dry Docks: Capacity 30,000 tons. *Airport:* Michelena International at Valencia, 45 minutes by road.

Puerto Cabezas, Nicaragua: 14.01 N. 83.23 W. **69**
Max. Size: LOA 400 ft., draft 19 ft. 6 in. *Fuel:* Gasoline, diesel oil and lubricants are supplied. *Airport:* 2 km., connects Managua.

Puerto Calbuco, Chile: 41.47 S. 73.12 W. **77**
Max. Size: 70,000 d.w.t., LOA 230 m., Draft 11.5 m.

Puerto Carupano, see Carupano.

Puerto Castilla, Honduras: 16.01 N. 86.03 W. **69**
Max. Size: LOA 225 m., draft 10.97 m.
Airport: San Pedro Sula, 440 km.

Puerto Chacabuco, Chile: 45.28 S. 72.50 W. **77**
Max. Size: LOA 165 m., draft 32 ft. *Fuel:* Available.
Airport: Balmaceda, 120 km.

Puerto Chicama, Peru: 7.42 S. 79.26 W. **72**
Max. Size: Anchorage port.

Puerto Colombia, Colombia: 11.00 N. 74.53 W. **69**

Puerto Corral, Chile: 39.52 S. 73.21 W. **77**
Max. Size: 60,000 d.w.t., LOA 229 m., draft 12.2 m.
Fuel: By road tanker. *Airport:* Pichoy, 1 hour by car.

Puerto Cortes, Honduras: 15.51 N. 87.56 W. **69**
Max. Size: Draft 28 ft. – 40 ft. *Fuel:* Available. *Airport:* San Pedro Sula, 70 km.

Puerto Cumaribo, Venezuela: 11.29 N. 69.21 W. **74**

Puerto de Hierro, Venezuela: 10.38 N. 62.05 W. . . **71, 72, 75**
Max. Size: Depth 30 ft. (LW), 33 ft. (HW) 690 ft. LOA, 90 ft. beam. Bauxite Terminal: Draft 37 ft., 40,000 d.w.t.
Fuel: Diesel in an emergency. *Airport:* Guiria, 1 hour voyage on launch – connects with Caracas.

Puerto de la Luz, see Las Palmas.

Puerto de Raos, see Santander.

Puerto de Santa Maria, Spain: 36.36 N. 6.12 W. **20**

Puerto de Soller, see Soller.

Puerto de Velez, Spain: 36.47 N. 4.06 W. **20, 22**

Puerto del Musel, see Musel.

Puerto del Rosario, (Fuerteventura), Canary Is. (Spain):
28.30 N. 13.51 W. **27**
Max. Size: LOA 194.32 m., draft 6.7 m. *Airport:* 10 km.

Puerto Deseado, Argentina: 47.46 S. 65.54 W. **77**
Max. Size: Depth 27 ft. *Fuel:* By road tanker.

Puerto Duarte, see Samana.

Puerto Galvan, see Bahia Blanca.

Puerto Granaderos, see San Lorenzo.

Puerto Guarello, see Madre de Dios Is..

Puerto Honduras, see Santa Cruz de Tenerife.

Puerto Ingeniero Rocca, see La Plata.

Puerto Iradier, Equatorial Guinea: 1.02 N. 9.41 E. . . . **29**

Puerto Isabel, see Prinzapolca.

Puerto Jimenez, Costa Rica: 8.40 N. 83.15 W. **69**

Puerto La Cruz, Venezuela: 10.13 N. 64.38 W. . . . **69, 71, 75**
Max. Size: LOA 950 ft., draft 51 ft. or LOA 920 ft., draft 55 ft.
Fuel: Most grades available to ships loading.

Puerto Las Minas, see Bahia Las Minas.

Puerto Lempire, Honduras: 15.15 N. 83.35 W. **69, 70**

Puerto Libertador, see Manzanillo.

Puerto Limon, Costa Rica: 10.00 N. 83.01 W. **69**
Max. Size: Depth 30 ft. Tankers: See Puerto Moin.
Fuel: Available. *Airport:* 5 miles, connects with San Jose.

Puerto Local, see Gijon.

Puerto Lopez, Colombia: 11.58 N. 71.18 W. **69, 74**

Puerto Macias, see Bata.

Puerto Madero, Argentina, see Buenos Aires.

Puerto Madero, Mexico: 14.44 N. 92.25 W. **69**
Max. Size: LOA 165 m., beam 25 m., draft 8 m.
Fuel: Small quantities. *Airport:* Tapachula, 10 km.

Puerto Madryn, Argentina: 42.46 S. 65.02 W. **77**
Max. Size: Depths to 55 ft. *Fuel:* By truck from Comodoro Rivadavia or Bahia Blanca. *Airport:* Trefew, 64 km.

Puerto Magdalena, Mexico: 24.38 N. 112.09 W. **57**

Puerto Maritime, see Guayaquil.

Puerto Mexico, see Coatzacoalcos.

Puerto Miranda, Venezuela: 10.46 N. 71.34 W. **69, 74**
Max. Size: 90,000 d.w.t., LOA 910 ft., beam 147 ft., draft 39.5 ft.
Fuel: Available. *Airport:* Maracaibo.

Puerto Moin, Costa Rica: 10.00 N. 83.05 W. **69**
Max. Size: Depth 9.0 m. Tankers: Depth 9.6 m.
Also see Puerto Limon.

Puerto Montt, Chile: 41.28 S. 72.57 W. **77**
Max. Size: LOA 200 m., draft 9.3 m. plus height of tide.
Tankers: 15,000 g.r.t. *Fuel:* Diesel.
Airport: 17 km., connects with Santiago.

Puerto Morelas, Mexico: 20.50 N. 86.55 W. **69**

Puerto Natales, Chile: 51.44 S. 72.32 W. **77**

Puerto Nuevo, Argentina, see San Nicolas.

Puerto Nuevo, Equatorial Guinea: 1.49 N. 9.44 E. **29**
Max. Size: Depth 14 m.
Also see Bata.

Puerto Ordaz, Venezuela: 8.21 N. 62.43 W. **69, 72, 75**
Max. Size: 115,000 d.w.t., LOA 289.5 m., beam 39 m.
Draft authorised by Port Captain. *Fuel:* Bunker "C" and diesel.

Puerto Ordaz Terminal, see Punta Cuchillo.

Puerto Padre, (Cayo Juan Claro), Cuba: 21.17 N. 76.32 W. **69, 70**
Max. Size: LOA 565 ft., draft 24 ft. Draft 25 ft. if LOA less than 500 ft. Max. LOA permitted 557 ft.

Puerto Palenque, see Palenque.

Puerto Percy, see Punta Arenas.

Puerto Plata, Dominican Republic: 19.49 N. 70.41 W. . . **69, 70**
Max. Size: LOA 700 ft., beam 100 ft., draft 30 ft.
Fuel: Diesel and fuel oil by truck. *Airport:* La Union, 20 km.

Puerto Princesa, (Palawan Is.), Philippines:
9.44 N. 118.43 E. **46, 47**
Max. Size: Draft 27 ft. (8.2 m.). *Fuel:* Diesel oil, gasoline and kerosene in drums. *Airport:* 2 miles, connects with Manila.

Puerto Prodeco, see Santa Marta.

Puerto Quetzal, Guatemala: 13.55 N. 90.47 W. **69**
Max. Size: LOA 210 m., beam 32 m., draft 10.5 m.
Fuel: Available. *Airport:* Local airport, 8 km. International airport at Guatemala City, 98 km.

Puerto Real, Spain: 36.32 N. 6.11 W. **20**

Puerto Rico (U.S.A.) **69, 70, 71**

Puerto Rosales, see Bahia Blanca.

Puerto San Blas, Argentina: 40.34 S. 62.14 W. **77**

Puerto San Martin, see San Martin.

Puerto Sandino, Nicaragua: 12.12 N. 86.46 W. **69**
Max. Size: Cargo vessels work at anchorage. Tankers at Sea Line Terminal up to 850 ft. LOA and 41 ft. draft. *Airport:* Managua, 75 km.

Puerto Sauce, Uruguay: 34.26 S. 57.27 W. **78**

Puerto Somoza, see Puerto Sandino.

Puerto Suarez, Bolivia: 18.58 S. 57.52 W. **72, 77**

Puerto Sucre, Venezuela: 10.28 N. 64.12 W. **71, 72, 75**
Max. Size: Least depth 8 m. (HW). *Fuel:* Diesel oil is brought from Puerto La Cruz by road.

Puerto Tarafa, see Nuevitas.

Puerto Vallarta, Mexico: 20.39 N. 105.15 W. **57**
Max. Size: Depth 5.0 m. – 10.0 m., LOA up to 300 m.
Airport: 1.25 miles.

Puerto Ventanas, see Quintero.

Puerto Viejo, see Azua.

Puerto Villamil, (Galapagos Is.), Ecuador: 0.55 S. 91.00 W. **72**

Puerto Williams, Chile: 54.56 S. 67.37 W. **77**
Max. Size: LOA 80 m., draft 15 ft., 2,500 g.r.t.
Airport: Local, 4 miles.

Puerto Zuniga, see Santa Marta.

Puget Sound, Washington, U.S.A. **56**
Max. Size: Limit 125,000 d.w.t.

Pugwash, N.S., Canada: 45.50 N. 63.40 W. **60**

Puhos, see Saimaa Canal.

Puka Puka, French Polynesia (France): 14.48 S. 138.49 W. . **49**

Pukou, China: 32.05 N. 118.40 E. **42**

Pula, Croatia: 44.52 N. 13.50 E. **9, 21, 24**
Max. Size: Depth 17 ft. – 31 ft. *Fuel:* Available by barge from Rijeka. *Airport:* Local.

Pulang Pisau, Indonesia: 2.45 S. 114.15 E. **38**

Pulantien, China: 39.25 N. 128.00 E. **42**

Pulap Is., (Caroline Is.), Micronesia: 7.38 N. 149.24 E. . **46**

Pulau Ayer Chawan, Singapore: 1.17 N. 103.42 E. **41**
Max. Size: Esso: 110,000 tons displacement (90,000 d.w.t. – 140,000 d.w.t.), LOA 1,000 ft., depth 51.8 ft.
Esso/Mobil SBM: 285,000 d.w.t., draft 67 ft.

Pulau Ayer Merbau, see Singapore.

Pulau Baai, see Bengkulu.

Pulau Besak, see Singapore.

Pulau Brani, see Singapore.

Pulau Bukom, Singapore: 1.14 N. 103.46 E. 41
   Max. Size: Shell: 135,000 d.w.t., LOA 245 m., depth 15.6 m.
   SBM: 353,784 d.w.t., LOA 457 m., depth 24.6 m.
Pulau Busing, see Singapore.
Pulau Herek, see Sibolga.
Pulau Merlimau, Singapore: 1.18 N. 103.43 E. 41
   Max. Size: Singapore Refining Co.: 105,000 tonnes
   displacement, LOA 290 m., depth 15.4 m.
   PSA SPM: 320,000 tonnes displacement, depth 23 m.
Pulau Naira, Indonesia: 4.32 S. 129.55 E. 46
Pulau Sambu, Indonesia: 1.09 N. 103.54 E. 39, 40, 41
   Max. Size: 29,500 d.w.t., LOA 175 m., depth 10.5 m.
   Fuel: Advise suppliers at least 15 days before ETA.
   Bunkers available: Fuel oil and MDO.
   Airport: Hang Nadim on Batam Island.
Pulau Samulun, see Singapore.
Pulau Sebarok, see Singapore.
Pulau Sebuku, see Sebuku.
Pulau Senang, see Singapore.
Pulau Seraya, see Singapore.
Pulau Sudong, see Singapore.
Pulau Tekong, see Singapore.
Pulau Tekukor, see Singapore.
Pulau Tiga, Sarawak, Malaysia: 5.43 N. 115.33 E. 39
Pulau Ubin, see Singapore.
Pulawat Is., (Caroline Is.), Micronesia: 7.22 N. 149.11 E. . . . 46
Pulmoddai, Sri Lanka: 8.55 N. 80.59 E. 37
   Max. Size: Open roadstead.
   Also see Trincomalee.
Pulo Anna, Palau: 4.39 N. 131.58 E. 46
Pulp, see Saimaa Canal.
Pulupandan, (Negros Is.), Philippines: 10.32 N. 122.48 E. . . . 47
   Max. Size: LOA 200 m., draft 30 ft. *Fuel:* Available.
   Airport: Bacolod, 30 km.
Pulusuk Is., (Caroline Is.), Micronesia: 6.40 N. 149.19 E. . . . 46
Puna, Ecuador: 2.45 S. 79.55 W. 72
Punta Ancla, see Bahia Blanca.
Punta Arenas, Chile: 53.10 S. 70.54 W. 77
   Max. Size: Pier: LOA 170 m., depth 22 ft. – 27 ft.
   Lenadura: LOA 175 m., draft 23 ft., 20,000 tons displacement.
   Magellan Straits: Draft 70 ft., except with authority's permission.
   Fuel: Only diesel oil ex-barge.
   Airport: 18 km., connects with Santiago.
Punta Bustamente, see Rio Gallegos.
Punta Cardon, Venezuela: 11.38 N. 70.14 W. 74
   Max. Size: 62,000 tons displacement, LOA 900 ft., draft 45 ft.
   6 in. or 70,000 tons displacement, LOA 900 ft., draft 44 ft. 6 in.
   Fuel: Available with notice.
   Also see Puerto Cabello.
Punta Charambira, Colombia: 4.18 N. 77.30 W. 69
Punta Chavez, see Puerto Cabello.
Punta Ciguena, see Bahia Blanca.
Punta Colorada, Argentina: 41.41 S. 65.00 W. 77
   Max. Size: Draft 11.58 m., LOA 230 m., 70,000 d.w.t.
Punta Cuchillo, Venezuela: 8.20 N. 62.47 W. 69, 75
   Max. Size: Draft 43 ft., half of high tide required at Bar.
   Fuel: Available.
Punta de la Almina, Spain: 35.54 N. 5.17 W. 23
Punta de Palmas, Venezuela: 10.24 N. 71.34 W. 69, 74
   Max. Size: LOA 890 ft., draft 42 ft., 100,000 d.w.t. *Fuel:* Heavy
   and medium marine diesel, intermediate fuel, and Bunker "C".
Punta del Este, see Maldonado.
Punta el Gancho, see Rio Gallegos.
Punta Europa Marine Terminal, Equatorial Guinea:
   3.47 N. 8.43 E. 28, 29
   Max. Size: 80,000 d.w.t., LOA 750 ft., no restriction on beam or
   draft. *Airport:* Malabo, flights to Madrid and Zurich.
Punta Gorda, Cuba, see Moa.
Punta Gorda, Nicaragua: 11.30 N. 83.45 W. 69
Punta Gorda, Venezuela, see Caripito.
Punta Grossa, see Koper.
Punta Indio Channel, River Uruguay 78
Punta Loyola, see Rio Gallegos.
Punta Mapam, see Topolobampo.
Punta Marieta, see Caripito.
Punta Marroqui, Spain: 36.00 N. 5.34 W. 23
Punta Medanos, Argentina: 36.50 S. 56.40 W. 77
Punta Molino, see Gaeta.
Punta Penasco, Mexico: 31.20 N. 113.35 W. 57
Punta Penna, see Vasto.
Punta Quilla, Argentina: 50.07 S. 68.25 W. 77
   Max. Size: Quay length 160 m., depth 40 ft. *Fuel:* Available.
Punta Salinas, see Antilla.
Punta Santiago, Equatorial Guinea: 3.12 N. 8.40 E. 29
Punta Tablones, see Ilo.
Puntarenas, Costa Rica: 9.58 N. 84.49 W. 69
   Max. Size: Depth 9 m. (All cargo operations handled at Caldera).
Punto Fijo, see Amuay Bay.
Purcell, see Road Harbour.
Purfleet, see London.

Puri, India: 19.47 N. 85.50 E. 37
Purmerend, Netherlands: 52.30 N. 5.03 E. 8
Punta Marroqui, Spain: 36.00 N. 5.34 W. 23
Pushthrough, Newfoundland, Canada: 47.38 N. 56.11 W. . . . 60
Puttalam, Sri Lanka: 8.13 N. 79.42 E. 37
Puttgarden, (Fehmarn Is.), Germany: 54.28 N. 11.15 E. . . 11, 12, 14
Puumala, see Saimaa Canal.
Pwllheli, U.K.: 52.53 N. 4.25 W. 5, 7
Pyarnu, Estonia: 58.23 N. 24.29 E. 10, 11
   Max. Size: Draft 4 m. *Fuel:* Available.
Pyeong Taek, South Korea: 36.57 N. 126.01 E. 42
   Max. Size: LOA 249.8 m., draft 13.12 m., 100,000 d.w.t.
Pylos, Greece: 36.55 N. 21.42 E. 24, 25
   Max. Size: Any size vessel can anchor in Navarino Bay. Pylos is
   only suitable for small vessels up to 15 ft. draft. *Fuel:* Fuel oil
   and diesel oil by small tankers. *Airport:* Kalamata, 40 km.
Pyongyang, North Korea: 39.00 N. 125.40 E. 42
Pyramid Is., see Chatham Is..
Pyrmont, see Sydney.

NOTES, ADDITIONS, CORRECTIONS

Please also advise Shipping Guides Ltd.
75 Bell Street, Reigate, RH2 7AN, United Kingdom
Tel: +44 1737 242255   Fax: +44 1737 222449
Email: updates@portinfo.co.uk   Web: www.portinfo.co.uk

Q

Qaboos, see Port Sultan Qaboos.
Qadima, see Al Qadimah.
Qalhat Marine Terminal, Oman: 22.40 N. 59.25 E. 31
Max. Size: LNG: Displacement 125,845 tonnes, LOA 310 m.,
draft 12.1 m. Condensate: Displacement 13,000 tonnes,
LOA 140 m., draft 7.7 m.
Qantara, see Kantara.
Qaqortoq, Greenland (Denmark): 60.43 N. 46.02 W. 17
Max. Size: Largest to berth – LOA 110 m., draft 7.0 m.
Fuel: Gas oil. *Airport:* Heliport.
Qasim, see Port Muhammad Bin Qasim.
Qasr Ahmed, see Misurata.
QATAR 31, 35
Qeis Is., Iran: 26.30 N. 54.00 E. 35
Qeqertarsuaq, Greenland (Denmark): 69.14 N. 53.32 W. . . . 17
Max. Size: Largest to berth – LOA 100 m., draft 6.5 m.
Qeshm, Iran: 26.58 N. 56.16 E. 31, 35
Qeshm Anchorage, Iran: 26.33 N. 55.45 E. 35
Max. Size: S-T-S/Bunkering anchorage. *Fuel:* Available.
Qeshm Is., Iran 31, 35
Qingdao, China: 36.04 N. 120.19 E. 42, 46
Max. Size: LOA 265 m., beam 39 m., draft 14 m.
Tankers: Draft 20.5 m. *Fuel:* Available. *Airport:* Qingdao.
Qinhuangdao, China: 39.55 N. 119.37 E. 42
Max. Size: General cargo: LOA 200 m., draft 11.5 m.
Tankers and coal: LOA 230 m., beam 22.5 m., draft 12.5 m.
Fuel: Available. *Dry Docks:* 2 available, max. 240 m. x 6.0 m.
over sill.
Qinzhou, China: 21.43 N. 108.35 E. 39
Max. Size: Depth 9.4 m. *Fuel:* Available.
Qornuq, Greenland (Denmark): 64.32 N. 51.06 W. 17
Qua Iboe, Nigeria: 4.20 N. 7.59 E. 29
Max. Size: 312,000 d.w.t., draft 72 ft.
Quang Ngai, Vietnam: 15.15 N. 109.00 E. 39
Quang Ninh, Vietnam: 21.02 N. 107.22 E. 39
Also see Cam Pha, Hon Gay and Van Gia.
Quanzhou, China: 24.53 N. 118.41 E. 42, 46
Max. Size: Draft 9.5 m. in channel. Tankers: 100,000 d.w.t., draft
16.0 m. at Xiaocud Terminal. *Fuel:* Available.
Quatsino, B.C., Canada: 50.32 N. 127.37 W. 56
Quebec, Canada 59, 60, 61
Quebec, Quebec, Canada: 46.49 N. 71.12 W. 60
Max. Size: Draft limit: 47 ft. Winter, 51 ft. Summer. No limit on
LOA and beam. *Fuel:* Available.
Dry Docks: 350.5 m. x 36.6 m. at gate entrance. *Airport:* 20 km.
Queen Charlotte, B.C., Canada: 53.15 N. 132.03 W. 56
Queen Charlotte Is., B.C., Canada 56
Queen Charlotte Sound, B.C., Canada 56
Queen Maud Land, Antarctica 80
Queenborough, U.K.: 51.26 N. 0.44 E. 6
Max. Size: Depth 5.8 m. (MHWS).
Also see Medway Ports.
Queens, see New York.
Queenscliff, Vic., Australia: 38.16 S. 144.40 E. 51
Queensferry, see Rosyth.
Queensland, Australia 50, 51
Queenstown, see Cobh.
Quelimane, Mozambique: 17.53 S. 36.53 E. 30
Quellon, Chile: 43.08 S. 73.38 W. 77
Quelpart Is., South Korea 42, 46
Quemchi, Chile: 42.09 S. 73.28 W. 77
Quemoy, see Chin Men.
Quepos, Costa Rica: 9.25 N. 84.10 W. 69
Quequen, Argentina: 38.35 S. 58.42 W. 77
Max. Size: LOA 175 m. and draft 31 ft. 1 in. or LOA 215 m. and
draft 27 ft. 1 in. LOA 215 m. – 220 m. with permission.
Fuel: By truck from Buenos Aires, Mar del Plata,
or Bahia Blanca. *Airport:* 5 miles, domestic.
Quezon, (Palawan Is.), Philippines: 9.05 N. 118.00 E. 47
Quiberon, France: 47.30 N. 3.08 W. 19
Quiliano Terminal, Italy: 44.17 N. 8.28 E. 9, 23, 24
Max. Size: Draft 21.4 m. *Fuel:* By barge at anchorage.
Quillebeuf, France: 49.28 N. 0.31 E. 7, 8
Quilon, India: 8.52 N. 76.35 E. 37
Quimper, France: 47.58 N. 4.07 W. 7, 19
Max. Size: At Spring tides: LOA 78 m., beam 12 m., draft 4.95 m.
At neap tides: LOA 72 m., beam 12 m., draft 3.40 m.
Fuel: By road tanker. *Airport:* 4 km.
Quincy, Massachusetts, U.S.A.: 42.15 N. 70.58 W. 60, 63
Also see Boston.
Quinfuquena, see Essungo.
Quinga, Mozambique: 15.50 S. 40.15 E. 30
Quintell Beach, Qld., Australia: 13.54 N. 143.41 E. 51

Quintero, Chile: 32.46 S. 71.31 W. 77
Max. Size: SBM: LOA 342 m., draft 25.5 m., 215,000 tons
displacement. Quay: LOA 240 m., draft 14.3 m.
Chemicals: Draft 41 ft. Puerto Ventanas (Private): 70,000 d.w.t.,
draft 14.0 m. *Fuel:* Only available by truck at Ventenas Quay.
Airport: Nearest Santiago.
Quirpon, Newfoundland, Canada: 51.36 N. 55.29 W. 60
Quoin Island, Oman: 26.31 N. 56.31 E. 31, 35
Quonset, Rhode Is., U.S.A.: 41.35 N. 71.24 W. 63
Quseir, Egypt: 26.06 N. 34.17 E. 32
Qutdligssat, Greenland (Denmark): 70.02 N. 53.00 W. 17
Quy Nhon, Vietnam: 13.46 N. 109.14 E. 39
Max. Size: LOA 180 m., draft 7.5 m. *Fuel:* Available.
Airport: Pha Chat, 35 km.

NOTES, ADDITIONS, CORRECTIONS

Please also advise Shipping Guides Ltd.
75 Bell Street, Reigate, RH2 7AN, United Kingdom
Tel: +44 1737 242255   Fax: +44 1737 222449
Email: updates@portinfo.co.uk   Web: www.portinfo.co.uk

R

Raa, Sweden: 56.00 N. 12.45 E. **12**
Raahe, Finland: 64.41 N. 24.29 E. **10, 15**
  Max. Size: Depth 9.1 m. *Fuel:* Small quantities.
  Airport: Oulu, 60 km.
Rab, Croatia: 44.45 N. 14.46 E. **24**
Rabac, Croatia: 45.05 N. 14.10 E. **24**
Rabat, Morocco: 34.03 N. 6.49 W. **27**
Rabaul, Papua New Guinea: 4.12 S. 152.10 E. . . **46, 49**
  Max. Size: Depth at LAT 10.2 m. *Fuel:* Diesel and distillate.
  Airport: 4 km.
Rabigh, Saudi Arabia: 22.44 N. 38.59 E. **32**
  Max. Size: Tankers: LOA 400 m., draft 23.5 m. Dry cargo: Depth 6.5 m. *Airport:* Jeddah, 150 km.
Rabon Grande, Mexico: 18.14 N. 94.23 W. **69**
  Max. Size: Arrival draft if over LOA 300 m.: Forward 20 ft., aft 32 ft.
Racine, Wisconsin, U.S.A.: 42.43 N. 87.47 W. **62**
Rade, see Schirnau.
Rades, see La Goulette.
Radicatel, see Tancarville.
Rafah, Egypt: 31.19 N. 34.13 E. **26, 32**
Rafina, Greece: 38.01 N. 24.01 E. **25**
Rafnes, see Heroya.
Rafti, see Porto Rafti.
Ragged Is., Bahamas: 22.15 N. 75.45 W. **69, 70**
Raglan, New Zealand: 37.53 S. 174.54 E. **52**
Raha, Indonesia: 4.51 S. 122.45 E. **46**
Raheita, Eritrea: 12.45 N. 43.05 E. **31, 32**
Raiatea, (Society Is.), French Polynesia (France) . . **49**
Rainham Creek, see Medway Ports.
Rainier, Oregon, U.S.A.: 46.05 N. 122.56 W. **56, 57**
Rairi, see Port Redi.
Raivavae, (Austral Is.), French Polynesia (France):
  23.52 S. 147.41 W. **49**
Rajang, Sarawak, Malaysia: 2.09 N. 111.15 E. . . **38, 39**
  Also see Tanjung Manis.
Rakahanga Is., Cook Is. (N.Z.): 9.58 S. 161.01 W. . . **49**
Raleigh Bay, North Carolina, U.S.A. **63**
Ramallo, Argentina: 33.32 S. 59.59 W. **78**
  Max. Size: LOA 200 m., depths to 30 ft.
Ramba, Indonesia: 2.37 S. 104.08 E. **38**
  Max. Size: Jetty: 10,000 d.w.t., LOA 90 m., depth 6 m. Tankers: Depth 16.5 m. – 22 m. *Fuel:* Available at jetty.
  Airport: Palembang.
Ramea Is., Newfoundland, Canada: 47.30 N. 57.23 W. . **60**
Ramsburg, see Georgetown.
Ramsey, (Isle of Man), U.K.: 54.19 N. 4.21 W. **5**
  Max. Size: LOA 70 m., beam 13 m., depth 5.5 m. (MHWS).
  Fuel: Available at 24 hours notice. *Airport:* 25 km.
Ramsgate, U.K.: 51.20 N. 1.24 E. **6**
  Max. Size: Royal Harbour: LOA 80 m., draft 4.8 m.
  Western Terminal: Depth 6.5 m. – 7.5 m. *Fuel:* Available.
  Airport: Gatwick.
Ramshall, see Norrkoping.
Ramvik, see Gustavsvik.
Randers, Denmark: 56.28 N. 10.04 E. **11, 12**
  Max. Size: 10,000 d.w.t., LOA 145 m., beam 19 m., draft 6.2 m.
  Fuel: All grades by road tankers. *Airport:* Tirstrup, 42 km.
Ranea, Sweden: 65.55 N. 22.20 E. **15**
Rang Dong, Vietnam: 10.01 N. 108.15 E. **39**
  Max. Size: 150,000 d.w.t.
Rangiora, New Zealand: 43.20 S. 172.35 E. **52**
Rangiroa, (Tuamotu Arch.), French Polynesia (France):
  15.05 N. 147.35 W. **49**
Rangoon, see Yangon.
Rankin Inlet, N.W.T., Canada: 62.48 N. 92.06 W. . . **59**
Raos, see Santander.
Raoul Is., (Kermadec Is.), New Zealand: 29.08 S. 177.52 W. . **49**
Rapa Is., French Polynesia (France) **49**
Rapallo, Italy: 44.21 N. 9.13 E. **23, 24**
Rapasaari, see Saimaa Canal.
Rapid Bay, S.A., Australia: 35.32 S. 138.12 E. . . . **50, 51**
  Port not used by commercial shipping since 1992
Raritan Bay, New Jersey, U.S.A. **63**
Raroia, (Tuamotu Arch.), French Polynesia (France):
  16.01 S. 142.26 W. **49**
Rarotonga Is., Cook Is. (N.Z.) **49**
Ras Abu Khomis, Saudi Arabia: 24.21 N. 51.36 E. . . **35**
Ras al Fasteh, Pakistan: 25.00 N. 61.39 E. **31**
Ras al Ghar, Saudi Arabia: 27.32 N. 49.13 E. **35**
Ras al Hadd, Oman: 22.29 N. 59.45 E. **31, 37**
Ras al Kuh, Iran: 25.48 N. 57.18 E. **35**
Ras al Mingar, see Benghazi.
Ras Al Mishab, Saudi Arabia: 28.13 N. 48.43 E. . . **31, 35**
  Max. Size: Draft 33 ft. (35 ft. planned).

Ras Al-Khafji, Saudi Arabia: 28.25 N. 48.32 E. **35**
  Max. Size: Draft 64 ft. – 66 ft., 300,000 d.w.t. *Fuel:* Available.
  Airport: Kuwait, 110 km. Dhahran, 325 km.
Ras Al-Khaimah, U.A.E.: 25.45 N. 56.01 E. **35**
  Max. Size: Depth 3 m.
  Also see Hulaylah Terminal and Mina Saqr.
Ras Alkatheeb, Yemen: 14.55 N. 42.53 E. **32**
  Max. Size: Max. draft of 26 ft. at HW.
Ras Bahregan, see Bahregan.
Ras Banas, Egypt: 23.55 N. 35.50 E. **32**
Ras Budran, Egypt: 28.56 N. 33.08 E. **26, 32**
  Max. Size: 250,000 d.w.t., LOA 1,130 ft., draft 18 m.
Ras Dubayyah, U.A.E.: 24.19 N. 54.08 E. **35**
Ras El Ish, Egypt: 31.09 N. 32.17 E. **33**
Ras Es Sider, see Es Sider.
Ras Fartak, Yemen: 15.40 N. 52.15 E. **31**
Ras Gharib, Egypt: 28.21 N. 33.06 E. **26, 32**
  Max. Size: Sea Berths: Draft 55 ft., LOA 980 ft.
Ras Isa Marine Terminal, Yemen: 15.08 N. 42.36 E. . . **32**
  Max. Size: 307,000 d.w.t., depth 38 m.
Ras Laffan, Qatar: 25.56 N. 51.37 E. **31, 35**
  Max. Size: Draft 12.5 m. *Airport:* Doha.
Ras Lanuf, Libya: 30.31 N. 18.35 E. **24**
  Max. Size: Conventional berths: 56 ft. draft; 130,000 d.w.t.
  SPM: 75 ft. draft, 300,000 d.w.t. RASCO: 50,000 d.w.t., LOA 250 m., draft 12.5 m.
Ras Madrakah, Oman: 18.55 N. 57.52 E. **31, 37**
Ras Selaata, Lebanon: 34.17 N. 35.40 E. **26**
  Max. Size: Up to 21 ft. draft. Sela'ata Terminal: Draft 13.0 m.
  Fuel: Diesel. *Airport:* Beirut or Kleiate (Tripoli).
Ras Shukheir, Egypt: 28.08 N. 33.17 E. **26, 32**
  Max. Size: Draft 64 ft., LOA 1,000 ft.
Ras Sudr, see Sudr.
Ras Tanura, Saudi Arabia: 26.39 N. 50.10 E. . . . **31, 35**
  Max. Size: Sea Island: Max. departure draft 19.48 m. plus height of tide. *Fuel:* Available at all berths. *Airport:* Dhahran.
Ras Zabarjad, (St. John's Is.), Egypt: 23.37 N. 36.12 E. **32**
Ras Zubayyah, see Ras Dubayyah.
Rasa, Croatia: 45.02 N. 14.03 E. **24**
  Max. Size: Depth 11 m.
  Also see Rijeka.
Rashau Is., (Kurile Is.), Russia: 47.40 N. 152.50 E. . . **43**
Rashid, see Port Rashid.
Rasht, Iran: 37.16 N. 49.34 E. **9**
Rasta, see Stockholm.
Rat Is., (Aleutian Is.), Alaska, U.S.A. **54**
Ratan, Sweden: 64.00 N. 20.54 E. **15**
Rathmullen, Ireland: 55.05 N. 7.31 W. **5**
  Max. Size: Draft 30 ft. *Fuel:* Available. *Airport:* 80 miles.
Ratnagiri, India: 16.58 N. 73.17 E. **37**
Raubergviga, Norway: 62.16 N. 7.02 E. **15**
Raufarhofn, Iceland: 66.27 N. 15.55 W. **17**
Rauma, Finland: 61.08 N. 21.30 E. **10, 11, 15**
  Max. Size: Draft 10 m. *Fuel:* By road tanker.
  Dry Docks: 280 m. x 80 m. x 10 m. *Airport:* Pori, 50 km.
Rautaruukki, see Raahe.
Ravenna, Italy: 44.25 N. 12.12 E. **9, 21, 24**
  Max. Size: San Vitale Basin: Draft 28 ft. ENEL: Draft 11.3 m.
  Fuel: By barge. *Dry Docks:* Floating dock 1,000 tons.
  Airport: Forli, 30 km. Rimini, 60 km. Bologna, 80 km.
Ravensbourne, see Dunedin.
Rawene, New Zealand: 35.25 S. 173.30 E. **52**
Raymond, see Willapa.
Rayong, Thailand: 12.38 N. 101.18 E. **39**
  Max. Size: Depth 19 m.
  Also see Map Ta Phut.
Raysut, see Port Salalah.
Razdolnoye, Ukraine: 45.40 N. 33.10 E. **26**
Real, see Puerto Real.
Ream, Cambodia: 10.32 N. 103.37 E. **39**
Reao, French Polynesia (France): 18.31 S. 136.22 W. . . **49**
Rebun Is., (Hokkaido), Japan: 45.25 N. 141.00 E. . . . **43**
Recalada Lightship, River Plate, Argentina:
  34.41 S. 56.16 W. **78**
Recanati, see Porto Recanati.
Recife, Brazil: 8.04 S. 34.52 W. **72**
  Max. Size: LOA 220 m., draft 31 ft. Tankers: Draft 30 ft. (HW).
  Fuel: Available. *Airport:* 9 miles.
Red Dog, Alaska, U.S.A.: 67.33 N. 164.12 W. . . . **54, 79**
  Max. Size: Anchorage port: 70,000 d.w.t., draft 45 ft.
Red Hook C.T., see New York.
Red Rock, Ontario, Canada: 48.56 N. 88.15 W. **62**
Red Sea **21, 31, 32, 33**
Red Tank, Panama Canal, Panama: 9.01 N. 79.36 W. . **73**
Redcar, U.K.: 54.37 N. 1.04 W. **6**
  Max. Size: Ore Terminal: 150,000 d.w.t. Dredged to 17.3 m. for vessels 305 m. LOA.
  Also see Teesport.
Redi, see Port Redi.
Redon, France: 47.39 N. 2.05 W. **19**

Redwood City, California, U.S.A.: 37.32 N. 122.12 W. 57, 58
  Max. Size: 30,000 d.w.t. Controlling depth 30 ft. (MLLW), depth alongside 34 ft. *Fuel:* Available.
  Also see San Francisco.
Reedham, U.K.: 52.34 N. 1.34 E. 7
Reedsport, Oregon, U.S.A.: 43.43 N. 124.05 W. 57
Reerso, Denmark: 55.31 N. 11.07 E. 12
Regencia, Brazil: 19.41 S. 39.50 W. 72, 77
  Max. Size: 30,000 d.w.t., LOA 200 m., beam 30 m., draft 13 m.
  Airport: Vitoria, 70 km.
Regensburg, Germany: 49.01 N. 12.07 E. 9
Reggio, Italy: 38.05 N. 15.35 E. 21, 24
Reine, Norway: 67.56 N. 13.06 E. 15
Rekefjord, Norway: 58.20 N. 6.16 E. 11
Rembang, Indonesia: 6.41 S. 111.21 E. 38
Remire, Guyane (France): 4.52 N. 52.11 W. 76
Rendsburg, Germany: 54.18 N. 9.40 E. 8, 12, 14
  Max. Size: Draft 9.5 m., air draft 40 m. *Fuel:* By truck or barge.
  Airport: Hamburg, 100 km.
Rene, Russia: 66.01 N. 178.50 W. 54
Renfrew, see Port Renfrew.
Reni, Ukraine: 45.26 N. 28.18 E. 9, 26
  Max. Size: Depth 7.5 m. *Fuel:* Available.
Rennell Is., Solomon Islands: 11.45 S. 160.15 E. 50, 51
Rensselaer, see Albany.
Reposaari, Finland: 61.37 N. 21.27 E. 15
  Max. Size: Draft 3.9 m. *Fuel:* Available.
  Also see Pori.
Repulse Bay, N.W.T., Canada: 66.30 N. 86.15 W. 59
Reserve, Louisiana, U.S.A.: 30.03 N. 90.33 W. 67
Resolution Is., N.W.T., Canada: 61.30 N. 67.00 W. 59
Resolution Is., (South Is.), New Zealand: 45.40 S. 166.40 E. . 52
Rethimnon, (Crete), Greece: 35.14 N. 24.38 E. 25, 26
Reunion (France) 18, 30
Reunion Port, (Reunion Is.), Reunion (France):
  20.55 S. 55.17 E. 30
  Max. Size: West Port: LOA 175 m., beam 24 m., draft 8.5 m. or LOA 160 m., beam 24 m., draft 9 m. East Port (Baie de la Possession): LOA 215 m., beam 34 m., draft 12 m.
  Fuel: Fuel and marine diesel. *Airport:* 30 km.
Revere, see Boston.
Revilla Gigedo Islands, Mexico. 49, 57
Revithousa Is., Greece: 38.58 N. 23.25 E. 23
Rey Malabo, see Malabo.
Reykjavik, Iceland: 64.09 N. 21.56 W. 17, 79
  Max. Size: Longest straight quay 315 m. Depth 26 ft. at MLWST. *Fuel:* Grade of fuel oil 200-400 sec. *Dry Docks:* Slipways available up to 2,000 metric tons. Length 85 m., breadth 13.6 m. *Airport:* 10 minute drive.
Rhine-Main-Danube Canal. 9
Rhoades, see Port Rhoades.
Rhode Island, U.S.A. 63
Rhodes, Greece: 36.25 N. 28.17 E. 21, 25, 26
  Max. Size: Up to 24 ft. draft. *Fuel:* By road tanker.
  Airport: 15 km.
Rhone-Fos Canal, France 23
Rhone-Rhine Canal 9
Rhum, U.K.: 57.02 N. 6.18 W. 5
Rhyl, U.K.: 53.19 N. 3.29 W. 6, 7
Riacho, see Aracruz.
Riachuelo, see Buenos Aires.
Ribadeo, Spain: 43.32 N. 7.02 W. 19, 20, 22
  Max. Size: Draft 15 ft. *Fuel:* Gas oil supply for small vessels.
  Airport: Corunna, 150 km.
Ribadesella, Spain: 43.28 N. 5.05 W. 19, 20
Ribe, Denmark: 55.20 N. 8.45 E. 11, 12
Ribnitz, Germany: 54.15 N. 12.25 E. 12
Riccione, Italy: 44.02 N. 12.40 E. 24
Richards Bay, South Africa: 28.48 S. 32.02 E. 30
  Max. Size: Beam 47.25 m., draft 17.5 m. *Fuel:* Available.
  Airport: 26 km., connects Johannesburg.
Richards Landing, Ontario, Canada: 46.18 N. 84.02 W. 62
Richborough, U.K.: 51.18 N. 1.12 E. 6
  Max. Size: LOA 60 m., draft 3.6 m.
Richibucto, N.B., Canada: 46.41 N. 64.52 W. 60
Richmond, New Zealand: 41.05 S. 173.10 E. 52
Richmond, California, U.S.A.: 37.56 N. 122.25 W. 58
  Max. Size: Channel depth 35 ft. Cargo vessels: Draft 16 ft. – 35 ft. Tankers: Draft 38 ft. – 43.2 ft. *Fuel:* Many grades.
  Also see San Francisco.
Richmond, New York, U.S.A., see Stapleton.
Richmond, Pennsylvania, U.S.A., see Philadelphia.
Richmond, Virginia, U.S.A.: 37.32 N. 77.25 W. 55, 63, 65
  Max. Size: Length recommended by Pilots 559 ft. – 564 ft., beam 85.5 ft., draft 22 ft. *Fuel:* Available. *Airport:* 10 miles.
Richmond River, see Ballina.
Ridham Dock, U.K.: 51.23 N. 0.46 E. 6
  Max. Size: LOA 102 m., beam 16.8 m., draft 6.7 m.
  Also see Medway Ports.

Riga, Latvia: 56.57 N. 24.06 E. 4, 10, 11
  Max. Size: LOA 225 m., draft 10 m. (FW). *Fuel:* Available.
  Airport: International.
Rigaih, see Calang.
Rigolet, Newfoundland, Canada: 54.10 N. 58.24 W. 59
Riishiri Is., (Hokkaido), Japan: 45.10 N. 141.10 E. 43
Rijeka, Croatia: 45.19 N. 14.26 E. 9, 21, 24
  Max. Size: LOA 200 m., draft 32 ft. 10 in. Containers: Draft 11 m. Bulk: Draft 42 ft. 6 in. *Fuel:* All grades. *Dry Docks:* 25,000 tons lifting capacity. *Airport:* Krk Island, 28 km.
Rijnpoort, see Rotterdam.
Rilaks, Finland: 59.57 N. 23.04 E. 11
Rimini, Italy: 44.05 N. 12.34 E. 24
Rimouski, Quebec, Canada: 48.28 N. 68.31 W. 60
  Max. Size: Depth 7.3 m. *Fuel:* Available. *Dry Docks:* Les Mechins, 70 miles. *Airport:* Rimouski.
Ringi Cove, Solomon Islands: 8.07 S. 157.06 E. 51
Ringkobing, Denmark: 56.05 N. 8.15 E. 11, 12
Rio, see Patras.
Rio Benito, Equatorial Guinea: 1.35 N. 9.35 E. 29
Rio Bueno, see Port Rhoades.
Rio Chico, Venezuela: 10.20 N. 66.00 W. 69, 71, 75
Rio Cullen, Argentina: 52.55 S. 68.22 W. 77
  Max. Size: 130,000 d.w.t., depth 115 ft.
Rio de Janeiro, Brazil: 22.54 S. 43.12 W. 76, 77
  Max. Size: Depths alongside to 13 m. Tankers (DTSE-GEGUA): Draft 15.8 m. (LW), 135,000 d.w.t. *Fuel:* At tanker terminal and by barge at anchorage.
  Dry Docks: Length 259 m., width 34 m., draft 14 m., 33,000 d.w.t. *Airport:* International.
Rio Gallegos, Argentina: 51.33 S. 68.59 W. 77
  Max. Size: 22 ft. in the pool at the port at LW. Height of tide up to 40 ft. Punta Loyola: New berth to receive vessels' length 375 m., depth 45 ft. Tankers: 60,000 d.w.t.
  Fuel: By road tanker. *Airport:* Daily to Buenos Aires.
Rio Grande, Brazil: 32.03 S. 52.05 W. 57, 66, 69, 77
  Max. Size: Draft 40 ft. Tankers: 25,000 d.w.t., draft 10.05 m.
  Fuel: Available. *Airport:* Rio Grande, 6 km. Nearest international airport at Porto Alegre.
Rio Grande do Sul, see Tramandai.
Rio Haina, Dominican Republic: 18.25 N. 70.01 W. 69, 70
  Max. Size: LOA 700 ft., beam 100 ft., draft 32 ft.
  Tankers: LOA 170 m. – 182 m., draft 7.3 m. – 8.5 m.
  CBM – LOA 170 m., draft 9.5 m. *Fuel:* Available.
  Airport: Santo Domingo, 25 miles.
Rio Marina, Italy: 42.49 N. 10.26 E. 23, 24
Rio Nunez, see Port Kamsar.
Rio Pacaja, Brazil: 2.48 S. 50.50 W. 72
Rio San Juan, see Caripito.
Rio Santiago, see La Plata.
Rio Tuba, (Palawan Is.), Philippines: 8.30 N. 117.26 E. . . . 47
  Max. Size: 41,000 d.w.t.
Rio Viejo, Panama Canal, Panama: 9.25 N. 79.49 W. 73
Rio Vista, California, U.S.A.: 38.08 N. 121.46 W. 58
Riohacha, Colombia: 11.50 N. 72.50 W. 69, 74
Rioverde, Ecuador: 1.00 N. 79.32 W. 72
Riposto, (Sicily), Italy: 37.44 N. 15.13 E. 24
Risan, Yugoslavia: 42.31 N. 18.42 E. 24
Risavika, see Sola.
Risdon, see Hobart.
Risor, Norway: 58.43 N. 9.14 E. 11, 12
  Max. Size: 10,000 d.w.t., draft 28 ft. *Airport:* 10 miles.
Ristiina, Finland: 61.32 N. 27.17 E. 13
  Also see Saimaa Canal.
Ritenbenk, Greenland (Denmark): 69.45 N. 51.16 W. 17
Riverdale, New Zealand: 41.00 S. 176.00 E. 52
Riverhead, (Long Is.), New York, U.S.A.: 41.00 N. 72.39 W. . 60, 63
  Max. Size: LOA 1,150 ft., draft 62 ft., 225,000 d.w.t. *Fuel:* Available if pipelines in black oil service, also available by barge. *Airport:* New York, 80 miles. Islip MacArthur, 35 miles.
  Also see New York.
Rivers:
  Amazon, Brazil 72
  Amite, Louisiana, U.S.A. 67
  Amur, Russia 43
  Arnaud, Quebec, Canada 59
  Arno, Italy 9, 24
  Atrato, Colombia 72
  Benin, Nigeria 29
  Brazos, Texas, U.S.A. 66
  Bug, Ukraine 26
  Cameroon, Cameroon 29
  Canche, France 7
  Caroni, Venezuela 75
  Casamance, Senegal 27
  Caura, Venezuela 75
  Chagres, Panama 73
  Chang Chiang, China 42
  Chao Phraya, Thailand 37, 39
  Charente, France 19

THE SHIPS ATLAS

Churchill, Manitoba, Canada	59
Clyde, U.K.	5
Colorado, California, U.S.A.	57
Columbia, Washington, U.S.A.	36, 57
Congo, Congo (D.R. of)	28
Courantyne, Guyana/Suriname	76
Cross, Nigeria	29
Cunene, Angola	28
Cuyuni, Guyana	75
Danube, Romania	26
Daugava, Latvia	10, 11
Dee, U.K.	6
Delaware, U.S.A.	63
Digul, Irian Jaya, Indonesia	46
Dnieper, Ukraine	26
Dniester, Ukraine	26
Don, Russia	9, 26
Dordogne, France	8
Douro, Portugal	20
Drina, Bosnia/Yugoslavia	9
Dudinka, Russia	16
Dvina, Russia	16
Eider, Germany	14
Elbe, Germany	8, 9, 11, 12, 14
Ems, Germany	7, 8, 14
Fraser, B.C., Canada	56
Gambia, Gambia	27
Ganges, India	37
Garonne, France	8, 19
George, Quebec, Canada	59
Gironde, France	8, 19
Godovari, India	37
Grande (Rio), Mexico/U.S.A.	57, 66, 69
Guadalquivir, Spain	20, 22
Guadiana, Portugal	22
Hong, Vietnam	39
Hooghly, India	37
Huang He, China	42
Hudson, New York, U.S.A.	60, 63
Humber, U.K.	5, 6
Indus, Pakistan	37
Irrawaddy, Myanmar	37
Jade, Germany	8, 10, 14
James, Virginia, U.S.A.	63, 65
Jordan, Israel/Jordan	26
Kolyma, Russia	54
Krishna, India	37
Lek, Netherlands	8
Loire, France	19
Maas, Netherlands	7, 8
Madeira, Brazil	72
Main, Germany	7
Marowijne, Guyane/Suriname	76
Mattapon, Virginia, U.S.A.	65
Medway, U.K.	6
Mekong, Cambodia/Vietnam	39
Mersey, U.K.	5, 6
Meuse, Belgium	7
Mezen, Russia	16
Mississippi, Louisiana, U.S.A.	66, 67
Montone, Italy	24
Muni, Equatorial Guinea	29
Murray, Vic., Australia	50, 51
Nadym, Russia	16
Napo, Peru	72
Neches, Texas, U.S.A.	66
Negro, Brazil	72
Nelson, Manitoba, Canada	59
Neretya, Bosnia/Croatia	24
Neuse, North Carolina, U.S.A.	63
Niger, Nigeria	28, 29
Nile, Egypt/Sudan	26
Nogat, Poland	11
Nottoway, Virginia, U.S.A.	65
Nyong, Cameroon	29
Ob, Russia	16
Oder, Germany	9
Onega, Russia	16
Orange, Namibia	28
Orinoco, Venezuela	69, 72, 75
Orne, France	7, 8
Ottawa, Canada	60, 61
Ouse, U.K.	6
Oyapock, Brazil/Guyane	76
Paira, Russia	16
Pamlico, North Carolina, U.S.A.	63
Parana, Argentina	77, 78
Parana Ibicuy, Argentina	78
Patuxent, Maryland, U.S.A.	63
Pechora, Russia	16
Pescara, Italy	24
Pitt, B.C., Canada	56
Plate, Argentina	77, 78
Po, Italy	9, 24
Potomac, Maryland, U.S.A.	60, 63, 65
Pruth, Romania	26
Pyasina, Russia	16
Rappahannock, Virginia, U.S.A.	63
Rhine, Germany/Netherlands	7, 8, 9
Rhone, France	9, 22, 23
Rovuma, Tanzania	30
Rufiji, Tanzania	30
Sacramento, California, U.S.A.	57, 58
Saguenay, Quebec, Canada	60
St. John's, Florida, U.S.A.	66
St. Lawrence, Canada	60, 61
St. Mary's, Canada/U.S.A.	62
Saloum, Senegal	27
San Francisco, Brazil	72
San Jacinto, Texas, U.S.A.	66
San Joaquin, California, U.S.A.	58
Sanaga, Cameroon	29
Saone, France	9
Sava, Yugoslavia	9
Schelde, Belgium	7
Seal, Manitoba, Canada	59
Seine, France	7, 8
Sepik, Papua New Guinea	46
Severn, Ontario, Canada	59
Severn, U.K.	5, 6
Shannon, Ireland	5, 8
Shatt Al Arab, Iran/Iraq	35
Skeena, B.C., Canada	56
Somme, France	7
Stor, Germany	8, 14
Sungari, China	43
Susquehanna, Maryland, U.S.A.	65
Swan, W.A., Australia	50
Tagus, Portugal	20
Tapajos, Brazil	72
Tay, U.K.	6
Taz, Russia	16
Tees, U.K.	5, 6
Thames, U.K.	5, 6
Tiber, Italy	9, 24
Tocantins, Brazil	72
Towy, U.K.	6
Trent, U.K.	5, 6
Tyne, U.K.	5, 6
Uguyali, Peru	72
Uruguay, Uruguay	77, 78
Ussuri, Russia	43
Villaine, France	19
Vistula, Poland	9, 11
Volga, Russia	9
Wareham, Massachusetts, U.S.A.	64
Weser, Germany	8, 10, 11, 14
Winisk, Ontario, Canada	59
Xingu, Brazil	72
Yalu, China	42
Yenisey, Russia	16
York, Virginia, U.S.A.	63, 65
Yukon, Canada/U.S.A.	54
Yung Ting, China	42
Zaire, Congo (D.R. of)	28
Zambeze, Mozambique	30

Riverton, New Zealand: 46.20 S. 168.00 E. ... 52

Riviere du Loup, Quebec, Canada: 47.49 N. 69.30 W. ... 60

Rize, Turkey: 41.03 N. 40.32 E. ... 26
  Max. Size: Draft 11 m. *Fuel:* Available.

Rizhao, China: 35.22 N. 119.17 E. ... 42, 46
  Max. Size: 25,000 d.w.t., depth 10.5 m. Coal: 125,000 d.w.t., depth 17 m. *Fuel:* Available. *Airport:* Qingdao, 140 km.

Road Bay, Anguilla (U.K.): 18.11 N. 63.01 W. ... 71
  Also see Blowing Point.

Road Harbour, (Tortola), Virgin Is. (U.K.): 18.25 N. 64.37 W. ... 69, 71
  Max. Size: Port Purcell: Draft 22 ft. *Fuel:* Diesel only for small vessels. *Airport:* Beef Island, 7 miles.

Roatan Is., Honduras: 16.18 N. 86.35 W. ... 69

Roberts Bank, B.C., Canada: 49.03 N. 123.09 W. ... 56
  Max. Size: Bulk: Depth 20.8 m. – 22.9 m.
  Container: Depth 15.8 m.
  Also see Vancouver.

Robertsport, Liberia: 6.45 N. 11.24 W. ... 27

Roca Partido Is., (Revilla Gigedo Is.), Mexico: 18.57 N. 112.08 W. ... 57

Rocas Is., Brazil: 4.00 S. 34.02 W. ... 72

Roche Bernard, France: 47.31 N. 2.18 W. ... 19

Roche Harbour, Washington, U.S.A.: 48.37 N. 123.10 W. ... 56

Rochefort sur Mer, France: 45.56 N. 0.57 W. **8, 19**
　Max. Size: LOA 115 m., beam 16.5 m., draft 6.5 m.
　Fuel: By road tanker. *Airport:* La Rochelle, 30 miles.
　Also see Tonnay Charente.
Rochester, U.K.: 51.27 N. 0.43 E. **6**
　Max. Size: LOA 122 m., draft 7.6 m. *Fuel:* Available.
　Airport: London Heathrow, London Gatwick and London
　Stansted.
　Also see Medway Ports.
Rochester, New York, U.S.A.: 43.17 N. 77.36 W. **55, 60, 62**
　Max. Size: Channel depth 20 ft. (LW).
　Depth alongside 10 ft. – 16 ft. *Fuel:* By road tanker.
　Airport: 10 miles.
Rochford, U.K.: 51.35 N. 0.44 E. **6**
Rock Sound, (Eleuthra Is.), Bahamas: 24.54 N. 76.12 W. . . **69, 70**
Rockhampton, Qld., Australia: 23.24 S. 150.33 E. **49, 50, 51**
　Max. Size: Channel depth 7.3 m. (LWOST). Berth: Depth 9.5 m.
　(LWOST). *Fuel:* All grades by road tankers. *Airport:* 43 miles.
Rockland, Maine, U.S.A.: 44.06 N. 69.07 W. **60**
　Max. Size: LOA 700 ft., draft 15 ft. *Fuel:* Available.
　Airport: Knox County.
Rockport, Ontario, Canada: 44.23 N. 75.56 W. **61**
Rockport, Florida, U.S.A., see Tampa.
Rockport, Texas, U.S.A.: 28.01 N. 97.03 W. **66**
Rocky Point, W.A., Australia: 33.30 S. 123.59 E. **50**
Rocky Point, Jamaica: 17.49 N. 77.08 W. **70**
　Max. Size: Draft 40 ft.
　Also see Salt River.
Rodby, Denmark: 54.39 N. 11.21 E. **11, 12, 14**
　Max. Size: Largest vessel: LOA 80 m., draft 4.5 m. *Fuel:*
　Available. *Airport:* Maribo, 14 km.
Roddickton, Newfoundland, Canada: 50.52 N. 56.08 W. . . **59, 60**
　Max. Size: Depth 6.2 m. – 7.5 m.
Rodosto, see Tekirdag.
Rodoy, Norway: 66.39 N. 13.05 E. **15**
Rodrigues Is., Mauritius: 19.40 S. 63.25 E. **30**
Rodvig, Denmark: 55.15 N. 12.23 E. **12**
Roes Welcome Sound, N.W.T., Canada **59**
Rogers City, Michigan, U.S.A.: 45.26 N. 83.49 W. **62**
Rognan, see Saltdal.
Roja, Latvia: 57.30 N. 22.48 E. **11**
　Max. Size: LOA 90 m., beam 15 m., draft 4 m. *Airport:*
　Riga, 120 km.
Rokko Is., see Kobe.
ROMANIA **4, 9, 21, 26**
Romanso do Pontal, see Altamira.
Romblon Is., Philippines: 12.35 N. 122.16 E. **47**
Rome, see Georgetown, Guyana.
Rome, Italy: 41.53 N. 12.30 E. **9**
Romo, Denmark: 55.10 N. 8.30 E. **12, 14**
Rompin, Malaya, Malaysia: 2.43 N. 103.30 E. **38, 39, 40**
　Max. Size: Anchorage port.
Roncador Cay, (Colombia): 13.35 N. 80.03 W. **69**
Rondeau, Ontario, Canada: 42.15 N. 81.55 W. **62**
Ronehamn, Sweden: 57.10 N. 18.30 E. **11**
Ronnang, see Stenungsund.
Ronne, Denmark: 55.06 N. 14.42 E. **10, 11, 12**
　Max. Size: LOA 600 ft. – 650 ft., draft 26 ft. Tankers: LOA 300 ft.,
　draft 22 ft. *Fuel:* Most grades. *Dry Docks:* Up to 350 tons.
　Airport: 3 miles, connects Copenhagen.
Ronneby, Sweden: 56.10 N. 15.17 E. **4, 11, 12**
　Max. Size: Limit is depth in fairway: 20 ft. 9 in. Tankers:
　Draft 20 ft. 6 in. *Fuel:* Diesel. *Airport:* 6 miles,
　connects with Stockholm, etc.
Ronnskarsverken, see Skelleftehamn.
Roomassaare, Estonia: 58.14 N. 22.31 E. **11**
　Max. Size: LOA 115 m., draft 4.7 m. *Fuel:* Available.
　Airport: Local airport, 1 km.
Roquetas del Mar, Spain: 36.45 N. 2.37 W. **22**
Rorvig, Denmark: 55.56 N. 11.45 E. **12**
Rorvik, Norway: 64.52 N. 11.15 E. **15**
Rosales, see Bahia Blanca.
Rosario, Argentina: 32.57 S. 60.33 W. **77, 78**
　Max. Size: Max. draft in river 27 ft. Up to 35 ft. depth at berths.
　Fuel: All grades. *Airport:* 16 km., connects with Buenos Aires.
Rosario, Philippines, see Manila.
Rosarito, Mexico: 32.22 N. 117.06 W. **57**
　Max. Size: CBM: LOA 210 m., draft 34 ft. SBM: LOA 215 m.,
　draft 50 ft.
Rosas, Spain: 42.14 N. 3.10 E. **9, 22**
　Max. Size: Depth in Commercial Port is 4 m. *Fuel:* Available to
　small vessels.
Roscoff, France: 48.43 N. 3.59 W. **7, 19**
　Max. Size: 5,000 d.w.t. *Fuel:* By road tanker.
　Airport: Morlaix, 13 miles, or Brest, 35 miles.
Rose Blanche, Newfoundland, Canada: 47.37 N. 58.44 W. . . **60**
Roseau, Dominica: 15.17 N. 61.24 W. **69, 71**
　Max. Size: Depths: Roseau Cruise Berth 40 ft. Woodbridge Bay
　32 ft. Tankers: Draft 12 ft. – 18 ft. (25 ft. with stern discharge).
　Fuel: Dieselene available in limited quantities.
　Airport: Melville Hall, 37 miles (Inter-island services).

Rosetta, Egypt: 31.20 N. 30.20 E. **26**
Rosfjord, see Lyngdal.
Roskilde, Denmark: 55.39 N. 12.05 E. **12**
Ross, New Zealand: 42.53 S. 170.49 E. **52**
Rossano, Italy: 39.36 N. 16.39 E. **24**
Rossel Is., Papua New Guinea: 11.21 S. 154.10 E. **50, 51**
Rosslare, Ireland: 52.16 N. 6.20 W. **5**
　Max. Size: Depth 6 m. (LWOST). *Airport:* Dublin 110 miles,
　Cork 134 miles, Waterford 51 miles.
Rostock, Germany: 54.09 N. 12.06 E. **4, 10, 11, 12, 14**
　Max. Size: LOA 250 m., beam 40 m., draft 13 m.
　Tankers: Draft 13 m. *Fuel:* All grades. *Airport:* Berlin, Hamburg
　and Rostock-Laage.
Rostov, Russia: 47.11 N. 39.42 E. **9, 26**
Rosyth, U.K.: 56.01 N. 3.26 W. **6**
　Max. Size: LOA 250 m., depth 4.9 m. – 8.3 m. *Fuel:* Available.
　Dry Docks: 252 m. x 30.78 m. x 40 ft. depth.
　Airport: Edinburgh, 10 miles.
Rota, Northern Mariana Is. (U.S.A.): 14.10 N. 145.10 E. . . **46**
Rota, Spain: 36.37 N. 6.21 W. **20, 22**
Rothesay Dock, U.K.: 55.53 N. 4.24 W. **6**
　Max. Size: LOA 535 ft., draft 9.4 m.
　Also see Clyde Port.
Roti, Indonesia **46, 50**
Rotterdam, Netherlands: 51.55 N. 4.24 E. **4, 7, 8, 9**
　Max. Size: Depths up to 13.5 m. Grain (Europoort): Depth 18 m.
　Bulk (Europoort): Draft 74 ft. Tankers: Europoort –
　depth 22.65 m. Maasvlakte – depth 24 m. Botlek – depth 14.5 m.
　Pernis – depth 12.6 m. *Fuel:* All grades.
　Dry Docks: 500,000 d.w.t. *Airport:* 6 km.
　Also see Europoort.
Rottnest Is., W.A., Australia: 32.00 S. 115.30 E. **50**
Rotuma Is., Fiji: 12.30 S. 177.09 E. **49**
Rouen, France: 49.28 N. 1.04 E. **4, 7, 8**
　Max. Size: Draft about 37 ft., LOA 280 m. *Fuel:* All grades by
　barge. *Dry Docks:* For vessels up to 14,000 tons.
　Airport: Rouen-Boos.
Rouge River, Michigan, U.S.A.: 42.17 N. 83.06 W. **62**
Rousay, U.K.: 59.10 N. 3.00 W. **5**
Rousse, see Ruse.
Rovinj, Croatia: 45.05 N. 13.38 E. **21, 24**
Rowan, see Port Rowan.
Rowhedge, see Wivenhoe.
Rowley Shoals, Australia: 17.10 S. 120.40 E. **51**
Roxas, (Palawan Is.), Philippines: 11.36 N. 122.43 E. . . . **47**
Royalist Haven, Indonesia: 2.30 N. 109.01 E. **38, 39**
Royan, France: 45.37 N. 1.02 W. **8, 19**
Roytta, Finland: 65.46 N. 24.10 E. **15**
Roytta Ijo, Finland: 65.16 N. 25.13 E. **15**
Rozelle Bay, see Sydney.
Rozi, see Bedi Bunder.
Ruapuke Is., (South Is.), New Zealand: 46.46 S. 168.32 E. . **52**
Ruby Princess, Vietnam: 10.23 N. 108.30 E. **39**
　Max. Size: 60,000 d.w.t. – 150,000 d.w.t.
Rudham Terminal, Yemen: 13.58 N. 47.55 E. **31**
　Max. Size: 50,000 d.w.t., draft 12.5 m.
Rudkobing, Denmark: 54.56 N. 10.42 E. **12, 14**
Rufisque, Senegal: 14.42 N. 17.17 W. **27**
Rugen Is., Germany **10, 11**
Ruhnu Is., Estonia: 57.49 N. 23.12 E. **11**
Ruhrort, see Duisburg-Ruhrort.
Ruisbroek, Belgium: 51.06 N. 4.20 E. **7**
　Max. Size: Draft 7.5 m.
Rum Cay, Bahamas: 23.40 N. 74.58 W. **70**
Rumoi, Japan: 43.57 N. 141.38 E. **43**
　Max. Size: Draft 10.0 m., LOA 150 m. *Fuel:* Available.
　Airport: 90 km.
Runanga, New Zealand: 42.23 S. 171.14 E. **52**
Runcorn, U.K.: 53.21 N. 2.44 W. **6**
　Also see Manchester.
Rundvik, Sweden: 63.33 N. 19.27 E. **15**
Rupat Is., Indonesia **40**
Ruse, Bulgaria: 43.45 N. 26.00 E. **9, 26**
Rushin, see Najin.
Russell, New Zealand: 35.14 S. 174.07 E. **52**
RUSSIA **4, 9, 10, 11, 13, 16, 21, 26, 43, 54, 79**
Russkya Gavan, Russia: 76.10 N. 62.20 E. **16**
Ruwais, see Jebel Dhanna - Ruwais.
Rya Harbour, see Gothenburg.
Rye, Australia, see Portsea.
Rye, U.K.: 50.56 N. 0.47 E. **7**
　Max. Size: LOA 235 ft. (278 ft. on request), draft 13 ft. 6 in.
　Fuel: Available.
Rynda, Russia: 68.58 N. 36.50 E. **16**
Ryotsu, Japan: 38.05 N. 138.26 E. **43**
Ryukyu Islands, Japan **42, 46**

S

S. Manitou Is., Michigan, U.S.A.: 45.02 N. 86.07 W. 62
Saaremaa, Estonia: 58.30 N. 23.00 E. 10, 11
Saba Is., Netherlands Antilles: 17.38 N. 63.16 W. 71
Sabagalet, Indonesia: 1.35 S. 98.40 E. 38
Sabah, Malaysia 38, 47
Sabang, Indonesia: 5.50 N. 95.20 E. 37, 38
   Max. Size: Berth: LOA 150 m., depth 8 m. LWS.
   Airport: 15 minutes drive.
Sabine, Texas, U.S.A.: 29.43 N. 93.52 W. 66
Sabine Pass, U.S.A. 66
Sablayan, (Mindoro Is.), Philippines: 12.49 N. 120.49 E. . . . 47
Sable, New Caledonia (France): 19.13 S. 159.57 E. 51
Sable Is., N.S., Canada: 43.56 N. 60.02 W. 60
Sacavem, see Lisbon.
Sacketts Harbor, New York, U.S.A.: 43.57 N. 76.07 W. 62
Sackville, N.B., Canada: 45.53 N. 64.22 W. 60
Saco, see Namibe.
Sacramento, California, U.S.A.: 38.32 N. 121.30 W. . . . 55, 57, 58
   Max. Size: LOA 800 ft., beam 106 ft., depth 30 ft. – 35 ft.
   (MLLW). *Fuel:* All grades. *Airport:* 16 miles.
Sacramento Ship Canal, California, U.S.A. 58
Sado Is., Japan: 38.15 N. 138.30 E. 43
Sadong, Sarawak, Malaysia: 1.30 N. 110.43 E. 38, 39
Saeby, Denmark: 57.20 N. 10.30 E. 12
Saeki, see Saiki.
Saetia, see Antilla.
Safaga, Egypt: 26.46 N. 34.00 E. 21, 26, 32
   Max. Size: Draft 30 ft. – 32 ft.
Safaga Is., Egypt: 26.42 N. 34.00 E. 32
Saffaniya, Saudi Arabia: 28.02 N. 48.49 E. 35
Saffle, Sweden: 59.08 N. 12.56 E. 12
Safi, Morocco: 32.18 N. 9.15 W. 21, 27
   Max. Size: Draft 30 ft. (HW). *Fuel:* Fuel oil, gas oil and diesel.
   Airport: Casablanca, 110 miles.
Saga, Japan: 33.02 N. 133.05 E. 45
Saganoseki, Japan: 33.15 N. 131.52 E. 45
   Max. Size: LOA 185 m., draft 9.45 m. *Fuel:* Available. *Airport:*
   Oita.
Saginaw, Michigan, U.S.A.: 43.26 N. 83.56 W. 62
Saginaw Bay, Lake Huron, U.S.A. 62
Saglek Bay, Newfoundland, Canada: 58.40 N. 62.50 W. 59
Sagres, Portugal: 37.00 N. 8.57 W. 20, 22
Sagunto, Spain: 39.39 N. 0.13 W. 22
   Max. Size: Depth 8.0 m. – 11.25 m. Bulk: Depth 14.0 m.
   Airport: Valencia, 40 km.
Saida, see Sidon.
Saigon, see Ho Chi Minh City.
Saiki, Japan: 32.59 N. 131.55 E. 43, 45
   Max. Size: Draft 9.0 m. – 12.0 m.
   Fuel: Available at 7 days notice. *Airport:* Oita.
Saimaa Canal, Finland: 60.34 N. 28.20 E. 10, 11, 13
   Max. Size: LOA 82.5 m., beam 12.8 m., draft 4.35 m.,
   height of mast 24.5 m. Larger by special permit. Time of transit
   through lock section of canal 5-8 hours.
Saimaa Lake, Finland 13, 15
   Also see Saimaa Canal.
St. Agnes, (Scilly Is.), U.K.: 49.54 N. 6.21 W. 19
St. Albans, Newfoundland, Canada: 47.52 N. 55.51 W. 60
St. Andrews, N.B., Canada: 45.10 N. 67.08 W. 60
   Max. Size: Draft 34 ft. (LWOST). *Fuel:* MDO and IFO.
   Airport: St. John, 45 miles.
St. Andrews, U.K.: 56.21 N. 2.48 W. 6
St. Anicet, Quebec, Canada: 45.08 N. 74.22 W. 61
St. Ann's Bay, see Ocho Rios.
St. Anne, (Channel Is.), U.K.: 49.43 N. 2.11 W. 19
St. Anne des Monts, Quebec, Canada: 49.07 N. 66.28 W. . . . 60
St. Anthony, Newfoundland, Canada: 51.22 N. 55.35 W. . . . 59, 60
St. Augustin, Quebec, Canada: 51.14 N. 58.39 W. 60
St. Augustin Bay, Madagascar: 23.28 S. 43.40 E. 30
St. Augustine, Florida, U.S.A.: 29.54 N. 81.20 W. 66
St. Barthelemy, Guadeloupe (France) 71
St. Brieuc, France: 48.32 N. 2.45 W. 7, 19
St. Catharines, Ontario, Canada: 43.10 N. 79.16 W. 62
   Max. Size: Welland Canal: LOA 730 ft. (222.51 m.), beam 76 ft.
   (23.15 m.), draft 8 m. *Fuel:* By road tanker.
   Airport: Toronto, 75 miles.
   Also see Port Weller.
ST. CHRISTOPHER AND NEVIS 71
St. Christopher Is., St. Christopher and Nevis 71
St. Clair, Michigan, U.S.A.: 42.49 N. 82.52 W. 62
St. Clair River, Lake Huron, U.S.A. 62
St. Croix, Virgin Is. (U.S.A.): 17.40 N. 64.43 W. 71
St. Davids, Newfoundland, Canada: 48.12 N. 58.53 W. 60
St. Davids, U.K., see Rosyth.

St. Davids Is., Bermuda (U.K.) 63
St. Denis, Reunion (France): 20.52 S. 55.28 E. 30
St. Estephe, France: 45.17 N. 0.46 W. 8
St. Eustatius, Netherlands Antilles: 17.29 N. 63.00 W. . . . 71
   Max. Size: South Berth: 175,000 d.w.t., draft 55 ft.
   SPM: 520,000 d.w.t., depth 64 m. *Fuel:* All grades.
   Airport: Connects with St. Maarten.
St. Gabriel, Louisiana, U.S.A.: 30.17 N. 91.07 W. 67
St. Genevieve Bay, Newfoundland, Canada:
   51.08 N. 56.48 W. 60
St. George Is., Florida, U.S.A.: 29.40 N. 84.55 W. 66
St. George's, (St. George's Is.), Bermuda (U.K.):
   32.22 N. 64.41 W. 63
   Max. Size: Length 704 ft., draft 28 ft. and depends on
   displacement and weather conditions. Tankers: 38,000 d.w.t.,
   LOA 700 ft., draft 34 ft. *Fuel:* Bunker "C" fuel and diesel oil.
   Airport: 2 miles.
St. George's, Newfoundland, Canada: 48.06 N. 58.28 W. . . . 60
St. George's, Grenada: 12.02 N. 61.46 W. 69, 71
   Max. Size: LOA 600 ft., draft 28 ft. (H.W.).
   Tankers: Min. depth 26 ft. *Fuel:* Available. *Airport:* Available.
St. George's Channel 5
St. George's Is., Alaska, U.S.A.: 56.38 N. 169.40 W. 54
St. Helen's, Oregon, U.S.A.: 45.52 N. 122.48 W. 56, 57
St. Helena (U.K.) 18, 28, 68
St. Helena Bay, South Africa 28
St. Helier, (Channel Is.), U.K.: 49.11 N. 2.07 W. 7, 19
   Max. Size: LOA 130 m., beam 22.6 m., draft 5.2 m.
   Fuel: By road tanker. *Airport:* St. Peter, 4 miles.
St. Ignace, Michigan, U.S.A.: 45.52 N. 84.43 W. 62
St. Ignace Is., Lake Superior, Canada 62
St. Ioni, Russia: 56.24 N. 143.20 E. 43
St. Ives, U.K.: 50.13 N. 5.28 W. 5, 7
St. James, Louisiana, U.S.A.: 29.59 N. 90.56 W. 67
   Also see Burnside.
St. James, Michigan, U.S.A.: 45.44 N. 85.31 W. 62
St. James Anchorage, (Agalaga Is.), Mauritius:
   10.20 S. 56.34 E. 30
St. Jean, Quebec, Canada: 45.20 N. 73.18 W. 60, 61
St. Jean de Luz, France: 43.24 N. 1.40 W. 19
St. Joe, see Port St. Joe.
Saint John, N.B., Canada: 45.16 N. 66.03 W. 60
   Max. Size: Depth in main channel is 30 ft. at LW.
   Containers: Depth 12.2 m. Bulk: Depth 10.7 m. – 12.2 m.
   Tankers: Depth 12.2 m. *Fuel:* Fuel oil and diesel.
   Dry Docks: 1,780 ft. × 125 ft. × 53 ft. deep with 42 ft. of water
   over sills at high tide. *Airport:* 12 miles.
   Also see Canaport.
St. John's, (Antigua), Antigua and Barbuda:
   17.07 N. 61.52 W. 69, 71
   Max. Size: At berth: Draft 32 ft. At anchor: Draft 45 ft. Tankers:
   CBM: Draft 43 ft. Sea Island: Draft 32 ft. *Fuel:* All grades.
   Airport: 4 miles.
St. John's, Newfoundland, Canada: 47.34 N. 52.41 W. 60
   Max. Size: Draft 36 ft. only limit. Tankers: See Holyrood.
   Fuel: Major grades. *Dry Docks:* Length of keel blocks 167.1 m.,
   width at coping 23.3 m., depth of water over sill 8.2 m.
   Airport: 4 miles.
St. John's Is., see Ras Zabarjad.
St. Johns, see Port St. Johns.
St. Joseph, Michigan, U.S.A.: 42.06 N. 86.29 W. 62
St. Joseph Is., Lake Huron, Canada 62
St. Kilda, New Zealand: 45.50 S. 170.30 E. 52
St. Kilda, U.K.: 57.49 N. 8.33 W. 5
St. Lambert Lock, see St. Lawrence Seaway.
St. Laurent, Guyane (France): 5.30 N. 54.02 W. 76
St. Lawrence, Qld., Australia: 22.21 S. 149.32 E. 50
St. Lawrence, Newfoundland, Canada: 46.55 N. 55.23 W. . . 60
St. Lawrence Is., Alaska, U.S.A. 54
St. Lawrence Seaway 53, 55, 60, 61
   Max. Size: LOA 225.5 m., beam 23.8 m., draft 8.0 m. Masts must
   not exceed 35.5 m. above water level.
St. Louis, Madagascar, see Port St. Louis.
St. Louis, Senegal: 16.01 N. 16.30 W. 27
St. Louis du Rhone, France: 43.23 N. 4.48 E. 9, 22, 23
   Max. Size: LOA 95 m., beam 16 m., draft 7.92 m.
   Fuel: Available. *Airport:* Marseilles, 70 km.
ST. LUCIA 69, 71, 72
St. Lunaire, Newfoundland, Canada: 51.30 N. 55.28 W. . . . 60
St. Maarten, (St. Maarten), Netherlands Antilles:
   18.01 N. 63.02 W. 71
St. Malo, France: 48.38 N. 2.02 W. 7, 19
   Max. Size: Cargo Vessels: LOA 150 m., beam 20 m., draft 9 m.
   at spring tides. Tankers: LOA 147.50 m., beam 20 m.,
   draft 9 m. *Fuel:* By road tanker. *Dry Docks:* Length 120 m.,
   breadth 16 m. and draft 8.0 m. *Airport:* 10 km.
St. Marc, Haiti: 19.07 N. 72.42 W. 70
St. Marks, Florida, U.S.A.: 30.10 N. 84.12 W. 66
St. Martin, France: 46.12 N. 1.22 W. 19
St. Martin Is., (France): 18.04 N. 63.02 W. 71
   Also see Philipsburg.

St. Martins, N.B., Canada: 45.22 N. 65.33 W. 60
St. Mary, see Port St. Mary.
St. Mary Is., Madagascar: 16.50 S. 50.00 E. 30
St. Mary Is., (Scilly Is.), U.K. 19
St. Mary's, U.K.: 58.54 N. 2.55 W. 5
St. Mary's, Georgia, U.S.A.: 30.44 N. 81.34 W. 66
St. Matthew Is., Alaska, U.S.A.: 60.20 N. 172.30 W. 54
St. Maxim, see St. Raphael.
St. Michael, Alaska, U.S.A.: 63.26 N. 162.10 W. 54
St. Michael's Bay, see Sint Michielsbay.
St. Nazaire, France: 47.17 N. 2.12 W. 19
   Max. Size: South Entrance Lock: Max. LOA 185 m., draft 8.5 m., beam 28 m. *Fuel:* Available. *Dry Docks:* Up to 240,000 d.w.t.
   Airport: Nantes.
   Also see Nantes.
St. Nicholas, see Aghios Nikolaos.
St. Nicolaas, see San Nicolas.
Saint Nicolas, Greece: 38.22 N. 22.41 E. 24, 25
   Max. Size: LOA 160 m., beam 22 m., draft 11 m.
   Fuel: By truck from Piraeus. *Airport:* Athens, 180 km.
St. Nikolo, see Aghios Nikolaos.
St. Palais, France: 45.39 N. 1.06 W. 8, 19
St. Paul Is., Alaska, U.S.A.: 57.10 N. 170.20 W. 54
St. Peter Port, U.K.: 49.27 N. 2.32 W. 7, 19
St. Petersburg, Russia: 59.54 N. 30.15 E. 10, 11, 79
   Max. Size: LOA 260 m., beam 40 m., draft 11.0 m.
   Tankers: 15,000 tonnes d.w.t., draft 9.6 m. *Fuel:* Available.
   Dry Docks: 6,000 d.w.t. – 15,000 d.w.t. *Airport:* 23 km.
St. Petersburg, Florida, U.S.A.: 27.46 N. 82.38 W. 66, 69
St. Pierre, Martinique (France): 14.45 N. 61.11 W. 71
St. Pierre, Reunion (France): 21.20 S. 55.30 E. 30
St. Pierre and Miquelon (France) 60
St. Pierre I., Seychelles: 9.19 S. 50.43 E. 30
St. Raphael, France: 43.25 N. 6.45 E. 22
St. Rose, Louisiana, U.S.A.: 29.56 N. 90.19 W. 67
   Max. Size: Depth 35 ft.
   Also see New Orleans.
St. Servan, see St. Malo.
St. Simeon, Quebec, Canada: 47.51 N. 69.54 W. 60
St. Stephens, N.B., Canada: 45.12 N. 67.17 W. 60
St. Thomas, Virgin Is. (U.S.A.): 18.20 N. 64.56 W. 69, 71
   Max. Size: Up to 25,000 g.t., depths 27 ft. – 30 ft.
   Fuel: Small craft only. *Airport:* 2 miles, connects with New York, Dallas – Fort Worth, Miami, etc.
St. Tropez, France: 43.17 N. 6.39 E. 22
St. Vaast, France: 49.35 N. 1.15 W. 7, 19
St. Valery-en-Caux, France: 49.52 N. 0.43 E. 7
St. Valery-sur-Somme, France: 50.11 N. 1.37 E. 7
St. Vincent, see Porto Grande.
ST. VINCENT AND THE GRENADINES 69, 71, 72
St. Vincent Gulf, S.A., Australia 50
St. Zotique, Quebec, Canada: 45.12 N. 74.18 W. 61
Saint-Pierre, St. Pierre and Miquelon (France):
   46.49 N. 56.10 W. 60
   Max. Size: LOA 200 m., draft 10 m. *Fuel:* Diesel.
   Dry Docks: Slipway, capacity 750 tons. *Airport:* Connects with Halifax and St. John's.
Saipan, Northern Mariana Is. (U.S.A.): 15.13 N. 145.44 E. . . 46
   Max. Size: LOA over 500 ft. requires special permission.
   Depth 30 ft. in channel and 35 ft. alongside. *Fuel:* Diesel.
   Airport: 9 miles.
Sakai, Japan: 34.34 N. 135.27 E. 44, 45
   Max. Size: LOA 181 m., draft 10.2 m. Tankers: 260,000 d.w.t., LOA 333 m., draft 14.5 m. *Fuel:* Most bonded fuels available.
   Dry Docks: Capacity 400,000 d.w.t. *Airport:* Kansai, 20 km.
Sakaide, Japan: 34.19 N. 133.51 E. 45
   Max. Size: LOA 275 m., draft 12.6 m., Tankers: 130,000 d.w.t., draft 19.6 m. *Fuel:* All grades lightered from nearest bunker stock ports. *Dry Docks:* 500,000 d.w.t.
   Airport: Takamatsu, connects with Osaka/Tokyo.
Sakaiminato, Japan: 35.32 N. 133.14 E. 43, 45
   Max. Size: Draft 7.1 m. – 11.5 m. *Fuel:* Bonded fuel from Moji.
Sakata, Japan: 38.55 N. 139.48 E. 43
   Max. Size: 40,000 d.w.t., LOA 270 m., draft 13.0 m.
   Tankers: Depth 7 m. – 7.5 m. *Fuel:* Bunkers lightered from Hakodate provided at least 7 days notice given.
   Airport: Shonai, 25 km.
Sakhalin Island, Russia 43
Sakihama, Japan: 33.25 N. 134.12 E. 45
Sakishima Is., Japan 46
Sakito, Japan: 33.01 N. 129.34 E. 45
Sakskobing, Denmark: 54.48 N. 11.38 E. 12, 14
Sal Is., Cape Verde: 16.45 N. 22.55 W. 27
Sal Rei, Cape Verde: 16.10 N. 22.57 W. 27
Sala y Gomez Is., Chile: 26.25 S. 105.28 W. 49
Salacgriva, Latvia: 57.45 N. 24.21 E. 11
   Max. Size: LOA 115 m., beam 20 m., draft 4.5 m.
   Airport: Riga, 100 km.
Saladin Marine Terminal, W.A., Australia: 21.24 S. 115.03 E. . 50, 51
   Max. Size: 180,000 tonnes displacement, beam 47 m.
   Minimum depth 15.6 m.

Salamaua, Papua New Guinea: 6.59 S. 147.05 E. 46
Salaminos Bay, Greece 23
Salamis, Greece: 37.57 N. 23.30 E. 23, 25
Salaverry, Peru: 8.13 S. 78.59 W. 72
   Max. Size: Approx. 25,000 d.w.t. with draft up to 29 ft. Tankers: Depth 26 ft.
Salawati, Indonesia: 1.21 S. 130.59 E. 46
   Max. Size: Up to 60,000 d.w.t. or 100,000 d.w.t. light loaded to equivalent of 60,000 d.w.t., draft 43 ft.
Salaya, India: 22.22 N. 69.36 E. 37, 46
Salaya Is., see Benteng.
Salayar, see Benteng.
Salazar, see Namibe.
Salcombe, U.K.: 50.14 N. 3.46 W. 5, 7
Saldanha Bay, South Africa: 33.02 S. 17.58 E. 28
   Max. Size: Ore and Oil: Draft 20.5 m. (inward) and 21.5 m. (outward), 21.25 m. (if swell running).
   General cargo: LOA 200 m., draft 11.5 m.
   Fuel: Not yet available ex-jetty. *Airport:* Cape Town.
Sale, Morocco: 34.05 N. 6.45 W. 27
Saleef, Yemen: 15.18 N. 42.41 E. 31, 32
   Max. Size: Draft 12 m., 50,000 d.w.t.
   Fuel: Barged from Hodeidah (80 km.).
Salekhard, Russia: 66.28 N. 66.34 E. 16
Salem, Massachusetts, U.S.A.: 42.31 N. 70.53 W. 55, 63, 65
   Max. Size: LOA 700 ft., beam 110 ft., draft 34 ft. Tankers: Depth 34 ft.
Salen, U.K.: 56.31 N. 5.50 W. 5
Salerno, Italy: 40.40 N. 14.45 E. 23, 24
   Max. Size: LOA 250 m., beam 35 m., draft 9.6 m. – 9.9 m.
   Fuel: From Naples by truck or barge. *Airport:* Naples, 50 km.
Salford, U.K.: 53.30 N. 2.16 W. 6
Salif, see Saleef.
Salina, see Kralendijk.
Salina Cruz, Mexico: 16.10 N. 95.12 W. 69
   Max. Size: 32,000 d.w.t., LOA 180 m., draft 10 m.
   Tankers: 250,000 d.w.t. *Fuel:* Available.
   Dry Docks: Capacity 21,000 tons displacement, draft 25 ft..
Salina Is., Italy: 38.35 N. 14.50 E. 24
Salinas, Ecuador: 2.10 S. 80.48 W. 72
Salinas, Netherlands Antilles, see Kralendijk.
Salinas, California, U.S.A.: 36.30 N. 121.40 W. 57
Salinas Bay, Costa Rica 69
Salineiro Offshore Terminal, see Areia Branca.
Salinopolis, Brazil: 0.41 S. 47.20 W. 72
Salipazari, see Istanbul.
Salisbury, Maryland, U.S.A.: 38.20 N. 75.38 W. 63
Salisbury Is., N.W.T., Canada: 63.30 N. 77.05 W. 59
Salomague, (Luzon Is.), Philippines: 17.48 N. 120.25 E. . . 47
   Max. Size: LOA 150 ft., draft 10 ft. *Airport:* 55 km.
Salomon Is., Chagos Arch. (U.K.): 5.24 S. 72.16 E. 30
Salonica, see Thessaloniki.
Salsaker, see Askja.
Salsbrucket, Norway: 64.48 N. 11.52 E. 15
Salt River, Jamaica: 17.50 N. 77.10 W. 69, 70
   Max. Size: Draft 30 ft. Tankers: See Rocky Point.
   Fuel: Can be arranged. *Airport:* Palisadoes, 50 miles.
Saltacaballo, see Castro-Urdiales.
Saltcoats, U.K.: 55.37 N. 4.47 W. 6
Saltdal, Norway: 67.06 N. 15.26 E. 15
Saltend, U.K.: 53.43 N. 0.15 W. 6
   Also see Hull.
Saltkallen, see Munkedal.
Salto, Uruguay: 31.23 S. 57.58 W. 77
Saltpond, Ghana: 5.05 N. 1.00 W. 28
   Max. Size: Depth 85 ft.
Saltsjobaden, see Stockholm.
Saltvik, Finland: 60.20 N. 20.25 E. 11
Salum, Egypt: 31.33 N. 25.11 E. 26
Salvador, Brazil: 13.01 S. 38.35 W. 72
   Max. Size: Access to the Port of Salvador: LOA 180 m., beam 30 m., draft 10 m. Tankers: 120,000 d.w.t., LOA 275 m., depth 13 m. – 22 m. *Fuel:* Available. *Airport:* Dois de Julio, 40 km.
   Also see Aratu.
Salwah, Qatar: 24.45 N. 50.51 E. 35
Sam Chuck, see Samcheog.
Samana, Dominican Republic: 19.12 N. 69.26 W. 69, 70
   Max. Size: LOA 700 ft., beam 120 ft., draft 34 ft.
   Fuel: By road tanker. *Airport:* Santo Domingo or Puerto Plata, 4-5 hours by car.
Samanco, Peru: 9.14 S. 78.29 W. 72
Samani, Japan: 42.05 N. 143.00 E. 43
Samar Is., Philippines 46, 47
Samarai, Papua New Guinea: 10.36 S. 150.39 E. 46, 49, 50, 51
   Max. Size: Depth at LAT 7.8 m. *Fuel:* Diesel available by pipeline. *Airport:* Alotau.
Samarang, see Semarang.

Samarinda, Indonesia: 0.30 S. 117.09 E. 38
Max. Size: 6,000 d.w.t., draft 6.0 m. (7.0 m. at HW). Coal loaded at anchorage. *Airport:* 6 km.
Sambas, Indonesia: 1.22 N. 109.17 E. 38, 39
Sambava, Madagascar: 14.15 S. 50.11 E. 30
Sambu, see Pulau Sambu.
Samcheog, South Korea: 37.30 N. 129.10 E. 42, 45
Max. Size: 5,000 d.w.t., depth 5.0 m. – 7.5 m.
Samcheon Po, South Korea: 34.52 N. 128.05 E. 42
Max. Size: 100,000 d.w.t., depth 18 m. *Fuel:* By barge from Busan. *Airport:* Nearest Busan.
Sami, Greece: 38.15 N. 20.39 E. 25
SAMOA 49
Samos, see Vathi.
Samos Is., Greece 25, 26
Samothraki Is., Greece 25, 26
Sampang, Indonesia: 7.11 S. 113.13 E. 38
Sampit, Indonesia: 3.06 S. 113.04 E. 38
Max. Size: Depth 4.5 m.
Samso Belt, Denmark 12
Samso Is., Denmark 10, 12
Samson Point, see Port Walcott.
Samsun, Turkey: 41.21 N. 36.34 E. 26
Max. Size: Depth 6 m. – 12 m.
Fuel: Available at 48 hours notice. *Airport:* 5 km.
San Andres Is., Colombia: 12.33 N. 81.43 W. 69
San Antioco Is., (Sardinia), Italy: 39.04 N. 8.30 E. . . . 24
San Antonio, Chile: 33.35 S. 71.37 W. 77
Max. Size: LOA 210 m., depth 35 ft. Tankers: Quay: Depth 36 ft. Buoys: Max. displacement 55,000 tons. *Fuel:* Marine diesel. *Airport:* Santiago, 1 hour by road.
San Antonio, Spain: 39.00 N. 1.20 E. 22
San Antonio Este, Argentina: 40.49 S. 64.54 W. 77
Max. Size: LOA 178 m., draft 26 ft.
Fuel: By truck from Bahia Blanca.
San Bartolome, Mexico: 27.41 N. 114.52 W. 57
San Benedetto, Italy: 42.57 N. 13.53 E. 24
San Benedicto Is., (Revilla Gigedo Is.), Mexico: 19.15 N. 110.48 W. 57
San Blas, Mexico: 21.32 N. 105.19 W. 57
San Bruno, California, U.S.A.: 37.37 N. 122.24 W. . . . 58
San Carlos, Equatorial Guinea: 3.28 N. 8.33 E. 29
San Carlos, Falkland Is. (U.K.): 51.30 S. 59.01 W. . . . 77
San Carlos, Mexico: 24.47 N. 112.08 W. 57
Max. Size: LOA 600 ft., beam 100 ft. and draft 30 ft.
Tankers: Depth 35 ft. *Fuel:* Moderate quantities of diesel oil. *Airport:* Nearest at La Paz.
San Carlos, Philippines, see Carlos.
San Carlos de la Rapita, see Sant Carles de la Rapita.
San Ciprian, Spain: 43.42 N. 7.27 W. 19, 20, 22
Max. Size: 62,000 d.w.t., draft 12.5 m. *Fuel:* Small quantities by road from Corunna.
San Clemente Is., California, U.S.A.: 32.50 N. 118.30 W. . 57
San Cristobal, Panama: 9.00 N. 80.50 W. 69
San Cristobal Is., (Galapagos Is.), Ecuador: 0.50 S. 89.30 W. . 69
San Cristobal Is., Solomon Islands 51
San Diego, California, U.S.A.: 32.42 N. 117.10 W. . . 55, 57
Max. Size: Draft 42 ft. Tankers: Draft 35 ft. *Fuel:* Diesel and bunker fuel. *Dry Docks:* Capacity 30,000 displacement tons. *Airport:* 5 miles.
San Esteban, Spain: 43.34 N. 6.05 W. 19, 20
San Felipe, Mexico: 31.00 N. 114.20 W. 57
San Feliu de Guixols, see Sant Feliu de Guixols.
San Felix, see Palua.
San Fernando, Argentina: 34.29 S. 58.30 W. 78
San Fernando, (Luzon Is.), Philippines: 16.37 N. 120.18 E. . 46, 47
Max. Size: Depth at quay 10 ft. – 54 ft. *Fuel:* Available. *Airport:* 3 km.
San Fernando, Spain: 36.28 N. 6.15 W. 20
San Fernando, Trinidad and Tobago: 10.18 N. 61.29 W. . 75
San Fernando de Apure, Venezuela: 7.55 N. 67.30 W. . . 75
San Filipe, (Fogo), Cape Verde: 14.56 N. 24.30 W. . . . 27
San Francisco, California, U.S.A.: 37.48 N. 122.25 W. . 55, 57, 58
Max. Size: Draft 40 ft. Tankers: Draft 35 ft. – 45 ft.
Fuel: Available. *Dry Docks:* 70,000 tons capacity. *Airport:* 10 miles.
San Isidro, (Leyte Is.), Philippines: 11.25 N. 124.20 E. . . 47
San Jorge Is., Azores (Portugal): 38.40 N. 28.05 W. . . . 20
San Jose, Guatemala: 13.55 N. 90.50 W. 69
Max. Size: Anchorage port (see Puerto Quetzal). *Airport:* Guatemala City, 108 km.
San Jose de Amacuro, Venezuela: 8.15 N. 60.30 W. . . . 75
San Jose de Buenavista, (Panay Is.), Philippines: 10.45 N. 121.56 E. 46
San Jose del Cabo, Mexico: 23.03 N. 109.41 W. 57
San Juan, Panama: 8.13 N. 81.47 W. 69
San Juan, Peru: 15.21 S. 75.10 W. 72

San Juan, Puerto Rico (U.S.A.): 18.28 N. 66.07 W. . . . 69, 70, 71
Max. Size: LOA 750 ft., depth 18 ft. – 35 ft. Tanker Berth: Depth 24 ft. *Fuel:* By barge. *Dry Docks:* Available. *Airport:* On outskirts of port area.
San Juan de la Costa, Mexico: 24.24 N. 110.40 W. . . . 57
Max. Size: Depth 32 ft.
San Juan del Norte, Nicaragua: 10.56 N. 83.43 W. . . . 69
San Juan del Sur, Nicaragua: 11.15 N. 85.53 W. 69
Max. Size: Anchorage: Depth 5 – 10 fathoms.
Airport: Managua, 2 hours by road.
San Julian, Argentina: 49.18 S. 67.43 W. 77
Max. Size: Depth 30 ft.
San Leandro, California, U.S.A.: 37.43 N. 122.13 W. . . 58
San Lorenzo, Argentina: 32.45 S. 60.38 W. 78
Max. Size: Up to 27 ft. draft. *Fuel:* Available.
San Lorenzo, Ecuador: 1.12 N. 78.51 W. 72
San Lorenzo, Honduras: 13.24 N. 87.22 W. 69
Max. Size: Draft 10 m. *Airport:* Tegucigalpa, 90 km.
San Lorenzo, Venezuela: 9.47 N. 71.05 W. 69, 74
Max. Size: LOA 665 ft., draft 34 ft. 6 in. *Fuel:* All grades.
San Lucas, Mexico: 22.52 N. 109.55 W. 57
San Luis, see Port San Luis.
San Marcos Is., Mexico: 27.12 N. 112.06 W. 57
San Martin, Argentina: 32.47 S. 60.43 W. 78
Max. Size: Depths up to 40 ft. alongside.
San Mateo, California, U.S.A.: 37.30 N. 122.23 W. . . 57, 58
San Miguel Is., (San Miguel Is.), Azores (Portugal):
37.43 N. 25.40 W. 20
San Nicolas, Argentina: 33.20 S. 60.13 W. 77, 78
Max. Size: Draft up to 24 ft. *Fuel:* By road tanker.
San Nicolas, Aruba (Netherlands): 12.26 N. 69.55 W. . . 69, 72, 74
Max. Size: Tankers: Reef Berths: Up to 550,000 d.w.t., LOA 1,400 ft., draft 95 ft. Inner Harbour: 50,000 d.w.t. – 90,000 d.w.t., LOA 740 ft. – 900 ft., beam 130 ft., draft 39 ft. – 41 ft. Dry cargo: LOA 650 ft., airdraft 95 ft., draft 31 ft.
Fuel: All grades.
San Nicolas, Peru: 15.14 S. 75.14 W. 72, 77
Max. Size: LOA 1,050 ft., beam 161 ft. – 174 ft. (depending on cargo), draft 57 ft. 5 in., airdraft 40 ft. 3 in. (12.26 m.).
San Nicolas Is., California, U.S.A.: 33.16 N. 119.30 W. . 57
San Nicolau Is., Cape Verde 27
San Pablo, Argentina: 54.20 S. 66.30 W. 77
San Pablo Bay, California, U.S.A. 58
San Pedrito, see Manzanillo.
San Pedro, Argentina: 33.42 S. 59.39 W. 77, 78
Max. Size: LOA 225 m., beam 32 m., draft over 30 ft.
San Pedro, Ivory Coast: 4.44 N. 6.38 W. 28
Max. Size: Draft 5.5 m. – 10.5 m., LOA 200 m.
Fuel: By road tanker. *Airport:* Daily flights to Abidjan.
San Pedro, California, U.S.A.: 33.55 N. 118.10 W. . . . 58
San Pedro, Venezuela: 7.00 N. 62.30 W. 75
San Pedro de Macoris, Dominican Republic:
18.26 N. 69.18 W. 70
Max. Size: LOA 600 ft., beam 100 ft., draft 24 ft.
Fuel: By road tanker. *Airport:* Santo Domingo, 30 km.
San Pietro Is., (Sardinia), Italy 24
San Quintin, Mexico: 30.23 N. 116.01 W. 57
San Rafael, California, U.S.A.: 37.58 N. 122.30 W. . . . 58
San Remo, Italy: 43.49 N. 7.47 E. 22, 23
San Roque, Spain: 36.13 N. 5.23 W. 23
San Salvador Is., Bahamas: 24.05 N. 74.25 W. 69, 70
San Salvador Is., (Galapagos Is.), Ecuador: 0.18 S. 90.45 W. . 69
San Sebastian, Argentina: 53.10 S. 68.30 W. 77
San Sebastian, Spain: 43.19 N. 1.58 W. 19, 22
San Sebastian Gomera I., Canary Is. (Spain):
28.05 N. 17.07 W. 27
San Tiago Is., Cape Verde 27
San Vasquez, Uruguay: 34.45 S. 56.25 W. 78
San Vicente, Chile: 36.44 S. 73.08 W. 77
Max. Size: Can berth ships greater than 200 m. LOA and 42 ft. draft. *Fuel:* Diesel. *Dry Docks:* ASMAR for large vessels. *Airport:* Internal flights only.
San Vicente, (Luzon Is.), Philippines: 18.31 N. 122.08 E. . . 47
Also see Aparri.
San Vicente Barquera, Spain: 43.24 N. 4.24 W. . . . 19, 20
San Vitale, see Ravenna.
Sanak Is., Alaska, U.S.A.: 54.29 N. 162.49 W. 54
Sanana, Indonesia: 2.03 S. 125.59 E. 46
Sanchez, Dominican Republic: 19.14 N. 69.36 W. . . . 70
Sand, Norway: 59.28 N. 6.15 E. 11
Sand Point, (Popof Is.), Alaska, U.S.A.: 55.20 N. 160.32 W. . 54
Sandakan, Sabah, Malaysia: 5.48 N. 118.05 E. 38, 47
Max. Size: 20,000 d.w.t. Draft restriction is 24 ft. on the Bar, plus the height of tide. (MHW about 6 ft.).
Depth alongside 6.1 m. – 11.0 m. Tankers: Depth 24 ft. – 31 ft.
Sandarne, Sweden: 61.16 N. 17.11 E. 15
Max. Size: Depth 7.2 m.
Also see Langror.
Sandaunhafen, see Hamburg.
Sanday, U.K.: 59.13 N. 2.28 W. 5, 15

Sandefjord, Norway: 59.07 N. 10.14 E. **8, 12**
  Max. Size: LOA 250 m., draft 8 m. – 12 m. *Airport:* Torp.
Sandhamn, Sweden: 59.17 N. 18.56 E. **11**
  Also see Stockholm.
Sandino, see Puerto Sandino.
Sandnes, Norway: 58.51 N. 5.45 E. **11**
Sandness, U.K.: 60.17 N. 1.38 W. **5**
Sandnessjoen, Norway: 66.03 N. 12.38 E. **10, 15**
Sando, Sweden, see Svano.
Sandoway, Myanmar: 18.31 N. 94.22 E. **37**
Sandoy, Faroe Is. (Denmark). **5**
Sandspit, B.C., Canada: 53.15 N. 131.49 W. **56**
Sandusky, Ohio, U.S.A.: 41.27 N. 82.43 W. **62**
Sandvig, Denmark: 55.30 N. 14.45 E. **11, 12**
Sandvik, (Seskaro Is.), Sweden: 65.44 N. 23.47 E. . . **15**
Sandviken, see Kramfors.
Sandwich, U.K.: 51.16 N. 1.21 E. **7**
Sandwich, Vanuatu, see Port Sandwich.
Sandwich Harbour, Massachusetts, U.S.A.:
  41.46 N. 70.29 W. **64**
Sandwich Oil Terminal, Massachusetts, U.S.A.:
  41.46 N. 70.31 W. **64**
  Max. Size: Draft 40 ft. (SW).
  Also see Cape Cod Canal.
Sandwick, U.K.: 60.00 N. 1.13 W. **5**
Sandy Hook, New Jersey, U.S.A.: 40.28 N. 74.00 W. . . **63**
Sangatta, Indonesia: 0.22 N. 117.34 E. **38**
  Max. Size: LOA 220 m., depth 21 m., 36,500 d.w.t.
  Airport: Samarinda.
Sangi, (Cebu Is.), Philippines: 10.23 N. 123.39 E. . . **47**
  Max. Size: 50,000 d.w.t., depth 16 m. (LW). *Fuel:* By
  road tanker. *Airport:* Cebu.
Sangi Is., Indonesia **46**
Sangkapura, Indonesia: 5.51 S. 112.41 E. **38**
Sangkulirang, Indonesia: 0.59 N. 117.58 E. **38**
Sanilac, see Port Sanilac.
Sanlucar de Barameda, Spain: 36.46 N. 6.21 W. **20, 22, 27**
Sans Souci, see Santo Domingo.
Sant Antioco, (Sardinia), Italy: 39.02 N. 8.26 E. **24**
  Max. Size: Anchorage. *Airport:* Cagliari, 85 km.
Sant Carles de la Rapita, Spain: 40.36 N. 0.36 E. . . **22**
  Max. Size: Draft 17 ft. *Fuel:* Available at 24 hours notice.
  Airport: Reus, 90 km.
Sant Feliu de Guixols, Spain: 41.46 N. 3.01 E. **22**
  Max. Size: Draft for berthing 22 ft. and up to LOA 115 m.
  Fuel: Can be supplied in small quantities.
Sant Martaan, Netherlands Antilles **71**
Santa Antonia, Sao Tome and Principe: 1.30 N. 7.45 E. . . **28**
Santa Barbara, Chile, see Huasco.
Santa Barbara, California, U.S.A.: 34.26 N. 119.40 W. . . **57**
Santa Catalina Is., California, U.S.A.: 33.24 N. 118.30 W. . . **58**
Santa Clara, California, U.S.A.: 37.20 N. 122.00 W. . . **57**
Santa Cruz, Argentina, see Punta Quilla.
Santa Cruz, (Flores Is.), Azores (Portugal): 39.27 N. 31.08 W. . . **20**
Santa Cruz, (Graciosa Is.), Azores (Portugal):
  39.00 N. 28.00 W. **20**
Santa Cruz, (Palma), Canary Is. (Spain): 28.40 N. 17.45 W. . . **27**
Santa Cruz, (Marinduque Is.), Philippines: 13.30 N. 122.04 E. . **46, 47**
Santa Cruz, California, U.S.A.: 36.58 N. 122.03 W. . . **57**
Santa Cruz de Tenerife, Canary Is. (Spain):
  28.28 N. 16.14 W. **27**
  Max. Size: Honduras Buoy: Up to 240,000 d.w.t.
  Dique del Este: 300 m. LOA limitation, draft up to 60 ft.
  Fuel: All grades. *Dry Docks:* Lifting capacity 6,000 tons.
  Airport: Reina Sofia, 65 km.
Santa Cruz del Sur, Cuba: 20.42 N. 77.59 W. **70**
Santa Cruz Is., (Galapagos Is.), Ecuador: 0.40 S. 90.25 W. . . **69**
Santa Cruz Is., Solomon Islands. **49**
Santa Cruz Is., California, U.S.A.: 34.00 N. 119.45 W. . . **57**
Santa Elena Bay, see La Libertad.
Santa Eugenia de Ribeira, Spain: 42.33 N. 8.59 W. . . **20**
Santa Fe, Argentina: 31.40 S. 60.37 W. **77, 78**
  Max. Size: Depths to 26 ft. *Fuel:* By road tanker. *Airport:* 17 km.
Santa Iria, see Lisbon.
Santa Isabel, see Malabo.
Santa Liberta, Italy: 42.25 N. 11.09 E. **24**
Santa Lucia, Cuba: 22.39 N. 83.59 W. **70**
  Max. Size: No draft limit at anchorage.
  Also see Mariel.
Santa Lucia Is., Cape Verde: 16.48 N. 24.46 W. **27**
Santa Lucia Oriente, see Vita.
Santa Margharita Ligure, Italy: 44.20 N. 9.13 E. . . . **23, 24**
Santa Maria, (Sal Is.), Cape Verde: 16.35 N. 22.54 W. . . **27**
Santa Maria, Cuba: 21.17 N. 78.31 W. **70**
  Also see Jucaro.
Santa Maria, Spain, see Puerto de Santa Maria.
Santa Maria Is., Azores (Portugal) **20, 27**

Santa Marta, Colombia: 11.15 N. 74.14 W. **69, 72**
  Max. Size: LOA 730 ft., 40 ft. draft. Puerto Prodeco: Depth 18 m.
  Tankers: See Pozos Colorados. *Fuel:* By road tanker.
  Airport: 19 miles.
Santa Panagia, Italy: 37.07 N. 15.16 E. **24**
  Max. Size: 600,000 d.w.t., LOA 1,200 ft., draft 78 ft.
  Also see Augusta.
Santa Rosa Is., California, U.S.A.: 34.00 N. 120.15 W. . . **57**
Santa Rosalia, Mexico: 27.20 N. 112.17 W. **57**
Santan Terminal, Indonesia: 0.06 S. 117.32 E. **38**
  Max. Size: 125,000 d.w.t. Calling for full cargo;
  minimum 35,000 d.w.t., LOA 275 m., depth 28 m.
  LPG: 4,100 tonnes, draft 7.5 m., LOA 60 m. – 110 m.
Santana, Brazil: 0.03 S. 51.11 W. **72**
  Max. Size: Along floating ore pier: Depth ranges from
  35 ft. – 90 ft. (at LW). *Airport:* Macapa, 25 km.
Santander, Spain: 43.28 N. 3.49 W. **19, 20, 21, 22**
  Max. Size: Max. advisable draft to enter port is 35 ft.
  Tankers: Depth 11.6 m. – 12.5 m. *Fuel:* Ordinary fuel, diesel
  and gas oil are available. *Dry Docks:* 722 ft. x 105 ft. x 38 ft.
  Airport: 4 miles.
Santarem, Brazil: 2.25 S. 54.43 W. **72**
  Max. Size: Draft 10 m. *Fuel:* Available.
Santiago de Cuba, Cuba: 19.50 N. 75.52 W. **69, 70**
  Max. Size: LOA 702 ft., draft 36 ft. *Fuel:* Fuel oil and diesel.
Santo, Vanuatu: 15.31 S. 167.11 E. **49**
  Max. Size: Depth 10.5 m. (LWS). *Fuel:* Available.
  Airport: 6 km.
Santo Antao Is., Cape Verde: 17.04 N. 25.12 W. **27**
Santo Antonio, Sao Tome and Principe: 1.39 N. 7.26 E. . . **29**
Santo Domingo, Dominican Republic: 18.28 N. 69.53 W. . . **70**
  Max. Size: LOA 610 ft., beam 100 ft., draft 29 ft.
  Tankers: Draft 29 ft. *Fuel:* Fuel and diesel oil.
  Dry Docks: Vessels up to LOA 400 ft., beam 50 ft., draft 20 ft.
  Airport: 18 miles.
Santo Stefano, see Porto Santo Stefano.
Santo Tomas de Castilla, Guatemala: 15.42 N. 88.37 W. . . **69**
  Max. Size: LOA 750 ft., draft 27 ft. – 30 ft. *Fuel:* Available.
  Airport: Puerto Barrios, 8 km.
Santona, Spain: 43.26 N. 3.27 W. **19**
Santorini, see Thira.
Santos, Brazil: 23.56 S. 46.19 W. **76, 77**
  Max. Size: Draft 34 ft. – 38 ft. Containers: Draft 11.2 m. – 12 m.
  Fuel: Available. *Dry Docks:* Vessels of 65 m. LOA, 12 m. beam
  and max. drafts of 4.20 m. aft and 3.90 m. forward. *Airport:* Sao
  Paulo, 60 km.
Santuao, China: 26.37 N. 119.40 E. **42**
Santurce, see Portugaleta.
Sanya, China: 18.14 N. 109.30 E. **39**
  Max. Size: Anchorage: Depth 10 m. – 16 m., 50,000 d.w.t.
Sao Francisco do Sul, Brazil: 26.10 S. 48.34 W. . . . **76, 77**
  Max. Size: Depths alongside 7 m. – 10 m. Tankers: 18 m. draft,
  200,000 d.w.t. *Fuel:* Available by truck from Itajai.
  Airport: Joinville, 40 km.
Sao Luis, Brazil: 2.30 S. 44.07 W. **72**
  Max. Size: Anchorage: Draft 18 ft. – 21 ft.
  Fuel: Fuel oil available. *Airport:* 13 km.
Sao Paulo, Brazil: 4.15 S. 68.10 W. **72**
Sao Sebastiao, Brazil: 23.48 S. 45.24 W. **76, 77**
  Max. Size: Depth 8.2 m. Tankers: Up to 300,000 d.w.t., with draft
  of 23 m. (75 ft. 05 in.). *Fuel:* All grades. *Airport:* Sao Paulo.
Sao Tome, Sao Tome and Principe: 0.21 N. 6.44 E. . . . **28, 29**
  Max. Size: Anchorage. *Airport:* 3.5 miles. Flights to Africa and
  Lisbon.
SAO TOME AND PRINCIPE **28, 29**
Sapangar Bay, see Kota Kinabalu.
Sapele, Nigeria: 5.55 N. 5.42 E. **28, 29**
  Max. Size: LOA 170 m., draft 6.4 m. at Escravos Bar.
  Fuel: Available from Warri. *Airport:* Benin or Warri.
Sapri, Italy: 40.03 N. 15.37 E. **24**
Sarajevo, Bosnia: 43.52 N. 18.26 E. **9**
Sarande, Albania: 39.52 N. 20.02 E. **24, 25**
  Max. Size: Anchorage port.
Sarasota, Florida, U.S.A.: 27.19 N. 82.29 W. **66, 69**
Sarawak, Malaysia **38, 39**
Sardinia, Italy **21, 24**
Saria Is., Greece: 35.52 N. 27.16 E. **25**
Sarikei, Sarawak, Malaysia: 2.08 N. 111.32 E. **39**
  Max. Size: Depth 7.6 m.
  Also see Sibu.
Sariyer, Turkey: 41.11 N. 29.04 E. **23**
Sark, (Channel Is.), U.K.: 49.25 N. 2.20 W. **7, 19**
Sarkoy, Turkey: 40.37 N. 27.08 E. **25, 26**
Sarnate, Latvia: 57.06 N. 21.29 E. **11**
Sarnia, Ontario, Canada: 42.59 N. 82.25 W. **62**
  Max. Size: LOA 730 ft., beam 75 ft. 6 in., draft 25 ft. 6 in.
  Fuel: All grades.
Saro, Sweden: 57.30 N. 11.53 E. **11, 12**
Sarpsborg, Norway: 59.17 N. 11.07 E. **8, 11, 12**
  Max. Size: Draft 24 ft. *Fuel:* By road tanker.
  Dry Docks: 3,100 d.w.t. *Airport:* Oslo, 110 km.

Sarroch, (Sardinia), Italy: 39.05 N. 9.01 E. 24
  Max. Size: Tankers: Draft 68 ft., 380,000 d.w.t.
  Also see Cagliari.
Sas van Gent, Netherlands: 51.14 N. 3.50 E. 8
  Max. Size: Draft 7.5 m.
  Also see Terneuzen.
Sasa, see Davao.
Sasebo, Japan: 33.06 N. 129.43 E. 42, 45
  Max. Size: General Cargo: Depths to 36 ft.
  Tanker: Depths to 45 ft. *Fuel:* Lightered from other ports.
  Dry Docks: Largest 300,000 d.w.t. *Airport:* Nagasaki, 70 km.
Sassandra, Ivory Coast: 4.56 N. 6.07 W. 28
Sassari, see Porto Torres.
Sassnitz, Germany: 54.30 N. 13.40 E. 12
Sasuna, Japan: 34.38 N. 129.24 E. 42, 45
Satawal, (Caroline Is.), Micronesia: 7.21 N. 147.02 E. . . . 46
Satawan, see Nomoi Is..
Sattahip, Thailand: 12.35 N. 100.55 E. 37, 39
  Max. Size: Chuk Samet: Draft 30 ft. (LWOST), LOA 600 ft.
  Tungprong: Anchorage: Depth 60 ft.
  Sattahip: LOA 180 m., draft 9.0 m. Map Pier: Depth 38.8 ft.
  POL Jetty: 50,000 d.w.t., LOA 820 ft., draft 30 ft.
  Fuel: Available.
Sauce, see Puerto Sauce.
Sauda, Norway: 59.40 N. 6.22 E. 10, 11
  Max. Size: Draft 30 ft. *Airport:* Stavanger and Haugesund.
SAUDI ARABIA 21, 26, 31, 32, 35
Saugatuck, Michigan, U.S.A.: 42.40 N. 86.12 W. 62
Saulkrasti, Latvia: 57.15 N. 24.30 E. 11
Sault Ste. Marie, Ontario, Canada: 46.28 N. 84.22 W. . . . 62
  Max. Size: Depth alongside 21 ft. 6 in. – 26 ft. 3 in. *Fuel:* Diesel.
Sault Ste. Marie, Michigan, U.S.A.: 46.27 N. 84.22 W. . . . 62
  Also see Sault Ste. Marie.
Saumlaki, Indonesia: 7.58 S. 131.19 E. 46
Saunders, see Port Saunders.
Saundersfoot, U.K.: 51.43 N. 4.42 W. 6
Saunsilta, see Uusikaupunki.
Savaii Is., Samoa: 13.30 S. 172.30 W. 49
Savanna la Mar, Jamaica: 18.12 N. 78.09 W. 69, 70
  Max. Size: Draft 19 ft. *Fuel:* Available.
  Airport: Montego Bay, 32 miles.
Savannah, Georgia, U.S.A.: 32.02 N. 81.07 W. 55, 66
  Max. Size: Depth 36 ft. – 42 ft. Draft 31 ft. at any time.
  Tankers: Draft 32 ft. – 38 ft. *Fuel:* Most grades.
  Dry Docks: 540 ft. x 72 ft. x 21 ft. *Airport:* 5 miles.
Savigsssvik, Greenland (Denmark): 76.01 N. 64.52 W. . . . 17
Savona, Italy: 44.18 N. 8.29 E. 9, 21, 23, 24
  Max. Size: Depths up to 51 ft. Savona Silos: Depth 23 ft. – 36 ft.
  Tankers: See Vado Ligure. *Fuel:* All grades. *Airport:* Genoa, 40 km.
Savonetta, see Point Lisas.
Savonlinna, Finland: 61.52 N. 28.53 E. 13
  Also see Saimaa Canal.
Savoonga, Alaska, U.S.A.: 63.47 N. 170.35 W. 54
Savu Savu, Fiji: 16.47 S. 179.21 E. 49
Savu Sea, Indonesia 46
Sawakin, Sudan: 19.07 N. 37.20 E. 32
  Max. Size: Draft 12.2 m.
Sawqirah, Oman: 18.05 N. 56.35 E. 31, 37
Sawu, Indonesia 50
Sayhut, Yemen: 15.10 N. 51.12 E. 31
Sayreville, New Jersey, U.S.A.: 40.28 N. 74.22 W. 63
Scalasaig, U.K.: 56.04 N. 6.12 W. 5
Scalea, Italy: 39.50 N. 15.45 E. 24
Scalloway, U.K.: 60.08 N. 1.16 W. 5
  Max. Size: LOA 90 m., draft 6.5 m. *Fuel:* Marine gas oil.
  Airport: Sumburgh, 25 miles.
Scapa Flow, (Orkney Is.), U.K.: 58.53 N. 3.05 W. 5
Scarborough, (Tobago), Trinidad and Tobago:
  11.11 N. 60.44 W. 69, 71, 75
Scarborough, U.K.: 54.17 N. 0.23 W. 5
Scarinish, U.K.: 56.29 N. 6.48 W. 5
Scarpanto, see Karpathos Is..
Scheerhafen, see Kiel.
Schestedt, Germany: 54.22 N. 9.49 E. 14
Scheveningen, Netherlands: 52.06 N. 4.16 E. 7, 8, 9
  Max. Size: LOA 160 m., draft 7.2 m. minus 10% U.K.C.
  Fuel: Available. *Airport:* Amsterdam, 58 km. Rotterdam, 16 km.
Schiedam, Netherlands: 51.54 N. 4.25 E. 7, 8
  Max. Size: Draft 24 ft. Private: LOA 305 m., draft 33 ft.
  Fuel: Available. *Dry Docks:* Largest: 160,000 tons capacity.
  Airport: Rotterdam, 6.4 km.
Schirnau, Germany: 54.21 N. 9.45 E. 14
  Also see Kiel.
Schleswig, Germany: 54.31 N. 9.34 E. 12, 14
Schouten Is., Indonesia 46
Schreiber, Ontario, Canada: 48.45 N. 87.20 W. 62
Schulau, Germany: 53.34 N. 9.42 E. 8, 14
Sciacca, (Sicily), Italy: 37.30 N. 13.05 E. 24
Scilla, Italy: 38.05 N. 15.50 E. 24

Scilly Is., U.K. 19
Scituate, Massachusetts, U.S.A.: 42.12 N. 70.43 W. 63
Scoresbysund, Greenland (Denmark): 70.25 N. 21.55 W. . . 17
Scotland, U.K. 4, 5
Scrabster, U.K.: 58.37 N. 3.33 W. 5
  Max. Size: LOA 90 m., draft 6.0 m. *Fuel:* Available.
  Airport: Wick, 32 km.
Seaforth, see Liverpool.
Seaham, U.K.: 54.50 N. 1.19 W. 6
  Max. Size: Largest vessel: LOA 120 m., beam 16.5 m.
  Fuel: Available. *Airport:* Newcastle, 32 km.
Seahorse Point, N.W.T., Canada: 63.48 N. 80.09 W. 59
Seal Cove, (Grand Manan Is.), N.B., Canada:
  44.36 N. 66.52 W. 60
Seal Sands, U.K.: 54.37 N. 1.11 W. 6
Searsport, Maine, U.S.A.: 44.28 N. 68.56 W. 55, 60
  Max. Size: Draft 38 ft. Tankers: Depth 34 ft. (LW).
  Fuel: No. 6 oil at dock. Light oils by tank truck.
  Airport: Bangor, 30 miles.
Seas:
  Sea of Azov 21, 26
  Sea of Crete, Greece 25, 26
  Sea of Japan 42, 43, 45
  Sea of Marmara, Turkey 23, 25, 26
  Sea of Okhotsk, Russia 36, 43
  Sea of Pechorskaya, Russia 16
Seattle, Washington, U.S.A.: 47.36 N. 122.20 W. 55, 56
  Max. Size: Depths alongside 10.6 m. – 21 m. (MLLW).
  Airdraft – 155 ft. *Fuel:* Available. *Dry Docks:* Up to
  20,000 tons. *Airport:* Sea-Tac International.
Seba, Indonesia: 10.29 S. 121.51 E. 38, 46, 50
Sebarok, see Singapore.
Sebuku, Indonesia: 3.42 S. 116.24 E. 38
  Max. Size: Anchorage – Depth 15 m.
Secretary Is., (South Is.), New Zealand: 45.15 S. 166.56 E. . 52
Seddon Island, see Tampa.
Segond, see Santo.
Seguam Is., (Aleutian Is.), Alaska, U.S.A. 54
Seguntur, Indonesia: 2.00 N. 117.52 E. 38
Sejero Is., Denmark: 55.55 N. 11.10 E. 12
Sejingkat, Sarawak, Malaysia: 1.35 N. 110.26 E. 38, 39
  Max. Size: Vessels up to 580 ft. LOA and 25 ft. draft
  regularly use anchorage.
Sekiu, Washington, U.S.A.: 48.17 N. 124.19 W. 56
Sekondi, see Takoradi.
Sekupang, Indonesia: 1.07 N. 103.55 E. 39, 40, 41
  Max. Size: Depth 12 m.
Selat Lalang, see Lalang Marine Terminal.
Selawik, Alaska, U.S.A.: 66.30 N. 160.09 W. 54
Selby, U.K.: 53.47 N. 1.04 W. 6, 7
Seldovia, Alaska, U.S.A.: 59.25 N. 151.45 W. 54
Seletar, see Singapore.
Selfs Point, see Hobart.
Selimye, Turkey: 36.40 N. 31.50 E. 26
Selvegen Is., (Portugal): 30.10 N. 15.55 W. 27
Selvik, see Svelvik.
Semangka Bay, see Teluk Semangka.
Semarang, Indonesia: 7.01 S. 110.27 E. 38
  Max. Size: Depth 9 m. Tankers (SBM): Draft 9 m.
  Fuel: Only for coasters (Fuel oil and diesel). *Airport:* 5 miles.
Sembawang, see Singapore.
Seme Terminal, Benin: 6.18 N. 2.39 E. 29
  Max. Size: Draft 14.0 m., 120,000 d.w.t. (Part load), depth 18 m.
Semisopochnoi, (Aleutian Is.), Alaska, U.S.A.:
  51.58 N. 179.40 E. 54
Semporna, Sabah, Malaysia: 4.29 N. 118.37 E. 38, 47
  Max. Size: Depth alongside 7.9 m.
  Also see Kudat.
Senboku, see Sakai.
Senbong, see Sonbong.
Sendai, Japan: 38.13 N. 141.06 E. 43
  Max. Size: Draft 11.5 m. Tankers: Draft 15.45 m.
  Fuel: Available. *Airport:* Sendai, 50 minutes by car.
SENEGAL 27
Senigallia, Italy: 43.42 N. 13.12 E. 24
Senipah Terminal, Indonesia: 1.03 S. 117.13 E. 38
  Max. Size: Up to 150,000 d.w.t. at SBM, loading 125,000 tons
  cargo (Minimum 33,000 d.w.t.). LOA: Minimum 195 m.,
  maximum 275 m. Depth 28 m. *Airport:* Senipah.
Senj, Croatia: 44.59 N. 14.53 E. 24
Senja Is., Norway 10, 15
Sentosa, see Singapore.
Senyavin Is., Micronesia: 7.01 N. 158.12 E. 49
Senzaki, Japan: 34.24 N. 131.11 E. 45
Sepasu, Indonesia: 1.00 N. 117.50 E. 38
Sepen, see Rijeka.
Sepetiba Bay, (Guaiba Is.), Brazil: 22.56 S. 43.50 W. . . . 76, 77
  Max. Size: Ore: Draft 22 m. Coal: Depth 15 m., 90,000 d.w.t.
Sepetiba Terminal, see Sepetiba Bay.
Sepinggan, see Lawi Lawi.

Sept Iles, Quebec, Canada: 50.12 N. 66.23 W. 60
  Max. Size: Iron ore – loading: LOA 1,600 ft., beam 175 m.,
  draft 57 ft. Tankers: LOA 775 ft., draft 40 ft. *Fuel:* Available.
  Airport: 12 km.
Seram Is., Indonesia 46
Serasan Is., see Royalist Haven.
Seria, Brunei: 4.43 N. 114.19 E. 38, 39
  Max. Size: SBM 1: 320,000 d.w.t., draft 17.4 m.
  Airport: Bandar Seri Begawan, 1.5 hours by car.
Serifos Is., Greece 25, 26
Sermata Is., Indonesia: 8.11 S. 128.50 E. 46
Serrana Bank, Colombia: 14.25 N. 80.20 W. 69, 70
Serui, Indonesia: 1.54 S. 136.15 E. 46
Sestao, see Portugaleta.
Sestoretsk, Russia: 60.10 N. 30.00 E. 11
Sestri, Italy: 44.16 N. 9.23 E. 23, 24
Sete, France: 43.24 N. 3.42 E. 9, 21, 22
  Max. Size: Commercial Port: Draft 11 m. Ore: LOA 259 m.,
  draft 13.18 m. Tankers: CBM: 100,000 d.w.t., draft 13.1 m.
  Basin: 40,000 d.w.t., LOA 225 m., draft 11 m. *Fuel:* All qualities
  available. *Airport:* Montpellier, 30 km.
Setubal, Portugal: 38.30 N. 8.55 W. 20, 22
  Max. Size: Draft 31.5 ft. *Fuel:* Available.
  Dry Docks: Up to 700,000 d.w.t. *Airport:* Lisbon, 50 km.
Sevastopol, Ukraine: 44.37 N. 33.32 E. 21, 26
  Max. Size: Passenger Ships: Length 200 m., draft 9.1 m.
  Cargo Ships: Length 185 m., draft 8.6 m. Tankers: LOA 185 m.,
  draft 9.1 m. *Fuel:* Available. *Dry Docks:* Max. LOA 280 m.
  Airport: Simpheropol (55 miles).
Seven Islands, see Sept Iles.
Severn, Ontario, Canada, see Waubaushene.
Severnaya Zemlya, Russia: 80.00 N. 95.00 E. 79
Severodvinsk, Russia: 64.34 N. 39.47 E. 16
Severomorsk, Russia: 69.05 N. 33.27 E. 16
Seville, Spain: 37.25 N. 6.00 W. 20, 21, 22, 27
  Max. Size: Beam 24.2 m., draft 23 ft. (Lock: Length 200 m.,
  width 5 m.) *Fuel:* All grades. *Dry Docks:* Length 149 m.,
  breadth 25 m. *Airport:* 12 km., connects with Madrid.
Seward, Alaska, U.S.A.: 60.07 N. 149.26 W. 54
  Max. Size: Depth 35 ft. (MLLW). *Fuel:* Marine Gas oil and diesel
  fuel (Summer only) from pipeline. *Airport:* 1 mile, charter
  service.
SEYCHELLES 30
Seydhisfjord, Iceland: 65.15 N. 14.00 W. 17
Sfaktiria, see Pylos.
Sfax, Tunisia: 34.43 N. 10.46 E. 24
  Max. Size: LOA 185 m. – 200 m., beam 26 m., draft 10.5 m.
  Fuel: Available. *Airport:* 10 km.
Sha Lun, see Keelung.
Shadwan Is., Egypt: 27.30 N. 34.00 E. 32
Shahid Rejaie, Iran: 27.04 N. 56.06 E. 35
  Also see Bandar Abbas.
Shaibara Is., Saudi Arabia: 25.25 N. 36.49 E. 32
Shakhtersk, Russia: 49.10 N. 142.02 E. 43
Shakir Is., see Shadwan Is..
Shaktolik, Alaska, U.S.A.: 64.10 N. 161.00 W. 54
Shallufa, Egypt: 30.05 N. 32.35 E. 33
Shalung, see Keelung.
Shanghai, China: 31.14 N. 121.28 E. 42, 46
  Max. Size: Draft 9.5 m. (F.W.). *Fuel:* Available. *Airport:* 30 km.
Shanhaiguan, see Qinhuangdao.
Shannon Airport Jetty, Ireland: 52.41 N. 8.55 W. 5
  Max. Size: 6,500 tonnes d.w.t., LOA 107 m., draft 7.0 m.
Shannon Estuary, Ireland: 52.36 N. 9.05 W. 5, 8
  Also see Aughinish Island Marine Terminal, Money Point, Foynes
  Harbour, Foynes Island, Tarbert Island Oil Terminal and Shannon
  Airport Jetty.
Shannon Is., Greenland (Denmark): 75.00 N. 18.00 W. . . 17
Shantou, China: 23.21 N. 116.40 E. 42
  Max. Size: Draft 6.0 m. in channel, 16,000 d.w.t.
Shanwei, China: 22.47 N. 115.22 E. 42
Shapinsay Is., (Orkney Is.), U.K.: 59.03 N. 2.55 W. 5
Sharak, Iran: 26.44 N. 54.11 E. 35
Sharjah, U.A.E.: 25.22 N. 55.24 E. 31, 35, 37
  Max. Size: Draft 11.5 m. Tankers: Draft 9.5 m. *Fuel:* Fuel oil,
  gas oil or blends. *Airport:* Sharjah, 15 km.
Shark Bay, see Carnarvon.
Sharm el Sheikh, Egypt: 27.53 N. 34.15 E. 32
Sharma, see Al Wajh.
Sharpness, U.K.: 51.43 N. 2.29 W. 6, 7
  Max. Size: Beam 55 ft. (16.76 m.), draft 21 ft. 6 in. (6.55 m.). Also
  see Gloucester and Sharpness Canal. *Fuel:* Most grades.
  Dry Docks: 360 ft. x 47 ft. x 14 ft. over blocks. *Airport:* London
  or Birmingham within 2 hours.
Shatt al Arab, Iraq/Iran 35
Sheboygan, Wisconsin, U.S.A.: 43.45 N. 87.42 W. 62
Shediac, N.B., Canada: 45.13 N. 61.32 W. 60
Sheerness, U.K.: 51.27 N. 0.43 E. 5, 6, 7
  Max. Size: LOA 230 m., draft 11.0 m. *Fuel:* Available.
  Also see Medway Ports.

Sheet Harbour, N.S., Canada: 44.50 N. 62.30 W. 60
  Max. Size: Depth 6.4 m. *Fuel:* Available. *Airport:*
  Halifax, 75 miles.
Sheikh Shuaib, see Lavan Island.
Shekou, see Chiwan.
Shelburne, N.S., Canada: 43.45 N. 65.19 W. 60
Sheldons Point, Alaska, U.S.A.: 62.15 N. 165.00 W. 54
Shelikhova Gulf, Russia 54
Shelikof Strait, Alaska, U.S.A. 54
Shell Harbour, see Port Kembla.
Shellhaven, see Coryton.
Shelton, Washington, U.S.A.: 47.13 N. 123.06 W. 56
Shen Ao, see Keelung.
Shenao, see Keelung.
Shengjin, Albania: 41.49 N. 19.35 E. 9, 24, 25
  Max. Size: Draft 18 ft.
Shenjiamen, China: 30.00 N. 122.18 E. 42
Shenzhen, China: 22.31 N. 114.08 E. 48
Shepstone, see Port Shepstone.
Sherbro, Sierra Leone: 7.32 N. 12.30 W. 27
  Max. Size: Draft 7.31 m. at anchorage.
Sherbro Is., Sierra Leone: 7.32 N. 12.30 W. 27
Sherbrooke, N.S., Canada: 45.08 N. 61.59 W. 60
Sherm Rabegh, see Rabigh.
Sheskharis, see Novorossiysk.
Shetland Islands, U.K. 4, 5
Shiashkotan Is., (Kurile Is.), Russia 43
Shibushi, Japan: 31.28 N. 131.07 E. 45
  Max. Size: LOA 240 m., draft 11.5 m. Tankers: Draft 21 m.
  (crude). *Airport:* Kagoshima.
Shibushi Bay, (Kyushu), Japan 45
Shidao, China: 36.53 N. 122.25 E. 42
  Max. Size: 5,000 d.w.t., depth 6.4 m. *Fuel:* Available.
Shido, Japan: 34.18 N. 134.10 E. 45
Shih Pu, China: 29.13 N. 121.57 E. 42
Shihr, Yemen: 14.45 N. 49.36 E. 31
Shijiu, see Rizhao.
Shijiusuo, see Rizhao.
Shika, Japan: 24.30 N. 124.00 E. 42
Shikama, Japan: 34.45 N. 134.39 E. 45
  Max. Size: Draft 10 m.
  Also see Himeji.
Shikoku, Japan 43, 45
Shikotan Is., (Kurile Is.), Russia 43
Shimabara, Japan: 32.47 N. 130.21 E. 45
Shimanzi, see Mombasa.
Shiminato, Japan: 34.10 N. 132.15 E. 45
Shimizu, (Honshu), Japan: 35.00 N. 138.30 E. 43, 45, 46
  Max. Size: Dry-cargo: Draft 12 m. Tankers: Draft 20 m.,
  250,000 d.w.t. *Fuel:* All grades. *Dry Docks:*
  Largest: 122 m. x 18.5 m. Capacity 5,700 tons. *Airport:* 263 km.
  to Narita (Tokyo).
Shimizu, (Shikoku), Japan: 32.46 N. 132.57 E. 45
Shimoda, Japan: 34.40 N. 138.57 E. 45
Shimogo, Japan: 34.03 N. 131.20 E. 45
Shimoni, Kenya: 4.37 S. 39.20 E. 30
Shimonoseki, Japan: 33.57 N. 130.58 E. 44, 45
  Max. Size: LOA 200 m., depth 10 m. Tankers: LOA 245 m., draft
  14 m. 95,000 d.w.t. *Fuel:* All grades lightered from
  nearest bunker stock ports. *Dry Docks:* Largest vessel
  size: 160 m. x 22.5 m. x 5.5 m. *Airport:* Fukuoka or Kitakyushu.
Shimotsu, Japan: 34.06 N. 135.08 E. 45
  Max. Size: Tankers: Up to 18.8 m. draft, LOA 349 m., 260,000
  d.w.t. Sea Berth: 259,999 d.w.t., draft 21 m.
  Fuel: Most grades. *Dry Docks:* At Yura. *Airport:* New Kansai.
Shinagawa, see Tokyo.
Shinas, Oman: 24.45 N. 56.29 E. 35
Shingu, Japan: 33.41 N. 135.59 E. 43, 45
  Max. Size: LOA 185 m., draft 9.6 m. *Fuel:* From Shimotsu
  or Yokkaichi. *Airport:* 200 km.
Shiogama, Japan: 38.20 N. 141.03 E. 43
  Max. Size: LOA 160 m., draft 8.5 m. *Fuel:* Bonded oil will be
  brought from Yokohama or Sendai.
Ship Harbour, N.S., Canada: 44.49 N. 62.53 W. 60
  Max. Size: HWOST 2.2 m. above CD. Wharf unusable. *Airport:*
  Halifax, 120 km.
Ship Is., Mississippi, U.S.A.: 30.14 N. 88.57 W. 67
Shippegan Harbour, N.B., Canada: 47.45 N. 64.42 W. . . . 60
  Max. Size: Depth 25 ft. *Airport:* Chatham, 70 miles.
  Also see Caraquet.
Shishimi, Japan: 34.32 N. 129.20 E. 45
Shishmaref, Alaska, U.S.A.: 66.15 N. 166.05 W. 54
Shizuki, Japan: 34.30 N. 134.58 E. 45
Shodoshima, see Tonosho Is..
Shokalski Is., Russia: 73.00 N. 74.10 E. 16
Shoreham, U.K.: 50.50 N. 0.15 W. 7
  Max. Size: LOA 105.9 m., beam 16.4 m., draft 6.7 m., subject
  tide. East Arm: LOA 120 m., beam 20 m., draft 6.7 m.
  West arm: LOA 82.3 m., beam 14.3 m., draft 5.5 m. (tidal).
  Fuel: By road tanker. *Airport:* Gatwick, 48 km.

Shortland Harbour, Solomon Islands: 7.04 S. 155.52 E. 49
  Port not operational. Operations moved to Malloco Bay
Shotton, see Flint.
Shoyna, Russia: 67.55 N. 44.15 E. 16
Shuaiba, Kuwait: 29.02 N. 48.10 E. 31, 35
  Max. Size: Draft up to 13 m. Tankers: Up to 13.71 m. draft.
  Fuel: Marine fuel and diesel oil. *Airport:* 35 km.
Shubertovo, Russia: 56.03 N. 161.58 E. 54
Shuidong, China: 21.28 N. 111.07 E. 39
  Max. Size: 20,000 d.w.t., depth 11 m. Tankers: 250,000 d.w.t.
  or max. draft 19.2 m. *Fuel:* Available.
Shumagin Is., Alaska, U.S.A. 54
Shuwaikh, Kuwait: 29.21 N. 47.56 E. 31, 35
  Max. Size: Draft 9.5 m., LOA 225 m. *Fuel:* Light bunker fuel oil,
  marine diesel oil and gas oil. *Dry Docks:* Floating dock with
  capacity 35,000 tons. *Airport:* 17 km.
Siak, Indonesia: 0.48 N. 102.04 E. 38, 39, 40
Siam Seaport, Thailand: 13.08 N. 100.53 E. 39
  Max. Size: LOA 300 m., draft 11.2 m.
Siargao Is., Philippines 47
Siasi, Philippines: 5.33 N. 120.49 E. 47
Sibenik, Croatia: 43.44 N. 15.53 E. 9, 21, 24
  Max. Size: Depth to 33 ft. alongside. *Fuel:* Diesel and gas oil in
  small quantities. *Airport:* Split.
Siberut Is., Indonesia 38, 40
Sibolga, Indonesia: 1.44 N. 98.45 E. 37, 38, 40
  Max. Size: Draft 5.3 m.
Sibu, Sarawak, Malaysia: 2.24 N. 111.56 E. 38, 39
  Max. Size: Largest vessel to berth: 10,077 gross tons.
  Deepest drafted vessel to berth was 7.1 m. Tankers: Sungai
  Merah – depth 4.6 m. *Dry Docks:* Slipway – 2,000 tons.
Sibuco, (Mindanao Is.), Philippines: 7.18 N. 122.08 E. 47
Sibuti, Sarawak, Malaysia: 4.04 N. 113.48 E. 38, 39
  Max. Size: Anchorage: Depth 30 ft., 3.5 miles offshore.
  Also see Miri.
Sicilian Channel, Italy 24
Sicily, Italy 21, 24
Siderno, Italy: 38.16 N. 16.17 E. 24
Sidi Ifni, Morocco: 29.26 N. 10.12 W. 27
Sidi Kerir, Egypt: 31.06 N. 29.37 E. 26
  Max. Size: SBM: Up to 350,000 d.w.t. (400,000 d.w.t. with
  SUMED approval), draft 75 ft. *Dry Docks:* Alexandria.
Sidney, B.C., Canada: 48.40 N. 123.23 W. 56
Sidon, Lebanon: 33.30 N. 35.21 E. 26
  Max. Size: Tankers up to 100,000 d.w.t., or approx. 55 ft. draft
  (Summer). Winter – 80,000 d.w.t. Sidaco Terminal: LOA 200 m.,
  draft 15 m. Jieh (Cogigo): LOA 200 m., beam 30 m., draft 12 m.
  (Summer). 10 m. (Winter). *Fuel:* Available.
Sidor, see Matanzas.
SIERRA LEONE 27
Sifnos Is., Greece 25
Siglap, see Singapore.
Sigli, Indonesia: 5.24 N. 95.59 E. 38, 40
Siglufjord, Iceland: 66.10 N. 18.50 W. 17
  Max. Size: Depths up to 8.5 m. LW. *Fuel:* Available.
  Airport: Small airport nearby.
Signy Is., see South Orkney Is..
Sigri, Greece: 39.13 N. 25.52 E. 25
Sigtuna, Sweden: 59.36 N. 17.44 E. 11
Sihanoukville, Cambodia: 10.38 N. 103.29 E. 39
  Max. Size: Cargo vessels: draft 7.60 m. plus tide.
  Tankers: LOA 80 m., draft 4.2 m. *Fuel:* Small quantities.
  Airport: Ream (Domestic), 18 km.
Siilinjarvi, Finland: 63.05 N. 27.41 E. 13
  Also see Saimaa Canal.
Sikea, Sweden: 64.09 N. 20.59 E. 10, 15
  Shipping has ceased at the port
Sikinos Is., Greece: 36.40 N. 25.07 E. 25
Sikka, India: 22.34 N. 69.42 E. 37
  Max. Size: Fertiliser Berth: LOA 180 m., draft 8.0 m. *Airport:* 1.5
  hours by car.
Silam, Sabah, Malaysia: 4.58 N. 118.15 E. 38
  Max. Size: Anchorage.
  Also see Kudat.
Silay, (Palawan Is.), Philippines: 10.48 N. 122.58 E. 47
Sile, Turkey: 41.10 N. 29.35 E. 23, 25, 26
Silistra, Bulgaria: 44.07 N. 27.15 E. 26
Silivri, Turkey: 41.04 N. 28.16 E. 23, 25
Silloth, U.K.: 54.52 N. 3.24 W. 5
  Max. Size: LOA 85 m., beam 13 m., draft 6 m. (Springs).
  Fuel: Available. *Airport:* Carlisle, 39 km.
Silver Bay, Minnesota, U.S.A.: 47.30 N. 91.02 W. 62
Silverdale, Washington, U.S.A.: 47.39 N. 122.42 W. 56
Simeulue Is., Indonesia 38, 40
Simi Is., Greece: 36.37 N. 27.51 E. 25
Simonstown, South Africa: 34.11 S. 18.26 E. 28
Simpson, see Port Simpson.
Simrishamn, Sweden: 55.33 N. 14.21 E. 11, 12
Simushir Is., (Kurile Is.), Russia 43
Sinabang, Indonesia: 2.27 N. 96.24 E. 38, 40

Sinco, see Houston.
Sines, Portugal: 37.57 N. 8.52 W. 20, 22
  Max. Size: Tankers: LOA 350 m., draft 22.5 m.
  Petrochemical: Draft 9.0 m. Multipurpose: Draft 15.5 m.
  Coal: Draft 12.5 m. – 17.0 m. Containers/Ro-Ro: Draft 15.0 m.
  Fuel: Available. *Airport:* Lisbon, 165 km.
SINGAPORE 38, 39, 40, 41
Singapore, Singapore: 1.16 N. 103.50 E. 38, 39, 40, 41
  Max. Size: Keppel Terminal: Depth 9.6 m. – 15.1 m.
  Jurong: Depth 4 m. – 18 m.
  Tanjong Pagar: Depth 4.2 m. – 14.8 m. Singapore Cruise
  Centre: Depth 8.9 m. – 12 m. Brani
  Terminal: Depth 11 m. – 14.6 m. Sembawang: Depth 9.3 m. –
  11.9 m. Pasir Panjang: Depth 2.6 m. – 15.3 m.
  Pulau Sakra: Depth 12.2 m. – 14.1 m.
  Pulau Seraya: Depth 12.6 m. – 15.4 m.
  Pulau Sebarok: Depth 5.5 m. – 17 m. Pulau
  Busing: Depth 14.6 m. – 17 m. *Fuel:* All grades.
  Dry Docks: 400,000 d.w.t. super graving dock
  Airport: International.
Singapore/Malacca Straits 36, 40
  Max. Size: Transit draft 20.5 m.
Singkep Is., Indonesia 38, 40
Singkil, Indonesia: 2.16 N. 97.47 E. 38, 40
Sinoe Bay, see Granville.
Sinop, Turkey: 42.01 N. 35.08 E. 26
  Max. Size: Draft 7.5 m. *Airport:* Samsun, 190 km.
Sinpo, North Korea: 40.03 N. 128.10 E. 42, 43
Sint Michielsbay, (Curacao), Netherlands Antilles: 12.09 N.
  69.01 W. 74
  Max. Size: Anchorage with buoy for vessels up to 350,000 d.w.t.
Sinucane Is., see Port Hedland.
Sinuiju, North Korea: 40.00 N. 124.30 E. 42
Sinuk, Alaska, U.S.A.: 64.30 N. 166.05 W. 54
Sipitang, Sabah, Malaysia: 5.03 N. 115.31 E. 38, 39
  Max. Size: 15,000 d.w.t.
Siporex, see Skelleftehamn.
Sippican Harbour, see Marion.
Sipura Is., Indonesia 38
Sir Abu Nu'ayr Is., U.A.E.: 25.13 N. 54.13 E. 35
Sir Bani Yas Is., U.A.E.: 24.19 N. 52.36 E. 35
Sir Edward Pellow Group, Australia 50
Siracusa, see Syracuse.
Sirna Is., Greece: 36.22 N. 26.42 E. 25
Sirri Island, Iran: 25.54 N. 54.33 E. 31, 35, 37
  Max. Size: LOA 365 m., draft 24.00 m., 330,000 d.w.t.
  Airport: Service to Tehran.
Sirte, Libya: 31.13 N. 16.35 E. 24
Sirtica Terminal, see Ras Lanuf.
Sisal, Mexico: 21.10 N. 90.03 W. 69
Sisimiut, Greenland (Denmark): 66.56 N. 53.40 W. 17
  Max. Size: LOA 136 m., beam 20 m., draft 7.2 m.
  Fuel: Arctic grade available. *Airport:* Heliport.
Sitia, (Crete), Greece: 35.13 N. 26.08 E. 25
Sitka, Alaska, U.S.A.: 57.03 N. 135.20 W. 56
  Max. Size: Harbour depth 22 ft. (MLLW).
Sitra, Bahrain: 26.09 N. 50.40 E. 31, 35
  Max. Size: Tankers: Sailing draft 12.85 m.
  Alba Marine Facilities: Up to 35,000 d.w.t., LOA 200 m.,
  depth 37 ft. (max. draft 35 ft.).
  G.I.I.C.: 60,000 d.w.t. – 100,000 d.w.t., LOA 240 m. – 290 m.,
  draft 12.8 m. G.P.I.C.: 52,000 d.w.t. (Urea), depth 13.5 m.
  Fuel: Available. *Airport:* 15 miles.
  Also see Mina Sulman.
Six Is., see Egmont Is..
Sjaelland, see Zealand Is..
Sjovegan, Norway: 68.53 N. 17.50 E. 15
Skadovsk, Ukraine: 46.06 N. 32.55 E. 26
Skaelskor, Denmark: 55.15 N. 11.18 E. 12
  Max. Size: Draft 4.2 m., LOA 60 m., beam 10 m.
  Fuel: Available. *Airport:* Nearest at Copenhagen.
Skaerbaek, Denmark: 55.31 N. 9.37 E. 12
  Max. Size: LOA 250 m., draft 36 ft. *Fuel:* By barge.
Skagastrond, Iceland: 65.50 N. 20.20 W. 17
  Max. Size: Max. draft 19 ft. *Fuel:* Available.
  Airport: Blonduos, 20 km.
Skagen, Denmark: 57.43 N. 10.36 E. 11, 12
  Max. Size: LOA 125 m., beam 18 m., draft 6.7 m.
  Fuel: By barge or road tanker. *Airport:* Aalborg, 100 km. Sindal,
  45 km.
Skagerrak 4, 10, 11, 12
Skagway, Alaska, U.S.A.: 59.27 N. 135.18 W. 56, 79
  Max. Size: Harbour depth 30 ft. Tides diurnal range 16.7 ft.
  Fuel: Available. *Airport:* Internal, daily flights.
Skandia Harbour, see Gothenburg.
Skanevik, Norway: 59.44 N. 5.57 E. 11
Skanor, see Falsterbo.
Skantzoura Is., Greece: 39.05 N. 24.06 E. 25
Skaramanga, Greece: 37.59 N. 23.35 E. 23, 26
  Dry Docks: Capacity 500,000 tons. *Airport:* Athens.
  Also see Eleusis.

Skarvik Harbour, see Gothenburg.
Skegness, U.K.: 53.10 N. 0.20 E. ... 5, 7
Skeldon, Guyana: 5.58 N. 57.21 W. ... 76
Skelleftea, Sweden: 64.45 N. 20.58 E. ... 15
Skelleftehamn, Sweden: 64.41 N. 21.15 E. ... 10, 15
  Max. Size: Depth 17.5 ft. – 42 ft. Tankers: LOA 200 m., draft 11 m. *Fuel:* All grades. *Airport:* 18 km.
Skelskor, see Gulfhavn.
Skeppsviken, see Uddevalla.
Skerries, Ireland: 53.35 N. 6.06 W. ... 5
Skerryvore, U.K.: 56.15 N. 7.02 W. ... 5
Skiathos Is., Greece: 39.10 N. 23.30 E. ... 25
Skidegate, see Queen Charlotte.
Skien, Norway: 59.12 N. 9.38 E. ... 8, 10, 11, 12
  Max. Size: Between Merstad and Skien: Grain Silo for vessels LOA 363 ft., draft 18 ft. 6 in. At Skien: LOA 280 ft., draft 17 ft. *Dry Docks:* Capacity 2,000 tons. *Airport:* Oslo and Sandefjord.
Skikda, Algeria: 36.53 N. 6.54 E. ... 22
  Max. Size: Draft 6.0 m. – 10.0 m., LOA 125 m. – 290 m. Tankers: Draft 10.0 m. – 14.0 m., LOA 140 m. – 260 m. *Fuel:* By barge. *Airport:* Constantine, 100 km. Annaba, 130 km.
Skinnarvik, Finland: 60.03 N. 22.29 E. ... 11
Skiros Is., Greece: 38.55 N. 24.34 E. ... 25, 26
Skive, Denmark: 56.34 N. 9.03 E. ... 11, 12
Skjervoy, Norway: 70.02 N. 20.58 E. ... 10, 15
Skogby, Finland: 59.55 N. 23.19 E. ... 11
  Max. Size: Depth 7 m., LOA 165 m. *Airport:* Helsinki, 120 km.
  Also see Ekenas.
Skoghall, Sweden: 59.21 N. 13.29 E. ... 12
Skogn, see Fiborgtangen.
Skoldvik, Finland: 60.18 N. 25.33 E. ... 13
  Max. Size: Up to about 260,000 d.w.t., draft 15.3 m. *Fuel:* Marine fuel oil and marine diesel oil. *Airport:* Helsinki, 50 km.
  Also see Porvoo.
Skonvik, see Sundsvall.
Skopelos Is., Greece: 39.07 N. 23.44 E. ... 25
Skredsvik, Sweden: 58.25 N. 11.30 E. ... 11, 12
  Max. Size: LOA 180 m. – 190 m., draft 10.0 m. *Fuel:* Can be supplied. *Airport:* Nearest at Gothenburg.
Skudeneshavn, Norway: 59.09 N. 5.16 E. ... 11
  Max. Size: LOA 90 m., depth 5.5 m. *Fuel:* Available. *Dry Docks:* 74 m. x 14 m. x 4.4 m. *Airport:* Karmoy.
  Also see Kopervik.
Skulte, Latvia: 57.19 N. 24.24 E. ... 11
  Max. Size: LOA 110 m., draft 4 m. *Airport:* Riga, 60 km.
Skuratov Point, Russia: 72.56 N. 69.23 E. ... 16
Skuthhamn, see Pitea.
Skutskar, Sweden: 60.35 N. 17.25 E. ... 11
Skutvik, Norway: 68.00 N. 15.30 E. ... 15
Skye, U.K.: 57.12 N. 6.10 W. ... 5
Skyros, see Skiros Is..
Slagen, Norway: 59.20 N. 10.31 E. ... 8, 11, 12
  Max. Size: Tankers up to 350 m. LOA and 66 ft. draft can be berthed. *Fuel:* All main grades. *Airport:* Oslo (Gardermoen), 150 km. Torp, 30 km.
Slano, Croatia: 42.47 N. 17.53 E. ... 24
Slate Is., Lake Superior, Canada. ... 62
Slavyanka, Russia: 42.53 N. 131.25 E. ... 43
Sleeper Is., N.W.T., Canada ... 59
Slemmestad, Norway: 59.47 N. 10.30 E. ... 8, 12
Sligo, Ireland: 54.17 N. 8.30 W. ... 5
  Max. Size: LOA 92 m. (100 m. with bow thruster), draft 5 m. spring tides, 4.3 m. neap tides. *Fuel:* All grades. *Airport:* Strandhill, Sligo.
Slite, (Gotland Is.), Sweden: 57.42 N. 18.50 E. ... 11
  Max. Size: LOA 215 m., draft 10 m. Tankers: 42,000 d.w.t., LOA 215 m., draft 10.2 m. *Fuel:* Practically all grades bunker oil. *Airport:* Visby, 40 km.
SLOVAKIA ... 4, 9
SLOVENIA ... 9, 21, 24
Sluiskill, Netherlands: 51.17 N. 3.50 E. ... 8
  Max. Size: Draft 10 m. – 10.15 m.
  Also see Terneuzen.
Smalkalden, Suriname: 5.37 N. 55.05 W. ... 76
  Port closed
Smiths Bluff, Texas, U.S.A.: 30.00 N. 93.59 W. ... 66
  Max. Size: Depth at berth 40 ft. *Fuel:* All grades.
  Also see Port Arthur.
Smithton, Tas., Australia: 40.51 S. 145.07 E. ... 51
Smogen, Sweden: 58.22 N. 11.13 E. ... 12
Smoky Bay, S.A., Australia: 32.23 S. 133.55 E. ... 50
Snails Bay, see Sydney.
Snares Is., New Zealand: 48.01 S. 166.32 E. ... 52
Snasa, Norway: 64.15 N. 12.10 E. ... 15
Snekkersten, Denmark: 56.00 N. 12.36 E. ... 12
Snell Lock, see St. Lawrence Seaway.
Snodland, U.K.: 51.19 N. 0.25 E. ... 6
Snug Cove, see Horseshoe Bay.
Soalala, Madagascar: 16.05 S. 45.20 E. ... 30

Soares Dutra Terminal, see Tramandai.
Sobo, Trinidad and Tobago: 10.15 N. 61.37 W. ... 71, 75
Soby, Denmark: 54.57 N. 10.16 E. ... 12, 14
Sochi, Russia: 43.35 N. 39.43 E. ... 26
  Max. Size: Draft 7.5 m., LOA 190 m., beam 25 m.
Society Islands, French Polynesia (France) ... 49
Socony, see Carteret.
Socorro Is., (Revilla Gigedo Is.), Mexico: 18.45 N. 111.00 W. ... 57
Socotra, Yemen ... 18, 31, 37
Soderhamn, Sweden: 61.18 N. 17.05 E. ... 10, 11, 15
  Max. Size: Orrskar: Depth 12.8 m. ML. Stugsund: Depth 6 m. ML. Soderhamn: Depth 3.5 m. ML. *Fuel:* Any normally used grades. *Airport:* Stockholm.
Soderkoping, Sweden: 58.30 N. 16.20 E. ... 11
Sodertalje, Sweden: 59.12 N. 17.38 E. ... 10, 11
  Max. Size: LOA 200 m., beam 32 m., draft 9 m. *Fuel:* Available. *Airport:* Stockholm, 60 km.
Sodus Bay, New York, U.S.A.: 43.15 N. 77.00 W. ... 62
Soervaag, Faroe Is. (Denmark): 62.04 N. 7.18 W. ... 5, 15
  Max. Size: Largest vessel: 12,000 cu.m. tanker. Depth at pier 8 m. *Fuel:* Marine diesel fuel, turbo-jet A1-100, gasoline-petroleum. *Dry Docks:* Up to 1,500 d.w.t. *Airport:* 3 km.
Sofia, Bulgaria: 42.40 N. 23.18 E. ... 9
Sogod, (Leyte Is.), Philippines: 10.23 N. 124.59 E. ... 47
Sohar, Oman: 24.22 N. 56.46 E. ... 35
Sokhna, Egypt: 29.40 N. 32.21 E. ... 32
  Max. Size: 170,000 d.w.t., depth 17 m.
Sola, Norway: 58.55 N. 5.35 E. ... 10, 11
  Max. Size: Depth 7 m. – 11 m. *Fuel:* All grades. *Airport:* Sola, 3 km.
  Also see Stavanger.
Solander Is., New Zealand: 46.36 S. 166.54 E. ... 52
Soledad, Venezuela: 8.10 N. 63.39 W. ... 75
Solenzara, (Corsica), France: 41.53 N. 9.25 E. ... 24
Solito, Venezuela: 9.05 N. 71.55 W. ... 69, 74
Soller, (Majorca), Spain: 39.47 N. 2.46 E. ... 22
  Max. Size: LOA 60 m., draft 4.50 m. *Airport:* 40 km.
Solombala, Russia: 64.35 N. 40.30 E. ... 16
Solomon, Alaska, U.S.A.: 64.33 N. 164.24 W. ... 54
SOLOMON ISLANDS ... 49, 51
Solomon Sea, Papua New Guinea ... 46
Solomons Is., Maryland, U.S.A.: 38.19 N. 76.27 W. ... 63, 65
Solta Is., Croatia ... 24
Solund, Norway: 61.08 N. 4.45 E. ... 5, 11, 15
Solvesborg, Sweden: 56.03 N. 14.35 E. ... 10, 11, 12
  Max. Size: LOA 170 m., breadth 30 m., draft 7.7 m. *Fuel:* Available. *Dry Docks:* 341 ft. x 51 ft. x 14.5 ft. deep on sill (HWOST). *Airport:* Kristianstad, 50 km.
Solway Firth, U.K. ... 5
Soma, Japan: 37.50 N. 140.58 E. ... 43
  Max. Size: 5,000 d.w.t., draft 7.2 m.
SOMALIA ... 30, 31
Sombra, Ontario, Canada: 42.43 N. 82.29 W. ... 62
Sombrero Channel, (Nicobar Is.), India ... 37
Sombrero Is., (U.K.): 18.36 N. 63.29 W. ... 71
Sombrero Key, Florida, U.S.A.: 24.38 N. 81.07 W. ... 66
Somerset, (Somerset Is.), Bermuda (U.K.): 32.18 N. 64.51 W. ... 63
Somoza, see Puerto Sandino.
Sonbong, North Korea: 42.20 N. 130.24 E. ... 43
  Max. Size: Depth 7.5 m. Tankers: Berth at SPM. *Fuel:* Available.
Sonderborg, Denmark: 54.55 N. 9.47 E. ... 11, 12, 14
  Max. Size: 30,000 g.r.t., draft 9.5 m., air draft 33 m., LOA 200 m. *Fuel:* Available. *Airport:* Connects with Copenhagen.
Sondre Stromfjord, see Kangerlussuaq.
Sondre Upernavik, Greenland (Denmark): 72.09 N. 55.32 W. ... 17
Songjin, see Chungjin.
Songkhla, Thailand: 7.14 N. 100.35 E. ... 37, 38, 39
  Max. Size: LOA 173 m., beam 25 m., draft 8.23 m. *Airport:* Had Yai, near city.
Sonora, N.S., Canada: 45.04 N. 61.55 W. ... 60
Sonsorol, Palau: 5.20 N. 132.19 E. ... 46
Sooke, B.C., Canada: 48.22 N. 123.44 W. ... 56
Sopot, Poland: 54.28 N. 18.32 E. ... 11
Soraker, Sweden: 62.31 N. 17.30 E. ... 15
  Max. Size: Tankers: LOA 200 m., draft 7 m.
  Also see Sundsvall.
Sorel, Quebec, Canada: 46.02 N. 73.07 W. ... 60
  Max. Size: Draft 35 ft. (10.67 m.). *Fuel:* All grades. *Dry Docks:* Up to 12,000 d.w.t. *Airport:* Montreal, 70 miles.
Soriano, Uruguay: 33.25 S. 58.20 W. ... 78
Sorol, (Caroline Is.), Micronesia: 8.09 N. 140.24 E. ... 46
Sorong, Indonesia: 0.53 S. 131.15 E. ... 46
  Max. Size: Draft 11.0 m. at Springs. Tankers: 21,000 d.w.t., LOA 175 m., depth 11 m. *Fuel:* Available. *Airport:* 8 miles.
Soroosh Terminal, Iran: 29.01 N. 49.28 E. ... 35
  Not operational

THE SHIPS ATLAS

Soroy Is., Norway **10, 15**
Sorrento, Australia, see Portsea.
Sorrento, Italy: 40.38 N. 14.25 E. **23, 24**
Sorsogon, (Luzon Is.), Philippines: 12.58 N. 124.00 E. . . **47**
Sortland, Norway: 68.42 N. 15.25 E. **15**
Sorvaer, Norway: 70.38 N. 21.58 E. **15**
Soskua, see Saimaa Canal.
Souda, (Crete), Greece: 35.29 N. 24.04 E. **25, 26**
  Max. Size: Depth 7 m. – 12 m. *Fuel:* By road tanker.
  Airport: 15 km.
Souellaba, Cameroon: 3.50 N. 9.31 E. **29**
Soulange Section, see St. Lawrence Seaway.
Sour, Lebanon: 33.16 N. 35.12 E. **26**
  Max. Size: Draft 5.3 m.
Souris, P.E.I., Canada: 46.21 N. 62.15 W. **60**
Sousakion, see Isthmia.
Soussa, see Sousse.
Sousse, Tunisia: 35.49 N. 10.39 E. **24**
  Max. Size: LOA 170 m., draft 8.7 m. *Fuel:* Available.
  Airport: Skanes Monastir, 15 km.
SOUTH AFRICA **28, 30, 80**
South Amboy, New Jersey, U.S.A.: 40.29 N. 74.16 W. . . **63**
South Andaman Is., (Andaman Is.), India **37**
South Australia, Australia **50, 51**
South Bend, see Willapa.
South Boston, see Boston.
South Brewer, see Bangor.
South Cape, (Spitsbergen), Norway: 76.31 N. 16.25 E. . . **17**
South Carolina, U.S.A. **66**
South China Sea, South China Sea **38, 39, 46, 47**
South Dakota, U.S.A. **57**
South East Farallon, California, U.S.A. **58**
South East Pass, (Mississippi Delta), Louisiana, U.S.A. . **67**
South Georgia, (U.K.) **68, 77, 80**
South Haven, Michigan, U.S.A.: 42.23 N. 86.18 W. **62**
South Is., New Zealand **52, 80**
South Louisiana, Louisiana, U.S.A.: 30.06 N. 90.29 W. . **66, 67**
  Max. Size: Channel: Depth 45 ft. Berths: Depth 15 ft. – 100 ft.
  Bulk/Tankers: Depth 25 ft. – 90 ft.
South Orkney Is., (U.K.): 60.40 S. 45.30 W. **68, 80**
South Pagai, Indonesia: 3.00 S. 100.20 E. **38**
South Pass, (Mississippi Delta), Louisiana, U.S.A. . . **66, 67**
South Pulau Laut Coal Terminal, see Mekar Putih.
South Riding Point, (Grand Bahama Is.), Bahamas:
  26.37 N. 78.14 W. **66, 69, 70**
  Max. Size: Up to 500,000 d.w.t., depth 100 ft.
South Ronaldsay, U.K.: 58.45 N. 3.00 W. **5**
South Sandwich Islands, (U.K.): 57.00 S. 27.00 W. . . . **68, 80**
South Shetland Is., U.K. **68**
South Shields, U.K.: 54.59 N. 1.25 W. **6**
  Also see Tyne District.
South Uist, U.K.: 57.12 N. 7.09 W. **5**
South West Cape, (South Is.), New Zealand:
  47.16 S. 167.31 E. **52**
Southampton, U.K.: 50.54 N. 1.24 W. **4, 5, 7, 19**
  Max. Size: Depth 4.1 m. – 15.0 m. Tankers: See Fawley and
  Hamble. *Fuel:* All grades. *Dry Docks:* 1,141 ft. length overall,
  132.5 ft. wide and 34 ft. over the blocks. *Airport:* Southampton
  International.
Southampton Is., N.W.T., Canada **59**
Southend, U.K.: 51.32 N. 0.43 E. **6**
Southport, U.K.: 53.38 N. 5.01 W. **5, 7**
Southport, North Carolina, U.S.A.: 33.56 N. 77.59 W. . . **66**
  Max. Size: ADM: 50,000 d.w.t. *Fuel:* Available.
Southwest Pass, (Mississippi Delta), Louisiana, U.S.A. . **66, 67**
  Max. Size: Project depth 45 ft.
Southwold, U.K.: 52.20 N. 1.40 E. **7**
Sovetskaya Gavan, Russia: 48.59 N. 140.17 E. **43**
Sovetsky, Russia: 60.32 N. 28.35 E. **11, 13**
Soyak, see Ambarli.
Soyo, Angola: 6.07 S. 12.22 E. **28**
SPAIN **19, 20, 21, 22, 23, 27, 69**
Spalding, U.K.: 52.46 N. 0.10 W. **7**
Spangareid, Norway: 58.03 N. 7.09 E. **11, 12**
Spanish, Ontario, Canada: 46.11 N. 82.20 W. **62**
Sparrows Point, Maryland, U.S.A.: 39.13 N. 76.29 W. . . **63, 65**
  Also see Baltimore.
Speightstown, Barbados: 13.15 N. 59.38 W. **71**
Spencer Gulf, S.A., Australia **50, 51**
Spetsai Is., Greece: 37.15 N. 23.10 E. **25**
Spezia, see La Spezia.
Spitsbergen, Norway **17**
Split, Croatia: 43.31 N. 16.26 E. **9, 21, 24**
  Max. Size: Draft 29 ft. (8.8 m.) (passenger ships), 35 ft. (10.6 m.)
  (general cargo) and 37 ft. (11.3 m.) (grain). Tankers: Draft 38 ft.
  (11.9 m.). *Fuel:* Available. *Dry Docks:* Up to 28,000 d.w.t.
  Airport: 23 km.
Spodsbjerg, Denmark: 54.56 N. 10.50 E. **12, 14**
Spragge, Ontario, Canada: 46.14 N. 82.41 W. **62**
  Max. Size: 10,000 d.w.t.

Sprangviken, see Gustavsvik.
Spratly Is., South China Sea: 8.40 N. 111.55 E. **39**
Spring Bay, Tas., Australia: 42.33 S. 147.56 E. **50, 51**
  Max. Size: Depth 10.7 m., vessels up to LOA 243.8 m. can be
  handled. *Fuel:* In emergency, by road tankers from Hobart.
  Airport: Hobart, 49 miles.
Springdale, Newfoundland, Canada: 49.30 N. 56.05 W. . . **60**
  Max. Size: Depth to 10 m.
Spurn Point, U.K.: 53.36 N. 0.07 E. **6**
Squamish, B.C., Canada: 49.41 N. 123.10 W. **56**
  Max. Size: LOA 700 ft., depth 38 ft. – 40 ft.
  Airport: Vancouver, 50 miles.
  Also see Vancouver.
SRI LANKA **37**
Sriracha, Thailand: 13.07 N. 100.52 E. **37, 39**
  Max. Size: MBK Bulk berth: 150,000 d.w.t., draft 14.3 m.
  Harbour: 124,000 d.w.t., LOA 257 m., depth 11.6 m. at LLW.
  Tankers: Thai Oil (CBM): 120,000 d.w.t., LOA 900 ft., depth 48 ft.
  Thai Oil (SBM): 230,000 d.w.t. (part load), draft 17.6 m.
  Esso (CBM): 105,000 d.w.t., LOA 274 m., draft 15.24 m.
  PTT jetties: 100,000 d.w.t., LOA 281 m., depth 15 m.
  Fuel: By barge. *Airport:* Bangkok.
Srivardhan, India: 18.02 N. 73.03 E. **37**
Stade, see Stadersand.
Stadersand, Germany: 53.37 N. 9.32 E. **8, 12, 14**
  Max. Size: LOA 230 m., beam 32 m., draft 11.50 m. (MHW).
  Size 60,000 d.w.t. *Fuel:* By barge.
Stadhafen, see Lubeck.
Stag Marine Terminal, W.A., Australia: 20.17 S. 116.15 E. . . **50, 51**
  Max. Size: 150,000 d.w.t., depth 47.0 m.
Stamford, Connecticut, U.S.A.: 41.02 N. 73.33 W. **63**
Stamsund, Norway: 68.08 N. 13.52 E. **10, 15**
Stanford le Hope, see Coryton.
Stanley, Tas., Australia: 40.46 S. 145.18 E. **50, 51**
  Max. Size: Depth 9.0 m. (LWOST). *Fuel:* By road tanker.
Stanlow, see Ince.
Stann Creek, Belize: 16.58 N. 88.12 W. **69**
Stanvac, see Port Stanvac.
Stapleton, U.S.A.: 40.38 N. 74.04 W. **63**
  Also see New York.
Starbuck Is., Kiribati: 5.37 S. 155.55 W. **49**
Staten Is., Argentina: 54.50 S. 64.00 W. **77**
Staten Is., U.S.A., see New York.
Stavanger, Norway: 58.58 N. 5.44 E. **10, 11**
  Max. Size: New Deep Water Berths: Depth 15 m.
  Tankers: Depth 25 ft. – 27 ft. *Fuel:* Normal grades available.
  Dry Docks: 545 ft. x 75 ft. x 24 ft. *Airport:* 10 km.
  Also see Sola.
Stavros, Greece: 40.40 N. 23.42 E. **25**
Ste. Maxime, France: 43.19 N. 6.39 E. **22**
Stebbins, Alaska, U.S.A.: 63.30 N. 162.16 W. **54**
Steenkool, Indonesia: 2.07 S. 133.34 E. **46**
Stege, Denmark: 54.59 N. 12.17 E. **11, 12**
  Max. Size: LOA 80 m., draft 3.8 m. *Fuel:* Available.
  Airport: Copenhagen, 110 km.
Steinkjer, Norway: 64.00 N. 11.30 E. **15**
Steno Straits, see Evripos Strait.
Stenungsund, Sweden: 58.04 N. 11.49 E. **12**
  Max. Size: Power Station: LOA 250 m., draft 10.5 m. – 12.5 m.
  Tankers: Borealis – LOA 240 m., draft 13.0 m.
  Hydro – LOA 100 m., draft 9.3 m. *Fuel:*
  Gothenburg, etc., by barge. *Airport:* Gothenburg, 75 km.
Stephens, see Port Stephens.
Stephenville, Newfoundland, Canada: 48.30 N. 58.33 W. . . **60**
  Max. Size: Depth 9.2 m. *Fuel:* Marine diesel. *Airport:* 5 miles.
Sterno, Sweden: 56.06 N. 14.58 E. **11**
  Max. Size: Water depth 6 m. *Fuel:* Available.
  Airport: Karlshamn.
  Also see Karlshamn.
Stettin, see Szczecin.
Steveston, B.C., Canada: 49.08 N. 123.11 W. **56**
Stewart, Australia, see Port Stewart.
Stewart, B.C., Canada: 55.56 N. 130.00 W. **56**
Stewart Is., New Zealand **52**
Stignaesvaerkets, Denmark: 55.12 N. 11.15 E. **12**
  Max. Size: Coal Berth: LOA 300 m., beam 43 m., draft 17 m.
  Tankers: Draft 15 m. *Airport:* Copenhagen, 120 km.
Stikkisholm, Iceland: 65.05 N. 22.43 W. **17**
Stilleryd, Sweden: 56.10 N. 14.50 E. **12**
  Max. Size: LOA 220 m., depth 11 m., 40,000 d.w.t.
  Fuel: Available. *Airport:* Karlshamn.
  Also see Karlshamn.
Stirling, U.K.: 56.08 N. 4.01 W. **6**
Stjernoy Is., Norway **10**
Stjordalshalsen, Norway: 63.30 N. 10.58 E. **15**
Stocka, Sweden: 61.54 N. 17.22 E. **15**
  Max. Size: Draft 4.9 m. MW, LOA 110 m.
  Also see Hudiksvall.

Stockholm, Sweden: 59.19 N. 18.03 E. **4, 10, 11**
  Max. Size: LOA 185 m., beam 26 m. draft 10 m.
  Tankers: Draft 12.4 m., 65,000 d.w.t. *Fuel:* All grades.
  Airport: 22 miles.
  Also see Sandhamn.
Stockton, U.K.: 54.35 N. 1.20 W. **6**
  Also see Teesport.
Stockton, California, U.S.A.: 37.57 N. 121.19 W. **58**
  Max. Size: Draft 35 ft. (LW) – 37 ft. (HW). *Fuel:* All grades.
  Airport: Stockton Metropolitan, 6 miles.
  Also see San Francisco.
Stockvik, see Sundsvall.
Stokes Bay, Ontario, Canada: 45.00 N. 81.20 W. **62**
Stokkseyri, see Eyrarbakki.
Stokmarknes, Norway: 68.34 N. 14.57 E. **15**
Stomion, Greece: 39.50 N. 22.45 E. **24, 25**
Stonehaven, U.K.: 56.58 N. 2.12 W. **5**
Stonington, Connecticut, U.S.A.: 41.20 N. 71.54 W. **63**
Stony Point Dyke, Massachusetts, U.S.A.: 41.42 N. 70.40 W. . . **64**
Stora Hoggarn, see Stockholm.
Storby, Finland: 60.13 N. 19.31 E. **10, 11**
Stormskar, see Umea.
Stornoway, U.K.: 58.12 N. 6.22 W. **5**
  Max. Size: 400 ft. × 60 ft. × 22 ft. draft to berth.
  Tankers: Draft 15 ft., LOA 220 ft. *Fuel:* Available at 24 hours
  notice. *Dry Docks:* One slipway of 750 tons displacement.
  Airport: 3 miles.
Storugns, (Gotland Is.), Sweden: 57.50 N. 18.48 E. **11**
  Max. Size: Draft 9.2 m. *Fuel:* Most grades from Visby.
  Airport: Visby.
Stott, Norway: 66.55 N. 13.27 E. **15**
Strahan, Tas., Australia: 42.10 S. 145.20 E. **50, 51**
  Max. Size: Depth 3.7 m. – 5.5 m. *Fuel:* By road tanker.
  Airport: Strahan 3 miles, connects to Hobart.
Straits:
  Strait of Bonifacio **24**
  Strait of Canso, N.S., Canada **60**
  Strait of Georgia, B.C., Canada **56**
  Strait of Gibraltar **20, 21, 22, 23, 27**
  Strait of Hormuz **31, 35, 37**
  Strait of Malacca **38**
  Strait of Messina, Italy **24**
  Strait of Otranto **24**
  Straits of Bab el Mandeb **32**
  Straits of Macassar, Indonesia **38**
  Straits of Magellan, Chile **77**
Stralsund, Germany: 54.19 N. 13.06 E. **11, 12**
  Max. Size: Vessels up to 17 ft. draft. *Fuel:* Gas oil and lube oil.
  Airport: Berlin and Barth.
Strand, Norway: 59.05 N. 5.57 E. **11**
Strandby, Denmark: 57.30 N. 10.31 E. **12**
Strangford, U.K.: 54.23 N. 5.34 W. **5**
Strangnas, Sweden: 59.22 N. 17.01 E. **11**
Stranraer, U.K.: 54.55 N. 5.02 W. **4, 5**
  Max. Size: Largest vessel handled: LOA 130 m., working
  draft 5 m. *Fuel:* Limited quantities of fuel oil.
Strasbourg, France: 48.34 N. 7.42 E. **9**
  Max. Size: Max. draft on Rhine is 4.0 m. *Fuel:* Can be
  arranged. *Airport:* Strasbourg-Entzheim: 15 km.
  Strasbourg-Mulhouse: 130 km. (airport Mulhouse Bale).
  Strasbourg-Frankfort: 220 km.
Stratoni, Greece: 40.31 N. 23.50 E. **25, 26**
Straumsvik, Iceland: 64.03 N. 22.03 W. **17**
  Max. Size: Berth: Length 220 m., depth 12 m. *Fuel:* Available.
  Airport: Reykjavik, 15 km.
Streaky Bay, S.A., Australia: 32.48 S. 134.13 E. **50, 51**
Stremoy, Faroe Is. (Denmark) **5, 15**
Strib, Denmark: 55.32 N. 9.46 E. **12**
Stromboli Is., Italy: 38.48 N. 15.13 E. **24**
Stromeferry, U.K.: 57.20 N. 5.35 W. **5**
Stromma, Finland: 60.11 N. 22.53 E. **11**
Stromnas, see Gustavsvik.
Stromness, U.K.: 58.58 N. 3.18 W. **5**
  Max. Size: LOA 130 m., beam 20 m., draft 6 m.
  Fuel: By road tanker. *Airport:* Kirkwall, 20 miles.
Stromstad, Sweden: 58.56 N. 11.10 E. **8, 11, 12**
  Max. Size: Cargo ships 3,000 d.w.t. *Airport:* Taxiplane connects
  with Gothenburg, 200 km.
Stronsay, U.K.: 59.10 N. 2.40 W. **5**
Strood, see Rochester.
Struer, Denmark: 56.30 N. 8.36 E. **11**
Stuart Is., Alaska, U.S.A.: 63.35 N. 162.25 W. **54**
Stubbekobing, Sweden: 54.53 N. 12.03 E. **12**
Studstrup, Denmark: 56.15 N. 10.21 E. **11, 12**
  Max. Size: LOA 245 m., draft 36 ft. Tankers: LOA 245 m.,
  draft 33 ft. *Fuel:* By road tanker.
Stugsund, see Soderhamn.
Sture, Norway: 60.37 N. 4.51 E. **5, 10, 11**
  Max. Size: 300,000 d.w.t., draft 23 m. *Airport:* Bergen, 60 km.
Sturgean Bay Canal, Wisconsin, U.S.A. **62**

Sturgeon Bay, Wisconsin, U.S.A.: 44.50 N. 87.23 W. **62**
Stuttgart, Germany: 48.47 N. 9.12 E. **9**
Stylis, Greece: 38.55 N. 22.37 E. **24, 25**
  Max. Size: Draft 18 ft. 6 in. *Fuel:* By barge or road tanker.
  Airport: Athens, 250 km.
Suai, Sarawak, Malaysia: 3.43 N. 113.34 E. **38, 39**
Suakin, see Sawakin.
Suances, Spain: 43.26 N. 4.02 W. **19, 20**
Suao, Taiwan: 24.36 N. 121.52 E. **42**
  Max. Size: LOA 260 m., draft 14.5 m.
  Fuel: By barge or road tanker. *Airport:* 3.5 hours by car.
Suape, Brazil: 8.24 S. 34.57 W. **72**
  Max. Size: Products: LOA 250 m., draft 13.9 m.
  LPG: LOA 190 m., draft 13 m. Dry cargo: Max. draft 14.0 m.
  Fuel: Diesel by road tanker.
Suarez, see Puerto Suarez.
Suba Nipa, (Mindanao Is.), Philippines: 7.17 N. 122.51 E. . . **46, 47**
Subi, Indonesia: 2.55 N. 108.52 E. **38, 39**
Subic Bay, (Luzon Is.), Philippines: 14.47 N. 120.14 E. . . **46, 47**
  Max. Size: Dry cargo: LOA 520 m., draft 13 m.
  Tankers: 68,600 d.w.t., LOA 253 m., draft 12 m.
  Tanker Terminal: 100,000 d.w.t., LOA 744 ft., draft 41 ft.
  Fuel: Available. *Dry Docks:* 350 m. × 65 m. × 12.5 m.,
  300,000 d.w.t. *Airport:* Cubi (Subic) or Manila, 47 km.
Sucre, see Cumana.
Suda Bay, see Souda.
SUDAN **32**
Sudan, see Port Sudan.
Sudr, Egypt: 29.35 N. 32.42 E. **26, 32**
Suduroy, Faroe Is. (Denmark) **5, 15**
Suez, Egypt: 29.58 N. 32.33 E. **21, 26, 32, 33, 34**
  Max. Size: Depth 40 ft. at Adabiya Quay. Tankers: LOA 750 ft.,
  depth 38 ft. (LWOST). *Fuel:* By barge.
  Also see Suez Canal.
Suez Canal, Egypt: 30.36 N. 32.17 E. **21, 26, 32, 33, 34**
  Max. Size: Max. draft 62 ft. Max. beam 254 ft. but dependant on
  draft. Average transit time 13 – 14 hours. *Fuel:* Available at
  Suez and Port Said. *Dry Docks:* 50,000 d.w.t. at Port Said.
  8,000 d.w.t. at Suez. *Airport:* Cairo (2.5 hours drive).
Sugluk, Quebec, Canada: 62.19 N. 75.33 W. **59**
Suhoza, see Paramaribo.
Sukadana, Indonesia: 1.13 S. 109.58 E. **38**
Sukhumi, Georgia: 42.57 N. 41.00 E. **26**
  Max. Size: Draft 6 m., LOA 190 m. *Fuel:* By barge.
Sukkertoppen, see Maniitsoq.
Sukumo, Japan: 32.56 N. 132.44 E. **45**
Sula Is., Indonesia **46**
Sulawesi, see Celebes.
Sulima, Sierra Leone: 6.56 N. 11.31 W. **27**
Sulina, Romania: 45.11 N. 29.45 E. **9, 26**
  Max. Size: Draft at Sulina Bar is 23 ft. (7.01 m.). Any other
  changes of official draft are broadcast daily. LOA 180 m.
  Airport: Tulcea, 70 km.
Sullom Voe, (Shetland Is.), U.K.: 60.27 N. 1.17 W. **4, 5**
  Max. Size: Cargo Pier: 100 m. long, depths 3.9 m. – 9.9 m.
  Tankers: LOA 365 m., 350,000 d.w.t., draft 24 m. LPG: LOA
  286 m., draft 15.7 m., 75,000 cu.m. *Fuel:* Available to shuttle
  tankers only. *Airport:* Nearby.
Sulphur, see Port Sulphur.
Sulu Archipelago, Philippines **38, 46, 47**
Sulu Sea **38, 46, 47**
Sumatra, Indonesia **38, 39, 40**
Sumba Is., Indonesia **38, 46, 50**
Sumbawa, Indonesia: 8.28 S. 117.28 E. **38**
Sumbawa Is., Indonesia **38, 46**
Sumbe, see Novo Redondo.
Sumbo, Faroe Is. (Denmark): 61.20 N. 6.30 W. **5, 15**
Sumenep, Indonesia: 7.03 S. 113.53 E. **38**
Suminoe, Japan: 33.12 N. 130.12 E. **45**
Sumisu, Japan: 31.25 N. 140.02 E. **43, 46**
Summerside, P.E.I., Canada: 46.23 N. 63.47 W. **60**
  Max. Size: LOA 550 ft., beam 75 ft., draft 24 ft. *Fuel:* Limited
  quantities by road. *Airport:* Charlottetown, 39 miles.
Sumoto, Japan: 34.20 N. 134.55 E. **45**
Sund, see Sundsvall.
Sunda Strait, Indonesia **36, 38**
Sundahofn, see Reykjavik.
Sunderland, U.K.: 54.55 N. 1.21 W. **6**
  Max. Size: South Dock: LOA 141 m., beam 18.9 m., draft 8.08 m.
  with Spring tides. Harbour: LOA 213 m., draft 8.18 m.
  Fuel: All grades. *Dry Docks:* Length 112 m., breadth 16.5 m.
  Airport: Teesside (International), 45 minutes. Newcastle
  (International), 35 minutes.
Sundsvall, Sweden: 62.25 N. 17.20 E. **4, 10, 11, 15**
  Max. Size: Draft 10.5 m. Tankers: LOA 250 m., draft 11.3 m.,
  70,000 d.w.t. *Fuel:* Available.
  Dry Docks: Lunde Varv (Kramfors). *Airport:* 22 km.
Sungai Gerong, see Plaju.
Sungai Merah, see Sibu.
Sungai Pakning, Indonesia: 1.20 N. 102.09 E. **38, 39, 40**
  Max. Size: 61,000 d.w.t., LOA 220 m., depth 15.3 m.

THE SHIPS ATLAS

Sungai Udang, Malaya, Malaysia: 2.14 N. 102.08 E. . . . **38, 39, 40**
  Max. Size: Tankers: Berth – 120,000 d.w.t., LOA 297 m., draft 17.3 m. SBM – 300,000 d.w.t., LOA 347.6 m., draft 22 m. LPG: 6,000 d.w.t., LOA 116 m., draft 7.5 m. Bulk: 5,000 d.w.t., LOA 95 m., draft 5.5 m. *Airport:* Kuala Lumpur, 200 km.
Sungailiat, Indonesia: 1.51 S. 106.07 E. **38**
Sungei Sarawak, see Sejingkat.
Sunndalsora, Norway: 62.41 N. 8.36 E. **10, 15**
  Max. Size: Draft 33 ft. *Fuel:* Available in small quantities. *Airport:* Kristiansund and Molde, 60 miles.
Suo Sea, Inland Sea, Japan. **45**
Supe, Peru: 10.48 S. 77.45 W. **72**
  Max. Size: Anchorage port.
Superior, Wisconsin, U.S.A.: 46.44 N. 92.05 W. . . . **62**
  Dry Docks: 831 ft. x 95 ft.
  Also see Duluth-Superior.
Supsa Marine Terminal, Georgia: 42.01 N. 41.43 E. . . **26**
  Max. Size: 150,000 d.w.t., LOA 290 m., depth 50 m. *Airport:* 350 km.
Sur, Oman: 22.35 N. 59.30 E. **31, 37**
Surabaya, Indonesia: 7.12 S. 112.44 E. **38**
  Max. Size: Draft for entering access channel is 9.5 m., depth alongside 4 m. – 10.5 m., LOA 210 m. Tankers: Depth 9 m. – 12 m. *Fuel:* Available. *Dry Docks:* 15,500 ton floating dock.
Surat, India: 21.10 N. 72.55 E. **37**
Surat Thani, Thailand: 9.07 N. 99.20 E. **39**
Surgidero de Batabano, see Batabano.
Surigao, (Mindanao Is.), Philippines: 9.49 N. 125.29 E. . . . **46, 47**
  Max. Size: LOA 150 m., draft 8.0 m. *Fuel:* Available. *Airport:* 4 km.
SURINAME **72, 76**
Surte, Sweden: 57.50 N. 12.01 E. **12**
Susak, see Rijeka.
Susaki, Japan: 33.24 N. 133.18 E. **45**
  Max. Size: Limestone: LOA 240 m., draft 12.5 m. Cement: LOA 165 m., draft 8.9 m. Logs: LOA 185 m., draft 8.7 m. *Airport:* Kochi, 70 km.
Susoh, Indonesia: 3.44 N. 96.48 E. **38, 40**
Sutton, see Tampa.
Sutton Bridge, U.K.: 52.46 N. 0.12 E. **7**
  Max. Size: Draft 6.0 m. *Fuel:* Available. *Airport:* Norwich.
Suttsu, Japan: 42.47 N. 140.14 E. **43**
Sutudden, see Karlshamn.
Suva, Fiji: 18.08 S. 178.26 E. **49**
  Max. Size: Largest vessel regularly entering is 42,000 tons. Depth alongside 11.6 m. (MLWS). Tankers: Depth 42 ft. *Fuel:* Furnace fuel oil, diesel fuel oil and gas oil. *Airport:* 15 miles.
Suvorov Is., Cook Is. (N.Z.): 13.10 S. 163.00 W. **49**
Suwadi Point, Oman: 23.48 N. 57.48 E. **35**
Suwannee, Florida, U.S.A.: 29.10 N. 83.10 W. **66**
Suza, see Sousse.
Suzaki, see Susaki.
Suzuka, see Yokkaichi.
Svalbard, see Spitsbergen.
Svaneke, Denmark: 55.08 N. 15.09 E. **11, 12**
Svano, Sweden: 62.55 N. 17.52 E. **15**
Svartvik, see Sundsvall.
Sveagruva, (Spitsbergen), Norway: 77.52 N. 16.48 E. . . . **17**
Svelgen, Norway: 61.45 N. 5.15 E. **15**
Svelvik, Norway: 59.37 N. 10.25 E. **8, 12**
Svendborg, Denmark: 55.03 N. 10.37 E. **12, 14**
  Max. Size: LOA 180 m., draft 22 ft. 4 in. Depth alongside 4.3 m. – 7.5 m. *Fuel:* Diesel by road tanker. *Dry Docks:* Floating dock with capacity 10,000 tons. *Airport:* Beldringe, 50 km. by road.
Sverdrup Is., Russia: 74.28 N. 79.21 E. **16**
Svolvaer, Norway: 68.14 N. 14.35 E. **10, 15**
  Max. Size: LOA 520 ft., draft 30 ft. *Fuel:* All grades. *Dry Docks:* Slipways for ships up to 240 ft. *Airport:* 4 km.
Swabue, see Shanwei.
Swains Is., American Samoa (U.S.A.): 11.04 S. 171.05 W. . . . **49**
Swakopmund, Namibia: 22.40 S. 14.31 E. **28**
Swan Is., (U.S.A.): 17.25 N. 83.56 W. **69, 70**
Swanage, U.K.: 50.37 N. 1.58 W. **7**
Swansboro, North Carolina, U.S.A.: 34.41 N. 77.08 W. . . . **63**
Swansea, Tas., Australia: 42.09 S. 148.05 E. **50, 51**
Swansea, U.K.: 51.37 N. 3.56 W. **4, 5, 6, 7**
  Max. Size: LOA 655 ft., beam 88 ft., draft 32 ft. 6 in. (HW) *Fuel:* Various grades of gas oil and diesel. *Dry Docks:* 670 ft. x 92 ft. *Airport:* 8 miles.
Swatou, see Shantou.
SWAZILAND **30**
SWEDEN **4, 10, 11, 12, 15, 79**
Swettenham, see Port Klang.
Swinemunde, see Swinoujscie.
Swinoujscie, Poland: 53.55 N. 14.15 E. **11, 12**
  Max. Size: LOA 240 m., draft 12.8 m. *Fuel:* All grades. Also see Szczecin.
SWITZERLAND **9, 21**

Sydney, N.S.W., Australia: 33.51 S. 151.12 E. **49, 50**
  Max. Size: Depth 8.4 m. – 12.0 m. at Glebe Island, 10.5 m. at Sydney Cove Passenger Terminal, 9.9 m. – 11.1 m. at Darling Harbour and 9.8 m. – 11.0 m. at White Bay. Tankers: Depth 9.1 m. – 14.0 m. *Fuel:* All grades. *Dry Docks:* Garden Island: Capacity 110,000 tonnes d.w.t. *Airport:* Sydney, 9 km.
Sydney, N.S., Canada: 46.09 N. 60.12 W. **60**
  Max. Size: Draft 11.6 m. – 15.0 m. Tankers: Depth 23 ft. (LW). *Fuel:* Marine diesel and galley fuels are obtainable. *Airport:* Internal.
Sydney Is., (Phoenix Is.), Kiribati: 3.30 S. 171.32 W. **49**
Sylt Is., Germany: 54.50 N. 8.20 E. **10, 12, 14**
Syracuse, Italy: 37.03 N. 15.17 E. **21, 24**
SYRIA **9, 21, 26**
Syriam, Myanmar: 16.45 N. 96.20 E. **37**
Syros, Greece: 37.26 N. 24.56 E. **21, 25, 26**
  Max. Size: LOA 200 m. *Fuel:* Available. *Dry Docks:* Floating dock 75,000 d.w.t.
Syros Is., Greece: 37.26 N. 24.56 E. **25**
Szczecin, Poland: 53.25 N. 14.32 E. **9, 10, 11, 12**
  Max. Size: LOA 160 m., draft 9.15 m. *Fuel:* All grades. *Dry Docks:* Lifting capacity of 15,000 tons. *Airport:* 45 km., connects with Warsaw. Berlin, 140 km.

NOTES, ADDITIONS, CORRECTIONS

*Please also advise Shipping Guides Ltd.
75 Bell Street, Reigate, RH2 7AN, United Kingdom
Tel: +44 1737 242255   Fax: +44 1737 222449
Email: updates@portinfo.co.uk   Web: www.portinfo.co.uk*

T

Tabaco, (Luzon Is.), Philippines: 13.21 N. 123.43 E. **46, 47**
  Max. Size: LOA 300 m., draft 40 ft. *Fuel:* All grades.
  Airport: At Legazpi City.
Tabangao, see Batangas.
Tabangao Bauan, see Batangas.
Tabar Is., Papua New Guinea: 2.50 S. 152.00 E. **46**
Tabarka, Tunisia: 36.57 N. 8.46 E. **24**
Tabatinga, Brazil: 4.50 S. 69.50 W. **72**
Tablas, Philippines: 12.22 N. 122.05 E. **47**
Table Bay, see Cape Town.
Taboga Is., Panama: 8.47 N. 79.33 W. **73**
Tabou, Ivory Coast: 4.28 N. 7.19 W. **28**
Tabuka, Japan: 33.38 N. 131.40 E. **45**
Tachibana, see Anan.
Tacloban, (Leyte Is.), Philippines: 11.15 N. 125.00 E. . . **47**
  Max. Size: Draft 6 m. (LW). *Fuel:* Available to small vessels.
  Airport: 9 km.
Tacoma, Washington, U.S.A.: 47.14 N. 122.28 W. . . . **55, 56**
  Max. Size: LOA over 305 m., depths to 21.34 m. (MLLW).
  Tankers: Depth 26 ft. – 41.5 ft. *Fuel:* Available.
  Airport: Seattle – Tacoma, 16 miles.
Taconite Harbour, Minnesota, U.S.A.: 47.31 N. 90.54 W. . **62**
Tadine, (Mare Is.), New Caledonia (France):
  21.33 S. 167.54 E. **49**
  Max. Size: Depth 3 m.
  Also see Noumea.
Tadjoura, Djibouti: 11.50 N. 42.53 E. **31, 32**
Tadoussac, Quebec, Canada: 48.09 N. 69.43 W. **60**
Taft, Louisiana, U.S.A.: 29.59 N. 90.25 W. **67**
Taganrog, Russia: 47.12 N. 38.57 E. **26**
Tagbilaran, (Cebu Is.), Philippines: 9.39 N. 123.51 E. . . **47**
  Also see Cebu.
Tagoloan, (Mindanao Is.), Philippines: 8.32 N. 124.44 E. . **47**
  Max. Size: Draft 10.0 m., 40,000 d.w.t.
Tagonoura, Japan: 35.08 N. 138.42 E. **43, 45**
  Max. Size: LOA 600 ft., beam 100 ft., draft to 9 m.
  Tankers: Draft 5.5 m. *Fuel:* All grades and lubricants
  available from Chiba and Tokyo. *Airport:* Tokyo (Narita).
Tagula Is., Papua New Guinea: 11.37 S. 153.50 E. . . **46, 50, 51**
Tahaa, (Society Is.), French Polynesia (France):
  16.36 S. 151.31 W. **49**
Tahanea Is., French Polynesia (France): 16.50 S. 144.46 W. **49**
Taharoa, New Zealand: 38.11 S. 174.42 E. **52**
  Max. Size: S.B.M.: Depth 30 m.
Taheri, see Bandar Taheri.
Tahiti, French Polynesia (France). **49, 68**
Tahkoluoto, Finland: 61.38 N. 21.25 E. **15**
  Max. Size: Draft 10.0 m. *Fuel:* Available.
  Also see Pori.
Tahsis, B.C., Canada: 49.55 N. 126.40 W. **56**
Tahuata, see Hiva Oa.
Tahuna, (Sangi Is.), Indonesia: 3.37 N. 125.28 E. . . **46, 47**
Tai Nan, Taiwan: 23.02 N. 120.00 E. **42**
Tai Tung, Taiwan: 22.45 N. 121.05 E. **42**
Taicang, China: 31.34 N. 121.16 E. **42**
  Max. Size: LOA 224 m., draft 9.0 m. *Fuel:* Available.
  Airport: Shanghai.
Taichung, Taiwan: 24.18 N. 120.29 E. **42, 46**
  Max. Size: LOA 295 m., draft 13.0 m. *Fuel:* Available.
  Airport: Taipei, 200 km.
Taiohae, (Marquesas Is.), French Polynesia (France):
  8.56 S. 140.04 W. **49**
Taipale, see Saimaa Canal.
Taipalsaari, see Lappeenranta.
TAIWAN **42, 46**
Taizhou, China: 32.17 N. 119.51 E. **42**
  Max. Size: 25,000 d.w.t., depth 17 m. *Fuel:* Available.
TAJIKISTAN **9**
Takamatsu, Japan: 34.21 N. 134.02 E. **45**
  Max. Size: 30,000 g.r.t., LOA 200 m., draft 10.0 m.
  Airport: Takamatsu.
Takaroa, (Society Is.), French Polynesia (France):
  14.26 S. 145.00 W. **49**
Takehara, Japan: 34.18 N. 132.58 E. **45**
  Max. Size: 85,000 d.w.t., depth 13.7 m.
Takoradi, Ghana: 4.53 N. 1.45 W. **28**
  Max. Size: Draft 9.5 m. alongside, 10.36 m. (forward) and
  10.97 m. (aft) at buoys. Tankers: LOA 183 m., draft 10.0 m.
  Fuel: Fuel and Gas Oil. *Dry Docks:* For vessels 100 ft. long,
  25 ft. wide and 8.5 ft. draft. *Airport:* 2 miles.
Taku Bar, China: 38.56 N. 117.53 E. **42**
  Max. Size: Draft 34 ft. *Fuel:* Brought from Dairen.
  Also see Tianjin Xingang.
Takua Pa, Thailand: 9.17 N. 98.20 E. **37**

Takuma, Japan: 34.14 N. 133.41 E. **45**
  Max. Size: Draft 7 m. *Airport:* Takamatsu.
Talamone, Italy: 42.33 N. 11.08 E. **24**
Talara, Peru: 4.35 S. 81.17 W. **72**
  Max. Size: 35,000 tons displacement, LOA 190 m., draft 12 m.
  Buoy berth: 55,000 d.w.t., LOA 228.65 m., draft 10.67 m.
  Fuel: Available. *Airport:* 4 km.
Talasea, Papua New Guinea: 5.20 S. 150.02 E. **46**
Talaud Is., Indonesia: 4.30 N. 127.10 E. **46, 47**
Talbot, see Port Talbot.
Talcahuano, Chile: 36.41 S. 73.06 W. **77**
  Max. Size: Draft 29 ft. and LOA 180 m. Vessels with LOA 230 m.
  and draft 27 ft. can dock at Mole 500 (Naval Base).
  Fuel: Small quantities. *Dry Docks:* 250 m. long by 40 m. wide.
  Airport: 7 km.
Taliabu Is., Indonesia **46**
Talien, see Dalian.
Taliwang, Indonesia: 8.48 S. 116.48 E. **38**
Tallaboa Bay, see Guayanilla.
Tallbacken, see Norrkoping.
Tallinn, Estonia: 59.27 N. 24.46 E. **4, 10, 11**
  Max. Size: Tallinn: LOA 200 m., draft 10.7 m. Muurga: LOA 280
  m., beam 40 m., draft 16.5 m. Kopli: LOA 190 m., draft 8.6 m.
  Fuel: Available. *Airport:* 7 km.
Taltal, Chile: 25.24 S. 70.29 W. **77**
  Max. Size: Anchorage port: No limit. Tankers: Depth 47 ft.
Talvik, Norway: 70.05 N. 23.00 E. **15**
Taman, Russia: 45.13 N. 36.42 E. **26**
Tamano, see Uno.
Tamara, see Conakry.
Tamaram Is., see Pulap Is..
Tamatave, see Toamasina.
Tambey, Russia: 71.30 N. 71.50 E. **16**
Tambo de Mora, Peru: 13.28 S. 76.10 W. **72**
Tammisaari, see Ekenas.
Tampa, Florida, U.S.A.: 27.57 N. 82.28 W. **55, 66, 69**
  Max. Size: Draft 41 ft. Airdraft 149 ft. (MHW). Depths: 28.5 ft.
  – 40 ft. Tankers: Depth 11 ft. – 40 ft. *Fuel:* All grades.
  Dry Docks: Max. 150,000 d.w.t. *Airport:* 15 miles.
Tampa Bay, Florida, U.S.A. **66, 69**
Tampico, Mexico: 22.16 N. 97.47 W. **69**
  Max. Size: LOA 225 m., depth 27 ft. – 33 ft. *Fuel:* Available.
  Dry Docks: 55,000 d.w.t. *Airport:* 10 km.
Tan-Tan, Morocco: 28.29 N. 11.01 W. **27**
  Max. Size: Depth 6 m.
Tana, Norway: 70.28 N. 28.14 E. **15**
Tana Is., Vanuatu: 19.30 S. 169.20 E. **49**
Tanabe, Japan: 33.44 N. 135.21 E. **45, 46**
  Max. Size: Draft 10.5 m. *Fuel:* Bonded oil will be brought
  from Shimotsu or Kobe. *Airport:* Nanki Shirahama, 25 km.
Tanaga Is., (Aleutian Is.), Alaska, U.S.A.: 51.45 N. 178.05 W. . **54**
Tanah Merah, Kalimantan, Indonesia: 1.47 S. 116.07 E. . . **38**
  Max. Size: 60,000 d.w.t., LOA 200 m., beam 35 m., draft 10 m.
Tanah Puteh, see Kuching.
Tanahgrogot, see Tanah Merah.
Tanahmerah, Irian Jaya, Indonesia: 6.22 S. 140.19 E. . . **46**
Tanamo, Cuba: 20.44 N. 75.20 W. **69, 70**
  Max. Size: If berthing, draft 6.71 m., LOA 157 m. If anchoring,
  draft 8.53 m. Tankers: LOA 163 m.
Tananger, see Sola.
Tanauan, (Leyte Is.), Philippines: 11.06 N. 125.01 E. . . **47**
  Max. Size: LOA 1,000 ft., beam 90 ft., draft 31 ft.
  Airport: Tacloban.
Tancarville, France: 49.29 N. 0.28 E. **8**
Tandag, (Mindanao Is.), Philippines: 9.05 N. 126.11 E. . . **47**
Tandoc, (Luzon Is.), Philippines: 14.04 N. 123.18 E. . . **47**
Tandu Batu, (Jolo Is.), Philippines: 6.01 N. 121.19 E. . . **47**
Tanega Is., Japan **42, 46**
Tanga, Tanzania: 5.04 S. 39.08 E. **30**
  Max. Size: Mainly anchorage port; berth for bulk vessels
  up to 20,000 d.w.t.
Tanggu, see Tianjin Xingang.
Tangier, Morocco: 35.47 N. 5.48 W. **20, 21, 22, 23, 27**
  Max. Size: Depth 8.5 m. Tankers: Depth 9 m. *Fuel:* Only
  fishing vessels. *Airport:* 12 km.
Tangimoana, New Zealand: 40.30 S. 175.10 E. **52**
Tangku, see Tianjin Xingang.
Tangshan, China: 39.13 N. 119.01 E. **42**
  Max. Size: Draft 9.5 m. – 11.0 m. *Fuel:* Diesel.
Tanimbar Is., Indonesia **46**
Tanjong Berlayer, Singapore: 1.16 N. 103.49 E.
Tanjong Bruas, see Singapore.
Tanjong Gul, see Singapore.
Tanjong Kling, see Singapore.
Tanjong Pagar, see Singapore.
Tanjong Pandam, see Sibu.
Tanjong Penjuru, see Singapore.
Tanjong Po, see Kuching.
Tanjong Salirong, Brunei: 4.53 N. 115.06 E. **39**
  Max. Size: 21 ft. draft to cross Bar at HW.

Tanjung Balai, Indonesia: 2.57 N. 99.48 E. **38, 39, 40**
Tanjung Bara, Indonesia: 0.33 N. 117.48 E. **38**
  Max. Size: 200,000 d.w.t, LOA 300 m., beam 50 m., draft 17.8 m.
Tanjung Berhala, see Kemaman.
Tanjung Gelang, see Kuantan.
Tanjung Gerem, Indonesia: 5.58 S. 105.59 E. **38**
  Max. Size: 35,000 d.w.t., depth 13 m.
Tanjung Lepee, Indonesia: 4.14 S. 121.32 E. **38, 46**
  Also see Pomalaa.
Tanjung Manis, Sarawak, Malaysia: 2.09 N. 111.21 E. **38, 39**
  Max. Size: 20,000 d.w.t., LOA 183 m., draft 8.4 m.
Tanjung Pandan, Indonesia: 2.45 S. 107.38 E. **38**
  Max. Size: Anchorage: Depth 11 m. – 12 m. Berth: Draft 3.0 m.
  Fuel: Available.
Tanjung Pelepas, Malaya, Malaysia: 1.21 N. 103.33 E. **41**
  Max. Size: Draft 13.5 m. *Fuel:* By barge. *Airport:* Senai (Johor), 70 km. and Changi (Singapore), 70 km.
Tanjung Pemancingan, Indonesia: 3.12 S. 116.17 E. **38**
  Max. Size: North Pulau Laut Coal Terminal: 150,000 d.w.t. Max. LOA 320 m., max. beam 46 m. Depth of water 18 m.
Tanjung Perak, see Surabaya.
Tanjung Pinang, Indonesia: 0.56 N. 104.27 E. **39**
Tanjung Priok, see Jakarta.
Tanjung Selor, Indonesia: 2.52 N. 117.23 E. **38**
Tanjung Uban, Indonesia: 1.04 N. 104.13 E. **39, 40**
  Max. Size: LOA 240 m., depth 17.4 m. *Fuel:* Medium fuel oil and heavy fuel oil. *Airport:* Kijang or Hang Nadim (Batam Island).
Tanjungredep, Indonesia: 2.10 N. 117.29 E. **38**
Tanoura, see Moji.
Tanshui, Taiwan: 25.10 N. 121.24 E. **42, 46**
Tantawan, Thailand: 10.05 N. 101.25 E. **39**
  Max. Size: 110,000 d.w.t., depth 74 m. *Airport:* Bangkok.
Tantung, see Dandong.
Tanysk, Russia: 59.30 N. 149.30 E. **43**
TANZANIA **30**
Taongi Is., Marshall Is.: 14.38 N. 168.58 E. **49**
Taormina, (Sicily), Italy: 37.51 N. 15.17 E. **24**
Tapaktuan, Indonesia: 3.15 N. 97.11 E. **38, 40**
Tapia, Spain: 43.36 N. 6.56 W. **19, 20**
Tappahannock, Virginia, U.S.A.: 37.56 N. 76.51 W. **63, 65**
Tarabulus, see Tripoli.
Tarafa, see Nuevitas.
Tarahan Terminal, see Panjang.
Taraika Bay, (Sakhalin Is.), Russia **43**
Tarakan, Indonesia: 3.17 N. 117.35 E. **38, 47**
  Max. Size: Jetty: Depth 5.5 m. Tankers: CBM: 55,000 d.w.t., LOA 230 m., depth 10.5 m. Jetty: 6,000 d.w.t, LOA 120 m., depth 7.0 m. *Fuel:* By road tanker. *Airport:* Juata, 7 km.
Taranaki, see New Plymouth.
Taranto, Italy: 40.29 N. 17.13 E. **21, 24**
  Max. Size: Draft 6 m. – 13.5 m. Coal: Draft 23 m. Tankers: Draft 22 m. *Fuel:* Available. *Airport:* Bari or Brindisi.
Tarawa, Kiribati: 1.25 N. 172.54 E. **49**
  Max. Size: Any vessel drawing up to 26 ft. may enter at LWOST and 30 ft. HW. Vessels over 600 ft. to navigate with extreme care. Tankers: Up to 14 ft. draft. *Fuel:* Diesel only, in restricted quantities. *Dry Docks:* 150 tons displacement. *Airport:* 13 miles, connects with Fiji, Nauru and Honolulu.
Tarbaek, Denmark: 55.47 N. 12.36 E. **12**
Tarbert, (Kintyre), U.K.: 55.55 N. 5.25 W. **6**
Tarbert, (Lewis), U.K.: 57.54 N. 6.49 W. **5**
Tarbert Island Oil Terminal, Ireland: 52.35 N. 9.21 W. . . . **5, 8**
  Max. Size: 60,000 tonnes d.w.t., LOA 250 m., draft 14 m. *Airport:* Shannon.
Tarfaya, Morocco: 27.56 N. 12.55 W. **27**
Tarif, U.A.E.: 24.05 N. 53.49 E. **35**
Tarifa, Spain: 36.00 N. 5.36 W. **20, 23**
Tarno, see Sterno.
Taroa, Marshall Is.: 8.45 N. 171.15 E. **49**
Tarpon Springs, Florida, U.S.A.: 28.09 N. 82.45 W. **66**
Tarragona, Spain: 41.05 N. 1.14 E. **21, 22**
  Max. Size: Draft 18.0 m. Tankers: Jetty: Draft 18.0 m. SBM: 325,000 d.w.t., draft 42.8 m. *Fuel:* Fuel oil and gas oil. *Airport:* 12 km, connects with Madrid. Barcelona (International), 60 miles.
Tartary Straits, Russia. **43**
Tartous, Syria: 34.53 N. 35.45 E. **21, 26**
  Max. Size: Draft 13 m. Tankers: LOA 280 m., draft 52 ft., 115,000 d.w.t. *Fuel:* Very limited. *Airport:* Damascus, 280 km.
Tasinge Is., see Troense.
Tasiussaq, Greenland (Denmark): 73.21 N. 56.00 W. **17**
Tasman Bay, New Zealand **52**
Tasman Sea **36, 50, 52**
Tasmania, Australia **50, 51, 80**
Tasu, B.C., Canada: 52.46 N. 131.58 W. **56**
Tasucu, Turkey: 36.20 N. 33.55 E. **26**
Tateyama, Japan: 34.59 N. 139.52 E. **43, 45**
Tau, see Strand.
Taufiq, see Port Taufiq.

Tauranga, New Zealand: 37.39 S. 176.11 E. **52**
  Max. Size: LOA 290 m., draft 13 m. at HW, 11.7 m. at LW. Tankers: Draft 12.0 m. *Fuel:* Most grades. *Airport:* 1.6 km.
Tavani, N.W.T., Canada: 62.08 N. 93.31 W. **59**
Taveuni, see Vanua Levu.
Tavira, Portugal: 37.07 N. 7.40 W. **20**
Tavoy, Myanmar: 14.03 N. 98.13 E. **37**
Tawas City, Michigan, U.S.A.: 44.15 N. 83.30 W. **62**
Tawau, Sabah, Malaysia: 4.14 N. 117.52 E. **38, 47**
  Max. Size: Depth 9.14 m. Tankers: Depth 9.75 m. *Fuel:* Diesoline in drums. *Airport:* Nearby.
Tawi Tawi Is., Philippines **47**
Taya Wan, Japan **48**
Tayport, U.K.: 56.27 N. 2.53 W. **6**
Taytay, (Palawan Is.), Philippines: 10.48 N. 119.30 E. . . . **47**
Tazerka, Tunisia: 36.36 N. 11.41 E. **24**
  Max. Size: LOA 297 m. (minimum 170 m.), 140,000 d.w.t.
Tazovskoye, Russia: 67.40 N. 77.40 E. **16**
Tchatamba Marine Terminal, Gabon: 2.05 S. 9.10 E. . . . **28**
  Max. Size: 135,900 tonnes d.w.t., depth 45 m.
Tebar, see Sao Sebastiao.
Tebig, see DTSE/GEBIG Oil Terminal.
Tecarmo, see Carmopolis.
Tedut, see Tramandai.
Teesport, U.K.: 54.39 N. 1.08 W. **5, 6**
  Max. Size: LOA 305 m., beam 48 m., draft 17 m. *Fuel:* All grades. *Dry Docks:* Max. 26,000 tons capacity. *Airport:* Teesside, 12 miles.
Tefran (S.B.M.) Terminal, see Sao Francisco do Sul.
Tegal, Indonesia: 6.52 S. 109.10 E. **38**
  Max. Size: Anchorage port. Draft above 25 ft. will be 2-3 miles offshore.
Teignmouth, U.K.: 50.33 N. 3.30 W. **7, 19**
  Max. Size: LOA 119 m., draft 5.0 m., 5,000 d.w.t. and beam 17.0 m.
Tekirdag, Turkey: 40.58 N. 27.31 E. **9, 25, 26**
  Max. Size: Depth 3.7 m. – 12 m. *Fuel:* Available. *Airport:* Istanbul, 138 km.
Tel Aviv, Israel: 32.05 N. 34.45 E. **26**
Tela, Honduras: 15.47 N. 87.27 W. **69**
  Port closed – awaiting re-development.
Telegrafberget, see Stockholm.
Teller, Alaska, U.S.A.: 65.15 N. 166.24 W. **54**
Tellicherry, India: 11.45 N. 75.30 E. **37**
Telo, Indonesia: 0.03 S. 98.17 E. **38, 40**
Telok Anson, Malaya, Malaysia: 4.02 N. 101.00 E. . . . **38, 39**
Telok Ayer, Indonesia: 0.44 S. 109.05 E. **38**
  Max. Size: Depth 6 fathoms at loading point.
Telok Ewa, see Langkawi.
Teluk Bayur, Indonesia: 0.58 S. 100.20 E. **37, 38, 40**
  Max. Size: Depth up to 10 m. *Fuel:* Available. *Dry Docks:* Up to 500 d.w.t. *Airport:* Tabing, 15 km.
Teluk Betung, Indonesia: 5.27 S. 105.16 E. **38**
Teluk Bungus, Indonesia: 1.04 S. 100.24 E. **38, 40**
  Max. Size: Tankers: Depth 15 m. *Airport:* Tabing, 25 km.
Teluk Semangka, Indonesia: 5.34 S. 104.37 E. **38**
  Max. Size: Vessels berth alongside 262,000 d.w.t. tanker. *Fuel:* By barge.
Telukdalem, Indonesia: 0.33 N. 97.50 E. **38, 40**
Tema, Ghana: 5.38 N. 0.01 W. **28**
  Max. Size: Depth 9.7 m. *Fuel:* Fuel oil, diesel oil. *Dry Docks:* Length 277.4 m., width 45.4 m., capacity 100,000 d.w.t. *Airport:* 29 km.
Temadre, see Salvador.
Tembelan Is., see Lepu.
Tembladora, Trinidad and Tobago: 10.41 N. 61.35 W. . . **71, 75**
  Max. Size: Draft 23 ft. – 36 ft. *Fuel:* Available.
Temryuk, Ukraine: 45.19 N. 37.21 E. **26**
Temse, see Hemiksem.
Tenakee Springs, Alaska, U.S.A.: 57.47 N. 135.12 W. . . . **56**
Tenasserim, Myanmar: 12.05 N. 99.05 E. **37**
Tenby, U.K.: 51.41 N. 4.41 W. **6**
Tenerife, Canary Is. (Spain): 28.28 N. 16.13 W. **27**
Tenes, Algeria: 36.35 N. 1.18 E. **22**
  Max. Size: Depth 7.2 m.
Tennessee, U.S.A. **66**
Tepa, (Babar Is.), Indonesia: 7.52 S. 129.36 E. **46**
Tepre, see Esmeraldas.
Terampa, Indonesia: 3.13 N. 106.13 E. **38, 39**
Terceira Is., Azores (Portugal) **20**
Teriberka, see Gavrilovo.
Termini Imerese, Italy: 38.00 N. 13.42 E. **24**
Termoli, Italy: 42.00 N. 15.00 E. **24**
Ternate, Indonesia: 0.46 N. 127.22 E. **46**
  Max. Size: Draft 10.0 m. *Fuel:* By road tanker. *Airport:* 4 km.
Terneuzen, Netherlands: 51.20 N. 3.50 E. **7, 8, 9**
  Max. Size: Draft 40 ft. 6 in. can reach Terneuzen in most circumstances. To pass through West Lock and Canal: LOA 265 m., beam 34 m., draft in fresh water (canal) 12.25 m. *Fuel:* Fuel oil and lubricating oil.

Terno, see Sterno.
Terracino, Italy: 41.13 N. 13.16 E. **23, 24**
Terrenceville, Newfoundland, Canada: 47.43 N. 54.46 W. **60**
Terrington Basin, see Goose Bay.
Tetney Marine Terminal, U.K.: 53.32 N. 0.07 E. **6, 7**
  Max. Size: Mono-buoy in 60 ft. of water at LW.
  Tidal range 7 ft. – 22.5 ft.
Tetyukhe, Russia: 44.22 N. 135.51 E. **43**
Texas, U.S.A. **57, 66**
Texas City, Texas, U.S.A.: 29.22 N. 94.53 W. **66**
  Max. Size: Depths up to 40 ft. *Fuel:* Bunker "C",
  other grades by barge from Houston. *Airport:* Houston.
THAILAND **37, 38, 39**
Thames, New Zealand: 37.08 S. 175.33 E. **52**
Thames Estuary, U.K. **5, 6**
Thamesport, U.K.: 51.26 N. 0.42 E. **6**
  Max. Size: Depth 13.5 m.
  Also see Medway Ports.
Thamshamn, see Thamshavn.
Thamshavn, Norway: 63.20 N. 9.52 E. **10, 15**
  Max. Size: LOA 200 m., depth 24 ft. (MLW) at Import Quay,
  beamn 23 m. *Airport:* Vaernes, 62 miles.
Thanh Hoa, Vietnam: 19.48 N. 105.49 E. **39**
  Max. Size: Anchorage – Depth 5 m. – 14 m. Berth – Depth 6 m.
  Airport: Sao Vang, 60 km.
Thasos, Greece: 40.48 N. 24.42 E. **25**
The Bight, (Cat Is.), Bahamas: 24.19 N. 75.24 W. **69, 70**
The Dalles, Oregon, U.S.A.: 45.37 N. 121.11 W. **57**
The Dardanelles, Turkey **25, 26**
The Gulf **31, 35**
The Hague, Netherlands: 52.05 N. 4.14 E. **7, 8**
The Minch, U.K. **5**
The Narrows, New York, U.S.A. **63**
The Naze, U.K. **5**
The River Plate, Argentina: 35.10 S. 56.15 W. **77, 78**
The Sisters, (Chatham Is.), New Zealand **52**
The Skaw, Denmark **11, 12**
The Sound **11, 12**
The Wash, U.K. **5, 7**
Theodosia, Ukraine: 45.04 N. 35.24 E. **26**
  Max. Size: LOA 150 m., draft 6.8 m. Tankers: Draft 12.6 m.
  Fuel: By barge or road tanker. *Airport:* Simpheropol, 117 km.
Thessalon, Ontario, Canada: 46.15 N. 83.34 W. **62**
Thessaloniki, Greece: 40.38 N. 22.56 E. **21, 24, 25**
  Max. Size: Depth 5.5 m. – 12 m. Tankers: Draft 32 ft. – 44 ft.
  Fuel: Available. *Airport:* 12 km.
Thevenard, S.A., Australia: 32.09 S. 133.39 E. **50**
  Max. Size: LOA 180 m., beam 28 m., depth 32 ft.
  Fuel: Available. *Airport:* Connects with Adelaide.
Thingeyri, Iceland: 65.53 N. 23.28 W. **17**
Thio, New Caledonia (France): 21.37 S. 166.15 E. **51**
  Max. Size: LOA 170 m., draft 10.8 m.
  Also see Noumea.
Thira, (Thira Is.), Greece: 36.23 N. 25.27 E. **25**
Thisted, Denmark: 57.00 N. 8.42 E. **11, 12**
Thitu Is., South China Sea: 11.03 N. 114.23 E. **39**
Thorold, Ontario, Canada: 43.05 N. 79.10 W. **60, 62**
  Max. Size: Max. draft in Welland Canal 8.0 m.
  Also see Port Weller.
Thorshofn, Iceland: 66.12 N. 15.19 W. **17**
Thousand Islands Section, see St. Lawrence Seaway.
Three Rivers, see Trois Rivieres.
Thule, see North Star Bugt.
Thunder Bay, Ontario, Canada: 48.25 N. 89.13 W. **62**
  Max. Size: Draft 26 ft. *Fuel:* Light diesel available. Bunker C
  only in emergencies. *Dry Docks:* Length 227.69 m. x 29.87 m.
  Airport: Served by regular airlines.
Thurrock, U.K.: 51.29 N. 0.24 E. **6**
Thursday Island, Qld., Australia: 10.35 S. 142.13 E. . . . **46, 50, 51**
  Max. Size: Depth 3.4 m. – 5.0 m. alongside. *Fuel:* Bulk distillate
  available. *Airport:* 2 miles by launch.
Thurso, U.K.: 58.36 N. 3.31 W. **5**
  Also see Scrabster.
Thyboron, Denmark: 56.42 N. 8.13 E. **11, 12**
Tia Juana, Venezuela: 10.15 N. 71.22 W. **74**
Tianjin Xingang, China: 39.06 N. 117.10 E. **42**
  Max. Size: Channel: Draft 11.0 m. Berths: Depths up to 12.0 m.
  at container berths and 13.5 m. at oil berths. *Fuel:* Available.
  Airport: Tianjin, 54 miles.
Tiburon Is., Mexico: 29.00 N. 112.25 W. **57**
Ticho, Eritrea: 14.41 N. 40.55 E. **32**
Tiden, (Nicobar Is.), India: 7.05 N. 93.45 E. **37**
Tiel, Netherlands: 51.53 N. 5.26 E. **8**
Tientsin, see Tianjin Xingang.
Tierra Colerada, see Paita.
Tierra del Fuego, Chile/Argentina **77**
Tignish, P.E.I., Canada: 46.57 N. 64.01 W. **60**
Tijuana, Mexico: 32.28 N. 117.12 W. **57**
Tiko, Cameroon: 4.00 N. 9.24 E. **29**
  Also see Douala.

Tilburg, Netherlands: 51.30 N. 5.05 E. **8, 9**
Tilbury, U.K.: 51.28 N. 0.23 E. **5, 6, 7**
  Max. Size: LOA 262 m., beam 32.2 m., draft 11.4 m.
  Grain: Depth 12.8 m. *Fuel:* All grades. *Airport:* London
  (Heathrow), London (Gatwick), London (City) and Stansted.
  Also see London.
Tilichiki, Russia: 61.05 N. 166.05 E. **54**
Tilos Is., Greece: 36.27 N. 27.27 E. **25**
Tilt Cove, Newfoundland, Canada: 49.53 N. 55.37 W. **60**
Timaru, New Zealand: 44.24 S. 171.19 E. **52**
  Max. Size: LOA 220 m., longer vessels by arrangement.
  Draft 10.5 m. (HWOST). *Fuel:* MDO available. *Airport:* 8 km.,
  connects with Wellington and Christchurch.
Timor Is., Indonesia **46, 50**
Timor Sea **38, 46, 50, 51**
Tin Can Island, Nigeria: 6.26 N. 3.23 E. **29**
  Max. Size: Draft 9.5 m.
  Also see Lagos.
Ting Hai, China: 30.01 N. 122.06 E. **42**
Tingmiarmiut, see Kutdlek.
Tinian, Northern Mariana Is. (U.S.A.): 15.00 N. 145.40 E. **46**
Tinos, (Tinos Is.), Greece: 37.33 N. 25.09 E. **25, 26**
Tioga Terminal, see Philadelphia.
Tioman, Malaya, Malaysia: 3.43 N. 104.11 E. **40**
Tirana, Albania: 41.20 N. 19.49 E. **9**
Tiree Is., U.K. **5**
Tiruchendir, India: 8.30 N. 78.09 E. **37**
Tivat, Yugoslavia: 42.26 N. 18.42 E. **24**
Tiverton, Rhode Is., U.S.A.: 41.38 N. 71.13 W. **63**
Tjilatjap, see Cilacap.
Tjirebon, see Cirebon.
Tjorn Is., Sweden **10**
Tjotta, Norway: 65.49 N. 12.26 E. **15**
Toamasina, Madagascar: 18.08 S. 49.22 E. **30**
  Max. Size: Cargo vessels: LOA 180 m., draft 31 ft. 2 in. (9.5 m.).
  Tankers: LOA 230 m., beam 31 m., draft 12.20 m.
  Fuel: Available. *Airport:* Served by regular airlines.
Toau, (Tuamotu Arch.), French Polynesia (France):
  15.55 S. 146.05 W. **49**
Toba, Japan: 34.29 N. 136.51 E. **45**
Tobago, Trinidad and Tobago **69, 71, 75**
Tobata, Japan: 33.55 N. 130.51 E. **44**
  Max. Size: 160,000 d.w.t. or 250,000 d.w.t. part load,
  LOA 327 m., draft 16 m. LNG: Up to 125,000 d.w.t., LOA 286 m.,
  draft 12 m. *Fuel:* Bonded oil will be brought from Moji, Ube or
  Ohita. *Airport:* Fukuoka or Kitakyushu.
Tobelo, Indonesia: 1.45 N. 127.59 E. **46**
Tobermory, Ontario, Canada: 45.14 N. 81.40 W. **62**
Tobermory, U.K.: 56.38 N. 6.05 W. **5**
Tobi, Palau: 3.02 N. 131.10 E. **46**
Toboali, Indonesia: 3.01 S. 106.27 E. **38**
Toboli, Indonesia: 0.38 S. 120.05 E. **46**
Tobruk, Libya: 32.04 N. 24.00 E. **26**
  Max. Size: Draft 29 ft., LOA 400 ft.
  Tankers: See Marsa al Hariga.
Tocopilla, Chile: 22.05 S. 70.11 W. **77**
  Max. Size: Buoys: Draft 45 ft. Wharf: Draft 11.0 m. Tankers:
  Draft 13.5 m. *Airport:* Antofagasta, 180 km.
Todd, Alaska, U.S.A.: 57.28 N. 135.03 W. **56**
Toft Voe, see Burravoe.
Togiak, Alaska, U.S.A.: 59.04 N. 160.31 W. **54**
TOGO **28, 29**
Tokachi, Japan: 42.15 N. 143.18 E. **43**
  Max. Size: 15,000 d.w.t., depth 9.0 m.
  Airport: Obihiro, 80 minutes.
Tokara Is., (Ryukyu Is.), Japan: 29.50 N. 129.55 E. **46**
Tokelau Islands, (New Zealand) **49**
Tokomaru, New Zealand: 38.08 S. 178.20 E. **52**
Tokushima-Komatsushima, Japan: 34.00 N. 134.36 E. **45**
  Max. Size: 42,000 d.w.t., LOA 200 m., draft 10.0 m.
  Fuel: All grades of bonded bunkers.
  Airport: Tokushima, 10 miles.
  Also see Osaka.
Tokuyama, Japan: 34.02 N. 131.48 E. **45**
  Max. Size: Depth 6 m. – 12 m. Tankers: Largest vessel at
  sea berth: 275,000 d.w.t., draft 19.5 m. *Fuel:* All grades. *Dry
  Docks:* 90,000 tonnes. *Airport:* Hiroshima or Ube, about
  40 minutes.
Tokyo, Japan: 35.43 N. 139.46 E. **43, 44, 45, 46**
  Max. Size: Depth 10.0 m. Containers: Depth 12.0 m. – 14.0 m.
  Tankers: 36,000 d.w.t. *Fuel:* All grades. *Dry Docks:*
  Largest: 180 m. x 24 m. x 7.27 m.
  Airport: Tokyo (Narita), 60 km.
Tolagnaro, see Fort Dauphin.
Toledo, Ohio, U.S.A.: 41.42 N. 83.28 W. **55, 62**
  Max. Size: LOA 730 ft., draft 26 ft. Height restriction of
  104 ft. for grain berths only. Tankers: Depth 22 ft. – 23 ft.
  Fuel: All grades. *Dry Docks:* 641 ft. x 78 ft.
Toledo, Oregon, U.S.A.: 44.37 N. 123.57 W. **57**
Toliara, see Toliary.

Toliary, Madagascar: 23.22 S. 43.40 E. 30
  Max. Size: Depth 6.7 m. – 9.29 m. *Fuel:* Available.
Tolkis, see Tolkkinen.
Tolkkinen, Finland: 60.20 N. 25.35 E. 11, 13
  Max. Size: Depth 6.5 m. *Fuel:* Small quantities.
Tolle, see Porto Tolle.
Tolo Harbour, Hong Kong (SAR), China: 22.18 N. 114.10 E. . . . 48
Tolong, (Negros Is.), Philippines: 9.20 N. 122.51 E. 47
  Max. Size: Depth 10.0 m. after dredging.
  Airport: Dumaguete, 100 km.
Tolu, Colombia: 9.30 N. 75.40 W. 69
Tomakomai, Japan: 42.35 N. 141.35 E. 43
  Max. Size: Up to 65,000 d.w.t., depth 14 m. Tankers: Up to
  250,000 d.w.t., depth 24 m. *Fuel:* Bonded oil will be brought
  from Hakodate. *Airport:* Sapporo, 25 km.
Tomari, Russia: 47.46 N. 142.03 E. 43
Tome, Chile: 36.37 S. 72.57 W. 77
Tomil Harbour, (Yap Is.), Micronesia: 9.31 N. 138.10 E. . . . 46
  Max. Size: 10,000 d.w.t., depth 30 ft. *Fuel:* Available.
  Airport: 2.5 miles.
Tomini Gulf, (Celebes), Indonesia 38, 46
Tomioka, Japan: 33.55 N. 134.42 E. 45
  Max. Size: Draft 5.2 m.
  Also see Anan.
Tommy's Arm, Newfoundland, Canada: 49.27 N. 55.46 W. . . . 60
Tomo, Japan: 34.23 N. 133.23 E. 45
Tomoni, Indonesia: 0.30 N. 120.28 E. 46
Tomoura, Japan: 33.36 N. 134.20 E. 45
Tompkinsville, see Stapleton.
Tonawanda, New York, U.S.A.: 43.02 N. 78.53 W. 62
Tonda, Japan: 34.02 N. 131.44 E. 45
  Max. Size: Depth 10.5 m. *Fuel:* Available at 7 days notice.
  Airport: Hiroshima or Ube, 40 minutes.
Tondi, India: 9.45 N. 79.02 E. 37
TONGA 49
Tongareva Is., Cook Is. (N.Z.): 9.05 S. 157.57 W. 49
Tonghae, South Korea: 37.29 N. 129.08 E. 42, 43, 45
  Max. Size: Draft 11.8 m. (SW) *Fuel:* Available.
  Airport: Nearest at Soeul.
Tongjiang, China: 47.44 N. 132.43 E. 43
Tongling, China: 30.57 N. 117.45 E. 42
Toningtao, China: 22.28 N. 114.37 E. 48
Tonnay Charente, France: 45.57 N. 0.53 W. 8, 19
  Max. Size: LOA 120 m., draft 5.7 m. – 6.6 m. *Fuel:* Obtained by
  truck from La Pallice (20 miles). *Airport:* La Rochelle, 30 miles.
  Also see Rochefort sur Mer.
Tonning, Germany: 54.19 N. 8.57 E. 11, 12, 14
Tonosho Is., Harima Sea, Japan. 45
Tonosi, Panama: 7.30 N. 80.15 W. 69
Tonsberg, Norway: 59.16 N. 10.25 E. 8, 10, 12
  Max. Size: (24 ft. draft for West entrance). Up to 30,000 tons
  in ballast. *Fuel:* By road tanker. *Airport:* Torp, 20 km.
  Oslo, 150 km.
Topolly, see Varna.
Topolobampo, Mexico: 25.35 N. 109.03 W. 57
  Max. Size: 50,000 d.w.t., LOA 240 m., draft 12 m. Tankers:
  Depth 14 m. *Airport:* Los Mochis, 12 miles.
Toppila, see Oulu.
Topsham, U.K.: 50.41 N. 3.25 W. 5, 7
Tor Harbour, see El Tur.
Tore, Sweden: 65.55 N. 22.40 E. 15
  Max. Size: Draft 6 m.
  Also see Karlsborgsverken.
Torefors, see Tore.
Torekov, Sweden: 56.24 N. 12.37 E. 12
Torgua, see Rio de Janeiro.
Tori, Japan: 30.27 N. 140.19 E. 43, 46
Tornio, Finland: 65.51 N. 24.09 E. 10, 15
  Max. Size: Draft 8 m. *Fuel:* Ordinary fuel by lorries.
  Airport: Kemi, 20 km.
Toronto, Ontario, Canada: 43.40 N. 79.25 W. 60, 62
  Max. Size: Size of vessels permitted to transit the Seaway: Not
  exceeding 730 ft. LOA and 75 ft. 6 in. extreme breadth, masts
  must not exceed 117 ft. above the water level. Draft 26 ft.
  Fuel: Available, but in most cases vessels bunker in Montreal.
  Airport: Toronto, 15 miles.
Torquay, U.K.: 50.27 N. 3.31 W. 5, 7, 19
Torre Annunziata, Italy: 40.45 N. 14.27 E. 23, 24
  Max. Size: LOA 472 ft., draft 29 ft. *Fuel:* By barge or road
  tanker. *Airport:* Naples, 23 km.
Torre del Greco, see Torre Annunziata.
Torremolinas, Spain: 36.37 N. 4.30 W. 20, 22
Torres, see Porto Torres.
Torres Is., Vanuatu: 13.18 S. 166.38 E. 49
Torres Strait, Qld., Australia: 10.36 S. 142.05 E. . . 46, 50, 51
  Max. Size: Draft 12.2 m. (40 ft.).
Torrevieja, Spain: 37.58 N. 0.40 W. 22
  Max. Size: LOA 150 m. Draft on entry 21 ft., and departure
  draft 29 ft. 6 in.
Torridon, U.K.: 57.31 N. 5.26 W. 5

Tors Harbour, see Gothenburg.
Torshalla, Sweden: 59.25 N. 16.29 E. 11
Torshamnen, see Gothenburg.
Torshavn, Faroe Is. (Denmark): 62.00 N. 6.45 W. 4, 5, 15
  Max. Size: LOA 280 m., 74,136 g.r.t. *Fuel:* All grades.
  Dry Docks: Slipway for vessels up to 2,000 tons. *Airport:*
  2 hours by car.
Torsminde, Denmark: 56.28 N. 8.10 E. 11, 12
Torsvag, Norway: 70.15 N. 19.30 E. 10, 15
Tortola Is., Panama: 8.52 N. 79.34 W. 73
Tortola Is., Virgin Is. (U.K.) 71
Tortuga Harbour, (Dry Tortugas), Florida, U.S.A.:
  24.38 N. 82.54 W. 66, 70
Tortuga Is., Venezuela 69, 71, 75
Tory Is., Ireland: 55.16 N. 8.14 W. 5
Tosa, Japan: 33.28 N. 133.25 E. 45
Tosa Bay, Japan 45
Tosa-Shimizu, Japan: 32.46 N. 132.57 E. 45
Tou, see Strand.
Toulon, France: 43.07 N. 5.55 E. 9, 21, 22
  Max. Size: Ships up to 250 m. LOA and 9.5 m. draft.
  Fuel: By road tanker. *Dry Docks:* Can accommodate vessels in
  excess of 250 m. *Airport:* Toulon-Nyeres, 23 km.
Tourane, see Da Nang.
Tournai, Belgium: 50.34 N. 3.26 E. 7
Toussoum, Egypt: 30.30 N. 32.20 E. 33
Townsend, see Port Townsend.
Townsville, Qld., Australia: 19.15 S. 146.50 E. 50, 51
  Max. Size: LOA 152 m. – 238 m., beam 34 m.,
  depth 9.7 m. – 12.4 m. Tankers: Depth 12.2 m.
  Fuel: Bunker fuel oil and distillate is available. *Dry
  Docks:* Slipway capacity of 800 tonnes d.w.t. *Airport:* 6.5 km.
Toyahashi, see Toyohashi.
Toyama, Japan: 36.46 N. 137.13 E. 43, 45
  Max. Size: 32,500 d.w.t., LOA 170 m., draft up to 9.5 m.
  Tankers: 264,658 d.w.t., draft 20.78 m. (Summer).
  Fuel: Bonded oil will be brought from Moji.
  Dry Docks: Shipbuilding docks only. *Airport:* 10 km.
Toyama Shinko, Japan: 36.47 N. 137.10 E. 43, 45
  Max. Size: 60,000 d.w.t., draft 12.0 m. *Fuel:* Bonded oil
  will be brought from Kanmon area. *Airport:* Toyama, 25 km.
Toyohashi, Japan: 34.43 N. 137.20 E. 45
  Max. Size: LOA 250 m., draft 9.8 m. *Fuel:* From Yokkaichi or
  Nagoya.
Trabzon, Turkey: 41.01 N. 39.46 E. 26
  Max. Size: Draft 9.5 m. Tankers: Depth at buoys – 31 m.
  Fuel: Fuel oil in limited quantities.
Tracadie, N.B., Canada: 47.30 N. 64.55 W. 60
Tralee, Ireland: 52.15 N. 9.40 W. 5, 8
Tramandai, Brazil: 29.59 S. 50.08 W. 77
  Max. Size: SBM-2 (E.): Designed for 200,000 d.w.t. tankers,
  draft 19 m. (62 ft.).
Trangan Is., (Aru Is.), Indonesia 46
Trangisvaag, see Tvoroyri.
Tranmere, U.K.: 53.22 N. 2.57 W. 6
Tranoy, Norway: 68.12 N. 15.42 E. 15
Trapani, (Sicily), Italy: 38.00 N. 12.30 E. 21, 24
  Max. Size: 35,000 d.w.t., LOA 202 m., draft 8.5 m.
  Fuel: By barge or road tanker.
  Dry Docks: Largest: 130 m. x 20 m. x 6.5 m.
  Airport: Birgi, 16 km. and Punta Raisi, 76 km.
Travemunde, Germany: 53.58 N. 10.53 E. 12, 14
  Max. Size: Depth 7 m. – 9.5 m.
  Also see Lubeck.
Traverse City, Michigan, U.S.A.: 44.45 N. 85.38 W. 62
Trebisacci, Italy: 39.52 N. 16.32 E. 24
Treguier, France: 48.48 N. 3.14 W. 7, 19
Trelleborg, Sweden: 55.21 N. 13.09 E. 11, 12
  Max. Size: Depths to 8 m. Tankers: LOA 570 ft., depth 8 m.
  Fuel: All grades.
Trenton, Ontario, Canada: 44.08 N. 77.34 W. 60, 62
Trenton, Michigan, U.S.A.: 42.05 N. 83.06 W. 62
Trenton, New Jersey, U.S.A.: 40.12 N. 74.46 W. 65
Trepassey, Newfoundland, Canada: 46.44 N. 53.25 W. 60
Tresco Is., (Scilly Is.), U.K.: 49.57 N. 6.20 W. 19
Trevor, U.K.: 53.00 N. 4.25 W. 5, 7
Triabunna, see Spring Bay.
Trial Bay, N.S.W., Australia: 30.51 S. 153.03 E. 50
Trieste, Italy: 45.39 N. 13.45 E. 9, 21, 24
  Max. Size: Tankers up to 328 m. LOA, draft 16.5 m. and
  215,000 S.d.w.t. Other vessels: Up to 52 ft. draft.
  Fuel: All grades by barge or road tanker. *Dry Docks:* A new
  dock at Arsenale San Marco takes vessels 297 m. LOA,
  56 m. moulded breadth, 19.0 m. moulded depth.
  Airport: 15 miles.
Trincomalee, Sri Lanka: 8.33 N. 81.13 E. 37
  Max. Size: Grain: LOA 227 m., draft 13.0 m.
  Tankers: LOA 200 m., draft 9.75 m. *Fuel:* Available.
  Airport: Colombo, 250 km.
Trinidad, Cuba, see Casilda.
Trinidad, Panama, see Porto Trinidad.

TRINIDAD AND TOBAGO 71, 72, 75
Trinidad Bay, Panama Canal, Panama 73
Trinity, Newfoundland, Canada: 48.22 N. 53.22 W. 60
Trinity Is., Alaska, U.S.A. 54
Trinkitat, Sudan: 18.42 N. 37.47 E. 32
Tripoli, Lebanon: 34.28 N. 35.49 E. 26
  Max. Size: Draft 22 ft. 6 in. Tankers: Up to 62 ft. draft at buoys. Up to 35,000 tonnes d.w.t., draft 7.5 m. at Petro-Store. *Fuel:* Available. *Airport:* Beirut.
Tripoli, Libya: 32.54 N. 13.13 E. 21, 24
  Max. Size: Draft 28 ft. *Fuel:* Available. *Dry Docks:* Lifting capacity 5,000 tons. *Airport:* Tripoli, 27 km.
Triso, see Lingga.
Tristan da Cunha (U.K.) 18, 28, 68
Tristan Island, see Edinburgh.
Triton Is., (Paracel Is.), South China Sea: 15.55 N. 111.13 E. . . . 39
Trivandrum, India: 8.29 N. 76.59 E. 37
Trobriand Is., Papua New Guinea 46
Troense, Denmark: 55.02 N. 10.39 E. 12, 14
Trogir, Croatia: 43.31 N. 16.16 E. 24
Trois Rivieres, Quebec, Canada: 46.22 N. 72.34 W. 60
  Max. Size: Draft 11.0 m. Tankers: Depth 10.6 m. *Fuel:* Fuel oil and diesel. *Airport:* Charter only, 5 miles.
Trollhattan, Sweden: 58.15 N. 12.20 E. 12
Trollhatte Canal, Sweden: 58.00 N. 12.00 E. 11, 12
  Max. Size: Locks: 87 m. x 13 m. x 5.3 m., airdraft 27 m. Also see Karlstad.
Trombetas, see Porto Trombetas.
Trompeloup, France: 45.14 N. 0.45 W. 8, 19
  Also see Pauillac.
Tromso, Norway: 69.39 N. 18.58 E. 10, 15, 79
  Max. Size: Depth 4.5 m. – 11 m. Tankers: Depth 6.4 m. – 11.9 m. *Fuel:* All grades. *Dry Docks:* 4 slipways, 80 ft. – 222 ft. *Airport:* 5 km.
Trondheim, Norway: 63.25 N. 10.24 E. 10, 15
  Max. Size: Depth 3.0 m. – 10.6 m. Cruise ships: Depth 13.0 m. Tankers: Depth 9 m. – 12 m. *Fuel:* Available. *Airport:* 30 km.
Troon, U.K.: 55.33 N. 4.40 W. 6
  Max. Size: Depth 6 m. *Fuel:* Available. *Dry Docks:* 112 m. x 17 m. x 4.6 m. Also see Ayr.
Trosa, Sweden: 58.55 N. 17.35 E. 11
Trout River, Newfoundland, Canada: 49.28 N. 58.08 W. . . 60
Trouville-Deauville, France: 49.23 N. 0.05 E. 7, 8
  Max. Size: Depth 2.80 m., dries out at LW. *Fuel:* Small quantities by road tankers. *Airport:* 3 miles.
Troy, New York, U.S.A.: 42.44 N. 73.42 W. 63
Trujillo, Honduras: 15.54 N. 86.00 W. 69
Truk Is., (Caroline Is.), Micronesia 46, 49
Truong Sa Sea Product Port, see Vung Tau.
Truro, U.K.: 50.15 N. 5.05 W. 7
Tsamkong, see Zhanjiang.
Tsi Nan, see Jinan.
Tsing Yi Is., see Hong Kong.
Tsingtao, see Qingdao.
Tsinkiang, see Zhangzhou.
Tsu, Japan: 34.40 N. 136.33 E. 43, 45
  Max. Size: Depth 4.5 m. – 5.5 m. *Airport:* Nagoya.
Tsuen Wan, Hong Kong (SAR), China: 22.22 N. 114.07 E. . . 48
Tsugaru Strait, Japan 43
Tsuiyama, Japan: 35.39 N. 134.50 E. 43, 45
Tsukumi, Japan: 33.05 N. 131.54 E. 45
  Max. Size: 23,000 d.w.t., draft 10.5 m. Cement: Draft 15 m., 100,000 d.w.t. *Fuel:* Bonded oil brought from Moji or Matsuyama. *Airport:* Oita, 1 hour by train.
Tsuruga, Japan: 35.40 N. 136.03 E. 43, 45
  Max. Size: Draft 12.6 m. *Fuel:* Bonded oil will be brought from Moji. *Airport:* 1 hour by train.
Tsurumi, see Yokohama.
Tsurusaki, Japan: 33.15 N. 131.42 E. 45
Tsushima Is., Japan 42, 43, 45
Tual, (Kai Is.), Indonesia: 5.38 S. 132.44 E. 46
Tuamotu Archipelago, French Polynesia (France) 49
Tuapse, Russia: 44.06 N. 39.04 E. 21, 26
  Max. Size: LOA 220 m., draft 12 m. Tankers: LOA 230 m., draft 12 m. *Fuel:* Fuel and gas oil. *Airport:* Sochi, 120 km.
Tuas, see Singapore.
Tuban Marine Terminal, Indonesia: 6.44 S. 112.09 E. 38
  Max. Size: 140,000 d.w.t.
Tubang, Indonesia: 1.45 S. 125.06 E. 46
  Max. Size: Depth 18.0 m.
Tubarao, Brazil: 20.17 S. 40.15 W. 77
  Max. Size: LOA 220 m. – 350 m., draft 11.3 m. – 20 m. plus tide. Tankers: LOA 181 m., draft 11.35 m. *Fuel:* Bunkers and diesel available at Oil Terminal and by truck or barge. *Airport:* 8 km. (Internal).
Tuborg Havn, Denmark: 55.44 N. 12.35 E. 12
Tubuai Is., French Polynesia (France) 49
Tucacas, Venezuela: 10.45 N. 68.20 W. 69, 74
Tuckerton, New Jersey, U.S.A.: 39.36 N. 74.20 W. 63

Tucurui, Brazil: 3.43 S. 49.43 W. 72
Tudy, see Port Tudy.
Tufi, Papua New Guinea: 9.05 S. 149.19 E. 46
Tugur, Russia: 53.45 N. 136.45 E. 43
Tulcea, Romania: 45.10 N. 28.49 E. 26
  Max. Size: Draft 23 ft. *Fuel:* Small quantities. *Airport:* Tulcea, 10 km.
Tulear, see Toliary.
Tumaco, Colombia: 1.49 N. 78.45 W. 72
  Max. Size: Depth 22 ft. Tankers: 100,000 d.w.t., LOA 250 m. and draft 20 m. *Fuel:* By barge. *Airport:* 4 km.
Tumany, Russia: 60.50 N. 156.00 E. 54
Tumby Bay, S.A., Australia: 34.23 S. 136.06 E. 51
Tumpat, Malaya, Malaysia: 6.11 N. 102.12 E. 38, 39
Tunadal, see Sundsvall.
Tunadalshamnen, see Sundsvall.
Tunas de Zaza, Cuba: 21.37 N. 79.32 W. 69, 70
  Max. Size: Draft 29 ft. Also see Cienfuegos.
Tunb Is., Iran: 26.15 N. 55.17 E. 35
Tung Ling, see Tongling.
Tungprong Port, see Sattahip.
Tunis, Tunisia: 36.46 N. 10.16 E. 21, 24
  Max. Size: Draft 6 m. Also see La Goulette.
TUNISIA 21, 24
Turbo, Colombia: 8.06 N. 76.43 W. 69, 72
  Max. Size: Anchorage port – draft 13 m.
Turf Point, see St. George's.
Turiamo, Venezuela: 10.28 N. 67.51 W. 74
Turkeli Is., Turkey: 40.30 N. 27.31 E. 25
TURKEY 9, 21, 23, 25, 26
Turkmenbashy, Turkey: 40.00 N. 53.00 E. 9
TURKMENISTAN 9
Turks and Caicos Islands (U.K.) 69, 70
Turku, Finland: 60.26 N. 22.13 E. 4, 10, 11
  Max. Size: Draft 11 m. (FW). Tankers: Draft 9 m. (FW). *Fuel:* Most grades. *Dry Docks:* Graving dock: Length 183 m., width of sluice gate 25.6 m., depth on sill 8.3 m. *Airport:* 10 km.
Turtle Is., Australia: 19.52 S. 119.00 E. 51
Turukhansk, Russia: 65.51 N. 87.40 E. 16
Tuticorin, India: 8.45 N. 78.13 E. 37
  Max. Size: Draft 10.7 m., LOA 235 m. *Fuel:* By road tanker. *Airport:* Madurai, 100 miles.
Tutoia, Brazil: 2.47 S. 42.17 W. 72
Tutuila Is., see Pago Pago.
Tutuncifilik, Turkey: 40.45 N. 29.47 E. 23
  Max. Size: Draft 18 m. *Fuel:* Available with notice.
TUVALU 49
Tuxpan, Mexico: 20.57 N. 97.24 W. 69
  Max. Size: LOA 190 m., depth 15 ft. – 23 ft. Tankers: Draft 55 ft. at SBM's. *Fuel:* Small quantities of diesel.
Tuzla, Turkey: 40.48 N. 29.19 E. 23
Tvaeraa, see Tvoroyri.
Tvedestrand, Norway: 58.37 N. 8.57 E. 11, 12
Tvoroyri, Faroe Is. (Denmark): 61.33 N. 6.50 W. 5, 15
  Max. Size: Draft 7 m. *Fuel:* Diesel. *Airport:* Vagar, 50 miles.
Tweed Heads, N.S.W., Australia: 28.10 S. 153.33 E. 50
Twillingate, Newfoundland, Canada: 49.40 N. 54.45 W. . . . 60
  Max. Size: Depth 21 ft. – 34 ft. *Airport:* Gander, 100 miles.
Two Harbours, Minnesota, U.S.A.: 47.01 N. 91.39 W. 62
Two Rivers, Wisconsin, U.S.A.: 44.09 N. 87.33 W. 62
Twofold Bay, see Eden.
Tybee Roads, see Savannah.
Tyne District, U.K.: 55.01 N. 1.24 W. 6
  Max. Size: Harbour entrance, draft 11 m. at HW. Tankers: Depth 6 m. – 10.5 m. (MHWS). *Fuel:* All grades. *Dry Docks:* Largest 217.9 m. x 32 m. x 8.8 m. *Airport:* Newcastle.
Tynemouth, see Tyne District.
Tyr, see Sour.
Tyrrhenian Sea 21, 24

U

Ua Hika, (Marquesas Is.), French Polynesia (France):
8.54 S. 139.33 W. 49
Ua Pou, see Nuku Hiva.
Ube, Japan: 33.56 N. 131.15 E. 45
Max. Size: Depth 13 m. – 13.6 m. Tankers: 285,000 d.w.t., draft 19.9 m. *Fuel:* All grades of bonded bunkers lightered from nearest stock ports. *Airport:* 20 minutes.
Ubu, see Ponta Ubu.
Uchiumi, Japan: 31.44 N. 131.28 E. 45
Uchiura, Japan: 35.32 N. 135.30 E. 45
Max. Size: Berth: 15,000 d.w.t., depth 9.0 m. Buoys: 15,000 d.w.t., depth 20.0 m.
Ucluelet, B.C., Canada: 48.57 N. 123.33 W. 56
Udbyhoj, Denmark: 56.37 N. 10.19 E. 12
Uddevalla, Sweden: 58.21 N. 11.56 E. 10, 12
Max. Size: Draft 11 m., height 43 m. Tankers: Draft 6.0 m. – 8.5 m. *Fuel:* All grades. *Airport:* Gothenburg, 100 km.
Ueckermunde, Germany: 53.45 N. 14.03 E. .. 11, 12
Uelen, Russia: 66.05 N. 169.46 W. 54
Uelkal, Russia: 65.31 N. 179.18 W. 54
Ugashik, Alaska, U.S.A.: 57.30 N. 157.25 W. .. 54
Ugborodo, Nigeria: 5.33 N. 5.03 E. 29
Uglegorsk, Russia: 49.04 N. 142.02 E. 43
Ugue, see Baie Ugue.
Uig, U.K.: 57.35 N. 6.22 W. 5
Ujang Pandang, see Ujung Pandang.
Ujelang Atoll, Marshall Is.: 9.49 N. 160.53 E. .. 49
Ujung Pandang, Indonesia: 5.08 S. 119.24 E. .. 38, 46
Max. Size: 30,000 d.w.t., draft 12.0 m. Tankers: 18,000 d.w.t., LOA 160 m., depth 9.0 m. *Fuel:* Available. *Airport:* 21 km.
Uka, Russia: 57.45 N. 162.00 E. 54
Ukpokiti, Nigeria: 5.44 N. 4.50 E. 29
Max. Size: 150,000 tonnes d.w.t., depth 85 ft.
UKRAINE 4, 9, 21, 26
Ulchin, South Korea: 37.00 N. 129.15 E. 42, 43
Ulcinj, Yugoslavia: 41.56 N. 19.11 E. 24
Uleaborg, see Oulu.
Uleeheue, Indonesia: 5.34 N. 95.17 E. 38, 40
Ulithi Is., (Caroline Is.), Micronesia. 46
Ulladulla, N.S.W., Australia: 35.22 S. 150.28 E. .. 50
Ullanger, see Askja.
Ullapool, U.K.: 57.54 N. 5.09 W. 5
Ullung-Do, South Korea: 37.30 N. 130.50 E. ... 45
Ulsan, South Korea: 35.27 N. 129.23 E. ... 42, 43, 45, 46
Max. Size: Depth 5 m. – 13 m. Tankers: SBM – Draft 22.65 m., 325,000 d.w.t. Dolphin – 150,000 d.w.t., draft 16.5 m. *Fuel:* By barge. *Airport:* Ulsan.
Ulsta Bay, see Burravoe.
Ulsteinvik, Norway: 62.21 N. 5.51 E. 10, 11, 15
Ulverstone, Tas., Australia: 41.10 S. 146.11 E. .. 51
Ulya, Russia: 59.08 N. 142.00 E. 43
Um Al Qiwain, see Ahmed Bin Rashid.
Umaiso, see Matsuyama.
Umanak, Greenland (Denmark): 70.41 N. 52.09 W. .. 17
Umba, see Lesnoy.
Umboi Is., Papua New Guinea. 46
Umea, Sweden: 63.42 N. 20.21 E. 10, 15
Max. Size: LOA 215 m., draft 10 m. Tankers: 42,000 d.w.t., LOA 215 m., draft 10.2 m. *Fuel:* All grades. *Airport:* 20 km.
Umm Al Nar, Abu Dhabi, U.A.E.: 24.27 N. 54.30 E. .. 35
Max. Size: 30,000 d.w.t., draft 9.5 m.
Umm al Qaiwain, see Ahmed Bin Rashid.
Umm Lajj, Saudi Arabia: 25.02 N. 37.25 E. 32
Umm Qasr, Iraq: 30.04 N. 47.57 E. 35
Max. Size: Draft 10.0 m. *Airport:* Basrah, 50 miles. Also see Basrah.
Umm Said, see Mesaieed.
Umnak Is., Alaska, U.S.A. 54
Unalakleet, Alaska, U.S.A.: 63.55 N. 160.45 W. .. 54
Unalaska, Alaska, U.S.A.: 53.54 N. 166.30 W. .. 54
Max. Size: Channel depth 24 ft., depth alongside 18 ft. – 50 ft. *Fuel:* Available. *Airport:* 4.5 miles.
Unalaska Is., (Aleutian Is.), Alaska, U.S.A. 54
Unga, Alaska, U.S.A.: 55.11 N. 160.30 W. 54
Ungalik, Alaska, U.S.A.: 64.34 N. 160.56 W. ... 54
Ungava Bay, Quebec, Canada: 17, 59
Unggi, North Korea: 42.20 N. 130.25 E. 43
Unimak, Alaska, U.S.A.: 54.30 N. 164.30 W. 54
Unimak Passage, (Aleutian Is.), Alaska, U.S.A. ... 54
Union Bay, B.C., Canada: 49.36 N. 124.53 W. .. 56
UNITED ARAB EMIRATES 31, 35
UNITED KINGDOM 4, 5, 7, 19, 79

UNITED STATES OF AMERICA 54, 55, 56, 57, 58, 60, 61, 62, 64, 65, 69, 70, 79
Uno, Japan: 34.29 N. 133.57 E. 45
Max. Size: LOA 176 m., draft 10.9 m. *Fuel:* Bonded fuel is available from main ports. *Dry Docks:* Up to 46,000 d.w.t. *Airport:* Okayama, 42 km.
Unst, U.K.: 60.52 N. 0.53 W. 5
Unye, Turkey: 41.07 N. 37.17 E. 26
Upernavik, Greenland (Denmark): 72.46 N. 56.09 W. .. 17
Upnor, see Rochester.
Upolu Is., Samoa 49
Upper Bay, New York, U.S.A. 63
Upper Beauharnois Lock, see St. Lawrence Seaway.
Uraba Is., Panama: 8.47 N. 79.32 W. 73
Uraga, Japan: 35.14 N. 139.43 E. 45
Uragami, Japan: 33.34 N. 135.52 E. 45
Urangan, Qld., Australia: 25.18 S. 152.54 E. 50
Closed to shipping.
Urangel, see Nakhodka.
Urdiales, see Castro-Urdiales.
Urinj, Croatia: 45.17 N. 14.32 E. 24
Max. Size: Tankers up to 200,000 d.w.t. Also see Rijeka.
Ursumco, Philippines: 9.41 N. 123.09 E. 47
Max. Size: Draft 30 ft.
URUGUAY 77, 78
Useless Loop, W.A., Australia: 26.05 S. 113.24 E. .. 50, 51
Max. Size: LOA 180 m., beam 28 m., depth 10.06 m. (LWOST). Also see Carnarvon.
Ushant, France: 48.25 N. 5.05 W. 7, 19
Ushibuka, Japan: 32.13 N. 130.01 E. 45
Ushuaia, Argentina: 54.49 S. 68.18 W. 77
Max. Size: Depth 18 ft. – 30 ft. Tankers: Depth 35 ft. *Fuel:* Available. *Airport:* Flights to Buenos Aires.
Usiba, see Salvador.
Uskudar, see Haydarpasa.
Ust Chaun, Russia: 68.17 N. 170.32 E. 54
Ust Dunaysk, Ukraine: 45.28 N. 29.42 E. 9, 26
Max. Size: LOA 226 m., draft 12 m. *Fuel:* Available with notice. *Airport:* Izmail, 100 km.
Ust Port, Russia: 69.40 N. 84.26 E. 16, 79
Ust Tigil, Russia: 58.00 N. 158.10 E. 54
Ust-Kara, see Kara.
Ustica Is., Italy: 38.43 N. 13.11 E. 24
Ustka, Poland: 54.35 N. 16.52 E. 10, 11
Ustkamchatka, Russia: 56.12 N. 162.28 E. 54
Ustluga, Russia: 59.38 N. 28.19 E. 11
Usuki, Japan: 33.08 N. 131.48 E. 45
Usunkum, see Eregli.
Utah, U.S.A. 57
Utansjo, Sweden: 62.46 N. 17.57 E. 15
Utersen, see Schulau.
Utila Is., Honduras: 16.06 N. 86.58 W. 69
Utirik, Marshall Is.: 11.20 N. 169.50 E. 49
Uto Is., Sweden: 58.57 N. 18.18 E. 11
Utrecht, Netherlands: 52.02 N. 5.08 E. 7, 8
Uturoa, (Society Is.), French Polynesia (France):
16.44 S. 151.25 W. 49
Utvuren-vuk, see Egvekinot.
Uusikaarlepyy, see Nykarleby.
Uusikaupunki, Finland: 60.48 N. 21.24 E. 10, 11
Max. Size: Depth 10 m. *Fuel:* Available. *Airport:* Turku, 90 km.
Uvea Is., see Wadrilla.
Uwajima, Japan: 33.13 N. 132.33 E. 45
Uyedinyeniya Is., Russia: 77.30 N. 82.22 E. 16
Uzava, Latvia: 57.12 N. 21.23 E. 11
UZBEKISTAN 9

V

Vaag, Faroe Is. (Denmark): 61.28 N. 6.48 W. **5, 15**
Vaago, Faroe Is. (Denmark) **5**
Vaasa, Finland: 63.06 N. 21.36 E. **4, 10, 15**
  Max. Size: Depth 9.0 m. Tankers: LOA 185 m., depth 9.0 m.
  Fuel: All grades. *Airport:* 8 miles.
Vacamonte, Panama: 8.51 N. 79.40 W. **73**
  Max. Size: Up to 3,000 tons, LOA 120 m., draft 7 m.
  Fuel: Available. *Airport:* Panama City.
Vada, Italy: 43.21 N. 10.27 E. **9, 23, 24**
  Max. Size: Draft 8.2 m.
Vadinar, India: 22.31 N. 69.42 E. **37**
  Max. Size: SBM: 285,000 d.w.t. – 300,000 d.w.t., LOA 343 m., draft 23 m.
Vado Ligure, Italy: 44.16 N. 8.26 E. **23, 24**
  Max. Size: Depth 10 m. – 15 m. Tankers: Up to 260,000 d.w.t. at buoys. Depth at piers 31 ft. – 39 ft. *Fuel:* Available.
  Airport: Genoa, 50 km.
  Also see Savona.
Vadso, Norway: 70.04 N. 29.45 E. **10, 16, 79**
  Max. Size: Depth 7 m. *Fuel:* Gas and diesel oil. *Airport:* 4 km.
Vagur, see Vaag.
Vaigach, Russia: 70.15 N. 58.45 E. **16**
Vaitape, (Society Is.), French Polynesia (France):
  16.31 S. 151.45 W. **49**
  Max. Size: Depth 4.0 m.
  Also see Bora Bora.
Vaja, see Kramfors.
Vaksdal, Norway: 60.29 N. 5.44 E. **11**
Val de Caes, see Belem.
Valdermarsvik, Sweden: 58.12 N. 16.37 E. **11**
Valdez, Alaska, U.S.A.: 61.07 N. 146.21 W. **54, 79**
  Max. Size: Dock: Depth 26 ft. MLLW. Tankers: Depth 36 ft. at dock. *Fuel:* Available. *Airport:* Connects with Anchorage.
  Also see Valdez Marine Terminal.
Valdez Marine Terminal, Alaska, U.S.A.: 61.05 N. 146.24 W. . . . **54**
  Max. Size: 265,000 d.w.t.
Valdivia, Chile: 39.49 S. 73.15 W. **77**
Vale, U.K.: 49.32 N. 2.32 W. **7, 19**
Valencia, Spain: 39.27 N. 0.18 W. **21, 22**
  Max. Size: Depth 7 m. – 16 m. Tankers: Depth 12 m. *Fuel:* By pipelines. *Dry Docks:* Lifting capacity 8,000 tonnes (floating dock). *Airport:* 15 km.
Valentia, Ireland: 51.55 N. 10.18 W. **5**
Valko, see Valkom.
Valkom, Finland: 60.25 N. 26.16 E. **13**
  Also see Lovisa.
Vallarta, see Puerto Vallarta.
Vallcarca, Spain: 41.14 N. 1.52 E. **22**
Vallejo, California, U.S.A.: 38.05 N. 122.15 W. **58**
Valletta, Malta: 35.54 N. 14.31 E. **21, 24**
  Max. Size: Depth 7 m. – 15 m. *Fuel:* Gas oil, fuel oil, thin fuel oil. *Dry Docks:* Length 360 m., beam 62 m., depth 10.72 m., capacity 300,000 d.w.t. *Airport:* Luqa, 4 miles.
Valleyfield, Quebec, Canada: 45.15 N. 74.08 W. **61**
Vallgrund, Finland: 63.15 N. 21.10 E. **15**
Vallvik, Sweden: 61.11 N. 17.11 E. **10, 11, 15**
  Max. Size: Draft in fairway 7.5 m. Depth alongside 5.2 m. – 8.3 m. *Fuel:* By road tanker.
  Airport: Arlanda, 15 miles.
Valona, see Vlore.
Valparaiso, Chile: 33.02 S. 71.38 W. **77**
  Max. Size: Depth 6.19 m. – 11.4 m. *Fuel:* Available.
  Dry Docks: Floating dock with lifting capacity of 10,000 tons.
  Airport: Pudahuel, 90 km.
Valverde, Canary Is. (Spain): 27.55 N. 18.00 W. **27**
Van Diemens Gulf, N.T., Australia **50**
Van Gia, Vietnam: 21.24 N. 107.57 E. **39**
  Max. Size: 10,000 d.w.t. *Airport:*
  No Bai, 350 km. Cat Bai, 230 km.
Van Hoa, Vietnam: 21.12 N. 107.34 E. **39**
Van Phong Bay, Vietnam: 12.31 N. 109.23 E. **39**
  Max. Size: S-T-S operation in anchorages with
  depths 21.5 m. – 34.5 m.
Vanasadam, Estonia: 59.27 N. 24.46 E. **11**
  Max. Size: LOA 230 m., beam 30 m., depth up to 10.7 m.
  Fuel: Available. *Airport:* 7 km.
Vancouver, B.C., Canada: 49.17 N. 123.07 W. **55, 56**
  Max. Size: Depth 7.3 m. – 18 m. Tankers: Depth 4.6 m. – 12.5 m. *Fuel:* Fuel and diesel oil. *Dry Docks:* Max. capacity 36,000 tons. *Airport:* Vancouver.
  Also see Roberts Bank.
Vancouver, Washington, U.S.A.: 45.36 N. 122.40 W. . . . **55, 56, 57**
  Max. Size: Depth 40 ft. *Fuel:* Available. *Airport:* 10 miles.
  Also see Portland.
Vancouver Is., B.C., Canada **56**

Vanersborg, Sweden: 58.25 N. 12.25 E. **11, 12**
Vanimo, Papua New Guinea: 2.41 S. 141.18 E. **46**
  Max. Size: LOA 81 m., draft 5.6 m. *Fuel:* Available.
  Airport: Local.
Vanino, Russia: 49.05 N. 140.14 E. **43**
  Max. Size: LOA 210 m., draft 11.3 m. Tankers: LOA 250 m., draft 15.5 m. *Fuel:* Available. *Airport:* Sovetskaya Gavan, 30 minutes by car.
Vankarem, Russia: 67.52 N. 175.55 W. **54**
Vannes, France: 47.40 N. 2.46 W. **7, 19**
Vansittart Is., N.W.T., Canada **59**
Vanua Lava, see Banks Is..
Vanua Levu, Fiji **49**
VANUATU **49**
Vanylven, Norway: 62.05 N. 5.35 E. **15**
Varanus Island Terminal, W.A., Australia: 20.38 S. 115.36 E. . **50, 51**
  Max. Size: 140,000 d.w.t. LOA 300 m., beam 46 m., draft 17 m.
Varberg, Sweden: 57.07 N. 12.15 E. **11, 12**
  Max. Size: LOA 215 m., beam 33 m., draft 10 m. *Fuel:* Fuel Oil No. 1 – 5 available. *Airport:* Landvetter Gothenburg, 60 miles.
Vardo, Finland: 60.18 N. 20.25 E. **11**
Vardo, Norway: 70.22 N. 31.05 E. **10, 16**
  Max. Size: LOA 150 m., draft 7 m. *Fuel:* Available.
  Airport: Vardo, 3 km.
Varkaus, Finland: 62.19 N. 27.52 E. **13**
  Also see Saimaa Canal.
Varlerhafn, Germany: 53.24 N. 8.08 E. **8, 14**
Varna, Bulgaria: 43.12 N. 27.57 E. **9, 21, 26**
  Max. Size: Draft up to 10.8 m., LOA 179 m. or draft 10 m. and LOA 204 m. Coal: Draft 11.5 m. Tankers: LOA 220 m., draft 10 m. *Fuel:* Bunker "C", diesel and gas oil available.
  Dry Docks: Up to 30,000 d.w.t. *Airport:* International.
Varneka, Russia: 69.43 N. 60.10 E. **16**
Varosha, Cyprus: 35.02 N. 34.00 E. **26**
Varton, see Stockholm.
Varzino, Russia: 68.30 N. 38.00 E. **16**
Vasalemma, Estonia: 59.15 N. 23.40 E. **11**
Vasklot, see Vaasa.
Vassiliko Bay, Cyprus: 34.43 N. 33.19 E. **26**
  Max. Size: LOA 175 m., draft 8.5 m. Tankers: 80,000 d.w.t., depth 32 m. *Fuel:* Available. *Airport:* Larnaca, 43 km. Paphos, 102 km.
Vasteras, Sweden: 59.37 N. 16.33 E. **10, 11**
  Max. Size: With beam of 18 m., draft 6.5 m. With beam 17 m., draft 7.0 m. LOA 124 m. Ship Canal: Lowest depth 7.6 m. Hammarby: LOA 110 m., draft 5.4 m. *Fuel:* All grades.
  Airport: Arlanda, 120 km.
Vastervik, Sweden: 57.46 N. 16.38 E. **11**
  Max. Size: Depth 4 m. – 8.3 m.
Vasto, Italy: 42.05 N. 14.40 E. **24**
Vathi, (Ithaca), Greece: 38.22 N. 20.43 E. **24, 25**
Vathi, (Samos), Greece: 37.45 N. 27.01 E. **26**
Vatomandry, Madagascar: 19.19 S. 49.00 E. **30**
Vaudreuil, Quebec, Canada: 45.24 N. 74.02 W. **61**
Vaukaus, see Varkaus.
Vava'u Group, Tonga **49**
Vavau, see Neiafu.
Vaxholm, Sweden: 59.24 N. 18.22 E. **11**
Vayenga Bay, see Severomorsk.
Vaygach Is., see Vaigach.
Vecchio, see Porto Vecchio.
Vedbaek, Denmark: 55.51 N. 12.35 E. **12**
Veitsiluoto, Finland: 65.42 N. 24.37 E. **10, 15**
  Max. Size: Depth 7.0 m. *Fuel:* Ordinary fuel, diesel and gas oil by lorry. *Airport:* Kemi, 15 km.
Vejle, Denmark: 55.42 N. 9.33 E. **11, 12**
  Max. Size: LOA 550 ft., draft 22 ft. 4 in. *Fuel:* All grades.
  Airport: Billund, 32 km.
Vela de Coro, see Coro.
Vela Luka, Croatia: 42.58 N. 16.42 E. **24**
Velikaya, Russia: 67.21 N. 47.52 E. **16**
Vellho, see Porto Velho.
Velsen, Netherlands: 52.27 N. 4.39 E. **8**
Venado Is., Panama: 8.53 N. 79.36 W. **73**
Venalum Terminal, Venezuela: 8.18 N. 62.50 W. **75**
  Max. Size: Depth 12 m.
Vendres, see Port Vendres.
VENEZUELA **69, 71, 72, 74, 75**
Vengurla, India: 15.51 N. 73.38 E. **37**
Venice, Italy: 45.26 N. 12.20 E. **9, 21, 24**
  Max. Size: Depth 3.66 m. – 10.67 m. Bulk: Draft 28 ft. Tankers: Draft 22 ft. – 45 ft. 3 in. *Fuel:* All grades.
  Dry Docks: Largest: 820.3 ft. x 117.8 ft. x 36 ft. on sill at HW.
  Airport: 10 km.
Ventry, Ireland: 52.07 N. 10.21 W. **5**
Ventspils, Latvia: 57.24 N. 21.33 E. **10, 11**
  Max. Size: LOA 240 m., draft 14.1 m. (FW).
  Tankers: LOA 270 m., draft 15.0 m. (FW). *Fuel:* All grades.
Ventura, California, U.S.A.: 34.16 N. 119.17 W. **57**

THE SHIPS ATLAS

Vera Cruz, Mexico: 19.12 N. 96.01 W. 69
  Max. Size: Depth 9 m. – 12 m. Tankers: Draft 31 ft., LOA 210 m. *Fuel:* Available. *Dry Docks:* Lifting capacity 80,000 d.w.t. *Airport:* 6 km.
Veraval, India: 20.55 N. 70.22 E. 37
  Max. Size: Anchorage – No restriction. *Airport:* Keshod, 30 miles.
Verdalsora, Norway: 63.47 N. 11.28 E. 15
Verdon, France: 45.33 N. 1.03 W. 8, 19
  Max. Size: LOA 290 m., draft 12.5 m.
  Also see Bordeaux.
Verkeback, see Vastervik.
Vermont, U.S.A. 60, 61
Vermsi, see Vormsi.
Verolme, see Angra dos Reis.
Vesme, see Porto Vesme.
Vestarelen Is., Norway 10, 15
Vesterohaven, Denmark: 57.25 N. 10.55 E. 12
Vestmanhavn, Faroe Is. (Denmark): 62.10 N. 7.10 W. . . . 5, 15
Vestmannaeyjar, Iceland: 63.30 N. 20.14 W. 17
  Max. Size: 5,000 g.r.t. *Fuel:* All grades. *Airport:* Local airport.
Vestvagoy, (Lofoten Is.), Norway: 68.10 N. 13.50 E. 15
Vesuvius Bay, Indonesia: 1.52 S. 125.22 E. 46
Viana do Castelo, Portugal: 41.41 N. 8.50 W. 20, 22
  Max. Size: LOA 180 m., draft 8.0 m. *Fuel:* Only small quantities of gas oil. *Dry Docks:* 203 m. x 34 m. x 18 ft. *Airport:* Oporto, 55 km.
Viareggio, Italy: 43.52 N. 10.14 E. 23, 24
Vibo Valentia, see Pizzo.
Victor Harbour, S.A., Australia: 35.33 S. 138.37 E. 50, 51
Victoria, Australia 50, 51
Victoria, Cameroon, see Limbe.
Victoria, B.C., Canada: 48.25 N. 123.22 W. 56
  Max. Size: Depth 33 ft. – 40 ft. *Fuel:* Available. *Airport:* Victoria, 32 km.
  Also see Esquimalt.
Victoria, P.E.I., Canada: 46.13 N. 63.30 W. 60
Victoria, Guinea, see Port Kamsar.
Victoria, Malaysia, see Labuan.
Victoria, (Gozo), Malta: 36.05 N. 14.15 E. 24
Victoria, Seychelles, see Port Victoria.
Victoria Harbour, Ontario, Canada, see Port McNicoll.
Victoria Harbour, China, see Hong Kong.
Victoria Point, see Kawthaung.
Vidlin, (Shetland Is.), U.K.: 60.22 N. 1.08 W. 5
Viejo, see Azua.
Vienna, Austria: 48.13 N. 16.22 E. 9
Vieste, Italy: 41.50 N. 16.14 E. 24
VIETNAM, SOCIALIST REPUBLIC OF 39
Vieux Fort, St. Lucia: 13.44 N. 60.58 W. 69, 71
  Max. Size: LOA 520 ft.
  Also see Castries.
Vigo, Spain: 42.14 N. 8.42 W. 20, 21, 22
  Max. Size: No limitation on LOA and beam. Depths up to 17 m. at Guixar Quay. Tankers: 40,000 d.w.t., LOA 220 m., draft 10.7 m. *Fuel:* Available. *Dry Docks:* One floating dock of 5,000 tons capacity. *Airport:* 8 km., connects with Madrid.
Vihreasaari, see Oulu.
Viko-Wochimex, Vietnam: 10.38 N. 106.50 E. 39
  Max. Size: LOA 162 m., draft 8.3 m. *Fuel:* Available. *Airport:* Tan Son Nhat, 85 km.
Vikram Ispat, India: 18.32 N. 72.56 E. 37
  Max. Size: LOA 100 m., draft 4 m.
Vila, see Port Vila.
Vila do Conde, Brazil: 1.33 S. 48.45 W. 72
  Max. Size: 60,000 d.w.t., LOA 250 m., draft 20 m. *Fuel:* Available. *Airport:* Belem, 9 km.
Vila do Porto, (Santa Maria Is.), Azores (Portugal): 36.56 N. 25.09 W. 20
Vila Nova, Azores (Portugal): 39.50 N. 31.05 W. 20
Vila Real de Santo Antonio, Portugal: 37.10 N. 7.26 W. . . 20, 22, 27
  Max. Size: Draft 5.5 m. (16 ft.) (HW). *Fuel:* Gas oil in small quantities.
Vilanculas, Mozambique: 22.00 S. 35.15 E. 30
Vilanova i la Geltru, Spain: 41.12 N. 1.43 E. 22
  Max. Size: LOA 426 ft., draft 22 ft. 11 in. *Fuel:* Available. *Airport:* Barcelona, 50 km.
Vilkitski, Russia: 73.30 N. 75.50 E. 16
Vilkovo, Russia: 45.15 N. 29.30 E. 26
Villa Cisneros, Morocco: 23.42 N. 15.55 W. 27
  Max. Size: LOA 100 m., beam 12 m., draft 5 m. *Fuel:* Available with notice. *Airport:* 1 km.
Villa Constitucion, Argentina: 33.15 S. 60.17 W. 77, 78
  Max. Size: Up to 25 ft. draft.
Villa Sanjurjo, see Al Hoceima.
Villa Urquiza, Argentina: 31.40 S. 60.22 W. 78
Villagarcia de Arosa, Spain: 42.36 N. 8.46 E. 19, 20, 22
  Max. Size: Depth 3 m. – 7 m. Bulk: Depth 7 m. – 11 m. *Fuel:* Gas oil. *Airport:* Santiago de Compostela, 50 km.
Village Cove, (Pribilof Is.), Alaska, U.S.A.: 57.08 N. 170.16 W. 54

Villanueva, (Mindanao Is.), Philippines: 8.35 N. 124.44 E. . . 46, 47
  Max. Size: LOA 351 m., beam 50 m., draft 25.0 m., 350,000 d.w.t. *Fuel:* By road tanker. *Airport:* Cagayan de Oro, 40 km.
Villaricos, Spain: 37.15 N. 1.47 W. 22
Villaviciosa, Spain: 43.30 N. 5.25 W. 19, 20
Villefranche, France: 43.42 N. 7.19 E. 22
Villequier, see Caudebec.
Vinalhaven, Maine, U.S.A.: 44.03 N. 68.50 W. 60
Vinaroz, Spain: 40.29 N. 0.29 E. 22
Vincent, see Port Vincent.
Vineyard Haven, Massachusetts, U.S.A.: 41.27 N. 70.36 W. . 63
Vinh, Vietnam: 18.45 N. 105.45 E. 39
Vinh Long, Vietnam: 10.16 N. 105.57 E. 39
  Max. Size: LOA 100 m., draft 5.5 m. *Fuel:* Available. *Airport:* Ho Chi Minh City, 120 km.
Vinh Thai, Vietnam: 10.21 N. 107.03 E. 39
  Max. Size: Draft 5 m.
Virac Catanduanes Is., Philippines: 13.35 N. 124.16 E. . . . 47
Virgin Gorda Is., Virgin Is. (U.K.): 18.28 N. 64.25 W. 71
Virgin Islands (U.K.) 71
Virgin Islands (U.S.A.) 71
Virginia, U.S.A. 60, 63, 65
Viru Harbour, (New Georgia), Solomon Islands: 8.30 S. 157.46 E. 51
Vis Is., Croatia: 43.03 N. 16.11 E. 24
Visakhapatnam, India: 17.41 N. 83.18 E. 37
  Max. Size: Outer Harbour: LOA 270 m., beam 42 m., draft 15.3 m. Inner Harbour: LOA 195 m., beam 32 m., draft 10.06 m. Tankers: LOA 260 m., draft 14.3 m. *Fuel:* Available. *Dry Docks:* Largest: 244 m. x 38 m., 70,000 d.w.t. *Airport:* 14 km.
Visby, Sweden: 57.38 N. 18.17 E. 11
  Max. Size: Draft 5.6 m. – 6.3 m. Tankers: LOA 160 m., depth 8 m. *Fuel:* By road tanker. *Airport:* 5 km.
Visgnaes, Denmark: 54.53 N. 11.39 E. 12, 14
Vita, Cuba: 21.05 N. 75.57 W. 69, 70
  Max. Size: Draft 7.92 m. (HW), LOA 150 m.
Viti Levu, see Suva.
Vitoria, (Terceira Is.), Azores (Portugal): 38.45 N. 27.05 W. . 20
Vitoria, Brazil: 20.19 S. 40.17 W. 77
  Max. Size: LOA 242 m., draft 39 ft. 9 in. with pontoons. Tankers: LOA 531 m., draft 27 ft. *Fuel:* Available. *Airport:* Internal, 8 km.
Vityaz Marine Terminal, Russia: 52.42 N. 143.33 E. 43
  Max. Size: Depth 30 m.
Vivero, Spain: 43.40 N. 7.35 W. 19, 20
Viviers, France: 44.28 N. 4.41 E. 9
Vivstavarv, Sweden: 62.29 N. 17.28 E. 15
  Max. Size: Draft 7.3 m.
  Also see Sundsvall.
Vlaardingen, Netherlands: 51.54 N. 4.20 E. 7, 8
  Max. Size: Draft 35 ft. (LW). *Fuel:* Available. *Dry Docks:* Capacity 5,300 tons. *Airport:* Rotterdam, 10 km.
Vladimir, see Port Vladimir.
Vladivostok, Russia: 43.07 N. 131.53 E. 43
  Max. Size: LOA 260 m., beam 36 m., draft 11.5 m. *Fuel:* Available. *Dry Docks:* 26,000 tonnes displacement (Dock 195 m. x 32.5 m.). *Airport:* Vladivostok, 40 km.
Vlissingen, see Flushing.
Vlore, Albania: 40.27 N. 19.29 E. 24, 25
Voer, Denmark: 56.31 N. 10.14 E. 12
Vohemar, Madagascar: 13.21 S. 50.00 E. 30
  Max. Size: Depth 5.8 m.
Volcano Is., Japan 46
Volgograd, Russia: 48.44 N. 44.30 E. 9
Vollsfjorden, see Skien.
Volonga, Russia: 67.05 N. 47.44 E. 16
Volos, Greece: 39.21 N. 22.56 E. 21, 24, 25
  Max. Size: Draft 30 ft. *Fuel:* Via tanker, capacity 182 tons.
Voltri, Italy: 44.24 N. 8.54 E. 23, 24
Vonitsa, Greece: 38.55 N. 20.54 E. 24, 25
Voorbaai, see Mossel Bay.
Vopnafjord, Iceland: 65.45 N. 14.50 W. 17
Vordingborg, Denmark: 54.50 N. 11.54 E. 11, 12, 14
  Max. Size: Draft 19 ft., beam 25 m. (depending on vessel's height). Width of bridge opening 25 m. At a height of 25 m., width of opening 22 m. due to angle of raised bridge. *Fuel:* All common fuels available. *Airport:* Kastrup, 96 km.
Vormsi, Estonia: 59.00 N. 23.15 E. 11
Vostochny, Russia: 42.44 N. 133.03 E. 43
  Max. Size: 250,000 d.w.t., draft 15 m. at Coal Pier, elsewhere 9.7 m. *Fuel:* Available.
Vostochny, (Sakhalin Is.), Russia: 53.30 N. 143.08 E. . . . 43
Vostochnyy, (Sakhalin Is.), Russia: 48.15 N. 142.36 E. . . . 43
Vostok Is., Kiribati: 10.05 S. 152.23 W. 49
Voudia Bay, Greece: 36.45 N. 24.32 E. 25
  Max. Size: LOA 610 ft., draft 36 ft.
  Also see Milos Island.
Vrangelya Is., Russia: 70.30 N. 179.58 E. 54

Vridi Canal, see Abidjan.
Vuda Point, see Lautoka.
Vulcano Is., Italy: 38.25 N. 14.58 E. 24
Vung Tau, Vietnam: 10.21 N. 107.04 E. 39
  Max. Size: LOA 200 m., draft 12.0 m. Tankers: 110,000 d.w.t., LOA 250 m., draft 15.0 m. *Fuel:* Available. *Airport:* Tan Son Nhat, International.
Vuoksi, see Saimaa Canal.
Vyborg, Russia: 60.42 N. 28.44 E. 10, 11, 13
  Max. Size: LOA 135 m., draft 6.5 m. *Fuel:* By barge.
Vysotsk, Russia: 60.42 N. 28.43 E. 11, 13
  Max. Size: Depth 9.5 m.
  Also see Vyborg.

NOTES, ADDITIONS, CORRECTIONS

Please also advise Shipping Guides Ltd.
75 Bell Street, Reigate, RH2 7AN, United Kingdom
Tel: +44 1737 242255   Fax: +44 1737 222449
Email: updates@portinfo.co.uk   Web: www.portinfo.co.uk

W

Wabana, Newfoundland, Canada: 47.37 N. 52.56 W. 60
Wachusett Reef: 32.00 S. 151.00 W. 49
Waddington, New York, U.S.A.: 44.51 N. 75.12 W. 61
Wadi Firan, Egypt: 28.44 N. 33.13 E. 26, 32
  Max. Size: 105,000 d.w.t., LOA 900 ft., draft 75 ft.
Wadrilla, (Uvea Is.), New Caledonia (France):
  20.35 S. 166.33 E. 49
  Max. Size: Depth 4 m.
  Also see Noumea.
Wageningen, Suriname: 5.46 N. 56.41 W. 76
  Max. Size: LOA 120 m., draft 5 m. *Airport:* New Nickerie, 50 km.
Wager Bay, N.W.T., Canada: 65.40 N. 89.00 W. 59
Wahai, Indonesia: 2.45 S. 129.32 E. 46
Wahran, see Oran.
Waigeo Is., Indonesia: 0.15 S. 130.40 E. 46
Waija, see Kramfors.
Waingapu, Indonesia: 9.38 S. 120.16 E. 38, 46, 50
  Max. Size: LOA 100 m., draft 10 m. *Fuel:* Available. *Airport:* 10 km.
Wainwright, Alaska, U.S.A.: 70.39 N. 160.00 W. 54
Waipipi, see Waverley Harbour.
Waipu, New Zealand: 36.00 S. 174.30 E. 52
Wairoa, New Zealand: 39.05 S. 177.25 E. 52
Waisarisa, Indonesia: 3.13 S. 128.16 E. 46
  Max. Size: Depth 85 m.
  Also see Ambon.
Waitangi, (Chatham Is.), New Zealand: 43.58 S. 176.31 W. . . . 52
Waitara, New Zealand: 39.00 S. 174.15 E. 52
Wajima, Japan: 37.28 N. 136.58 E. 43, 45
Wakamatsu, Japan: 33.54 N. 130.48 E. 44, 45
  Max. Size: LOA 166 m., draft 8.5 m. Dolphins: LOA 162 m., draft 9.0 m. *Fuel:* Bonded oil will be brought from Moji, Ube or Ohita. *Dry Docks:* Max. size: 160 m. x 22.5 m. x 5.5 m. draft. *Airport:* Fukuoka or Kitakyushu.
Wakayama, Japan: 34.13 N. 135.08 E. 45
  Max. Size: LOA 175 m., draft 9.0 m. Metals Pier: LOA 300 m., draft 14.0 m. 100,000 d.w.t. or 150,000 d.w.t. part-load. *Fuel:* All grades of bonded bunkers lightered from nearest stock ports. *Airport:* Itami, Osaka, 3 hours by car.
Wake Island, (U.S.A.): 19.15 N. 166.34 W. 49
Wakeham, see Maricourt.
Wakkanai, Japan: 45.25 N. 141.42 E. 43
  Max. Size: 15,000 d.w.t., depth 10.0 m.
Wakrah, Qatar: 25.10 N. 51.37 E. 35
Wala, (Art Is.), New Caledonia (France): 19.43 S. 161.19 E. . . . 51
  Max. Size: Depth 4 m.
  Also see Noumea.
Walcheren Is., Netherlands 7
Walcott, see Port Walcott.
Wales, U.K. 4, 5, 7
Wales, Alaska, U.S.A.: 65.40 N. 168.08 W. 54
Walkom, see Valkom.
Wallaceburg, Ontario, Canada: 42.37 N. 82.25 W. 62
Wallaroo, S.A., Australia: 33.56 S. 137.37 E. 50, 51
  Max. Size: LOA 200 m., beam 30 m., depth in approaches 8.4 m., depth alongside 7.3 m. – 9.45 m. *Fuel:* By road tanker.
Wallasey, U.K.: 53.26 N. 3.03 W. 6
Wallhamn, Sweden: 58.01 N. 11.42 E. 11, 12
  Max. Size: Draft 10 m. Stone loading berth: Depth 6.0 m. *Fuel:* Most grades. *Airport:* Gothenburg, 85 km.
Wallis and Futuna Islands (France) 49
Wallis Is., Wallis and Futuna (France): 13.20 S. 176.10 W. . . . 49
Walls, U.K.: 60.14 N. 1.34 W. 5
Wallsend, U.K.: 54.59 N. 1.30 W. 6
  Also see Tyne District.
Walpole Is., New Caledonia (France): 22.38 S. 168.55 E. . . . 49
Walsh Bay, see Sydney.
Walton, N.S., Canada: 45.14 N. 64.00 W. 60
Walvis Bay, Namibia: 22.57 S. 14.30 E. 28
  Max. Size: LOA 224 m., draft 12.8 m. Tankers: LOA 192 m., draft 10.0 m. *Fuel:* Gas oil. *Airport:* 14 km.
Wamsasi, Indonesia: 3.33 S. 126.09 E. 46
  Max. Size: Anchorage port: Depth 15 m. (600 m. offshore).
Wanapiri, Indonesia: 4.28 S. 135.51 E. 46
Wandoo Marine Terminal, W.A., Australia: 20.08 S. 116.25 E. . . 51
  Max. Size: 100,000 tonnes S.d.w.t., depth 54 m.
Wanganui, New Zealand: 39.57 S. 175.00 E. 52
  Max. Size: LOA 100 m., beam 20 m., draft usually 5.5 m. max. at HWS. *Fuel:* All grades available but ship has to pump out of road tankers. *Airport:* 6 miles.
Waratah, see Newcastle.
Wareham, Massachusetts, U.S.A.: 41.45 N. 70.43 W. . . . 64
Warkworth, U.K.: 55.20 N. 1.40 W. 5

THE SHIPS ATLAS

Warnemunde, Germany: 54.10 N. 12.05 E. **12, 14**
  Max. Size: Depth 27 ft. 6 in.
  Also see Rostock.
Warrenpoint, U.K.: 54.06 N. 6.16 W. **5**
  Max. Size: Depth 5.4 m. (LWOST). *Fuel:* Available. *Airport:* Belfast (Aldergove), 60 miles. Belfast (City), 50 miles. Dublin, 75 miles.
Warrenton, Oregon, U.S.A.: 46.10 N. 123.55 W. **56, 57**
Warri, Nigeria: 5.30 N. 5.44 E. **29**
  Max. Size: LOA 156 m., draft 6.4 m. due to Escravos Bar.
  Airport: Service to Lagos.
  Also see Burutu and Lagos.
Warrington, U.K.: 53.25 N. 2.37 W. **6**
  Also see Manchester.
Warrnambool, Vic., Australia: 38.24 S. 142.28 E. **50**
Warsaw, Poland: 52.15 N. 21.02 E. **9**
Warwick, Virginia, U.S.A.: 37.27 N. 77.25 W. **63**
Washburn, Wisconsin, U.S.A.: 46.39 N. 90.54 W. **62**
Washington, U.S.A. **56, 57**
Washington, D.C., U.S.A.: 38.55 N. 77.00 W. . . . **60, 63, 65**
Washington, North Carolina, U.S.A.: 35.34 N. 77.04 W. . **63**
Washington, Washington, U.S.A., see Port Washington.
Washington Is., Kiribati: 4.43 N. 160.25 W. **49**
Watchet, U.K.: 51.11 N. 3.20 W. **6, 7**
  Max. Size: LOA 90 m., beam 16 m., draft 12 ft. (neap). 14 ft. – 18 ft. (spring). *Fuel:* All grades. *Airport:* Bristol.
Waterford, Ireland: 52.15 N. 7.07 W. **4, 5**
  Max. Size: LOA 150 m., LOA 156 m. by arrangement, draft 6.8 m. (neap), 7.5 m. (spring). Belview: LOA 230 m., draft 10.0 m. Great Island Jetty: Tankers – 20,000 d.w.t. Cruise ships – LOA 240 m., depth 11.0 m.
  Fuel: By road tanker. *Airport:* Waterford, 5 miles.
Wates, Indonesia: 7.53 S. 110.06 E. **38**
Watling Is., see San Salvador Is..
Waubaushene, Ontario, Canada: 44.46 N. 79.43 W. . . . **62**
Waukegan, Illinois, U.S.A.: 42.22 N. 87.52 W. **62**
Waverley Harbour, New Zealand: 39.51 S. 174.36 E. . . **52**
Wayabula, Indonesia: 2.17 N. 128.12 E. **46**
We, (Lifou Is.), New Caledonia (France): 20.55 S. 167.17 E. . **49**
  Max. Size: Depth 5.5 m.
  Also see Noumea.
Weda, Indonesia: 0.25 N. 127.52 E. **46**
Weddell Is., Falkland Is. (U.K.): 51.50 S. 61.00 W. . . . **77**
Weddell Sea, Antarctica **80**
Wedgeport, N.S., Canada: 43.45 N. 66.00 W. **60**
Weehawken, U.S.A.: 40.47 N. 74.01 W. **63**
  Also see New York.
Weener, Germany: 53.08 N. 7.33 E. **8, 14**
Wei Chou Is., China: 21.03 N. 109.08 E. **39**
Wei Hai, China: 37.31 N. 122.08 E. **42**
  Max. Size: Draft 10.9 m.
Weipa, Qld., Australia: 12.42 S. 141.41 E. **46, 50, 51**
  Max. Size: LOA 254 m. (835 ft.), beam 35.41 m. Channel depth 10.8 m. (LAT). Depth alongside 9.5 m. – 12.3 m.
  Airport: 10 km., domestic.
Weld, see Port Weld.
Welland, Ontario, Canada: 42.58 N. 79.13 W. **62**
  Max. Size: Depth 27 ft.
Welland Ship Canal, Canada **60, 62**
  Max. Size: Draft 7.92 m. (26 ft.). Locks limit: Length 222.5 m. (730 ft.) and breadth 23.16 m. (76 ft.).
Weller, see Port Weller.
Wellington, Ontario, Canada: 43.55 N. 77.20 W. **62**
Wellington, New Zealand: 41.17 S. 174.47 E. **52**
  Max. Size: Draft 9.7 m. plus height of tide. Containers: Draft 11 m. Tankers: Draft 10.2 m. *Fuel:* Available. *Airport:* 7 km.
Wellington Is., Chile **77**
Wells, U.K.: 52.57 N. 0.51 E. **5, 7**
Welshpool, Vic., Australia: 38.42 S. 146.28 E. **51**
Wemelding, Netherlands: 51.31 N. 4.00 E. **8**
Wemyss, U.K.: 55.53 N. 4.53 W. **6**
Wenchow, see Wenzhou.
Wentworth, see Port Wentworth.
Wenzhou, China: 28.02 N. 120.39 E. **42, 46**
  Max. Size: Draft 6.0 m. Depth alongside 5 m. – 9 m.
Wesel, Germany: 51.39 N. 6.37 E. **9**
Wesiri, Indonesia: 7.30 S. 126.31 E. **46**
Wesleyville, Newfoundland, Canada: 49.10 N. 53.35 W. . **60**
West Bay, Louisiana, U.S.A. **67**
West Fayu Is., (Caroline Is.), Micronesia: 8.11 N. 146.48 E. . **46**
West Hartlepool, see Hartlepool.
West Kirby, U.K.: 53.22 N. 3.10 W. **6**
West Point, Virginia, U.S.A.: 37.33 N. 76.48 W. . . . **63, 65**
West Spitsbergen, (Spitsbergen), Norway **17**
West Thurrock, see London.
Western Australia, Australia **50, 51**
Western Channel, Korea Strait **45**
Western Port, see Hastings.
Westkapelle, Netherlands: 51.32 N. 3.26 E. **7, 8**
Westland Bight, New Zealand **52**

Weston, Sabah, Malaysia: 5.13 N. 115.35 E. **38, 39**
Weston Point, see Runcorn.
Weston-super-Mare, U.K.: 51.20 N. 2.59 W. **6, 7**
Westport, N.S., Canada: 44.16 N. 66.21 W. **60**
Westport, Ireland: 53.48 N. 9.32 W. **5**
Westport, New Zealand: 41.45 S. 171.40 E. **52**
  Max. Size: LOA 131.7 m., depth at bar 3.6 m. (12 ft.) at C.D.
  Fuel: Diesel and lube oil only.
Westport, Washington, U.S.A.: 46.48 N. 124.05 W. . . . **56**
Westray, (Orkney Is.), U.K.: 59.08 N. 3.00 W. **5**
Westview, see Powell River.
Westville, see Philadelphia.
Westwego, Louisiana, U.S.A.: 29.55 N. 90.09 W. **67**
  Max. Size: Depth 28 ft. – 40 ft.
  Also see New Orleans.
Wetar Is., Indonesia **46**
Wete, Tanzania: 5.14 S. 39.43 E. **30**
  Max. Size: LOA 240 ft., draft 25 ft.
Wevok, Alaska, U.S.A.: 68.50 N. 164.45 W. **54**
Wewak, Papua New Guinea: 3.34 S. 143.39 E. **46**
  Max. Size: Depth at LAT 6.7 m. *Fuel:* Diesel by road tanker.
  Airport: 5 km.
Wexford, Ireland: 52.20 N. 6.26 W. **5**
Weymouth, N.S., Canada: 44.27 N. 66.01 W. **60**
  Max. Size: LOA 375 ft., beam 55 ft., draft approx. 26 ft. (HW).
Weymouth, U.K.: 50.36 N. 2.27 W. **5, 7, 19**
  Max. Size: LOA 125 m., draft 5.2 m. *Fuel:* By road tanker.
  Airport: Hurn or Exeter.
Weymouth, U.S.A., see Boston.
Whakaaropai, New Zealand: 39.39 S. 173.18 E. **52**
  Max. Size: 100,000 d.w.t.
Whakatane, New Zealand: 37.57 S. 177.00 E. **49, 52**
Whampoa, see Huangpu.
Whangarei, New Zealand: 35.45 S. 174.21 E. **52**
  Max. Size: LOA 190 m., draft 9.45 m. *Airport:* 8 miles.
Whangaroa, New Zealand: 35.02 S. 173.46 E. **52**
Whiddy Island, see Bantry Bay.
Whiffen Head, Newfoundland, Canada: 47.46 N. 54.01 W. . **60**
  Max. Size: Max. displacement 181,000 tonnes, LOA 280 m., draft 17.2 m. *Airport:* St. John's, 152 km.
Whitby, Ontario, Canada: 43.52 N. 78.56 W. **62**
Whitby, U.K.: 54.30 N. 0.36 W. **5**
  Max. Size: LOA 80 m., beam 14 m., draft 5.2 m. *Fuel:* By road tanker. *Airport:* Teeside, 40 miles.
White Bay, Australia, see Sydney.
White Bay, Newfoundland, Canada **60**
White Is., N.W.T., Canada **59**
White Lake, Ontario, Canada: 43.23 N. 86.20 W. **62**
White Sea, Russia **16**
Whitegate, see Cork.
Whitehall, U.K.: 59.09 N. 2.36 W. **5**
Whitehaven, U.K.: 54.33 N. 3.36 W. **5**
  No longer considered a commercial port.
Whitehead, Northern Ireland, U.K.: 54.45 N. 5.43 W. . . **6**
Whitemark, Tas., Australia: 40.06 S. 148.00 E. **51**
Whitgift, U.K.: 53.42 N. 0.46 W. **6**
Whitianga, New Zealand: 36.46 S. 175.42 E. **52**
Whitley Bay, U.K.: 55.03 N. 1.25 W. **6**
Whitney Cove, Russia: 76.15 N. 68.00 E. **16**
Whitstable, U.K.: 51.21 N. 1.02 E. **6**
  Max. Size: LOA 95 m., draft 4.9 m. (Harbour dries out). *Fuel:* Available.
Whitsunday Is., Australia: 25.00 S. 148.55 E. **50, 51**
Whittier, Alaska, U.S.A.: 60.47 N. 148.40 W. **54**
  Max. Size: LOA 170 m., depth at pier 48 ft. – 80 ft.
  Airport: Small airstrip.
Whyalla, S.A., Australia: 33.02 S. 137.36 E. **50, 51**
  Max. Size: Max. LOA 250 m., depth 11.4 m. (LW).
  Fuel: Locally in emergency only or from Adelaide by road tanker. *Airport:* Connects with Adelaide.
Wiarton, Ontario, Canada: 44.44 N. 81.09 W. **62**
Wick, U.K.: 58.26 N. 3.05 W. **5**
Wicklow, Ireland: 52.59 N. 6.02 W. **5**
  Max. Size: LOA 100 m., draft 5.2 m. *Airport:* Dublin, 40 miles.
Widnes, U.K.: 53.22 N. 2.44 W. **6**
Widuri Terminal, Indonesia: 4.40 S. 106.39 E. **38**
  Max. Size: 178,000 d.w.t., draft 50 ft.
Wiesbaden, Germany: 50.05 N. 8.15 E. **9**
Wigtown, U.K.: 54.52 N. 4.27 W. **5**
Wiley Dondero Ship Channel, Ontario, Canada **61**
Wilhelmsburg, see Hamburg.
Wilhelmshaven, Germany: 53.31 N. 8.10 E. . . . **4, 7, 8, 11, 12, 14**
  Max. Size: River Jade: LOA 350 m. (1,150 ft.), draft 20 m. (65 ft. 7 in.). Keel clearance of at least 8.5% of draft required, beam 52 m. Berths: Draft 38 ft. Tankers: Draft 20.0 m.
  Fuel: All grades. *Airport:* Local airport. Nearest international at Bremen, 102 km.
Wilkes Land, Antarctica **80**
Willapa, Washington, U.S.A.: 46.42 N. 123.45 W. **57**
Willemsdorp, Netherlands: 51.44 N. 4.35 E. **8**

98

Willemstad, Netherlands: 51.42 N. 4.26 E. **7, 8**
Willemstad, (Curacao), Netherlands Antilles:
  12.06 N. 68.56 W. **69, 72, 74**
  Max. Size: LOA 875 ft. Draft 45 ft.
  Tankers (Emmastad): LOA 259 m., draft 12.8 m.
  Fuel: Available. *Dry Docks:* Graving dock 919 ft. long,
  entrance width 152 ft. and depth over sill 27 ft., 155,000 d.w.t.
  Airport: International.
William, see Port Stanley.
Williamsburg, Virginia, U.S.A.: 37.15 N. 76.45 W. **63, 65**
Williamsport, Newfoundland, Canada: 50.28 N. 56.22 W. **60**
Williamstown, see Melbourne.
Wilmington, California, U.S.A., see Los Angeles.
Wilmington, Delaware, U.S.A.: 39.45 N. 75.30 W. **55, 63, 65**
  Max. Size: Depth 38 ft. (MLW). *Fuel:* Available.
  Dry Docks: Penn Ship Yard, Chester, Pa.
  Airport: Philadelphia and Wilmington.
Wilmington, North Carolina, U.S.A.: 34.14 N. 77.57 W. . . **55, 63, 66**
  Max. Size: Draft limit is present channel project depth of 38 ft.
  Fuel: Bunker ''C'' and diesel. *Dry Docks:* 1 x 1,000 ton lift
  floating dry dock. *Airport:* Internal, 7 miles.
Windsor, N.S., Canada: 45.00 N. 64.09 W. **60**
Windsor, Ontario, Canada: 42.19 N. 83.03 W. **62**
  Max. Size: See St. Lawrence Seaway. Tankers: Depth 27 ft.
  Fuel: Available. *Airport:* 5 miles.
Windward Islands, South China Sea **71**
Windward Passage, Cuba/Haiti. **69, 70**
Wing, see Port Wing.
Winisk, Ontario, Canada: 55.22 N. 85.16 W. **59**
Winisk River, Ontario, Canada **59**
Winneba, Ghana: 5.22 N. 0.37 W. **28**
Winslow, Washington, U.S.A.: 47.37 N. 122.31 W. **56**
Wintam, see Brussels.
Wisbech, U.K.: 52.39 N. 0.09 E. **7**
Wisconsin, U.S.A. **62**
Wismar, Germany: 53.54 N. 11.27 E. **10, 11, 12, 14**
  Max. Size: LOA up to 205 m., beam 28.0 m., draft 7.65 m.
  (5.0 m. on water gauge). *Fuel:* Diesel and fuel by truck or
  barge. *Airport:* Lubeck, 50 km. Hamburg, 100 km.
Withnell Bay Terminal, see Dampier.
Wivenhoe, U.K.: 51.51 N. 0.58 E. **7**
  Max. Size: LOA 250 ft., draft 14 ft. 6 in. spring tides, 10 ft. neap
  tides. *Fuel:* By road tanker.
  Airport: London, 70 miles. Stansted, 30 miles.
  Also see Colchester.
Wladyslawowo, Poland: 54.47 N. 18.25 E. **11**
Wokum Is., (Aru Is.), Indonesia **46**
Woleai, (Caroline Is.), Micronesia: 7.22 N. 143.54 E. **46**
Wolf Rock, U.K.: 49.57 N. 5.48 W. **19**
Wolfville, see Port Williams.
Wolgast, Germany: 54.03 N. 13.47 E. **11, 12**
Wolin, Poland: 53.50 N. 14.38 E. **12**
Wollongong, see Port Kembla.
Wolloomooloo, see Sydney.
Womens Bay, see Kodiak.
Wonsan, North Korea: 39.10 N. 127.26 E. **42, 43**
Woodbridge, U.K.: 52.05 N. 1.20 E. **7**
Woodfibre, B.C., Canada: 49.40 N. 123.15 W. **56**
  Max. Size: Depth 30 ft. *Airport:* Vancouver.
Woodlands, see Singapore.
Woodlark Is., Papua New Guinea **46**
Woods Hole, Massachusetts, U.S.A.: 41.31 N. 70.40 W. **63**
Woody Is., (Paracel Is.), South China Sea: 16.45 N. 112.21 E. . . **39**
Woody Point, Newfoundland, Canada: 49.30 N. 57.55 W. **60**
Woolwich, U.K.: 51.30 N. 0.04 E. **6**
  Max. Size: Depth 5 m. (MHWS).
  Also see London.
Workington, U.K.: 54.39 N. 3.34 W. **5**
  Max. Size: 10,000 d.w.t., LOA 137.2 m., draft 8 m.,
  beam 20.4 m. *Fuel:* Available.
Wotho Is., Marshall Is.: 10.08 N. 166.00 E. **49**
Wotje Is., Marshall Is.: 9.40 N. 170.00 E. **49**
Wowoni Is., Indonesia: 4.10 S. 123.05 E. **46**
Wrangell, Alaska, U.S.A.: 56.28 N. 132.22 W. **56**
  Max. Size: Harbour depth 32 ft. (MLLW). Depth at berths 32 ft. –
  40 ft. Tides: Mean range 13.7 ft. *Fuel:* Small quantities.
  Airport: Airstrip.
Wreck, see Barqueriza.
Wright Point, see Port Hawkesbury.
Wrightsville, North Carolina, U.S.A.: 34.13 N. 77.49 W. **63**
Wroclaw, Poland: 51.05 N. 16.59 E. **9**
Wu Chou, see Wuzhou.
Wu Tao, China: 39.20 N. 121.30 E. **42**
Wuhan, China: 30.34 N. 114.17 E. **42**
  Max. Size: Draft Nov. – Apr. 4.5 m., Mar. – Oct. 8.0 m.
  Depth alongside 4.5 m. – 9 m. *Fuel:* Available.
Wuhu, China: 31.22 N. 118.22 E. **42, 46**
  Max. Size: Channel: Draft 6.1 m. Berth: Draft 10 m.
Wulsan, see Ulsan.
Wurzburg, Germany: 49.46 N. 10.00 E. **9**

Wuzhou, China: 23.29 N. 111.18 E. **39**
Wyandotte, Michigan, U.S.A.: 42.12 N. 83.09 W. **62**
Wyk, Germany: 54.41 N. 8.35 E. **12, 14**
Wyndham, W.A., Australia: 15.28 S. 128.06 E. **46, 50**
  Max. Size: LOA 190 m., draft 8.8 m.
  Max. displacement 26,000 tonnes. *Fuel:* Small quantities.
  Airport: Connects with Darwin.
Wyoming, U.S.A. **57**

NOTES, ADDITIONS, CORRECTIONS

Please also advise Shipping Guides Ltd.
75 Bell Street, Reigate, RH2 7AN, United Kingdom
Tel: +44 1737 242255   Fax: +44 1737 222449
Email: updates@portinfo.co.uk   Web: www.portinfo.co.uk

X

Xeros, see Gemikonagi.
Xiamen, China: 24.30 N. 118.04 E. 42
  Max. Size: Dong Du: Draft 11.7 (Grain). *Fuel:* Available.
  Airport: Flights to major cities in China and Hong Kong (SAR), China.
Xiang Jiang, see Xingang.
Xiaohu, see Guangzhou.
Xiaohudao, see Guangzhou.
Xijiang Terminal, China: 21.18 N. 114.57 E. 39
  Max. Size: At FPSO: 120,000 d.w.t., depth 31 m.
Xili, see Plitra.
Xingang, China: 39.02 N. 117.41 E. 42
  Max. Size: Draft 9.0 m.
  Also see Tianjin Xingang.
Xinhai, China: 22.30 N. 113.01 E. 48
Xinhui, China: 22.31 N. 113.03 E. 39
Xinmin, see Fuzhou.
Xiuyu, China: 25.13 N. 118.59 E. 42
  Max. Size: Channel: Draft 13 m. Berth: 10,000 d.w.t., draft 9.6 m. *Fuel:* Available.
Xpila, see Ykspihlaja.
Xpili, see Ykspihlaja.
Xu Wen, China: 20.02 N. 110.05 E. 39

NOTES, ADDITIONS, CORRECTIONS

Please also advise Shipping Guides Ltd.
75 Bell Street, Reigate, RH2 7AN, United Kingdom
Tel: +44 1737 242255   Fax: +44 1737 222449
Email: updates@portinfo.co.uk   Web: www.portinfo.co.uk

Y

Yabucoa, Puerto Rico (U.S.A.): 18.02 N. 65.48 W. 71
  Max. Size: Draft 44 ft. 6 in. *Fuel:* Available.
Yahata, see Chiba.
Yakacik, see Isdemir.
Yakataga, Alaska, U.S.A.: 60.00 N. 142.45 W. 54
Yakutat, Alaska, U.S.A.: 59.33 N. 139.44 W. 56
Yali Island, Greece: 36.40 N. 27.08 E. 25, 26
  Max. Size: LOA 190 m., beam 24 m., draft 33 ft. *Airport:* At Kos.
Yalova, Turkey: 40.39 N. 29.16 E. 23, 25
Yalta, Ukraine: 44.30 N. 34.12 E. 26
  Max. Size: LOA 215 m. – 195 m., draft 6 m. – 8.6 m.
Yamagawa, Japan: 31.11 N. 130.38 E. 45
Yamaguchi Bay, see Iwakuni.
Yamba, N.S.W., Australia: 29.26 S. 153.21 E. 50
  Max. Size: LOA 110 m., draft 3.8 m. plus tide, *Fuel:* Available.
  Dry Docks: Slipway 1,100 tonnes. *Airport:* Grafton (1 hour), connects with Sydney.
Yambacoona, Tas., Australia: 39.44 S. 143.57 E. 51
Yampi Sound, W.A., Australia: 16.08 S. 123.38 E. 50, 51
  Port closed in 1993
Yanbu, Saudi Arabia: 24.05 N. 38.03 E. 21, 32
  Max. Size: Commercial Port: LOA 260 m., draft 34 ft., cement – draft 36 ft. Industrial Port: Crude Oil – 500,000 d.w.t., draft 95 ft. NGL – 200,000 cu.m., draft 53 ft. 2 in. Petromin – 80,000 d.w.t., depth 16.0 m.
  SAMREF – 150,000 d.w.t., draft 16.65 m.
  YANPET – 50,000 d.w.t., draft 12.15 m.
  Al Muajjiz: 500,000 d.w.t., draft 29.6 m. General Cargo – depth 14 m. Bulk – 60,000 d.w.t., draft 13.9 m. *Fuel:* Available.
  Airport: Yanbu, 15 km.
Yandina, Solomon Islands: 9.04 S. 159.14 E. 49, 51
  Max. Size: Depth 6 m. *Airport:* Flights to Honiara.
Yangjiang, China: 21.52 N. 111.52 E. 39
  Max. Size: Depth 9.0 m. – 9.5 m.
Yangon, Myanmar: 16.47 N. 96.15 E. 37
  Max. Size: LOA 180 m., draft 28 ft. Tankers: Draft 7 m.
  Fuel: Available. *Dry Docks:* Max. 2,000 tons.
Yangpu, China: 19.44 N. 109.11 E. 39
  Max. Size: LOA 200 m., draft 11.0 m. *Fuel:* Diesel.
  Airport: At Haikou.
Yangzhou, China: 32.16 N. 119.26 E. 42
  Max. Size: Channel 9.7 m. Berth: 15,000 d.w.t., depth 12 m.
  Fuel: Available.
Yantai, China: 37.33 N. 121.24 E. 42
  Max. Size: Channel: Eastern – Draft 8.5 m. Western – Draft 10.1 m. Berth: Depth 5.7 m. – 14 m. *Airport:* Flights to Shanghai and Beijing.
Yantian, China: 22.35 N. 114.15 E. 48
  Max. Size: Depth 4.2 m. – 13.0 m.
Yap Is., see Tomil Harbour.
Yapen Is., Irian Jaya, Indonesia 46
Yar Sale, Russia: 66.50 N. 70.50 E. 16
Yarimca, Turkey: 40.45 N. 29.45 E. 23, 25, 26
  Max. Size: Depth 12 m. – 13.5 m. Aygas: Depth 24 m. – 26 m.
  Fuel: By barge.
Yarmouth, N.S., Canada: 43.50 N. 66.07 W. 60
Yarmouth, U.K.: 50.42 N. 1.30 W. 7
Yarraville, see Melbourne.
Yashiro, Inland Sea, Japan 45
Yasuda, Japan: 33.28 N. 134.00 E. 45
Yatsushiro, Japan: 32.30 N. 130.05 E. 43, 45
  Max. Size: 40,000 d.w.t., draft 11.8 m.
  Airport: Kumamoto, 70 km.
Yavaros, Mexico: 26.41 N. 109.30 W. 57
Yawata, Japan: 33.52 N. 130.49 E. 44, 45
  Max. Size: LOA 200 m., draft 8.5 m. *Fuel:* Bonded oil will be brought from Moji, Ube or Ohita. *Airport:* Fukuoka, 70 km.
Yawatahama, Japan: 33.28 N. 132.25 E. 45
Ye, Myanmar: 15.15 N. 97.51 E. 37
Yell, U.K.: 60.37 N. 1.05 W. 5
Yelland, U.K.: 51.04 N. 4.09 W. 6
Yellow Sea 42
Yembo, see Yanbu.
YEMEN, REPUBLIC OF 31, 32
Yen Tai, see Yantai.
Yenbo, see Yanbu.
Yenikoy, Turkey: 41.08 N. 29.04 E. 25
Yeniseyski Bay, Russia 16
Yerakini, Greece: 40.16 N. 23.28 E. 25
Yerba Buena Is., California, U.S.A. 58
Yesilkoy, Turkey: 40.58 N. 28.50 E. 23
Yetagun Marine Terminal, Myanmar: 13.04 N. 96.51 E. . . . 37
  Max. Size: 88,000 d.w.t., depth 105 m.
Yevpatoriya, see Evpatoria.
Yeysk, Russia: 46.45 N. 38.15 E. 26

Yingkou, China: 40.41 N. 122.15 E. **42**
Max. Size: Anchorage: Depth 9.0 m. – 12.0 m., 30,000 d.w.t.
Berth: Draft 6.5 m. – 11.3 m. Tankers: Draft 11.3 m.

Yioura Is., Greece: 39.23 N. 24.10 E. **25**

Yithion, Greece: 36.45 N. 22.34 E. **25**

Ykspihlaja, Finland: 63.49 N. 23.06 E. **15**
Also see Kokkola.

Ymuiden, Netherlands: 52.28 N. 4.34 E. **7, 8, 9**
Max. Size: LOA 350 m. or draft 54 ft. *Fuel:* By barge.

Yoichi, Japan: 43.14 N. 140.46 E. **43**

Yokkaichi, Japan: 34.57 N. 136.38 E. **43, 45**
Max. Size: Depth up to 14.0 m. LPG/LNG: Draft 11.0 m.
Tankers: Draft 19.95 m. at SBM. *Fuel:* Bonded oil available
ex-barge. *Airport:* Nagoya, 2 hours by car.

Yokohama, Japan: 35.27 N. 139.38 E. **43, 44, 45, 46**
Max. Size: Tankers: Draft 21 m. Cargo: LOA 350 m.,
draft 17.5 m. *Fuel:* Available. *Dry Docks:* Largest: Up to
270,000 d.w.t. *Airport:* Haneda International, 25 km.

Yokosuka, Japan: 35.17 N. 139.39 E. **44, 45**
Max. Size: Draft 10 m. *Fuel:* Most grades available from
Yokohama or Kawasaki. *Dry Docks:* Largest – 475 ft. x 19.5 ft.
Airport: Tokyo, 40 km.

Yombo, Congo (Rep. of): 4.27 S. 11.06 E. **28**
Max. Size: 155,000 d.w.t., LOA 280 m., beam 53.6 m.,
draft 15.0 m.

Yongdangpo, see Haeju.

Yonkers, New York, U.S.A.: 40.56 N. 73.52 W. **63**

York Factory, Manitoba, Canada: 57.02 N. 92.29 W. . . . **59**

Yorktown, Virginia, U.S.A.: 37.14 N. 76.30 W. . . . **55, 63, 65**

Yosu, South Korea: 34.44 N. 127.45 E. **42, 43, 46**
Max. Size: (a) LG Caltex – Crude Wharf: 320,000
d.w.t. draft 21 m. (b) LG Caltex – Products Wharf: 48,000 d.w.t.
(c) Nakpo Wharf: 50,000 d.w.t.
(d) LG Advanced Materials: 4,400 d.w.t., draft 5.5 m. (e)
Yosu Harbour – Bulk: 250,000 d.w.t., depth 20 m.
Containers: Depth 10.0 m. – 14.5 m.
(f) LG Caltex Gas: 100,000 cu.m., LOA 230 m., draft 13 m.
Fuel: Bunkers available by barge.

Youghal, Ireland: 51.58 N. 7.50 W. **5**

Youngstown, New York, U.S.A.: 43.15 N. 79.02 W. . . . **62**

Ystad, Sweden: 55.26 N. 13.50 E. **10, 11, 12**
Max. Size: About 5,500 d.w.t. Draft 6.7 m. (22 ft.).
Fuel: Available. *Airport:* 30 km.

Yu Lin, China: 18.14 N. 109.33 E. **39**

Yuasa, Japan: 34.07 N. 135.11 E. **45**

Yucatan Channel, South China Sea: 21.45 N. 85.30 W. . . . **69, 70**

Yugorski Strait, Russia **16**

YUGOSLAVIA **9, 21, 24**

Yukalpeten, see Progreso.

Yukon Delta, Alaska, U.S.A. **54**

Yukuhashi, Japan: 33.41 N. 131.02 E. **45**

Yunaska Is., (Aleutian Is.), Alaska, U.S.A. **54**

Yura, Japan: 33.57 N. 135.07 E. **45**
Max. Size: Length 110 m. *Dry Docks:* 350,000 d.w.t.
Also see Shimotsu.

Yuribei, Russia: 71.08 N. 76.59 E. **16**

Yuzhny, Ukraine: 46.39 N. 30.55 E. **26**
Max. Size: LOA 280 m., draft 13.0 m. Buoys: LOA 280 m.,
draft 14.2 m. *Fuel:* By barge. *Airport:* Odessa, 22 miles.

Yxpila, see Kokkola.

THE SHIPS ATLAS

Z

Zaafarana Terminal, Egypt: 29.10 N. 32.41 E. **21, 26, 32**
Max. Size: Side-by-Side Mooring: 130,000 tonnes d.w.t.,
LOA 850 ft., draft 55 ft.

Zaandam, Netherlands: 52.26 N. 4.49 E. **7, 8**
Max. Size: Draft 10.0 m. *Fuel:* Available. *Airport:*
Amsterdam, 20 km.
Also see Amsterdam.

Zaanstad, see Zaandam.

Zadar, Croatia: 44.07 N. 15.14 E. **9, 21, 24**
Max. Size: Draft 10.7 m. – 11.6 m. *Dry Docks:* Floating dock,
max. 8,600 tonnes. *Airport:* Connects with Zagreb.

Zafiro Offshore Terminal, Equatorial Guinea: 3.51 N. 8.07 E. . . **29**
Max. Size: 310,000 d.w.t.

Zagreb, Croatia: 45.49 N. 16.00 E. **9**

Zakinthos, Greece: 37.47 N. 20.54 E. **24, 25**

ZAMBIA **30**

Zamboanga, (Mindanao Is.), Philippines: 6.54 N. 122.04 E. . **38, 46, 47**
Max. Size: Draft 10 m. Tankers: Draft 18 ft. *Fuel:* Available.
Airport: 3 km., connects with Manila.

Zanimah, see Abu Zenima.

Zante, Greece: 37.45 N. 20.55 E. **24, 25**

Zanzibar, Tanzania: 6.09 S. 39.11 E. **30**
Max. Size: (Anchorage) LOA 1,100 ft., beam 110 ft., draft 32 ft.

Zanzibar Is., Tanzania **30**

Zarate, Argentina: 34.09 S. 59.05 W. **77, 78**
Max. Size: Up to 26 ft. draft, depending on river depth.

Zarubino, Russia: 42.34 N. 131.05 E. **43**
Max. Size: Depth 9.5 m.

Zarzis, Tunisia: 33.33 N. 11.07 E. **24**
Max. Size: Draft 10.5 m. *Airport:* Djerba, 50 km.

Zawia, Libya: 32.48 N. 12.42 E. **24**
Max. Size: C.B.M. No. 2: LOA 175 m., draft 10,0 m.,
25,000 d.w.t. S.A.L.M.: Draft 19.0 m., 140,000 d.w.t.

Zayed, see Mina Zayed.

Zealand Is., Denmark **11, 12, 14**

Zeballos, B.C., Canada: 49.58 N. 126.51 W. **56**

Zeballos Cue, see Asuncion.

Zeebrugge, Belgium: 51.20 N. 3.12 E. **7, 8**
Max. Size: Depths up to 16 m. and 18 m. Tankers: Depth 13.1
m. *Fuel:* All grades. *Airport:* Ostend, 30 km.

Zeila, Somalia: 11.19 N. 43.29 E. **31, 32**

Zeit Bay, Egypt: 27.50 N. 33.36 E. **26, 32**
Max. Size: S.B.M.: 250,000 d.w.t., LOA 1,300 ft., draft 18 m.
LPG: LOA 108 m., draft 5 m.
Also see East Zeit Terminal.

Zelenika, Yugoslavia: 42.27 N. 18.35 E. **9, 24**
Max. Size: LOA 120 m. *Fuel:* By road tanker.
Dry Docks: Floating dock with lifting capacity 33,000 tons.

Zhangjiagang, China: 31.58 N. 120.24 E. **42, 46**
Max. Size: 10,000 d.w.t.

Zhangzhou, China: 24.25 N. 118.02 E. **42**
Max. Size: 36,000 d.w.t., depth 12.5 m. *Fuel:* Available.

Zhanjiang, China: 21.11 N. 110.24 E. **39**
Max. Size: Cargo: Draft 11.4 m. Tankers: Draft 11.73 m.
Fuel: Available. *Airport:* Domestic flights and direct flights
to Hong Kong (SAR), China.

Zhapu, China: 30.35 N. 121.05 E. **42**
Max. Size: 25,000 d.w.t., depth 11.3 m. *Fuel:* Available.

Zhdanov, see Mariupol.

Zhenhai, China: 29.57 N. 121.43 E. **42**
Max. Size: Depth 9.5 m., 10,000 d.w.t. Tankers: 80,000 d.w.t.,
draft 14 m.
Also see Ningbo.

Zhenjiang, China: 32.13 N. 119.27 E. **42**
Max. Size: Draft 9.5 m. in channel. Berth: LOA 200 m.,
depth 11 m. *Fuel:* Available.

Zhoushan, China: 30.01 N. 122.06 E. **42**
Max. Size: Draft 15.0 m. in channel. Berth: LOA 170 m.,
draft 10 m. Tankers: Ao Shan – Depth 21 m.

Zhuhai, China: 22.18 N. 113.35 E. **39, 48**
Max. Size: Draft 6 m. – 8.2 m. *Fuel:* By truck.

Zierikzee, Netherlands: 51.39 N. 3.54 E. **8**

Ziguinchor, Senegal: 12.35 N. 16.20 W. **27**

Zikrit, Qatar: 25.30 N. 50.45 E. **35**

ZIMBABWE **30**

Zingst, Germany: 54.27 N. 12.41 E. **12**

Zinnowitz, Germany: 54.05 N. 13.55 E. **12**

Zirku Island, Abu Dhabi, U.A.E.: 24.52 N. 53.04 E. **35**
Max. Size: S.B.M.: 350,000 d.w.t., draft 21 m.

Zlitan, Libya: 32.31 N. 14.35 E. **24**

Zonguldak, Turkey: 41.28 N. 31.49 E. **25, 26**
Max. Size: Depths to 10 m.

Zorra Is., Panama Canal, Panama **73**

Zorritos, Peru: 3.40 S. 80.40 W. **72**

Zorrosa, see Bilbao.

Zuara, Libya: 32.55 N. 12.07 E. 24
  Max. Size: Draft 13 ft. LOA 65 m.   *Airport:* Tripoli, 127 km.
Zueitina, Libya: 30.51 N. 20.00 E. 24
  Max. Size: Tankers: 275,000 d.w.t., draft 20 m.
  LPG: 30,000 cu.m., draft 8.7 m.
Zula, Eritrea: 15.16 N. 39.38 E. 32
Zulayfayn, see Ju'aymah.
Zumaya, Spain: 43.18 N. 2.15 W. 19
Zuniga, see Santa Marta.
Zuqar Is., Yemen: 14.00 N. 42.40 E. 32
Zutphen, Netherlands: 52.08 N. 6.12 E. 8
Zuwarah, see Zuara.
Zwolle, Netherlands: 52.31 N. 6.07 E. 8
Zwyndrecht, see Antwerp.
Zyyi, see Vassiliko Bay.

NOTES, ADDITIONS, CORRECTIONS

Please also advise Shipping Guides Ltd.
75 Bell Street, Reigate, RH2 7AN, United Kingdom
Tel: +44 1737 242255   Fax: +44 1737 222449
Email: updates@portinfo.co.uk   Web: www.portinfo.co.uk

NOTES, ADDITIONS, CORRECTIONS

Please also advise Shipping Guides Ltd.
75 Bell Street, Reigate, RH2 7AN, United Kingdom
Tel: +44 1737 242255   Fax: +44 1737 222449
Email: updates@portinfo.co.uk   Web: www.portinfo.co.uk

NOTES, ADDITIONS, CORRECTIONS

*Please also advise Shipping Guides Ltd.
75 Bell Street, Reigate, RH2 7AN, United Kingdom
Tel: +44 1737 242255   Fax: +44 1737 222449
Email: updates@portinfo.co.uk   Web: www.portinfo.co.uk*

Map 81

Vessels may proceed to Prince Rupert (Which is Lat. 54° 19' N) by any route. Calls at Queen Charlotte Islands barred.

- BERING SEA ④
- ① D — 54° 30' N Prince Rupert
- Vancouver
- 130° 50' W
- San Francisco
- New Orleans
- ① B
- New York
- Greenland
- Cape Farewell
- ① C
- 52° 10' N — See Inset
- ① A
- Panama
- Recife
- Valparaiso
- Chile / Patagonia
- ⑤
- Falkland Islands
- Cape Horn

NORTH AMERICA (ATLANTIC)

- Quebec
- Baie Comeau — St. Lawrence
- Matane
- CANADA
- New Brunswick
- ① B
- Maine
- Montreal
- U.S.A.
- Gulf of St. Lawrence
- ① A
- Cape North
- Newfoundland
- Cape Ray
- Battle Harbour
- 52° 10' N
- Pistolet Bay
- 50° W
- Port Hawkesbury
- Port Mulgrave
- Nova Scotia
- Atlantic Ocean

The Shaded waters are Warranty-barred for Winter trading, i.e. East of Baie Comeau/Matane between 21st December and 30th April b.d.i. and West of Baie Comeau/Matane (but not West of Montreal) between 1st December and 30th April b.d.i.

**MAP 81
INSTITUTE WARRANTIES
10th Edition**

Reproduced by kind permission of WITHERBY & CO. LTD.,
32 - 36 AYLESBURY STREET, LONDON EC1R 0ET

© Shipping Guides Ltd., Reigate, United Kingdom